About the editors

Nalini Visvanathan, a native of India, is an independent researcher whose interests and publications cover women's health, population policies, women's movements and community-based participatory research. She has a doctoral degree in interdisciplinary communication studies with an emphasis on international development; and she has been active in women's movements. She was on the faculty of an experiential under-graduate programme in international studies for many years.

Lynn Duggan, professor of labour studies since 1997 and PhD economist, teaches at Indiana University Bloomington. She has written articles and book chapters on free trade and social policy, feminist comparative economic systems, family policy in East and West Germany, and reproductive rights in the Philippines.

Nan Wiegersma is professor of economics, emeritus, at Fitchburg State University, Massachusetts. She has published numerous articles on land tenure, gender and development. Her article 'Peasant patriarchy and the subversion of the collective in Vietnam' was reprinted in the research anthology *Gender and Development: Theoretical, Empirical and Practical Approaches*, vol. I (ed. Lourdes Beneria). She is author of *Vietnam: Peasant Land, Peasant Revolution* and is coauthor (with Joseph Medley) of *US Development Policies toward the Pacific Rim*. She was the women and development expert for the United Nations on a World Food Programme mission to Vietnam.

Nan was a Fulbright fellow in Nicaragua, studying women's work in export processing zones. The research from this study was published in *Women in the Age of Economic Transformation* (ed. Aslanbegui et al., 1994) and *Women in Globalization* (ed. Aguilar and Lacsamana, 2004).

Laurie Nisonoff, professor of economics, has taught economics, economic history and women's studies at Hampshire College in Amherst, Massachusetts, USA, since 1974. She is an editor of the *Review of Radical Political Economics*, and served as the coordinator of the RRPE 6th Special Issue on Women, 'Women in the international economy'. She has published alone and with Marilyn Dalsimer on women in China, and on the labour process.

THE WOMEN, GENDER AND DEVELOPMENT READER

second edition

edited by Nalini Visvanathan, Lynn Duggan,
Nan Wiegersma and Laurie Nisonoff

1, 2, 3, 5, 7, 8, 14, 19, 20, 35, 37

4, 6, 9, 10, 11, 12, 13, 15, 17, 18, 21, 22, 24, 25, 27...

Fernwood Publishing
HALIFAX | WINNIPEG

Zed Books
LONDON | NEW YORK

The Women, Gender and Development Reader was first published in 1997
This second edition was first published in 2011

Published in Canada by Fernwood Publishing Ltd, 32 Oceanvista Lane, Black Point, Novia Scotia B0J 1B0

www.fernwoodpublishing.ca

Published in the rest of the world by Zed Books Ltd, 7 Cynthia Street, London N1 9JF, UK and Room 400, 175 Fifth Avenue, New York, NY 10010, USA

www.zedbooks.co.uk

Set in OurType Arnhem, Monotype Gill Sans Heavy by Ewan Smith, London
Index: ed.emery@thefreeuniversity.net
Cover designed by Rogue Four Design
Printed and bound in Great Britain by the MPG Books Group, Bodmin and King's Lynn

Mixed Sources
Product group from well-managed forests and other controlled sources
www.fsc.org Cert no. SA-COC-1565
© 1996 Forest Stewardship Council
FSC

Distributed in the USA exclusively by Palgrave Macmillan, a division of St Martin's Press, LLC, 175 Fifth Avenue, New York, NY 10010, USA

A catalogue record for this book is available from the British Library
Library of Congress Cataloging in Publication Data available

Library and Archives Canada Cataloguing in Publication
  The women, gender and development reader / [edited by] Nalini Visvanathan ... [et al.]. -- 2nd ed.
Includes bibliographical references and index.
ISBN 978-1-55266-427-8
    1. Women--Developing countries--Social conditions. 2. Women--Developing countries--Economic conditions. 3. Women in development. I. Visvanathan, Nalini, 1945-
HQ1240.W67 2011   305.409172'4
C2011-901955-8

ISBN 978 1 84813 586 4 hb (Zed Books)
ISBN 978 1 84813 587 1 pb (Zed Books)
ISBN 978 1 55266 427 8 pb (Fernwood Publishing)

Contents

PART FIVE **Women organizing themselves for change: transnational movements, local resistance**

Tables and boxes

Tables

Boxes

Introductory note

In 1997, as members of the erstwhile New England Women and Development Discussion Group (see Acknowledgements), we collaborated in creating the first edition of this anthology. In 2008, Zed decided to produce a second edition of the reader, which has been well received and widely adopted. This second edition represents the evolvement of the field since the early 1970s, though the impact of the global financial crisis creates an important caveat to the collection. The reader is divided into the same five parts; however, we have retained only a small number of original readings, in order to accommodate a burgeoning literature that spans four decades. Within each part, important essays and significant studies outline and challenge established theories that have animated the field over time. An introduction to each part highlights the thematic issues and the conceptual frameworks, with readings grouped and discussed at the end. Space constraints have led us to exclude some important contributions to the literature, to which we refer in our introductions and further reading. Others are cited in the excerpts, whose unabridged texts have full bibliographies. And not all geographical regions could receive the coverage they merit. We recognize and regret these limitations.

We hope the selected excerpts will encourage you to read the unabridged essays cited in the list of sources (pages xiii–xv) and explore the related literature.

Acknowledgements

In 1978, Lourdes Benería, Hamideh Sedghi and Grace Horowitz organized the initial Women and Development Discussion Group composed of women students and teachers then residing on the East Coast, USA. These women were involved in empirical and theoretical research about women's roles in development and/or history and they gathered monthly on Saturdays in New York City to discuss their work-in-progress. They shared an understanding of the centrality of women's roles in political-economic development and a sense of the importance of class differences. The group self-consciously called its topic Women and Development, rather than Women in Development, to underline the importance of class distinctions in determining the impact of the development process on women.

In 1984, Laurie Nisonoff and Nan Wiegersma noted that an increasing number of women who were living or teaching in the New England region were also involved in similar research. They called these women together and the New England Women and Development Discussion Group began meeting. Three of the participants, Carmen Diana Deere, Jeanne Koopman and Nan Wiegersma, had been members of the New York group and they shared this experience with their New England colleagues.

Zed Books approached Betsy Hartmann in 1991 with the idea of a reader that would feature landmark articles and essays on the impact of development on women's lives. Betsy was too busy to work on this project, but Nalini Visvanathan, Brenda Wyss, Lynn Duggan and Laurie Nisonoff began to outline the book that summer. Nan joined the project in 1992 when Brenda had to withdraw because of other commitments.

We would like to thank the multiple incarnations of the Women and Development discussion groups for providing us with the inspiration and insights we needed to sustain us through the many trials we encountered in producing the first edition of this reader, published in 1997.

When Zed Books approached us concerning a new edition of the reader in 2008, we were living at a distance from one another: Washington, DC, Bloomington, Indiana, and Amherst and Northampton, Massachusetts. Nevertheless, through conference calling and Internet communications we have been able to pull this new edition together.

We would like to record our gratitude to the authors and editors whose works appear in the first and second editions of this reader and thank all of them. The two editions of the book could not have been completed without the cooperation and support we received from the authors and editors as we abridged their work. Some authors waived their copyrights and relinquished their royalties so that we could stay within a strictly defined budget. We appreciate their generosity and their commitment to making their writings available to a larger circle of readers.

We are grateful also to our colleagues and to the administrations at Fitchburg State University, Hampshire College and Indiana University. We would like to thank Hilary Kahn, Associate Director of the Center for the Study of Global Change at Indiana University Bloomington, and the Center itself, for reprint permissions support.

Nalini Visvanathan returned to the reader after a long hiatus from teaching and valued the suggestions and support she received from colleagues – academics, activists and practitioners – including Kanthie Athukorala, Arin Atilgan, Rajani Bhatia, Ayse Dayi, Lynette Dumble, Betsy Hartmann, Dan Moshenberg, Imrana Qadeer, Raj Patel, Ramaa Vasudevan, Kalpana Wilson and Elaine Zuckerman. In particular, she would like to gratefully acknowledge the insights and encouragement from Wendy Harcourt, Adetoun Ilumoka, Shirin Rai, Abha Sur and Karla Yoder. She is greatly indebted to authors and publishers for their generosity, which enabled her to cover the permissions costs for Parts 1 and 5. She would also like to acknowledge the support of the Department of Geography, Dartmouth College. Their consideration and assistance made it possible to condense critical readings and include a broader representation of the literature. And she thanks Mahita and Subodh for their understanding and patient endurance.

We are indebted to three anonymous reviewers who responded to our initial outline for the second edition with perceptive suggestions for retaining chapters and introducing fresh material and would like to thank them for their guidance.

There are many women and development anthologies and readers available for use by experts in the field. This reader is intended to be accessible to students and practitioners and we have chosen and excerpted articles and prepared the introductions with this in mind. Our selections have been made in order to represent the lives of women of many different regions. We hope that the reader will reach women worldwide and help expand the set of tools, concepts and frameworks available to share their experiences of development throughout our global community.

Lynn Duggan, Laurie Nisonoff, Nalini Visvanathan and Nan Wiegersma

Sources

Part One

1 'The history of international development: concepts and contexts', in S. M. Rai, *Gender and the Political Economy of Development*, Polity Press, Cambridge, 2002.

2 Jayati Ghosh, 'Financial crises and the impact on women', original essay, New Delhi, India, June 2010.

3 'Gender and development: theoretical perspectives', in S. M. Rai, *Gender and the Political Economy of Development*, Polity Press, Cambridge, 2002.

4 'Women's role in economic development', from Chapters 1 and 3 in E. Bose-rup, *Women's Role in Economic Development*, Earthscan, London, 1970.

5 'The invisible heart: care and the global economy', from Chapter 3 in the 1999 *Human Development Report*, Oxford University Press, Oxford, 1999.

6 'Feminist political ecology', in *Gender and Environment Series*, Zed Books, London, forthcoming.

7 Nalini Visvanathan and Karla Yoder, 'Women and microcredit: a critical introduction', original essay, Washington, DC, June 2010.

8 K. Kalpana, 'Negotiating multiple patriarchies: women and microfinance in south India', original essay, Chennai, India, June 2010.

9 'Gender as a social determinant of health', in G. Sen and P. Ostlin, *Gender Equity in Health: The Shifting Frontiers of Evidence and Action*, Routledge, New York, 2010.

10 'Peace-building and reconstruction with women: reflections on Afghanistan, Iraq, and Palestine', in V. M. Moghadam, *From Patriarchy to Empowerment*, Syracuse University Press, New York, 2007.

11 'Under Western eyes: feminist scholarship and colonial discourses', in C. Mohanty, A. Russo and L. Torres, *Third World Women and the Politics of Feminism*, Indiana University Press, Bloomington, 1991.

12 'Do Muslim women really need saving? Anthropological reflections on cultural relativism and its others', L. Abu-Lughod, *American Anthropologist*, 104(3), 2002, pp. 783–90.

13 'The "gender lens": a racial blinder?', S. C. White, *Progress in Development Studies*, 6(1), 2006.

14 'From missionaries to microcredit? "Race", gender and agency in neoliberal development', in K. Wilson, *'Race,' Racism and Development: Interrogating History, Discourse and Practice*, Zed Books, London, forthcoming.

30 Women's Environment and Development Organization (WEDO), *Gender, Climate Change and Human Security: Lessons from Bangladesh, Ghana and Senegal*, selections from 2 by Irene Dankelman and 4 by Yacine Diagne Gueye, 2008.

31 'The population bomb is back – with a global warming twist', *Women in Action*, 2, 2009.

32 'Caring for people with HIV: state policies and their dependence on women's unpaid work', *Gender and Development*, 17(1), 2009.

33 'The right to have rights: resisting fundamentalist orders', *openDemocracy*, www.opendemocracy.net, 2010.

34 'Women's movements negotiating peace', in A. M Tripp et al., *African Women's Movements: Transforming Political Landscapes*, Cambridge University Press, 2008.

35 Ruth Needleman, '"I am somebody!": Brazil's social movements educate for gender equality and economic sustainability', original essay, 2010.

36 'Capitalism and socialism: some feminist questions', in R. Rapp and M. B. Young (eds), *Promissory Notes: Women in the Transition to Socialism*, Monthly Review Press, New York, 1989.

Part Five

37 *The Global Women's Movements: Origins, Issues and Strategies*, Zed Books, London.

38 '"Under Western eyes" revisited: feminist solidarity through anti-capitalist struggles', *Signs: Journal of Women in Culture and Society*, 28(2), 2002, pp. 417–37.

39 'Challenges in transnational feminist mobilization', in M. M. Ferree and A. M. Tripp, *Global Feminism: Transnational Women's Activism, Organizing and Human Rights*, New York University Press, New York, 2006, pp. 296–312.

40 'Cooperation, collaboration and community', in *La Vía Campesina: Globalization and the Power of Peasants*, Fernwood Publishing, Halifax, NS, 2007, pp. 161–89.

41 'Birthing and growing the African Feminist Forum', *Development*, 52, 2009, pp. 167–74.

42 'Women's community organizing in Quito: the paradoxes of survival and struggle', in *Gendered Paradoxes*, Pennsylvania State University Press, University Park, 2005, pp. 93–112.

43 'Feminist nation-building in Afghanistan: an examination of the Revolutionary Association of the Women of Afghanistan', *Feminist Review*, 89, 2008, pp. 34–54.

44 'Struggle, perseverance, and organization in Sri Lanka's export processing zones', in K. Bronfenbrenner (ed.), *Global Unions: Challenging Transnational Capital through Cross-Border Campaigns*, Cornell University Press, Ithaca, NY, 2007, pp. 78–98.

History of international development; theories and discourse of women, gender and development

Introduction to Part One

Nalini Visvanathan

This introduction discusses significant historical events in the development arena since the mid-1990s, and links the narrative to the readings given in this section. While changes in the development establishment, mainly financial and multilateral institutions, are covered here, accounts of women's movements and organized responses to continuing gender inequities are found in an expanded Part 5. The sections that follow the history subsection address three major categories in development: Theories, Practice and Discourse. The last category presents an unconventional critique of development theory and practice.

A: Historical background

International development,[1] as an area of intellectual inquiry, can be traced to the 1950s and the post-World War II period of reconstruction. The success of the United States Marshall Plan convinced Western and Western-trained economic planners that aid-based strategic planning would enable developing countries to bridge the gap that separated them from the industrialized world.[2] High-income nations channeled monetary and technical aid through United Nations (UN) agencies, based on the theory that this aid would foster growth that would trickle down to the masses. This trickle-down approach to economic planning contributed to the failure of the development work in the first UN Development Decade (1961–70).[3] (See Rai, Ch. 1.)

Economic development (growth) is only one aspect of the human security and progress needed to lift the majority of the world's population out of poverty; however, it is external aid that often helps highlight and address deficits in national spending on health, education and vulnerable groups. The recent milestones covered here provide context for readings and references.

Reforming aid architecture From the setting up of the Bretton Woods institutions, the International Monetary Fund (IMF) and the International Bank for Reconstruction (IBRD) (World Bank), the United States took leadership of the international financial system and assumed a dominant role in decision-making within the international financial institutions (IFIs) for the first fifty years. The impact of the oil crisis (1973) and the restructuring of national economies in an interdependent world economy created national financial crises in Mexico, Russia and East Asian countries with consequences far beyond their borders (see Ghosh, Ch. 2). Initially the IFIs viewed these crises as instances of individual state failures that could be set right by stringent prescriptions. However, the Asian crisis commencing in 1998 moved the singular country focus to a regional stage and precipitated a reformation of the international financial system. The year 1999 marked a milestone in the evolution of international political and financial governance, when IFIs introduced reforms for strengthening transparency and regulation (Germain 2002). The Group of 20 was constituted to include the emerging high-growth economies of Brazil, Russia, India and China (BRIC) to assume greater responsibility in crisis prevention. Despite these changes critics see little done to dispel the selectiveness of the club or its accountability to the majority of the countries.[4]

Emerging economies as donors A longstanding history of South-to-South Cooperation (SSC) is being reshaped by new donors China, India and Brazil, accounting for almost 10 percent of aid flowing to developing countries in 2006 (ODI 2010). China's aid, which topped two billion dollars that year, is widely spread over the African continent. Brazil follows India, with one billion dollars in aid, and targets mainly lusophone countries. All three countries still receive aid and appear to follow in Japan's path from recipient to donor nation.

World Bank and global governance Structural Adjustment Programs (SAPs) initiated in the 1980s for fiscal discipline undermined social and economic development and imposed severe hardships on the most vulnerable groups; responding to their critics, the IMF and the World Bank replaced conditionality-tied loans for Heavily Indebted Poor Countries (HIPCs) with a broader strategy ostensibly promoting poverty reduction through greater self-governance. Poverty Reduction Strategy Papers (PRSPs) enjoin participatory consultation processes and were designed as strategic interventions for the HIPCs to bring transparency and accountability in highlighting neglected issues and marginalized groups. However, initial evaluation showed little evidence of women's participation and limited attention to the root causes of gender disparities.[5] A recent evaluation indicated that women, indigenous populations and the role of gender status in discriminatory practices and relations are being overlooked.[6] Feminist critics of PRSPs underscore the gap between the Bank's rhetoric and women's reality; others view it as a tool that enables the IMF to dictate macroeconomic policy and the World Bank to align social and structural policies to that framework (Cammack 2002: 45).

Aid effectiveness Fostering partnerships between agencies and groups in the North and their counterparts in the South has now become a priority for donors. The High Level Forum on Harmonization convened in 2003 initiated the first efforts to harmonize funding activities aiming for a paradigmatic change in the relations between donors and recipients. In 2005, the Paris Declaration on AID Effectiveness was endorsed by countries around the world.[7] The Third High Level Forum, in Accra, Ghana (2008), through the Accra Agenda for Action (AAA), committed countries to the five principles of aid effectiveness: ownership; alignment; harmonization; managing for development; and mutual accountability.

Millennium Development Goals At the 2000 Millennium Summit, a gathering of world leaders signed a commitment that generated the eight Millennium Development Goals (MDGs) to be met by 2015.[8] At the summit in September 2010, a UN report stressed that many nations have made both absolute progress as well as progress relative to MDG goals.[9] Three goals focus on women and girls and include gender equality and women's health. The MDGs represent an unprecedented effort to mobilize the world community to recognize the urgency of eradicating poverty and its related issues.

United Nations Agency for Gender Equality and the Empowerment of Women As we complete work on the reader, the United Nations has announced the creation of a new agency for women that consolidates the work of four longstanding UN agencies working on different aspects of women's development.[10] The 1995 Beijing Platform of Action calling for Women's Equality is in effect the agenda for the new agency, which opens next year.

Global crisis The 2008 global financial crisis has deepened across the world, undermining economic and food security, destroying livelihoods in urban and rural areas, and affecting particularly women workers.[11]

It exacerbates the triple crisis in climate, food and energy that activists had long exposed (Shiva 2008). Financial crises have multiplied during this period of neoliberal globalization, sometimes threatening the foundations of state and society as was the case in Argentina in 2001; the IMF has tallied 158 financial crises between 1975 and 1997 (Young 2003: 103). Governments are responding with social provisioning strategies such as cash transfers and legislative actions like India's National Rural Employment Guarantee Act (NREGA) as we await the emergence of a more just and equitable order for women.

Readings In Chapter 1 Shirin Rai's historical overview encompasses the role of the newly emerging post-colonial states, their elite leaders and their vision for national development. Her account frames political events and economic processes that joined visionary leaders and their liberated people in a quest for material and human progress, rendering a rich contextual introduction to the development project.

In Chapter 2, Jayati Ghosh provides a concise overview of the history of financial crises during the last few decades, the conditions that precipitate them and their impact on countries in the global South. Her essay discusses the ramifications of a financial crisis brought about by a dominant neoliberal growth model and emphasizes the gendered nature of the detrimental impact, particularly for women, drawing on historical experiences and the current economic situation.

B: Theories

In 1997, an exposition of the radical political economy approach was critical in distinguishing progressive philosophy from the capitalist paradigm and elucidating the polarized ideologies that shaped the preceding decades. This edition of the reader is broadly grounded in feminist political economy (FPE) and variants from discipline-specific theorizing.[12] Riley (2008) clarifies and defines FPE: 'Feminist political economy is one among several heterodox economics that challenge the reigning orthodox neo-liberal economic model which emphasizes the market economy with growth and accumulation as its primary goals. FPE, in contrast, focuses on the provisioning of human needs and human well-being.'[13] She underscores the stress placed on gendered analysis in FPE frames.

In their introduction to a special issue of *Signs* dedicated to feminist political economy, Bedford and Rai (2010) decry the continuing absence of gendered concerns within mainstream international political economy. They underscore a critical feminist analysis of systems of production and exchange and also examine gendered governance, the neglect of women's role in social reproduction and the dominance of normative heterosexuality even within feminist political economy discourse and debate.

The concept of social reproduction has evolved from its early interpretation, as biological reproduction and household work for reproducing and sustaining the labor force, found in multidisciplinary historical Marxist feminist theorizing.[14] Folbre (2001) broadens the theoretical frame for 'Care,' to include 'reproduction' work services provided in the market (private) and by the state (public). Razavi's (2007) 'care diamond,' which builds on this view, depicts the four providers of Care as the family, community, market and state. Feminist scholars (Truong et al. 2006) see the growing complexity of caring labor and recognize it as a manifestation of social relation with grounding in 'ethical and political practice.'

The migration of healthcare workers from South to North has created critical shortages in countries of sub-Saharan Africa and spotlighted the care economy. Whether in local and national settings or in the care chains binding the global economy of the two hemispheres, care workers are predominantly women, vulnerable to sexual and labor exploitation (see Part 3). Lately, changing condi-

6

tions of care workers in low-income countries, where they are concentrated, are being highlighted[15] and particularly within areas of the AIDS epidemic where family caregivers are the care workers (see Part 4). In many spheres feminist scholars are re-examining social reproduction as a critical area for making progress in gender justice (Bakker and Gill 2003).

Readings Chapter 3 provides a comprehensive overview of the principal theories and frameworks that guide research and practice in the field of women, gender and development. Going beyond the political bifurcation in the theoretical domain during the Cold War period, Rai examines the emergence of critical theories and methodologies that enable progressive feminist theorizing and analyses.

Chapter 4 presents a short extract from Ester Boserup's *Women's Role in Economic Development*, which is said to have launched the subfield of women and development within development studies. The classic text is exemplified by her discussion of male and female farming systems, a widely recognized aspect of her pioneering work.[16]

Chapter 5 is an excerpt from Nancy Folbre's 'The invisible heart: care and the global economy' that explicates the concept of care as social reproduction and links it to the formal economy. Her lucid exposition of the concept is central to understanding how much of the labor produced by the world's women remains undervalued and largely uncounted.

Chapter 6 on feminist political ecology traces the fluid transformations that characterize the sustainable development arena when feminist environmentalist activists, scholars and writers steer a progressive path. Reacting to the mainstreaming of this concept after its universal acceptance in the 1990s, feminists in the South and the North have engendered an inclusive vision that encompasses those at the margins and those who are customarily excluded.

C: Practice

Tinker (1990) documents the major role that advocates and practitioners played, no less than scholars, in launching the women and development field and determining its course. The distinction between these groups is blurred when women and men practitioners, within institutions of development, seize strategic moments to address male bias in policymaking (Miller and Razavi 1998). The movement for gender equality gained momentum at the 1995 Fourth UN World Conference on Women at Beijing, and placed women's rights on the agenda for action. Since then, gender mainstreaming within the UN, the IFIs and other agencies overseeing development has gained little ground in changing deeply embedded cultural mores (see Chapter 9). This subsection highlights three major themes that have engaged practitioners in recent years: empowerment; gender equality; and violence against women.

A UN survey links gender inequalities to women's lack of resources and the consequent implications for them.[17] Among its recommendations for women's economic empowerment is the inclusion of gender in macroeconomic policies, access to full employment and decent work, greater access to productive resources such as land and housing and access to financial resources and social protection. Women's empowerment has become a ubiquitous goal for development programs at all levels, with the concept often misinterpreted or diluted. In tandem with empowering women, practitioners have worked to reduce poverty and the widespread violence against women in post-conflict environments.

In a meticulous analysis, Kabeer (1999) reviews the measurement of the multidimensional empowerment concept and separates the process view of empowerment, emphasizing decision-making, from the instrumentalist approach that requires a quantitative measurement. Kabeer (ibid.) also traces discrepant findings about microfinance's impact on women's empowerment to differences in measurement, indicator and organizational strategy.[18]

Violence against women (VAW) is viewed as a major public health problem that is globally prevalent. It ranges from minor abuse to torture and homicide, from female infanticide to elder abuse. Sex inequality leads to violence and helps to maintain the 'unequal balance of power.'[19] In conflict arenas, where their physical security is threatened, women face an increased risk of sexualized violence. UN Resolution 1325, which highlights women's vulnerability and the need to bring them into peace negotiations and reconstruction, has received mixed reports (Anderlini et al. 2010). Women in post-conflict settings undergoing reconstruction and societal reformation are also at greater risk, which can be compounded by fundamentalist forces (Kandiyoti 2007). Beyond war, women challenge the national security paradigm that brings the violence of militarism into their communities (Fukumura and Matsuoka 2002). However, it is not only the lack of physical security but also the absence of economic and social security which endangers women. A recent UN report exposes the limitations of human rights discourse and practice and recommends a political economy approach, paying attention to the structures of entitlement and to oppressive neoliberal policy environments, for understanding and eliminating VAW.[20]

Readings Chapter 7 is an overview of the phenomenal growth of microfinance in development and includes a critical feminist assessment. Nalini Visvanathan and Karla Yoder survey the historical origins of microcredit, the shifts in practice and the conditions conducive to women's empowerment.

In Chapter 8, K. Kalpana examines the Indian microfinance model using self-help groups as a vehicle for women's empowerment, which she contrasts with the popular Grameen model. She argues that group membership provides protective benefits for women and the solidarity to selectively challenge bank functionaries who manipulate their vulnerable status.

In Chapter 9, Gita Sen and Piroska Ostlin review how gender relations of power lead to gender inequalities that become powerful determinants of health. Because these unequal power relations are manifested in different settings, they argue that gender inequality must be addressed at many levels in multiple sectors and cite the success of strategic gender-sensitive policies and interventions.

Valentine Moghadam surveys women's roles and participation in peace-building and reconstruction processes in the post-conflict states of Afghanistan, Iraq and Palestine in Chapter 10. She argues for addressing the root causes of patriarchal violence against women and for bringing women into peace negotiations and state-building to ensure gender justice.

D: Discourse/language of WID

The critique of development begun in this section is continued in Part 5. This section briefly examines terminology and categories, embedded in development literature, and the neglect of race and class analysis in mainstream feminist thought. It also documents the institutionalization of heteronormative thinking in development projects and discourse.

The critique of development and its discourse has expanded over the last two decades. In his critique of WID discourse, Escobar (1995) finds that 'women' constitute a 'client category' analogous to 'peasant' and 'environment' in the mainstream development discourse. The journal *Development in Practice* critically examined the language and concepts of development in a 2007 issue; and a special issue of *Development* in 2002 was dedicated to the importance of place.

Since September 2001 the plight of Muslim women in authoritarian societies has focused much of the negative attention directed at a religious group and extended the critique of development discourse. Although they represent only a minor proportion of women workers in the South, factory workers have become the iconic symbol of capitalist exploitation generating a moralizing script among Western activists that is being challenged by critics.[21]

In development literature, race and racism have often been subsumed by colonialism, diluting the analysis and blurring distinctions of class and locally grounded hierarchies. Citing the disproportionate impact of the US subprime crisis on racial minority homeowners, Dymski (2010) argues that by not incorporating social exclusion and inclusion in their theorizing and practice development economists have misinterpreted significant aspects of the crisis.

Finally, with its origins in the mid-twentieth century, the development project has been slow to recognize new norms and diverse groups. Its orthodoxy is continually challenged by critics of heteronormativity, lesbian, gay and queer activists and scholars (Cornwall et al. 2008), as well as disability groups (Ghai 2002) and others excluded from the mainstream (Harcourt 2009). Their recognition within development discourse is growing but still far from mainstream.

Readings Chapter 11 presents a brief excerpt from Chandra Mohanty's classic essay 'Under Western eyes,' analyzing the dominance of Western economic rationalism in the WID literature. Citing examples, Mohanty shows how WID scholars have failed to differentiate between women of different classes and ethnic identity, have generalized women's subordination and have assumed that those women were a unified, coherent group.

In Chapter 12, Lila Abu-Lughod's acclaimed essay 'Do Muslim women really need saving?' critically examines the ethnocentric attitudes embedded in the Western depiction and treatment of women in the Islamic world. The author argues for sensitivity to differences and alternative pursuits of social justice.

In Chapter 13 Sarah White contends that racial disparities are conspicuous in the gender and development (GAD) project. Black feminism, which has much to offer development practitioners, has been marginalized and the expertise of international development experts is made the standard to the detriment of local staff.

In Chapter 14, Kalpana Wilson examines neoliberal cooptation of concepts such as 'agency' and 'empowerment' in GAD literature and the erasing of the place of movements in women's resistance.

Correa and Jolly explore the essentialist treatment of sexuality in society and within the development industry in Chapter 15 and argue for more progressive attitudes.

Notes

1 We recognize that 'development' is a problematic construct and use it reluctantly for lack of a better alternative.

2 The terms 'developing countries', 'lesser developed countries' (LDCs) and 'Third World' are used interchangeably. North and South refer to global regions of industrialized and non-industrialized nations.

3 See Tinker (1990) and Fraser and Tinker (2004) for accounts of the UN Development Decades and the landmark UN conferences.

4 J. Langmore and S. Fitzgerald, 'Global economic governance: addressing the democratic deficit', *Development*, 53(3), 2010, pp. 390–93.

5 E. Zuckerman and A. Garrett, 'Do Poverty Reduction Strategy Papers (PRSPs) address gender? A gender audit of 2002 PRSPs', Gender Action, Washington, DC, 2002, www.genderaction.org.

6 S. Liaquat Ali Khan, *Poverty Reduc-tion Strategy Papers: Failing minorities and indigenous peoples*, Minority Rights Group International, London, 2010.

7 www.oecd.org/document/18/0,3343, en_2649_3236398_35401554_1_1_1_1,00. html.

8 www.un.org/millenniumgoals/.

9 www.un.org/en/mdg/summit2010/.

10 UNIFEM, OSAGI, DAW and INSTRAW; www.un.org/apps/news/story. asp?NewsID=32066&Cr=women&Cr1.

11 B. Emmett, 'Paying the price for the economic crisis', Oxfam International Discussion Paper, Oxfam, Oxford, 2009.

12 Readings and literature cited have extensive bibliographies.

13 M. Riley, 'A feminist political economic framework', Center of Concern, Washington, DC, 2008.

14 See E. Edholm, O. Harris and K. Young, 'Conceptualising women', *Critique of Anthropology*, 9/10(3), 1977, pp. 101–30; L. Beneria, 'Reproduction, pro-

duction and the sexual division of labour', *Cambridge Journal of Economics*, 3(3), 1979, pp. 203–25.

15 S. Razavi and S. Staab, 'Underpaid and overworked – a cross-national perspective on care workers', *International Labor Review*, 149(4), December 2010.

16 See *The Women, Gender and Development Reader* (1997) for L. Benería and G. Sen's essay 'Accumulation, reproduction and women's role in economic development: Boserup re-visited', criticizing the lack of class analysis and historical specificity.

17 Division for the Advancement of Women (DAW), *World Survey on the Role of Women in Development: Women's Control over Economic Resources and Access to Financial Resources, including Microfinance*, United Nations, New York, 2009.

18 Ibid. N. Kabeer authored the report.

19 C. Watts and C. Zimmerman, 'Violence against women: global scope and magnitude', *Lancet*, 359, 2002, pp. 1232–7.

20 UN, 'Political economy and violence against women', Addendum to the Report of the Special Rapporteur on violence against women, its causes and consequences, Yakin Erturk, 2009, www2.ohchr.org/english/issues/women/rapporteur/docs/A.HRC.11.6.Add.6.pdf.

21 See D. M. Siddiqi, 'Do Bangladeshi factory workers need saving? Sisterhood in the post-sweatshop era', *Feminist Review*, 91, 2009, pp. 154–74; P. Ramamurthy, 'Material consumers, fabricating subjects: perplexity, global discourses and transnational feminist research practices', *Cultural Anthropology*, 18(4), 2003, pp. 524–50.

References and further reading

Abu-Lughod, L. (2010) 'The active social life of "Muslim women's rights": a plea for ethnography, not polemic, with cases from Egypt and Palestine', *Journal of Middle East Women's Studies*, 6(1): 1–45.

Afshar, H. and D. Eade (eds) (2004) *Development, Women, and War. Feminist Perspectives*, Oxford: Oxfam GB.

Agarwal, B. (1992) 'The gender and environment debate: lessons from India', *Feminist Studies*, 18(1).

— (1994) *A Field of One's Own: Gender and Land Rights in South Asia*, Cambridge: Cambridge University Press.

— (1998) 'Environmental action, equity and ecofeminism: debating India's experience', *Journal of Peasant Studies*, 25(4): 55–95.

Agustin, L. (2007) *Sex at the Margins: Migration, Labour Markets and the Rescue Industry*, London: Zed Books.

Anderlini, S. N. et al. (2010) 'What the women say: participation and UNSCR 1325', Cambridge: ICAN-MIT, web.mit.edu/cis/pdf/WomenReport_10_2010.pdf.

Bakker, I. (2007) 'Social reproduction and the constitution of a gendered political economy', *New Political Economy*, 12(4): 541–56.

Bakker, I. and S. Gill (eds) (2003) *Power, Production, and Social Reproduction: Human in/security in the global political economy*, New York: Palgrave Macmillan.

Bakker, I. and R. Silvey (eds) (2008) *Beyond States and Markets. The challenges of social reproduction*, New York: Routledge.

Bedford, K. and S. M. Rai (2010) 'Feminists theorize international political economy', *Signs*, 36: 1.

Bhavnani, K. (2001) *Feminism and Race*, Oxford: Oxford University Press.

Bhavnani, K., J. Foran and P. A. Kurian (eds) (2003) *Feminist Futures: Reimagining Women, Culture and Development*, London: Zed Books.

Cammack, P. (2002) 'The mother of all governments; the World Bank's matrix for global governance', in R. Wilkinson (ed.), *Global Governance: Critical Perspectives*, London: Routledge.

Chen, M. A. (ed.) (1998) *Widows in India: Social neglect and public action*, New Delhi: Sage Publications.

Chen, M. A., J. Vanek and M. Carr (2004) *Mainstreaming Informal Employment and Gender in Poverty Reduction*,

London: Commonwealth Secretariat and IDRC.

Cornwall, A. and A. Welbourn (2002) *Realizing Rights. Transforming Approaches to Sexual and Reproductive Well-being*, London: Zed Books.

Cornwall, A., S. Jolly and S. Correa (2008) *Development with a Body: Sexuality, Human Rights and Development*, London: Zed Books.

Dymski, G. A. (2010) 'Development as social inclusion: reflections on the US subprime crisis', *Development*, 53(3): 368–75.

Escobar, A. (1995) *Encountering Development: The Making and Unmaking of the Third World*, Princeton, NJ: Princeton University Press.

Fan, C. C. (2003) 'Rural–urban migration and gender division of labor in transitional China', *International Journal of Urban and Regional Research*, 27(1): 24–47.

Folbre, N. (2001) *The Invisible Heart*, New York: New Press.

Fraser, A. and I. Tinker (eds) (2004) *Developing Power. How Women Transformed International Development*, New York: Feminist Press.

Fukumura, Y. and M. Matsuoka (2002) 'Okinawa women's resistance to U.S. militarism', in N. Naples and M. Desai, *Women's Activism and Globalization*, New York: Routledge.

Germain, R. D. (2002) 'Reforming the international financial architecture: the new political agenda', in R. Wilkinson (ed.), *Global Governance: Critical Perspectives*, London: Routledge.

Ghai, A. (2002) 'Disabled women: an excluded agenda of Indian feminism', *Hypatia*, 17(3), Summer.

Ghosh, J. and C. P. Chandrasekhar (2003) *Work and Well-being in the Age of Finance*, New Delhi: Tulika Books.

Gilmartin, C., G. Hershatter, L. Rofel and T. White (2005) *Engendering China: Women, Culture and the State*, Cambridge, MA: Harvard University Press.

Grown, C., E. Braunstein and A. Malhotra (2006) *Trading Women's Health and Rights. Trade Liberalization and Reproductive Health in Developing Economies*, London: Zed Books.

Harcourt, W. (1994) *Feminist Perspectives on Sustainable Development*, London: Zed Books.

— (2009) *Body Politics in Development*, London: Zed Books.

Jackson, C. and R. Pearson (1998) *Feminist Visions of Development*, New York: Routledge.

Jaquette, J. S. and G. Summerfield (2006) *Women and Gender Equity in Development Theory and Practice*, Durham, NC: Duke University Press.

Kabeer, N. (1994) *Reversed Realities: Gender Hierarchies in Development Thought*, London: Verso.

— (1999) 'Resources, agency, achievements: reflections on the measurement of women's empowerment', *Development and Change*, 30: 435–64.

Kandiyoti, D. (2007) 'Old dilemmas or new challenges? The politics of gender and reconstruction in Afghanistan', *Development and Change*, 38(2): 169–99.

Kerr, J. and C. Sweetman (2003) *Women Reinventing Globalisation*, Oxford: Oxfam GB.

Lin, C. (2006) *The Transformation of Chinese Socialism*, Durham, NC: Duke University Press.

Lind, A. (2010) *Development, Sexual Rights and Global Governance*, New York: Routledge.

Marchand, M. H. and A. S. Runyan (2000) *Gender and Global Restructuring*, New York: Routledge

Meintjes, S., A. Pillay and M. Turshen (2005) *The Aftermath. Women in Post-Conflict Transformation*, London: Zed Books.

Menon, N. (1999) *Gender and Politics in India*, New Delhi: Oxford University Press.

— (2007) (ed.) *Sexualities*, London: Zed Books.

Miller, C. and S. Razavi (eds) (1998) *Missionaries and Mandarins*, London: Intermediate Technology Publications & UNRISD.

Moghadam V. M. (2010a) 'Gender, politics, and women's empowerment', in C. Jenkins and K. T. Leicht (eds), *Blackwell Handbook of Politics*, London and New York: Blackwell.

— (2010b) 'Women and democracy: reflections on the Middle East and North Africa', in G. Di Marco and C. Tabbush (eds), *Feminisms, Democratization and Radical Democracy*, Buenos Aires: UNSAMEDITA (University of San Martin Press, Argentina, in English and Spanish)

Moser, C. O. N. (1993) *Gender Planning and Development*, New York: Routledge.

ODI (2010) 'Brazil: an emerging aid player', *Briefing Paper* 64, London: Overseas Development Institute. www. odi.org.uk.

Porter, F. and C. Sweetman (2005) *Mainstreaming Gender in Development. A Critical Review*, Oxford: Oxfam GB.

Quisumbing, A. R. (2003) *Household Decisions, Gender, and Development*, Washington, DC: International Food Policy Research Institute.

Rai, S. (2002) *Gender and the Political Economy of Development*, Oxford: Polity Press.

Razavi, S. (2002) *Shifting Burdens. Gender and Agrarian Change under Neoliberalism*, Bloomfield, CT: Kumarian Press.

— (2007) 'Political and social economy of care in a development context; gender and development', Programme Paper 3, Geneva: UNRISD.

Sen, G. and C. Crown (1987) *Development, Crises and Alternative Visions: Third World Women's Perspectives*, New York: Monthly Review Press.

Sen, G. and P. Ostlin (2010) *Gender Equity in Health: The Shifting Frontiers of Evidence and Action*, Routledge: New York.

Shepherd, L. J. (2008) *Gender, Violence and Security*, London: Zed Books.

Shiva, V. (1988) *Staying Alive. Women, Ecology and Survival*, London, Zed Books.

— (2008) *Soil Not Oil. Climate Change, Peak Oil and Food Insecurity*, London: Zed Books.

Squires, J. (2007) *The New Politics of Gender Equality*, New York: Palgrave Macmillan.

Tinker, I. (1990) *Persistent Inequalities*, New York: Oxford University Press.

Tinker, I. and G. Summerfield (eds) (1999) *Women's Rights to House and Land: China, Laos, Vietnam*, Boulder, CO: Lynne Rienner Publishers.

Truong, T., S. Wieringa and A. Chhachhi (2006) *Engendering Human Security. Feminist Perspectives*, London: Zed Books.

UNDP (2010) *Power, Voice and Rights. A Turning Point for Gender Equality in Asia and the Pacific*, Delhi: Macmillan, http://hdr.undp.org/en/reports/regional/asiathepacific/RHDR-2010-AsiaPacific.pdf.

Young, B. (2003) 'Financial crises and social reproduction: Asia, Argentina and Brazil', in I. Bakker and S. Gill, *Power, Production and Social Reproduction*, New York: Palgrave Macmillan.

Young, K. (1993) 'Planning from a gender perspective', in *Planning Development with Women*, New York: St Martin's Press.

1 | The history of international development: concepts and contexts[1]

Shirin M. Rai

The origins of development

Development is a relatively recent concept but one burdened by history (Woolcock et al. 2009). Development was brought into focus in President Truman's speech in which he claimed for the West the geopolitical space of development with the rest marked as 'underdeveloped areas':

> ... we must embark on a bold new program for making the benefits of our scientific advances and industrial progress available for the improvement and growth of underdeveloped areas. More than half the people of the world are living in conditions approaching misery. Their food is inadequate. They are victims of disease. Their economic life is primitive and stagnant. Their poverty is a handicap and a threat both to them and to more prosperous areas ... I believe that we should make available to peace-loving peoples the benefits of our store of technical knowledge in order to help them realize their aspirations for a better life. (20 January 1949)[2]

Dividing up the world in this way laid the foundations of not only the policy terrain of development but also the theoretical frames within which development has been conceived as well as critiqued.

The origins of development can be studied within two overlapping contexts. The first was that of the Second World War and the emerging post-war world order with the deepening ideological fissures between the socialist and the capitalist worlds as well as the consolidation of post-war hierarchies of power in the international system. The second was the context of the nationalist struggles and of the processes through which post-colonial states came into being and approached modernizing and development agendas. Both contexts were deeply gendered and framed gender relations; in both contexts the assumptions of universality led to a gender blindness which translated into particular modalities of gendered modernities and development.

The international divide

The post-Second World War world was a divided world, where a cold war took over from the military conflict that preceded it. The (in)famous 'Domino

Theory' was the political articulation of this perceived threat, while at the economic level there was a recognition that the question of poverty would have to be tackled in response to this challenge. The Labour victory in the UK and the Marshall Plan were also indicative of the aspirations of the people in the post-war new world order, on the one hand, and the serious competition for influence to shape that world on the other. Through the 1950s, as the post-colonial world took shape, political alliances were based on the growing clash of ideologies. Revolutionary movements that culminated in the formation of socialist states, such as in China, were automatically seen as potential allies of the Soviet Union. Aid packages and trade regimes were often tied to perceived security concerns, making the attempts of the newly emerging nation-states to articulate their development plans contingent upon international politics. This state of affairs continued until 1991 when the Soviet Union imploded and with it also collapsed its satellite states in eastern Europe. In sum, the cold war between the two superpowers and the two ideological configurations had a direct impact on the alternatives that post-colonial elites felt able to consider and pursue. The ideological divide and the resulting security concerns led to different outcomes reflected in the institutionalization of the international economic and financial regimes, which continue to frame development policies on a global level. The Bretton Woods Conference was held in 1944, as the first phase of decolonization was about to begin with the independence of India in 1947. It resulted in the establishment of the two institutions that have played a central role in crafting development agendas in direct and indirect ways – the World Bank, and the International Monetary Fund. These institutions were set up to promote stable exchange rates, foster the growth of world trade, and facilitate international movements of capital. Their concern was to avoid the shortcomings of the pre-war international economic system such as protectionism, and competitive devaluations through the regulation of international financial markets. In the post-war period, the development focus of these institutions remained Europe and Japan. Their voting systems gave clear control to the larger contributors – the Western industrialized countries – thus marginalizing the emerging post-colonial nations (South Commission 1990). The Bretton Woods system was as much a response to the failures of the past as to the challenges of the present.

Together with the emergence of two ideological camps in the period of the Cold War, there also emerged 'Three Worlds'. The polarized worlds of the Western and the Soviet blocs were called the First and Second worlds, and the non-aligned countries trying to chart their own models of development, such as India and Tanzania, and later Yugoslavia, were the Third World. These countries came together for the first time at the Bandung Conference in 1955 to assert their identity, and to propose what we might today call a Third Way between capitalist and Marxist development models. The name

Group of 77 also described these states at the time of the setting up of the UN Conference on Trade and Development (UNCTAD) in 1964. However, the unity between these countries could not be maintained for long as pressures of ethnic, religious and cultural historical divisions led to conflict between some. Increasingly, in the 1970s, the term Third World came to mark post-coloniality, and also economic position within the world system. GNP per head became the determinant of which of the three worlds a country belonged to, with the lowest GNP per capita economies placed in the Third World category. What the countries belonging to this category shared then was a history of colonial exploitation that allowed them to identify with each other; however, different colonial histories and processes of decolonization also led to fracturing of a sense of solidarity among these nations.[3]

Development and/as modernization

However, there were also some unsurprising similarities between the two sides in their approaches to development. First, whether liberal or communist, both believed that development was a purposeful project – with 'resources, techniques and expertise ... brought together to bring about improved rates of economic growth ...' (Kabeer 1994: 69), which was the main target, and development agendas were geared to increasing its levels. There is a linearity that marks both types of development processes too. For the communists, development accrued when a country moved from a capitalist form to a socialist form of social relations, from the anarchy of the market to the certainty of planning. For the liberals, development occurred when human and physical resources could be developed through the force of rational individualism and the development of market-regulated competition. Second, for both sides, economic growth was tied to industrialization and urbanization of economies and societies. Mechanization of agriculture, the building of dams, and a general valorization of Science were common to both ideological camps. Both liberal and Marxist theories have in common elements of a reductionist methodology, with its determinate outcomes, its linearity, and hierarchies of knowledge leading to constructions of regimes of Truth. All these features, together with the political systems and ideologies arising out of this rationalizing discourse on development, had consequences for the relations of power within the newly emerging nations – especially relations between men and women, and between maginalized communities and the dominant groups. This is not to suggest that the differences between the two ideological frameworks were cosmetic. However, the similarities in the two approaches did create an international consensus around what development meant, even though the route by which this definition was arrived at was ideologically specific. Development became a metanarrative and, at the same time, a particular stage of economic viability.

These ideological frames of course also left an imprint on the study of development. For example, although by the 1960s China had developed an alternative model of development – alternative to both capitalism and Soviet-style socialism – this model is absent from the debates about development. No standard development texts explore the development experiments that were conducted in China – the land reform after 1949, the Great Leap Forward and the debates on development after its failure (Gray 1995) – which made a tremendous impact on other Third World states at the time. One reason, perhaps, was the absence of socialist China from international fora; Taiwan (Republic of China) took the 'Chinese' seat in the Security Council of the United Nations. A second reason for a refusal to engage with the Chinese model of development was its challenge – in terms of both rhetoric and politics – to both capitalist models of development and the Soviet-style centralized model. As an international pariah, China and its leadership were not taken seriously by either camp in the Cold War-dominated world.

What is clear in the brief outline of the origins of development is that it was insensitive to gendered power relations that are operative within its frame.[4] The successful post-colonial nationalist elites saw themselves as participants in the regeneration of their countries through gaining independence from the colonial rulers and envisioning a 'progressive', 'modern' 'industrialized' state (Rai 2002). Indeed, the role of the state, of planning, of regulation and of rationality, was constantly emphasized in the nationalist rhetoric (see Mao Zedong 1941; Nehru 1990; Nyerere 1973), while overlooking and marginalizing the alternative visions of development that were articulated by subaltern publics (Sarkar 1983). Such visions of modernity had direct consequences for structuring gender relations in post-colonial states. The emphasis on industrialization, for example, meant that the focus remained on male employment; the acceptance of commercialization and mechanization of agriculture meant the marginalization of women's work in rural societies, and the 'taming of nature' by construction of dams across rivers – Nehru called these the 'temples of modern India' – for the production of electricity meant the displacement of populations resulting in particular vulnerabilities for women. Other than in the Marxist nationalist states, private property was taken as given. In terms of agrarian gender relations it meant that women could rarely inherit under recognized or accepted 'cultural' regimes, and this further supported the 'traditional' or modified colonial legal arrangements.

The linear and gendered discourse of development was, as noted above, institutionalized through both state policies and international institutions with particular gendered outcomes. State-led development led to concentration of power in the hands of the elite and the marginalization of the subaltern publics; the North–South divide congealed in policy and development frameworks proposed and implemented by the Bretton Woods institutions. This made for a powerful alliance that was kept in place by the philosophical convergence that equated modernity with development. The challenges to this dominant discourse came from different quarters and were variously successful in disturbing its power. Development remains, however, bound to its originary moments even as it adjusts to the challenges posed by globalization.

Mapping development

Development continues to be linked to economics – growth, modernization, industrialization, trade, the income of nations and the poverty of populations map the development of countries in the World Bank annual reports. Critiques of this economic focus have stretched the boundaries of development to include education and health in the UNDP's Human Development Index (HDI) starting in 1990 and gendered critiques of development resulted in the introduction in 1995 of the Gender-related Development Index (GDI) and Gender Empowerment Measure, which measures achievement in the same basic capabilities as the HDI does, but takes note of inequality in achievement as well as agency between women and men (hdr.undp.org/en/statistics/indices/gdi_gem/). Time has been an important element in mapping economic development – the pace of change has been slow or rapid, leading to different challenges and outcomes; for colonized nations the introduction of industry and commercialization of agriculture were rapid, changing the social relations on the ground and creating both opportunities and tensions that were politically difficult to cope with.

The early articulations of economic development built upon capitalist social and political contexts – the argument was that capitalist growth was built upon the idea of democratic governance which allowed for the efficient functioning of market relations. Economic and political development then were seen to go hand in hand – first the challenge of the socialist bloc and then the 'third wave' of democratization consolidated arguments in this regard; political conditionalities of democratic or 'good' governance that were imposed on aid-receiving countries institutionalized this link (World Bank 1994). Political hierarchies were also mapped through the examination of the international system and how this impinged upon the development of the poor nations – the continued dependency of these countries on the powerful nations was articulated through the 'dependency theory', which suggested that it was the terms of trade of the international system which underpinned economic inequalities rather than any lack of democratic governance and that a 'delinking' from the capitalist world order was the key to the development of the poorer/ peripheral states (Frank 1969; Amin 1970). The oil crisis in 1972/73 that led to the debt crisis when Mexico defaulted on its debt payments in 1982, which in turn resulted in the economic bail-out of Third World states through the structural adjustment policies (SAPs) of the 1980s promoted and implemented by and through the Bretton Woods institutions, underlined this dependence for some and the importance of liberalizing economies for others. That in hindsight SAPs are seen to have failed to stimulate sustainable growth in the affected countries did not change these political positions. In face of the sharp critiques of SAPs, the 1990s saw a shift to Poverty Reduction Strategy Papers (PRSPs), which focused on the role of the state, good governance, 'country ownership' of liberalization policies and poverty alleviation. While this shift suggested nothing new in terms of relations of dependence in the international economy for the critics of market liberalization, PRSPs were put forward as the 'human face' of market economies by their proponents.

Development thus came to be associated with particular discursive frames, the unpacking of which led to struggles over meanings of development and its translations into policy – underdeveloped, developing, Third World, the global South are all terms that are used to describe the poorer nations of the world. The struggles over terms were about the way in which development was envisioned. The development imaginary reflected the dominant power relations as well as the challenges to these. The questions that were posed suggested that poverty can be as much of the economy as of ideas and culture; formal democratic politics that does not encourage direct participation in setting development agendas can only be limited in its scope. With globalization and the rise of 'emerging markets' that had been lumped together as 'developing countries' the distinctions between the first, second and third worlds began to crumble and new discursive challenges arose – the term global South suggested a greater interdependence between different geopolitical spaces (Escobar 1995; Crush 1995). Questions were also raised about whether development itself was a concept whose time had gone – post-development literature challenged the value of development as we know it, with its state-led, top-down approach to market-led economic growth (Pieterse 2000).

Feminist critiques of development also found voice during these phases of critiques. They built on Marxist analyses of how women's work subsidizes capital accumulation (Mackintosh 1984), they pointed to how the invisibility of women in development processes led to policy imbalances (Boserup 1970), how the non-accounting of women's domestic work secured their dependence on men and bolstered the 'family wage' model with the male breadwinner assumed as the head of household (Waring 1988) and how male bias in development was institutionalized (Elson 1995). Despite these significant gains in institutional politics, the indicators of economic inequality pertaining to gender have continued to persist and even grow (Rai 2008). The International Labour Organization estimates that GDP growth did not translate into decent employment – 'of the more than 2.8 billion workers in the world, 1.4 billion still did not earn enough to lift themselves and their families above the US$2 a day poverty line – just as many as 10 years ago'.[5] Women's employment continues to lag behind that of men; the fact that women's work within the home is not counted as part of a nation's income underlines the gap between male and female employment. Gender segregation of work and wage differentials between men and women continue to haunt the labour market, despite women making up around 40 per cent of the global workforce; 2 per cent of farmers are registered as women, despite the full participation of women in farming, especially among poor peasant households. Oxfam has reported that over ninety countries did not meet the deadline of 2005 for eliminating gender disparity in primary and secondary education. Reviewing the progress on the Millennium Development Goals, the UN secretary-general admitted that the least progress was made on gender equality and that 'there has been little progress in reducing maternal deaths; maternal mortality declined only marginally, from 480 deaths per 100,000 live births in 1990 to 450 in 2005. At this rate, the target of 120 deaths per 100,000 live births by 2015 cannot be achieved' (www.un.org/ga/search/view_doc.asp?symbol=A/64/665).

The context of development – economic and political as well as discursive – has therefore shifted over a period of time with significant outcomes for different groups of nations and peoples. The initial concern of development with poverty and growth remains relevant today even though critics continue to point to the dangers of increasing inequalities in the world and to the injuries that these cause. Despite a strong gender critique of development and some progress in mainstreaming this in development frameworks, policies and institutions, women continue to bear the brunt of poverty, ill health and lack of opportunities. Alternative development agendas proliferate at a time when the convergence of liberal agendas of development also strengthens. The challenge of and to development remains.

Notes

1 This chapter builds on Chapter 2 of *Gender and the Political Economy of Development*, Polity Press, Cambridge, 2002.

2 The post-colonial elites too bought into this discourse of developed versus underdeveloped nations. Nehru writes in *Discovery of India*: 'India, as well as China, must learn from the West for the modern West has much to teach, and the spirit of the age is represented by the West' (1990: 384–5).

3 I use the term Third World, as well as the more recently crafted term South, to denote post-colonial and poor countries of the world. This is as much to indicate their economic position as to acknowledge their evolving histories.

4 There is also of course the absence of the subaltern approaches to development, which have been so well critiqued by the 'subaltern studies' school of historians (Guha 1982).

5 'ILO annual jobs report says global unemployment continues to grow, youth now make up half those out of work'; www-lomirror.cornell.edu/public/english/bureau/inf/pr/2006/1.htm.

References

Amin, S. (1970) *L'accumulation à l'échelle mondiale; critique de la théorie du sous-développement*, Dakar: IFAN. Translated by Brian Pearce as *Accumulation on a World Scale: A Critique of the Theory of Underdevelopment*, New York: Monthly Review Press, 1974.

Boserup, E. (1970) *Woman's Role in*

Economic Development (new edn 1989), London: Earthscan.

Crush, J. (ed.) (1995) *The Power of Development*, London: Routledge.

Elson, D. (1995) *Male Bias in the Development Process*, Manchester: Manchester University Press.

Escobar, A. (1995) 'Imagining a post-development era', in J. Crush (ed.), *Power of Development*, London: Routledge.

Frank, A. G. (1969) *Capitalism and Underdevelopment in Latin America: Historical Studies of Chile and Brazil*, New York: Monthly Review Press.

Gray, J. (1995) *Enlightenment's Wake*, London: Routledge.

Guha, R. (ed.) (1982) *Subaltern Studies: Writings on South Asian history and society*, Delhi and Oxford: Oxford University Press.

Kabeer, N. (1994) *Reversed Realities: Gender Hierarchies in Development Thought*, London: Verso.

Mackintosh, M. (1984) 'Gender and economics: the sexual division of labour and the subordination of women', in K. Young, C. Wolkowitz and R. McCullah (eds), *Of Marriage and the Market: Women's Subordination Internationally and Its Lessons*, London: Routledge and Kegan Paul.

Mao Zedong (1941) 'On contradictions', in *Selected Works*, vol. 2, Beijing: People's Publishing House.

Nehru, J. L. (1990) *The Discovery of India*, Oxford: Oxford University Press.

Nyerere, J. K. (1973) *Freedom and Development: A Selection from Writings and Speeches*, Dar es Salaam: Oxford University Press.

Pieterse, J. N. (ed.) (2000) *Global Futures: Shaping Globalization*, London: Zed Books.

Rai, S. (2002) *Gender and the Political Economy of Development*, Oxford: Polity Press.

— (2008) *The Gender Politics of Development*, London, Zed Books.

Sarkar, S. (1983) *Modern India, 1885–1947*, Delhi: Macmillan India Ltd.

South Commission (1990) *The Challenge to the South: The report of the South Commission*, Oxford: Oxford University Press.

Waring, M. (1988) *If Women Counted: A New Feminist Economics*, San Francisco, CA: Harper and Row.

Woolcock, M., S. Szreter and V. Rao (2009) 'How and why does history matter for development policy', BWPI Working Paper 68, Manchester: Brooks World Poverty Institute, University of Manchester.

World Bank (1994) *Good Governance*, Washington, DC: World Bank.

2 | Financial crises and the impact on women: a historical note

Jayati Ghosh

The nature of financial crises

A financial crisis is, in essence, a situation in which a group of economic agents have liabilities (such as debt) that they cannot repay, and this inability to pay then affects the financial viability of those holding these claims. National financial crises can result when depositors lose confidence in their banks and start a panicked rush to withdraw money, thereby starting a spiralling movement; they are created when the stock market collapses, especially after soaring to dramatic heights, or when a government defaults on a loan from external sources (Chandrasekhar 2010).

The proliferation of financial crises actually reflects the rise to dominance of finance, which in turn can be seen as part of a wider political economy process, a result of the attempt in developed capitalism to use the expansion of finance in the economy or 'financialization' (Epstein 2005; Fine 2010; Foster 2010) to counter the inherent tendencies towards periods of slow economic growth or no growth (stagnation) in mature capitalism. Financialization enables and encourages the greater frequency of speculative bubbles in which asset prices rise and create the illusion of greater wealth. This keeps effective demand growing, even when wage incomes are stagnating. At the same time, the dominance of finance also contributes to overall stagnationary tendencies that are concealed by the periodic bubbles that it generates (Patnaik 2003). When finance is mobile across countries, it constrains the economic policies of nation-states, making it harder to raise tax rates or run large government deficits because of fear of capital flight. This in turn means that governments find it harder to spend money that would directly and indirectly increase employment and economic activity in the system as a whole, and also makes it more difficult to pull the economy out of a slump through more government spending.

It is no accident that the period of the rise to dominance of finance is also the period of the hegemony of neoliberal ideology, which has pushed a shift in the nature of state involvement away from attempting to provide social and economic rights of citizens to ensuring conditions of profitability for large capital, especially finance. Even though the hegemony of finance is associated with greater instability and economic injustice, its political power

22

and ability to affect state policies tend to be largely unconstrained, as the current global crisis shows.

Periodic financial crises have marked the history of some regions such as Latin America for more than a century (Eichengreen and Kindert 1992). They have become more widespread across the developing world since the early 1980s, especially in more financially open and deregulated developing economies. Financial liberalization has resulted in an increase in financial fragility in developing countries, making them prone to periodic financial and currency crises (Ghosh 2005). In addition, the emergence of universal banks or financial supermarkets increases the degree of entanglement of banks with other financial companies such as mutual funds, hedge funds and insurance companies, which in turn increases the possibility of domino effects of individual financial failures.[1] The major financial crises of the recent past in the developing world – the 1982 Latin American debt crisis, the 1994 Mexican crisis, the Southeast Asian financial crisis of 1997/98, the 2001 Argentine crisis – can be described as resulting from under-regulated financial markets (Palma 1998).

The global financial crisis that started in 2008 was relatively novel in that it originated in the core of capitalism (specifically in the USA), although its ramifications were rapidly felt across the world, even in developing countries that had tried to impose greater discipline upon their own domestic financial systems. This occurred first through declines in exports, since the USA was the main source of demand for global exports. This led to job losses in export production and then in related sectors as the negative effects of those job losses were felt in domestic demand. Private capital flows became volatile and caused stock markets to fall and banks in developing countries to face problems. As tax revenues fell, governments were less able to spend more, and some even cut back on their expenditure, especially in critical areas like health, sanitation and nutrition. The period was also one of very great volatility in food and fuel prices, and the increases in these prices were transmitted to developing countries, affecting the real incomes of most citizens.

The gendered impact of financial crises

The effects of the crisis tend to be disproportionately distributed among the population, with certain vulnerable groups, including women and girls, much worse affected than more secure or privileged sections. Financial crises tend to deliver the most harm to those who had usually gained the least from the preceding boom, by reducing wages and chances of employment, destroying livelihoods, and constraining public provision of essential goods and services.

Gender discrimination tends to be intertwined with other forms of social and economic disparity, such that region, location, community, social category and occupation also typically determine the extent of deprivation of women and girls. Even so, there are critical differences in the impact of such crises on men and women, determined largely by the greater significance of women in social reproduction and the care economy as well as their greater involvement in more vulnerable forms of paid work. The impact of financial crises on women can therefore be considered in terms of their roles as paid workers, unpaid workers, members of households, citizens with rights and individuals with needs, wants and aspirations.

The most immediate direct impact of the crisis is usually on employment [see Part 4]. Where exports are hit and more women are involved in export-oriented production, it is only to be expected that women will be disproportionately affected. But usually the impact extends beyond this.

During the Asian financial crisis of 1997/98, women workers were the first to be laid off even in non-exporting sectors, because of the job segregation that put them in the low-paying and more 'flexible' activities unlike the more diversified and relatively more secure occupations of male workers. For example, women were laid off at seven times the rate of men in South Korea in 1998/99 (Seguino 2009), and evidence from the crisis of 2008/09 also points to a similar tendency in other Asian countries (Chibber et al. 2009).

Wages are hit for a number of reasons. The pressure on employers to compete in an increasingly hostile environment gets associated with attempts to reduce labour costs by driving down wages and forcing remaining workers to work for longer hours, often for less pay. This is made easier by the expansion of open unemployment. Two other categories of women workers deserve special mention: women cultivators and women working in the informal sector and as home-based workers.

Farming sector

In the developing world as a whole, the majority of women workers are in farming, either as cultivators or agricultural workers. The impact of the crisis on agriculture is often much more severe than is recognized, also because the patterns of late capitalist development since the last two decades of the twentieth century have been associated with more or less continuous agrarian crisis. Such crises were related to public policies from the early 1990s onwards that systematically reduced the protection afforded to farmers and exposed them to import competition and market volatility. Trade liberalization meant that farmers had to operate in a highly uncertain and volatile international environment. Volatile crop prices also generated misleading price signals, causing large and often undesirable shifts in cropping pattern which ultimately rebounded on the farmers themselves. The associated increase in debt (often to private moneylenders) then became a major drag on the viability of cultivation.

All these difficulties are heightened in the case of women farmers, because in many countries, especially in the developing world, lack of land titles and other recognition has tended to deprive them of benefits such as access to institutional credit, extension services and subsidized inputs. They therefore tend to have higher costs of cultivation than their male counterparts, and less state protection; they are also likely to be deprived of the benefits of any crisis relief packages in the absence of specific measures.

Informal work

Women in informal work are especially badly affected in periods of crisis. As opportunities for paid employment dwindle, in many countries women workers turn to home-based subcontracting activities, or work in very small units that do not even constitute manufactories, often on a piece-rate basis and usually very poorly paid and without any known non-wage benefits. This was evident in all the countries that suffered from the Asian crisis (Ghosh and Chandrasekhar 2009) and was repeated during the 2008/09 recession, as the economic downswing tends to be directly reflected in both declining orders or contracts and falling rates of remuneration. There is typically also a decline in access to credit for self-employed women, as the meagre institutional credit that they could earlier access tends to dry up and non-institutional sources of credit become more precarious, difficult and expensive. This causes costs to increase even as small producers are forced to reduce prices of their goods and services in order to compete in increasingly adverse market conditions. Floro and Dymski (2000) have shown how financial crises can change gender relations through intra-household adjustments.

Migrant workers

Women migrant workers have been growing in quantitative importance throughout the past half-century, both within and across borders, and for both short-term and long-term periods. Crises have less of a direct impact on female migrant workers than on men, because of the gendered nature of migration, especially cross-border migration. Male migrants go in dominantly for employment in manufacturing and construction sectors, while women migrants are concentrated in the service sectors, such as the care economy broadly defined (including activities such as nursing and domestic work) and 'entertainment'. Thus job losses in the North during the 2008/09 crisis were concentrated in construction, financial services and manufacturing, all dominated by male workers. By contrast female migrants workers' incomes are more stable over the cycle and do not immediately rise or fall to the same extent (Ghosh 2009). However, migrant workers are often targeted in periods of heightened economic instability, when local residents feel that they are taking away jobs in a difficult labour market.

Informal sector and the care economy

The unpaid labour of women is directly and indirectly affected by financial crisis. The extent of unpaid work and the conditions of such work are crucially affected by the state of physical and social infrastructure, access to natural resources such as water and fuel and to basic public services such as health and care services. This is why unpaid work typically tends to be more common and involve greater drudgery in poor developing countries where infrastructure is relatively undeveloped and public services are limited and inadequate.

In times of crisis it is the care economy and social reproduction in general which often acts as a socio-economic buffer (Elson 1995). [See also Part 4.] This occurs for several reasons. As household incomes decline, families are forced into different survival strategies, including the use of women's labour to provide necessities sold in the market. Financial crises tend very quickly to become fiscal crises of the state, either because of the large bail-outs that governments are forced to undertake to save major financial firms and other corporate entities, or because periods of recession involve lower tax revenues that affect fiscal deficits. Quite often, especially in the developing world, adjustment is then sought to be forced by measures such as fiscal austerity and cutting back on public spending. This typically involves raising user charges for public health, sanitation and education services and on utilities providing energy and transport. The withdrawal or reduction of access to such public services usually puts a greater burden on unpaid labour within the household, which is typically performed by women.

The same processes also affect women as members of households and as citizens, often depriving them of what may be seen as fundamental socio-economic rights. As incomes fall, access to food becomes more difficult, and in many countries this means that within the household women and girls are relatively more deprived. This has been exacerbated in the most recent crisis by the global volatility of fuel and food prices, which has caused substantial increases in food prices in many countries. Higher user charges for health and education often result in reduction or denial of access to women and girls. In most post-crisis situations, as well as the most recent one, there have been reports of withdrawal of girls from school and reduced access to medical care, including for reproductive health (King and Sweetman 2010; Chibber et al. 2009). Initial analyses (UN 2010; WHO 2009) suggest that the financial crisis and the associated cutbacks on public health expenditure and rise in food prices have all impacted adversely on the health of women and children, especially infants.

Finally, there is the impact on the physical security of women, through increased proclivity to gender-based violence and domestic violence as worsening material conditions combine with a sense of helplessness among men, who then look for outlets for their anger and frustration. The increase in violence and insecurity of women in periods of economic crisis has been noted and documented (United Nations – Human Settlements Programme 2008).

Note

1 Greater freedom to invest, including in sensitive sectors such as real estate and stock markets, ability to increase exposure to particular sectors and individual clients and increased regulatory forbearance all lead to increased instances of financial failure.

References

Chandrasekhar, C. P. (2010) 'Financial crises', in K. Basu (ed.), *Concise Oxford Companion to Economics in India*, New Delhi: Oxford University Press.

Chibber, A., J. Ghosh and T. Palanivel (2009) *The Global Financial Crisis and the Asia-Pacific Region*, Colombo: UNDP.

Eichengreen, B. and P. H. Kindert (eds) (1992) *The International Debt Crisis in Historical Perspective*, Cambridge, MA: The Press.

Elson, D. (1995) *Male Bias in the Development Process*, Manchester: Manchester University Press.

Epstein, G. (ed.) (2005) *Financialization and the World Economy*, Cheltenham: Edward Elgar.

Fine, B. (2010) 'Looking at the crisis through Marx: or is it the other way about?', in S. Kates (ed.), *The Meltdown of the World Economy: Alternative Perspectives on the Global Financial Crisis*, Northampton, MA: Edward Elgar, pp. 51–64.

Floro, M. and G. Dymski (2000) 'Financial crises, gender and power: an analytical framework', *World Development*, 28(7): 1269–83.

Foster, J. B. (2010) 'The age of monopoly finance capital', *Monthly Review*, 61(9).

Galbraith, J. K. (2010) *A Short History of Financial Euphoria*, New York: Penguin (reprint).

Ghosh, J. (2005) 'The social and economic effects of financial liberalization: a primer for developing countries', DESA Working Paper, New York: United Nations, www.un.org/esa/desa/papers/2005/wp4_2005.pdf.

— (2009) 'Migration and gender empowerment: recent trends and emerging issues', Human Development Background Paper, New York: UNDP.

Ghosh, J. and C. P. Chandrasekhar (2009) *After Crisis – Adjustment, Recovery and Fragility in East Asia*, New Delhi: Tulika Books.

King, R. and C. Sweetman (2010) 'Gender perspectives on the global economic crisis', Oxford: Oxfam International.

Palma, G. (1998) 'Three and a half cycles of "mania, panic, and [asymmetric] crash": East Asia and Latin America compared', *Cambridge Journal of Economics*, 22: 789–808.

Patnaik, P. (2003) *The Retreat to Unfreedom: Essays on the emerging world order*, New Delhi: Tulika Books.

Seguino, S. (2009) 'The global economic crisis and women', Presentation to the UN Commission on Status of Women, 53rd Session, New York, 3–15 March.

UN (United Nations) (2010) *Rethinking Poverty: Report on the World Social Situation*, New York: UN.

United Nations – Human Settlements Programme (2008) *The Global Assessment on Women's Safety*, Nairobi: UN-Habitat.

WHO (2009) *Women and Health: Today's Evidence, Tomorrow's Agenda*, Geneva: WHO.

3 | Gender and development: theoretical perspectives

Shirin M. Rai

Women in development

Women first came into focus in development as objects of welfare concerns (Moser 1993). Programmes of birth control, nutrition projects for women and children and for pregnant and lactating mothers were the focus of aid programmes. Patriarchal and liberal discourses, at both nationalist and international level, left unchallenged the question of gender relations in society, and often made these attendant upon a sexual division of labour and individual negotiation within the family. The welfarist approach remained dominant in the first phase of development practices.

Challenging the growth agenda

The predominance of the liberal paradigm was continually challenged by both internal liberal critics and by the alternative development model of state socialism. After the optimism of the 1960s, the oil crisis of the 1970s and 1980s focused attention on the issue of consumption of non-renewable natural resources, and the UN World Food Conference emphasized the need to address the question of food production rather than emphasizing the production of tradable cash crops to address the fact that violence, hunger and poverty were showing no sign of abating in the Third World. The shift in thinking about development came from three different quarters. The first was from within the liberal framework. The ILO initiated the work on development which sought to shift the focus of development from growth to fulfilment of basic human needs. In the 1980s Amartya Sen built on Basic Needs theory in his work on poverty and the concept of human entitlements and capabilities (1987) and during the 1980s there also emerged the discourse of sustainable development. The 'women in development' (WID) approach was first articulated during the 1970s and became a starting point for feminist engagements with development as discourse and as practice. The second challenge was from Marxism – alternative models of state socialist development, especially in China but also in Cuba, as well as neo-Marxist theorists who focused on the role of the post-colonial state in development and localized class struggles (Amin 1976; Sen 1982). Marxist feminists critiqued and contributed to these debates

(Mies et al. 1988). Third, there emerged in the 1980s a sustained questioning by post-structuralist critics of the development paradigm as a narrative of progress and as an achievable enterprise.

The liberal critiques: access and enablement In 1962 the UN General Assembly asked the Commission on Women's Status to prepare a report on the role of women in development. Boserup's pathbreaking study on *Women's Role in Economic Development* was published in 1970. Boserup powerfully combined an argument for equality with one for efficiency. She argued that women are marginalized in the economy because they gain less than men in their roles as wage workers, farmers and traders and that mechanization of agriculture, generally equated with economic development, has resulted in the separation of women's labour from waged agricultural labour, which in turn undermines their social status, while shifting agriculture and irrigated agriculture regimes showed high levels of women's participation in production as well as their social status. Building on Boserup's work other feminists analysed how women continued to be adversely affected by development and cultural practices such as mechanization of agriculture (Whyte and Whyte 1982). Rogers (1982) emphasized the importance of women to the development process itself; it was not only women who would benefit from expansion of opportunity, but the development process itself would better achieve its targets. This was an appeal to efficiency as much as to a better deal for women. Together, this liberal feminist analysis became the basis upon which the women in development (WID) agenda was crafted. The project was to ensure that the benefits of modernization accrued to women as well as men in the Third World.

However, WID's focus on access overlooked the importance of social and political structures within which women were located and acted. As Benería and Sen have argued, Boserup presumed that 'modernization is both beneficial and inevitable in the specific form it has taken in most Third World countries ... [She] tends to ignore processes of capital accumulation set in motion during the colonial period, and ... does not systematically analyse the different effects of capital accumulation on women of different classes' (1997: 45). What Boserup and other WID scholars offered in terms of policy insights were prescriptions regarding improving women's standards of education and skills so that they might compete more effectively with men in the labour market; the privileging of the male productive norm – which women, in this analysis, need to participate in – led to a 'truncated understanding of their lives' (Kabeer 1994: 30). By 1980 feminist scholars and activists were criticizing this access-based framework by focusing on gender relations rather than women's status and challenging the eliding of gender issues with the practice of development agencies (Pearson and Jackson 1998: 2). Despite all its problems, however, the WID theorists' work made an important correlation between work and status, which had thus far been ignored by the development agencies and governments in the West.

Meeting needs, developing capabilities, sustaining development The Basic Needs (BN) approach, which was first articulated in the 1970s, was an important contribution to the debates on development and influenced Sen and Nussbaum's capability approach, which was more gender sensitive than BN. BN queried the focus on growth and income as indicators of development. Methodologically, it put forward the idea that poverty is not an 'end' which can be eradicated by the 'means' of a higher income (Kabeer 1994: 138–40) and challenged the view that the liberal 'trickle down' approach to development resulted in a reduction of poverty and unemployment. At the World Employment Conference of 1976, the ILO proposed that *'development planning should include, as an explicit goal, the satisfaction of an absolute level of basic needs'* (1977: 31, emphasis in the original).

It was argued by BN theorists that basic needs are both physical – minimum levels of calorie consumption, for example – as well as intangible, what Sen was to call 'agency achievements' – of participation, empowerment and community life (1987). Thus development economics, in emphasizing longevity and neglecting the quality of life, was flawed and redistributing resources and addressing issues of inequalities – state provisioning of health and education and access to public infrastructure – were integral to delivering on development. Finally, BN proposed a participatory approach to development (ILO 1977: 32), which was expanded to include basic human rights 'which are not only ends in themselves but also contribute to the attainment of other goals' (ibid.). However, while BN allowed for a context-bound analysis of labour issues, it remained embedded in a gender ideology that did not unpack the relations of power obtaining within families. Women's work, too, remained on the margins of ILO analysis.

BN theory found reflection in debates on human capabilities and the Human Development Index of the UNDP through the work of Amartya Sen and Martha Nussbaum. Sen's work moved beyond an understanding of basic human needs and capabilities to a discussion of the required entitlements for the development of these capabilities. Following the work of feminist scholars such as Hannah Papanek, Sen challenges a 'culture'-based acceptance of women's entitlements. For Sen the basic parameters of entitlements are 'endowment' (what is initially possessed) and 'exchange entitlements mapping' (which reflects the possible exchanges through production and trade). In terms of endowment, Sen argues that, for the vast majority of people, it is their labour which is most important, and therefore the conditions of labour should be central to any analysis of entitlements. Nussbaum and Sen include legal, political and human rights that govern the domain of freedom needed to maximize labour-based entitlements (Nussbaum 1999). Sen argues that while these freedoms are instrumental to (means of) development, they are also an end of development, and therefore constitutive of it (Sen 1999).

An analysis of the importance of development as freedom to make decisions led capability theorists to challenge the assumptions of the model of altruistic family distribution of resources (Becker 1981). Drèze and Sen argued that the family was not, as Becker had delineated, an altruistic space of harmonious distribution of resources, but a deeply contested space where women suffered owing to the patriarchal social relations obtaining within the home and in the public sphere (Drèze and Sen 1990: 56–61; Sen 1999: 189–203). This analysis of the household followed the feminist critiques of the family and the analysis of the way women negotiate spaces within it through making 'patriarchal bargains' (see Kandiyoti 1988). Unlike BN, the capability theory espoused by Sen and Nussbaum has given prominent attention to gender relations within the household through the examination of intra-household transfers and the critique of the altruistic nature of the family.

Intergenerational justice and sustainable development debates emerged in the 1980s; ecofeminist scholars, among others, challenged both the policies of modernization and the paradigm of modernism. They pushed further the sustainable development argument to incorporate the relations between social and biological life on the one hand, and the relations of power that structure these on the other. Ecofeminism reasserts the 'age-old association' between women and nature (Merchant 1980; Mies and Shiva 1993: 16). Ecofeminists have made direct links between colonialism and the degradation of the environment and of women's lives themselves (Shiva 1989). Ecofeminism's anti-modernism provides a radical edge to its critique of growth. The alternative model of development that ecofeminists espouse is anti-patriarchal, decentralized, interdependent and sustainable (Braidotti et al. 1994). The critics of these attacks upon modernism, however, point to the essentialism at the heart of ecofeminist articulations about women and nature and challenge 'the dismantling of scientific rationality into social and cultural discourses ...' which deprives the poor and the marginalized of strategies to reclaim the fruits of scientific advances (Nanda 1999).

The BN, human capability and ecofeminist theories all have an interest in sustainable development, a term that entered the development discourse with the publication of the 1987 report of the World Commission on Economic Development, *Our Common Future*. It defined sustainable development as: 'development that meets the needs of the present without compromising the ability of future generations to meet their own needs' (p. 43) and identified two key concepts, 'needs', and limits to growth for sustaining environment's ability to meet future needs. In doing so it clearly built upon the BN discourse, but by focusing on the needs of future generations it also supported the ecological concerns of the long-term sustainability of our environment.

The attractions of these critiques of modernization are manifold. First, they are challenges from within the liberal paradigm. Second, they speak in the language of feasible politics – NGOs can lobby, the economists and philosophers can persuade, the social movements can pressure and challenge dominant discourses – which makes change possible. Third, perhaps the most attractive feature of these approaches is that they bring together the concerns and viewpoints of various social movements and positions on development, creating a counter-hegemonic consensus in development.

However, the critique of this liberal challenge to the mainstream development model was also trenchant. First, it was pointed out that in all these theoretical interventions, while group-differentiated needs meant a disaggregation of requirements of development processes and outcomes, the disaggregated groups themselves remained relatively closed categories as intersections of class and identities were overlooked. Second, the focus of the liberal critiques, while interrogating the growth agendas, has been limited in its challenge to offering 'public action' for the provision of 'public goods' as an alternative to the growing globalizing of market-led development.

From WID to gender and development

By the 1980s, the feminist critique of WID had led to a shift in the discursive focus from the inclusion of women in development towards the transformation of gender relations as the major concern. While some saw, and continue to see, this shift as depoliticizing and de-centring the claims of women, the gender and development (GAD) theorists have argued that a focus on the relationships that position women within society must be at the heart of political activity (see Young 1997: 51–4). A focus on the gender division of labour within the home and in waged work, access to and control over resources and benefits, material and social position of women and men in different contexts all form part of the GAD perspective on development (Parpart et al. 2000: 141). GAD theorists also distinguished between practical, more immediate and strategic or long-term and transformative needs of women in their specific social and political contexts (Molyneux 1985; Moser 1993). This concern with interests was also being reflected in the later debates about empowerment (Moser 1989; Rowlands 1997; Parpart et al. 2002).

However, the GAD framework has not been able to influence development planning: 'Gender planning, with its fundamental goal of emancipation is by definition a more "confrontational" approach [than WID]' (Moser 1993: 4). I would argue, however, that while this challenge of 'gender and development' remains *potentially* a powerful one, in practical policy terms it too has been depoliticized. Institutionalization of gender, as integration of women before it, poses critical practical and political questions for feminist activists and theorists (Baden and Goetz 1997: 10).

Deconstruction and representation: the politics of post-development Building
on the WID/GAD debates, but extending them in different directions, there
emerged in the 1980s and 1990s the postmodernist feminist critique of state-
based strategies of development leading to a disillusionment with 'the project
of development' itself. Postmodern critics of development argued that 'Development has been the primary mechanism through which the Third World has
been imagined and imagined itself, thus marginalizing or precluding other
ways of seeing and doing' (Escobar 1995: 212). Development, they argued, shares
this framing characteristic with Orientalism (Said 1978). The modern/traditional
binary was rejected, as were articulations of planned development. 'Science'
became one of many legitimate modes of understanding our worlds. 'The
local' as a political and conceptual space then became important – not to be
reconfigured by the nation-state but to be the site of multiple, life-improving
initiatives (Escobar 1995).

As Marchand and Parpart comment, it is unsurprising that the feminist
focus on difference and attraction to postmodernism coincided with the critique of middle-class, white Western feminism by women who did not recognize
themselves and their experiences in these early articulations of feminism (1995:
7). The displacement of Feminism by various feminisms was a starting point
for self-examination for many feminists, creating a space within which their
subject positions came under scrutiny. The intellectual complicity of modernizing elites was brought into focus by post-development feminists, as was
the hierarchical relationship between donors and recipients of aid, the NGO
worker and the 'clients' of the Third World.

Several questions have been raised about this postmodern critique and the
post-development framework. First, there is the question of agency: if all power
is diffuse and all hierarchies redundant, how are we to approach the question of political activism? The question of organization – political, social and
economic – also becomes unanswerable as the question of achievable goals is
brought into question. Harstock (1990) points to the postmodern view of power
as one in which 'Resistance rather than transformation dominates ... thinking
and consequently limits ... politics' (ibid.: 167) and Lehman suggests that the
constant deconstruction of discourse leaves difficult questions of power relations
and immediate questions of crises management unanswered and unanswerable
(1997). Postmodern perspective is also criticized for leading to relativism and
political nihilism (Moghissi 1999: 50–51). Post-colonial feminists have pointed out
that the postmodernist critique 'Would indeed dismiss the current strategies and
visions of African women whose struggles for gender-sensitive democratization
hinge upon universalist feminist ideals' (Nzomo 1995: 141).

The structuralist challenge to liberal development The structuralist opposition
to the modernization model of development, while entirely gender-blind, was

a powerful critique. Dependency theorists argued that the liberal development model was in fact the 'development of underdevelopment' (Frank 1969) and disassociated (and even counterpoised) capitalism and development. What was less clear was what this critique offered in terms of feasible politics, and incremental development. Upon this view, 'delinking' from the global capitalist system was the only strategy that Third World countries could pursue, which was not an option for most countries. Further, the focus on the world capitalist system took away the focus on local struggles of the working peoples of Third World countries. There was also no attempt to distinguish between the marginalized within societies on the basis of ascriptive, gendered or non-economic indicators. In response to some of these criticisms, Wallerstein (1979) developed the 'world-system' theory. While the first two categories corresponded to the dependency theorists' characterizations of core and periphery, the third – semi-periphery – was a group of 'emerging markets'. Wallerstein emphasized the role of politics, ideology and the state in the working of this three-tiered world-system. Taking their cue from Marx's analysis of the 'Asiatic Mode of Production', some neo-Marxist theorists, writing in the 1970s and early 1980s, argued that state elites played an important economic role in post-colonial societies as a monopolizer of political infrastructures of violence and coercion, as well as an economic actor (O'Leary 1989).

A strong intervention was made in the structuralist debate by Marxist and socialist feminists. Mies et al. argued that primitive accumulation remained essential to capitalist growth, and that both international and national capital and state systems exploited the Third World as well as women in its pursuit of profit. They identified several commonalties between 'women and the colonies' (1988: 4): '... they are treated as if they were means of production or "natural resources" such as water, air, and land ... the relationship between them is one of *appropriation*' (ibid.: 4–5). They argued that capitalist exploitation of wage labour was based upon the male monopoly of violence in a modified form; that patriarchal violence at home and in the public space was intrinsic to the lives of women and to their exploitation. They suggested that the state institutionalized the 'housewifisation' of women's labour within marriage and through work legislation (ibid.). As an alternative, Mies argued for a society based on '... autonomy for women over their lives and bodies, and rejection of any state or male control over their reproductive capacity; and finally men's participation in subsistence and nurturing work ...' (Kabeer 1994: 66). Again, while this was a powerful critique of existing social relations, and its focus on the gendered nature of capitalist accumulation provided a critical development of structural analysis, its utopian radicalism remained both politically essentializing of women and men, and its rejection of any engagement with the state made it difficult to translate this critique into policy agendas of development.

Taking on this challenge of 'transforming practice' has been an increasingly influential group of feminists who have drawn inspiration from Marxist critiques of capitalist development, but have been largely eclectic in their theoretical approach. They have argued against the 'male bias in the development process' (Elson 1995) and for initiating an engagement with institutions on the 'inside' of the policy processes – at both national and global levels (Elson 1998). Two areas have been at the core of this critique of development – the non-recognition of women's work, and the gendered nature of structural adjustment policies of the 1980s and 1990s (Waring 1988; Elson 1995). They have built upon Sen's critique of the altruistic family, to show how women's contributions to the household income are being appropriated without acknowledgement. They have also incorporated Sen's work on capability and developed sophisticated analyses of provisioning of human needs (Cagatay et al. 1995). In disaggregating the impact of structural adjustment policies on the household and focusing on the disproportionate burden of the privatization of social welfare that women are being forced to carry, this powerful critique has resulted in some important shifts within the economic discourse of international institutions. They have also further developed the interventions of Third World feminist and development groups, such as DAWN, which have advocated a strategic engagement with the policy community, and with state and international economic institutions in order to challenge the assumptions of neutral goals of development (Sen and Grown 1985). Because they have engaged actively with the policy machineries, especially at the international level, their influence in the field of development studies, and their interventions in the debates on development, have been significant.

Conclusion

Interrogating the theoretical debates on gender and development in the context of world politics allows us to reflect upon the complex and often contradictory nature of these debates, and therefore the impact that these have on policy and institutional issues, directly as well as indirectly: the Human Development Index adopted by the UNDP now measures the 'quality of life' rather than simple economic growth rates; many national statistical agencies now produce gender-disaggregated data; and the Human Development and the World Development Reports show the impact of WID/GAD theorizing and research. The various world conferences on women, from Mexico to Beijing, organized by the UN allowed gender and development agendas to be articulated, reassessed, critiqued and pushed forward. Bi- and multilateral aid and assistance programmes have also been affected by these wider debates on development (Staudt 2002). And yet, gendered inequality continues to be high and gender justice remains an aspiration. The struggle for gender justice and equality thus continues; the debates discussed in this chapter reflect as well as shape these struggles.

References

Amin, S. (1970) *L'accumulation à l'échelle mondiale; critique de la théorie du sous-développement*, Dakar, IFAN. Translated by Brian Pearce as *Accumulation on a World Scale: A Critique of the Theory of Underdevelopment*, New York: Monthly Review Press, 1974.

— (1976) *Unequal Development: An essay on the social formations of peripheral capitalism*, Brighton: Harvester Press.

Baden, S. and A. M. Goetz (1997) 'Who needs [sex] when you can have [gender]? Conflicting discourses of gender at Beijing', *Feminist Review*, 56, Summer, pp. 3–25.

Becker, G. (1981) *A Treatise on the Family*, Cambridge, MA: Harvard University Press.

Benería, L. and G. Sen (1997) 'Accumulation, reproduction and women's role in economic development: Boserup revisited', in N. Visvanathan et al. (eds), *The Women, Gender and Development Reader*, London: Zed Books.

Braidotti, R., E. Charkiewicz, S. Hausler and S. Wieringa (1994) *Women, the Environment and Sustainable Development: Towards a Theoretical Synthesis*, London: Zed Books in association with INSTRAW.

Cagatay, N., D. Elson and C. Grown (1995) 'Introduction', *World Development*, 23(11): 1827–36.

Drèze, J. and A. Sen (eds) (1990) *The Political Economy of Hunger*, vol. 2: *Famine Prevention*, Oxford: Clarendon.

Elson D. (1995) 'Male bias in macro economics: the case of structural adjustment', in D. Elson (ed.), *Male Bias in the Development Process*, Manchester: Manchester University Press, pp. 164–90.

— (1998) 'Talking to the boys: gender and economic growth models', in C. Jackson and R. Pearson (eds), *Feminist Visions of Development*, London: Routledge.

Escobar, A. (1995) 'Imagining a post-development era', in J. Crush (ed.), *Power of Development*, London: Routledge.

Frank, A. G. (1969) *Capitalism and Underdevelopment in Latin America: Historical Studies of Chile and Brazil*, New York: Monthly Review Press.

Harstock, N. (1990) 'Foucault on power: a theory for women?', in L. J. Nicholson (ed.), *Feminisim/Postmodernism*, London: Routledge.

ILO (International Labour Organization) (1977) *Employment, Growth and Basic Needs: A One-World Problem*, London: Praeger.

Kabeer, N. (1994) *Reversed Realities: Gender Hierarchies in Development Thought*, London: Verso.

Kandiyoti, D. (1988) 'Bargaining with patriarchy', *Gender and Society*, 2(3), September.

Lehman, D. (1997) 'An opportunity lost: Escobar's deconstruction of development', *Journal of Development Studies*, 33(4): 568–78.

Marchand, M. H. and J. L. Parpart (eds) (1995) *Feminism, Postmodernism, Development*, London: Routledge.

Merchant, C. (1980) *The Death of Nature: Women, Ecology and the Scientific Revolution*, New York, Harper and Row.

Mies, M. and V. Shiva (1993) *Ecofeminism*, London: Zed Books.

Mies, M., V. Bennholdt-Thomsen and C.von Werlhof (1988) *Women: The Last Colony*, London: Zed Books.

Moghissi, H. (1999) *Feminism and Islamic Fundamentalism: The Limits of Postmodern Analysis*, London: Zed Books.

Molyneux, M. (1985) 'Mobilization without emancipation? Women's interests and the state in Nicaragua', *Feminist Studies*, 11(2): 227–54.

Moser, C. O. N. (1989) 'The impact of recession and structural adjustment on women: Ecuador', *Development*, 1: 75–83.

— (1993) *Gender, Planning and Development: Theory, Practice and Training*, London: Routledge.

Nanda, M. (1999) 'In search of an epistemology for Third World peoples' science movements', *Rethinking Marxism*, June.

Nussbaum, M. (1999) 'Women and equality: the capabilities approach', *International Labour Review*, 138(3): 227–45.

Nussbaum, M. and A. Sen (eds) (1993) *The Quality of Life: A Study Prepared for the World Institute for Development Economics Research (WIDER) of the United Nations University*, Oxford: Clarendon Press.

Nzomo, M. (1995) 'Women and democratization struggles in Africa: what relevance to post-modernist discourse?', in M. Marchand and J. Parpart (eds), *Feminism, Postmodernism, Development*, London: Routledge.

O'Leary, B. (1989) *The Asiatic Mode of Production: Oriental Despotism, Historical Materialism and Indian History*, Oxford: Blackwell.

Parpart, J. L. and M. Marchand (1995) 'Exploding the canon: an introduction/ conclusion', in M. Marchand and J. Parpart (eds), *Feminism, Postmodernism, Development*, London: Routledge.

Parpart, J. L., P. M. Connelley and V. E. Barriteau (eds) (2000) *Theoretical Perspectives on Gender and Development*, Ottawa: IDRC.

Parpart, J. L., S. M. Rai and K. Staudt (2002) *Rethinking Empowerment: Gender and Development in a Local/Global World*, London: Routledge.

Pearson, R. and C. Jackson (1998) 'Introduction: interrogating development, feminism, gender and policy', in C. Jackson and R. Pearson (eds), *Feminist Visions of Development*, London: Routledge.

Rogers, B. (1982) *The Domestication of Women*, London: Tavistock.

Rowlands, J. (1997) *Questioning Empowerment: Working with Women in Honduras*, Oxford: Oxfam.

Said, E. (1978) *Orientalism*, London: Routledge & Kegan Paul.

Sen, A. (1982) *The State, Industrialization and Class Formations in India: A Neo-Marxist Perspective on Colonialism, Underdevelopment and Development*, London: Routledge & Kegan Paul.

— (1987) 'Gender and cooperative conflicts', Working Paper no. 18, World Institute for Development Economics Research (WIDER).

— (1999) *Development as Freedom*, Oxford: Oxford University Press.

Sen, G. and C. Grown (1985) *Development, Crises and Alternative Visions: Third World Women's Perspectives*, London: Earthscan.

Shiva, V. (1989) *Staying Alive*, London: Zed Books.

Staudt, K. (2002) 'The uses and abuses of empowerment discourse', in J. L. Parpart et al. (eds), *Rethinking Empowerment: Gender and Development in a Local/Global World*, London, Routledge.

Wallerstein, I. (1979) *The Capitalist World-Economy*, Cambridge: Cambridge University Press.

Waring, M. (1988) *If Women Counted: A New Feminist Economics*, San Francisco, CA: Harper and Row.

WCED (World Commission on Economic Development) (1987) *Our Common Future*, New York: Oxford University Press.

Whyte, R. O. and P. Whyte (1982) *The Women of Rural Asia*, London: Westview.

Young, K. (1997) 'Gender and development', in N. Visvanathan, L. Duggan, L. Nisonoff and N. Wiegersma (eds), *The Women, Gender and Development Reader*, London: Zed Books.

4 | Women's role in economic development

Ester Boserup

Male and female farming systems (Chapter 1)

A main characteristic of economic development is the progress towards an increasingly intricate pattern of labour specialization. In communities at the earliest stages of economic development, practically all goods and services are produced and consumed within the family group, but with economic development more and more people become specialized in particular tasks and the economic autarky of the family group is superseded by the exchange of goods and services.

Both in primitive and in more developed communities, the traditional division of labour within the farm family is usually considered 'natural' in the sense of being obviously and originally imposed by the sex difference itself. In fact, an important distinction can be made between two kinds or patterns of subsistence agriculture: one in which food production is taken care of by women, with little help from men, and one where food is produced by the men with relatively little help from women. As a convenient terminology I propose to denote these two systems as the male and the female systems of farming.

The division of labour within African agriculture Africa is the region of female farming par excellence. In many African tribes, nearly all the tasks connected with food production continue to be left to women. In most of these tribal communities, the agricultural system is that of shifting cultivation: small pieces of land are cultivated for a few years only, until the natural fertility of the soil diminishes.

We may identify three main systems of subsistence farming in Africa according to whether the field work is done almost exclusively by women, predominantly by women, and predominantly by men.

Before the European conquest of Africa, felling, hunting and warfare were the chief occupations of men in the regions of female farming. Gradually, as felling and hunting became less important and intertribal warfare was prevented by European domination, little remained for the men to do. The Europeans, accustomed to the male farming systems of their home countries, looked with little sympathy on this unfamiliar distribution of the workload between the sexes and, understandably, the concept of the 'lazy African men' was firmly fixed in the minds of settlers and administrators. European extension agents in many parts of Africa tried to induce the underemployed male villagers to cultivate commercial crops for export to Europe, and the system of colonial taxation by poll tax on the households was used as a means to force the Africans to produce cash crops. In many other cases, however, European penetration in Africa resulted in women enlarging their part in agricultural work in the villages, because both colonial officers and white settlers recruited unmarried males for work, voluntary or forced, in road building or other heavy constructional work, in mines and on plantations. As a result of all these changes, the present pattern of sex roles in African agriculture is more diversified than the one which gave rise to the European concept of the 'lazy African men'.

In Asia, too, many examples of female farming systems are known. They are widespread among tribal peoples in India, where districts are found with women working more hours in farming than men. In all the countries of South-East Asia many tribal peoples subsist by shifting cultivation with female farming.

The plough, the veil and the labourer In the regions of plough cultivation, agricultural work is distributed between the two sexes in a very different way. The main farming instrument in those regions, the plough, is used by men helped by draught animals. Women contribute mainly to harvest work and to the care of domestic animals. Because village women work less in agriculture, a considerable proportion of them are completely freed from farm work. Sometimes such women perform only purely domestic duties, living in seclusion within their own home, and appearing in the village street only under the protection of the veil, a phenomenon associated with plough culture.

But there is an additional and very important difference between the distribution of work in African shifting cultivation and in Asian plough cultivation. The plough is used in regions with private ownership of land and with a comparatively numerous class of landless families in the rural population. Therefore, in many regions of plough cultivation, the farm family gets more help from hired labourers than is usual in regions of shifting cultivation.

Population pressures and sex roles in farming Female farming systems seem most often to disappear when farming systems with ploughing of permanent fields are introduced in lieu of shifting cultivation. In a typical case, this change is the result of increasing population density, which makes it impossible to continue with a system necessitating long fallow periods when the land must be left uncultivated. In recent decades, the rapid population increase in developing countries has prompted a change to plough cultivation in many regions of shifting cultivation with a predominantly female pattern of work.

And the advent of the plough usually entails a radical shift in sex roles in agriculture; men take over the ploughing even in regions where the hoeing had formerly been women's work.

Loss of status under European rule (Chapter 3)

The responsibility of the Europeans European settlers, colonial administrators and technical advisers are largely responsible for the deterioration in the status of women in the agricultural sectors of developing countries. It was they who neglected the female agricultural labour force when they helped to introduce modern commercial agriculture to the overseas world and promoted the productivity of male labour.

As a result of the attitudes of the extension services, the gap between labour productivity of men and women continues to widen. Men are taught to apply modern methods in the cultivation of a given crop, while women continue to use the traditional methods in the cultivation of the same crop, thus getting much less out of their efforts than the men. The inevitable result is that women are discouraged from participating in agriculture, and are glad to abandon cultivation whenever the increase in their husband's income makes it possible.

It is the men who do the modern things. They handle industrial inputs while women perform the degrading manual jobs; men often have the task of spreading fertilizer in the fields, while women spread manure; men ride the bicycle and drive the lorry, while women carry head loads, as did their grandmothers. In short, men represent modern farming in the village, women represent the old drudgery.

5 | The invisible heart: care and the global economy

Nancy Folbre

Studies of globalization and its impact on people focus on incomes, employment, education and other opportunities. Less visible, and often neglected, is the impact on care and caring labour – the task of providing for dependants, for children, the sick, the elderly and all the rest of us. Human development is nourished not only by expanding incomes, schooling, health, empowerment and a clean environment but also by care. Care, sometimes referred to as social reproduction, is also essential for economic sustainability.

Globalization is putting a squeeze on care and caring labour. Changes in the way that men and women use their time put a squeeze on the time available for care. The fiscal pressures on the state put a resource squeeze on public spending on care services. And the wage gap between the tradable and non-tradable sectors puts an incentive squeeze on the supply of care services in the market. Gender is a major factor in all these impacts, because women the world over carry the main responsibility for these activities, and most of the burden.

Human development, capabilities and care

The role of care in the formation of human capabilities and in human development is fundamental. Without genuine care and nurturing, children cannot develop capabilities and adults have a hard time maintaining or expanding theirs. But the supply of care is not merely an input into human development. It is also an output, an intangible yet essential capability – a factor of human well-being. A clear manifestation of this is the positive effect of social support and social relationships on life expectancy. The difference that care makes for child health and survival is also well documented.

In almost all societies the gender division of labour hands the responsibility for caring labour to women, much of it without remuneration – in the family or as voluntary activity in the community. The hours are long and the work physically hard – fetching water and fuel – especially in rural areas of developing countries. These inequalities in burden are an important part of the obstacles women face in their life choices and opportunities. Women also make up a disproportionate share of workers in domestic service and in professions such as childcare, teaching, therapy and nursing.

Globalization and care

Economic analysis of care offers three insights into the impact of globalization on human development:

- Women's increased participation in the labour force and shifts in economic structures are transforming the ways care services are provided. Needs once provided almost exclusively by unpaid family labour are now being purchased from the market or provided by the state.
- Increases in the scope and speed of transactions are increasing the size of markets, which are becoming disconnected from local communities.
- Perhaps most important, the expansion of markets tends to penalize altruism and care. Both individuals and institutions have been free-riding on the caring labour that mainly women provide.
- Globalization is dominated by the expansion of markets and rewards profitability and efficiency. While economic growth reflects increasing private and public incomes, human development needs people to provide goods and services that fall outside the market – such as care and other unpaid services. The traditional restrictions on women's activities once guaranteed that women would specialize in providing care. Globalization's shifts in employment patterns have promoted and to some extent enforced the participation of women in wage employment. Nonetheless, women in most countries continue to carry the 'double burden' of care services – ending up exhausted.

Care and market rewards

The market gives almost no rewards for care. Much of it is unpaid – most of it provided by women, some by men. The market also penalizes individuals who spend time in these activities, which take time away from investing in skills for paid work or from doing paid work. Care services are also provided in the market, usually under-remunerated.

And global economic competition has tended to reinforce these trends, as the wage gap increases between the tradable and non-tradable sectors. Care produces goods with social externalities – widespread benefits for those who do not pay for them. It creates human and social capital – the next generation, workers with human and social skills who can be relied on, who are good citizens. But mothers cannot demand a fee from employers who hire their children. This care will be under-produced and overexploited unless non-market institutions ensure that everyone shares the burden of providing it.

[Ed.: This chapter is an excerpt from Chapter 3 of the 1999 *Human Development Report*. The complete report can be downloaded from hdr.undp.org/en/reports/global/hdr1999/.]

6 | Feminist political ecology

Gender and Environment Series Editorial
Committee (GESEC)[1]

Introduction

Feminist Political Ecology (FPE) is an interdisciplinary academic field and a critical framework to challenge uneven power relations in everyday ecologies. It is based on a strong but not exclusive focus on gender and an assumption of intersectionality and interrelationality. FPE continues to engender debates on political and economic development, agricultural transformations, technologies and environmental change. It highlights the importance of gendered knowledges, rights and politics in the analysis of environmental issues and addresses ecologically based political struggles at the intersection of multiple levels from individual to global.

A brief positioning of the FPE approach

Framed in the context of debates over ecofeminism (Shiva 1988) and socialist feminism (Warren 1987), FPE emerged as a viable third analytical position in the 1990s. Critical meetings and debates that framed FPE were positioned within critiques of sustainable development. While political ecology provided a strong and useful critique of corporate and state-driven sustainable development in the 1990s, FPE advanced a series of feminist critiques and innovations (Rocheleau et al. 1996). It built on the work on women, environment and development (WED) (Harcourt 1993; Braidotti et al. 1994), feminist environmentalism (Agarwal 1986), post-structuralist and social movement literature (Alvarez et al. 1998) and post-colonial writings on environment, post-development, science, gender and culture (Sundberg 2004).

FPE draws on all these approaches, to critique rampant and accelerating processes of modernization. These include privatization of land, water and forests; eviction of rural communities; and state and corporate projects of social, environmental and production engineering under the umbrella of development. The FPE approach recognizes gender differences in interests, knowledges, abilities and labour, based not in biology but in socialization and everyday experience of socially constructed spaces, work and social life. It joins theory, politics and practice by working from case studies, with a focus on complex interlinkages among gender, environment, culture and economy 'in place'.

The evolving analysis of FPE

The first wave of FPE writings in the 1990s concentrated on three dimensions of gender and environment: knowledge and authority, rights and tenure, and social organizations and movements, including gendered labour within each of these. FPE writings often used gendered life stories and social movement histories, connecting complex lives in place, within larger histories and geographies of culture, nature and power. Cases ranged from gendered drought and famine responses in Kenya, to the Chipko movement to save the Himalayan forests.

The second wave of FPE in the 2000s advocated for a situated and scaled analysis of the gendered dimensions of globalization, imperialism and modernist frameworks of nature and culture. Cultural, post-structural and post-colonial studies, as well as feminist scholarship, introduced a critique of state- and corporate-driven development as assaults on diversity of every kind. Feminist scholarship on social movements also generated robust frameworks to deal with situated knowledges, complex identities and affinities, complex ecologies, and the cultural politics of place (Underhill-Sem 2003).

A growing focus on bodies in society and in environments has led to reconceptions of gender, environment and development (Harcourt 2009). A resurgence of place-based social movements has led to more detailed studies of gender and ecologies entwined with the growing networks of peoples' movements (Harcourt and Escobar 2005). Scholarship on social and ecological complexity and network theories, combined with feminist post-structural thought (Haraway 1989; Harding 1986), has generated new relational formulations of genders, ecologies, technologies and communities and has resulted in new understandings of social movements linking culture/nature networks to territories (Rocheleau 2010; Escobar 2008; Rocheleau and Roth 2007).

Motherhood, culture and nature are also being revisited within FPE. The predominant Western concept of motherhood is challenged for its anthropomorphic and sexist associations with nature and culture. Biomedical notions of reproduction and indigenous understandings of maternities can coexist so that people can recognize spiritual and symbolic dimensions of motherhood and maternities as well as their materiality, at multiple scales.

Contemporary FPE is shaped by current debates on climate change and climate justice, land grabbing, forced displacement of rural people, and the role of food, energy and financial crises in cascading damage to ecologies and peoples across the planet (Di Chiro 2009; Seager 2009). Gendered experience of each of these crises is entangled with ecological processes and assaults upon them by prevailing powers and state/corporate-driven science, politics, militarization and development. By engaging with these issues FPE builds on the experience of women's leadership in social movements that proposes alternative visions of nature, culture and power.

FPE: A transformational agenda

FPE provides a lens to articulate new approaches to science(s), knowledge(s) and socially just and ecologically viable futures. It interrogates the dominant ecological and social imaginaries driving technological innovations and responses to environmental change. FPE advocates for democratically engendered and diverse technological alternatives. It seeks to advance bio-political debates on bodies and ecology and to continue to subvert male/female and nature/culture binaries. FPE also explores the emergence of new subjects and elaborates feminist perspectives on the proliferation of new biotechnologies and reproductive technologies.

FPE continues to address gendered land, territory and resource rights, knowledges and socio-ecological relations. Emerging issues in this domain include the global land grabbing and runaway expansion of industrial monocultures for food, energy and carbon sequestration.

FPE is also well positioned to tackle new challenges to society stemming for example from development and commercialization of new technologies such as synthetic biology, geo-engineering, and industrial production systems driven by technological convergence at the nano scale.

FPE's major challenge is to move beyond critique, and affirm the resistance, resilience and rights of multiple actors to imagine and create diverse futures. FPE seeks to map out alternative ecologies and economies that simultaneously protect the rights of people and the health of the earth. A convergence of multiple efforts is needed to restructure social and ecological relations and reclaim principles of love, compassion, reciprocity and diverse spiritualities towards gender, racial, economic, environmental and erotic justice.

Note

1 This essay emerges from the collective work of the Zed Books GESEC: Giovanna Di Chiro (Five College Women's Studies Research Center, and Nuestras Raices, Inc.), Niclas Hällström (What Next Forum), Wendy Harcourt (Society for International Development), Khawar Mumtaz (Shirkat Gah), Anita Nayar (Development Alternatives with Women for a New Era – DAWN), Dianne Rocheleau (Clark University), and Yvonne Underhill-Sem (University of Auckland). Particularly the last third of the piece is based on the discussion at a What Next feminist seminar held in Uppsala at the Dag Hammarskjöld Foundation in January 2008 where GESEC was also working with Nidhi Tandon (Networked Intelligence for Development) to review our individual and collective experiences and writings as feminist political ecologists. The meeting produced a short statement on feminist political ecology on which this chapter draws.

References

Agarwal, B. (1986) *Cold Hearths and Barren Slopes: The Woodfuel Crisis in the Third World*, London: Zed Books.

Alvarez, S., E. Dagnino and A. Escobar (1998) *Cultures of Politics/Politics of Cultures: Revisioning Latin American Social Movements*, Boulder, CO: Westview Press.

Braidotti, R. et al. (1994) *Women, the Environment and Sustainable Development*, London: Zed Books.

Di Chiro, G. (2009) 'Sustaining everyday life: bringing together environmental, climate, and reproductive justice', *DifferenTakes*, 58.

Escobar, A. (2008) *Territories of Difference: Place – Movements – Life – Redes*, Durham, NC, and London: Duke University Press.

Haraway, D. (1989) *Primate Visions: Gender, Race, and Nature in the World of Modern Science*, New York: Routledge.

— (1991) *Simians, Cyborgs and Women: The Reinvention of Nature*, New York: Routledge.

Harcourt, W. (ed.) (1993) *Feminist Perspectives on Sustainable Development*, London: Zed Books.

— (2009) *Body Politics in Development*, London: Zed Books.

Harcourt, W. and A. Escobar (eds) (2005) *Women and the Politics of Place*, Bloomfield, CT: Kumarian Press.

Harding, S. (1986) *The Science Question in Feminism*, Ithaca, NY: Cornell University Press.

Rocheleau, D. (2010) 'Rooted networks, webs of relation, and the power of situated science: bringing the models back down to earth in Zambrana', in M. Goldman, P. Nadasdy and M. Turner (eds), *Knowing Nature, Transforming Ecologies: A Conversation between Science and Technology Studies and Political Ecology*, Chicago, IL: University of Chicago Press.

Rocheleau, D. and R. Roth (2007) 'Rooted networks, relational webs and powers of connection: rethinking human and political ecologies', *Geoforum*, 38: 433–7.

Rocheleau, D., B. Thomas-Slayter and E. Wangari (eds) (1996) *Feminist Political Ecology: Global Perspectives and Local Experiences*, London: Routledge.

Seager, J. (2009) 'Death by degrees: taking a feminist hard look at the 2 Degrees climate policy', *Kvinder, Kon & Forskning* (Denmark) [Women, gender & research], 18(3/4): 11–22.

Shiva, V. (1988) *Staying Alive*, London: Zed Books.

Sundberg, J. (2004) 'Identities-in-the-making: conservation, gender, and race in the Maya Biosphere Reserve, Guatemala', *Gender, Place and Culture*, 11(1): 44–66.

Underhill-Sem, Y. (2003) '"Tragedies" in out-of-the-way places: oceanic interpretations of another scale', in K.-K. Bhavani, J. Foran and P. Kurian (eds), *Feminist Futures: Reimagining Women, Culture and Development*, London: Zed Books, pp. 43–54.

Warren, K. J. (1987) 'Feminism and ecology: making connections', *Environmental Ethics*, 9(1): 3–20.

7 | Women and microcredit: a critical introduction

Nalini Visvanathan and Karla Yoder

As of December 31, 2007, 3,552 microcredit institutions reported reaching 154,825,825 clients, 106,584,679 of whom were among the poorest when they took their first loan. Of these poorest clients, 83.4 percent, or 88,726,893, are women.[1]

Microcredit, the advancing of small loans without collateral to the poor to enable them to start entrepreneurial activities, has become a central poverty alleviation strategy in neoliberal development programs directed at women. Loans are expected to generate or support self-employment, and with that outcome empower women as well as alleviate their experience of poverty. Why has microfinance (loans, savings and insurance) assumed an important place in development planning, particularly directed at women? What are the historical bases for the increased emphasis on microcredit for women in the low-resource countries of the global South? And how is this trend related to global development policy? This chapter briefly responds to these questions.

By the 1970s, the failure of the development establishment to improve the lives of the poor, particularly women, was clearly manifest (see Rai, Part 1). Planners at UN agencies then shifted their focus downwards from macro-level economic development and industrial promotion to meeting basic needs, initially through small business development, and then eventually to the informal sector and micro-level. After first emphasizing business development and training, planners concluded that what was needed most was capital (Dichter 2007). Concurrently, a shift in the aid paradigm among donors in the North prioritized individual self-employment and privatization rather than structural changes for the benefit of the population (McMichael 2000).

When soaring oil prices created national debt crises, multilateral financial institutions such as the IMF addressed these crises through advancing loans contingent on the institution of structural adjustment programs (SAPs). The cutbacks in the public sector reduced and eliminated welfare services, and many public sector agencies were privatized to increase efficiency. Multilateral agencies promoted microfinance programs to cushion the harsh measures imposed by SAPs (Mayoux 2002). In addition, the scaling back of employment in the public sector led to an unregulated expansion of the informal economy, which became the principal source of income for millions of displaced workers, women and marginalized groups.

Mounting empirical evidence that women were the more responsible members of households supported the targeting of women for microcredit. Data from population surveys and child health and nutrition studies showed mothers' work status could enhance children's nutritional status and extend their schooling (Engle 1989). Equally critical in dispelling regressive beliefs were studies demonstrating that women's employment had no deleterious impact on their children's health status (Leslie 1989). The uncovering of women's critical role in family welfare and resource allocation was clearly influential in the creation of lending schemes that targeted women. They were seen to use money for household survival and child welfare purposes to a greater extent than men and had better loan repayment rates, being more compliant or more easily coerced than men (Rahman 1999). Consequently, gathering women into solidarity groups for lending purposes, along with providing them with access to micro-loans, was seen as giving them increased power and thus meeting other development goals of gender equality and women's empowerment.

Historical and sociocultural origins

Historically, informal savings and credit associations were found in most regions of the world. The eighteenth-century writer Jonathan Swift created the Irish Loan Fund to provide small loans without collateral to the rural poor. In nineteenth-century Europe, the rural and urban poor organized formal savings and credit institutions that emerged as people's banks, credit unions, and savings and credit cooperatives.[2] In the global South, there were similar groups and associations engaged in dispensing loans and amassing savings for rural and urban clientele. Centuries before Muhammad Yunus founded Grameen Bank and the Self Employed Women's Association of India established its credit union, there were *chit funds* and *hundis* in India, *tontines* in Cameroon and Senegal, *susus* in Ghana, *esusu* in Nigeria, *tandas* in Mexico, *huis* in China, *kyes* in Korea and scores of similar groups across the continents.[3]

Anthropologists have documented the structures and functions of rural savings and loans groups, including their purposive origins and pervasive impact on community life. Geertz (1962) emphasizes the sociocultural nature of the traditional 'rotating credit associations' whose periodical gatherings foster and strengthen mutual support among villagers. In the 'arisan,' of eastern Java, whose literal meaning is 'cooperative endeavor' or 'mutual help,' the social functions were an integral aspect of the group's economic activity. Ardener's (1964) comparative study of these associations also recognized the role of social prestige, kinship ties and other non-economic factors in the constitution of these groups. In sum, the early forms of microfinance emphasized mutual assistance, cooperative initiatives and organized worker unions. In transplanting these economic practices of the poor to the protocols for micro-finance, the microfinance institutions (MFIs) restructured them to serve a profit-making industry viewing the informal economy as new territory for exploration (Elyachar 2002).

MFI models

The microfinance models currently promoted represent a broad spectrum of group-based lending structures (Table 7.1), as well as less commonly offered individual lending popular with clients. An underlying neoliberal philosophy has created a market-driven credit system in which indicators of success are quantified in terms of repayment rates, loan recovery and timeliness, repre-senting the bottom line for lenders. Though the individual is central to these systems and emphasis is placed on her economic independence, solidarity groups remain, as borrowed trappings from longstanding indigenous models, serving as an alternative to collateral and as a means of making microcredit profitable to MFIs. In the group lending model, borrowers take on the func-tions of the banker. They assume liability for screening peers, monitoring their behavior and enforcing timely payments, thereby reducing or removing administrative costs incurred by bankers with individual lending. This approach helps the lending agency to stay financially solvent and even make profits. Notably, it increases the appeal of microfinance in an era when neoliberal economic principles are dominant.

Traditional forms of savings and loans groups – termed Rotating Savings and Credit Associations (ROSCAs) – form the basis for most of the microfinance models promoted today. A ROSCA is the simplest of systems which requires no management, records, or interest. All group members contribute the same amount at a regular meeting and the sum collected is given in its entirety to a different member each time. A number of NGOs working in microfinance promote Accumulating Savings and Credit Associations (ASCAs), which are more complex ROSCAs requiring management (either by members or an outside organization) and in which interest is charged and profit earned by members. Village banking refers to a variant of the ASCA developed by FINCA in which the NGO provides external capital as a loan to the group for which the members act as one another's guarantee. The NGO's capital is lent out in small amounts to members who repay with interest and the group repays the lump sum some months later. The Indian Self-Help Group (SHG) is an ASCA notable for its relationship with a formal bank, which usually provides external capital to the group as a loan after it has established a savings account. Savings and credit cooperatives (SACCOs) are formalized ASCAs that operate at a much larger scale.

The Grameen Bank is one of the most widely known MFIs and its lend-ing model has spread globally and been adapted widely. In this model, the

TABLE 7.1 Major microfinance lending models: an overview

Model	Type	Sponsor	Structure	Regions/countries	Notable features
ROSCA (Rotating Savings and Credit Associations)	Traditional group-based finance system based on social/cultural ties.		Informal groups of community or neighborhood women in rural and urban areas, contributing small amounts for predetermined time for savings or loans. One member takes all contributions at each meeting.	Asia, Africa, Latin America. Immigrant groups in UK, USA	*Independent and autonomous *Members known to each other *Formed and disbanded easily *Small contributions *Promote mutual assistance and solidarity *Short lifespan
ASCA (Accumulating Savings and Credit Associations)	Complex version of ROSCA, where members or an external MFI undertake management of savings, profit calculation and repayment. Variants include Village Savings and Lending Associations (VSLAs) and Savings and Internal Lending Communities (SILCs).	NGOs include CARE International and Catholic Relief Services	Group forms and operates like a ROSCA except that interest is charged on loans and so members earn profit when paid back their capital. NGOs often promote enhanced versions of ASCAs with improved governance, internal rules, cash controls, etc.	Africa, India, Latin America, Caribbean	*Independent and autonomous *Membership larger and heterogeneous *Multiple loans per member possible *Short- and long-term loans *Bookkeeping and record maintenance *Administrative overheads *Interest on loans *Contributions can be irregular *Funds deposited in banks for safe-keeping *Short life cycles

Village banking	Variant of ASCA that usually includes external funding.	FINCA Pro Mujer	NGO or MFI lends sum to operating ASCA which is on-lent to members in smaller amounts and repaid as a lump sum in a moderate time period.	Latin America, Caribbean, Africa	*Group may be self- or NGO-managed *Group members act as collateral to ensure repayment *External funding allows for larger loan sizes
Grameen I & II	Bank officials initiate groups of 5 to 8 peers. After screening, individuals are given credit.	Grameen Bank	Under Grameen I, individuals couldn't receive credit if other members of their group were delinquent on loans. Grameen II reforms removed this provision.	Bangladesh (adapted around the world)	*Provider directs group lending *Use of group members as collateral to ensure repayment *External funding (from MFI) allows for larger loan size
Self-help groups	Variant of ASCA with external funding from a bank.	Central and state governments, NGOs, MFIs, banks	The savings money of members in a self-managed ASCA is deposited in a bank account out of which small loans are regularly made. Eventually, the group receives a loan from the bank which it on-lends to members.	India	*Group is self-managed *Group members act as collateral to ensure repayment of bank loan *External funding (from bank) allows for larger loan sizes
Individual lending	Loans given to individuals with or without collateral or guarantors.	Banks and non-bank finance institutions	While liability is individual, clients often still meet regularly in groups with a loan officer for repayment.	Asia, Latin America	*Small loans are provided without collateral

MFI approves loans to individuals in solidarity groups of five to eight peers, often formed by MFI staff. Individuals receive credit based on the screening of their peers, their own and group members' repayment of loans, and savings accumulated. In recent years, a number of MFIs have begun offering individual liability loans more widely as competition grows within the microfinance sector.

Microcredit and women's empowerment

The debate over microcredit is underscored by the evangelistic zeal of its promoters being matched by the outright rejection of its opponents (Kabeer 2005). Critics often fail to look beyond its ideological underpinnings to the specific local context and the denial of credit to poor women by the formal banking sector. Research over the last decades shows a gap between the program rhetoric and the reality found on the ground.

In the 1990s, the diffusion and adoption of the Grameen Bank model across continents led to numerous studies by researchers seeking to understand the phenomenon (Goetz and Sen Gupta 1996; Harper 1998). Both feminist and mainstream critics examined the twin claims of women's empowerment and poverty alleviation. Recent attempts to gain a more nuanced and localized understanding of the impact of credit on the lives of the poor, one qualitative (Collins et al. 2009) and another using a randomized controlled trial design (Banerjee et al. 2009), have challenged common beliefs about loan use among the poor and the inevitably positive impact of microcredit.

Microfinance promotes empowerment as the desired goal for women, interpreting the term as a discrete outcome and separating it from its original meaning of transformed power relations in the household or in public spaces that mark separation by caste, class and religion. In the 1960s and 1970s, the concept signified the transformative processes wrought by radical movements and politicized groups working for social justice and breaking traditional hierarchical barriers to build solidarity in regions of Latin America and South Asia (Batliwala 2007). The cooptation of the term originally applied to a complex process and its treatment as an outcome in an individual-centered program distort and undermine its original meaning. Feminist critic Chakravarti (2008) finds this a problematic aspect of the neoliberal strategy to gain wider acceptance for microcredit and calls for a re-engagement with the issues of poverty and the struggle against all forms of oppression that once engaged the Indian women's movement.

Goetz and Sen Gupta (1996) noted that husbands and male kinfolk (in-laws), not the woman borrower, tended to take control of loans. In patriarchal households, where wives defer to household males for financial decisions, such findings questioned whether targeting women could necessarily lead to goals of equality and empowerment when gender hierarchies are left unaddressed.

Mayoux (1999) faulted the uncritical assumptions of loan providers that view empowerment as a 'natural offshoot' and suggested that strategies for empowerment be made explicit.

Isserles (2003) argues that it is the support network among women, formed at group meetings, which leads to empowerment and not the acquisition of a loan. She concludes that women are at the center of this development project because they are treated as instruments for ensuring household survival to compensate for the male householder's failure to care for the family.

Program designs, particularly Grameen-based, use group members as social collateral and exert undue pressure on borrowers to make payments on time. These pressures result in women borrowing from moneylenders so they do not fall behind and get penalized. The recourse to new loans to repay old ones on time creates a spiral of indebtedness for women struggling to survive and improve their lot. In Bangladesh, debt recycling leads to untenable debt liability in poor households (Rahman 1999); and in Bolivia, food consumption is reduced to make loan payments (Brett 2006).

Kabeer (2005) argues that strategic gender interests that mire women in a dependency relationship, without access to assets and vulnerable to violence and exploitation, cannot change during the short term. She acknowledges, however, the positive aspects of microcredit for marginalized women. In socially stratified societies, where gender prejudice is compounded by longstanding practices of stigma and ostracism, microcredit could constitute a channel for upward mobility. Few microfinance programs reach marginalized women at the bottom. An exception Kabeer finds is Murthy's study of Dalit members participating in SHGs who registered greater physical mobility and social interactions across castes.[4]

Self-help groups working within a context of social justice have the potential to advance women's interests. It is noteworthy that Indian women's organizations have strongly criticized SHGs as a government program that is failing to deliver in its objective to change women's unequal status (Sharma and Parthasarathy 2007).

Notes

1 State of the Microcredit Summit Campaign Report 2009, p. 3, www.micro creditsummit.org/uploads/socrs/SOCR 2009_English.pdf, accessed 10 June 2010.

2 For a descriptive overview of the origins of modern credit unions and co-operatives, see *The History of Microfinance*, www.globalenvision.org, accessed 6 June 2010.

3 Many of these indigenous forms of financial self-help groups have been transplanted and diffused by refugees and immigrants.

4 Broader positive impact appears linked to the type of group surveyed; women in groups within a larger institution such as BRAC gained more decision-making powers within the household than women members in limited organizational structures.

References

Ardener, S. (1964) 'The comparative study of Rotating Credit Associations', *Journal of the Royal Anthropological Institute of Great Britain and Ireland*, 94(2): 201–29.

Banerjee, A., E. Duflo, R. Glennerster and C. Kinnan (2009) 'The miracle of microfinance? Evidence from a randomized evaluation', Cambridge, MA: Abdul Latif Jameel Poverty Action Lab and MIT Department of Economics.

Batliwala, S. (2007) 'Taking the power out of empowerment – an experiential account', *Development in Practice*, 17(4/5).

Brett, J. A. (2006) '"We sacrifice and eat less": the structural complexities of microfinance participation', *Human Organization*, 65(1), Spring.

Chakravarti, U. (2008) 'Beyond the mantra of empowerment: time to return to poverty, violence and struggle', *IDS Bulletin*, 39(6).

Collins, D., J. Morduch, S. Rutherford and O. Ruthven (2009) *Portfolios of the Poor*, Princeton, NJ: Princeton University Press.

Dichter, T. (2007) 'Introduction', in T. Dichter and M. Harper (eds), *What's Wrong with Microfinance?*, Rugby: Practical Action Publishing, pp. 1–6.

Elyachar, J. (2002) 'Empowerment money: the World Bank, non-governmental organizations, and the value of culture in Egypt', *Public Culture*, 14(3): 493–513.

Engle, P. (1989) 'Child care strategies of working and non-working women in rural and urban Guatemala', in J. Leslie and M. Paolisso (eds), *Women, Work, and Child Welfare in the Third World*, Washington, DC: American Association for the Advancement of Science.

Geertz, C. (1962) 'The Rotating Credit Association: a "middle rung" in development', *Economic Development and Cultural Change*, 1(3).

Goetz, A. M. and R. Sen Gupta (1996) 'Who takes the credit? Gender, power and control over loan use in rural credit programs in Bangladesh', *World Development*, 24(1): 45–63.

Harper, M. (1998) *Profit for the Poor – Cases in Micro-finance*, London: ITDG Publications.

Isserles, R. (2003) 'Microcredit: the rhetoric of empowerment, the reality of development as usual', *Women's Studies Quarterly*, 31(3/4).

Kabeer, N. (2005) 'Is microfinance a "magic bullet" for women's empowerment? Analysis of findings from South Asia', *Economic and Political Weekly*, 29 October.

Leslie, J. (1989) 'Women's work and child nutrition in the Third World', in J. Leslie and M. Paolisso (eds), *Women, Work, and Child Welfare in the Third World*, Washington, DC: American Association for the Advancement of Science.

Mayoux, L. (1999) 'Questioning virtuous spirals: microfinance and women's empowerment in Africa', *Journal of International Development*, 11(7): 957–84.

— (2002) *Women's Empowerment or Feminization of Debt? Towards a new agenda in African microfinance*, London: One World Action.

McMichael, P. (2000) *Development and Social Change: A Global Perspective*, 2nd edn, Thousand Oaks, CA: Pine Forge.

Rahman, A. (1999) 'Micro-credit initiatives for equitable and sustainable development: who pays?', *World Development*, 27(10): 67–82.

Sharma, J. and S. Parthasarathy (2007) 'Examining self-help groups: empowerment, poverty alleviation, education; a qualitative study', New Delhi: Nirantar.

8 | Negotiating multiple patriarchies: women and microfinance in South India

K. Kalpana

Introduction

The UN declaration of 2005 as the International Year of Microcredit and the award of the 2006 Nobel Peace Prize to Muhammad Yunus and the bank he founded – the Grameen Bank of Bangladesh – have reinforced the perceived status of microfinance as a strategy for combating poverty, particularly focused on women. The widespread perception that microfinance programs are empowering their female clientele while alleviating their poverty, even as they ensure the financial sustainability of lending agencies, underpins the global appeal of microfinance as a development strategy (Mayoux 1998). The belief that access to financial services enhances a woman's role in household decision-making, increases her confidence level, improves her participation in wider social networks and fosters her engagement in political activity has conceptually linked women's credit and female empowerment (Mayoux 1999). Discussions around the UN Millennium Development Goals reinforce this linkage (Littlefield et al. 2003).

Microfinance programs have demonstrated their capacity to organize women en masse and facilitate their access to safe savings opportunities and collateral-free microloans at interest rates lower than those of local moneylenders, although usually higher than those of the formal banking sector. However, the magnitude of the claims of poverty reduction and female empowerment attributed to an intervention that addresses survival needs of women is excessive. Researchers argue that these claims need to be carefully examined in diverse regional and institutional contexts (Goetz 2001; Johnson 2005). Research has shown the relationship between access to credit and the empowerment of female borrowers is often constrained by and contingent upon the organizational arrangements through which microfinance services are delivered; it is also influenced by the broader social and economic structures in which such programs are embedded. Consequently, the ability of women microfinance clients to effectively challenge structures of power at household and community levels is not an automatic outcome of access to microfinance.

This chapter examines a model of microfinance delivery in India wherein poor women own, manage and control grassroots savings and credit organizations or self-help groups (SHGs). Structurally, SHGs can be distinguished from

55

microfinance programs in which lending agencies set the terms of savings, credit and other financial services. Although women members of SHGs exercise control over the microfinance program, they are simultaneously involved in unequal relationships with more powerful institutional actors that include commercial banks, state development bureaucracies and NGOs. By documenting the challenges women face in securing access to institutional credit, this chapter illustrates how microfinance is embedded in and shaped by existing institutional and societal structures and practices. At the same time, it shows how women deploy a range of strategies that challenge institutional practices they perceive as disadvantageous to their interests and seek to reshape program objectives to better fit their needs and lived realities.

The chapter draws on an ethnographic study of twenty-seven SHGs in three villages in the South Indian state of Tamil Nadu. The groups studied ranged from three to seven years in age and consist of fifteen to twenty members each. All were exclusively women's groups and were, for the most part, caste-segregated. Of the twenty-seven SHGs, fifteen were composed entirely of the Scheduled Castes (SCs), ten of the Other Backward Classes (OBCs) and two were mixed-caste (both SC and OBC).[1]

Indian SHGs: women-owned and -managed collectives

The Grameen Bank of Bangladesh and Grameen-modeled programs worldwide typify the 'provider' model of microfinance delivery (Rutherford 2000), which involves the direct provision of financial services to the poor by professionally managed, specialized financial institutions. In this model, borrowers (organized into neighborhood-based peer groups) save with the local branch of the microfinance institution (MFI) and borrow funds from it. MFIs source funds for on-lending to their borrower groups from a variety of sources including donor organizations, microfinance wholesalers and borrowers' savings.

The Grameen Bank and Grameen-modeled programs have been criticized for offering savings and loan products that are rigidly designed and limited in scope (Cohen 2002; Dunn 2002) as well as for the non-participation of clients in deciding the terms of credit and other financial services (Jain and Moore 2003). Program features that have circumscribed the efficacy of microfinance in combating household poverty include standardized credit packages, the absence of easy-access loans during emergencies, inflexible weekly loan repayments incompatible with the income fluctuations of the poor, constraints placed upon consumption-related borrowing, and savings that remain inaccessible to the poor even during a period of great need. Importantly, protests from borrowers directed at rigid program features were, in part, responsible for a reinvention of the original Grameen Bank model leading to 'Grameen II' in 2001, providing greater choice in repayment terms and savings plans (Yunus 2002).[2]

In contrast to Grameen-modeled programs, the SHG model involves the promotion (by a variety of agencies) of grassroots village-level women's groups that *own the capital they generate* and function as user-owned and member-controlled entities. All members of an SHG save a certain amount on a regular basis. The promoter agency assists in the formation and smooth functioning of groups by providing services that include training in bookkeeping, periodic supervision of group accounts, financial auditing and troubleshooting, whenever required. Members save with the SHG (and *not* with the promoter agency) and borrow from it, and groups usually place no restriction on the purpose for which loans can be used by members. The women select leaders from within the group who help administer the funds and execute group decisions. While the terms of lending and borrowing are determined by the lending agency in the 'provider' model, SHGs are able to make policy decisions regarding the amount and frequency of savings, loan size, the duration of loan repayment and interest rates.

It needs to be emphasized that the potential for women, at local levels, to exercise control over the program is important for ensuring that the terms of savings and credit dovetail with livelihood conditions in the village and respond to their life circumstances. This study found that SHG women often decided to lower or increase interest rates in keeping with changes in their immediate economic environment and acted to a large extent autonomously of promoter agencies when doing so. In a context in which an overwhelming majority (83 percent) of SHG women's households was dependent on daily wage labor in agriculture or the urban informal sector for survival, women valued the unconstrained freedom to make decisions regarding the end-use of loans they borrowed. Women invested loans in income-generating activities only when they judged the environment favorable and their household circumstances conducive for the management of a microenterprise.

Institutional players in SHG promotion and financing

In addition to facilitating greater control by the poor vis-à-vis the terms of savings and credit, SHGs institutionalize financial linkages between informal groups of poor women and formal credit institutions, in particular India's nationalized commercial banks. Shortly after formation, an SHG opens a savings account in a commercial bank as a safe deposit for its funds. Subsequently groups apply for bank loans, in order to supplement their loanable resources. Thus, SHG women access two types of loans: *internal loans* borrowed from members' savings and *bank loans*.[3] Under the SHG–bank linkage scheme, banks make non-collateralized loans which SHG members can use for any purpose, including household consumption (RBI 2009: 2–4). Additionally, a central government-sponsored anti-poverty program provides a mix of bank credit and government subsidy to SHGs in order to finance self-employment-based livelihood activities of the poor.

Indian SHGs interact with a diverse range of institutional actors in order to realize their entitlements to institutional credit. These actors include nationalized commercial banks that play a critical role in SHG financing; the rural development administration of the Indian state at district and local levels, which sanctions the subsidy component of loan-cum-subsidy schemes targeted at SHGs; and development NGOs (which usually play a role in the promotion of SHGs). It would appear therefore that rural women members of SHGs are directly interfacing with state institutions in perhaps larger numbers than ever before in the history of post-independence India in order to press their claims to credit-based development resources earmarked for them by state policies.[4] SHGs' interface with more powerful institutional actors provides a site for studying bank lending practices and state-run poverty-alleviation programs.

Women and banks: gendered interfaces

Relations between SHG women and their banks are shaped by the legacy of poor repayment that characterized older, credit-based schemes implemented by banks as part of nationwide anti-poverty programs.[5] Bankers approved SHG loan applications, contingent on group members repaying delinquent loans. Members, or more commonly their male relatives, were responsible for these delinquent loans. Banks would threaten to stall loans to SHGs unless groups *expelled* individual members unable to repay overdues on individual-targeted loans. In three study villages, eight women under repayment pressure dropped out of their SHGs; only three were *direct* borrowers. An elderly widow quit her SHG when asked to repay her deceased husband's overdue loan to the bank. SHG women sometimes resisted bankers' loan recovery tactics and argued that assessment of creditworthiness should be based solely on the repayment record of their group. It is important to note that bankers were able to successfully invoke women's gendered and household-related identities for the instrumental purpose of loan recovery as they drew upon a shared understanding of women's responsibility for repayment of their husbands' loans – *an understanding that cut across institutions including government bureaucracies, NGOs and even households of SHG members*. Bank officials' insistence on the recovery of individual-targeted loans through SHGs triggered 'bank-induced drop-outs,' in addition to provoking intra-group conflicts (thereby threatening group solidarity) as well as creating household-level tensions when women pressured male relatives to repay overdues on long-lapsed loans.

To secure their loans, women had to make frequent visits to the bank. Group coordinators found this prospect unwelcome since bankers were impatient with women who had little or no formal schooling and lost their temper when a woman took time to understand bank procedure. Although some bank personnel treated SHG customers with civility, their assumption of zero opportunity costs of women's time and labor frustrated the women. A coordinator was once sent home on three consecutive visits as bank personnel were too busy to accept her deposit. While SHG banking opened doors to poor women from rural communities, this study found that it was not sensitive to the needs of the poor or the situation of women.

Spaces for maneuver

SHG women used diverse strategies to secure bank loans when facing pressure from banks to repay individual-targeted loans. Some groups deceived bank officials by providing a letter declaring that the women (with overdues on the loans of their male kin) had quit the group, even when they continued to remain members. Asked by the bank manager to provide the names of fathers-in-law of her co-members, a coordinator provided false names, foreseeing correctly that the enquiries pertained to unpaid bank loans. Women's strategies to secure bank loans even included their informal role as 'debt collectors' who launched repayment campaigns in their villages on behalf of the bank, required whenever bank officials made loans conditional on loan repayment by village residents who were *not* related to SHG members. When one coordinator was jocularly asked by a bank manager to recover overdues from the village community at large, she retorted: 'You are earning the salary. Will you pay me for this work?' Her response highlights the cynical manipulation by banks of SHGs' community-level social networks as well as bankers' exploitation of the unremunerated time and effort expended by coordinators to settle bank debt. Still, SHG women invested considerable resources in building close relationships with the branch manager of the bank, a crucial benefactor, taking pains to show their appreciation to those who were helpful.

Subverting enterprise-promotion loans: fitting policy to reality

Since April 1999, a nationwide, anti-poverty scheme[6] has used SHGs to deliver subsidy-bearing loans to targeted households to finance income-earning activities (GOI n.d.: 1.1). The enterprise-promotion loan scheme identifies a few key economic activities at the sub-district level and promotes self-employment of loan recipients based on those activities (ibid.: 3.19). Each SHG receiving the loan is expected to set up and collectively manage an enterprise since the scheme anticipates greater success from group-based economic activities (ibid.: 3.21).

All groups interviewed firmly asserted that collectively managed group enterprises held no prospect for advancement of the SHG and, in fact, could endanger their existence. If enterprises failed, the group could collapse and the women's accumulated savings would be lost. Nonetheless, the enterprise-promotion scheme was sought after on account of the coveted subsidy component (ranging from one third to half of loan value). As a result, SHGs distributed the total amount (loan and subsidy) equally among all members and collectively repaid the loan to the bank.[7] The loans were used by the women to meet household consumption or livelihood-related needs.[8]

The case of an SHG which proposed to manage a brick kiln business illustrates the modus operandi groups used to show proof of business ownership and management. The group struck a deal with a local brick kiln owner who provided a false document to the bank stating that the SHG had acquired a kiln and leased it to him to manage. The SHG paid the kiln owner Rs 4,000 for this service and for his cooperation when bank staff inspected the work place thrice for verification purposes. However, as the coordinator put it, 'Of course the bank knew that we were not managing the brick kiln.' Importantly, the fiction of make-believe enterprises, owned and operated by women, was sustained by SHGs with the full knowledge of promoter NGOs, financing banks and the rural development administration, all required by state policy to ensure the smooth operation of the enterprise-promotion scheme. As the case of the brick kiln demonstrates, groups incurred costs through bribes to business owners who supplied the documents to help SHGs feign productive use of the loans.

SHGs' costs increased when rural development administration officials sought illegal remuneration for approving the subsidy component of the loan.[9] While the local bureaucracy was perceived by women as corrupt and primarily interested in securing bribes, it could also be an important ally when required to 'manage' difficult bank managers who tried to actively supervise enterprises ostensibly managed by women's groups. It was also the case that the moral support provided by a few empathetic bank officers helped groups reduce the amount of bribes paid to the bureaucracy. SHGs frequently appealed to one institution to help mitigate the excesses of the other.

Women's strategies for survival and change

As this chapter shows, SHGs seeking credit are vulnerable to the institutional imperatives of banks, the systemic corruption of the rural development administration and the policy mandates of a developmental state, which legitimizes women's access to institutional credit, even as it imposes an enterprise-promotion agenda widely perceived as irrelevant to their life circumstances. However, women are not merely manipulated by institutional actors; they maneuver to secure bank credit, defend their interests and resist instrumentalist pressures. As has been argued in other contexts (Jackson 1997: 163), women participants of development programs are active agents who subvert policies and shape programs.

This study found that SHG women deployed tact and skill, even subterfuge and lies where necessary, besides investing time and resources cultivating business owners and bank managers in order to optimize their chances of securing bank loans. However, the ample evidence of SHG women's agency should not blur the underlying fact that poor women continue to strategize and act within institutional contexts in which the 'rules of the game' are set against them. Their exercise of agency in such contexts is limited and likely to invite negative consequences. For instance, women's ingenious efforts to manufacture evidence of enterprise activity secured their access to subsidy-bearing loans, even as it extracted a price. For the most part, groups were unable to resist the demand for bribes by the development administration when women's subversion of the enterprise-promotion scheme was well known to all actors involved. Apart from the coping or 'survival' strategies that SHG women fashioned in response to pressures from promoter and financing agencies, this study also found evidence of what may be described as 'transformative agency.'

SHGs proactively sought to extend their relationship with institutions of the state beyond the intended goal of securing credit access. Women used their SHGs to gain access to state institutions such as the police. Some women threatened to report cases of sexual harassment and marital violence to the police through the group ('file a complaint using the SHG's letterhead') in order to keep abusive husbands or sons-in-law in check. The official invitation that is routinely extended to SHGs to participate in all public events relating to local governance such as *Panchayat*[10] meetings has, in some villages, been seized upon by women to initiate a dynamic engagement with local development issues. In one village, SHGs drew up petitions listing the names of the elderly poor excluded from old-age pensions and women denied the widow's pension and demanded the immediate allotment of house sites to the homeless SC poor. When the village headman, outraged by the seriousness with which women (SC women in particular) engaged the *Panchayat*, verbally abused the women, these women took the matter up with the head of the district administration and successfully defended their right to participate in the *Grama Sabha* (village assembly). In this case, the women used the links they developed with state institutions strategically to challenge local vested interests and power structures.

In the study region, state commitment to the promotion of women's SHGs was popularly interpreted as official endorsement of a gender equality agenda. A disgruntled husband informed the researcher that men often discussed with each other that SHGs had eroded women's respect for their husbands, taught them to speak a 'language of rights' at home and spawned the idea that women have power too. As he put it, 'Women tell their husbands: even the government says we have equal rights.' Thus it appeared that the visibility of state support for SHGs was creatively used by rural women to advance their interests and defy household and community-level patriarchies in small but significant ways *that were recognized as transgressive by men and local community leaders.* We note that advantages that derive from the presence of multiple institutional actors such as the possibility of appealing to one to intercede with another or using the legitimacy bestowed by state institutions to negotiate with other actors are likely to be absent in Grameen-modeled programs in which women's groups interact exclusively with the MFI.

Conclusion

My study corroborates earlier findings that microfinance programs do not inherently empower their women clients or alleviate poverty. It reinforces the importance of institutional context and the socio-economic landscapes of the regions in which programs operate. In the case of the Indian experience, SHGs' close engagement with state institutions entailed costs for women even while it created possibilities for successfully challenging entrenched structures of patriarchy. Finally, insights from this study should help policymakers design microcredit programs that respond to conditions that burden women borrowers.

Notes

1 The Indian government classifies caste groups as SCs and OBCs in decreasing order of social oppression and deprivation. The two groups usually live in segregated fashion in separate hamlets in rural Tamil Nadu.

2 In recent times, the 'provider' model of microfinance delivery has faced a series of crises in several parts of the world including India. Issues such as over-lending by the MFI, spiraling indebtedness of borrowers and coercive loan recovery tactics adopted by MFI staff have surfaced, seriously questioning the poverty alleviation and empowerment objectives of microfinance programs (New York Times 2011).

3 The Reserve Bank of India (the central bank) has promoted SHG banking to optimize utilization of commercial banks by sections of the poor formerly perceived as uncreditworthy.

4 As of end-March 2008, over five million SHGs maintained savings worth Rs37.85 billion with the banking sector (NABARD 2009: 4).

5 From 1980 to 1999, the Indian government implemented the Integrated Rural Development Programme (IRDP), which provided financial assistance to targeted poor households to undertake self-employment activities. The IRDP was plagued by poor institutional incentives

for loan repayment (Kabeer and Murthy 1996: 2.3).

6 The scheme in question is the government-sponsored SwarnaJayanti Gram Swarozgar Yojana (SGSY). This scheme is henceforth referred to as the enterprise-promotion loan scheme.

7 The majority of groups in this study received loans ranging in size from Rs100,000 to Rs200,000.

8 The SGSY scheme has been criticized for poor conceptualization and flawed implementation in enterprise selection, market linkage and beneficiary capacity assessment (Banerjee and Sen 2003).

9 Such demands are widespread in Tamil Nadu and are not unique to the study villages.

10 The *Panchayat* is the lowest (village-level) unit of self-governance in India.

References

Banerjee, N. and J. Sen (2003) 'The Swarnajayanti Gram Swarozgar Yojana: a policy in working', Kolkata, www.idrc.ca/uploads/user-S/11138471151Swarnajayanti__Gram_Swarozgar_Yojana.pdf.

Cohen, M. (2002) 'Making microfinance more client-led', *Journal of International Development*, 14(3): 335–50.

Dunn, E. (2002) 'It pays to know the customer: addressing the information needs of client-centered MFIs', *Journal of International Development*, 14(3): 325–34.

Goetz, A. M. (2001) *Women Development Workers: Implementing Rural Credit Programmes in Bangladesh*, New Delhi, Thousand Oaks, CA, London: Sage Publications.

GOI (Government of India) (n.d.) 'Swarn-Jayanti Gram Swarozgar Yojana Guidelines', Ministry of Rural Development, New Delhi.

Jackson, C. (1997) 'Actor orientation and gender relations at a participatory project interface', in A. M. Goetz (ed.), *Getting Institutions Right for Women in Development*, London and New York: Zed Books, pp. 161–75.

Jain, P. and M. Moore (2003) 'What makes microcredit programmes effective? Fashionable fallacies and workable realities', IDS Working Paper 177, Brighton: Institute of Development Studies.

Johnson, S. (2005) 'Gender relations, empowerment and microcredit: moving on from a lost decade', *European Journal of Development Research*, 17(2): 224–48.

Kabeer, N. and R. K. Murthy (1996) 'Compensating for institutional exclusion? Lessons from Indian government and non-government credit interventions for the poor', IDS Discussion Paper 356, Brighton: Institute of Development Studies.

Littlefield, E., J. Morduch and S. Hashemi (2003) 'Is microfinance an effective strategy to reach the Millennium Development Goals?', Focus Note 24 (January), Washington, DC: Consultative Group to Assist the Poor (CGAP).

Mayoux, L. (1998) 'Women's empowerment and microfinance programmes: approaches, evidence and ways forward', Discussion Paper, Open University, Milton Keynes.

— (1999) 'Questioning virtuous spirals: micro-finance and women's empowerment in Africa', *Journal of International Development*, 11(7): 957–84.

NABARD (National Bank for Agriculture and Rural Development) (2009) *Annual Report 2008–2009*, Mumbai: NABARD.

New York Times (2011) 'Microlenders, honored with Nobel, are struggling', 6 January, www.nytimes.com/2011/01/06/business/global/06micro.html?_r=1&pagewanted=2.

RBI (Reserve Bank of India) (2009) 'Master circular on micro credit', rbidocs.rbi.org.in/rdocs/notification/PDFs/40MCMC010709_F.pdf.

Rutherford, S. (2000) *The Poor and Their Money*, New Delhi: Oxford University Press.

Yunus, M. (2002) 'Grameen Bank II: designed to open new possibilities', *Grameen Dialogue*, Newsletter published by the Grameen Trust, Bangladesh.

9 | Gender as a social determinant of health: evidence, policies, and innovations[1]

Gita Sen and Piroska Ostlin

Gender relations of power constitute the root causes of gender inequality and are among the most influential of the social determinants of health. They operate across many dimensions of life affecting how people live, work, and relate to each other. They determine whether people's needs are acknowledged, whether they have a voice or a modicum of control over their lives and health, whether they can realize their rights. Addressing the problem of gender inequality requires actions both outside and within the health sector because gender power relations operate across such a wide spectrum of human life and in such interrelated ways. In particular, intersectoral action to address gender inequality is critical to the realization of the Millennium Development Goals (MDGs).

It can be difficult, however, to understand how gender power relations work to reproduce health inequity without also understanding how gender intersects with economic inequality, racial or ethnic hierarchy, caste domination, differences based on sexual orientation, or a number of other social markers. Focusing only on economic inequalities among households can seriously distort our understanding of how inequality works and who actually bears much of its burden. Gender analysis itself has been challenged more recently by work deriving from social movements for sexual rights, in particular the lesbian/gay/bisexual/transgender (LGBT) movement. These movements have challenged feminist movements to be more inclusive and to recognize sexual and gender orientation as an important source of discrimination, bias, violence, and challenges to health. If the feminist movement has challenged masculinist norms, the LGBT movement challenges heterosexual norms that are also sources of discrimination and bias.[2]

The right to health is affirmed in the Universal Declaration of Human Rights (United Nations 1948) and is part of the WHO's core principles. Yet the egregious violation of women's human rights through violence was globally recognized only at the World Conference on Human Rights in Vienna in 1993. Even after this, gender equality remains in a limbo where everyone agrees publicly about the need to act but resources are not allocated and follow-up action is weak or nonexistent. The heart of the problem is that gender discrimination, bias, and inequality permeate the organizational structures of governments and international organizations, and the mechanisms through which strategies and policies are designed and implemented. People within these structures are themselves often deeply invested in the gender status quo.

Gendered structural determinants of health

Gender systems have a variety of different features, not all of which are the same across different societies. Women have less land, wealth, and property in almost all societies; yet they have higher burdens of work in the economy of 'care' – ensuring the survival, reproduction, and security of people, including young and old. Girls, in some contexts, are fed less, educated less, and more physically restricted; and women are typically employed and segregated in lower-paid, less secure, and 'informal,' occupations. Gender hierarchy governs how people live, and what they believe, and claim to know about what it means to be a girl or a boy, a woman or a man. Restrictions on their [girls' and women's] physical mobility, sexuality, and reproductive capacity are perceived to be natural; and, in many instances, accepted codes of social conduct and legal systems condone, and even reward, violence against them (Garcia-Moreno et al. 2006).

Women are thus seen as objects rather than subjects (or agents) in their own homes and communities, and this is reflected in norms of behavior, codes of conduct, and laws that perpetuate their status as lower beings and second-class citizens.

Intersecting inequalities The other side of the coin of women's subordinate position is that men typically have greater wealth, better jobs, more education, greater political clout, and fewer restrictions on behavior. Moreover, men in many parts of the world exercise power over women, making decisions on their behalf, regulating and constraining their access to resources and personal agency, and sanctioning and policing their behavior through socially condoned violence or the threat of violence. Again not all men exercise power over all women; gender power relations are intersected by age and life-cycle, as well as the other social stratifiers, such as economic class, race, or caste. The impact of gender power for physical and mental health – of girls, women, and transgender/intersex people, and also of boys and men – can be profound.

Education deficits Despite recent advances, a gender gap in literacy and education persists in many parts of the world (Herz and Sperling 2004). Significant numbers of women reach adulthood with no education, especially in South Asia, where the literacy rate for women (equal to and over fifteen years of age) in 2004 was as low as 48 percent, only two-thirds the rate for men (HDR 2006). The children of women who have never received an education are 50 percent more likely to suffer from malnutrition or to die before the age of five (UNFPA 2002). Children and especially girls with low levels of schooling assume the work burdens of adults prematurely. In many countries millions of girls 'disappear' into early traditional marriages, hazardous labor, or even combat roles (UNICEF 2006).

Barriers to the education of girls include negative perceptions about women that devalue their capabilities, strong beliefs about the division of labor that places inequitable burdens on females, gender-biased beliefs about the value of educating girls, and curricula that are seen as inappropriate for girls (Abane 2004). Such beliefs are exacerbated by structural barriers such as school fees or school-going costs; distance from schools; perceived or actual lack of safety for girls going to school; absence of female teachers; lack of gender sensitivity in schools, including absence of decent toilet facilities for adolescent girls; and inflexibility of classroom programs.

Demographic changes and women's burdens Changes in the demand for and supply of education have been fueled in part by the demographic transition in birth rates and death rates. Some countries have seen falls in death rates without corresponding declines in birth rates. In regions seriously affected by the HIV/AIDS pandemic, the age pyramid appears hollowed out in the middle ages owing to the high infection rates among women and men in the reproductive ages. In regions with endemic son-preference, the availability of ultrasound technologies has significantly altered the sex ratio in the population as a whole, and particularly the child sex ratio, against girls and women (UNFPA 2006).

These processes have important implications for girls and women as the first-line providers of all forms of care, including healthcare within and outside the home. When mothers work for low incomes, girls are often recruited to care for siblings at the expense of their own education (Herz and Sperling 2004). The aging of populations also increases women's care-work burdens in supporting the elderly. Widows tend to be poorer, and their rates of impoverishment and destitution higher than those of widowers and many other subsets of the population.

The extent to which the needs of young populations, as well as older populations, have to be met through the unpaid 'care' work of women is exacerbated by crumbling health services and vanishing paid health staff.

Globalization During the last four decades, the effect of demographic transitions and of increased education have been crosscut by technological and other changes that have brought local, national, and regional economies ever closer. Fueled by the revolution in information technology and its penetration to the core of economic and production systems, this globalization, which has been driven by the rising dominance of highly volatile finance capital, has also given birth to social movements that are more global in scope.

Three implications of globalization are of particular significance for our focus on gender relations. The *first* is how it has transformed the composition of workforces, and the resulting impacts on women's health. Feminization of workforces has gone hand in hand with increased casualization, and continuing unequal burdens for unpaid work in the household, with serious implications for women's occupational health and the consequences of insufficient rest and leisure (Joekes 1995; Standing 1997; Messing and Ostlin 2006).

A *second* gendered consequence of globalization is through its narrowing of national policy space resulting in reducing funds for health and education with negative impacts on girls' and women's access (Stiglitz and Charlton 2005; Herz and Sperling 2004). In the 1990s, these harsh structural adjustment policies springing from the so-called Washington Consensus began to be somewhat modified. Commitment to Poverty Reduction Strategies (PRS) or equivalent National Development Strategies (NDS) by countries were made the basis of foreign lending. But while program lending for health increased in a number of cases, it has often been associated with pressures for privatization and increases in user fees.

A *third* aspect of globalization of importance for health is the rise in violence linked to the changing political economy of nation-states in the international order. Petchesky and Laurie [see Sen and Ostlin 2010, ch. 4] argue(s) that a human rights approach to gender and health equity is especially critical in 'sites of exclusion' – refugee camps, detention areas for undocumented migrants or trafficked persons, spaces on the margins of national regimes or under contested international jurisdiction. Importantly, gendered violence does not only affect girls and women in these sites, but includes violence against boys and men, as well as transgender and intersex persons, and all those who do not meet heterosexual norms.

Deepening the human rights agenda Some of the negative consequences of globalization contrast with the deepening, during recent decades, of the normative framework of human rights. This deepening has been important in altering values, beliefs, and knowledge about gender systems and their implications for health and human rights.

The explicit recognition of lived realities, for example of rape as a violation of women's human rights (United Nations 1993), or racism as a violation of the human rights of specific racial or ethnic groups (United Nations 2001), was critical to their being acknowledged as needing legal and policy remedies. One important precursor at the global level was the adoption of the Convention on the Elimination of All Forms of Discrimination against Women (CEDAW) in 1979. CEDAW provided a broad framework for women's rights that has been used in a number of countries to advance action at the national level.

A further important way in which the human rights framework has been deepened is through interpreting the right to health to include reproductive and sexual health and reproductive rights (United Nations 1994) and sexual rights (United Nations 1995). In 2007, international human rights experts launched the Yogyakarta Principles on the application of international human rights law to sexual orientation and gender identity.[3]

Transforming the gendered structural determinants of health Deepening the recognition of human rights is, however, only half the needed action. The other half is to turn such norms into reality through mechanisms for implementation and accountability.

Intermediary factors – discriminatory values, norms, practices and behaviors

Direct causal relationships, linking cultural biases against girls and women to health outcomes, vary widely across regions and cultures, and over time. These biases include differential access to nutrition and healthcare for boys versus girls, and women versus men. Norms of masculinity vary, as do models of what represents perfect femininity.

Challenging gender stereotypes and how they affect health No single or simple action or policy intervention can be expected to provide a panacea for the problem. Multilevel interventions are therefore needed. We identify three sets of actions.

The first is creating formal agreements, codes, and laws to change norms that violate women's human rights, and then implementing them. The cardinal rule for this is that there must be local groups of advocates, especially women's organizations or human rights groups.

Recent years have seen a number of legal changes in different countries. A milestone was the change in the personal status law in Tunisia. This legislation has brought about a profound change in the norms regarding women's position in society and within marriage. In Egypt the revision in 2000 of the 1979 law on formal marriage contracts gave a woman much wider rights to ask for divorce unilaterally provided she is willing to renounce her financial rights. A remarkable combination of coalition politics, legal activism, and an intelligent reclaiming of Islam by women's rights advocates made this possible.

Yet another example was the act against domestic violence in India. As a result of strong lobbying by women's groups, and effective redrafting by feminist lawyers, a considerably improved act has recently come into force as the Protection of Women from Domestic Violence Act 2005.

Once laws are there, they need to be enforced, and this requires that appropriate institutions and budgets be assigned for this. One of the most thorough attempts to date to delineate a multilevel and multisectoral strategy for an important manifestation of unequal gender norms is in WHO's report on violence against women (WHO 2005), based on a multi-country study.

Complementing legal changes and multilevel actions is the third action priority – working with boys and men towards male transformation. Program H, an innovative educational program that was pioneered by Latin American NGOs, attempts to create a safe space in which young men can question manhood norms and learn alternatives through group activities and processes. Another example is Stepping Stones in South Africa, a behavioral intervention that approaches HIV prevention and reduction in violence against women from the perspective of gender inequality, relationships, and skills, and broader reproductive health concerns (Jewkes et al. 2007). Stepping Stones provides evidence of success in reducing sexually transmitted infections in women, changing men's sexual risk-taking behavior, and reducing their violence against women.

Intermediary factors – differential exposures and vulnerabilities In a wide range of countries male survival at all ages is inferior to that of females and this is reflected in lower life expectancy for men. Even where men die earlier than women, most studies on morbidity from both high- and low-income countries show higher rates of illness among women.

Many health conditions reflect a combination of biological sex differences and gendered social determinants. Gender differentials in exposure and vulnerability to health risks can arise from two main reasons: the interplay of biological sex with the social construction of gender, and the direct impacts of structural gender inequalities. Vulnerability reflects an individual's capacity to avoid, respond to, cope, and/or recover from exposures. As such, one's ability to deflect or absorb exposures with differing health effects and social consequences depends on a range of normative and structural social processes.

Biological differences are important, but they do not always have sufficient power to determine health outcomes on their own. Yet women's health concerns are often understood as being mainly determined by biology. Tuberculosis increases poor health outcomes during pregnancy for both mother and child. For men, however, it is behavior in the form of smoking which influences TB's disease progression.

In unprotected heterosexual intercourse, females are about twice as likely as males to contract HIV from an infected partner.[4] Most significant are the power relations that influence sexual behavior and constrain health-seeking behavior and social support. Increasingly, men at risk of HIV have been initiating sex with younger and younger female partners, and this places young girls at increasing risk (Brown et al. 2001). At a policy level, women are also more vulnerable to HIV owing to the conservative hierarchy of policy options that does not acknowledge women's realities or rights.

There are health risks and conditions that are determined primarily by gender structures and relations. For example, an outcome of masculinity norms as manifested through risk behavior is that, globally, 2.7 times as many men as women die from road traffic injuries. Violence against women is another consequence of macho male behavior and unequal power relationships between women and men (Garcia-Moreno 2002).

Reducing the health risks of being women and men Where biological sex differences interact with social determinants to define different needs for women and men in health, policy efforts must address these different needs. Two intertwined strategies to address social bias are: tackling the social context of individual behavior, and empowering individuals and communities for positive change. For strategies to succeed they must provide positive alternatives that support individuals and communities to take action against the status quo.

Intermediary factors – biased health systems The WHO defines health systems as 'all the activities whose primary purpose is to promote, restore, or maintain health' (WHO 2001). Action priorities include supporting improvements in women's access to services, recognition of women's role as healthcare providers, and building accountability for gender equality and equity into health systems, and especially in ongoing health reform programs and mechanisms.

Changing how we care and cure Minimizing gender bias in health systems requires systematic approaches to building awareness and transforming values among service providers, steps to improve access to health services, and effective mechanisms for accountability.

Transforming the medical curriculum is a key measure for building capacity of healthcare providers in gender analysis and responsiveness. Improving women's access to healthcare requires ensuring that user fees are not collected at the point of access to the service. Profamilia's *Clinica Para El Hombre* in Colombia represents one of the most successful attempts to increase men's access to comprehensive reproductive health services through the introduction of men-only clinics. Finally, absence of effective accountability mechanisms for available, affordable, acceptable, and high-quality health services and facilities may seriously hinder women and their families in holding government and other actors accountable for violations of their human rights to health.

Intermediary factors – biased health research Gender imbalances in research content include the following dimensions: slow recognition of health problems that particularly affect women; misdirected or partial approaches to women's and men's health needs in different fields of health research; and lack of recognition of the interaction between gender and other social factors. Mechanisms and policies need to be developed to ensure that gender imbalances in both the content and processes of health research are avoided and corrected.

Changing what we know Without sex-disaggregated data gender analysis of health is not possible. The importance of having good-quality data and indicators for health status disaggregated by sex and age from infancy through old age cannot be overstated. The Women and Health Program of WHO's Center for Health Development (Kobe, Japan) has produced a detailed evaluation of indicators for Gender Equity and Health that is an important resource in this area (WHO 2003).

Removing organizational plaque

Gender mainstreaming came to the forefront of gender equity and equality policies after the Beijing Conference on Women in 1995. It was understood to mean systematic integration of gender perspective at all relevant levels. Insufficient resources, weak organizational mechanisms, and poor political commitment have resulted in fragmented efforts, significant mismatches between stated gender policy and these efforts, and serious gaps between political rhetoric and actual practice.

Many of the organizational structures of government and other social and private institutions, through which gender norms have to be challenged and practices altered, have been in existence for decades, even centuries. Working towards gender equality challenges longstanding male-dominated power structures, and patriarchal social capital (old boys' networks) within organizations. Resistance to gender-equal policies may take the form of trivialization, dilution, subversion, or outright resistance, and can lead to the evaporation of gender equitable laws, policies, or programs.

Gender mainstreaming in government and nongovernment organizations has to be owned institutionally, funded adequately, and implemented effectively. It needs to be supported by an action-oriented gender unit with strong positioning and authority, and civil society linkages to ensure effectiveness and accountability.

The way forward

Gender relations of power exist both within and outside the health sector, and they exercise a pernicious influence on the health of people. The consequences for people's health are not only unequal and unjust, but also ineffective and inefficient. While there are still only a few countries that have taken comprehensive multisectoral actions backed by policies and legislation and supported by civil society, there are many smaller cases and examples from which all actors can learn, and which can be the basis for moving forward.

Notes

1 This chapter is based on the Final Report of the Women and Gender Equity Knowledge Network of the WHO Commission on Social Determinants of Health.

2 'On February the 11th, the Andalusian Parliament had the representatives of Identidad de Genero as guests for the discussion of a motion introduced by the PSOE [Socialist Party] about transsexual people's rights. The motion was passed with no votes against' (Euro-Letter, 68, March 1999).

3 See www.yogyakartaprinciples.org/docs/File/Yogyakarta_Principles_EN.pdf.

4 See www.unaids.org/en/IIssues/Affected_communities/women.asp, accessed 9 April 2007.

References

Abane, H. (2004) 'The girls do not learn hard enough so they cannot do certain types of work – experiences from an NGO-sponsored gender sensitization workshop in a southern Ghanaian community', Community Development Journal, 39: 49–61.

Brown, A., S. Jejeeboy, I. Shah and K. Yount (2001) Sexual Relations among Young People in Developing Countries: Evidence from WHO Studies, Geneva: Department of Reproductive Health Research, World Health Organization.

Garcia-Moreno, C. (2002) 'Violence against women: consolidating a public health agenda', in G. Sen, A. George and P. Ostlin (eds), Engendering International Health: A Challenge of Equity, Cambridge, MA: MIT Press.

Garcia-Moreno, C., H. Jansen, M.Ellsberg, L. Iese, C. H. Watts (2006) 'Prevalence of intimate partner violence: findings from the WHO multi-country study on women's health and domestic violence', Lancet, 368: 1260–69.

HDR (2006) Human Development Report 2006; Beyond Scarcity: Power, Poverty and the Global Water Crisis, New York: UNDP.

Herz, B. and D. Sperling (2004) What Works in Girl's Education: Evidence and Policies from the Developing World, New York: Council on Foreign Relations.

Jewkes, R., M. Nduna, J. Levin, N. Jama, K. Dunkle, K. Wood, M. Koss, A. Puren and N. Duvvury (2007) Evaluation of Stepping Stones: A Gender Transformative Prevention Intervention. Policy Brief, South Africa: MRC, March.

Joekes, S. (1995) 'Gender and livelihoods in northern Pakistan', IDS Bulletin, 26: 66–74.

Messing, K. and P. Ostlin (2006) Gender Equality, Work and Health: A Review of the Evidence, Geneva: World Health Organization.

Sen, G. and P. Ostlin (2010) Gender Equity in Health. The Shifting Frontiers of Evidence and Action, New York: Routledge.

Standing, H. (1997) 'Gender and equity in health sector reform programmes: a review', Health Policy Plan, 12: 1–18.

Stiglitz, J. E. and A. Charlton (2005) Fair Trade for All. How Trade Can Promote Development, Oxford: Oxford University Press.

UNFPA (2002) State of World Population 2002 – People, Poverty and Possibilities: Making Development Work for the Poor, New York: United Nations Population Fund.

— (2006) State of the World Population 2006. A Passage to Hope: Women and International Migration, New York: United Nations Population Fund.

UNICEF (2006) The State of the World's Children: Excluded and Invisible, New York: UNICEF.

United Nations (1948) Universal Declaration of Human Rights, New York: United Nations.

— (1993) The Report of the UN World Human Rights Conference in Vienna, Vienna: United Nations.

— (1994) Report of the International Conference on Population and Development (ICPD), Cairo, 5–13 September.

— (1995) Report of the fourth World

Conference on Women, Beijing, 4–15 September.

— (2001) Report of the World Conference against Racism, Racial Discrimination, Xenophobia and Related Intolerances, Durban, 21 August–7 September.

WHO (2001) *World Health Report*, Geneva: World Health Organization.

— (2003) *Comparative Evaluation of Indicators for Gender Equality and Health*, Women and Health Programme, Center for Health Development, World Health Organization, Kobe, Japan.

— (2005) *WHO's Multi-Country Study on Women's Health and Domestic Violence against Women*, Geneva: World Health Organization.

10 | Peace-building and reconstruction with women: reflections on Afghanistan, Iraq, and Palestine

Valentine M. Moghadam

Violence against women is multifaceted and occurs in different contexts. From domestic violence to 'date rape,' from assaults on the streets to war crimes, violence is often sexualized and occurs at times of 'peace' as well as during armed conflict. All too often, armed conflict exacerbates violence against women. Rapes may occur on a large scale, men may institute controls over the women of their community, and women may suffer at the hands of husbands or male kin who feel humiliated or emasculated by occupying powers. Conditions are worsened when states lack the capacity or the will to protect the human rights of citizens, and especially the human rights of women.

Afghanistan and Iraq have seen some twenty-five years of conflict, starting at roughly the same time, and both countries have experienced invasions and occupation by foreign troops.[1] They also are beset by ethnic, communal, and sectarian divisions. Palestine has been in conflict since at least the early 1970s, when its armed struggle for national recognition took shape. The first intifada (uprising) of the late 1980s paved the way to a peace process and the establishment of the Palestine Authority, but the outbreak of the second intifada in 2001 led to more fighting and many deaths on both sides. In addition to the infrastructural damage caused by punitive Israeli military action, a consequence of the second intifada has been a collapsed economy and exceedingly high unemployment.

The situation is even more dire in Afghanistan, where hardly any of the elements of a modern economy were in place prior to 'reconstruction' following the ouster of the Taliban in late 2001. In a country that is predominantly rural and underdeveloped, with a majority of its population illiterate, economic development is the major requirement – along with nation-building, state formation, and the building of civil society. Iraq is a more economically and socially developed country than Afghanistan, but major infrastructure was destroyed, and health and literacy seriously damaged, as a result of the punitive sanctions of the 1990s as well as during the Iran–Iraq war in the 1980s and the military invasion of 2003.

Violence against women is common in all three cases. In Afghanistan's highly patriarchal society, women have been long subjected to violence by husbands and male kin. 'Honor killings' occur with some frequency in certain Iraqi and Palestinian communities. As feminist scholarship has shown, constructions of masculinity and femininity have tended to 'normalize' and 'naturalize' violence against women. On top of that, wars, and especially occupations by foreign powers, have been accompanied by crises of masculinity that have led to restrictions on women's mobility and increases in violence against women (Breines et al. 2000; Enloe 1990). In all three countries, women are caught between weak states, occupying powers, armed opposition movements, and patriarchal gender arrangements. Moreover, politics have been masculine and male-dominated, with women largely excluded from political decision-making.

In October 2000, the landmark Security Council Resolution 1325 was adopted.[2] It reaffirms the important role of women in the prevention and resolution of conflicts, and the need to implement fully international humanitarian and human rights law that protects the rights of women and girls during and after conflicts. However, despite the adoption of this important resolution, we continue to see the sidelining of both women actors and gender issues in many contemporary conflicts, peacekeeping initiatives, and reconstruction efforts.[3] In Israel/Palestine, Afghanistan, and Iraq, a culture of 'hegemonic masculinity' prevails among the major political actors, be they the occupiers, the resistance, or the state.

In such a context, what are the prospects for women's empowerment? How to reconstruct – or in the case of Afghanistan and Palestine, construct – political and economic systems while also ensuring human security and human rights, especially for women?

Afghanistan

Afghanistan was once considered a model of post-conflict reconstruction, yet women can hardly be said to be enjoying security, participation, and rights. Reports by various international agencies have cited harassment, violence, illiteracy, poverty and extreme repression as characterizing women's social reality. These circumstances are the result of the persistence of patriarchal gender relations and the absence of a strong, centralized state with the capacity or will to implement a wide-ranging program for women's rights.

Afghanistan's 2004 constitution mandates compulsory education up to grade 9, but the majority of girls remain out of school. Secondary school enrollments remained extremely low, especially for girls; only 9 percent of girls attending primary school continued to secondary school. The country's Supreme Court barred married women from attending high school – in a country where girls as young as ten are married off, often to far older men. Afghan girls and women still learn to read and write in secret classrooms – girls because of attacks on schools or because their fathers will not send them to a state school; women because the government prohibits married women from attending school.[4]

Patriarchal practices, attitudes and policies prevail. Approximately 57 percent of girls are married before the age of sixteen, according to a study by the Ministry of Women's Affairs and Afghan women's nongovernmental organizations (NGOs) (www.hrw.org/campaigns/afghanistan/facts.htm). Health statistics remain dire for citizens as a whole, but UNICEF figures show that women also suffer very high rates of maternal mortality. In a culture where a woman without a *sarparast* (male household head) is often shunned, widows face many prejudices. Under the Taliban, widows were denied employment opportunities and many had to resort to begging to provide for their families.

Women experience considerable violence in the country. Son-preference is still strong, and mothers can be abused by husbands and in-laws for not producing sons (UNIFEM 2004). An Amnesty International report noted that girls and women in many parts of the country are prosecuted for *zina* crimes such as adultery, running away from home, and premarital sex. Self-immolations appear to be on the rise in Afghanistan and are tied to forced marriage; the typical victim is fourteen to twenty years old and is trying to escape a marriage arranged by her father (Los Angeles Times 2002). Under such conditions, it is not surprising that the vast majority of women continue to wear the all-encompassing burqa. Veiling is determined not only by custom and tradition, but also by social pressure within the family, and fear of harassment in the street.

What is behind the persistence of violence, patriarchy, and insecurity in post-Taliban Afghanistan? A tribal social structure, warlordism, and state compromises are key factors. The contemporary Afghan state seems to be the result of social and ideological compromise between modernists and traditionalists, feminists and fundamentalists, and Islamists and Muslims with more moderate religious views. As a result, the state cannot take a definitively pro-woman stance.

Despite serious obstacles, or perhaps because of them, women's organizations continue to work with each other, transnationally, and with global feminist groups to bring pressure to bear on the Karzai government, to raise funding for women's projects, and to make women's rights a reality and not merely a formality.

Iraq

The record of women's rights in pre-war Iraq was a mixed one, beginning with gains as a result of the Baathist ideology of Arab socialism and progress in the 1960s and 1970s, but with setbacks following the Gulf wars, the sanctions, and Saddam Hussein's attempt to curry favor with tribes and religious forces by assuming an Islamic mantle and reinstating patriarchal family practices.[5]

But after the invasion of 2003 and the escalation of conflict, women's human security or human rights could not be guaranteed, as neither the post-Saddam Coalition Provisional Authority (CPA) nor the US military was able, or perhaps even willing, to protect women in their everyday lives. Reports showed that many more women were appearing in public in hijab, for fear of harassment or worse. It was an ironic but tragic consequence of the US invasion and occupation that Iraq was experiencing a breakdown in public order, with reports of increases in domestic violence, honor killings, kidnapping, and rapes.

Although a quota system was established to guarantee a 25 percent share of women in the country's parliament, the legal framework for women's rights had serious limitations. There remained provisions in the Iraqi Penal Code allowing a man to escape punishment for abduction by marrying the victim, and allowing for significantly reduced sentences for so-called honor killings.[6]

Unlike Afghanistan, Iraq has a relatively large and well-educated middle class, with many strong and highly educated women, some of them in or around the government, others working independently. This is why, when the Iraqi Governing Council tried to return family affairs to religious courts through the notorious Resolution 137 in early 2004, large numbers of Iraqi women mobilized opposition inside and outside the country. The result was that the resolution was withdrawn. It was an important victory for Iraqi women leaders, and they went on to demand greater representation in government bodies.

Despite the growth of women's NGOs and their collective action, the violence surrounding the women's leadership is considerable. The violence began with the assassination in 2003 of Akila Hashemi, a member of the Interim Governing Council, and has continued with targeted killings of other prominent women, unveiled women, and women who work in services associated with the occupation or government. Iraqi activists note the rise of honor killings and domestic violence, as well as targeted assassinations and the kidnappings, rapes, and killings of ordinary Iraqi women and girls.

Any plans for reconstruction must include the mobilization of the country's human resources, including its women – who in turn must be included in decision-making and planning for the rebuilding and upgrading of the country's physical and social infrastructure, and its public sector and civil service.

Palestine

The problems that Palestinian women face – early marriage and high fertility; the poverty of female-headed households; difficulties in daily life; domestic violence and sexual abuse; low political participation and representation; and absence of a legal framework for rights – originate in the persistence of patriarchal gender relations, the Israeli military occupation and non-resolution of the national problem, and the conservative nature of the main political forces. Patriarchal relations are particularly acute in the refugee camps and small towns. There, Palestinian women tend to be married young, at about nineteen, often to close cousins. Studies also show that the high rates of unemployment, loss of livelihood, homelessness, and the frustrations of the occupation have resulted in an increase in domestic violence. According to Nahla Abdo (2000), research on Palestinian refugee camps, particularly in Gaza, has shown that refugee women and girls bear the brunt of increased physical, mental, psychological, and sexual domestic violence, including incest rape.

Women face serious obstacles in their efforts to provide food and other basic necessities for their families. Thousands of women have lost husbands and male kin to the intifada, exile, emigration in search of work, Israeli imprisonment, or death. Half of all refugee families are headed by women, and female-headed households have been disproportionately affected by the rise in poverty that has accompanied the second intifada and the closures and curfews (UNIFEM 2005b). Meanwhile, women's participation in the labor force, while remaining persistently low, has been affected by the rise in unemployment since the second intifada began. The conflict, curfews, and checkpoints have also adversely affected girls' access to schooling.[7]

Settlers have been known to be verbally abusive to Palestinian women residents of East Jerusalem, who have also experienced physical harassment by them. One example of graffiti in Hebron read: 'Watch out Fatima – we will rape all Arab women.'[8] Settlers also attacked Palestinian homes while women and their families were inside. The Israeli human rights organization B'Tselem has collected personal testimonies describing such attacks. All of these events have compounded the difficulties Palestinian women already face in meeting their family and household responsibilities and have increased their dependence on assistance.

It is perhaps because of all the violence, frustration, and humiliation Palestinians have faced that an unprecedented and certainly unexpected development has occurred: the participation of a number of women in suicide bombings since the second intifada began. Although Palestinian women have been strongly nationalist even when engaged in peace-building initiatives, violent action seemed to be outside the scope of their activities until relatively recently.

Palestinian women's political participation has been consistent and often significant, though usually unacknowledged. The Palestine Authority has not demonstrated any strong support for women's rights. Throughout the Arafat era, clientelism and patronage were often criteria for political appointments, and women have occupied fewer than 10 percent of leadership positions. A grassroots feminist push for quotas resulted in about a 17 percent female representation in the municipal elections of 2004.

The record of Palestinian–Israeli interaction across the years exemplifies the importance of bridge-building among women and the illogic of ignoring women in negotiations and post-conflict political developments. Palestinian and Israeli women have met and talked and negotiated in informal settings for years, and the Jerusalem Link – the main partners of which are Bat Shalom and the Jerusalem Center for Women – was set up to bring together a number of progressive Israeli and Palestinian women's groups in a more formal network of communication.

Since SCR 1325 was adopted, Palestinian and Israeli women have studied it with a view to making it a reality in the 'peace process.' In early February 2005, the Ad Hoc Coalition of Palestinian and Israeli Women wrote to Condoleezza Rice, pointing out that women have been at the forefront of peace-building and that '... only one Palestinian woman [Hanan Ashrawi] has held an official role at any Middle East peace summit. This is not only in violation of UN Security Resolution 1325 ... but a squandering of formidable skill, talent, and experience that both nations can ill afford.'[9]

Peace-building, reconstruction, and gender justice

What do the three cases presented here offer by way of lessons of a wider relevance regarding the gender dynamics of conflict, peace-building, and reconstruction? And how may feminist frameworks and insights contribute to the success of peace and reconstruction processes in Afghanistan, Iraq, Palestine, and elsewhere?

A gender perspective puts the spotlight on the social relations that exist between women and men, and on the laws and actions of states. It places women at the center of analysis because of the fact that, across history and cultures, women have been denied equality, autonomy, and power. Women as a group have experienced diverse forms of violence from men as a group, because women have lacked power and because states or communities have failed to protect them or have in fact punished them. Gender analysis also demonstrates that conflict, peace-building, and reconstruction processes may reflect and reinforce forms of masculinity and femininity.

It was not until the 1990s that violence against women and the problem of wartime rape acquired global prominence and action. Armed conflicts in Yugoslavia and Rwanda showed that women, like men, are victims of military onslaughts and terrorist actions; they lose life and limb, and join the ranks of refugees or internally displaced persons. Unlike men, however, they also are the special victims of sexual violence, especially rape.

All too often, women – their legal status, social positions, and bodies – have been pawns during conflicts or in post-conflict agreements. States have been known to make compromises or accommodations at the expense of women's integrity, autonomy, and rights (Kandiyoti 1991).

What do we know about gender and conflict? We know that women's subordinate roles in peacetime render them vulnerable in wartime. Conflicts can be anticipated – so can the fact that women will be violated. Survivors of wartime trauma face inadequate services.[10] International outcries rarely succeed in bringing perpetrators to justice. The message is that women's lives matter less. Sexualized violence is implicated in armed violence but it also exists during so-called times of peace – hence the need to recognize the gender dynamics of peace as well as conflict.

For women, peace does not mean only the formal end of war and its concomitants, such as the demobilization, disarmament, and reintegration of armed combatants. It also means the enjoyment of human security and human rights, including the right not to be beaten at home or assaulted on the streets. Ending gender and other social inequalities and bringing about human security, including women's security, is at the heart of feminist analyses of peace-building.

The concept of human security has been defined in different ways, but some aspects are: personal security, water and food security, rights to healthcare and political participation, and economic security. Reconstruction should therefore be viewed not only in terms of the repair or building of physical and social infrastructure, but also in terms of the establishment of participatory and egalitarian social and gender relations.

Women's role in peace movements is well known, and 'maternalist politics' has a long history. Women peace-builders have often deployed the discourse of motherhood and emphasized feminine values of nurturing and care in their efforts to build bridges, mediate, or encourage reconciliation. Maternalist politics constitutes one model of women's activism, seen largely in peace, anti-militarist, and human rights movements.

Peace-building requires justice, including gender justice. Gender justice has at least three components parts. One is the participation of women in peace-building, reconstruction, and decision-making. Another is the establishment of laws and institutions for the realization of women's human rights. A third pertains to redress for sexualized or other forms of violence against women during conflict or war. A major international achievement was the designation of rape as a war crime when carried out in the context of armed conflict.

Women must be involved in formal processes of peace-building and reconstruction for at least five reasons. The first and most basic reason is that women constitute half, and in some cases a majority, of any population. Second, because women are often the special victims of armed conflict, their experiences, perspectives, and aspirations need to be incorporated into negotiations, mediation, and peace-building processes. For the same reason, women experts and leaders must be involved in processes of demilitarization, demobilization, and reintegration of fighters. Third, women often play a key role in bridge-building and peace-making at the local level. Fourth, women are major stakeholders and actors in the reconstruction or building of infrastructure, the state, and civil society. Fifth, exclusion/marginalization of women is part of the logic of authoritarian, patriarchal state systems. This is why including women is so important – *it helps to change the nature of the state.*

Research has shown that how women fare in a post-conflict situation depends on a number of factors, both internal and external. Internal factors include: (1) pre-existing gender relations and women's legal status and social positions before the conflict; (2) the extent of women's mobilizations before and during the conflict, including the number and type of women's organizations and other institutions; (3) the ideology, values, and norms of the ruling group; and (4) the state's capacity and will to mobilize resource endowments for rights-based reconstruction and development. The salience of these factors has been well illustrated by the cases of Afghanistan, Iraq, and Palestine. In an era of globalization, however, we can expect external factors to play an important part. In particular, transnational feminist monitoring and advocacy can make a difference in terms of laws, policies, and resources available for women's participation and rights (Moghadam 2005).

Reconstruction with women: concluding thoughts

In Afghanistan, compulsory and quality schooling for girls right through grade 12 will be absolutely necessary if the country is to make the transition from patriarchy to modernity and build its human resources as well as women's capabilities. The expansion of girls' education must be at the center of a rights-based development strategy in Afghanistan. In Iraq, the legal reforms and quotas for political participation that have been established are important, but women leaders must be equally involved in issues of security, constitution-building, reconstruction, and development. In Palestine, SCR 1325 must be fully implemented. Proactive policies such as quotas and affirmative action must redress women's longstanding marginalization from decision-making, and international agencies and negotiators must bring Palestinian women to the table.

Notes

1 The armed uprising against the government of the Democratic Republic of Afghanistan (DRA) began in the latter part of 1978 and saw the military support of the United States and Pakistan in the summer of 1979, six months before the intervention of the Soviet army at the request of the Kabul government. The civil conflict raged until 1992, when the left-wing government was overthrown. It resumed when erstwhile partners of the Islamic Mujahidin alliance waged war against each other (1992–94) and the Taliban emerged to fight the Mujahidin (1994–96). Afghanistan was invaded by American troops, and the Taliban removed from power, in October 2001. Iraq was at war with Iran from 1980 to 1988, and with Kuwait, Saudi Arabia, and the United States in 1990/91. It was invaded and occupied by US/UK troops in April 2003, and at this writing (March 2005) conflict and insecurity were pervasive.

2 See www.un.org/docs/scres/2000/sc2000/htm.

3 The study *Women, Peace and Security:*

Study submitted by the Secretary-General pursuant to Security Council Resolution 1325 (2000) (United Nations, New York, 2002) acknowledged that much remained to be done in the realization of the resolution, while also drawing attention to the importance of women's informal peace networking.

4 Sources of the data in this chapter are UNICEF, UNIFEM, UNESCO, Amnesty International, and Human Rights Watch.

5 Comments by Prof. Naba al-Barak and Mrs Mahdieh, Helsinki, 6 and 9 September 2004 (seminar on 'Family, society, and the empowerment of women: North African women meeting Finnish women', Helsinki, 6–10 September 2004). They described how the war with Iran changed the legal status of women. From 1981 to 2003, no woman could travel abroad without a *mahram* (husband or close male kin).

6 These are Articles 398 and 427. See Human Rights Watch, 15(7), July 2003, hrw.org/reports/2003/iraq0703/l.htm.

7 Rema Hammami, personal communication, East Jerusalem, 22 February 2005.

8 For testimonials, see www.wclac.org/stories/shield.html.

9 I am grateful to Pamela Pelletreau of Search for Common Ground for bringing this matter to my attention, in a conversation in East Jerusalem, 21 January 2005, and via an e-mail message.

10 One response was the formation of Medica Mondiale, founded after the Bosnian conflict to treat women victims of sexual violence, as well as Women for Women International. See www.medica-mondiale.org and www.womenforwomen-international.org.

References

Abdo, N. (2000) 'Engendering compensation: making refugee women count!', Prepared for the Expert and Advisory Services Fund, International Development Research Center, Ottawa, March.

Breines, I., R. Connell and I. Eide (eds) (2000) *Male Roles, Masculinities and Violence: A Culture of Peace Perspective*, Paris: UNESCO.

Enloe, C. (1990) *Bananas, Beaches and Bases: Making Feminist Sense of International Politics*, Berkeley: University of California Press.

Hasso, F. (1998) 'The "Women's Front": nationalism, feminism, and modernity in Palestine', *Gender and Society*, 12(4): 441–65.

Human Rights Watch (2004) 'The status of women in Afghanistan', www.hrw.org/campaigns/afghanistan/facts.htm, accessed September 2005.

Kandiyoti, D. (ed.) (1991) *Women, Islam, and the State*, London: Macmillan.

Moghadam, V. M. (1997) 'Gender and revolutions', in J. Foran (ed.), *Theorizing Revolutions*, London: Routledge, pp. 137–65.

— (2005) *Globalizing Women: Transnational Feminist Networks*, Baltimore, MD: Johns Hopkins University Press.

Los Angeles Times (2002) 'Self-immolations on the rise in Afghanistan', 18 November, posted on the RAWA website, www.rawa.fancymarketing.net/immolation.htm.

UNIFEM (2004) *Afghanistan: Women in the News*, 35, 10–15 July, Kabul: UNIFEM.

— (2005a) *Women, War, Peace. Country Profile: Afghanistan*, www.womenwarpeace.org/afghanistan/afghanistan.htm, accessed September 2005.

— (2005b) *Women, War, Peace. Country Profile: Occupied Palestinian Territory*, www.womenwarpeace.org/opt/opt.htm, accessed September 2005.

11 | Under Western eyes: feminist scholarship and colonial discourses

Chandra Talpade Mohanty

Any discussion of the intellectual and political construction of 'Third World feminisms'[1] must address itself to two simultaneous projects: the internal critique of hegemonic 'Western' feminisms, and the formulation of autonomous, geographically, historically and culturally grounded feminist concerns and strategies. The first project is one of deconstructing and dismantling; the second, one of building and constructing.

It is to the first project that I address myself. What I wish to analyse is specifically the production of the 'Third World woman' as a singular monolithic subject in some recent (Western) feminist texts. The definition of colonization I wish to invoke here is a predominantly discursive one, focusing on a certain mode of appropriation and codification of 'scholarship' and 'knowledge' about women in the Third World by particular analytic categories employed in specific writings on the subject which take as their referent feminist interests as they have been articulated in the USA and western Europe. If one of the tasks of formulating and understanding the locus of 'Third World feminism' is delineating the way in which it resists and works against what I am referring to as 'Western feminist discourse', an analysis of the discursive construction of 'Third World women' in Western feminism is an important first step.

Clearly Western feminist discourse and political practice is neither singular nor homogeneous in its goals, interests or analyses. However, it is possible to trace a coherence of effects resulting from the implicit assumption of 'the West' (in all its complexities and contradictions) as the primary referent in theory and praxis. My reference to 'Western feminism' is by no means intended to imply that it is a monolith. Rather, I am attempting to draw attention to the similar effects of various textual strategies used by writers which codify Others as non-Western and hence themselves as (implicitly) Western. It is in this sense that I use the term *Western feminist*. Similar arguments can be made in terms of middle-class urban African or Asian scholars producing scholarship on or about their rural or working-class sisters, which assumes their own middle-class cultures as the norm, and codifies working-class histories and cultures as Other.

My critique is directed at three basic analytic principles which are present in (Western) feminist discourse on women in the Third World.

The first analytic presupposition I focus on is involved in the strategic location of the category 'women' vis-à-vis the context of analysis. The assumption of women as an already constituted, coherent group with identical interests and desires, regardless of class, ethnic or racial location, or contradictions, implies a notion of gender or sexual difference or even patriarchy which can be applied universally and cross-culturally. The second analytical presupposition is evident on the methodological level, in the uncritical way 'proof' of universality and cross-cultural validity are provided. The third is a more specifically political presupposition underlying the methodologies and the analytic strategies, i.e. the model of power and struggle they imply and suggest. I argue that as a result of the two modes – or, rather, frames – of analysis described above, a homogeneous notion of the oppression of women as a group is assumed, which, in turn, produces the image of an 'average Third World woman'. This woman leads an essentially truncated life based on her feminine gender (read: sexually constrained) and her being 'Third World' (read: ignorant, poor, uneducated, tradition-bound, domestic, family-oriented, victimized, etc.). This, I suggest, is in contrast to the (implicit) self-representation of Western women as educated, as modern, as having control over their own bodies and sexualities, and the freedom to make their own decisions.

The distinction between Western feminist representation of women in the Third World and Western feminist self-presentation is a distinction of the same order as that made by some Marxists between the 'maintenance' function of the housewife and the real 'productive' role of wage labour, or the characterization by developmentalists of the Third World as being engaged in the lesser production of 'raw materials' in contrast to the 'real productive activity' of the First World. These distinctions are made on the basis of the privileging of a particular group as the norm or referent. Men involved in wage labour, First World producers, and, I suggest, Western feminists who sometimes cast Third World women in terms of 'ourselves undressed' (Michelle Rosaldo's [1980] term), all construct themselves as the normative referent in such a binary analytic.

'Women' as category of analysis, or: we are all sisters in struggle

By women as a category of analysis, I am referring to the crucial assumption that all of us of the same gender, across classes and cultures, are somehow socially constituted as a homogeneous group identified prior to the process of analysis. This is an assumption which characterizes much feminist discourse. The homogeneity of women as a group is produced not on the basis of biological essentials but rather on the basis of secondary sociological and anthropological universals. Thus, for instance, in any given piece of feminist analysis, women are characterized as a singular group on the basis of a shared oppression. What binds women together is a sociological notion of the 'sameness' of their oppression. It is at this point that an elision takes place between 'women' as a discursively constructed group and 'women' as material subjects of their own history.[2] Thus the discursively consensual homogeneity of 'women' as a group is mistaken for the historically specific material reality of groups of women. This results in an assumption of women as an always already constituted group, one which has been labelled 'powerless', 'exploited', 'sexually harassed', etc., by feminist scientific, economic, legal and sociological discourses.

In this section I focus on specific ways in which 'women' as a category of analysis is used in Western feminist discourse on women in the Third World. Each of these examples illustrates the construction of 'Third World women' as a homogeneous 'powerless' group often located as implicit victims of particular socio-economic systems.

This mode of defining women primarily in terms of their object status (the way in which they are affected or not affected by certain institutions and systems) is what characterizes this particular form of the use of 'women' as a category of analysis. In the context of Western women writing on/studying women in the Third World, such objectification (however benevolently motivated) needs to be both named and challenged. As Valerie Amos and Pratibha Parmar argue quite eloquently, 'Feminist theories which examine our cultural practices as "feudal residues" or label us "traditional", also portray us as politically immature women who need to be versed and schooled in the ethos of Western feminism. They need to be continually challenged ...' (1984: 7).

Women and the development process

The best examples of universalization on the basis of economic reductionism can be found in the liberal 'Women in Development' literature. Proponents of this school seek to examine the effect of development on Third World women, sometimes from self-designated feminist perspectives. At the very least, there is an evident interest in and commitment to improving the lives of women in 'developing' countries. Scholars such as Irene Tinker and Michelle Bo Bramsen (1972), Ester Boserup (1970), and Perdita Huston (1979) have all written about the effect of development policies on women in the Third World.[3] All three women assume 'development' is synonymous with 'economic development' or 'economic progress'. Women are affected positively or negatively by economic development policies, and this is the basis for cross-cultural comparison.

For instance, Perdita Huston (1979) states that the purpose of her study is to describe the effect of the development process on the 'family unit and its individual members' in Egypt, Kenya, Sudan, Tunisia, Sri Lanka and Mexico. She states that the 'problems' and 'needs' expressed by rural and urban women in these countries all centre around education and training, work and wages, access to health and other services, political participation and legal rights.

Huston relates all these 'needs' to the lack of sensitive development policies which exclude women as a group or category. Here again, women are assumed to be a coherent group or category prior to their entry into 'the development process'. Huston assumes that all Third World women have similar problems and needs. Thus, they must have similar interests and goals. However, the interests of urban, middle-class, educated Egyptian housewives, to take only one instance, could surely not be seen as being the same as those of their uneducated, poor maids? Development policies do not affect both groups of women in the same way. Practices which characterize women's status and roles vary according to class. Women are constituted as women through the complex interaction between class, culture, religion and other ideological institutions and frameworks. They are not 'women' – a coherent group – solely on the basis of a particular economic system or policy. Such reductive cross-cultural comparisons result in the colonization of the specifics of daily existence and the complexities of political interests which women of different social classes and cultures represent and mobilize.

Thus, it is revealing that for Perdita Huston, women in the Third World countries she writes about have 'needs' and 'problems', but few if any have 'choices' or the freedom to act. This is an interesting representation of women in the Third World, one which is significant in suggesting a latent self-presentation of Western women which bears looking at. She writes: 'What surprised and moved me most as I listened to women in such very different cultural settings was the striking commonality – whether they were educated or illiterate, urban or rural – of their most basic values: the importance they assign to family, dignity and service to others' (ibid.: 115). Would Huston consider such values unusual for women in the West?

What is problematical about this kind of use of 'women' as a group, as a stable category of analysis, is that it assumes an ahistorical, universal unity between women based on a generalized notion of their subordination. Instead of analytically *demonstrating* the production of women as socio-economic political groups within particular local contexts, this analytical move limits the definition of the female subject to gender identity, completely bypassing social class and ethnic identities. What characterizes women as a group is their gender over and above everything else, indicating a monolithic notion of sexual difference. Because women are thus constituted as a coherent group, sexual difference becomes coterminous with female subordination, and power is automatically defined in binary terms: people who have it (read: men), and people who do not (read: women). Men exploit, women are exploited. Such simplistic formulations are historically reductive; they are also ineffectual in designing strategies to combat oppressions. All they do is reinforce binary divisions between men and women.

What would an analysis which did not do this look like? Maria Mies's work illustrates the strength of Western feminist work on women in the Third World which does not fall into the traps discussed above. Mies's study of the lacemakers of Narsapur, India (1982), attempts to analyse carefully a substantial household industry in which 'housewives' produce lace doilies for consumption in the world market. Through a detailed analysis of the structure of the lace industry, production and reproduction relations, the sexual division of labour, profits and exploitation, and the overall consequences of defining women as 'non-working housewives' and their work as 'leisure-time activity', Mies demonstrates the levels of exploitation in this industry and the impact of this production system on the work and living conditions of the women involved. In addition, she is able to analyse the 'ideology of the housewife', the notion of a woman sitting in the house, as providing the necessary subjective and sociocultural element for the creation and maintenance of a production system that contributes to the increasing pauperization of women, and keeps them totally atomized and disorganized as workers. Mies's analysis shows the effect of a certain historically and culturally specific mode of patriarchal organization, an organization constructed on the basis of the definition of the lacemakers as 'non-working housewives' at familial, local, regional, statewide and international levels. The intricacies and effects of particular power networks are not only emphasized but form the basis of Mies's analysis of how this particular group of women is situated at the centre of a hegemonic, exploitative world market.

This is a good example of what careful, politically focused, local analyses can accomplish. It illustrates how the category of women is constructed in a variety of political contexts that often exist simultaneously and are overlaid on top of one another. There is no easy generalization in the direction of 'women' in India, or 'women in the Third World'; nor is there a reduction of the political construction of the exploitation of the lacemakers to cultural explanations about the passivity or obedience that might characterize these women and their situation. Finally, this mode of local, political analysis which generates theoretical categories from within the situation and context being analysed also suggests corresponding effective strategies for organizing against the exploitation faced by the lacemakers. Narsapur women are not mere victims of the production process, because they resist, challenge and subvert the process at various junctures. Mies delineates the connections between the housewife ideology, the self-consciousness of the lacemakers, and their interrelationships as contributing to the latent resistances she perceives among the women [see Mies 1982: 157].

It is only by understanding the *contradictions* inherent in women's location within various structures that effective political action and challenges can be devised.

As discussed earlier, a comparison between Western feminist self-presentation and Western feminist representation of women in the Third World yields significant results. Universal images of 'the Third World Woman' (the veiled woman, chaste virgin, etc.), images constructed from adding the 'Third World difference' to 'sexual difference', are predicated upon (and hence obviously bring into sharper focus) assumptions about Western women as secular, liberated and having control over their own lives. Similarly, only from the vantage point of the West is it possible to define the 'Third World' as underdeveloped and economically dependent. Without the overdetermined discourse that creates the *Third* World, there would be no (singular and privileged) First World. Without the 'Third World woman', the particular self-presentation of Western women mentioned above would be problematical. I am suggesting, then, that the one enables and sustains the other. It is time to move beyond the Marx who found it possible to say: they cannot represent themselves; they must be represented.

Notes

1 Terms such as *Third* and *First World* are problematical both in suggesting oversimplified similarities between and among countries thus labelled, and in reinforcing implicitly existing economic, cultural and ideological hierarchies which are conjured up using such terminology. I use the term 'Third World' with full awareness of its problems, only because this is the terminology available to us at the moment.

2 Elsewhere I have discussed this particular point in detail in a critique of Robin Morgan's construction of 'women's herstory' in her introduction to *Sisterhood Is Global: The Internatinal Women's Movement Anthology* (Anchor Press/Doubleday, New York, 1984). See my 'Feminist encounters: locating the politics of experience', *Copyright*, 1, 'Fin de Siècle 2000', pp. 30–44, especially pp. 35–7.

3 These views can also be found in differing degrees in collections such as Wellesley Editorial Committee (ed.), *Women and National Development: The Complexities of Change* (University of Chicago Press, Chicago, IL, 1977), and *Signs*, Special Issue, 'Development and the sexual division of labor', 7(2) (Winter 1981). For an excellent introduction to WID issues, see ISIS, *Women in Development: A Resource Guide for Organization and Action* (New Society Publishers, Philadelphia,

1984). For a politically focused discussion of feminism and development and the stakes for poor Third World women, see Gita Sen and Caren Grown, *Development Crises and Alternative Visions: Third World Women's Perspectives* (Monthly Review Press, New York, 1987).

References

Amos, V. and P. Parmar (1984) 'Challenging imperial feminism', *Feminist Review*, 17: 3–19.

Boserup, E. (1970) *Women's Role in Economic Development*, New York/London: St Martin's Press/Allen and Unwin.

Huston, P. (1979) *Third World Women Speak Out*, New York: Praeger.

Lazreg, M. (1988) 'Feminism and difference: the perils of writing as a woman on women in Algeria', *Feminist Issues*, 14(1): 81–107.

Mies, M. (1982) *The Lace Makers of Narsapur: Indian Housewives Produce for the World Market*, London: Zed Books.

Rosaldo, M. A. (1980) 'The use and abuse of anthropology: reflections on feminism and cross-cultural understanding', *Signs*, 53: 389–417.

Tinker, I. and M. B. Bramsen (eds) (1972) *Women and World Development*, Washington, DC: Overseas Development Council.

12 | Do Muslim women really need saving? Anthropological reflections on cultural relativism and its others

Lila Abu-Lughod

What are the ethics of the current 'War on Terrorism,' a war that justifies itself by purporting to liberate, or save, Afghan women? Does anthropology have anything to offer in our search for a viable position to take regarding this rationale for war?

I was led to pose the question of my title in part because of the way I personally experienced the response to the US war in Afghanistan. Like many colleagues whose work has focused on women and gender in the Middle East, I was deluged with invitations to speak. Why did this not please me, a scholar who has devoted more than twenty years of her life to this subject and who has some complicated personal connection to this identity?

My discomfort led me to reflect on why, as feminists in or from the West, or simply as people who have concerns about women's lives, we need to be wary of this response to the events and aftermath of 11 September 2001. I want to point out the minefields of this obsession with the plight of Muslim women. I hope to show some way through them using insights from anthropology, the discipline whose charge has been to understand and manage cultural difference. At the same time, I want to remain critical of anthropology's complicity in the reification of cultural difference.

Cultural explanations and the mobilization of women

It is easy to see why one should be skeptical about the focus on the 'Muslim woman' if one begins with the US public response. I will analyze two manifestations of this response: some conversations I had with a reporter from the *PBS NewsHour with Jim Lehrer* and First Lady Laura Bush's radio address to the nation on 17 November 2001. The presenter from the *NewsHour* show first contacted me in October to see if I was willing to give some background for a segment on Women and Islam. I agreed to look at the questions she was going to pose to panelists. The questions were hopelessly general. I asked her: If you were to substitute Christian or Jewish wherever you have Muslim, would these questions make sense? There was a consistent resort to the cultural, as if knowing something about women and Islam or the meaning of a religious ritual would help one understand the tragic attack on New York's World Trade Center and the US Pentagon, or how Afghanistan had come to be ruled by the Taliban.

The question is why knowing about the 'culture' of the region, and particularly its religious beliefs and treatment of women, was more urgent than exploring the history of the development of repressive regimes in the region and the US role in this history. Such cultural framing, it seemed to me, prevented the serious exploration of the roots and nature of human suffering in this part of the world.

Laura Bush's radio address on 17 November reveals the political work such mobilization accomplishes. On the one hand, her address collapsed important distinctions that should have been maintained. There was a constant slippage between the Taliban and the terrorists. Then there was the blurring of the very separate causes in Afghanistan of women's continuing malnutrition, poverty, and ill health, and their more recent exclusion under the Taliban from employment, schooling, and the joys of wearing nail polish. On the other hand, her speech reinforced chasmic divides between the 'civilized people throughout the world' whose hearts break for the women and children of Afghanistan and the Taliban-and-the-terrorists, who want to 'impose their world on the rest of us.'

The speech enlisted women to justify American bombing and intervention in Afghanistan. As Laura Bush said, 'Because of our recent military gains in much of Afghanistan, women are no longer imprisoned in their homes. They can listen to music and teach their daughters without fear of punishment. The fight against terrorism is also a fight for the rights and dignity of women' (US Government 2002).

These words have haunting resonances for anyone who has studied colonial history. Many who have worked on British colonialism in South Asia have noted the use of the woman question in colonial policies where intervention into sati (the practice of widows immolating themselves on their husbands' funeral pyres), child marriage, and other practices was used to justify rule. As Gayatri Chakravorty Spivak (1988) has cynically put it: white men saving brown women from brown men. The historical record is full of similar cases, including in the Middle East. In turn-of-the-century Egypt, what Leila Ahmed (1992) has called 'colonial feminism' was hard at work. This was a selective concern about the plight of Egyptian women that focused on the veil as a sign of oppression but gave no support to women's education and was professed loudly by the same Englishman, Lord Cromer, who opposed women's suffrage back home. Sociologist Marnia Lazreg (1994) has (also) offered some vivid examples of how French colonialism enlisted women to its cause in Algeria.

Just as I argued above that we need to be suspicious when neat cultural icons are plastered over messier historical and political narratives, so we need to be wary when Lord Cromer in British-ruled Egypt, French ladies in Algeria, and Laura Bush, all with military troops behind them, claim to be saving or liberating Muslim women.

Politics of the veil

I want now to look more closely at those Afghan women Laura Bush claims were 'rejoicing' at their liberation by the Americans. This necessitates a discussion of the veil, or the burqa, because it is so central to contemporary concerns about Muslim women.

First, it should be recalled that the Taliban did not invent the burqa. The burqa, like some other forms of 'cover,' has, in many settings, marked the symbolic separation of men's and women's spheres, as part of the general association of women with family and home, not with public space where strangers mingled.

Twenty years ago the anthropologist Hanna Papanek (1982), who worked in Pakistan, described the burqa as 'portable seclusion.' She noted that many saw it as a liberating invention because it enabled women to move out of segregated living spaces while still observing the basic moral requirements of separating and protecting women from unrelated men. Such veiling signifies belonging to a particular community and participating in a moral way of life in which families are paramount in the organization of communities and the home is associated with the sanctity of women.

What had happened in Afghanistan under the Taliban is that one regional style of covering or veiling, associated with a certain respectable but not elite class, was imposed on everyone as 'religiously' appropriate, even though previously there had been many different styles popular or traditional with different groups and classes.

Second, not only are there many forms of covering, which themselves have different meanings in the communities in which they are used, but also veiling itself must not be confused with, or made to stand for, lack of agency. As I have argued in my ethnography of a Bedouin community in Egypt in the late 1970s and 1980s (Abu-Lughod 1986), one of the ways women show their standing is by covering their faces in certain contexts. They decide for whom they feel it is appropriate to veil.

We need to work against the reductive interpretation of veiling as the quintessential sign of women's unfreedom, even if we object to state imposition of this form, as in Iran or with the Taliban. And we must take care not to reduce the diverse situations and attitudes of millions of Muslim women to a single item of clothing.

Ultimately, the significant political-ethical problem the burqa raises is how to deal with cultural 'others.' How are we to deal with difference without the cultural relativism for which anthropologists are justly famous – a relativism that says it's their culture and it's not my business to judge or interfere, only to try to understand. Cultural relativism is certainly an improvement on ethnocentrism and the racism, cultural imperialism, and imperiousness that underlie it; the problem is that it is too late not to interfere. The forms of lives we find around the world are already products of long histories of interactions.

I want to explore the issues of women, cultural relativism, and the problems of 'difference' from three angles. First, I want to consider what feminist anthropologists are to do with strange political bedfellows. I used to feel torn when I received the e-mail petitions circulating for the last few years in defense of Afghan women under the Taliban. I was not sympathetic to the dogmatism of the Taliban; I do not support the oppression of women. But the provenance of the campaign worried me. I had never received a petition from such women defending the right of Palestinian women to safety from Israeli bombing or daily harassment at checkpoints, asking the United States to reconsider its support for a government that had dispossessed them, closed them out from work and citizenship rights, refused them the most basic freedoms. I do not think it would be easy to mobilize so many of these American and European women if it were not a case of Muslim men oppressing Muslim women – women of cover for whom they can feel sorry and in relation to whom they can feel smugly superior.

To be critical of this celebration of women's rights in Afghanistan is not to pass judgment on any local women's organizations, such as RAWA, whose members have courageously worked since 1977 for a democratic secular Afghanistan in which women's human rights are respected, against Soviet-backed regimes or US-, Saudi-, and Pakistani-supported conservatives. Their documentation of abuse and their work through clinics and schools have been enormously important. It is also not to fault the campaigns that exposed the dreadful conditions under which the Taliban placed women. It is, however, to suggest that we need to look closely at what we are supporting (and what we are not) and to think carefully about why.

Suspicion about bedfellows is only a first step; we need to confront two more big issues. First is the acceptance of the possibility of difference. Can we only free Afghan women to be like us or might we have to recognize that even after 'liberation' from the Taliban, they might want different things than we would want for them? Second, we need to be vigilant about the rhetoric of saving people because of what it implies about our attitudes.

What I am advocating is the hard work involved in recognizing and respecting differences – precisely as products of different histories, as expressions of different circumstances, and as manifestations of differently structured desires. We may want justice for women, but can we accept that there might be different ideas about justice and that different women might want, or choose, different futures from what we envision as best (see Ong 1988)?

We must be careful not to fall into polarizations that place feminism on the side of the West, because those many people within Muslim countries who are trying to find alternatives to present injustices, who do not accept that being feminist means being Western, will be under pressure to choose: Are you with us or against us? Yet we must remain aware of differences, respectful of other paths toward social change that might give women better lives. Can there be a liberation that is Islamic? And, beyond this, is liberation even a goal for which all women or people strive? Are emancipation, equality, and rights part of a universal language we must use? In other words, might other desires be more meaningful for different groups of people? Living in close families? Living in a godly way? Living without war? I have done fieldwork in Egypt over more than twenty years and I cannot think of a single woman I know, from the poorest rural to the most educated cosmopolitan, who has ever expressed envy of US women, women they tend to perceive as bereft of community, vulnerable to sexual violence and social anomie, driven by individual success rather than morality, or strangely disrespectful of God.

Mahmood (2001) has pointed out [...] that there seems to be a difference in the political demands made on those who work on or are trying to understand Muslims and Islamists and those who work on secular humanist projects. We need to have as little dogmatic faith in secular humanism as in Islamism, and as open a mind to the complex possibilities of human projects undertaken in one tradition as the other.

Beyond the rhetoric of salvation

The second issue to confront is the deeply problematic construction of the Afghan woman as someone in need of saving. When you save someone, you imply that you are saving her from something. You are also saving her to something. What violences are entailed in this transformation, and what presumptions are being made about the superiority of that to which you are saving her? Projects of saving other women depend on and reinforce a sense of superiority by Westerners, a form of arrogance that deserves to be challenged. All one needs to do to appreciate the patronizing quality of the rhetoric of saving women is to imagine using it today in the United States about disadvantaged groups such as African-American women or working-class women. We now understand them as suffering from structural violence. We have become politicized about race and class, but not culture.

As anthropologists, feminists, or concerned citizens, we should be wary of taking on the mantles of those nineteenth-century Christian missionary women who devoted their lives to saving their Muslim sisters. Speaking of the ignorance, seclusion, polygamy, and veiling that blighted women's lives across the Muslim world, the missionary women spoke of their responsibility to make these women's voices heard. One can hear uncanny echoes of their virtuous goals today, even though the language is secular, the appeals not to Jesus, but to human rights or the liberal West.

Could we not leave veils and vocations of saving others behind and instead train our sights on ways to make the world a more just place? The reason respect for difference should not be confused with cultural relativism is that it does not preclude asking how we, living in this privileged and powerful part of the world, might examine our own responsibilities for the situations in which others in distant places have found themselves. We do not stand outside the world; we are part of that world. Islamic movements themselves have arisen in a world shaped by the intense engagements of Western powers in Middle Eastern lives. Our task is to critically explore what we might do to help create a world in which those poor Afghan women, for whom 'the hearts of those in the civilized world break,' can have safety and decent lives.

[Author's note: This is a highly abridged version of the article that appeared in the *American Anthropologist*. Full acknowledgments can be found in the original.]

References

Abu-Lughod, L. (1986) *Veiled Sentiments: Honor and Poetry in a Bedouin Society*, Berkeley: University of California Press.

Ahmed, L. (1992) *Women and Gender in Islam*, New Haven, CT: Yale University Press.

Lazreg, M. (1994) *The Eloquence of Silence: Algerian Women in Question*, New York: Routledge.

Mahmood, S. (2001) 'Feminist theory, embodiment, and the docile agent: some reflections on the Egyptian Islamic revival', *Cultural Anthropology*, 16(2): 202–35.

Ong, A. (1988) 'Colonialism and modernity: feminist re-presentations of women in non-Western societies', *Inscriptions*, 3/4: 79–93.

Papanek, H. (1982) 'Purdah in Pakistan: seclusion and modern occupations for women', in H. Papanek and G. Minault (eds), *Separate Worlds*, Columbus, MO: South Asia Books, pp. 190–216.

Spivak, G. C. (1988) 'Can the subaltern speak?', in C. Nelson and L. Grossberg (eds), *Marxism and the Interpretation of Culture*, Urbana: University of Illinois Press, pp. 271–313.

US Government (2002) Electronic document, www.whitehouse.gov/news/releases/2001/11/20011117.

13 | The 'gender lens': a racial blinder?

Sarah C. White

Introduction

This paper comes out of two abiding concerns: with gender and with race. Since researching my PhD on women's work and power in rural Bangladesh, 1984 to 1988, gender has occupied a central place in my consciousness, academic life, and practical work as (occasional) consultant for development agencies. Alongside this, much more muted but nonetheless insistent and recurring, has been a second motif, of race. As a white person in 1980s Bangladesh, I found myself in a position of marked racial privilege which, in typical middle-class liberal fashion, made me profoundly uncomfortable, even as I benefited significantly from it. What I observed and experienced was a whole system in which advantage and disadvantage were patterned by race. While in terms of political struggle gender and race have had an equal focus, in development the high profile accorded to gender contrasts with an almost total silence on race in official publications. Asking how race has figured in the theory and practice of WID/GAD, this paper explores three dimensions: the charge of cultural imperialism; the intellectual reference points that inform core approaches; and the construction of development expertise.

Defining terms

I use 'development' in a restricted way, to refer to the 'industry' of aid agencies, government ministries and non-governmental organizations (NGOs). Like other industries, development is committed at once to producing an output, and to reproducing itself. While it foregrounds materiality – the construction of roads, hydroelectric projects, schools, hospitals and factories – it also comprises regimes of power/knowledge. New infrastructure provides services to local people, but also enables the extension of state and market structures, and more efficient extraction of raw materials and profits (Ferguson 1990). Development discourses assume and inscribe notions of difference, between here and there, now and then, us and them, developed and developing. This is reflected in the notion of expertise, which constitutes the 'class-marker' of the development industry.

A paradoxical relationship

GAD has long faced criticism on grounds of cultural imperialism. At worst, internal inequalities are denied as nationalist appeals invoke images of Western woman as folk devil, symbol of chaos and threat to the natural (patriarchal) order. This is easily allied with retrogressive elements in development patriarchies, and may ironically deflect attention from the more significant forms of economic and political domination they embody. This notwithstanding, there *is* a danger that GAD implies that 'West is best' as it decries gender inequalities in Third World societies (see Mohanty 1988, 1991; Goetz 1991; Schech and Haggis 2000). There *is* a tendency to transfer uncritically Western analytical models to other contexts. The challenge is to see these facts as points of entry into further questioning of the development industry, rather than an excuse for jettisoning a commitment to gender equity.

The gender 'lens'

The most celebrated achievement of the WID/GAD project is to bring 'women' in to development. The new marking of 'women' as a distinct group required the creation of new thinking, labelled 'gender awareness'. The description of gender analysis as a 'gender lens' suggests a new way of seeing the world, in which gender (for which read sexual difference) is magnified and constituted as the primary power relation. This carries the danger of inappropriately 'reading in' gender difference, and/or blocking the exploration of other inequalities. At its worst, the common GAD phrase 'using a gender lens' could therefore mean that gender dimensions of difference are magnified, while all others are screened out.

Race in GAD

One aspect of this is the lack of black feminism as intellectual reference point within core GAD frameworks. Black feminism is clearly diverse, with many points of contestation and difference. I concentrate here on African-American theorists who spearheaded black feminism in the 1980s. They question the categories of both 'women' and 'race' as offering automatic solidarity (hooks 1981). Instead, intersectional paradigms configure the connectedness of race, class, and gender as critical to a political economy that takes women's lives seriously (Hill Collins 2000). While admitting black patriarchy, they insist their struggle must involve alliances with men. Critical examination of men and masculinity was therefore a part of bell hooks' seminal work *Ain't I a Woman?* as far back as 1981. Second, they questioned identifying paid work with women's liberation, emphasizing employment as a key site of contradiction for women. Third, black feminists rejected seeing the family as the primary location of oppression. While admitting sexism in the home, they see it also as a place of resistance, and labour there as humanizing and affirming of the humanity often denied in workplace experience, especially within slavery (Davis 1982). Rather than dividing work and family, considering the 'work/family nexus' offers new directions for understanding black women's poverty (Hill Collins 2000: 45). Finally, black feminists have maintained the primacy of the personal as the place from which theory is made sense.

As time passes, none of these points looks controversial: all find some echoes within contemporary GAD. Their relatively recent arrival, however, suggests the absence of black feminist voices in development circles. Much of this is due to ignorance: black feminist writers and activists were simply not the reference points of those who forged the GAD project.

Race and expertise

The ignoring or erasure of black voices is one form in which racism can operate. Paradoxically, racism also works by 'marking' 'others' as hypervisible, often in ways that obscure or devalue. Discussions of the 'corruption' of 'African governments', for example, can easily draw on elements of racist discourse, which suggest that black people are somehow morally inferior to white. This may have profound material as well as discursive outcomes, in the form of the withholding or circumscribing of aid programmes.

While the marking is often negative, however, it is not always so. An ambivalence is evident in relation to those black women who have been heard within GAD. These have largely been feminists from the South, such as the socialist feminist DAWN group (e.g. Sen and Grown 1987); the post-colonial critic Chandra Mohanty (1988, 1991) or the ecofeminist Vandana Shiva (1987). There is no doubt that such women have made a significant contribution to GAD theory and practice. Nevertheless, while feminists of the South may speak on a global stage, their legitimacy is at least partially invested in their 'localized' status. Whether the designation of 'local' serves to add or diminish value is not in the end the key question. The play of power lies not in *what* valuation is accorded others, but in the assumption that the development international is the reference point against which others are judged.

Divisions of rank and influence among national staff in development agencies often turn on their capacity to engage with the international rather than their skills, knowledge or experience in development practice. The 'international elite' is no longer composed almost exclusively of white faces; its primary characteristics are etched in class rather than racial terms. However, the racial distributions which result from the definition of 'expertise' in development remain highly unequal. This shows materially in the very different pay and conditions provided to 'international experts' and 'local counterparts', even when working in parallel on the same project. These forms of identification run deep. In an international gender training workshop women from Africa, Latin America and Asia divided into regional groups without difficulty. The

European women, however, insisted on being called 'the global group' (Matlanyane-Sexwale 1994).

Development and the construction of difference

In its refusal to identify gender issues only with 'the field' and its insistence that they must be considered also 'back home' in the office, GAD raised a challenge to the neutrality of development. To take race seriously similarly involves critical reflection on the development project itself, and the ways that racial difference is both assumed by and reproduced through it. However, these broader political perspectives expose a key contradiction that while a large part of the GAD critique concerns the bias within the development apparatus, GAD protagonists have largely relied on precisely those same flawed institutions to implement sound gender policies. To move beyond this means we need to recognize that those institutions and the habits of thought and behaviour they express are part of the problem, not the solution. The way forward lies ultimately not in more and better planning, but in more inclusive and people-centred politics.

References

Davis, A. (1982) *Women, Race and Class*, London: The Women's Press.

Ferguson, J. (1990) *The Anti-Politics Machine: 'Development', Depoliticisation, and Bureaucratic Power in Lesotho*, Cambridge: Cambridge University Press.

Goetz, A.-M. (1991) 'Feminism and the claim to know: contradictions in feminist approaches to women in development', in R. Grant and K. Newland (eds), *Gender and International Relations*, Milton Keynes: Open University Press.

Hill Collins, P. (2000) 'Gender, black feminism, and black political economy', *Annals of the American Academy of Political and Social Science*, 568: 41–53.

hooks, b. (1981) *Ain't I a Woman? Black Women and Feminism*, Boston, MA: South End Press.

Matlanyane-Sexwale, B. M. (1994) 'The politics of gender training', *Agenda* (Cape Town), 23: 57–63.

Mohanty, C. T. (1988) 'Under Western eyes: feminist scholarship and colonial discourses', *Feminist Review*, 30.

— (1991) 'Cartographies of struggle: Third World women and the politics of feminism', in C. Mohanty, A. Russo and L. Torres (eds), *Third World Women and the Politics of Feminism*, Bloomington and Indianapolis: Indiana University Press.

Schech, S. and J. Haggis (2000) *Culture and Development: A Critical Introduction*, Oxford: Blackwell.

Sen, G. and C. Grown (1987) *Development, Crises, and Alternative Visions*, London: Earthscan.

Shiva, V. (1987) *Staying Alive*, London: Routledge.

White, S. C. (2002) 'Thinking race, thinking development', *Third World Quarterly*, 23(3): 407–19.

14 | From missionaries to microcredit? 'Race', gender and agency in neoliberal development

Kalpana Wilson

[...] Partly in response to critiques by Third World feminists, Gender and Development theorists have increasingly highlighted women's 'agency'. Women in the global South are no longer invariably seen as passive victims; there is an increased focus on women's ability to make decisions and choices under given circumstances. But rather than challenging the racialized power relationships inherent in development, this has decisively shifted attention away from material and ideological structures of power (see Wilson 2007).

Much recent GAD literature has been concerned with constructing a rational self-interested basis for what are described as women's 'choices' to conform to gendered expectations, or to collude in the oppression of other women. The individual exercising 'free will' reappears here, albeit acting within the material constraints imposed by patriarchal power. For example, it is argued that 'women may sacrifice their immediate welfare for future security; this would be perfectly in keeping with self-interested behavior' (Agarwal 1994: 434–5). Analysis of gendered constructions and ideologies has been actively delegitimized by suggesting that such a focus attributes 'false consciousness' to women.

Further, the use of the concept of 'agency' in these texts frequently has the effect of reassuring us that women do in fact exercise choice in situations where structural constraints mean that women are simply 'choosing' survival – for example, when it is argued that women victims of wartime rape exercise agency by choosing to remain silent about their experiences because to speak out would endanger their own lives (Kelly 2000: 54; Parpart 2010).

These approaches have contributed to the elaboration of neoliberal models of development based on the further intensification of the labour of 'poor' women in the global South as a buffer against the ravages of economic reforms and financial crisis. Thus the concept of agency is regularly mobilized in inherently racialized constructions of 'women in the global South' as enterprising subjects with limitless capacity to 'cope'; women's potential for exercising agency is fulfilled, we are told, in the context of the state's withdrawal from social provision and, most frequently, in the context of the remarkable rise of microfinance initiatives.

Underpinning this version of agency is the construction of women in the global South as 'more efficient' than their male counterparts because women have better repayment rates on microcredit loans, work harder, and expend less resources (including time) on themselves than their male counterparts, and women's income therefore has a far greater impact on children's well-being. These well-documented gender disparities in the use of income and resources clearly stem from specific patriarchal structures, institutions and ideologies (such as women's primary responsibility for children, or expectations that women will 'make sacrifices' for their families). Further, when women engage in collective movements for social transformation, they often question precisely those gendered inequalities which make women more 'efficient' neoliberal subjects (see Wilson 2007 for a discussion of Dalit women agricultural labourers' experiences of this in Bihar, India).

The moralistic overtones of the development literature's oft-cited contrasts between women's 'good' spending and men's 'bad' spending are distinct echoes of the Victorian discourses of the 'deserving' and 'undeserving' poor, and like them are also deeply racialized in their reinscription of essentialized constructions of men in the global South as inherently 'lazy' and irresponsible. While masculinities have been recognized as an important focus of GAD theory and practice, the role of constructions of 'race' in shaping perceptions of masculinities *within* GAD frameworks is yet to be addressed.

The few existing accounts of 'race' and racism in development have tended to emphasize the Eurocentrism of a monolithic developmentalism based on planning and characterized by 'the construction of roads, hydroelectric projects, schools, hospitals and factories' (White 2006: 56). What are the implications for 'race', then, of the decisive shift from the 'developmental state' to neoliberal 'market-led' development, which is more likely to entail unplanned and untrammelled incursions by footloose corporate capital, and the destruction of these public services and infrastructure?

Post-structuralist notions of 'difference' and of multiple subjectivities have, like the notion of agency, been increasingly appropriated, transformed and redeployed within neoliberal discourses of gender and development. They reappear in the context of an emphasis on 'choice', 'empowerment' through the market and 'participation' in (and responsibility for) social provision.

Ideas of difference have also been mobilized in recent GAD work that argues that concepts of emancipation are always external impositions, with women in 'developing' countries invariably being more concerned with notions of 'security', 'responsibility' and 'respect'. Thus Judy El-Bushra suggests that 'exploitation is a price they are willing to pay for the public acknowledgement that they make important contributions to society, and for the removal of doubt about the security of their marital and other relationships' (El-Bushra 2000: 83). Increasingly, then, any desire for structural change is constructed as not only irrelevant, but culturally alien in these contexts. This contributes to the process of rendering movements which involve collective visions of social transformation invisible within development discourses. Such movements frequently run counter to the neoliberal model, demanding the redistribution of resources, challenging the operation of markets, or confronting the violence of the neoliberal state.

References

Agarwal, B. (1994) *A Field of One's Own: Gender and land rights in South Asia*, Cambridge: Cambridge University Press.

El-Bushra, J. (2000) 'Transforming conflict: some thoughts on a gendered understanding of conflict processes', in S. Jacobs, R. Jacobson and J. Marchbank (eds), *States of Conflict: Gender, Violence and Resistance*, London: Zed Books.

Kelly, L. (2000) 'Wars against women: sexual violence, sexual politics and the militarised state', in S. Jacobs, R. Jacobson and J. Marchbank (eds), *States of Conflict: Gender, Violence and Resistance*, London: Zed Books.

Parpart, J. L. (2010) 'Choosing silence: rethinking voice, agency and women's empowerment', in R. Ryan-Flood and R. Gill (eds), *Secrecy and Silence in the Research Process*, Abingdon: Routledge.

White, S. (2006) 'The "gender lens": a racial blinder?', *Progress in Development Studies*, 6(1): 55–67.

Wilson, K. (2007) 'Agency', in G. Blakeley and V. Bryson (eds), *The Impact of Feminism on Political Concepts and Debates*, Manchester: Manchester University Press.

15 | Development's encounter with sexuality: essentialism and beyond

Sonia Correa and Susie Jolly

Conceptualizing 'sex': essentialism and constructivism

Exploring the connections between sexuality, development and human rights requires that the dominant conceptualization of sex as a natural force be critically revisited. As is widely recognized, in the Western philosophical and religious tradition this view of sex has been and remains pervasive and compelling. Suffice to remind: the essentialist conception of sex underlies Aristotle's and Kant's ideas – which are foundational references to contemporary ethics and human rights. It is also of crucial relevance to Darwinist and post-Darwinist interpretations of social realities, and to the recurrent imbrications of sex and sin in Christian doctrine.

Though from the late eighteenth century onwards sexuality became a highly contested political terrain, this natural conception of sex was not so easily shaken. Rather, the development of science reinforced naturalistic assumptions, further crystallizing the widespread idea that sex is a unified domain of human experience (Weeks 1985, 2003).

Over the past few decades, however, sex essentialism has been systematically challenged by a wide range of philosophers, historians, social anthropologists and interactionist sociologists, and also feminists and queer theorists (Plummer 2000; Weeks 1985, 2003). They argue that sexuality interweaves in complex ways with several crucial dimensions of human lives and is transformed by economic and political processes (Parker and Gagnon 1994; Parker and Aggleton 1999).

Conceptualizing women, men and sex as fundamentally determined by unchangeable natural laws leaves no room for transformation, plasticity or re-creation. This greatly compromises the articulation of sexuality, social change, democracy and human rights, and of 'development' conceived as the cumulative improvement of human subjectivities and relations. It also obscures the ways in which power operates through sex both through the construction of sex hierarchies on the basis of 'natural' sexual conducts and by a still-resonant colonial discourse on sexuality which affirms the civilized nature of the colonizer. Anthropological research since the 1970s on same-sex relations throughout Western history and in a wide variety of cultural contexts (Parker and Aggleton 1999; Weeks 1985, 2003) has also revealed how sex hierarchies intersect with other forms of stratification – such as race, class, ethnicity and age – and translate into power differentials, socio-economic inequalities, stigma, discrimination and abuse.

A constructivist approach to sexuality, on the other hand, challenges the hierarchy of 'natural' and 'unnatural' itself, instead of just shifting the place of certain sexualities within that hierarchy. Most importantly it creates a solid ground for sexual pluralism as a democratic value, and for the expansion of sexual rights claims as in the 1990s and early 2000s.

Development's encounters with sexuality

Sex essentialism, often interpreted as silence on the subject, has been and continues to be a recurrent subtext of development theories, values and applications. In the post-Second World War period, for example, much thinking was devoted to understanding and promoting fertility decline. It is not possible to intervene in fertility without acknowledging the complexities of heterosexuality, in particular power inequalities between women and men. Yet for more than forty years population policy recommendations managed to ignore these, as if they were a part of the natural order that could not be challenged or changed. Thousands of pages have been written on population that address complex demographic and macroeconomic aspects without ever mentioning the word sexuality, even when women's status eventually began to be taken into account. In terms of policy prescriptions, an obsession with technological fixes to bypass naturalized fertility preferences has dominated the field.

Related to this is the implied assumption in liberal economic thinking that sexuality is a natural and individual preference which does not need to be factored in. The classic household model, for example, assumes a heterosexual family, with the man as the head, hence invisibilizing other kinds of relationships. If a woman lives in a lesbian relationship, the household would be likely to be categorized as a 'female-headed household' – a term which generally applies to single women with children/other dependants since it is assumed a woman cannot head a household in which a man is present.

Reflections and recommendations

Development–sexuality intersections have become more explicit in the past two decades. Public health is one such crossroads. But here again initiatives have served to regulate sexualities by keeping them in line with naturalized hierarchies, as much as to improve people's quality of life.

HIV/AIDs work has created further openings. Here the struggle continues between essentialist hierarchies of natural and unnatural behaviours, innocent and guilty victims, and constructivist approaches that see the challenge as combating stigma and promoting safety in the wide diversity of behaviours. This has meant new resources and visibility for men who have sex with men, at the same time as new regulation of this population.

Human development discourses have been slow to address sexuality. Yet they have paved the way for seeing sexuality as part of development, not just a frivolity to be enjoyed once the serious issues of poverty have been tackled. This opens the way for a consideration of how poverty and sexuality intersect, not just in terms of sexual ill health, but around the norms, social rules, economic and legal structures that regulate our lives, integrating some people into oppressive systems, and marginalizing others.

Human rights and sexual rights offer the most promising potential for progress, although rights-based approaches to development have yet to incorporate sexuality as a core dimension of freedom and well-being. More development funding for community building, social inclusion and justice work should be directed at empowering women in their sexuality, to increase possibilities for them to make their own choices, including to engage in same-sex sexual relations if they wish to do so.

Identities are also not necessary as a basis for rights. We need to seek rights for people in all our diversity, including the diversity in each individual; make universal claims to rights that recognize the cultural variation in sexual identities; call for rights for women to be free of violence without pandering to discourses on innocence and chastity. And in all of this we need to remember that sex can be a good thing, a source of well-being and joy, not just of violence, disease, discrimination and poverty.

References

Parker, R. G. and P. Aggleton (eds) (1999) *Culture, Society and Sexuality: A Reader*, London: UCL Press.

Parker, R. and J. Gagnon (1994) *Conceiving Sexuality Approaches to Sex Research in a Postmodern World*, London: Routledge.

Plummer, K. (2000) 'Sexualities in a runaway world: utopian and dystopian challenges', Paper presented at the conference on Sexuality and Social Change, ABIA (Brazilian Interdisciplinary AIDS Association), Rio de Janeiro.

Weeks, J. (1985) *Sexuality and Its Discontents: Meanings, Myths and Modern Sexualities*, London: Routledge & Kegan Paul.

— (2003) *Sexuality*, 2nd edn, New York: Routledge.

PART TWO

Households, families and work

Introduction to Part Two

Lynn Duggan

The domestic sphere is arguably the main site of women's subordination. Gender hierarchies established in homes determine and structure opportunities throughout household members' lives. The readings in Part 2 of this book focus on power dynamics in caring for family members across different systems and times as well as geographic space in the global South. It is impossible to do justice to this topic in so few pages, but, together with the readings included in the references section, it is a start.

As noted in Part 1, modernization proponents emphasize that capitalism releases women from feudal restrictions and that men's power over women and children is reduced when these latter have options outside the extended family. However, although the forms of male privilege may change, new systems bring new power constellations.

We begin this section with the invisibility of unpaid work, move from there to the gender division of caring work, follow this with households' and household members' allocations of income, then shift to constraints placed on women's movements outside households. From here we move to violence and threats of violence within the household, and end with policy concerns in light of women's share of the responsibility for families' care.

A: Women's unpaid work

The work performed within households usually earns no direct income. Women perform the lioness's share of such work, including food preparation, sewing, cleaning, and child- and relative-care, all of which often involve carrying water and finding firewood or other fuel. Typically, unpaid work is overlooked or not considered to be 'productive' activity by economic analysts and policymakers.

In 1995, as part of the Beijing Platform for Action, the UN assigned member governments the responsibility of estimating the value of non-market work and including such estimates in satellite accounts to augment national income accounts and other official measures of economic activity. As Benería (2003) notes, the purposes of such estimates of unpaid work include increasing the visibility of household work and evaluating its contributions to social well-being and the reproduction of labor; evaluating the extent to which total work is shared at the household and society levels; providing information on the allocation of work and leisure; increasing gender neutrality of government budgets; and analyzing trends in paid and unpaid work over time.

Reading Chapter 16 is an excerpted piece by Lourdes Benería that provides a brief history of the 'discovery' of unpaid work with an overview of the ways in which subsistence, informal, domestic, and volunteer work have been dealt with or ignored, conceptually and in practice.

B: Households and capitalism

As noted in the Introduction to Part 1 and excerpted there, Ester Boserup (1970) was the first to hypothesize that capitalist economic development tends to increase the productivity of tasks within men's work as they acquire access to new methods, tools and machinery, thus shifting the household balance of power away from women. Margaret Mead (1976) also called attention to the power inequalities that arise from the tendency for men to control markets and mechanization while women work in unpaid subsistence agriculture.

As Cohen (1985) subsequently noted in her work on Canadian economic history, agricultural production for trade has tended to expand women's workload, because the responsibility for families' subsistence needs is usually assigned to women. Production for exchange and export also increases households' vulnerability to the world market.

Benería and Sen (1981) supported and gave class content to Boserup's conclusion that development benefits men disproportionately, and Sen and Grown (1987) noted that families offer a vantage point from which to resist the encroachment of capitalist values and individual-based organizations of production. With increased migration and urbanization, extended families that acted as insurance systems against old age and other types of insecurity tend to be replaced by nuclear and female-headed units (Becker 1981; Brown 1981; Folbre 1994; Abraham 1993; D'Amico 1993; Blumberg 1993; Castro 1993; Islam 1993; Mencher and Okungwu 1993).

Research by Deere (1977, 1978) and Wiegersma (1981) on Peruvian and Vietnamese peasant households, by contrast, supported the Marxist perspective that the destruction of feudal constraints may afford women more degrees of freedom, challenging the notion that capitalism exacerbates gender inequality. This debate regarding the impact of markets on women may illuminate patterns and experiences common to women in different regions and nations.

In the early 1980s Marxist and socialist-feminist economists also debated the usefulness of the concept of a 'patriarchal mode of production,' seeking to extend Marxism beyond its market- and production-centric focus to include reproductive care and homemaking work (Folbre 1986; Koopman 1991; Wiegersma 1991). On the one hand, this theoretical framework draws on extensive evidence of unequal exchanges between men and women in work and consumption. On the other hand, a 'modes of production' approach focuses attention on material exploitation, putting physical productive and reproductive work in the center of the analysis and providing no framework to value the emotional effort involved in caring work, implicitly ranking psychological and emotional dimensions of male domination lower than other dimensions.

As with Marxian theory, an evolving feminist literature critiques mainstream economic models of households and gender divisions of labor. Such models include the school of 'New Home Economics,' founded by Becker (1965), which views households as tiny factories that make efficient use of inputs to 'produce' children and maximize the well-being of family members. According to such models, men specialize in labor-force work because returns to their investments in education and training are higher than they are for women, implying, for example, that households will have higher income if resources are channeled disproportionately into boys' and men's education.

Mainstream (neoclassical) economists neglect power dynamics in access to education and other resources, relegating this topic to sociologists and anthropologists. As a result, the mainstream economic theory of gendered labor is tautological: women are held to earn less in the labor force because they specialize in child-rearing, yet they specialize in child-rearing because they earn less in the labor force. Mainstream economic theory also assumes that household members pool income and behave altruistically toward one another (Becker 1981). However, empirical studies show that consumption spending on women's and children's needs and allocations of food and medical care vary with the shares of income earned by women and men (Hoddinott 1992). Women tend to allocate more income to children's needs.

In the last several decades, economists have turned increasingly to bargaining models to interpret expenditure patterns and other household decisions (Manser and Brown 1979; McElroy 1992; Seiz 1991; Agarwal 1994; Friedmann-Sanchez 2007). This stream of research makes use of the concepts of 'threat points' and fall-back positions (defined as the income, skills, and resources individuals would have access to if the household dissolves). Such research may frame individuals' fall-back positions within parameters such as cultural practices, laws, and enforcement of laws structuring men's and women's options, such as with regard to marital property, child custody, child-support payments and domestic violence (McElroy 1992). For early empirical studies of gender dynamics in household decisions see, for example, Blumberg (1993), Hoddinott (1992) and the studies cited in Dwyer and Bruce (1988), as well as the special issues of *Development and Change* (1987) and *World Development* (1989).

Readings In Chapter 17 Kavita Datta examines fathering in Botswana households during the time when the HIV/AIDS epidemic has intensified caring work, using focus groups to examine possible sources of change in the construction of men's roles. Diana Wolf's sociological comparison of two Asian countries (Chapter 18) challenges the notion of a unified household survival strategy. Gita Sen's landmark piece (Chapter 19) examines the control of Indian women's sexuality. Sen explores the way in which pervasive threats of sexual harassment and rape impact women's place in families, communities, and labor markets.

C: Violence in households

Perhaps the most graphic expression of unequal household power relations is physical violence against family members. In the absence of institutions that equalize men's and women's access to income and property, women are frequently unable to divorce or leave abusive partners, especially if they have children to support. An in-depth look at spouse abuse is provided in Counts et al. (1992), an edited collection that examines aspects of social organization in countries with varying degrees of wife-beating. Cultural practices associated with less violence against women include a larger role for women in choice of marital partners, bonds of solidarity among village women, cultural norms that disdain expressions of anger, a greater role for women as principal food providers, and the near-absence of alcohol.

As Kandiyotti (1988) points out, women's compromises with male power structures often have the effect of pitting generations of women against one another. Tensions between mothers-in-law and daughters-in-law are endemic in many Asian cultures, where a mother's main bond is with her sons as her main source of security. In turn, sons' emotional ties with mothers may be stronger than with their wives, depending on the extent to which marriages are arranged or based on filial choice. Wolf (1972) provides a detailed examination of patrilocal marriage and its implications for women.

Reading Chapter 20 is an excerpted article by Aysan Sev'er that traces the practice of dowry and infant sex selection in India historically and provides a current account, analyzing the growing incidence of dowry-related deaths.

D: Female-headed households

As markets bring rapid change, options for women in traditional societies may increase, as noted above. Adding to this, improvements in birth control and medical technology, increasing education requirements for children, and diminishing acreage in family-based agriculture have contributed to falling birth rates and family size. As Folbre (1983, 1994) shows, this trend is reinforced by adult children's rising employment and falling land ownership, reducing the power of fathers to control children by threatening disinheritance and thus reducing men's incentives to increase family size.

In the face of women's transformed options and men's reduced stake in children's labor, both influenced by markets and globalization, the incidence of female-headed households has grown. Ostergard (1992) estimates that, at any point in time, one third of the world's households are headed by women, either temporarily, owing to a spouse's migration, or permanently.

Reading Chapter 21 is an excerpted article by Sylvia Chant in which she examines several questions related to female headship and the 'feminization of poverty' thesis, concluding that it is not so much poverty as responsibility and obligation which have been feminized. Examining policy implications, Chant notes that the equation of 'women' with 'gender' in anti-poverty initiatives has all too often (re)masculinized advantage.

References and further reading

Abraham, E. (1993) 'Caught in the shift: the impact of industrialization on female-headed households in Curacao, Netherlands Antilles', in J. P. Mencher and A. Okongwu (eds), *Where Did All the Men Go?*, Boulder, CO: Westview Press.

Agarwal, B. (1990) 'Neither sustenance nor sustainability: agricultural strategies, ecological degradation and Indian women in poverty', in B. Agarwal (ed.), *Structures of Patriarchy*, New Delhi: Kali for Women.

— (1994) *A Field of One's Own: Gender and Land Rights in South Asia*, Cambridge: Cambridge University Press.

Becker, G. S. (1965) 'A theory of the allocation of time', *Economic Journal*, 75(299).

— (1981) *A Treatise on the Family*, Cambridge, MA: Harvard University Press.

Benería, L. (2003) 'Paid and unpaid labor: meanings and debates', in *Gender, Development, and Globalization: Economics as If All People Mattered*, New York: Routledge.

Benería, L. and G. Sen (1981) 'Accumulation, reproduction, and women's role in development: Boserup revisited', *Signs*, 8(2).

Blumberg, R. L. (1993) 'Power versus "purse power": the political economy of the mother-child family III,' in J. P. Mencher and A. Okongwu (eds), *Where Did All the Men Go?*, Boulder, CO: Westview Press.

Boserup, E. (1970) *Women's Role in Economic Development*, New York: St Martin's Press.

Brown, C. (1981) 'Mothers, fathers, and children: from private to public patriarchy', in L. Sargent (ed.), *Women and Revolution*, Boston, MA: South End.

Castro, M. G. (1993) 'Similarities and differences: female-headed households in Brazil and Colombia', in J. P. Mencher and A. Okongwu (eds), *Where Did All the Men Go?*, Boulder, CO: Westview Press.

Clark, M. H. (1984) 'Women-headed households and poverty: insights from Kenya', *Signs*, 10(2).

Cohen, M. (1985) 'The razor's edge invisible: feminism's effect on economics', *International Journal of Women's Studies*, 8(3).

Collins, J. L. and M. Giminez (eds) (1990) *Work without Wages: Comparative Studies of Domestic Labor and Self-Employment*, Albany, NY: SUNY.

Counts, D., J. Brown and J. Campbell (eds) (1992) *Sanctions and Sanctuary: Cultural Perspectives on the Beating of Wives*, Boulder, CO: Westview Press.

D'Amico, D. (1993) 'A way out of no way: female-headed households in Jamaica reconsidered', in J. P. Mencher and A. Okongwu (eds), *Where Did All the Men Go?*, Boulder, CO: Westview Press.

Deere, C. D. (1977) 'Changing relations of production in Peruvian peasant women's work', *Latin American Perspectives*, 4.

— (1978) 'The difference of the peasantry and family structure: a Peruvian case study', *Journal of Family History*, 3.

Deshmukh-Ranadive, J. (2005) 'Gender, power, and empowerment: an analysis of household and family dynamics,' in D. Narayan (ed.), *Measuring Empowerment: Cross-Disciplinary Perspectives*, Washington, DC: World Bank.

Development and Change (1987) 18(2).

Dube, L. and R. Patriwala (eds) (1990) *Structures and Strategies: Women, Work and Family*, New Delhi: Sage.

Duvvury, N. and M. Nayak (2003) 'The role of men in addressing domestic violence: insights from India', *Development*, 46(2).

Dwyer, D. and J. Bruce (eds) (1988) *A Home Divided: Women and income in the third world*, Stanford, CA: Stanford University Press.

Fapohunda, E. R. (1988) 'The nonpooling household: a challenge to theory', in D. Dwyer and J. Bruce (eds), *A Home Divided: Women and income in the third world*, Stanford, CA: Stanford University Press.

Floro, M. S. (1991) 'Market orientation and the reconstitution of women's role in Philippine agriculture', *Review of Radical Political Economics*, 23(3/4).

Folbre, N. (1983) 'Of patriarchy born: the political economy of fertility decisions', *Feminist Studies*, 9(2).

— (1986) 'Hearts and spades: paradigms of household economics', *World Development*, 14(2).

— (1991) 'Women on their own: global patterns of female headship', in R. Gallin and A. Fergeson (eds), *Women and Development Annual*, vol. 2, Boulder, CO: Westview Press.

— (1994) *Who Pays for the Kids? Gender and the Structures of Constraint*, London: Routledge.

Friedmann-Sanchez, G. (2007) 'Assets in intrahousehold bargaining among women workers in Colombia's cut-flower industry', in C. Deere and C. Doss, *Women and the Distribution of Wealth*, London: Routledge.

Gawaya, R. (2009) 'Investing in women farmers to eliminate food insecurity in southern Africa: policy-related research from Mozambique', *Gender and Development*, 16(1).

Guyer, J. (1984) 'Women in the rural economy: contemporary variations', in M. J. Hay and S. Stichter (eds), *African Women South of the Sahara*, Harlow: Longman Group.

Hoddinott, J. (1992) 'Household economics and the economics of households', Paper presented at the International Food Policy Research Institute–World Bank Conference on Intrahousehold Resource Allocation, International Food Policy Research Institute, Washington, DC, 12–14 February.

Islam, M. (1993) 'Female-headed households in rural Bangladesh: a survey', in J. P. Mencher and A. Okongwu (eds), *Where Did All the Men Go?*, Boulder, CO: Westview Press.

Jahan, R. (1988) 'Hidden wounds, visible scars: violence against women in Bangladesh', in B. Agarwal (ed.), *Structures of Patriarchy*, New Delhi: Sage.

Jones, A. (2006) *Men of the Global South: A Reader*, London: Zed Books.

Kandiyotti, D. (1988) 'Bargaining with patriarchy', *Gender and Society*, 2(3).

Katz, E. (1991) 'Breaking the myth of harmony: theoretical and methodological guidelines to the study of rural Third World households', *Review of Radical Political Economics*, 23(3/4).

Kisseka, M. and H. Standing (eds) (1989) *Sources of Sexual Behaviour: A Review and Annotated Bibliography*, London: Overseas Development Administration.

Koopman, J. (1991) 'Neoclassical household models and modes of household production: problems in the analysis of African agriculture households', *Review of Radical Political Economics*, 23(3/4).

— (1992) 'The hidden roots of the African food problem: looking within the rural household', in N. Folbre, B. Bergmann, B. Agarwal and M. Floro (eds), *Women's Work in the World Economy*, New York: New York University Press.

Manser, M. and M. Brown (1979) 'Bargaining analyses of household decisions', in E. A. Lloyd and C. Gilroy (eds), *Women in the Labor Market*, New York: Columbia University Press.

McCrate, E. (1987) 'Trade, merger and employment: economic theory on marriage', *Review of Radical Political Economics*, 19(1).

McElroy, M. (1992) 'The policy implications of family bargaining and marriage markets'. Paper prepared for the International Food Policy Research Institute–World Bank Conference on Intrahousehold Resource Allocation: Policy Issues and Research Methods, International Food Policy Research Institute, Washington, DC, 12–14 February.

Mead, M. (1976) 'A comment on the role of women in agriculture', in I. Tinker and M. B. Bramen (eds), *Women and World Development: The Complexities of Change*, Washington, DC: Overseas Development Council.

Mencher, J. (1989) 'Women agriculture labourers and land owners in Kerala and Tamil Nadu: some questions about gender and autonomy in the household', in M. Crisnaraj and K. Chanana (eds), *Gender and the Household Domain*, New Delhi: Sage.

Mencher, J. P. and A. Okongwu (eds) (1993) *Where Did All the Men Go?*, Boulder, CO: Westview Press.

Ostergard, L. (ed.) (1992) *Gender and Development: A Practical Guide*, London: Routledge.

Seiz, J. (1991) 'The bargaining approach and feminist methodology', *Review of Radical Political Economics*, 23(1/2).

Sen, G. and C. Grown (1987) *Development, Crises, and Alternative Visions: Third World Women's Perspectives*, New York: Monthly Review.

Singh, A. and K. Viitaen (eds) (1987) *Invisible Hands: Women in Home-based Production*, New Delhi: Sage.

Wiegersma, N. (1981) 'Women in the transition to capitalism: nineteenth to mid-twentieth century Vietnam', *Research in Political Economy*, 4.

— (1988) *Vietnam: Peasant Land, Peasant Revolution, Patriarchy and Collectivity in the Rural Economy*, New York: St Martin's Press.

— (1991) 'Peasant patriarchy and the subversion of the collective in Vietnam', *Review of Radical Political Economics*, 23(3/4).

Wolf, M. (1972) *Women and the Family in Rural Taiwan*, Stanford, CA: Stanford University Press.

World Development (1989) 17(7).

16 | Accounting for women's work: the progress of two decades[1,2]

Lourdes Benería

The problem of underestimation of women's work in labour force statistics and national income accounts has been pointed out repeatedly since the 1970s (Boserup 1970: Wainerman and Lattes 1981; Benería 1982; Dixon-Mueller and Anker 1988; Folbre and Abel 1989; UN 1989). This underestimation has been observed particularly in four general areas of activity: (a) subsistence production; (b) informal paid work; (c) domestic production and related tasks; (d) volunteer work. Even by accepted definitions of labour force, there has been a tendency to underestimate female labour force participation rates in the first and second areas – as with the case of unpaid family workers in agriculture or with participants in the informal labour market; the main problem in this case consisted in designing more comprehensive and accurate methods of data collection although some conceptual issues regarding the definition of subsistence production also had to be dealt with. In the case of domestic production and related tasks, the problem has been more conceptual; in the conventional view, this type of production was not included in any national accounting statistics because it was defined as falling outside of the economic realm unless performed as some form of remunerated activity. Similarly, in the case of volunteer work, the problem has also been conceptual and definitional.

Boserup (1970) was one of the first authors to point out the importance of women's subsistence activities, particularly in rural areas in predominantly agricultural countries, and the underestimation of such activities in the conventional methods of national income accounting. The influence of the international women's movement since the 1970s, however, and the subsequent work carried out in international organizations and academic institutions have been instrumental in providing the impetus to analyse and emphasize all aspects of the invisibility of women's work, including domestic production.

The need to deal with the undercounting of women's work at all levels was given important recognition in the 1985 Nairobi Conference that ended the UN Decade for Women, as was reflected in its report *Forward-looking Strategies for the Advancement of Women*. By strongly recommending appropriate efforts to measure the contribution of women's paid and unpaid work 'to all aspects and sectors of development', the report officially sanctioned the process by which the underestimation of women's economic activities had been analysed while the conceptual and practical obstacles to overcoming the problem had gradually weakened. Since then, strong support for a more systematic inclusion of statistics on women's work in national accounts has been expressed by other international organizations, many government officials and non-governmental institutions (United Nations office in Vienna 1989). The effort has been undertaken at the two levels which are most relevant – that is, labour force and production statistics.

Assessing the problem

Labour force statistics and national income accounts were historically designed to gather information about the level of economic activity and changes over time, and to provide a basis for economic policy and planning. In capitalist economies, the market has always been viewed as the core of economic activity. Similarly, participation in the labour force and the inclusion of production in national accounts have been defined in relation to their connection to the market or to the performance of some work for 'pay or profit' (as defined by the International Conference of Labor Force Statisticians in 1954). The typical story about the decrease in GNP when a man marries his housekeeper is well known by readers of introductory economics textbooks, even if, as a wife, her household activities might not have changed or might even have increased. The reason for this is the notion that unremunerated work was not to be included in national income, and the person performing it not to be counted as a member of the labour force because they were not part of the market or paid exchanges of goods and services and therefore not viewed as economically significant. The notion, however, has been applied differently to various areas of economic activity:

Subsistence production

An important exception to this rule was subsistence production. As early as 1947, Kuznets had warned about the need to improve the then still quite young system of national income accounts to include subsistence production: methods to estimate its value and the proportion of people engaged in it were recommended by the UN system of national income accounts during the 1950s, particularly for countries in which this sector had a relatively important weight in the economy. Thus, countries such as Nepal, Papua New Guinea, Tanzania and others developed methods of estimating subsistence production in varying degrees during this period. By 1960 a working party of African statisticians recommended that estimates of rural household activities would be useful and could be added to those of subsistence production in agriculture, forestry and fishing (Waring 1988).

This effort was consolidated with the 1966 definition of labour force recommended by the International Conference of Labor Statisticians which included *all persons of either sex who furnish the supply of economic goods and services* (ILO 1976; emphasis mine). Whether this supply was furnished through the market was not relevant. This exception to the market criterion was addressed particularly to the case of subsistence production, although what constituted 'economic goods and services' was not entirely clear.

For the purpose of recording women's economic activities, the 1966 definition of labour force did not end the problem. Despite the conceptual and practical progress made to include subsistence production in national accounting, the statistical information on women working in this sector was problematic for a variety of reasons having to do with methods of data collection, enumeration procedures as in cases of application of concepts such as 'family labour', and the perception of respondents – men and women – regarding women's work and their primary area of concentration (Benería 1982).

National income accounts likewise differed in their definition of economic goods and services regarding unremunerated production. As Blades (1975) showed based on a survey of seventy countries, an effort to incorporate subsistence production *in agriculture* in GDP accounts was gradually made in most countries but the statistical estimation of subsistence activities was subject to a great variation by country. Once the market criteria did not apply clearly, what was considered an economic activity became arbitrary, and differences between countries developed regarding their inclusion in national accounts of activities such as home gardening, water carrying and food processing (Dixon-Mueller and Anker 1988).

All of these factors resulted in a tendency to undercount the proportion of the population in the labour force and the value of goods and services included in national accounts. The problem has affected women in particular, given their high concentration in subsistence activities and their specific role in the domestic sphere – which often makes difficult the drawing of a clear line between domestic and subsistence activities.

Over the years, this has resulted in significant statistical disparities between countries – creating difficulties for comparative analysis. Given the general acceptance of the need to include subsistence production in labour force and national income statistics, the problem presently could be identified as one of defining with greater clarity what are 'economic goods and services', a task that has been taken up by experts and appropriate organizations.

The informal sector

A different type of problem is represented by the lack of statistical information on workers engaged in the underground and informal sector of the economy or any form of paid work not registered statistically. The absence of appropriate and systematic data collection can in this case be overcome only through an effort to recognize the importance of this sector in many countries and, in the case of women, the high participation of the female population in it. Projects have been undertaken, but they have been of an ad hoc nature (SSP/UCECA 1976; Portes et al. 1987; Roberts 1991).

The difficulties of such a task are not to be underestimated; they derive from the underground character of a [substantial] proportion of this sector as well as from its unstable, precarious and unregulated nature. Periodic and more systematic country surveys could, however, realistically be elaborated to provide estimates of this sector's weight in labour force and GNP statistics. Along these lines, the UN has prepared general conceptual and methodological guidelines for the measurement of women's work in the sector – industry, trade and services – and carried out useful pilot studies in Burkina Faso, Congo, the Gambia and Zambia (United Nations Statistical Office/ECA/INSTRAW 1991a, 1991b). In each case, microeconomic survey data have been combined with macroeconomic data.

Domestic work

In the case of domestic production and related activities, the problem was of a different nature; unlike subsistence production, this type of work was not viewed as a substitute for market-oriented goods and services and not defined as an 'economic activity'. Until recently there was therefore no attempt to include it in national accounts and labour force statistics because it was seen as falling outside the boundary of these accounts.

The practice was not questioned until the late 1970s. Boserup (1970), for example, argued strongly for the inclusion in national accounts 'of food items obtained by collecting and hunting, of output of home crafts such as clothing, footwear, sleeping and sitting mats, baskets, clay pots, calabashes, fuel collected by women, funeral services, hair cuts, entertainment, and traditional administrative and medical services' together with 'pounding, husking and grinding of foodstuffs and the slaughtering of animals' (pp. 162–3). She saw these activities, however, mostly as subsistence production, not as domestic work; although she mentioned the omission of the 'domestic services of housewives' from national accounts, she was less vociferous about it than in the case of subsistence production. Thus, she emphasized the need to include production for own consumption, which she pointed out was larger in the economically less developed and agricultural countries than in the more industrialized countries. Yet, as labour has become more expensive in the high-income countries, self-help activities such as construction, carpentry and repairs have increased considerably; this is likely to result in an increase in the number of hours spent on unpaid household work.

Production therefore shifts out of the household at some stages in the economic development process while at least part of it might return to the domestic sphere later – regardless of who performs it. If household production is not being accounted for, growth rates are likely to be overestimated when this production shifts to the market (and) underestimated when it shifts from the market to the household. Given the predominant division of labour and women's role in the household the problem affects women's work in particular. Self-help work, however, such as construction and repairs, also involves men. In any case, the problem of over- or underestimation would disappear if all domestic work and related activities were accounted for. This includes tasks that are carried out simultaneously – as when a housewife cleans the house or goes shopping and takes care of children at the same time.

Since the late 1970s, the absence of statistical information about domestic work has been under scrutiny in many circles and for a variety of reasons. What seemed to be a far-fetched and quite unacceptable notion a decade earlier has become a matter of serious and constructive work, with specific practical implications, even though much remains to be done.

Volunteer work

A different area of undercounted work by women is that of volunteer work. The wide range of tasks in this category creates both conceptual and methodological problems. Conceptually, it refers to work whose beneficiaries must not be members of the immediate family. In addition, there cannot be any direct payment and the work must be part of an organized programme. That is, volunteer work is different from domestic work even though there might be some close connections between the two – such as in the case of voluntary work performed in one's neighbourhood – which might make the boundaries difficult to draw. In addition, while some voluntary tasks might easily be viewed as production, such as that of free job training and voluntary home-building organizations, others are more difficult to classify, such as some of those associated with charitable work. Even in the latter case, some accounting of these tasks seems important, particularly if these tasks are free substitutes for what would otherwise be remunerated market work. Gender asymmetries with regard to volunteer work are abundant. As argued by women in New Zealand when they mobilized around this issue in 1984, while (mostly male) monetary contributions to charity are tax-deductible, time contributions (mostly female) are not. The result of this mobilization was the inclusion of a question about time dedicated to volunteer work in the 1986 Census of Population (Waring 1988).

Much remains to be done to account for women's volunteer work, particularly given that in many areas it has been increasing significantly. Such is the case with survival activities among the poor resulting from the drastic deterioration of living standards of countries with structural adjustment packages. The participation in collective kitchens, for example, raises questions about the conventional definition of volunteer work since the beneficiaries often include both immediate family and neighbourhood members.

Conclusion

Numerous reasons have been given for recording unremunerated production and improving the accuracy of statistical information in other areas. These range from the need to base national and international policies and planning on the most accurate assessment of reality, to recognizing the contribution of women to all aspects of development, to constructing more comprehensive indices of welfare. A variety of studies carried out in many countries over the years indicates that the value of unrecorded activities, a high proportion of which are performed by women, might range between one third to one half of measured GNP (Goldschmidt-Clermont 1983, 1989). Different UN documents have repeatedly pointed out that statistics on women's contribution to the economy can be useful for human-resources planning and estimations of potential output, agricultural policies, measures to be taken with regard to the informal sector, and the different adjustment and stabilization policies designed at times of economic crisis. Likewise, they can be useful for the study of savings and consumption patterns, the analysis of household dynamics, regional and comparative studies of men's and women's participation in production and studies of time use by gender (United Nations Office in Vienna 1989). More accurate data can be useful to design appropriate policies regarding employment, income distribution, social security provisions, pay equity and others.

Systematic information about domestic production and related subsistence activities would shed light on the estimation of welfare levels and on the current discussion about the intensification of women's work resulting from the structural adjustment policies implemented in many countries during the past decade (Elson 1991; Floro 1992; Benería 1992).

Conceptually at least, the battle against the invisibility of women's work seems largely to have been won, at least among those working on these issues; the remaining difficulties appear to be mostly of a practical nature even though, here too, some progress has clearly been made.

Notes

1 The original version of this chapter includes a summary of the 'contributions of two decades'.

2 Editor's note (2nd edn): An updated version of the original chapter is 'Paid and unpaid labor: meanings and debates', in L. Benería, *Gender, Development and Globalization*, Routledge, London, 2003.

References

Benería, L. (1982) 'Accounting for women's work', in L. Benería (ed.), *Women and Development, the Sexual Division of Labour in Rural Societies*, New York: Praeger.

— (1992) 'The Mexican debt crisis: restructuring the economy and the household', in L. Benería and

S. Feldman (eds), *Economic Crises, Persistent Poverty and Women's Work*, Boulder, CO: Westview Press.

Benería, L. and C. Stimpson (eds) (1987) *Women, Households and the Economy*, New Brunswick, NJ: Rutgers University Press.

Blades, D. W. (1975) *Non-monetary (Subsistence) Activities in the National Accounts of Developing Countries*, Paris: OECD.

Boserup, E. (1970) *Woman's Roles in Economic Development*, London: George Allen & Unwin.

Carrasco, C. et al. (1992) *El Trabajo Doméstico y la Reproducción Social*, Madrid: Instituto de la Mujer.

Chadeau, A. (1989) 'Measuring household production: conceptual issues and results for France', Paper presented at the Second ECE/INSTRAW Joint Meeting on Statistics of Women, Geneva, 13–16 November.

Dixon-Mueller, R. and R. Anker (1988) *Assessing Women's Economic Contribution to Development*, Training in Population, Human Resources and Development Planning, World Employment Programme Paper no. 6, Geneva: ILO.

Elson, D. (1991) 'Male bias in macroeconomics: the case of structural adjustment', in D. Elson (ed.), *Male Bias in the Development Process*, Manchester: Manchester University, pp. 164–90.

Floro, M. S. (1992) 'Work intensity and women's time: a conceptual framework', Paper presented at the URPE/ASSA conference, New Orleans, 3–5 January.

Folbre, N. and M. Abel (1989) 'Women's work and women's household: gender bias in the US Census', *Social Research*, 56(3): 545–69.

Goldschmidt-Clermont, L. (1983) *Unpaid Work in the Household*, Geneva: ILO.

— (1989) 'Valuing domestic activities', Paper submitted to the the Second ECE/INSTRAW Joint Meeting on Statistics of Women, Geneva, 13–16 November.

ILO (International Labour Office) (1976) *International Recommendations on Labour Statistics*, Geneva: ILO.

Kuznets, S. (1954) *National Income and Its Composition 1919–1938*, New York: National Bureau of Economic Research.

Langfeldt, E. (1987) 'Trabajo no remunerado en el contexto familiar', *Revista de Estudios Economicos*, 1: 131–46.

Portes, A. et al. (1987) *La Mujer Rural Dominicana*, Santo Domingo: CIPAE.

Roberts, B. (1991) 'Urban labor services and structural adjustment', in G. Standing and V. Tokman (eds), *Towards Social Adjustment*, Geneva: International Labour Office, pp. 115–40.

SSP/UCECA (Secretaria de Programación y Presupuesto/Unidad Coordinadora de Empleo, Capacitación y Adriestramiento) (1976) *La Ocupación Informal en Areas Urbanas*, Mexico, DF, December.

United Nations (1989) *Improving Statistics and Indicators on Women using Household Surveys,* Studies in Methods, Series F, No. 48, New York: Statistical Office/ INSTRAW.

United Nations Office in Vienna (1989) *World Survey on the Role of Women in Development*, New York: United Nations.

United Nations Statistical Office/ECA/INSTRAW (1991a) *Handbook on Compilation of Statistics on Women in the Informal Sector of Industry, Trade and Services in Africa*, Santo Domingo and New York: United Nations.

—— (1991b) 'Synthesis of pilot studies on compilation of statistics on women in the informal sector in industry, trade and services in four African countries', Santo Domingo and New York: United Nations.

Wainerman, C. H. and Z. R. de Lattes (1981) *El Trabajo Femenino en el Banquillo de los Acusados*, Mexico, DF: Population Council/Terra Nova.

Waring, M. (1988) *If Women Counted*, New York: Harper & Row.

17 | 'In the eyes of a child, a father is everything': changing constructions of fatherhood in urban Botswana?

Kavita Datta

Research on parenting in the global South reflects a bias towards capturing the practices and experiences of motherhood, which is justifiable given prevalent gender ideologies (Bowlby et al. 1997; Doucet 1995; Engle and Leonard 1995; Lawler 1996). In turn, a depiction of fatherhood as oppositional to, and in conflict with, motherhood has led to a focus on a 'deficit' model of fatherhood (Greene and Biddlecom 1997: 36). Viewed from such a vantage point, men are either providers and disciplinarians or absent, irresponsible fathers (Fox 1999).

More recent work has challenged such homogeneous understandings and is exploring temporal and spatial differences in fathering and fatherhood (Chopra 2001; Fox 1999; Morrell 2005; Simpson 2005; Townsend 1997, 2001). In turn, this appreciation that fatherhood is socially constructed and hence malleable is vitally important for three interrelated reasons. First, the potential to reshape fatherhood is critical for the achievement of gender equality both within the productive *and* reproductive spheres (Morrell 2005). A second imperative to consider fatherhood as malleable emerges from the sexual and reproductive health agenda (Bruce 1995). The HIV/AIDS crisis has lent a particular urgency to the need to engage with men as sexual and reproductive beings given the consensus that they are critical for the prevention of the disease (Bujra 2002). A third and final reason emerges from a focus on the rights of the children. There is increased consensus that children benefit from having active fathers in their lives which in turn entails a reconstruction of fatherhood (Morrell 2005).

Yet, having illustrated the importance of recognizing that fatherhood is socially constructed and hence negotiable, one has to recognize that change does not naturally follow (Bujra 2002). This article seeks to critically explore temporal changes in the construction of fathering and fatherhood in urban Botswana. It draws upon focus group discussions held with a range of men of differing age, marital and parental status which examined both the parental histories of the men as well as their own child-raising practices. The location of this work in Botswana is especially pertinent given the HIV/AIDS epidemic in the country.

Rethinking fatherhood? Gender, HIV/AIDS and the rights of children

It is perhaps instructive to begin with a definition, and in particular the distinction between fathers, fathering and fatherhood. 'Fathers' and 'fathering' are defined in relation to reproduction such that fathers contribute half of a child's genetic material, while 'fatherhood' is a more complex term embracing a broader range of parenting functions (Engle and Leonard 1995). Perhaps most critically, it is agreed that fatherhood is a role which is socially constructed and negotiated and played out in relation to particular children, in specific community circumstances and cultural milieus (Roggman et al. 2002).

In turn, fathering and fatherhood are critical to the constructions of masculinities. Hegemonic constructions of masculinities are intimately related to sexual prowess such that the biological fathering of children is a vital marker of male virility and masculinity, as is the ability to provide for the economic needs of children, and families at large.

Furthermore, fatherhood is a role which is constructed not only by men but also women and children, and in relation to motherhood and childhood. A gendered division of parenting work is the product of particular economic production structures and gender organization which facilitates a separation of fathers from children (Townsend 2001). Within this context, it is also important to recognize that motherhood is also constructed in relation to fatherhood. In spite of the fact that fatherhood varies spatially and temporally, it has certain universal characteristics in that it is a gendered role which is invested with power, both in relation to motherhood, and within the household (Engle and Leonard 1995). The linking of motherhood and the traits associated therein with nature sets up an unalterable link between women bearing children *and* assuming primary responsibility for bringing them up (Lawler 1996). Unsurprisingly, then, mothers are what Townsend (2001) refers to as 'default parents' and the rights of mothers and children are sometimes conflated.[1] Feminists argue that in order to reclaim their rights over motherhood, women need to reclaim control over their bodies, sexualities and motherhood, which must be valued and validated without slipping into essentialism, which presupposes that all women have an intrinsic capacity to nurture (Lawler 1996).

The HIV/AIDS epidemic, and the discovery that it is a gendered disease, has led to a focus on men and masculinities within sexual and reproductive health discourse and policies (Bujra 2002; Gosine 2004). Although women were primarily blamed for spreading the disease in parts of the global South such as Africa (and have therefore become the main targets of intervention), there has been a gradual realization that the HIV/AIDS epidemic is driven by men who are identified as a 'core group' in the transmission of the disease, be this through sharing needles for drug injection, hetero- or homosexual sex (Foreman 1999: 4). In Africa, the main form of HIV/AIDS transmission is heterosexual sex, which is deeply affected by imbalances of gender power.

Men often determine the frequency and type of sexual encounters that take place which, in turn, may be characterized by risk such as unprotected sex as well as multiple sexual partners. This is partly attributable to the fact that male identities are predicated upon the performance of high-risk behaviour which exposes them to HIV/AIDS given their refusal to protect themselves, and sometimes deliberately so. Unlike men, women are vulnerable to HIV infection because they have limited opportunities to protect themselves.

Furthermore, the HIV/AIDS epidemic demands that fatherhood is reconstructed such that men take on new gender parenting roles such as caring for the sick and dying, jobs which are traditionally assigned to women and mothers but which men have to perform so that HIV/AIDS-torn societies can cope with the epidemic. As such, men as fathers (but also brothers and sons) must become carers for both family members afflicted by AIDS *and* their own children and younger siblings (Morrell 2005). Their failure to do so has serious repercussions. For example, children who have lost their mothers to the disease often also lose their fathers as they are sent to live with other female relatives.

Recent research has also begun to call for a re-examination of fathers and fatherhood within the framework of the rights-based literature (Jabeen and Karkara 2005; Mayo 2001).

There is some debate about the importance of fathers to children. On the one hand, researchers argue that a father's presence within a family signifies stability, 'normality' and leads to the healthy adjustment of children (Lloyd and Duffy 1995). Children, and especially sons, raised in households where fathers are absent are likely to face psychological stress and stigmatization. On the other hand, there is also research which does not fully endorse the importance of fathers to children. Researchers argue that children raised in households where fathers are absent may *not* be at such a disadvantage. For one, female-headed households are less prone to violence than those in which fathers reside, as men who beat their wives often also beat their children (Chant 1997). The distribution of resources such as clothes and education may also be fairer in female-headed households. Furthermore, sons are often raised in contravention to prevailing gender norms and roles, as mothers are anxious that their sons are not socialized in the same masculine traditions as their fathers (ibid.; O'Connell 1994).

Fatherhood in Botswana: across time and space

While research on fathers and fatherhood per se remains scarce in Botswana (although see Townsend 1997, 2001, 2002), that which exists can be divided into two broad groups. The first is largely anthropological and looks at fathering within the general context of sexuality, marriage and parenting (Comaroff and Roberts 1977; Garey and Townsend 1996; Gulbrandsen 1996; Van Driel 1996). The second examines fatherhood through the legal lens and addresses issues such as legal pluralism, child maintenance and the rights of mothers (Armstrong 1992; Armstrong and Ncube 1987; Molokomme 1996). While the general picture which emerges out of this research is that fathers are, at best, distant and, at worst, absent and irresponsible, there is some attempt to try to understand such perceptions within the cultural constructions and practices of fatherhood in Botswana (Garey and Townsend 1996; Townsend 1997, 2001).

Dealing first with the evidence which supports the thesis of male irresponsibility, a striking feature of the social landscape of Botswana is the significant number of female-headed households, with 50 per cent of rural and 44 per cent of urban households headed by women (Ministry of Labour and Home Affairs 1996: 8). Furthermore, dependency ratios within these households are high, with almost a third of all female-headed households having between seven and ten dependent members, some of whom were the biological children of other women (ibid.: 8).

The explanations for these family forms lie in the increased separation of sexuality, marriage and parenting (O'Laughlin 1998; van Driel 1996). Traditionally, marriage was a process beginning with the decision to marry and culminating in the payment of *bogadi* (bridewealth) when a woman could move into a man's family home (Molokomme 1996; Schapera 1940). However, even before *bogadi* was paid, a period of living together (*go ralala*) took place, and this stage usually lasted until a child was born (van Driel 1996). Therefore, premarital sexual relations and the birth of children were culturally sanctioned albeit within the broad process of marriage, as *go ralala* implied that the conditions necessary for the expression of sexuality had been met (MacDonald 1996; Townsend 1997; van Driel 1996). At the same time, the payment of *bogadi* remained crucial for the control of a woman's fertility as it was at this point that her reproductive capacity was transferred to her husband's family. All of a woman's children became the legal responsibility of her husband upon payment of *bogadi* (van Driel 1996). So, a primary function of marriage was also to provide a social position for children.[2]

This link between premarital sex, the birth of children and marriage was broken in the early part of the nineteenth century owing to various factors. First, the growing influence of missionaries led to the abolition of 'pagan' traditional customs such as *bogadi*. Second, the commercialization of traditional economies and the imperative to earn wage incomes led to the increased migration of (mostly) men to the South African mines and farms for fairly prolonged periods (ibid.). This led to more flexible and early sexual relations occurring increasingly outside the context of marriage (Datta 1996; Datta and McIlwaine 2000; Jewkes et al. 2001; Mturi and Moerane 2001; Schapera 1940). Furthermore, the high social status conferred on women with children in Tswana[3] culture, coupled with social opprobrium faced by women who were infertile, continued such that birth outside of marriage became a statistical norm which has continued to the present day (McIlwaine and Datta 2004; Molokomme 1996; Upton 2001). Yet marriage remains a long-term goal because bachelors are not classified as adults until they marry. Until such time as marriage takes place, however, they are able to pursue a series of relationships, or indeed even multiple relationships at the same time, as they are not held responsible for either the women they are involved with or any children who result from such unions (Suggs 1987). As such, the separation that has occurred between the roles of wife and mother in the case of women has not occurred in the case of men who have to be husbands in order to be fathers. Men may pay *bogadi* when their children are grown up, or indeed, not at all (Garey and Townsend 1996).

The formulation of family law in Botswana exhibits state attempts to address issues such as male abandonment of women and children while also promoting certain types of idealized family arrangements (Ministry of Labour and Home Affairs 1996). In turn, these laws have been criticized by feminists for various reasons. While supposedly dealing with absentee fathers, laws such as the Affiliation Act of 1971 in fact stipulate that men are not obliged to look after 'illegitimate' children unless they accept parentage of these children and bring them to live with their families (ibid.). Furthermore, the onus is on women to prove the paternity of their children, which many women are unwilling to do (Molokomme 1996). As such, few women claim maintenance; most who do experience long delays in payment; the sum of money involved is paltry and dependent upon the age of a child (ibid.; van Driel 1996). The 1971 Act is also criticized for being based upon Western family norms such that it focuses on biological rather than social children.

This leads us to counter-arguments against the construction of fatherhood as deviant. The separation of men into biological and social fathers is an outcome of Tswana cultural norms such that biological paternity is not an ongoing relationship unless it is coupled with social paternity (Garey and Townsend 1996). Upon marriage, men take responsibility for not only their own biological children but also any other children that their wife may have. Thus, Garey and Townsend (ibid.) argue that perceptions of irresponsible fathers are culturally inappropriate as men do make important contributions to their social children. The failure by men to acknowledge children born outside of marriage is also not necessarily harmful to children. Instead, it falls on maternal grandfathers and maternal uncles to incorporate such children into their own lineage, thus guaranteeing them a social position as well as ritual, political, jural and economic rights and responsibilities (ibid.).

Furthermore, men also make important contributions to other children. A man's responsibility to support children is divided between his family of origin and his family of marriage and depends upon his own position along a marriage continuum (ibid.). He has to contribute to his family of origin and particularly his sisters' children so that in time his family will contribute to his *bogadi*, which will enable him to set up his own household. Indeed, the expectation that men will look after their parents and sisters' children can conflict with the active caring that men are able to give their own children (Townsend 2001).

The construction of fatherhood as distant is also attributable to Tswana culture, which prohibits men's contact with (especially young) children. The distance between fathers and children in Botswana is also due to the spatial and economic organization of traditional living, which is gendered and age-specific and spread out over three distinct locations: the village, lands and the cattle posts (van Driel 1996). Gendered divisions of labour mean that older people and young children live in the villages, women and children work on the lands, while men and older sons (from the age of nine or ten) herd the cattle at the cattle posts (ibid.). Some researchers posit that, with urbanization, a fourth zone has been added to this spatial organization such that fathers are likely to migrate to urban areas in search of jobs, returning to the villages seasonally.

Exploring changing constructions of fatherhood in Gaborone, Botswana

Methodological framework Feminist research methodologies have offered new, and improved, ways of conducting research with women and by women. However, such research has had rather less to say about the particular challenges of researching men in general (although see Hutchinson et al. 2002), of women researching men (Grønnerød 2004; Lee 1997) or of men researching men (Schwalbe and Wolkomir 2001). Indeed, some of the very advances offered by feminist research methodologies, such as the deconstruction of hierarchical relationships between the researcher and the researched and the investment of the researcher's own personal identity in the research process, can raise challenges when women conduct research on men (Lee 1997).

While aware of these limitations, this research utilized a feminist methodological framework which entailed the following. The first stage was a mapping of the organizations involved in women and gender issues in Botswana. This was followed by in-depth interviews with women activists and government officials working within this sector in order to explore the place of men and masculinities in local gender and development discourses and practice (Datta 2004). The next stage of the research involved focus group discussions with diverse groups of men, and this article draws primarily on these.

In total, seven focus group discussions were held, with individual groups ranging in size from four to six participants with a total of twenty-seven respondents taking part.[4] Each focus group included men who varied in their age, marital and parental status. Eleven of the men said that they were fathers.

All but two of these men were married, these two being a widower (Joel) and a man who lived with his partner. These fathers identified the number of children they had. Eight of the respondents were raised in female-headed households which obviously had an important bearing on their experiences as children (see below). Occupations ranged from being students to working in the public sector as teachers, drivers or in low-level clerical jobs, while a couple of men worked in the private sector. Seven respondents were unemployed at the time of the discussions.

Sons and fathers: retelling parental histories I begin the empirical discussion by first examining the parental histories of the participants as this enables us to both trace temporal changes as well as gain an insight into socialization processes. The key issues which arose in the men's retelling of their parental histories were the existence of distant fathers; the pivotal roles played by mothers in their upbringing; and, perhaps contradictorily, their continued subscription to an ideology that fathers were very important in raising children, especially sons. The latter was particularly developed in relation to discipline and the socialization of sons.

Taking each of these in turn, most of the focus group discussions began with an observation that (biological) fathers were generally distant from children, which was justified first in terms of work commitments. While older men such as Joel reported that his father had been away at the South African mines through much of his childhood, the younger men spoke about the migration of their fathers to Botswana towns, thus reflecting broader migration patterns in the country and the region (Datta 1996). The spatial organization of rural living (see above) also contributed to a lack of contact, as reported by Morake: 'I grew up in the village, my father was out looking after the cattle, my mother was there for me, she provided everything for me.'

Equally implicated in this distance was the social construction of fatherhood in Tswana culture. The initial discussion in a couple of groups highlighted the fact that both mothers and fathers were distant, with Cornelius arguing that parents merely 'disciplined, corrected [children] but not to assist, or even to say that you have done well'. Fathers were then particularly identified as being socialized to be largely distant from the lives of their children with one participant in this research quoting a Tswana proverb which she loosely translated as meaning: 'your mother is your friend, I am your father'. As John explained in one group discussion, 'there is a line of communication for children, for sons. They cannot question their fathers directly, they must go to their uncles and he intervenes and questions father.'

If fathers were distant or remote, mothers were then identified as being a constant presence or as 'default parents' (see above). Perhaps unsurprisingly, the importance of mothers was first raised by the participants who had grown up in *de jure* female-headed households. Before elaborating upon this, it is important to note that although the majority of men involved in the study had been raised in de facto female-headed households, they drew a clear distinction between their own situation and that of children raised in *de jure* female-headed households, which they referred to as 'households with no men'. Two participants, Morake and Selewa, who had been raised in *de jure* female-headed households, opened the discussion in rather defensive terms and argued that 'you don't miss anything if your father is not around' (Morake). They went on to say how important their mothers were.

This led to a general discussion about the importance of mothers, irrespective of whether households were headed by men or women. There was general agreement that 'in some households, children do not have fathers who live with them' and that this may not be a bad thing as a 'mother brings more peace than the man' (John).

Having acknowledged the importance of their mothers, the men then went back to talk about the importance of fathers to children, and particularly sons. Werner appeared to be speaking for his group when he said: '... [we had] tremendous respect for him. No matter who they are, in the eyes of a child a father is everything.'

Thus, in order to learn how to be a man, the respondent had to be in the company of men, and especially their fathers. Indeed, it was at this stage that the lack of a father, as in *de jure* female-headed households, became a problem, at least for some of the participants, such as Ernest:

> Boys brought up by single mothers have no idea of a complete household, when he gets married, he has no one to look up to, he does not know how to behave with his wife, how to head his house. There are no initiation schools any more so such children have a difficult start in life. Sometimes, they hunt down their fathers for a sense of belonging, of identity, they want to change their surnames to their father's. [A] surname is very important here, you have to discuss things with your fathers and uncles in the *kgotla*.[5] You find that a father is a figurehead to start off the marriage arrangements. At the beginning of primary school, children also begin to question about their fathers, it leads to depression in boys.

Again, this led to fairly heated discussions with participants raised in *de jure* female-headed households arguing that they did not suffer owing to the absence of their fathers as his role was assumed by other adult men in the family.

A second reason why fathers were deemed as being important in the lives of their sons was discipline. None of the men questioned their father's right to physically punish them but seemed to view it instead as a rite of passage that they, as sons, had to pass through.

The association of discipline with fathers led once again to a questioning of what happened in *de jure* female-headed households. There were particularly animated discussions around an implicit assumption that children raised in these households were likely to be undisciplined and delinquents (see also Datta and McIlwaine 2000). Yet Selewa, who had been raised by his mother, counter-argued that 'discipline is associated with men, society believes that men are disciplinarians. But if you compare me with children from married couple, maybe my mother is a woman and a man ... if I compare myself with boys who have fathers, I find myself more disciplined.'

His reference to the fact that his mother is a 'woman and a man' reflects the extent to which he thought his mother fulfilled the role of both mother and father by not only taking care of him but also being a tough disciplinarian. It is also illustrative of the extent to which motherhood may be being reconstructed in Botswana owing to the absence of fathers. While the experiences of most of the men as children suggested that they had limited contact with their fathers, it was striking that few of the respondents attributed such absences to male abandonment or irresponsibility in their retelling of their parental histories. Instead, they explained these distant relationships in terms of work commitments and cultural constructions of fatherhood, thus exempting their own fathers from any blame. However, there was more dissent within groups between participants who had been raised in *de jure* female-headed households and those raised in de facto female- or male-headed households. The main point of contention was the importance of fathers in the upbringing of children, with the former arguing that neither had they missed out on a male role model (owing to other older men assuming these roles) nor were they undisciplined.

Fathers and sons: child-raising practices I turn now to focus on the child-raising practices of the men. The purpose of this discussion is to explore temporal changes in the practices and experiences of fatherhood, particularly in relation to the HIV/AIDS epidemic in the country as well the rights of the child. The men articulated highly complex understandings which incorporated both a continuation of deviant and irresponsible fathering and fatherhood practices as well as a potential for change.

Deviant and irresponsible fatherhood continued Having discussed their parental histories, many of the men were keen to place their child-raising practices within the context of change. This was perhaps best exemplified by Morake's pronouncement in one group that '[we] want to be part of our children's lives'. However, having identified what seemed to signal a significant change, some discussants almost immediately qualified this desire and, in so doing, justified a range of (unchanging) irresponsible fathering and fatherhood practices.

Focusing first on fathering practices, there was agreement among some participants that men had to be given a choice regarding when they became fathers. Young men like Selewa were particularly keen to stress this point. Thus, he argued: 'I want to have children when I am ready for them, not unexpected children ... then I will run away ...'

Indeed, discussants in this group argued that, according to their culture, men were under no obligation to look after such 'unexpected' children who were born out of wedlock. To this end, Phinius said that: 'no shame is attached to fathers who are not looking after their children'.

This was qualified by Selewa, who felt that the pressure to look after children was dependent upon class. Thus, 'we fragment ourselves into classes, if a girl from a richer family gets pregnant, then there is more pressure [to look after the children]'.

By and large, these men continued to draw a clear distinction between biological fathering and social fatherhood, as well as linking fatherhood to marriage. In turn, the time which elapsed between biological fathering and social fatherhood was significant owing to the pursuit of multiple casual sexual relationships which continued to be fundamentally important to the construction of masculinities.

The men sought to justify this period of 'prolonged youth' by referring to peer pressure and culture. Male peer groups pressurized men to enact their masculinities through numerous casual sexual relationships such that men who pursued monogamous relationships were accused of being bewitched. Such relationships were also naturalized by being presented as part of culture. John, for example, argued that 'sleeping around' was culturally sanctioned such that: '[The] African tradition still accepts polygamy. That context still moves from one generation to the next.'

When asked to consider the implications of these sexual practices, most of the men spoke exclusively in terms of HIV/AIDS. What is perhaps more important to highlight here is that while the men were tentatively beginning to identify a link between sexual practices and HIV/AIDS, they were *not* relating either to fathering or fatherhood. This was despite a recognition that the disease was leading to 'this problem of AIDS orphans' (Jonas) as well as the break-up of families owing to the stigma attached to the disease. As such, it was not surprising that when asked to propose solutions to the HIV/AIDS epidemic, they largely failed to acknowledge the role that they could play as fathers. Instead, they argued that it was ultimately the responsibility of the state to look after the orphans through welfare schemes.

Participants were asked to identify the key characteristics they associated with women and men. Women were overwhelmingly defined in relation to motherhood, thus establishing the link between women and children. In turn, men were more likely to be defined in relation to women and the family rather than children.

Discipline was also a parenting role which was especially associated with men, as evident in Joel's pronouncement that 'fathers are the beaters more than the mothers'.

This gendering of parenting roles also meant that most of the men involved in this research did little reproductive work associated with child-raising, which was seen as being the preserve of women.

Joel, one of the older widowed respondents in the study, argued that 'I will not work in the house ... our culture does not expect us to cook for a woman, or wash children, you get married for that and you just go out and get drunk.' Furthermore, hegemonic masculinities would not allow men to do more reproductive work. Thus, even when they wanted to do more, married men were pressured not to participate in child-rearing by older generations including their own fathers and uncles, as evidenced by this exchange in one focus group:

MALELA: [even if you work before you get married], when you get married you change. Your uncle would not expect it. When they go home, they will say things. Parents still believe that men should not do anything in the house.

ERNEST: They would feel that the guy has lost control of his household. Would hold meetings and would watch the guy.

JOEL: If I start to wash or look after the children, and my father sees it, he will go to the traditional court and say my son is working, he will say there is witchcraft going on, that is why a man is doing the washing.

ERNEST: When I was growing up, my mother would say that being a boy does not mean that you are a cripple, you can help your sisters. But there are no role models ... Motswana men can help wife during the week, if no one else is there, if your father is there, they will expect you to stay away from the kitchen.

Finally, culture was also held responsible for exerting other demands on men such that they did not have the time to be engaged, active fathers. Some of the discussants such as Selewa spoke about the demands that their own parents made on their time: 'there is also a conflict between mothers and wives, mothers expect a lot, they leave little time for your own family'. Thus, men's responsibilities to their own children were contested and negotiated through their obligations to their wider families.

This discussion highlights some of the constraints on the potential for fathering and fatherhood to be transformed even in the face of HIV/AIDS. The men themselves implicitly attributed what could be labelled as deviant fathering and fatherhood practices to the patriarchal dividend as well as hegemonic masculinities which policed their behaviour and prescribed a separation between men and their children.

Potential for change? There was a questioning among some participants of why masculinities were constructed without reference to children. Werner was one participant who spoke at length about the pressures that men came under:

> men suffer from low self-esteem, strict system where there is a lot expected of men ... career not going where it supposed to be going, drink, depressed, not what they want to be, don't know how to get there. Society does not allow men to express themselves. At the workplace you don't talk about your children and families.

The gendering of parenting roles was also seen as potentially harmful to the relationship between men and their children.

It is perhaps predictable that women were held responsible for causing these rifts as they placed fathers in a position of authority. This was exemplified by Phinius, who argued that: '[Men are the] second level of command, the court of appeal, children are told: "Your father will be coming home so you better behave."'

At the same time, however, some participants began to distinguish between the kind of physical chastisement which was associated with men and the more subtle discipline associated with women. Joel, in particular, argued that: 'if your wife dies and leaves you with the children, they [i.e. the children] would be less respectful than if their mother was around. Man by himself cannot handle a family ...'

Perhaps more importantly, it was in these discussions on discipline that the issue of children's rights arose. While many groups spoke about how men were primary disciplinarians and that this was a role which was foisted on men by women, one participant in a group, Morake, began to argue that perhaps it was wrong to physically chastise children in the first place. There was wry agreement with his observation that 'disciplining children is also changing, now we have Child Line, you are not supposed to beat children'. Child Line is an NGO which deals with issues relating to children. It was clear from this discussion that societal and young people's perceptions of physical punishment or disciplining were undergoing a change such that parents', and in particular fathers', right to discipline their children was being questioned.

The gendering of productive and reproductive work was also challenged. Many of the participants agreed that women had to work, which Jonas attributed to the fact that 'financially you need two incomes because the cost of living is so high, you need two incomes today'. However, there was much more debate about whether women's increased participation in the workplace should be matched by men's participation in the reproductive sphere and in the assumption of caring roles (see also above). Nonetheless, John and Morake argued that 'men's participation in home chores is increasing', albeit at 'a very slow pace and only in urban areas where women go to schools'. Although many of the men attributed their lack of participation in child-raising and reproductive work to socialization and lack of male role models, participants who had been raised in *de jure* female-headed households argued that they were more ready to participate in household chores than others. Selewa argued that: '[where] a mother is the head of a family, there is not going to be much difference between the [upbringing] of sons and daughters. Married women come from the context of a man. [In my case] there is no distinctive difference between my sisters and myself.'

In his case, this meant that he did his fair share of housework and shared domestic chores, such as cooking, with his sister.

Finally, returning to the HIV/AIDS epidemic, some of the participants challenged the sense that the epidemic was not resulting in any change in sexual behaviour. Phinius argued that: 'HIV/AIDS will change sexual behaviour,' although he qualified that this would occur in the distant future as 'at the moment, things are getting worse'. The Church was then identified as a key institution, both in relation to the fight against HIV/AIDS and changing fathering practices. Cornelius and Ernest both agreed that: 'the Church is important for those who are not married. We have this problem of HIV and the Church tells us not to have more than one relationship and the importance of being faithful. Children should also be born after marriage.' There was also a greater appreciation of personal responsibility among some participants, albeit not specifically as fathers, that men had a role to play in combating HIV/AIDS. As such, Jonas and John, who had both raised the issue of AIDS orphans and the break-up of families, agreed that men had to work with women to deal with the HIV/AIDS epidemic in the country.

Conclusions

A recognition that the practices and experiences of fatherhood are temporally variable is significant both because it challenges stereotypical notions of deviant fatherhood as well as having potentially beneficial consequences for the achievement of gender equality, HIV/AIDS prevention and the rights of children. Yet, as this article has illustrated, the extent to which fatherhood and masculinities are malleable and subject to change is debatable. On the one hand, fatherhood appears to have changed very little. Many of the men in this study assumed the same gendered parenting roles and responsibilities that their fathers had fulfilled and justified a range of irresponsible fathering and fatherhood practices by drawing upon prevalent gender ideologies and pressures from both men and women to conform to established gender norms. Indeed, even the HIV/AIDS epidemic had done little to change sexual behaviour and there was very little evidence that it was leading to more responsible fathering and fatherhood practices.

On the other hand, it is important also to highlight the few changes that were evident. For a start, some of the men questioned the gendered parenting roles that they were expected to perform, arguing, for example, that the role of disciplinarian harmed their relationship with their children. They even raised the prospect that such disciplining was in contravention of the rights of children. Furthermore, there was evidence that wider structural and social changes were precipitating changes in household form. As such, some men spoke about a tendency for parents to bring their children to live with them in the towns so as to take advantage of better education prospects, as well as to conform to nuclear household ideologies propagated by the Church. While the men were failing to explicitly link HIV/AIDS and fatherhood, there was an appreciation that the epidemic was having a fundamental impact on children and family forms as well as an appreciation that the prevention of the disease required collective action from men and women.

Notes

1 This conflation is also evident in government institutions such as the Department of Women and Child Development in India and the Ministry of Women and Children's Affairs in Bangladesh (Jabeen and Karkara 2005).

2 Some of these issues were addressed by the International Conference on Population and Development (ICPD) in 1994. Particularly important was the appreciation that women should be treated as agents and not passive recipients of sexual and reproductive health interventions (Cornwall and Welbourn 2002). Yet it has been problematic to translate some resolutions into action and it has been recognized that women are still often cast as victims and not as actors in their own right (UNFPA 2005).

3 The Tswana are the dominant ethnic group in Botswana (Motswana, singular; Batswana, plural).

4 Five focus groups had four participants; one had five participants and one had six participants. A total of thirty-one men were interviewed. The paper draws upon the contributions of twenty seven participants as four participants left the discussions before they were completed owing to work commitments.

5 The *kgotla* is the traditional court which is traditionally dominated by older men and where decisions pertaining to ethnic groups were made in the past.

References

Armstrong, A. (1992) 'Maintenance payments for child support in Southern Africa: using law to promote family planning', *Studies in Family Planning*, 23(4).

Armstrong, A. and W. Ncube (eds) (1987) *Women and the Law in Southern Africa*, Harare: Zimbabwe Publishing House.

Bowlby, S., S. Gregory and L. McKie (1997) '"Doing home": patriarchy, caring and space', *Women's Studies International Forum*, 20(3).

Bruce, J. (1995) 'Family policy: supporting the parent-child link', in J. Bruce, C. Lloyd, A. Leonard, P. Engle and N. Duffy (eds), *Families in Focus: New Perspectives on Mothers, Fathers and Children*, New York: Population Council.

Bujra, J. (2002) 'Targeting men for a change: AIDS discourse and activism in Africa', in F. Cleaver (ed.), *Masculinities Matter! Men, gender and development*, London: Zed Books.

Chant, S. (1997) *Women Headed Households: Diversity and dynamics in the developing world*, Basingstoke: Macmillan.

Chopra, R. (2001) 'Retrieving the father: gender studies, "father love" and the discourse of mothering', *Women's Studies International Forum*, 24.

Comaroff, J. and S. Roberts (1977) 'Marriage and extramarital sexuality: the dialectics of legal change among the Kgatla', *Journal of African Law*, 21(1).

Connell, R. (1995) *Masculinities*, Cambridge: Polity.

Cornwall, A. and A. Welbourn (eds) (2002) *Realizing Rights: Transforming approaches to sexual and reproductive well-being*, London: Zed Books.

Datta, K. (1996) 'Rural homes and urban dwellings?', *International Journal of Population Geography*, 1(2).

— (2004) 'A coming of age? Reconceptualising gender and development in urban Botswana', *Journal of Southern African Studies*, 30(2).

Datta, K. and C. McIlwaine (2000) '"Empowered leaders"? Perspectives on women-headed households in Latin America and Southern Africa', *Gender and Development*, 8(3).

Doucet, A. (1995) 'Gender equality and gender differences in household work and parenting', *Women's Studies International Forum*, 18(3).

Engle, P. and A. Leonard (1995) 'Fathers as parenting partners', in J. Bruce, C. Lloyd, A. Leonard, P. Engle and N. Duffy (eds), *Families in Focus: New Perspectives on Mothers, Fathers and Children*, New York: Population Council.

Foreman, M. (1999) *AIDS and Men: Taking risks or taking responsibility?*, London: Panos Institute and Zed Books.

Fox, D. J. (1999) 'Masculinity and fatherhood re-examined: an ethnographic account of the contradictions of manhood in a rural Jamaican town', *Men and Masculinities*, 2(1).

Garey, A. and N. Townsend (1996) 'Kinship, courtship and child maintenance law in Botswana', *Journal of Family and Economic Issues*, 17(2).

Gosine, A. (2004) 'Sex for pleasure, rights to participation, and alternatives to AIDS: placing sexual minorities and/or dissidents in development', IDS Working Paper 228, Brighton: Institute of Development Studies.

Greene, M. and A. Biddlecom (1997) 'Absent and problematic men: demographic accounts of male reproductive roles', Paper no. 103, Population Council.

Grønnerød, J. S. (2004) 'On the meanings and uses of laughter in research interviews: relationships between interviewed men and a woman interviewer', *Young: Nordic Journal of Youth Research*, 12(1).

Gulbrandsen, O. (1996) *Poverty in the Midst of Plenty*, Bergen: Norse Publications.

Hutchinson, S., W. Marsiglio and M. Cohan (2002) 'Interviewing young men about sex and procreation: methodological issues', *Qualitative Health Research*, 12(1).

Jabeen, F. and R. Karkara (2005) 'Government support to parenting in Bangladesh and India', Save the Children Discussion Paper, Kathmandu: Format Printing Press.

Jewkes, R., C. Vundule, F. Moforah and E. Jordaan (2001) 'Relationship dynamics and teenage pregnancy in South Africa', *Social Science and Medicine*, 52.

Lawler, S. (1996) 'Motherhood and identity', in T. Cosslett, A. Easton and P. Summerfield (eds), *Women, Power and Resistance*, Buckingham and Philadelphia, PA: Open University.

Lee, D. (1997) 'Interviewing men: vulnerabilities and dilemmas', *Women's Studies International Forum*, 20(4).

Lloyd, C. and N. Duffy (1995) 'Familial risk factors for children', in J. Bruce, C. Lloyd, A. Leonard, P. Engle and N. Duffy (eds), *Families in Focus: New Perspectives on Mothers, Fathers and Children*, New York: Population Council.

MacDonald, D. (1996) 'Notes on the socio-economic and cultural factors influencing the transmission of HIV in Botswana', *Social Science Medicine*, 42(9).

Mayo, M. (2001) 'Children's and young people's participation in development in the South and urban regeneration in the North', *Progress in Developmental Studies*, 1(4).

McIlwaine, C. and K. Datta (2004) 'Endangered youth? Youth, gender and sexualities in urban Botswana', *Gender, Place and Culture*, 11(4).

Ministry of Labour and Home Affairs (1996) *National Women in Development Policy*, Gaborone: Government Printer.

Molokomme, A. (1996) 'State intervention in the family: a case-study of the child maintenance law in Botswana', in R. Palriwala and C. Risseeuw (eds), *Shifting Circles of Support: Contextualising gender and kinship in South Asia and sub-Saharan Africa*, London and Thousand Oaks, CA: Sage.

Morrell, R. (2005) 'Youth, fathers and masculinity in South Africa today', *Agenda: Special focus on gender, culture and rights*, pp. 84–7.

Mturi, A. and W. Moerane (2001) 'Premarital childbearing among adolescents in Lesotho', *Journal of Southern African Studies*, 27(2).

O'Connell, H. (1994) *Women and the Family*, London: Zed Books.

O'Laughlin, B. (1998) 'Missing men? The debate over rural poverty and women-headed households in Southern Africa', *Journal of Peasant Studies*, 25(2).

Roggman, L., H. Fitzgerald, R. Bradley and H. Raikes (2002) 'Methodological, measurement and design issues in studying fathers: an interdisciplinary perspective', in C. Tamis-LeMonda and N. Carrera (eds), *Handbook of Father Involvement: Multidisciplinary perspectives*, New Jersey: Laurence Erlbaum Associates.

Schapera, I. (1940) *Married Life in an African Tribe*, London: Faber and Faber.

Schwalbe, M. and M. Wolkomir (2001) 'The masculine self as problem and resource in interview studies of men', *Men and Masculinities*, 4(1).

Simpson, A. (2005) 'Sons and fathers/boys to men in the time of AIDS: learning masculinity in Zambia', *Journal of Southern African Studies*, 23(3).

Suggs, D. (1987) 'Female status and role transition in the Tswana life cycle', *Ethnology*, 26(2).

Townsend, N. (1997) 'Men, migration and households in Botswana: an exploration of connections over time and space', *Journal of Southern African Studies*, 23(3).

— (2001) 'Fatherhood and the mediating role of women', in C. Brettell and C. Sargent (eds), *Gender in Cross-cultural Perspective*, New Jersey: PrenticeHall.

— (2002) 'Cultural contexts in father involvement', in C. Tamis-LeMonda and N. Cabrera (eds), *Handbook of Father Involvement: Multidisciplinary perspectives*, New Jersey: Lawrence Erlbaum Associates.

UNFPA (2005) *State of the World's Population 2004: The Cairo Consensus at Ten: Population, Reproductive Health and the Global Effort to End Poverty*, New York: UNFPA.

Upton, R. (2001) '"Infertility makes you invisible": gender, health and the negotiation of fertility in Northern Botswana', *Journal of Southern African Studies*, 27(2).

Van Driel, F. (1996) 'Marriage – from rule to rarity? Changing gender relations in Botswana', in R. Palriwala and C. Risseeuw (eds), *Shifting Circles of Support: Contextualising gender and kinship in South Asia and sub-Saharan Africa*, New Delhi and Thousand Oaks, CA: Sage.

18 | Daughters, decisions and domination: an empirical and conceptual critique of household strategies[1]

Diana L. Wolf

Feminists have cut through romantic assumptions about family and household unity, arguing that there exist instead multiple voices, gendered interests and an unequal distribution of resources within families and households (Hartman 1981; Thorne and Yalom 1982). Attention is slowly turning to intra-household processes, conflicts and dynamics, particularly within poor Third World peasant and proletarian households. Indeed, Third World household studies appear to be the only context in which the myth of family solidarity and unity is perpetuated, and this is seen most clearly in the concept of household strategies.

Those researching the conditions of poor people – both in social histories of advanced industrialized and in contemporary Third World countries – often refer to the sum total of behaviours at the household level as family or household survival strategies (hereafter referred to as household strategies) (de Janvry 1987; Hareven 1982; Tilly and Scott 1978; Stern 1987; Sorensen 1988; Findley 1987). All demographically related acts, from the urban migration of household members in the Philippines, in Latin America and elsewhere (Arizpe 1982; Findley 1987; Harbison 1981; Trager 1981) to the allocation of labour in poor Javanese households (Firman 1988; Guest 1989; Hart 1986; White 1976), the early marriage of a daughter in rural Bangladeshi families (Abdullah and Zeidenstein 1982) or the allocation of more food to male than female children in Indian families (Rosenzweig 1986) are attributed to household strategies.

This chapter will focus on intra-household relations between parents and daughters in a South-East and East Asian setting where gender relations differ considerably. This focus will further demystify 'the household', revising notions about internal household relations. Additionally, this analysis of intra-household processes will be utilized to illustrate the inadequacy of the concept of household strategies, and a number of erroneous assumptions therein. While not denying the utility of understanding what poor people or domestic groups must do in order to survive, I argue that, owing to certain unwarranted assumptions about individuals and households, the concept of household strategies misrepresents intra-household behaviour, obscures intra-household stratification by gender and generation, and stifles the voices of the empowered – usually females and the young.

The chapter will focus on women and their households in two Asian settings affected by the new international division of labour. Specifically, I will analyse the decision-making process in the family with regard to the young women and factory employment in Java, Indonesia and Taiwan, and critically examine to what extent these processes reflect a household strategy.

Problems in household research

One of the main points in this article is that in household research, whether based on a neoclassical economic framework or a neo-Marxist one, individuals and households are merged and are discussed interchangeably, as though they are one and the same unit, and this problem is most clearly reflected in the concept of household strategies. The household is treated as 'an individual by another name', as though it has a logic and interests of its own (Folbre 1986: 5). On the other hand, any behaviour exhibited by an individual is de facto interpreted as motivated by household interests. The individual is treated like a household in miniature as though (s)he is directed by a gene of household interests with any and all behaviour assumed to reflect household needs.

A second and serious problem with the current usage of household strategies is that most individual or household-level behaviour is assumed by researchers to be part of a strategy without consulting the views of the social actors involved. Researchers rarely elicit respondents' explanations, motives for their behaviour, or the reasoning behind their decisions (Guest 1989).

Researchers otherwise sensitive to the structural constraints faced by the poor often impose their own interpretations about strategies, extrapolating from household-level and individual-level data. Without empirical information from those involved, they have had a free hand in interpreting behaviour in ways that reflect romantic and ideological views of the family or of family solidarity.

Before it is assumed that any and all individual- or household-level behaviour reflects certain motives, it is imperative to explore the expressed intentions of social actors. My point of departure, drawing upon Giddens's theory of structuration, is that social structures are both 'enabling and constraining' (1984: 169) – social actors are both affected by structural features of the political economy and in turn, through the process of reproduction, affect those very structures. Central to my argument is that social actors 'know a great deal about the conditions and consequences of what they do in a day-to-day life' (ibid.: 281) and understand a good deal about 'the conditions of reproduction' (ibid.: 5) in their society. If asked, social actors can explain their behaviour and desires (Scott 1985). The problem is that such responses might not fit models in which individual interests are already assumed.

Setting of research in Java My research site is a rural district (*kecametan*) in central Java with a population of 83,500, located approximately sixteen miles south of Semarang, a large port city. In the early 1970s provincial and district-level government officials encouraged foreign and domestic urban investment in this area. Factories began locating in this rural district in 1972 and continue to do so.[2] The site is not a free trade zone, but has a mixture of multinational and domestically owned firms that are oriented towards both the national and global markets. The area is still rural, with the majority of the population engaged in some form of agricultural production.

Part of the continued attraction to this site is the low cost of available, docile female labour. In 1982, three-fourths of the approximately six-thousand-person industrial labour force consisted of females. Most of these women were single, between the ages of fifteen and twenty-four, and lived at home with their parents in the village. The familial context of workers allowed a more in-depth view of interactions between worker-daughters and their families.

Research design and analysis I lived in an agricultural village, Nuwun, located several miles from the factories with easy access to public transportation so as to study commuting workers, their non-factory village peers and their peasant families.[3] The decision to leave family, home, hearth and village on a daily basis to enter the industrial labour force represents an important individual transition which can also have a considerable impact on the family economy (Hareven 1982; Tilly and Scott 1978). To discern the determinants of factory employment, I interviewed all factory workers (n = 39) and all non-factory females ages fifteen to twenty-four (n = 90) and their families from Nuwun and a neighbouring village. In this unusual rural and industrial setting, households (co-residential groups sharing food and the kitchen) consisted of nuclear and extended families.

Class status interacted with individual and family life-cycle conditions in affecting the probability of seeking factory employment. If intra-household conditions were such that a productive member could be released for full-time work at a distance from home, it appeared that poor families allowed a daughter – or much less frequently a wife – to seek employment in the industrial capitalist sector. These conditions usually included few or no small children, and the availability of at least one other able-bodied female in the household, indicating a later stage of the family life cycle, when children no longer needed constant care. The poorest families – those in poverty at an early, expanding stage of the family life cycle – could not afford to forgo the daily labour or returns to the labour of one female productive member needed at home or on the farm.

From the quantitative analysis alone it could easily be concluded that if certain demographic and economic conditions exist within a household daughters seek factory employment to fortify the family economy. We could conclude that dutiful and sensible factory daughters in Java are driven by the 'family economy ideology' (Tilly and Scott 1978) – altruism towards the family that persists even though the family and work are separate and work is remunerated; in addition, that factory employment is part of a household survival strategy for poor rural families who have few choices. Any notion of industrial employment as part of the household strategy collapses, however, when the household is opened up and the actors, and in this case actresses, speak.

Factory employment and household decision-making I asked the parents (mostly mothers) of factory workers in Nuwun: 'In Java, who decides where an unmarried daughter should work?' Ten out of twenty parents said the child should decide, nine felt that the parents together with the child should decide, and only one parent felt that the parent alone should decide. However, when asked 'Who in your household decided where *your* daughter should work?' *all* twenty parents responded that their daughter had decided alone, on her own.

Daughters had various ways of balancing parental approval with factory employment. Normatively, the ideal decision-making process was to ask parental permission (*minta ijin*) first and then apply for factory positions. While permission from the father seemed to be somewhat more important, most asked both parents. The more common sequence was to apply for positions first, receive a job, and *then* ask parental permission. While most parents agreed, not all consented to their daughter's decision. Parents who disagreed were either fathers or widowed mothers – both of whom are considered heads of households. At that point, daughters either went along with or went against their parents' wishes.

Many of the non-factory single females in 1982 belonged to the group of daughters whose parents would not consent to their factory employment. In situations where the household could not afford to release her labour, parents emphatically forbade a daughter's factory employment. This particular group of daughters, most of whom were about thirteen or fourteen years old, obeyed their parents. However, at about age fifteen these young women did become factory workers, often when another sister took their place doing housework but, more importantly, when they became brave enough (*berani*) to defy parental orders.[4]

I found that dutiful daughters were the exception, not the rule. Surinah's widowed mother told this story:

> Actually, I didn't allow her to work in a factory but she forced it anyway. Her older brother also forbade it. I didn't even know when she went looking for a

job; I only found out after she started working. She said she wanted to have her own money. In my opinion, it's better if a daughter works at home, helping in the rice-fields [*sawah*].

Ratmi, a commuting factory daughter, recounted the common story of starting factory work against her father's wishes; he was so angry that he didn't speak to her for one month.[5] Another worker in Nuwun who had been forbidden by her parents to work in a factory secretly had sought work on her own:

I saw my friends work in the factories and then I wanted to work there too. Before, my parents wouldn't allow it. I didn't ask their permission and I started work right away. I went secretly because if my parents had known, they would have gotten angry with me because they told me to go work in the *sawah*.

Qualitative data from a sample of fifteen migrant workers boarding in an industrialized village[6] revealed similar but even more dramatic dynamics, with daughters leaving home against parental wishes. Yularikah was told by a friend about the jobs at the biscuit factory. She signed up for work and received a job immediately. When asked how her parents felt, she said, 'Well, Father and Mother were forced to agree; they didn't have any choice since I decided to take the job.'

Clearly, seeking factory employment – an important transition normally assumed to greatly affect the family economy – was not necessarily made in tandem with parental visions of a daughter's role or a family economic plan. While younger daughters (ages thirteen to fourteen) accepted parental disapproval of factory employment, older daughters usually disobeyed and rebelled.[7] In not one case did a parent suggest to a daughter that she seek factory employment. Rather, most parents were on the defensive, responding and adapting to a daughter's decision.[8]

There is, of course, a class basis to this lack of parental control. Better-off families – a small minority in the village – controlled their children's activities and labour by giving them education. Poor families had less ability to control grown offspring (White 1976).

Motives for seeking factory employment An important and unexpected finding was that most young women were motivated to seek factory employment for individual social and economic reasons, not for the betterment of the family economy.[9] 'I wanted to be like my friends,' said five workers. 'Almost all of my friends here work in a factory. In the late morning [*siang*], it's very quiet because they've all gone to work. I wanted to work too.'

Factory work was a higher-status job than agricultural labour or trade because, according to one worker, their skin remained lighter, reflecting non-manual work. 'I wanted to work in a factory because it's not hot and you don't work hard,' said one woman. This particular situation reflects some of the ideological contradictions of capitalist development. On the one hand, employment in an industrial capitalist firm was easier and economically more lucrative compared with agricultural labour or domestic service. In terms of workers' personal lives, industrial capitalism was a progressive change as it loosened familial control over their behaviour, brought them into contact with males and females from other villages, often led to romances, and gave them some earnings of their own. However, while factories were perceived as a more desirable work environment, workers in factories had far less autonomy in the production process compared with traders in the market or agriculturalists, owing to the highly disciplined and controlled atmosphere of industrial capitalist production (Ong 1987).[10]

Many workers sought factory employment to gain some financial autonomy from their families. The economic rewards for such employment were, however, meagre and could not attempt to satisfy workers' needs. Although such employment offered young women independence, low wages forced workers to remain economically dependent on their families.

Workers did not mention helping the family economy as a reason for their employment; rather they mentioned buying soap for themselves. Most villagers purchased blocks of inexpensive, unscented soap. If the family was poor, the same soap was used for bathing, washing clothing and dishes. Factory workers bought bars of scented soap for bathing only, costing more than half a day's wage. Buying their own bar of luxury bath soap somehow signified independence and high status, differentiating them from other poor villagers. Comments such as 'I wanted to work in a factory so that I could buy my own soap, like Parjiah', or 'It's nice to be able to buy my own soap', underscore the poverty of workers and their families.

Given such poverty, I expected high remittances from factory wages to the family economy. My findings of a high degree of income retention rather than income pooling have been documented elsewhere (Wolf 1998b). Unlike their Taiwanese counterparts who turned over 50 to 80 per cent of factory wages to families, these Javanese factory daughters controlled their own income, remitting little if anything from their weekly wages to the family till, and often *asked* their parents for money. Most participated in rotating savings association through which they accumulated substantial sums of capital. That money was used to buy their clothing, consumer goods for the household, and was made accessible to parents for life-cycle events (birth, death, circumcision, marriage), emergencies and debts.

In 1986 I returned to Nuwun to find out if increasing participation in the family economy by daughters was matched by a greater role in their life decisions, the timing of marriage and the ability to choose one's own spouse (Wolf 1988a). Traditionally, Javanese females are married at a young age in arranged marriages. I found that the majority of factory daughters had chosen their own spouse. However, in not one case did a daughter mention considering her family's economy in terms of the timing of her marriage or her spouse (Tilly and Scott 1978).

The relative autonomy of young Javanese females and their somewhat self-centred concerns are far from resembling our image of docile Asian females. Why might parents of a grown adolescent daughter not direct her labour? Why might they tolerate her rebellious decisions?

The Javanese kinship system traditionally accorded women some economic autonomy. Because of this tradition, parents expect daughters to engage in economic activities and may not attempt to regulate strongly the economic motions of young and female members as they would in a more rigid, patri-archal system. In addition, factory females exhibited more autonomous and plucky behaviour than their mothers would have dared at the same age, because these young women are experiencing a new life-cycle state in Java for which there are few traditional norms – prolonged adolescence. Certainly, the mothers of these young women would have been more controlled by parents and would not have risked dissenting from them, but they would also have been married by age thirteen or fourteen. Increased education, the increasing age at mar-riage, a new period of adolescence and a young adulthood without economic dependants may well be encouraging more assertive behaviour among young women. Class position also affects behaviour. Since poor parents have little to bequeath to their children, they have less control over them compared with better-off landed families who can orchestrate children's movements more fully because of an eventual inheritance.[11]

To summarize, from a household perspective, economic-demographic char-acteristics were clearly important but not sufficient in explaining a daughter's employment trajectory. Parents appeared to react and adapt to daughters' deci-sions rather than direct or orchestrate them. The qualitative data argue against the assumption that poor Javanese households make decisions and develop a strategy, or that members of poor households automatically repress their own desires and needs for the collective good. This is not to argue that Javanese household members never adapt to each other (as did parents in this case) or pursue a united goal. When crop failure occurred in the mid-1980s, factory daughters' savings were used to sustain the family and prevent migration. The data suggest, then, that the economic behaviour of household members is fluid and dynamic and should be analysed rather than assumed. These findings challenge an overly structural or materialist approach to household behaviour.

Taiwanese household strategies From research on Taiwanese daughters and the Chinese family economy, we can see more clearly the formulation and execu-tion of a parental strategy at the household level which draws heavily upon the organization of a patriarchal kinship system. Within this patrilineal and patrilocal system, daughters are socialized to be filial and to pay back the debt they incurred to parents for bringing them up.[12] Parents socialize daughters 'to believe that they themselves [are] worthless, and that literally everything they [have] – their bodies, their upbringing, their schooling – belong[s] to their parents and [has] to be paid for' (Greenhalgh 1985: 277; Wolf 1972; Gates 1987). While male and female children are born owing their parents debt, males pay it off later in life by taking care of elderly parents. Since daughters permanently leave their natal home upon marriage, they must pay back their debt early in life. Because daughters were seen as 'short-term members' of the family, parents did not 'waste' resources in schooling them (Greenhalgh 1985: 270).

Without question, historically, parents controlled a daughter's labour – the decision to work, where to work and her wages. In the 1920s and 1930s in Taiwan and elsewhere, parents controlled their daughters' labour and received her wage directly.[13] Fathers often signed labour contracts, turning their daughters into factory workers who were then treated as indentured servants (Kung 1983: 17–27; Salaff 1981: 40).[14]

Since daughters have been socialized to feel that they must pay back their debt to parents, it is not a question of whether to work, but when and where. While parents in the 1950s were hesitant to allow a daughter to leave home for factory work, eventually, factory employment became automatic for young women (Wolf 1972: 99; Arrigo 1980; Diamond 1979).

In contemporary Taiwan, parents are still involved in a daughter's work-related decisions and parental opinions are obeyed. Indeed, Kung (1981, 1983) and Greenhalgh (1985) found that parents make the decisions as to when a daughter will stop schooling and where and when she will start working. When an occupation is selected, 'parents are insistent about having daughters abide by their decision' (Kung 1983: 54). Parents exert authority over which factory she should work in if she is seeking employment or attempting to change factories, particularly if there is a wage differential between factories or if it involves living away from home (ibid.: 54).

Workers' stories, such as: 'going to company Y was my father's idea; being just out of primary school I really didn't have many choices anyway', or 'it was decided by my mother that I should go to the fish-net factory' (ibid.: 58), demonstrate the difference in parental involvement and deference to parental authority in Chinese families compared with Javanese.[15] Since a daughter's labour and returns to it are seen as economic resources which families control (Salaff 1981), parents do not demand money from daughters; there is an implicit contract and daughters fulfil their obligation by remitting 50–100 per cent of their wage.[16]

Javanese and Taiwanese factory daughters compared Changes in the international division of labour have not greatly changed female status within the family in either the Javanese or Taiwanese case, but have fortified the previous position of each, building upon the gender relations which existed before industrial capitalism. Javanese daughters operate within a context of a relatively higher level of female autonomy and they are able to bypass, resist and defy parental control over their labour. Compared with the Javanese case, Taiwanese parents appropriate a daughter's labour as part of the family portfolio for the benefit of their brothers, who will eventually provide for parents in their old age. Chinese daughters adhere to a high degree of subordination and deference to parents. As dutiful daughters they are controlled and used as a resource and, according to Greenhalgh (1985) and Niehoff (1987), even more exploited by parents owing to changes in the global economy.[17]

While Chinese families may superficially fit the household strategy metaphor Hareven (1982: 6) suggested, of the movement of a school of fish, or perhaps even a flock of birds, it is clear that not all fish or birds are equal or willing, nor do they necessarily benefit from flying in a flock or swimming in a school. It is also obvious that Javanese families fall short of the bird or fish analogy. Let us now turn to the broader analytical implications of household strategies with these two different cases in mind.

Implications of household strategies

Definition How are household strategies defined?

For a household strategy to be created, a decision must be made. Since such decisions are made with the collective good in mind, other household members must accept those decisions and carry them out. Individuals must sublimate their own wishes for this larger goal; 'personal autonomy is subsumed under the constraints imposed by family needs' (Fernandez-Kelly 1982: 13).

Decision-making for household strategies Certain people within the household make decisions and other less-empowered household members follow them. Since few family systems operate in democratic fashion (Todd 1985), household strategies necessarily embody relationships of power, domination and subordination. We saw that Taiwanese parents, not households, make decisions about their daughters' education, labour and marriages, and that those daughters, because of a lifelong socialization into their inferior positions, obey dutifully. We saw that neither Javanese households nor Javanese parents control or decide how to allocate an adolescent daughter's labour.

Fathers as benevolent dictators Although we know rarely how it is that 'the household' makes its decisions, household economic theory carries a sexual bias in that the individual orchestrating this strategy is implicitly assumed to be male. He does the calculations and makes policy decisions, as the family economy manager and accountant (Findley 1987: 31). Sorensen's (1988: 63) description of how Korean peasants make cropping decisions provides yet another example. Certainly this particular patriarchal power structure drives certain family systems, but as we saw in the Javanese case, not all (Todd 1985).

In the new home economics models, Becker's concept of a benevolent dictator assumes that altruism is inherent in such decision-making power (Folbre 1988: 248; Hannan 1982; Becker and Murphy 1988) – a wise Solomonian father-judge internalizes all family members' needs and rules with justice over his brood (Hart 1978: 35).

The collective good, however defined by the father or mother, reflects particular interests which are not necessarily the interests of household members. Nerlove (1974: 207) noted that in patriarchal societies this often leads to more benefits for sons, particularly elder sons, and less education, food and healthcare for daughters, sometimes leading to higher female mortality. In her research on Mexican households, Roldan asks if their survival strategies provide the maximum benefit to each and every member of the household. From the perspective of the female industrial workers (engaged in industrial homework), 'the answer to this question must be negative' (1985: 271).

In our case study we saw that Chinese parents control a daughter's labour and attempt to extract as much capital as possible from her before she marries in *their* own interest. A Taiwanese factory daughter is exploited by patriarchal interests for as long as ten years. She is coerced and terrorized into drudgery and sometimes dangerous working conditions for fear of sanctions and loss of her one piece of security – the uterine family. Taiwanese factory daughters hand over their income to their parents and postpone their marriages, all for the interests of a household whose lineage doesn't recognize them.

The moral economy of the household In general, the lack of analysis of household relations, particularly in peasant studies, reflects a romanticized view of automatic and inevitable mechanical solidarity between members of poor families. Such an approach assumes that cohesion and coherence rather than conflict are at the basis of intra-household relationships. The peasant or semi-proletarian household is assumed to be a 'wholly co-operative unit' with its own 'moral economy' (Folbre 1988: 253; Sorensen 1988: 130). Those from both a neoclassical economic or Marxist economic background often assume that the competition, struggle or economic self-interest that pervades the capitalist marketplace is left on the doormat, and never enters the household. In the new home economics, 'altruism dominates family life; it drives out selfishness' (Hannan 1982: 69). Pre-capitalist norms of mutual voluntary aid and concern for the group's good are thought to persist inside the house even as the cold winds of capitalism whip around its outer walls. According to Folbre, in peasant economy models and in Marxian analyses, the 'vision of pure altruism within the family' resembles nothing short of 'utopian socialism' (1988: 9). These assumptions allow neoclassical studies to be based on another assumption – a joint utility function – while more Marxist studies 'assume that reciprocity rules within the household' (Folbre 1986: 254).

Portraying Third World households or families as cohesive units perpetuates the 'romantic mist' (Hannan 1982), from the world we have lost. The problem with these comforting consensual images is that they miss entirely intra-household relations of power, subordination and perhaps conflict and dissent. Such research also tends to ignore everyday acts of resistance such as income retention, non-compliance and conflict. Assumptions of household cooperation prevent researchers from considering (and therefore observing) that individual members may not exhibit altruism and may engage in passive non-strategic or overtly resistant, antagonistic, ambivalent, anti-strategic or even multi-strategic behaviour such as laziness, greed, selfishness, revenge or egocentrism.

Whose rationality? Pronouncing household behaviour 'strategic' carries ethnocentric strains and imposes a particular world-view on conditions vastly different from whence the concept came. It implies the kind of calculation, rationalization and cost–benefit analysis financial advisers apply to our taxes and investments, or we apply to buying a car or a washing machine. The peasant, formerly the 'bumbling idiot of modernization theory enslaved by tradition, is here transformed into a hyper-rational strategist, playing the social game according to optimal strategies' (Gupta 1987: 44). This is not to say that peasants don't calculate, but that we shouldn't assume that they do or that they calculate in the same way a Westerner might.

The term strategy itself implies militaristic reasoning and echoes language of the capitalist firm. Firms are individual, closed entities, economically independent of each other, competing with each other for a piece of the limited market and profit. However, poor households in the Third World are remarkably fluid in their boundaries and in their economic relations with other households. The struggle for household survival, unlike market profits, is not a zero-sum game. Additionally, the use of 'adaptive household strategies' reflects a Darwinistic ecological approach which portrays household behaviour in a manner similar to a sociobiological perspective (Sorensen 1988). Clearly the language used to describe household behaviour also needs serious remodelling.

The view from below Since researchers have tended to assume that most individual behaviour is part of a household strategy, the views and explanations of social actors are rarely elicited. In addition, researchers may have felt that respondents could not adequately explain their own behaviour. One reason why respondents' explanations are rarely investigated may be due to the assumption that household strategies tend to operate at the subconscious level, rendering empirical analysis difficult if not impossible. However, Giddens argues that the actions required in daily life and social reproduction (household strategies are one form of social reproduction) are not unconscious but lie within the realms of practical and discursive consciousness. Social actors *can* discuss their intentions, reasoning, choices and motives (Giddens 1984: 6); Javanese daughters and parents of Taiwanese parents were well able to express their motives and reactions.

Another reason why we rarely hear the voices of the strategists may be due to an assumption that, even if social actors can discuss their decisions, they cannot sufficiently understand or explain them. Put rather forcefully, social actors are often perceived either as 'cultural dopes' or mere 'bearers of a mode of production' (Giddens 1979: 71).

A final and related explanation for this gap is that even if social actors can explain and discuss their behaviour, researchers may feel that respondents do not fully understand what they're doing, or do not understand it correctly. In other words, they may have 'false consciousness'.[18] These three reasons for the exclusion of those involved are paternalistic, and give researchers licence to impose their own interpretation upon the data.

Beyond tautologies

'Peasants', a colleague once said to me, 'are by definition rational.' Similar tautological reasoning has led researchers to label all household behaviour 'strategic', echoing a functionalist, biological and ecological approach to adaptation. Whatever members of poor households do is necessarily a strategy, and strategies are whatever households do; nothing is presented comparatively as irrational, non-strategic or anti-strategic behaviour. Indeed Gupta (1987) points out that this approach severely circumscribes the complexity of behaviour and the range of individual responses. I am not suggesting that we focus solely on individuals, or that household-level research be abandoned. Javanese daughters may indeed repress their own wishes and adapt to household needs, but such conditions should be analysed more specifically in terms of age, family life-cycle stage, and type of problem or decision, and need to be seen more fluidly.

While sociologists and historians are beginning to recognize the need to examine differential power and divergent interests within the household (Salaff 1988: 272, fn. 9), economists are considering ways to integrate power and control into the neoclassical household model (Lesthaeghe and Surkyn 1988; Rosenzweig 1986; Hannan 1982). Indeed, Ellis's (1988) excellent text on *Peasant Economics* fully integrates Folbre's feminist critique (1986) of household models, an encouraging change which should affect future rural studies.

The question then becomes: how is it that Taiwanese parents can push a daughter into working selflessly for them to the extent that she will postpone her marriage, sell her youth to the company and still feel worthless? We need to better understand the social mechanisms, the struggles and the process within households which perpetuate domination or engender resistance. This will entail analysing gender ideology and relationships of power, particularly the processes through which power is exerted within the family or household, and linking these intra-household asymmetries and processes with political economic structural change. Benería and Roldan (1987), and Kandiyoti (1988), have succeeded in viewing such intra-household relationships dynamically in terms of a continuous process of negotiations, contracts, renegotiations and exchange within a broader political economic context. While such analyses represent a significant departure from the stasis in past studies, it is important to analyse empirically whether appropriating yet another set of economic terms accurately portrays intra-household dynamics.

While the deconstruction of households and analysis of intra-household asymmetries has emerged in African and Latin American studies, considerable work is yet to be done in Asia, particularly South-East Asia (Guyer and Peters 1987; Watts 1988). Qualitative and comparative data are needed, representing the voices, decisions, desires and acts of resistance of the unempowered, particularly females and the young. We also need a more appropriate and less static conceptual language which takes into account power differentials, different types of decisions and changes over the life cycle. A comparative approach can help illuminate the differences among and commonalities between women and household practices, and can avert assumptions about the homogeneity of Third World women, Asian women or 'the patriarchal family' (Mohanty 1988: 70). Opening up the household and analysing the interactions between social actors will erode the image of Third World women as passive victims (Moore 1988: 79; Mohanty 1988) and contribute to a portrayal of Third World women as active participants in social change in their own right.

Notes

1 This chapter is a revised version of 'Father knows best about all in the household: a feminist critique of household strategies', presented at the Sex and Gender session of the annual meeting of the American Sociological Association, 1988. Field research in Java was sponsored by LIPI and supported by a Title XII grant administered through the Program in International Agriculture, Cornell University (1981–83) and the Graduate School Research Fund, University of Washington (1986).

2 When I conducted research in

1981–83 there were nine large-scale factories operating and three under construction. When I returned in 1986 three additional factories had been built and all fifteen seemed untouched by national and global economic crises. The largest factories (by number of workers) were two textile firms, followed by garments and food processing (bread, cookies, bottling), furniture and buses.

3 I conducted fieldwork for fifteen months from 1981 to 1983, and returned for a two-month follow-up in 1986.

4 In situations where a father is

not present, an older brother or cousin takes over the patriarchal role, making decisions for, and attempting to protect, younger females in the household.

5 Silence and withdrawal are a more common way to express anger in Java, rather than openly and directly expressing discontent.

6 This industrialized village is different and separate from the agricultural villages studied – Nuwun and a neighbouring village.

7 This age difference in daughters' willingness to rebel may partially relate to the age requirements at most factories. Most only accepted females fifteen years old and above.

8 Certainly, better-off families had made calculations about their financial capabilities and, whenever possible, sent their children on to middle school and, in the rare case, to high school. Parents had hopes for one child becoming a civil servant and earning a steady wage unrelated to the agricultural cycle, which would help support parents in their old age. In these few families, parents made decisions about which child could continue schooling (and it was often a male child if a choice had to be made), and about their children's labour. With the prospect of a future inheritance in mind, grown children from better-off households tended to follow parental wishes.

9 It should be noted that young women's choices for income-earning were limited and usually less desirable compared with factory work: trade or agricultural labour, both of which were considered hard and seasonal labour, or domestic service, which was poorly paid and perceived as close to serfdom.

10 On the other hand it is important to note that domestic service was detested by young village women because of the high degree of control exerted by the employers, coupled with extremely low wages. Former domestics described a situation in which they had to be prepared to work at any time of the day or night their employer demanded, for long hours, at very low pay.

11 While I am arguing that controls over the female within the family have weakened, working in a capitalist factory means that other, new forms of control over females outside the household have been reconstituted (Elson and Pearson 1981; Ong 1987). Such forms of control draw upon traditional generational and patriarchal relationships in Java as elsewhere in the world.

12 Margery Wolf (1972) points out that, before factory employment was common, some filial daughters took this burden to the extreme and became prostitutes, which parents accepted. See her chapter on 'Filial daughters'.

13 Honig's historical research on women in the Shanghai cotton mills found that, in some cases, women received their wages directly at least in the 1930s, but most simply turned over all of their wages to their parents (1986: 170–71).

14 Honig writes that, in Shanghai in the 1920s and 1930s, young girls aged nine and ten were sent to work partly so that their brothers could go to school (1986: 168).

15 Although Chinese culture is on the whole patriarchal, there are regional differences.

16 This particular economic relationship has been carefully studied by several researchers, because even a 5 per cent increase in income retention by a factory daughter would indicate social change (Thornton et al. 1984).

17 Salaff (1981) suggests that the nature of the Chinese family in Hong Kong creates values and practices which then in turn create a docile and disciplined workforce. This benefits the state, capitalists and the male working class (Roldan 1985: 272).

18 I am not suggesting that anything and everything expressed by respondents be taken simplistically as data without analysis of ideology, consciousness or structure, but that women's voices and respondents' intents and explanations

be included in the structural analyses of household behaviour.

References

Abdullah, T. and S. A. Zeidenstein (1982) *Village Women of Bangladesh*, Oxford: Pergamon.

Arizpe, I. (1982) 'Relay migration and the survival of the peasant household', in H. Safa (ed.), *Towards a Political Economy of Urbanization in Third World Countries*, Delhi: Oxford University Press.

Arrigo, L. G. (1980) 'The industrial work force in young women in Taiwan', *Bulletin of Concerned Asian Scholars*, 12(2).

Becker, G. and K. Murphy (1988) 'The family and the state', *Journal of Law and Economics*, 31.

Benería, L. and M. Roldan (1987) *The Crossroads of Class and Gender*, Chicago, IL: Chicago University Press.

De Janvry, A. (1987) 'Peasants, capitalism and the state in Latin American culture', in T. Shanin (ed.), *Peasants and Peasant Society*, London: Blackwell.

Diamond, N. (1979) 'Women and industry in Taiwan', *Modern China*, 5.

Ellis, F. (1988) *Peasant Economics*, Cambridge: Cambridge University Press.

Elson, D. and R. Pearson (1981) 'Nimble fingers make cheap workers: an analysis of women's employment in Third World export manufacturing', *Feminist Review*, 7 (Spring).

Fernandez-Kelly, M. P. (1982) *For We Are Sold, I and My People: Women and Industry in Mexico's Frontier*, Albany, NY: SUNY.

Findley, S. (1987) *Rural Development and Migration: A Study of Family Choices in the Philippines*, Boulder, CO: Westview Press.

Firman, T. (1988) 'Labor flows and the construction industry: the case of housing development in Bandung, Indonesia', Unpublished PhD dissertation, University of Hawaii.

Folbre, N. (1986) 'Cleaning house: new perspectives on households and economic development', *Journal of Development Economics*, 22.

— (1988) 'The black four of hearts: toward a new paradigm of household economics', in J. Bruce (ed.), *A Home Divided: Women and Income in the Third World*, Stanford, CA: Stanford University Press.

Gates, H. (1987) *Chinese Working Class Lives: Getting By in Taiwan*, Ithaca, NY: Cornell University Press.

Giddens, A. (1979) *Central Problems in Social Theory*, Berkeley: University of California Press.

— (1984) *The Constitution of Society*, Berkeley: University of California Press.

Greenhalgh, S. (1985) 'Sexual stratification: the other side of "growth with equity" in East Asia', *Population and Development Review*, 11(2).

Guest, P. (1989) *Labor Allocation and Rural Development: Migration in Four Javanese Villages*, Boulder, CO: Westview Press.

Gupta, A. (1987) 'The choice of technique and theories of practice', Unpublished paper, Jackson School of International Studies, University of Washington, Seattle.

Guyer, J. and P. Peters (eds) (1987) 'Conceptualising the households: issues of theory and policy in Africa', *Development and Change*, 13(2).

Hannan, M. (1982) 'Families, markets, and social structures: an essay on Becker's treatise on the family', *Journal of Economic Literature*, 20.

Harbison, S. (1981) 'Family structure and family strategy in migration decision-making', in G. de Jong and R. Gardner (eds), *Migration Decision Making*, New York: Pergamon.

Hareven, T. (1982) *Family Time and Industrial Time*, New York: Cambridge University Press.

Hart, G. (1978) 'Labor allocation strategies in rural Javanese households', Unpublished PhD dissertation, Cornell University.

— (1986) 'Power, labor and livelihood: processes of change in rural Java',

Berkeley: University of California Press.

Hartman, H. (1981) 'The family as the locus of gender, class and political struggle', *Signs*, 6(3).

Honig, E. (1986) *Sisters and Strangers: Women in the Shanghai Cotton Mills, 1919–1949*, Stanford, CA: Stanford University Press.

Kandiyoti, D. (1988) 'Bargaining with patriarchy', *Gender and Society*, 2(3).

Kung, I. (1981) 'Perceptions of work among factory women', in E. Ahern and H. Gates (eds), *The Anthropology of Taiwanese Society*, Stanford, CA: Stanford University Press.

— (1983) *Factory Women in Taiwan*, Ann Arbor: University of Michigan Press.

Lesthaeghe, R. and J. Surkyn (1988) 'Cultural dynamics and economic theories of fertility change', *Population and Development Review*, 14.

Mohanty, C. (1988) 'Under Western eyes: feminist scholarship and colonial discourses', *Feminist Review*, 30.

Moore, H. I. (1988) *Feminism and Anthropology*, Cambridge: Polity.

Nash, J. (1983) 'Implications of technological change for household level and rural development', Working Paper no. 37, Women in International Development, Michigan State University.

Nerlove, M. (1974) 'Household and economy: toward a new theory of population and economic growth', *Journal of Political Economy*, 82.

Niehoff, J. (1987) 'The villagers as industrialist: ideologies of household factories in rural Taiwan', *Modern China*, 13(3).

Ong, A. (1987) *Spirits of Resistance and Capitalist Discipline: Factory Women in Malaysia*, Albany, NY: SUNY.

Roldan, M. (1985) 'Industrial outworking, struggles for the reproduction of working class families and gender subordination', in N. Redclift and M. Enzo (eds), *Beyond Employment*, New York: Blackwell, pp. 248–85.

Rosenzweig, M. (1986) 'Program interventions, intrahousehold distribution and the welfare of individuals: modeling household behavior', *World Development*, 14(2): 233–43.

Salaff, J. (1981) *Working Daughters of Hong Kong*, New York: Cambridge University Press.

— (1988) *State and Family in Singapore*, Ithaca, NY: Cornell University Press.

Scott, J. (1985) *Weapons of the Weak*, New Haven, CT: Yale University Press.

Sheridan, M. and J. Salaff (1984) *Lives: Chinese Working Women*, Bloomington: Indiana University Press.

Smith, J., I. Wallerstein and H. Evers (eds) (1984) *Households and the World Economy*, Beverly Hills, CA: Sage.

Sorensen, C. (1988) *Over the Mountains Are Mountains*, Seattle: University of Washington Press.

Stern, M. J. (1987) *Society and Family Strategy*, Albany, NY: SUNY.

Thorne, B. and M. Yalom (1982) *Rethinking the Family*, New York: Longman.

Thornton, A., Ming Cheng Chang and Te Hsiung Sun (1984) 'Social and economic change, intergenerational relationships, and family formation in Taiwan', *Demography*, 21(4).

Tilly, L. (1978) 'Women and family strategies in French proletarian families', Michigan Occasional Paper no. 4, Department of History, University of Michigan.

Tilly, L. and J. Scott (1978) *Women, Work and Family*, New York: Holt, Rinehart & Winston.

Todd, E. (1985) *The Explanation of Ideology: Family Structures and Social Systems*, New York: Blackwell.

Trager, I. (1981) 'Rural–urban linkages and migration: a Philippines case study', in G. Hainsworth (ed.), *Southeast Asia: Women, Changing Social Struture and Cultural Continuity*, Ottawa: University of Ottawa.

Watts, M. (1988) 'Putting Humpty-Dumpty back together again? Some comments on studies of households, gender and work in rural Africa', Paper prepared for SSRC Workshop on 'Socio-economic transformations, demographic changes and the family in Southeast Asia', Honolulu.

White, G. (1976) 'Production and reproduction in a Javanese village', Unpublished PhD dissertation, Columbia University.

Wolf, D. L. (1984) 'Making the bread and bringing it home: female factory workers and the family economy in rural Java', in G. Jones (ed.), *Women in the Urban and Industrial Workforce*, Development Studies Center Monograph no. 33, Canberra: Australian National University.

— (1988a) 'Factory daughters, the family, and nuptiality in Java', Paper presented to IUSSP conference on 'Women's position and demographic change in the course of development', Oslo, June.

— (1988b) 'Female autonomy, the family, and industrialization in Java', *Journal of Family Issues*, 9(1).

— (1992) *Factory Daughters: Gender, Household Dynamics and Rural Industrialisation in Java*, Berkeley: University of California Press.

Wolf, M. (1972) *Women and the Family in Rural Taiwan*, Stanford, CA: Stanford University Press.

19 | Subordination and sexual control: a comparative view of the control of women

Gita Sen

A view across cultures

Ask many an Indian man what he thinks of the movement for women's liberation in the West and his response would probably be, 'Oh, they need it there; Western women are treated as sex objects by their men, with little recognition of their intellectual, emotional, or moral worth. We in India give our women a special place of honour and dominance in the home and family life; we respect our women.' Encounters with variants of the above self-satisfied pronouncement have forced upon me the realization that, as feminists, we urgently need a cross-cultural examination of the control over female sexuality.

Most Indian women would say that while, perhaps, we are not made to feel we are sex objects in the same manner as women in the West, we are certainly made constantly aware of ourselves as embodiments of sexuality. Whatever the justification for this, the implications for the restrictions on women's mobility, dress, behaviour or interpersonal ties are very similar in many parts of the country.

What we have, then, is the following interesting duality. In the West, the female body is constantly used as an advertising medium for the sale of commodities – jeans, automobiles, washing machines, airlines – every consumer product where the choice of brand is believed to depend on the extent of sexual arousal of the consumer. The effect is to reinforce the objectification of woman as a purely sexual creature; all other human attributes are submerged. In India, on the other hand, use of the female anatomy for the purpose of selling commodities, while growing, is not quite so prevalent. Women are not turned into sexual objects principally *via the commodity form*. Sexual objectification is more direct and personal, its social roots lying in the historical antecedents of a peasant society.

In such a society, production has historically been privatized on the basis of patriarchal family units using family labour complemented by non-family labour. Patrilocality and patrilineality are the norm. Women of the landholding classes are secluded and their sexuality guarded not only as a mechanism to recruit and control their labour to the productive and reproductive tasks of the

154

family, but especially to ensure the paternity of children. Children represent labour potential and are the heirs of the next generation.

It is an interesting puzzle why the patriarchal family should be so concerned about the precise paternity of the children borne by its female members. If the concern of the patriarchs is over children as potential labourers or as heirs, what does it matter who the *biological* father is, so long as the children are *socially* recognized as belonging to the patriarchal family? One possible answer is the tension among brothers or between males of different generations within the family. Control over children may be a crucial aspect of such intra-family struggles for domination among males.

It is possible, however, that a more fundamental basis of the tension over biological paternity may lie in the relations between men and women. We have been accustomed to viewing paternity tensions as tensions among men, viz., 'to which man does this child belong?' However, if we examine the social origins of such 'appropriation' and treat it as historically evolved, we come to a different hypothesis about the social meaning of struggles over paternity.

This hypothesis states that in earlier, more egalitarian societies, it is most likely that women had both responsibility for *and* control over children. This would have been reinforced by the fact that, until recently, the only biological certainty in most societies was maternity, not paternity. However, as patriarchal household structures developed concomitant with the growth of economic surplus and the development of the state, the control of children (as over inanimate means of production) passed from women to some (if not all) men. This 'appropriation' of children by patriarchs occurred through the sexual control over women and was strongly reinforced by social and religious glorification of the 'chaste' woman. Indian religious mythology, for example, is full of stories of such embodiments of female 'chastity'; it is my hypothesis that many of these myths arose with the growth of patriarchal religious, cultural and economic domination over prior, more egalitarian, communities. Tensions over paternity therefore represent an ongoing assertion by patriarchs of their control over children. The expressed tension is really that between women and men, and only secondarily among men themselves.

It would be a mistake to infer from this that all women are in identical positions within the hierarchical structure of the patriarchal peasant household. Clearly, it is the sexuality of *young* women, daughters-in-law and daughters, which is most in question. Even here, the position is not symmetrical; daughters-in-law must be sexually controlled in the interests of reproducing the patriarchal hierarchy within the household.[1] Control of daughters on the other hand is undertaken to ensure their recruitment to other households via marriage, and thus to ensure the reproduction of the household within the nexus of the community's social life. The strictest guardians of the sexuality of young women are older women, mothers and mothers-in-law, whose own relative position within the hierarchy is based on their ability to recruit and channel the labour and sexuality of younger women so as to reproduce patriarchal domination.

It would be a great mistake to imagine that the control of women's sexuality is as rigid within the kin network as it is outside. The extent to which sexuality is expressed within the family varies in different regions of India, but its existence is undeniable. The best-known example is the relationship, involving a considerable degree of emotional and physical intimacy, between the daughter-in-law of the house and her husband's younger brothers in parts of North India. Much of this sexuality within kinship is unacknowledged as such, but there is a definite awareness among kin members about its nuances, the subtleties in tabooed relations, forms, etc. Sexuality is not therefore totally suppressed. Rather, it is channelled by and through the networks of the patriarchal family.

The role of men in such channelling is to dominate and control the public space. This control takes the form of a more or less aggressive occupation of the space in which women, especially young women, are tolerated only within very rigidly defined and strict limits of movement, dress and action. Any transgression of these limits by a woman brings down swift and sometimes harsh retribution in the form of physical, often sexual, molestation. Men police the limits, furthermore, by making women constantly aware of themselves as sexual object, through looks, gestures, laughter and ribaldry. Harkening back to the duality with which we began, women then are no less sexual objects in India than they are in the West, but the form of objectification is different.

In India, for the most part, sexual control is very direct and only peripherally through the commodity form. The economic and cultural conjuncture of a peasant society that is turning capitalist throws up strange and highly contradictory ideological forms. The messages transmitted by Indian cinema, for example, about women and sexuality are a fascinating study in inconsistency, as they attempt to interpret and glamorize life in the cities for the benefit of a largely rural and small-town audience.

The growth of the film image of Indian woman-as-sex-object presents a paradox for our argument that the commodity form is less responsible here for the sex objectification of women. There is a rapidly growing use of female nudity, molestation and rape to titillate and attract male audiences, as well as a sharp increase in pornographic film during the last decade. Commercial Indian film has been using female sexuality precisely in order to sell a commodity – itself. But the apparent paradox is easily resolved when we note that cinema, while a commodity, is of a very unusual type. It is what we may call an 'ideological commodity'. At its most successful, it draws out and mirrors the cultural unconscious of its audience. For better or worse, whether we as feminists like it or not, male control of the public space is part and parcel of the Indian male's image of his world today. And it is this peculiarly male vision of gender relations, with its corollaries of direct, personalized sexual control of women, which is projected on the Indian screen. The example of film therefore buttresses, if anything, our argument about the personalized nature of sexual objectification and control in India.

Class domination and sexual ideology

The direct control of women's sexuality in India, arising as it does from the social relations of patriarchal, family-based production, has its roots in the economics and culture of the landed classes.[2] Is sexual control unimportant, then, among those with no land? Women's experience appears to indicate otherwise. While seclusion and restrictions on mobility may not be as rigid among the class of landless wage-earners, they are not totally absent. Women agricultural labourers, construction workers or petty traders experience a degree of sexual control over their mobility that affects their entry into the market for wage labour and income-earning.

Within the home and community of the landless, female chastity and female virtue are preponderant values, guarded, as among the landholders, by older women and by men, young and old, in the public spaces. The relatively high incidence of free unions without formal marriage, or of wife-initiated separation, bespeaks a degree of female autonomy within the conjugal bond; but this in no way implies an absence of sexual control.

To what can we attribute this concern with women's chastity in a situation where inheritance is largely irrelevant? Srinivas's theory of Sanskritization (Srinivas 1969) hypothesizes an attempt by those at the lower ends of the social, particularly caste, hierarchy to move upwards through the adoption of upper-caste norms, values and practices. A variant of this concept, of special relevance to women, is the idea that as agricultural households acquire more land or other access to income, they imbibe 'middle-class' values and withdraw their women from work outside the home, and even from work on the family farm.[3]

A counter-theory is the orthodox Marxist one that the dominant ideology is that of the dominant class. Control by the ruling classes of the material means for the production of culture allows them to dominate and manipulate the ideas, beliefs and consciousness of the ruled. Such a domination fosters a more effective reproduction of the social hierarchy. Thus the two theories can be seen to approach the problems from opposing directions, the orthodox Marxist seeing the problem as one of domination and imposition, while Srinivas sees it as one of emulation and upward mobility.

Neither approach grants sufficient autonomy to the production of culture and beliefs by the ruled themselves. Neither can tell us enough about the material referents of the sexual control of women among the landless rural population in India. The orthodox Marxist theory of ideology cannot be simply applied in this case, since it is not at all clear what landholders have to gain from the sexual control of women among the landless. Arguments that it promotes divisions within the working class, thus lowering wages and militancy, are too general (perhaps tautological), and tend to confuse causality with factual assertion. Srinivas's theory of cultural assimilation, on the other hand, presumes an emulative pattern in the beliefs and culture surrounding sexuality that does not dissect the implicit hierarchies based on gender. The real question is *who* believes and *who* emulates and *why*? And why do poor, landless women submit to sexual restriction in a situation where they do not, indeed cannot, rely on men for economic survival?

The answer to these questions must be twofold. Male interest in the control of sexuality is probably rooted deep in the psychological make-up of oppressed manhood.[4] Common experience tells us that sex between human beings (like perhaps all human interaction) has dual, possibly dialectical, aspects – control appropriation versus communication. To the extent that male control of a woman's body is the dominant aspect (as opposed to the reciprocity inherent in communication), the sexual act is itself intrinsically linked to the transformation of woman into sexual object, not subject.

Though no formal studies have been done in India that I am aware of, the sharing of women's experiences tells us that such control/appropriation is the norm not only among the middle and upper classes, but also among poor people. For the latter, the absence of communication is compounded by very material problems such as lack of space and overcrowding. Perhaps, in addition, the extent of their oppression and subservience based on caste and class leads poor men to control and appropriate in the only sphere possible to them, the sexual.[5] Be that as it may, the consequent sexual objectification and control is experienced by poor women at various levels, from the conjugal bed to the village street. Sexual objectification and control in the public space has its counterpart, perhaps its roots, in objectification within the sexual act itself.

But why do poor, labouring women submit to this control? Responsibility for children under conditions of acute poverty makes women willing to submit to male sexual control in return for some economic resources, however meagre. Connection to a man also means a degree of protection, socially sanctioned and itself reflecting the community's control and channelling of women's sexuality, against sexual harassment by other men of the community. Such protection is much less effective against sexual molestation by members of the landed classes, a subject to which we will now turn.

Sexual demands by men from landed households are a regular and systematic aspect of the lives of poor women. Such oppression may take the form of regularized rape of women who are employed as casual agricultural labourers or as bonded permanent labourers on the owner's land. It may take the less onerous but no less demeaning form of undesired physical intimacy from landowners and supervisors who consider the women who work under them to be 'fair game'. The threat of joblessness and the ever-present spectre of hunger work effectively to ensure women's acceptance of molestation, unless there is a conscious attempt to organize against it.

This type of oppression is heightened during periods of class and caste tension. During times of militancy and organized resistance by either landless labourers or poor peasants, landowners and their hired goons often counter with organized orgies of gang rape and mass sexual violence. For poor women, their class is enmeshed with their gender in an unmistakable way, since class violence here takes precisely the form of sexual violence. It punishes the militant women in the most direct and brutal manner, and it violates the militant men by appropriating the only arena in which they exercise authority – 'their' women.

The class nature of sexual violence in India has been noted before (Mies 1980). Brutal as it is, the existence of such violence perpetrated by the ruling classes is perhaps easier to acknowledge than the sexual control inflicted by poor men upon the women of their own class. A socialist-feminist perspective does not allow us, however, to be blind to either, and even forces us to search out the links between the two.

In the course of organizing work among the women agricultural labourers in a district of Tamil Nadu, activists who were themselves village women found the medium of role-plays to be very useful in raising the consciousness of women in the village.

One such play dealt with the theme of sexual oppression by landowners. In the discussion that followed a debate ensued about the meaning and relevance of female chastity when it was a well-known, if unacknowledged, fact that such sexual impositions were fairly common. Some young village men on the periphery of the audience intervened, hotly demanding of the women how they could dare question 'chastity', and whether they all wished to be 'immoral'.

What had affected the men most was not the idea of the women having to face the violence of the landlords but the idea that the women might begin to question the notion of female 'virtue', thereby undermining their own, male, control over the women's sexuality.

Sexual control and the labour market

The theory of labour-market segmentation has been adopted without much modification to explain Indian women's 'secondary' position in [that] market (Mukhopadhyay 1981). In a Third World context, the explanatory power of theories developed for labour markets in the West is limited. For women workers, in particular, I would hypothesize that restrictions to mobility arising from the control of sexuality play a crucial role in defining their secondary place.

Two examples will illustrate this argument. Women agricultural labourers are traditionally considered among the freest and most mobile of women workers. Given that many of them are casual labourers who have to search for work, sometimes on a daily basis, it has been assumed that they are free to move considerable distances and to accept work with little restriction.

In fact, the picture above is a rather roseate version of reality. Women labourers generally tend to work fairly close to their homes, or in work situations where co-workers are other women, or men from their own family/community. Women tend to work more in the 'private' or 'semi-public' spaces, and do few tasks considered demeaning to modesty (Kala 1976).[6] The private space is defined, in the context of Kerala, as the house-site or owner's garden area, while semi-public space is that which involves a short walk from home.

Only part of this work definition is based on considerations such as proximity to childcare since most labouring women have either an older child, a neighbour or an older family member to look after small children. A significant part is the women's own, socially defined perceptions of 'virtue', and the importance they attach to it. Working in proximity to strange men often carries a moral stigma and a suspicion of promiscuity. Gulati (1981) documents such a perception for women construction workers in Kerala. Gangs of migrant labourers, who travel a great deal during the harvest periods, are often hired by contractors on a family basis. Usually, this is the only way in which women can be made to travel long distances from home.

A second illustration is derived from research on women petty traders in Madras city. Quite apart from the handicaps of insufficient capital and connections needed to obtain a stall in the market, women suffer significantly from the control of sexuality. Their inability to travel, to associate easily with male wholesalers, or to be in the market late at night, all act as barriers to their income-earning capacity. This is compounded by the daily sexual harassment faced by these women as a consequence of their being in the public space (Lessinger 1982).

My hunch is that the effect of the sexual control of women on their labour-market position and income-earning capacity needs to be taken more systematically into account. Certainly such phenomena are not entirely unknown in the history of industrialization in the West.

Our conceptual concern is that sexual control is such a 'normal' and accepted part of the work life of women that it has achieved the status of an axiom. Our task as feminists is to raise it to the level of a practical and theoretical problem.

Conclusion

In India today, the progressive feminist movement has two sections. Those who focus mainly on the economic and class problems of poor women, and those who focus more attention on issues like dowry and bride-burning, which seriously affect middle- and upper-class women. While neither side underplays the importance of the work done by the other, and while there are many points on which the two sides come together, there is an unease in the alliance around the issues of class and of the control of sexuality.

Facing up to the theoretical and practical importance of the control of sexuality may place the alliance on firmer ground. The problems of dowry, rape and bride-burning are the most visible and brutal effects of the social control of female sexuality. But this is only the tip of the iceberg. The way in which sexual control shapes gender relations among workers, rural and urban, and defines poor women's subordination within the family/community and in the workplace, is the iceberg itself.

Notes

1 Reproduction involves both physical reproduction and the maintenance of social relations, in this instance the patriarchal hierarchy.

2 There is a serious question of how to treat the rural semi-proletariat, i.e. those who have a little land, but who must do wage labour as well. Since children are more important as workers and as old-age security rather than as heirs in this case, the basis of the control of women's sexuality may be very similar to its basis among the landless poor.

3 This, of course, raises the question of the relation between sexual control and patriarchal control over land.

4 Frantz Fanon's work springs readily to mind in this context.

5 This does not mean that the sexual realm is 'a haven in the heartless world' in any sense. Rather, it is a realm where the hierarchy and the domination of gender relations are played out.

6 As is well known, 'modesty' itself is socially defined; clothes considered modest for women in one region of India are often immodest in another. This fact, in itself, points to the social functions of the notion of modesty; there is nothing natural about it.

References

Gulati, I. (1981) *Profiles in Female Poverty*, Delhi: Hindustan Publishing Company.

Kala, C. V. (1976) 'Female participation in farm work in central Kerala', *Sociological Bulletin*, 25(2).

Lessinger, J. (1982) 'On the periphery of trade: male–female competition in a South-Indian market place', Mimeo, Conference on Women and Income Control in the Third World, Columbia University.

Mies, M. (1980) 'Capitalist development and subsistence reproduction; rural women in India', *Bulletin of Concerned Asian Scholars*, 12(1).

Mukhopadhyay, S. (1981) 'Women workers in India: a case of market segmentation', in *Women in the Indian Labour Force*, Bangkok: ILO-ARTEP.

Srinivas, M. N. (1969) 'The caste system in India', in A. Beteille (ed.), *Social Inequality*, Harmondsworth: Penguin.

20 | Discarded daughters: the patriarchal grip, dowry deaths, sex ratio imbalances and foeticide in India[1]

Aysan Sev'er

India is a relatively new and vibrant democracy. With its numerous natural resources, an extremely large population (1.12 billion; CIA 2007) and emphasis on education, India is hastily taking its due place in a globalized world.

Yet a perusal of the daily news media shows a much darker reality that coexists with the economic and political gains the country has made (Prasad 1994; UNIFEM 2003a, 2003b). That dark reality is dowry murders and other crimes against women and girl children that take place within the family realm (UNIFEM 2004; ICRW 2002, 2004a, 2004b).[2]

The severe under-reporting of all crimes against women notwithstanding, statistics show that five women face severe cruelty in their homes every hour and eighteen cases of dowry deaths occur every day in India (CWDS 2002: 27; Hitchcock 2001; ICRW 2002; Rustagi 2004). Moreover, while total crime rates are falling, crimes against women in all categories (rape, molestation, sexual harassment, and cruelty at home which includes dowry harassment, dowry deaths and abduction) are on the rise (CWDS 2002; Dowry in India 2004; Singh 2004a). For all India, the dowry death rate has risen from 5 per million population to 7 per million population, and cruelty rates from 31 per million to 45 per million.

Since the 1980s, grassroots women's organizations, local and international NGOs and legal reformists have tried to dismantle dowry practices in order to curb violence against women. As a result of these efforts, numerous political and legal changes to protect women have emerged. Nevertheless, official statistics link 7,000 women's deaths [per year] to dowry murders (CWDS 2002). The official reports are only the peak of an iceberg. The actual numbers may be manyfold since the majority of the killings are disguised as accidents and many bodies are ritualistically burned on funeral pyres before any official investigation can take place. Moreover, no one knows how many women continue to live under dowry threats, harassment and abuse. Among the limited political action and the circular political rhetoric, dowry continues to be a deadly business.

In this paper, I will summarize the historical roots of dowry and the current debates about its continuing cultural relevance and I will review the reasons behind the emergence and escalating violence related to dowry. One of the dimensions I will stress is the close link between dowry and other patriarchal practices that vanquish the rights of women and girls, most notably the practices of foeticide and female infanticide which are still rampant in India. My aim is to establish a link between dowry and sex-selection practices and show that these form a deadly grid for the female population, young and old.

Dowry

Dowry is a form of property women bring with them when they marry. Dowry often consists of money, land, animals and other gifts like jewellery or household items the bridal family is expected to present to the groom's family.

Historical roots For centuries, the patriarchal, feudal and tribal regions that are now subsumed under the modern Indian state functioned within a rigid caste system wherein one's social location and opportunities are fixed at birth. Originally, dowry was a ritualized Hindu marriage practice confined to the highest caste (Brahmans). The heavily one-sided traffic of gifts was justified as a matter of reaffirming the honour and status of the receiving family (Puri 1998). Since arranged marriages were often hypergamous for the brides (meaning that men married down), acceptance into a family system higher in subcaste[3] than the woman's own standing was also considered an honour for the bridal clan.

In its earlier forms, dowries were paid in accordance with one's means and almost always constituted a one-time payment (gift) at the time of marital celebrations. Dowry was also considered as '*streedhan*' (translates to women's property; Gandhi and Shah 1992: 52). Land and other productive assets were not expected to change hands, thus protecting the bridal families from a serious economic setback (Palriwal 2003). Large families with multiple offspring also ensured that what was given out through daughters was to some degree recovered through the marriages of sons. However, since women married up, daughters were considered a net loss for most families. A son that married 'down' could not bring in enough to compensate for the dowry of a daughter who 'married up'.

Oldenburg (2002) blames British colonialism for the degeneration of the dowry system. In pre-modern India where dowry was widespread, she charges, the concept of land ownership was not established. Although patriarchy barred women from inheriting either from their fathers or from their husbands, there was not much to inherit in the first place. Although women who left their fathers' estate lost the use of the fathers' land, they gained the use of their husbands' estate. It was only through British colonization, and especially around the 1850s when land was privatized and parcelled out, that already patriarchal households were transformed into haves versus have-nots. By taxing the land without regard to the uneven harvest conditions, colonizers created a chronic indebtedness among the patriarchal households. The chronic indebtedness resurrected an old practice (dowry) as a mechanism to get out of debt. It is then that not only land but women who married out of their fathers' households became commodified and marginalized (ibid.). Like Oldenburg, Gandhi and Shah (1992: 52) also blame colonization and the ensuing overlay of a market economy on an existing feudal system. They argue that in Punjab, dowry has been transformed from being seen as 'greed' and avoided to being consistently utilized as a 'status symbol'. In Bihar, grooms are regularly put on display and brokers negotiate the best dowry from would-be bridal families (Gandi and Shah 1992).

Defenders of dowry argue that women's position in a society has to be historicized. The original dowry system is seen as a form of insurance for women. Within this context, for example, Oldenburg (2002) faults the British colonizers for transforming a once enabling social ritual for women into a practice that has turned to oppress them. Others reason that the wealth women brought from their fathers' house was to dignify their transition to the house of their husbands (Kishwar 1999). Moreover, in case of a misfortune such as the death of a husband, women had some personal insurance vested in their dowry (*streedhan*) since Indian cultural practices were not kind to widows (MacFarquhar 1994).

In reality, however, the dowry system always was contentious. Bridal families resented the diminished wealth through the marriage of a daughter, and male siblings saw their sisters' dowry as a competition to their inheritance rights. Young brides, who found themselves totally powerless within the patriarchal clan of their husbands, seldom if ever had access to their own dowry. Thus, rather than engendering dignity and freedom for women, the dowry system often demeaned their worth both as persons and as potential contributors to their husbands' estate.

Recent developments in dowry The first voices of protest against dowry were raised during the Indian nationalist struggle. Gandhi saw dowry as a corrupt social evil linked to the caste system and asked women and men to refuse dowry and break the system (Gandhi and Shah 1992: 52). Albeit weak, ambiguous and not enforceable, the 1961 Dowry Prohibition Act was the outcome of this new awareness. However, in the mid-seventies, the Committee on the Status of Women in India noted some alarming changes. For example, the dowry practice had spread much beyond the upper Hindu castes to all Hindus, many Sikhs, Christians, Muslims and animists from all socio-economic strata. In an extensive study conducted by Naik (1996), it was found that all respondents (with the exception of 1.3 per cent non-responders) had either given or received dowry in their marriage arrangements.

The spiralling of dowry has also been accompanied by new expectations. First, dowry expectations increased in size and the flow of dowry became even more one-sided than before. Moreover, land and other means of survival which were traditionally excluded from dowries became fair game. Second, what was once considered a one-time event took on a longitudinal quality. The one-sided flow of gifts and other commodities became associated not only with marriage but also with other events such as holidays, anniversaries, births, etc. Third, marriage became the most important life event, overshadowing all other life-cycle rituals. Even death ceremonies, once considered the most important Hindu *samskara* (rite of passage), became a distant second to the rights of marriage. Fourth, rather than accompanying sound marital choice/arrangements, the size of dowries became the most important incentive in men's choice of partners.

Another noteworthy change in the dowry practice is associated with increasing consumerism. For example, rather than items of necessity for the newlyweds, gifts have shifted to elaborate, expansive commodities such as luxury cars, motorcycles, boats, summer cottages, etc., in the lists of the wealthy. Microwaves, TVs, washing machines, etc., form the dowry lists of lower-caste/class counterparts, *even* in regions where running water and/or electricity are not available. Above all, the shift to consumerism has created an insatiable demand for hard cash. Young girls whose dowry is insufficient sometimes find themselves married off to men who are multiples of their own age, or men with severe mental or physical disabilities. A combined effect of all these changes is the further devaluation of girls. Moreover, expanding dowry demands have transformed girl children into an outright liability and dowry disputes into a fertile arena for intra-family (against girl children) and inter-family (against brides) violence.

Why, then, rather than shedding a controversial practice such as dowry, does there seem to be a notable increase in its demand and link with violence? The answer to this question is complex. At the official level, there is indeed a blatant condemnation of dowry. At the social level, increased access to global markets has made dowry a fast track to consumerism. I will now review these two competing changes and their net effect.

Official response The first dowry-related legislation in India was the Dowry Prohibition Act of 1961. However, this legislation was so full of loopholes that no case of dowry death has ever been successfully prosecuted under its coverage (Singh 2004b).

- In 1983, a new penal provision on cruelty against women (Section 498A) was introduced to the Indian Penal Code (IPC). Moreover, women's suicide after being subjected to dowry harassment was considered as suicide abetted by the husband (Singh 2004a).
- In 1984, an amendment to the Dowry Prohibition Act was passed. This

legislation defined anything given as an inducement to marriage, as well as during and after marriage, as dowry. Police were required to investigate all complaints about dowry harassment and the burden of proof that dowry exchange did not happen was shifted to the person being prosecuted. However, customary and traditional 'presents' were excluded from the definition, thus creating ambiguity in enforcement (ibid.).

- In 1986, Section 304B on any unnatural death of a woman within seven years after marriage, and Section 113B on forced suicides of women within a seven-year period after marriage, were added to the IPC (Goonesekere 2004; Singh 2004a).
- Currently, the government of India is cooperating with UNICEF to improve the status of children and women (UNICEF 2003–07).

Non-official situation Despite the undeniable gains at the official level and despite the galvanized women's movement at the grassroots as well as NGO levels (CEDAW 2004, n.d.; ICRW, 2004a; Magar 2003; UNIFEM 2003b, n.d.), the official gains hardly made a dent in the Indian dowry tragedies. Forces that work against the official gains are many:

- Remnants of colonialism and its imposition of market economy on pre-capitalist structures have widened the already existing inequality gaps in India (Oldenburg 2002).
- The caste-based society which was traditionally impermeable suddenly became permeable through the official renunciation of the caste system. However, the desire for stratification did not die (ibid.). Those ascending the capitalist ladder of wealth needed new symbols to affirm their recently acquired positions. Since opportunities for individual initiative remained modest, consumerism through exploitation of the traditional means (dowry) became all the more attractive.
- The emerging class system sometimes disenfranchised the earlier higher castes, creating families that wanted to preserve their status but which were reduced in wealth. Dowry became a tool to reassert their once unquestioned privileges.
- Caught in the tension between celebrating modernity and capitalism and holding on to traditions to preserve their Indian identity, younger generations resurrected traditional marriage rules and dowry. As dowry spread, so did its size and obligatory character (CWDS 2002; Dowry in India 2004; Mandal 2001).

Too expensive? Missing female children

Sex ratios, foeticide and infanticide If nature is allowed to take its course, viable female births are equal to or slightly outnumber male births in a given population. Moreover, when all is equal, females outlive men, sometimes for as much as five to seven years. In the developed world, these advantages translate into slightly more than 50 per cent of the population being female.

However, socio-demographic statistics show that more than fifty million girls/women are 'missing' from the Indian population (Abortion ... 2004; Bahatnagar 2005; Bagga 2004; Gandhi and Shah 1992; MacFarquhar 1994; Missing ... 2003). According to the World Bank (2007), women constitute only 48.7 per cent of the Indian population and the sex ratio at birth is 1.12 males per female (CIA 2007). This imbalance is on the rise in many regions of India. For example, in 1901 the sex ratio for all India was 972 per thousand men. In 2001, this ratio stood at 933 (Rustagi 2003: 6). The following are some reasons behind the sex imbalances:[4]

Maternal Mortality Rates (MMR) The MMR for India is 540 per 100,000 live births (World Bank 2007), although there is lots of regional variability in these numbers (see Rustagi 2003). CEDAW (n.d.) estimates MMR for India to be 707 per 100,000 live births since women also die shortly after delivery. Factors that victimize women are poor nutrition both during and prior to pregnancy, frequent and unplanned pregnancies without women's consent or choice, anaemia, tuberculosis, infections due to unsanitary conditions and lack of medical facilities and trained personnel during birth (Mukhopadhyay and Savithri 1998; Rustagi 2003). CEDAW (n.d.) estimates that 78 per cent of births take place without the attendance of skilled health personnel.

Infant Mortality Rates (IMR) India's 73 (per 100,000 live births) is one of the highest IMR in the world. For the purposes of the present paper, what is of great importance is that IMR are gendered. Baby girls in India are more likely to become victims of infant mortality.

Sharma (2001) estimates that between the ages of one and four, the number of deaths for female children is one and a half times higher than the number of deaths among boys of the same age. She explains this substantial disadvantage as a product of malnutrition and medical neglect of girls.

Female infanticide Mostly afflicting rural areas, and increasingly replaced by foeticide, infanticide still snuffs out the life of many female children shortly after birth (Abortion ... 2004; Sethuraman 2006). Elimination techniques include poisonous berries, pesticides, uncooked rice, stuffing the infant's mouth with black salt or urine, poison on mother's breasts, suffocation with a wet towel and starvation (Hegde 1999; Jones 1999).

Foeticide In India, easy access to new reproductive technologies has advanced the blatant misuse of these technologies (Luthra 1994; Sarna 2003). Although India has passed legislation to curb misuse (the Pre-Natal Diagnostic

Techniques [Regulation] Act, 1994; see ICRW 2004b; UNICEF: India 2007), the Indian Medical Association estimates that more than five million female foetuses are aborted annually (ICRW 2004b: 12; Luthra 1994). There are other disturbing trends of abuse of technologies such as ultrasound and amnio-centesis. Once basically confined to rich districts of the wealthy states, there is a visible proliferation of such technologies in the poor rural regions. Ultrasound clinics have mushroomed and have become 'mobile' (ICRW 2004a, 2004b). It is no longer necessary to travel to urban centres; sex selection services from the back of a van or a pick-up truck now reach the poor, rural clientele. Moreover, more sophisticated sex selection techniques such as sperm separa-tion and pre-implantation are increasingly made available to the traditional upper castes and the newly rich, despite the fact that these techniques have been regulated by the state since 2003 (ICRW 2004a, 2004b).

Dowry deaths, domestic cruelty and sex-ratio imbalances

Up to this point, I have reviewed a number of gendered social ills that afflict Indian society and provided available statistical comparisons to back my assertions. It is now time to show the link between dowry deaths, domestic cruelty and unbalanced sex ratios.

In India, one should keep in mind that there are substantial differences among the states and Union Territories. For example, twenty-three out of thirty-two states/Union Territories have official dowry death rates equal to or larger than one per million population [ranging up to fifteen in Haryana] which means that nine out of thirty-two show zero per million (not absolute zero). Readers might think that a few deaths per million might not be an alarming statistic until they are reminded that India has over 1.12 billion population and thus the totality of dowry-related deaths is in many thousands. Moreover, many deaths escape official recording.

Violence against Indian girls/women is not random, but more likely to cluster in certain regions. States that show dowry problems also seem to show problems in one or more other measures (dowry deaths, cruelty by husbands/ kin, and adult and child sex-ratio imbalances). Also worth underscoring is the fact that *all* states/Union Territories that show the highest levels of problems (Haryana, Chandigarh, Delhi, Daman & Diu, Madhya Pradesh, Punjab, Rajastan and Uttar Pradesh) are located in some of the most affluent north-east and north-central regions of India. In contrast, some of the lowest levels of violence in all measures seem to be found in the southern tip and north-eastern regions (Assam, Karnataga, Manipur, Meghalaya, Mizoram, Tamil Nadu, Lakshadweep, Pondicherri), which are much less affluent than their northern counterparts. In a way, the level of violence against women in India is not due to relative or absolute poverty, but seems to be exacerbated by the relative affluence of the region.

Low status of women in India Many scholars trace the low status of Indian women to the 2,000-year-old writings of Manu, according to which females must be subjected to their fathers when they are young, should obey and serve their husbands in adulthood and be subservient to their sons in the event that they are widowed. Manu orders that women should never be independent (cited in Wadley 1988).

In analysing the low status of women, Singh (2004a) highlights the state's failure to enforce existing legislation against dowry and dowry harassment. For example, dowry cases rarely reach the courts, first and foremost because of under-reporting. Reasons behind under-reporting are multilayered but linked to women's docility whereby female victims and their families remain in a tapestry of silence: 'The single largest factor which contributes to women's undoing is her submissiveness. She totally accepts her environment because she has internalized acceptance and submission as a goal in her life' (Gandhi and Shah 1992: 85). Others find fault with Indian marriage customs. Gandhi and Shah (ibid.) see marriage as a 'compulsion' which dominates all Indian women's lives. Mothers' self-worth gradually erodes after reaching the end of their reproductive years, and as Gandhi and Shah (ibid.: 59) observe, they bargain hard for sons (dowry) and take reflected glory from 'his value', which becomes a symbolic measure of the value of the mothers who brought them up (see also Rastogi and Therly 2006).

Once married, a woman is expected to stay married, regardless of the violence in her life. Natal families are often reluctant to see a married woman return home. Kishwar (1999, 1991) argues that the pressure to keep a marriage going at all costs is the real killer, rather than dowry or the lack of it. However, blaming the women themselves or blaming their natal families for the violence should not misdirect the critical gaze away from the failures of the state. In India, it is clear that the dowry prohibition attempts of the 1980s have not been accompanied by a serious political will to improve the status of women in or outside of marriage. The dowry prohibition attempts have not dismantled inheritance biases against women, not put a stop to dowry exchanges, are not focused on prevention and have not made the prosecution of cases easy for victims. The state has also failed to deal with the unnatural deaths of female foetuses, infants and children. Indian feminist and activist literatures carefully document examples of police bias, indifference and corruption, especially in crimes committed against women (Goonesekere 2004; Poonacha and Pandey 1999; Elizabeth 2000; Singh 2004a; Visaria 1999). Many perpetrators easily escape justice. For example, in 1997, out of the 1,133 cases of 'unnatural deaths' of women in Bangalore, only 157 were treated as murder, while 546 were considered 'suicide' and another 430 were written off as 'accidental' (Hitchcock 2001).

Looking to the future: forces for and against change

In this paper, dowry violence was not seen as a social evil on its own, but as an evil that is deeply linked with other gendered evils such as violence against and life and death disadvantages for females. In a country where patriarchal, feudal and patrilocal marriage rules reign, girls are still seen as a burden on their natal families and as an intruder in their families of procreation. Women, especially mothers-in-law, are socialized to stay silent, accept and also enforce discriminatory rules. In many cases, they themselves become the abusers and perpetrators of heinous acts (Rastogi and Therly 2006). Moreover, the following confounding factors make a unitary stance against gendered violence difficult, if not impossible:

1 India has fifteen official languages (CIA 2007), subsumes more than a hundred languages and dialects, has at least five separate religious groups (Hindu, Sikh, Muslim, Buddhist, Jain) and still-visible remnants of an entrenched caste hierarchy. The sheer number and the magnitude of social problems of a relatively new democracy with over a billion population are often insurmountable.
2 Given the size of the country, the regional variability is overwhelming. Costs associated with travel and communication are prohibitive. There are also security issues surrounding free travel and women travelling alone are at heightened peril.
3 Absolute poverty for a very large segment of the population exhausts efforts. Despite its natural richness and beauty, many parts of India are one step ahead of natural disasters, epidemic scares and racial/ethnic/religious unrest. Almost half of India's children are malnourished (World Bank 2007).
4 Despite its gargantuan information technology jump into the twenty-first century, in many regards India remains a traditional society. This traditionality is especially strong when it comes to family customs and rituals. Even Indian feminists, scholars and activists seem to seek solutions within the existing gender hierarchies and family customs rather than in their critical analysis or possible annihilation.

On the positive side, India is producing a highly educated workforce and, at least in the urbanized areas, women's paid labour force participation is on the rise (28 per cent of the workforce; ibid.). Eapen and Kodoth (2003) see Indian women's salvation in improved formal education and paid labour force participation. These two indices, in the long run, may create a slightly more balanced playing field for Indian girls/women in and outside of family relations. A second positive development is a vibrant grassroots women's movement in India which is also buttressed by national and international NGOs (Action India 2004; Gandhi and Shah 1992; Magar 2003; Malhotra et al. 2003; UNIFEM 1998, 2003a, 2003b, n.d.). As the third point, with its mega-population, massive manufacturing and information technologies and nuclear power status, India is now under the global gaze. It is quite possible that the state's historical shortcomings and failures in protecting its female population may be catapulted into a higher level of commitment and action under this global scrutiny. Let us hope that the positive developments will help remedy the continuing disadvantages of Indian women.

Notes

1 This work is generously supported by the Social Sciences & Humanities Research Council of Canada (SSHRC). An earlier version of the paper was presented at the International Sociology Association (ISA) meetings in Durban, South Africa (July 2006). I thank my colleagues from the University of North & South Delhi and University of Jawaharlal Nehru for their generous help with interviews. I would also like to thank the directors of numerous Delhi-based NGOs for helping me observe the difficult lives of countless women. Most particularly, I would like to thank the supervisors and directors of UNIFEM/Jorbagh, Shakti Shalini/Jangpura, Action India/Mathura, ICRW/Lodi Estate and CREA/Shantiniketan for sharing their extraordinary insights with me.

2 The original version of this article, in *Women's Health and Urban Life*, 7(1), 2008, is more extensive and includes Indian newspaper reports and several tables.

3 There were and continue to be strong taboos against cross-caste marriages. The hypergamy was usually in terms of subcastes where women with sufficient dowries married up.

4 In this paper, I am omitting a discussion of suttee (wife burning). This practice has now been outlawed for more than two decades and occurs extremely rarely in remote regions. However, the status of widows is still low in India and widows continue to be treated as social outcasts.

References

'Abortion, female infanticide, foeticide, son preference in India' (2004) www.indian child.com/abortion_infanticide_foeticide_india.htm, accessed 15 January 2008).

Action India (2004) 'Protection from domestic violence', New Delhi: Action India.

Bagga, C. (2004) 'Census shocker: child sex ratio takes a fall', *Times of India*, New Delhi, 8 September.

Bahatnagar, R. D. (2005) *Female Infanticide in India: A Feminist Cultural History*, New York: New York State University.

CEDAW (2004) *Restoring Rights to Women*, New Delhi: UNIFEM.

— (n.d.) 'From convention to action: monitoring women's rights under CEDAW in India', *Women's Voices*, Lucknow, UP: Sahayog.

CIA (2007) *The World Factbook. India*, www.cia.gov/library/publications/the_world_factbook/geos/in.html, accessed 16 January 2008.

CWDS (Center for Women's Development Studies) (2002) *Crimes against Women: Bondage and Beyond*, New Delhi: CWDS.

'Dowry in India' (2004) www.indianchild.com/dowry_in_india.htm, accessed 15 January 2008.

Eapen, M. and P. Kodoth (2003) 'Family structure, women's education and work: re-examining the high status of women in Kerala', in S. Mukhopadhyay and R. M. Sudarshan (eds), *Tracking Gender Equity under Economic Reforms*, Ottawa: International Development Research Centre.

Elizabeth, V. (2000) 'Patterns and trends of domestic violence in India: an examination of court records', in *Domestic Violence in India*, Washington, DC: ICRW.

Gandhi, N. and N. Shah (1992) 'The issues at stake: theory and practice in the contemporary women's movement in India', New Delhi: Kali.

Goonesekere, S. (ed.) (2004) 'Violence, law and women's rights in South Asia', New Delhi: Sage.

Hegde, R. S. (1999) 'Marking bodies, reproductive violence: a feminist reading of female infanticide in South India', *Violence Against Women*, 5(5): 507–24.

Hitchcock, A. (2001) 'Rising number of dowry deaths in India', www.wsws.org/articles/2001/jul2001/ind-j04_prn.shtml, accessed 19 January 2008.

ICRW (International Center for Research on Women) (2002) *Domestic Violence in India: Exploring Strategies, Promoting Dialogue*, Washington, DC: ICRW.

— (2004a) *Panchayat Involvement on Violence against Women*, New Delhi: ICRW.

— (2004b) *Violence against Women in India: A Review of Trends, Patterns and Response*, New Delhi: UNFPA.

Jones, A. (1999) 'Case study: female infanticide', Gendercide Watch, www.gendercide.org.

Kishwar, M. (1991) *In Search of Answers: Indian women's voices from Manushi*, New Delhi: Horizon India Books.

— (1999) *Off the Beaten Track: Rethinking gender justice for Indian Women*, London: Oxford University Press.

Luthra, R. (1994) 'A case of problematic diffusion: the use of sex determination techniques in India', *Knowledge: Creation, Diffusion, Utilization*, 15(3).

MacFarquhar, E. (1994) 'The echoes of Sita', *US News and World Report*, 116, 28 March.

Magar, V. (2003) 'Empowerment approaches to gender-based violence: women's courts in Delhi slums', *Women's Studies International Forum*, 26(6).

Malhotra, A., L. Nyblade, S. Parasuraman, K. MacQuarrie, N. Kashyap and S. Walia (2003) *Realizing Reproductive Choice and Rights*, New Delhi: ICRW.

Mandal, S. (2001) 'Modernization and women's status in India: a gender in developmental perspective on dowry deaths, sex ratios and sex-selective abortion', PhD dissertation, University of Texas at Austin.

Missing: Mapping the Adverse Child Sex Ratio in India (2003) Office of the Registrar General & Census Commissioner, India: UNFPA.

Mukhopadhyay, S. and R. Savithri (1998) *Poverty, Gender and Reproductive Choice*, New Delhi: Manohar.

Naik, R. D. (1996) *Marriage and Dowry in India*, Pune: Dastane-Ramachandra.

Oldenburg, V. T. (2002) *Dowry Murder: The Imperial Origins of a Cultural Crime*, London: Oxford University Press.

Palriwal, R. (2003) 'Dowry in contemporary India: an overview', in *Expanding Dimensions in Dowry*, New Delhi: AIDWA (All India Democratic Women's Association).

Poonacha, V. and D. Pandey (1999) 'Responses to domestic violence in Karnataka and Gujarat', in *Domestic Violence in India*, New Delhi: ICRW.

Prasad, B. D. (1994) 'Dowry-related violence: a content analysis of news in selected newspapers', *Journal of Comparative Family Studies*, 25(1).

Puri, D. (1998) 'Gift of a daughter: change and continuity in marriage patterns among two generations of North Indians in Toronto and Delhi', PhD dissertation, University of Toronto.

Rastogi, M. and P. Therly (2006) 'Dowry and its link to violence against women in India: feminist psychological perspectives', *Trauma, Violence and Abuse*, 7.

Rustagi, P. (2003) *Gender Biases and Discrimination against Women*, New Delhi: UNIFEM.

— (2004) 'Significance of gender-related development indicators: an analysis of Indian states', *Indian Journal of Gender Studies*, 11(3): 291–343.

— (2006) 'The deprived, discriminated and damned girl child: story of declining child sex ratios in India', *Women's Health and Urban Life*, 1.

Sarna, K. (2003) 'Female feticide on the rise in India', *Nursing Journal of India*, February.

Sethuraman, S. (2006) 'Female infanticide and foeticide', chennaionline.com/columns/variety/2006/12child.asp, accessed 15 January 2008.

Sharma, O. P. (2001) 'Census results mixed for India's women and girls', www.prb.org/Articles/2001/2001Census Results MixedforIndiasWomenand Girls.aspx.

Singh, K. (2004a) 'Violence against women and the Indian law', in S. Goonesekere (ed.), *Violence, Law and Women's Rights in South Asia*, New Delhi: Sage.

— (2004b) 'Where is the human face? Where are the reforms?', Op-ed., *Sunday Express*, 22 August.

UNICEF (2003–07) *A Programme of Co-operation for Children and Women in India: Masterplan of Operations*, New Delhi: UNICEF.

UNICEF: India (2007) 'Gujarat launches save the girl child campaign', www.unicef.org/india/media_3284.htm, accessed 15 January 2008.

UNIFEM (1998) *A Life Free of Violence: It's Our Right*, New Delhi: UNIFEM.

— (2003a) *Not a Minute More: Ending Violence against Women*, New York: UNIFEM.

— (2003b) *Women's Movement in India*, New Delhi: UNIFEM.

— (2004) Report of the 4th South Asia Regional Meeting, New Delhi: UNIFEM.

— (n.d.) *Only Her Word: A National Campaign for a Law on Domestic Violence*, New Delhi: Lawyers' Collective.

United Nations Economic and Social Council (1999) 'Integration of the human rights of women and the gender perspective: violence against women', www.unhchr.ch/Huridocda/Huridoca.nsf/0811fcbd0b9 f6bd58025667300306dea/72, accessed 21 January 2005.

Visaria, L. (1999) 'Violence against women in India: evidence from rural Gujarat', in *Domestic Violence in India*, New Delhi: ICRW.

Wadley, S. (1988) 'Women and the Hindu tradition', in R. Ghadially (ed.), *Women in Indian Society*, New Delhi: Sage.

World Bank (2007) *Gender Stats: Summary gender profile*, devdata.worldbank.org/genderstats/genderRpt.asp?rpt=profile&cty=IND,India&hm=home, accessed 16 January 2008.

21 | The 'feminization of poverty' and the 'feminization' of anti-poverty programmes: room for revision?[1]

Sylvia Chant

Introduction

This paper reflects on the relevance of the 'feminization of poverty' thesis to analysis and policy in developing countries. Informed in part by recent field research in The Gambia, the Philippines and Costa Rica,[2] it argues for reorienting the 'feminization of poverty' in a manner which more appropriately reflects trends in gendered disadvantage among the poor and which highlights the growing responsibilities and obligations women bear in household survival.

The 'feminization of poverty' was first coined in the 1970s (Pearce 1978) but did not make its major breakthrough into the development lexicon until the mid-1990s. A critical catalyst was the Fourth UN Conference on Women in 1995 at which it was asserted that 70 per cent of the world's poor were female. Disregarding the fact that the 70 per cent level was supposed to be rising and that, a decade on, no revision seems to have been made to the original estimate, this bold and largely untenable claim[3] seems to have brought women, if not gender, more squarely into the frame of international fora on poverty reduction (Chant 2007: ch. 1). According to Wennerholm (2002), the 'feminization of poverty' thesis has been responsible not only for drawing attention to the 'great number of women living in poverty' but for highlighting the impact of macroeconomic policies on women, calling for women to be recognized in the development process and promoting consciousness of the existence and vulnerability of female-headed households.

Yet there are various problems with the 'feminization of poverty' thesis, methodologically, analytically and in terms of its translation into policy. My paper is divided into five sections. The first explores common understandings of the 'feminization of poverty'. The second examines the purposes served by the popularization and adoption of this concept. The third summarizes some of the key problems with the 'feminization of poverty' analytically and in respect of how the construct has been taken up and responded to in policy circles. The fourth suggests some revisions to the 'feminization of poverty' concept, while the fifth points to possible directions for policy.

What is understood by the 'feminization of poverty'?

The term 'feminization of poverty' is often used without any elucidation of its meaning. In general terms, monetary privation is implied yet it is somewhat strange that this should be uppermost in 'feminization of poverty' discussions for two reasons. First, various authors, including Fukuda-Parr (1999), have stressed that the feminization of poverty is not 'just about lack of income'. Second, feminist research over the last twenty-five years has consistently stressed the importance of more holistic conceptual frameworks to encapsulate gendered privation. These include: (a) 'capability' and 'human development' frameworks, which identify factors such as education, health and infrastructure (ibid.; Sen 1999; Kabeer 2003; Klasen 2004); (b) 'livelihoods' frameworks, which emphasize social as well as material assets (Rakodi 1999; Rakodi with Lloyd-Jones 2002); (c) 'social exclusion' perspectives, which highlight the marginalization of the poor (Chen et al. 2004: 5–6; UNRISD 2005: 49); and (d) frameworks which stress the importance of subjective dimensions of poverty such as self-esteem, dignity, choice and power (World Bank 2000; Kabeer 2003; Rojas 2003; Johnsson-Latham 2004a; Painter 2004).

Another conundrum is that in the light of shrinking disparities between a number of women's and men's capabilities and opportunities – particularly in education, employment and politics – it is almost counterintuitive that gender gaps in income poverty should be widening (Chant 2007: ch. 1).

Yet a second problem attached to the 'feminization of poverty' is that relevant data are extremely scarce.

Despite the calls of the Convention on the Elimination of All Forms of Discrimination Against Women (CEDAW) for more sex-disaggregated statistics, there is still no international database which provides a comprehensive breakdown of the incidence and extent of women's income poverty in comparison with men's (UNIFEM 2002: 60). In terms of the South, only for Latin America is there a regional breakdown of the numbers of females and males within households which fall below national poverty lines (CEPAL 2002: Cuadros 6a, 6b; UNIFEM 2002: Table 15). While on the surface these data suggest that women are poorer than men and, indeed, in all rural areas of Latin America for which data are available a higher percentage of the female population seems to live in poverty, differences are, for the most part, fairly marginal. Moreover, in urban areas in ten out of seventeen countries, the proportion of men in poverty is actually on a par with or slightly higher than that of women. On the basis of this, UNIFEM (2002: 61) concludes that the 'feminization of poverty' is present only in some countries in Latin America and that women are nowhere near the level of 70 per cent of people in income poverty as popularly expounded.

Although a progressively greater share of households in extreme poverty in some parts of Latin America have become headed by women in the last decade (Arriagada 2002), a detailed quantitative study of Argentina, Bolivia,

Box 21.1 Common characterizations of the 'feminization of poverty'

- Women experience a higher incidence of poverty than men.
- Women experience greater depth/severity of poverty than men.
- Women are prone to suffer more persistent/longer-term poverty than men.
- Women's disproportionate burden of poverty is rising relative to men.
- Women face more barriers to lifting themselves out of poverty.
- The 'feminization of poverty' is linked with the 'feminization of household headship'.
- Women-headed households are the 'poorest of the poor'.
- Female household headship transmits poverty to children ('inter-generational transmission of disadvantage').

Sources: Chant (1997b, 2007); Moghadam (1997); Cagatay (1998); Baden (1999); Davids and van Driel (2005); Medeiros and Costa (2006)

Brazil, Chile, Colombia, Costa Rica, Mexico and Venezuela between the early 1990s and early 2000s by Medeiros and Costa (2006: 13) found 'no solid evidence of a process of feminization of poverty in the Latin American region' (ibid.: 13). This conclusion was drawn on the basis of an extremely comprehensive analysis which not only considered per capita income figures but examined women and men in general and according to household headship.

Moreover, within a wider geographical remit there is relatively little evidence to support the notion that women-headed households are poorer than their male counterparts in any systematic manner (Chant 1997b, 2003a; Moghadam 1997: 8, 1998; Fukuda-Parr 1999: 99; IFAD 1999; CEPAL 2001: 20; Chen et al. 2004: 37). Yet from the early 1990s onwards, categorical pronouncements about female-headed households being the 'poorest of the poor' have flowed thick and fast (see Box 21.1), added to which female heads have often become a crude proxy for women.

Irrespective of whether we consider households *or* individuals, another major problem in sustaining the 'feminization of poverty' thesis as a trend is the dearth of sex-disaggregated longitudinal panel data (Johnsson-Latham 2004b: 18; Nauckhoff 2004: 65). And, as Medeiros and Costa remind us:

In spite of its multiple meanings, the feminization of poverty should not be confused with the existence of higher levels of poverty among women or female-headed households ... The term 'feminization' relates to the way poverty changes over time, whereas 'higher levels' of poverty focuses on a view of poverty at a given moment. Feminization is a process, 'higher poverty' is a state. (Medeiros and Costa 2006: 3)

The importance of the feminization of poverty thesis in engendering poverty analysis and poverty reduction strategies

As mentioned earlier, growing circulation of the notion of a 'feminization of poverty' in academic and policy arenas has had a number of benefits.

The term may be poorly elaborated or substantiated but it is nonetheless a succinct and hard-hitting slogan. The 'feminization of poverty' has clearly proved persuasive enough to grab the attention of planners and policymakers beyond gender and development (GAD) circles. In the process this has helped to raise the status of women's concerns in national and international discourses on poverty and social development (Jassey 2002; Chant 2007: ch. 1).

The need to incorporate gender differences has not only increasingly been taken on board in poverty analysis but in policy and practice too. This is conceivably because the wedding of gender and poverty offers the tantalizing prospect that 'two birds may be killed with one stone' – that is, in the process of reducing poverty, gender equality goals can also be realized. In the 'South' more generally, women's 'economic empowerment' has progressively been deemed crucial not only in achieving gender equality but eliminating poverty and leading to development which is 'truly sustainable' (UNIFEM 2002: 1–2; see also Razavi 1999: 418; DfID 2000; UNDAW 2000; Rodenberg 2004). To this end, resources have been garnered for a range of interventions aimed at increasing women's literacy and education, facilitating their access to micro-credit, enhancing their vocational skills, and/or providing economic or infrastructural support to female-headed households (Kabeer 1997; Yates 1997; Chant 1999, 2003a; UNDAW 2000; Mayoux 2002, 2006; Pankhurst 2002).

In light of the above, widespread take-up of the 'feminization of poverty' thesis could be celebrated as something of a 'coup' for GAD stakeholders. Its bold (and surprisingly little-contested) claims have provided an important tactical peg upon which justification for directing resources to women may be hung (Baden and Goetz 1998: 23; Jackson 1998; Chant 2003a). The construction has managed to put 'gender on the agenda' in an unprecedented manner.

Yet although the 'feminization of poverty' has undeniably had some advantages, its current constitution and rather uncritical adoption pose a number of problems for analysis and policy alike.

Problems with the 'feminization of poverty' thesis for analysis and policy

Analytical problems

Lack of attention to differences among women Aside from the general problem of scant sex-disaggregated data on poverty, data which are disaggregated along other lines are also lacking. For example, attention has seldom been paid to other differences among women, such as age, which is arguably critical in determining whether and how poverty might be feminizing.

Given women's generally greater life expectancy, there is an increasing tendency for more women to feature in populations as a whole and among senior age groups in particular. Female senior citizens may be particularly prone to disadvantage for three main reasons. The first is a legacy of greater gender gaps – for example, in education, literacy, savings, pension coverage and so on. The second is a greater probability that older women will be widowed than men and/or live alone, and the third, the possibility that older women suffer greater social and economic discrimination than their younger counterparts or male peers (CELADE 2002: 17; Ofstedal et al. 2004: 166–7; UNMP/TFEGE 2005: 13).

Overemphasis on income A second major analytical problem with the 'feminization of poverty' thesis, as mentioned earlier, is its implicit privileging of income and neglect of other more complex and/or abstract dimensions of poverty.

The value of income data in supporting the 'feminization of poverty' is dubious for two main reasons. First, income is argued to be one of the few indicators which is less robust in confirming women's relative privation than other criteria, such as access to land and credit, decision-making power, legal rights within the family, vulnerability to violence, and (self-) respect and dignity (Johnsson-Latham 2004b: 26–7). In short, the privileging of income may underestimate the extent to which poverty is feminized or feminizing, and deflect attention from other factors pertinent to women's disadvantage.

Second, and related to this, unless we are able to get a handle on poverty's subjective dimensions or its multidimensionality, we cannot go very far in understanding gendered poverty and its dynamics, or make policy-oriented assessments more relevant to women at the grass roots. For example, while the level of household income is clearly important in any poverty diagnosis, this may bear no relation to *women's* poverty because women themselves may not necessarily be able to *access* it (Bradshaw 2002: 12; also Chant 1997a, 1997b).

The significance of subjectivities and the multidimensionality of poverty has perhaps been best illustrated in work on female household headship and the notion of 'trade-offs' whereby women make tactical choices between different dimensions of poverty in the interests of personal and/or household well-being (Kabeer 1996, 1997; Chant 1997b, 2003a). For example, being without a male partner may at one level exacerbate poverty for female heads – especially in respect of incomes – but this can be compensated by other gains. These may include female heads being able to use whatever income they themselves or other household members earn at their own discretion, to avoid the vulnerability attached to erratic support from spouses, or simply to enjoy a greater sense of well-being because their lives are freer from conflict, coercion or violence (van Driel 1994; Jackson 1996; Chant 1997b).[4]

While the choice of trade-offs may be limited (Kabeer 1997, 1999; also van Driel 1994), and the 'price' of women's independence may be high (Jackson 1996; Molyneux 2001: ch. 4), as Graham (1987: 59) has argued: '... single parenthood can represent not only a different but a preferable kind of poverty for lone mothers' (see also UNDAW 1991: 41; González de la Rocha 1994). Indeed, although women do not usually choose to stay single or to engineer the dissolution of their marriages or unions, in the interests of their own or others' well-being they may well opt to remain alone rather than return to ex-partners or form new relationships (Chant 1997a: ch. 7; see also Fonseca 1991: 156–7; Bradshaw 1996; van Vuuren 2003: 231).

Overemphasis on female-headed households A third major problem is an undue (if not exclusive) concentration on female-headed households, encapsulated by such statements as: '... the feminization of poverty is the process whereby poverty becomes more concentrated among individuals living in female-headed households' (Asgary and Pagan 2004: 97). It is increasingly evident that some women are actively *choosing* household headship as a means by which they are able to enhance the well-being of their households and/or exert more control over their own lives (Safa 1995; Baden 1999; van Vuuren 2003).

Another case against undue emphasis on female-headed households in the 'feminization of poverty' is that they are a highly heterogeneous group. Differentiation derives from a wide range of factors including routes into the status, stage in the life course and household composition. These, and other axes of difference, can exert mediating effects on poverty and thereby defy their categorical labelling as the 'poorest of the poor' (Chant 2003a).

Neglect of men and gender relations A fourth analytical problem with the 'feminization of poverty' is that its focus on women tends to deflect attention from men and gender relations, when it is perhaps precisely the latter which should come under greater scrutiny. Indeed, if poverty is feminizing, does this imply a counterpart 'masculinization' of power, privilege and asset accumulation? If so, how is this explained when there is talk of a 'crisis of masculinity' and mounting evidence that men in some countries are beginning to fall behind women in respect of educational attainment and access to employment (Kaztman 1992; Gutmann 1996; Escobar Latapi 1998; Silberschmidt 1999; Arias 2000; Chant 2000, 2002; Fuller 2000; Varley and Blasco 2000)? While UNRISD (2005: 12) endorses the idea that some men are disadvantaged, and this can exert costs such as higher suicide rates and stress- and alcohol-related health risks, they maintain that in general: 'Male underachievement has not led to parallel underachievements in wealth and politics.' In order to interrogate the

Box 21.2 Women's views on the unevenness of gendered responsibilities for dealing with poverty in The Gambia, Philippines and Costa Rica

Men are not doing anything – if they pay for breakfast, it's women who pay for lunch and dinner. Women pay for school lunches … [S]ome men are not working, and some men refuse to work, or if they work they don't do it for that [the family]. (Teeda, thirty-five, fruit seller and batik-maker, married mother of four, Cape Point, The Gambia)

If you are a woman you always have to think about having to spend it [money] on everyone else, whereas men will just use any surplus income to secure a second wife. (Satou, thirty-eight, fruit seller and batik-maker, divorced female head of nine-member extended household, Cape Point, The Gambia)

A poor man will say 'I do not have a job, I do not have some things', and usually most will resort to gambling or drinking … vices … to try and compensate them for what they don't have. Whereas a poor woman will … create something in order to have earnings. I have to have a *sari-sari* store [small grocery shop] to have earnings. I have to cook to eat, to sustain ourselves, different to a man. (Linda, forty-four, small shopkeeper and part-time hospice worker, married mother of four, Mandaue City, Philippines)

A poor woman doesn't only think of herself; she thinks about her family, her children, in getting ahead. In contrast, men are more selfish, only concerned with their own needs, unlike women … When men see a situation getting difficult, they tend to go off and leave the women to assume responsibility. (Ixi, forty, housewife, separated female head of five-member extended household, Liberia, Costa Rica)

Source: Chant (2007: chs 4–6)

validity of this claim, men and gender relations undoubtedly deserve closer attention in analysis of the feminization of poverty.

On top of these four already well-established criticisms, a fifth set of points, inspired mainly by the author's recent fieldwork in The Gambia, the Philippines and Costa Rica (see note 2), relates to the need to place emphasis on the inputs related to dealing with poverty, as on income.

Missing the major points about gendered poverty: a 'feminization of responsibility and obligation'? Although women are often income-poor, what is perhaps more important is that they are increasingly at the front line of *dealing* with poverty. While the burden of household survival has long been widely documented as falling disproportionately on women, the unevenness between women's and men's inputs and their perceived responsibilities for coping with poverty both seem to be growing. In some cases, the skew has reached the point of virtual one-sidedness. On top of this, women's mounting responsibilities do not seem to be matched by any discernible increase in rewards or entitlements.

Feelings about the injustice of these gendered disparities were remarkably consistent across the case study countries and across all age groups, as illustrated by an indicative sample of comments of female respondents in The Gambia, the Philippines and Costa Rica presented in Box 21.2. On the basis of respondents' views, the author had a strong sense not so much of a 'feminization of poverty' in the conventional sense but of a 'feminization of responsibility and obligation'.[5, 6]

In my proposed 'feminization of responsibility and/or obligation', there are three key elements:

1. *Diversification and intensification of women's inputs to household survival versus stasis or diminution of men's.* Growing numbers of women of all ages in the three case study countries are working outside the home, as well as performing the bulk of unpaid reproductive tasks for husbands, fathers, brothers and sons. Men, on the other hand, are not only finding it harder to be the sole or primary economic support for their households but are not increasing their participation in reproductive work either.

A study by the UNDP of nine developing and thirteen developed economies found that unpaid reproductive labour accounted for two-thirds (66 per cent) of women's work, compared with only one quarter to one third of men's (24–34 per cent) and that women spend 18 to 122 minutes more working per day than men (UNDP 2004: 28). Generally speaking, the disparity between hours of men's and women's work is most marked among low-income groups, and, as noted by Pineda-Ofreneo and Acosta (2001: 3), the '... poorer the household, the longer women work'. Certainly major disparities were found in my own fieldwork. In the Philippines, for example, female respondents usually worked fifteen hours or more a day, spending their 'time off' with their children. Men, on the other hand, felt entitled to 'down tools' after eight to nine hours of paid work, and did not seem to prioritize dedicated parenting, household labour, or even spending time at home thereafter.

At the same time as women are diversifying their activities in household survival, their reproductive labour also undergoes intensification as they come under the hammer of price liberalization and reduced subsidies on basic staples, as well as limited or declining investment by the public sector in essential infrastructure and basic services. This may imply more onerous or time-consuming domestic labour, greater efforts in self-provisioning, and/or more care or forethought in budgeting and expenditure (Chant 1996; UNMP/ TFEGE 2005: 7).

2. *Persistent and/or growing disparities in women's and men's capacities to negotiate obligations and entitlements in households.* Women's mounting responsibilities for coping with poverty do not seem to be giving them much leverage in respect of negotiating greater inputs to household survival on the part of men.

In all case study countries it was clear that men not only feel entitled but act on this perceived entitlement to escape from the daily hardship of family life. This ranges from withholding earnings (and/or appropriating those of their wives or other household members), to absenting themselves from the home to spend time with male friends, and/or consoling themselves with the transitory therapeutic fixes offered by drugs, drink, casual sex and gambling. While this by no means applies to all men, and some of these pursuits can be an important source of networking and securing resources, others add up to an evasion of core responsibilities, which can compound problems for the rest of their households.

As documented earlier, some women faced with negligible support from male partners are able to break away and set up their own households. However, others may not be in a position to do so and are rendered more vulnerable than ever to extremes of servitude and inequality. This may be endorsed by culturally condoned expectations of female altruism – a woman who opts for another, more egoistic, course is not deemed 'feminine' and the consequences can be severe, including non-marriageability, divorce or separation. The chances of women negotiating increased financial help or contributions of labour from their husbands, in or outside the home, seemed negligible in all my case study localities.

Most women in the survey expressed dissatisfaction about having to absorb heavier loads of labour, or bankrolling household subsistence with little or no male assistance (Box 21.2). Women also complain to one another about the injustice of performing the bulk of all domestic tasks when they are the economic mainstay of households. However, in accordance with the norms of feminine deference, they are much less open and vocal in expressing their grievances to men. Indeed, in some cases there was the sense that women were effectively 'redoubling' their efforts to live up to idealized norms of 'good wives' and 'dutiful daughters', maybe to defuse the conflict which so often erupts when men feel threatened by women's 'encroachment' on to 'male terrain' such as paid work (see also below).[7]

Summing up this second element of a 'feminization of responsibility and obligation', it is not only gender inequalities in incomes and consumption which are important but gender differences in *time and labour inputs*, and the fact that the *onus* on women to cope is increasing. This is not only because they cannot and/or do not *expect* to rely on men but because a growing number seem to be supporting men as well. Also disturbing is that women are forced into accepting rather than challenging these mounting responsibilities in a spirit of quiet and self-sacrificing acquiescence.

3. *Increasing disarticulation between investments/responsibilities and rewards/ rights.* Leading on from this, while responsibilities for dealing with poverty are becoming progressively feminized, there seems to be no corresponding increase in women's rights and rewards. Men, on the other hand, despite their lesser inputs, are somehow managing to retain their traditional privileges and prerogatives, such as control over income, licence for social freedom and power over household decision-making. This presents us with a rather puzzling scenario in which investments are becoming progressively detached from rights and rewards and conceivably evolving into a new and deeper form of female exploitation. Owing to a narrow and unproblematized focus on women and on incomes, the 'feminization of poverty' seems to have obscured rather than illuminated understanding of gendered poverty, and to have done little to engender effective policy approaches. Indeed, one of the main policy responses to date – which is to 'feminize' anti-poverty programmes – seems to have contributed to the problem it is supposedly attempting to solve – that is, to push more of the burden of dealing with poverty on to the shoulders of women. Some of the more specific issues associated with this dilemma are identified below.

Policy problems
Poverty reduction and reduction in gender inequality not one and the same Despite the fact that the 'feminization of poverty' seems to have commandeered some resources for women (see earlier), the emphasis on alleviating gender inequality and poverty simultaneously is misguided when these are distinct, albeit overlapping, forms of disadvantage (Jackson 1996). Two birds cannot necessarily be killed with one stone, and one major danger, if experience to date is anything to go by, is that poverty reduction imperatives may end up overshadowing commitments to change gender relations.

Competing/contradictory interests of GAD stakeholders and poverty stakeholders A related concern with the mounting alliance between gender equality and poverty reduction is the difference in goals motivating gender and poverty stakeholders. As pointed up by de Vylder (2004: 85), while the pursuit of gender equality has usually been regarded within the GAD community as an end in itself and from a human rights perspective, pursuing gender equality as a means to achieve poverty reduction – especially among economists – is grounded in efficiency considerations. One aspect of efficiency is the desire to cut costs, which often takes the form of scaling down universal programmes in favour of targeted initiatives. Focusing on poor female heads of household or poor women clearly presents a cost-effective option given the belief that resources directed to women maximize the well-being of families as a whole (Molyneux 2006, 2007). Indeed, repeated emphasis on the idea that investing in women is one of the most efficient routes to ensuring all-round development benefits seems to have translated into a generalized bid to alleviate poverty primarily, or even exclusively, *through* women (Razavi 1999: 419; Molyneux 2001: 184; Pankhurst 2002; Mayoux 2006). Here, we get the unfortunate but all too common scenario where instead of development *working for* women, women end up working *for* development (Elson 1989, 1991; Moser 1993: 69–73; Kabeer 1994: 8).

The tendency to orient anti-poverty programmes to, and through, women has been particularly marked under neoliberal restructuring, giving rise to the conclusion that while the 'feminization of poverty' has had a positive impact in terms of GAD, it has also served neoliberal interests in the shape of a rather instrumentalist agenda whereby the returns and 'pay-offs' from investing in women tend to prevail over women's rights (Jackson 1996: 490; Kabeer 1997: 2; Razavi 1999: 419; Molyneux 2001: 184, 2007; see also World Bank 1994, 2002). As summarized by Molyneux (2006: 49):

> Women have much to contribute to anti-poverty programmes ... This is not least because they also represent an army of voluntary labour, and can serve as potential guardians of social capital ... [G]endered assets and dispositions are being increasingly recognised by the international development agencies, but so far this has not brought significant material benefits to the women involved. The costs many women bear ... in terms of weak labour market links, lack of support for carework and long term security are rarely taken into account. Prevailing policy assumptions still tend to naturalise women's 'roles' and seek to make use of them and influence how they are developed and managed subjectively and situationally.

In light of this it is not hard to see how '... some programmes to combat poverty reproduce patterns of discrimination, since women are used as unpaid or underpaid providers of family or social welfare services, and are only marginally treated as autonomous individuals entitled to rights and benefits ...' (see Molyneux 2002, 2007).

Women as 'victims' Leading on from this, another unfortunate by-product of 'feminization of poverty' orthodoxy is that it tends to present women as 'victims', with Johnsson-Latham (2004b: 38) arguing that perceptions of the vulnerability of women often means they get 'special support', rather than 'equal rights' (see also Bibars 2001).

Neglect of domestic gender inequalities A further policy-related problem with the feminization of poverty is that its routine wedding to female household headship tends to either favour the targeting of women-headed households at the expense of women in general, or to address 'women's issues' as if domestic gender relations had no part to play in female privation (Kabeer 1996; Jackson 1996, 1997; Feijoó 1999: 165; May 2001: 50; Chant 2003a). As noted:

> What is implied is that female-headed households are poorer than male-headed households. The question that is not asked, however, is whether women are better-off in male-headed households. By making male-headed households the norm, important contradictions vanish within these households, and so too does the possibly unbalanced economical (sic) and social position of women compared to men. (Davids and van Driel 2001)

While poor female heads of household clearly have problems to contend with, their counterparts in male-headed households may actually end up in the same position owing to restricted access to and control over household assets (Bradshaw 2002; see also Budlender 2004: 8; Linneker 2003: 4). Yet despite this, and considerable evidence of 'secondary poverty' in male-headed households (Bradshaw 1996; Chant 1997a; Fukuda-Parr 1999; González de la Rocha and Grinspun 2001), intra-household power relations have rarely been broached in anti-poverty programmes.

Missing men ... (again) Beyond neglect of the heterogeneity of women is the fact that men and gender relations remain largely absent from policy responses to women's poverty (Chant and Gutmann 2000; Cornwall 2000; Cornwall and White 2000). Indeed, potential benefits all too easily become burdens when strategies to enhance women's access to material resources simply increase the loads they bear and/or the demands made upon them.

Additional dangers of excluding men are that this can fuel gender rivalry or hostility, with evidence indicating that growing pockets of male social, educational and economic vulnerability can manifest in violence in the home and in the community, in drug or alcohol abuse and other forms of disaffected behaviour (UNESCO 1997: 6; Chant and Gutmann 2000; Moser and McIlwaine 2004; Molyneux 2006).

In short, the 'feminization of poverty' thesis tends to have translated into single-issue and/or single-group interventions which have little power to destabilize deeply embedded structures of gender inequality in the home, the labour market and other institutions. As articulated by Baden (1999: 7), 'The "feminization of poverty" argument is not helpful if it is used to justify poverty reduction efforts which uncritically target women-headed households or even "women" in general, but which do not challenge the underlying "rules of the game".'

This leads me on to my final point regarding the problems of policy interventions which marry poverty reduction with women's empowerment, namely that women's power to negotiate their burdens is not being addressed.

Missing 'real' empowerment Although empowerment is a problematic and highly contested term (Kabeer 1999; Parpart 2002), the main thrust of empowerment interventions has been to increase women's access to material resources as a route to widening their choices (UNDP 1995; UNIFEM 2000). Yet as Johnson (2005: 77) points up on the basis of earlier work by ECLAC, most mainstream poverty programmes are rather more preoccupied with addressing the *condition* of poor women, than their *position*, the former referring to people's material state and the latter to their position in society. In turn, steps to improve women's poorer condition have rarely challenged men's condition *or* position (ibid.: 77).

Despite the best-intentioned efforts of even the most rounded programmes, there is clearly a long way to go in respect of enhancing women's ability to negotiate greater gender equality at the domestic level. If anything, it appears that women are encouraged to be even more altruistic and family-oriented as their education, skills and access to economic opportunities expand. As such, rather than finding themselves 'empowered' to strike new deals within their households, many women simply end up burdened with more obligations (Chant 2006, 2007). Women's duty towards others is rarely questioned, which is partly to do with an aforementioned resilience of culturally condoned expectations of female altruism and servility. Yet if we are to accept that poverty and human rights are integrally linked, women's rights to stand up for themselves and to negotiate social expectations of their roles are fundamental.

Room for revising the 'feminization of poverty' thesis

In terms of what the above implies for the 'feminization of poverty' thesis, it should be clear not only that there are insufficient data but few theoretical or practical inducements to continue using the term as it is currently construed and deployed – that is, with an implicit focus on women's monetary poverty and an overemphasis on female household headship.

The effective redundancy of the 'feminization of poverty' thesis methodologically and analytically presents two possible choices. Either the existing terminology is abandoned and perhaps substituted by the 'feminization of responsibility and/or obligation' or the 'feminization of survival' (see notes 5 and 6), or the term is retained with the proviso that the poverty part of the construct refers not just to income but other, albeit related, privations.

I feel we should stick with the 'feminization of poverty' for three main reasons. First, the term is already known and there is nothing to stop it evolving into a more substantiated and elaborate concept. Second, it has had proven impacts on going some way to 'engender' poverty reduction strategies. Third, it could be said that a 'feminization of poverty' is occurring if we embrace a broader take on poverty which comprises the notion that poverty is not just about *incomes* but *inputs* and which highlights not women's *level* or *share* of poverty, but their *burden* of dealing with it.[8]

The other aspect of the 'feminization of poverty' thesis in need of revision is its persistent bias towards female household headship. Among many persuasive reasons are, first, that female-headed households do not necessarily lack male members; second, free of a senior male 'patriarch', their households can become 'enabling spaces' in which there is scope to distribute household tasks and resources more equitably; and third, women in *male*-headed households may be in the position of supporting not only children but spouses as well, with some men moving from the position of 'chief breadwinner' to 'chief spender'.

Conclusion and possible policy directions

The widespread adoption of the 'feminization of poverty' thesis in academic and policy circles has probably been a 'good thing' insofar as it has made women visible in poverty discourses and raised their profile in anti-poverty initiatives. Yet in order to make it a more effective tool for analysis and policy it is necessary to recast the construct in such a way that the multidimensional nature of poverty and its gendered dimensions are taken on board. Improving the basis and scope of policy interventions is essential given that the present tendency to 'feminize' anti-poverty programmes seems merely to be exacerbating gender disparities.

While some interventions to reduce gender-differentiated poverty have clearly begun to respond to more holistic approaches to poverty analysis, and have arguably moved into a new gear through experimentation with 'gender budgets' at national and local levels (UNRISD 2005: 60), much remains to be done. As articulated by Gangopadhyay and Wadhwa (2003: 2–3):

> If poverty incidence reflects a gender bias it is important to investigate where it originates. If it is in the workplace, such biases have to be fought differently from the case where it originates within the household. If the bias is in [the] workplace, policy measures such as affirmative action may be a way out. On the other hand, if the bias against the girl child originates in the household, policies must aim at improving awareness within the family. To combat the first one requires a strict enforcement of laws. The second is a deeper social problem and laws alone may not help.

Subscribing to Jackson's (2003: 477) point that '... rather than wishing the family or household away, more detailed understanding of them is necessary', two 'family-oriented' strategies which might complement existing approaches to alleviating poverty among women while enhancing their empowerment are, first, greater public support for parenting and unpaid carework; and second, dedicated moves to equalize responsibilities and power at the domestic level (Chant 2003a, 2003b). Unfortunately, neither is likely to be easy. One of the major sticking points in addressing family matters, for example, is that it will require the greater involvement of men. Although there is growing recognition of the need to bring men on board in GAD initiatives on the part of some development agencies and national governments (such as Costa Rica[9]), the persistent equation of 'women' with 'gender', together with concerns about how to translate men's incorporation in practice, means that only limited progress has been made to date (for discussions, see Chant and Gutmann 2000; Cornwall 2000; Cornwall and White 2000; Ruxton 2004). Yet in continuing to talk about a 'feminization of poverty' (or even a 'feminization of responsibility and obligation'), we must not miss what is conceivably the main point, namely that even as women enjoy increased capabilities and opportunities, their potential gains are all too often cancelled out by men's seemingly infinite reservoir of props for asserting power and (re)masculinizing advantage. Attention needs to be paid not only to the 'female victims' but to the structures which uphold men's advantage. This not only involves taking into account men and gender relations but addressing the models which are guiding the direction of economic development nationally and internationally.

Notes

1 Funding for this research was provided by a Leverhulme Major Research Fellowship (2003–06) (Award no. F07004R), to whom the author is grateful for support. For assistance in the field, I would like to thank Baba Njie (The Gambia), Tessie Sato, Josie Chan and Fe Largado (Philippines), and Enid Jaen Hernandez, Luis Castellon Zelaya and Roberto Rojas (Costa Rica). For comments on an earlier draft of this paper, I am indebted to Cathy McIlwaine, Maxine Molyneux, Jane Parpart, Diane Perrons and Silvia Posocco.

2 The fieldwork has comprised individual interviews and focus group discussions with 223 low-income women and men in different age groups in The Gambia, the Philippines and Costa Rica between 2003 and 2005, and an additional forty interviews with professionals in

NGOs, government organizations and international agencies (see Chant 2007 for full methodological details).

3 Aside from lack of robust empirical evidence, as detailed later in the paper, Marcoux (1998a, 1998b) points out that the 70 per cent share of poverty assigned to women in 1995 is untenable in light of the age distribution of the global population and its household characteristics (see also Klasen 2004).

4 Violence tends to be statistically invisible despite the fact that it exacts a heavy toll in terms of economic costs and instability, not only on individual households but on society at large (World Bank 2003: 7; also WEDO 2005). As highlighted by ECLAC: 'A thorough understanding of poverty must include an analysis of violence as a factor that erodes personal

autonomy, the exercise of citizenship and social capital (social autonomy). On the one hand, poverty ... makes ... physical violence in the home more probable. In addition, violence produces more poverty, since it holds back economic development: (i) dealing with the effects of both social and domestic violence requires spending on the part of the police, judicial and social services systems, and (ii) in the case of women, those who suffer domestic violence are less productive at work, which leads to a direct loss to national production.'

5 This has some resonance with Sassen's (2002) notion of a 'feminization of survival' observed in the context of international migration. Sassen points out that not only households but whole communities, and states, are increasingly reliant on the labour efforts of women, within as well as across national borders.

6 The term 'feminization of responsibility and obligation' is not as succinct or 'catchy' as the 'feminization of poverty' or the 'feminization of survival' but it is useful in respect of working through the ways in which women are most affected by poverty. The 'feminization of responsibility' is intended to convey the idea that women are assuming greater liability for dealing with poverty and the 'feminization of obligation' that women have progressively less choice other than to do so. Women have less scope to resist the roles and activities imposed on them structurally (for example, through legal contracts or moral norms), or situationally (through the absence of spouses or male assistance), and this 'duty' often become 'internalized', perceived as non-negotiable and binding.

7 That an ostensible reaffirmation of femininity may be a short-term strategy for women to improve their longer-term 'fall-back' position has been noted by Gates (2002) in the context of Mexico, where some women offer to do more unpaid work in the home as a means of getting their husband's permission to take employment.

8 The notion that the 'feminization of poverty' should entail considering what people do, as well as the income they have, is at least being verbalized by some organizations. In their Framework Plan for Women, for example, the National Commission on the Role of Filipino Women (2002: 11) state that the current trend towards the feminization of poverty is because women '... are the ones mainly responsible for the welfare and survival of households under conditions of increasing poverty'.

9 Some discussion has taken place in Costa Rica, mainly driven by women at the grass roots, about including men in ancillary programmes in order to help ensure the exercise of women's and children's rights and to stimulate more cooperative family patterns. Thus far, however, this has not resulted in any concrete policy initiative.

References

Arias, O. (2000) *Are All Men Benefiting from the New Economy? Male Economic Marginalisation in Argentina, Brazil and Costa Rica*, Washington, DC: World Bank/LCSPR.

Arriagada, I. (2002) 'Cambios y desigualdad en las familias latinoamericanas', *Revista de la CEPAL*, 77.

Asgary, N. and J. Pagan (2004) 'Relative employment and earnings of female household heads in Mexico, 1987–1995', *Journal of Developing Areas*, 38(1).

Baden, S. (1999) 'Gender, governance and the "feminisation of poverty"', Background paper prepared for UNDP meeting on 'Women and political participation: 21st century challenges', New Delhi, 24–26 March.

Baden, S. and A. M. Goetz (1998) 'Who needs [sex] when you can have [gender]?', in C. Jackson and R. Pearson (eds), *Feminist Visions of Development: Gender Analysis and Policy*, London: Routledge.

Bibars, I. (2001) *Victims and Heroines: Women, welfare and the Egyptian state*, London: Zed Books.

Bradshaw, S. (1996) 'Female-headed households in Honduras: a study of their formation and survival in low-income communities', Unpublished PhD thesis, Department of Geography, London School of Economics.

— (2002) *Gendered Poverties and Power Relations: Looking Inside Communities and Household*, Managua: ICD/Embajada de Holanda/Puntos de Encuentro.

Budlender, D. (2004) *Why Should We Care about Unpaid Care Work?*, New York: United Nations Development Fund for Women.

Cagatay, N. (1998) *Gender and Poverty*, Working Paper 5, New York: Social Development and Poverty Elimination Division, United Nations Development Programme.

CELADE (Centro Latinoamericano y Caribeno de Demografía) (2002) *Los Adultos Mayores en América Latina y el Caribe: Datos e Indicadores*, Santiago de Chile: CELADE.

CEPAL (Comisión Económica Para América Latina) (2001) *Panorama Social de América Latina 2000–2001*, Santiago: CEPAL.

— (2002) 'América Latina y el Caribe: Indicadores Seleccionados con una Perspectiva de Género', *Boletín Demográfico*, 70, Santiago de Chile: CEPAL.

Chant, S. (1996) *Gender, Urban Development and Housing*, vol. 2, Publications Series for Habitat II, New York: United Nations Development Programme.

— (1997a) *Women-headed Households: Diversity and Dynamics in the Developing World*, Basingstoke: Macmillan.

— (1997b) 'Women-headed households: poorest of the poor? Perspectives from Mexico, Costa Rica and the Philippines', *IDS Bulletin*, 28(3).

— (1999) 'Women-headed households: global orthodoxies and grass roots realities', in H. Afshar and S. Barrientos (eds), *Women, Globalisation and Fragmentation in the Developing World*, Basingstoke: Macmillan.

— (2000) 'Men in crisis? Reflections on masculinities, work and family in north-west Costa Rica', *European Journal of Development Research*, 12(2).

— (2002) 'Families on the verge of breakdown? Views on contemporary trends in family life in Guanacaste, Costa Rica', *Journal of Developing Societies*, 18(2/3).

— (2003a) *Female Household Headship and the Feminisation of Poverty: Facts, Fictions and Forward Strategies*, Gender Institute, Working Paper no. 9, London: London School of Economics.

— (2003b) *Contributions to the Analysis of Poverty: Methodological and Conceptual Challenges to Understanding Poverty from a Gender Perspective*, Unidad Mujer y Desarrollo, Serie 47, Santiago de Chile: Comisión Económica para América Latina (CEPAL).

— (2006) *Revisiting the 'Feminisation of Poverty' and the UNDP Gender Indices: What Case for a Gendered Poverty Index?*, Gender Institute, Working Paper no. 18, London: London School of Economics.

— (2007) *Gender, Generation and Poverty: Exploring the 'Feminisation of Poverty' in Africa, Asia and Latin America*, Cheltenham: Edward Elgar.

Chant, S. and M. Gutmann (2000) *Mainstreaming Men into Gender and Development: Debates, Reflections and Experiences*, Oxford: Oxfam.

Chen, M. A., J. Vanek and M. Carr (2004) *Mainstreaming Informal Employment and Gender in Poverty Reduction: A Handbook for Policy-Makers and Other Stakeholders*, London: Commonwealth Secretariat.

Cornwall, A. (2000) 'Missing men? Reflections on men, masculinities and gender in GAD', *IDS Bulletin*, 31(2).

Cornwall, A. and S. White (2000) 'Men, masculinities and development: politics, policies and practice', *IDS Bulletin*, 31(2).

Davids, T. and F. van Driel (2001) 'Globalisation and gender: beyond dichotomies', in F. J. Schuurman (ed.), *Globalisation and Development*

Studies Challenges for the 21st Century, London: Sage, pp. 153–75.

— (2005) 'Changing perspectives', in T. Davids and F. van Driel (eds), *Local Gender Globalised*, Aldershot: Ashgate.

De Vylder, S. (2004) 'Gender in poverty reduction strategies', in G. Johnsson-Latham (ed.), *Power and Privileges: Gender Discrimination and Poverty*, Stockholm: Regerinskanliet.

DfID (Department for International Development) (2000) *Poverty Elimination and the Empowerment of Women*, London: DfID.

Elson, D. (1989) 'The impact of structural adjustment on women: concepts and issues', in B. Onimode (ed.), *The IMF, the World Bank and the African Debt*, vol. 2: *The Social and Political Impact*, London: Zed Books.

— (1991) 'Structural adjustment: its effects on women', in T. Wallace with C. March (eds), *Changing Perceptions: Writings on Gender and Development*, Oxford: Oxfam.

Escobar Latapi, A. (1998) 'Los hombres y sus historias: reestructuración y masculinidad en México', *La Ventana*, Universidad de Guadalajara.

Feijoó, M. del C. (1999) 'De pobres mujeres a mujeres pobres', in M. González de la Rocha (ed.), *Divergencias del Modelo Tradicional: Hogares de Jefatura Femenina en América Latina*, Mexico, DF: Centro de Investigaciones y Estudios Superiores en Antropología Social.

Fonseca, C. (1991) 'Spouses, siblings and sex-linked bonding: a look at kinship organisation in a Brazilian slum', in E. Jelin (ed.), *Family, Household and Gender Relations in Latin America*, London/Paris: Kegan Paul International/ UNESCO.

Fukuda-Parr, S. (1999) 'What does feminisation of poverty mean? It isn't just lack of income', *Feminist Economics*, 5(2).

Fuller, N. (2000) 'Work and masculinity among Peruvian urban men', *European Journal of Development Research*, 12(2).

Gangopadhyay, S. and W. Wadhwa (2003) *Are Indian Female-headed Households More Vulnerable to Poverty?*, Mimeo, Delhi: Indian Development Foundation.

Gates, L. C. (2002) 'The strategic uses of gender in household negotiations: women workers on Mexico's northern border', *Bulletin of Latin American Research*, 21(4).

González de la Rocha, M. (1994) *The Resources of Poverty: Women and Survival in a Mexican City*, Oxford: Blackwell.

González de la Rocha, M. and A. Grinspun (2001) 'Private adjustments: households, crisis and work', in A. Grinspun (ed.), *Choices for the Poor: Lessons from National Poverty Strategies*, New York: UNDP.

Graham, H. (1987) 'Being poor: perceptions and coping strategies of lone mothers', in J. Brannen and G. Wilson (eds), *Give and Take in Families: Studies in Resource Distribution*, London: Allen & Unwin.

Gutmann, M. (1996) *The Meanings of Macho: Being a Man in Mexico City*, Berkeley: University of California Press.

IFAD (International Fund for Agricultural Development) (1999) *The Issue of Poverty among Female-headed Households in Africa*, Rome: IFAD.

Jackson, C. (1996) 'Rescuing gender from the poverty trap', *World Development*, 24(3).

— (1997) 'Post-poverty, gender and development', *IDS Bulletin*, 28(3).

— (1998) 'Rescuing gender from the poverty trap', in C. Jackson and R. Pearson (eds), *Feminist Visions of Development: Gender Analysis and Policy*, London: Routledge.

— (2003) 'Gender analysis of land: beyond land rights for women?', *Journal of Agrarian Change*, 3(4).

Jassey, K. (2002) 'Active, visible women in poverty discourses – an impossibility?', Paper presented at the workshop 'Agency, power relations and globalization', Institute for Peace and

Development Research, Gothenberg University, 29 August.

Johnson, R. (2005) 'Not a sufficient condition: the limited relevance of the gender MDG to women's progress', in C. Sweetman (ed.), *Gender and the Millennium Development Goals*, Oxford: Oxfam.

Johnsson-Latham, G. (2004a) '"Ecce homo"? A gender reading of the World Bank study "voices of the poor"', in G. Johnsson-Latham (ed.), *Power and Privileges: Gender Discrimination and Poverty*, Stockholm: Regerinskanliet.

— (2004b) 'Understanding female and male poverty and deprivation', in G. Johnsson-Latham (ed.), *Power and Privileges: Gender Discrimination and Poverty*, Stockholm: Regerinskanliet.

Kabeer, N. (1994) *Reversed Realities: Gender Hierarchies in Development Thought*, London: Verso.

— (1996) 'Agency, well-being and inequality: reflections on the gender dimensions of poverty', *IDS Bulletin*, 27(1).

— (1997) 'Tactics and trade-offs: revisiting the links between gender and poverty', Editorial, *IDS Bulletin*, 28(3).

— (1999) 'Resources, agency, achievements: reflections on the measurement of women's empowerment', *Development and Change*, 30(3).

— (2003) *Gender Mainstreaming in Poverty Eradication and the Millennium Development Goals: A Handbook for Policymakers and Other Stakeholders*, London: Commonwealth Secretariat.

Kaztman, R. (1992) '¿Por qué los hombres son tan irresponsables?', *Revista de la CEPAL*, 46.

Klasen, S. (2004) 'Gender-related indicators of well-being', Discussion paper no. 102, Goettingen: GeorgAugust Universitat, Ibero-Amerika Institiit für Wirtschaftsforschung.

Linneker, B. (2003) 'Gender comparisons of capital influences on the well-being of women and households experiencing poverty in Nicaragua', Working draft report, Managua: Coordinadora Civil – Nicaragua (CCER).

Marcoux, A. (1998a) 'How much do we really know about the feminisation of poverty?', *Brown Journal of World Affairs*, 5(2).

— (1998b) 'The feminisation of poverty: claims, facts and data needs', *Population and Development Review*, 24(1).

May, J. (2001) 'An elusive consensus: definitions, measurement and the analysis of poverty', in A. Grinspun (ed.), *Choices for the Poor: Lessons from National Poverty Strategies*, New York: UNDP.

Mayoux, L. (2002) 'Women's empowerment or the feminisation of debt? Towards a new agenda in African micro-finance', Paper given at One World Action Conference, London, 21/22 March.

— (2006) 'Women's empowerment through sustainable micro-finance: rethinking "best practice"', Discussion paper, www.genfinance.net.

Medeiros, M. and J. Costa (2006) 'Poverty among women in Latin America: feminisation or overrepresentation?', Working Paper no. 20, Brasilia: International Poverty Centre.

Moghadam, V. (1997) 'The feminisation of poverty: notes on a concept and trend', Women's Studies Occasional Paper no. 2, Normal: Illinois State University.

— (1998) 'The feminisation of poverty in international perspective', *Brown Journal of World Affairs*, 5(2).

Molyneux, M. (2001) *Women's Movements in International Perspective: Latin America and Beyond*, Basingstoke: Palgrave.

— (2002) 'Gender and the silences of social capital: lessons from Latin America', *Development and Change*, 33(2).

— (2006) 'Mothers at the service of the new poverty agenda: PROGRESA/ Oportunidades, Mexico's conditional transfer programme', *Journal of Social Policy and Administration*, 40(4).

— (2007) *Change and Continuity in Social Protection in Latin America: Mothers at the Service of the State?*, Gender and

Development Paper no. 1, Geneva: UNRISD.

Moser, C. (1993) *Gender Planning and Development: Theory, Practice and Training*, London: Routledge.

Moser, C. and C. McIlwaine (2004) *Encounters with Violence in Latin America*, London: Routledge.

National Commission on the Role of Filipino Women (2002) *Framework Plan for Women*, Manila: NCRFW.

Nauckhoff, E. (2004) 'Poverty without poor', in G. Johnsson-Latham (ed.), *Power and Privileges: Gender Discrimination and Poverty*, Stockholm: Regerinskanliet.

Ofstedal, M. B., E. Reidy and J. Knodel (2004) 'Gender differences in economic support and well-being of older Asians', *Journal of Cross-Cultural Gerontology*, 19(3).

Painter, G. (2004) 'Gender, the millennium development goals, and human rights in the context of the 2005 review processes. Report for the Gender and Development Network', London: GADN.

Pankhurst, H. (2002) 'Passing the buck? Money literacy and alternatives to savings and credit schemes', *Gender and Development*, 10(3).

Parpart, J. (2002) 'Gender and empowerment: new thoughts, new approaches', in V. Desai and R. Potter (eds), *The Companion to Development Studies*, London: Edward Arnold.

Pearce, D. (1978) 'The feminisation of poverty: women, work and welfare', *Urban and Social Change Review*, 11.

Pineda-Ofreneo, R. and M. L. Acosta (2001) 'Integrating gender concerns in anti-poverty strategies', *Public Policy* (University of the Philippines), 5(2).

Rakodi, C. (1999) 'A capital assets framework for analysing household livelihood strategies: implications for policy', *Development Policy Review*, 17.

Rakodi, C. with T. Lloyd-Jones (eds) (2002) *Urban Livelihoods: A People-centred Approach to Reducing Poverty*, London: Earthscan.

Razavi, S. (1999) 'Gendered poverty and well-being: introduction', *Development and Change*, 30(3).

Rodenberg, B. (2004) 'Gender and poverty reduction: new conceptual approaches in international development cooperation', *Reports and Working Papers* 4/2004, Bonn: German Development Institute.

Rojas, M. (2003) 'The multidimensionality of poverty: a subjective well-being approach', Paper prepared for conference on 'Inequality, poverty and human well-being', World Institute for Development Economics Research, United Nations University, Helsinki, 30/31 May.

Ruxton, S. (ed.) (2004) *Gender Equality and Men*, Oxford: Oxfam.

Safa, H. (1995) *The Myth of the Male Breadwinner: Women and Industrialisation in the Caribbean*, Boulder, CO: Westview Press.

Sassen, S. (2002) 'Counter-geographies of globalisation: feminisation of survival', in K. Saunders (ed.), *Feminist Post-Development Thought*, London: Zed Books.

Sen, A. K. (1999) *Development as Freedom*, Oxford: Oxford University Press.

Silberschmidt, M. (1999) '"Women forget that men are the masters": gender antagonism and socioeconomic change in Kisii District, Kenya', Uppsala: Nordiska Afrikainstitute.

UNDAW (United Nations Division for the Advancement of Women) (1991) 'Women and households in a changing world', in E. Barbieri Masini and S. Stratigos (eds), *Women, Households and Change*, Tokyo: United Nations University.

— (2000) *Women 2000: Gender Equality, Development and Peace for the 21st Century*, New York: UNDAW.

UNDP (United Nations Development Programme) (1995) *Human Development Report 1995*, Oxford: Oxford University Press.

— (2004) *Human Development Report 2004*, Oxford: Oxford University Press.

UNESCO (United Nations Educational, Scientific and Cultural Organization)

(1997) 'Male roles and masculinities in the perspective of a culture of peace. Report, Expert Group Meeting', Oslo, 24–28 September, Paris: UNESCO.

UNIFEM (United Nations Development Fund for Women) (2000) *Progress of the World's Women 2000*, Biennial report, New York: UNIFEM.

— (2002) *Progress of the World's Women 2002*, vol. 2, New York: UNIFEM.

UNMP (United Nations Millennium Project) and TFEGE (Task Force on Education and Gender Equality) (2005) *Taking Action: Achieving Gender Equality and Empowering Women*, London: Earthscan.

UNRISD (United Nations Research Institute for Social Development) (2005) *Gender Equality: Striving for Justice in an Unequal World*, Geneva: UNRISD.

Van Driel, F. (1994) *Poor and Powerful: Female-headed Households and Unmarried Motherhood in Botswana*, Nijmegen Studies 16, Saarbrücken: Verlag für Entwicklungspolitik Breitenbach.

Van Vuuren, A. (2003) *Women Striving for Self Reliance: The Diversity of Female-headed Households in Tanzania and the Livelihood Strategies They Employ*, Leiden: African Studies Centre.

Varley, A. and M. Blasco (2000) 'Exiled to the home: masculinity and ageing in urban Mexico', *European Journal of Development Research*, 12(2).

WEDO (Women's Environment and Development Organization) (2005) *Beijing Betrayed: Women Worldwide Report that Governments Have Failed to Turn the Platform into Action*, New York: WEDO.

Wennerholm, C. J. (2002) *The 'Feminisation of Poverty': The Use of a Concept*, Stockholm: Swedish International Development Cooperation Agency.

World Bank (1994) *Enhancing Women's Participation in Economic Development*, Washington, DC: World Bank.

— (2000) *World Development Report 2000/2001: Attacking Poverty*, New York: Oxford University Press.

— (2002) *Integrating Gender into the World Bank's Work*, Washington, DC: World Bank.

— (2003) *Challenges and Opportunities for Gender Equality in Latin America and the Caribbean*, Washington, DC: Gender Unit, Latin America and the Caribbean Division, World Bank.

Yates, R. (1997) 'Literacy, gender and vulnerability: donor discourses and local realities', *IDS Bulletin*, 28(3).

Women in the global economy

Introduction to Part Three

Laurie Nisonoff with Lynn Duggan
and Nan Wiegersma

Women work. Women of all ages and marital statuses – single, married,
divorced or widowed – work. Women in nearly all circumstances of class
or status work, and have always worked. However, as explained by Lourdes
Benería in Chapter 16, much of the work that women have done and continue
to do is invisible, or is assumed to be either 'natural' or of little value. These
assumptions exist, in part, because most tasks, and even occupations, performed primarily by women take place within the household and are not seen
as productive (in economic terms, creating goods or services that are paid for)
or as making direct contributions to the economy of either a household or a
nation (Chapter 11). Over the last twenty-five years, there has been significant
debate about whether women's subordinated status influences how their work
is regarded, or whether the lack of respect for certain tasks reserves such jobs
for women, because of their relatively low status as workers. In any case, the
result is the degradation of women and their work.

As economies have industrialized, women have often followed 'traditionally
women's' tasks from the private household into the public industrialized sphere
of production. This can be seen in the predominance of women in transforming
raw material (cotton, flax, wool) into cloth and garments, planting crops and
preparing food, and educating or succouring younger, older and weaker members
of the community. Over the past two hundred years, the women in North America
and Europe who have performed such 'women's' tasks have received lower pay
for their work. This transformation of the work of women in many developing
nations has taken place more rapidly, however, owing to government-sponsored
development plans as well as to global economic phenomena.

In the years since World War II, governments of some developing nations
have sought to transform their countries from poor, stagnant economies dependent on the export of raw materials into industrialized nations capable
of rapid growth and material prosperity, which planners hoped would 'trickle
down' throughout societies. The two principal policies have been import substitution – the local production of formerly imported goods such as automobiles
and steel – and export-led industrialization, which employs local low-wage
workers to produce inexpensive export items such as clothing.

Since the consumption-goods markets in the Third World reflect tastes of the wealthy minorities of the population, import-substituting production is generally capital intensive, requiring expensive manufacturing processes and plants, as well as 'skilled' workers. Export-led growth is, by contrast, often a much less costly process to initiate, requiring fewer expensive materials, less manufacturing equipment, and lower-wage workers. Men have constituted the predominant labor force of import-substitution while women have been the labor force in the export-led sector.

While both these strategies were used often in the immediate post-war era, the 1980s and 1990s have witnessed a decided shift to the export-led method, especially under the impact of structural adjustment (see below). Studies of the implications for women of these processes have centered on their role in the global economy and their experiences in the informal sector. The latter (discussed below) falls between state-registered, taxed economic enterprises and household or farm-based production.

A: Women and industrialization

During the Industrial Revolution of the late eighteenth and nineteenth centuries, many European and North American women found employment in the industrial sector, particularly in the textile and garment industries. These women formed a visible section of the paid labor force, and often played a crucial role in organizing for regulations that were subsequently sanctioned by the state and established in legislation (e.g. wages, hours, working conditions, pensions and benefits). The firms subject to these regulations were (and are) often defined as the formal economy. Many other women produced goods and services in their homes, where their contributions were not always visible to census gatherers or policymakers (see Part 2).

The increasing post-World War II focus on export-led development in the Third World has had a profound impact on the working lives of women. Capital and production were increasingly internationalized, and transnational corporations (TNCs) began to subdivide the labor process. At one time, garment production was concentrated in centers such as New York or Paris to take advantage of many small support firms (e.g. button-makers, or subcontractors for part of the production process). By the 1930s, production had become more geographically diverse and union officials and scholars in these countries began to discuss the phenomenon of 'runaway shops.' Declines in transportation costs (airplanes and shipping), changes in tax codes and materials, and innovations in electronic communications meant that sales, design and skilled cutting of pieces could remain in the central location while the 'piecework' – the assembly and sewing of garments – could be done elsewhere to take advantage of cheaper labor and special development programs. The first of these schemes was the post-war 1948 Operation Bootstrap in Puerto Rico, which exploited the island's US commonwealth status for lower taxes, and also made land and capital available (at subsidized prices) (Acevedo 1990).

Helen Safa's (1981) classic article places this new phenomenon in its historic context. She notes that the US garment and textile industries had first employed displaced, but skilled, farm women and immigrant labor. This search for cheap labor continues: the history of the industrialization process can be traced by following these industries around the world from the nineteenth century when they originated in Lancashire, England, and the New England region of the USA to their present locations in the newest free trade zones.

Operation Bootstrap included, however, an explicit government role in this process. When the Puerto Rican experience with export-led development proved financially successful for mainland firms, although significantly less so for the long-term economic development of the island, US tariff laws were amended to make it feasible to export partially completed goods to take advantage of low wages and pay only import duties on the value added abroad (small, owing to low wages) when the goods returned to the USA for completion and marketing. Export processing zones were established in many regions of the Third World. Import duties and local and environmental laws were often suspended, and land, plants, capital, and infrastructure (such as airports and modern roads) were provided at low or no cost.

The zone along the US–Mexico border has been the subject of many studies by social scientists and business people. Some twin plants have been established wherein the US-side plant performs the capital-intensive tasks and provides high-wage jobs. The Mexican plant, called a *maquiladora*, offers low-wage employment that involves the labor-intensive tasks of electronic assembly or sewing garments. Many *maquiladoras* were eventually established while the more capital-intensive tasks continued to be performed in the USA, often outside the border region. The early *maquiladoras* employed a predominantly young female labor force; however, the 1990s have seen the growth of employment in automobile parts and electronic-components manufacturing, jobs usually reserved for men (Rendon and Salas 1995). The zone approach has been so successful in creating low-wage work in the Third World that, since the 1980s, Great Britain and the USA have established free enterprise zones within their own borders to encourage industrial investment in impoverished regions.

Throughout the 1980s, social scientists and activists debated whether jobs in the zones were good for women – liberating them from patriarchal homes and providing them with wages – or served as another level of exploitation. This question of whether women were 'pulled' to new opportunities or 'pushed' out of the home to provide wages for either their natal or marital families parallels historical debates over early industrialization in Europe and the United States, debates which remain unresolved.

The authors of our first selection, Diane Elson and Ruth Pearson, have written several of the earliest and most comprehensive analyses of this phenomenon, critiquing the idea that Third World women are 'unskilled' and therefore worthy of only low wages. Both in the selection below and in their 1981 article Elson and Pearson analyse the historical construction of men's tasks as skilled (i.e. learned in public apprenticeships on the job), in contrast to women's tasks, which are viewed as unskilled (learned at home from mothers or other women).

Several significant contributions to this literature were published in 1983: a key anthology by June Nash and María Patricia Fernández-Kelly, Fernández-Kelly's (1983a) monograph, Wendy Chapkis and Cynthia Enloe's (1983) edited collection, and an introductory pamphlet by Annette Fuentes and Barbara Ehrenreich (1983). The latter two provide short first-hand accounts of women's work experiences and resistance activities around the globe. A film of the same year, *The Global Assembly Line* (Gray 1983), illustrates the effect of the movement of jobs upon women in the Philippines, Mexico, and the USA. Kamel (1990) suggests methods to incorporate the film into classroom and community-organizing activities.

Among other important monographs that explore the complicated realities of women workers' lives, those of Aiwha Ong (1987) and John Humphrey (1987) reveal the worldwide nature of the global factory and provide details of the relationship between the home and work lives of factory women. Humphrey studies both men and women in seven Brazilian factories and explores the process by which gender roles established in the family are transmitted and maintained in the workplace. Ong's study of Malay peasant women in Japanese-owned factories in Malaysia portrays the multiple cultural influences of religion, patriarchy and modern capitalism encountered by these women. The women's working conditions are negotiated 'for them' by their fathers and brothers. These women are famous for generating demands: claims of 'spirit possession' that require time-consuming ceremonies to 'free' them or the machines. Women were thus able to negotiate the overlapping layers of culture and patriarchy to gain a modicum of control over their work lives. Bill Maurer (1991) contributes another ethnographic example, from Dominica, problematizing the distinction between sex as 'natural' and gender as 'cultural' in much feminist thought.

While most of the literature focuses on the poor conditions faced by women workers in the free trade zones and transnational firms, Linda Lim (1993) provides a contrasting perspective. While agreeing with many authors that TNCs subject women to multiple layers of exploitation, Lim suggests that within the interplay of these systems, young women's employment in the TNCs might expand their limited freedom to confront the restrictions of their lives, as TNCs have often provided higher wages and better employment opportunities relative to jobs with locally owned businesses or to women's uncompensated work in patriarchal households.

Boserup (1970) states that women appear to lose employment possibilities as larger industrial firms replaced home industries. As Benería (1989) argues, the prominence in the literature of the impact of TNC employment on young women had 'tended to exaggerate' its importance, at least statistically, as only a small proportion of total women's employment is in these firms. She also offers compelling arguments for the importance of this phenomenon: in some countries (especially the Asian NICs) TNC employment is prevalent. There are indirect effects including: subcontracting chains to domestic firms that also employ women (see below), discovery or acceptance of women as a new source of industrial labor by domestic firms, and the spread of capitalist consumerist behavior into new households. Benería argues that it is more than women's low wages which is leading to the 'feminization of global capital'; she points to three factors: labor control and malleability; productivity; and 'flexible labor', which 'women provide ... through their predominance in temporary contracts, as well as in part-time unstable work' (ibid.: 251). Guy Standing (1989) cites this flexibility as essential to both the formal and informal sectors, and in economic restructuring of industrialized economies.

The issues of 'push versus pull' explanations of employment in the export sector and of whether filial piety or independence accompanies factory work have been explored by Janet Salaff (1981, 1990) and Wolf (1990; see Part 2). Kathryn Ward (1990) includes pieces on the interconnections of formal and informal work by Diane Wolf and Cynthia Truelove. Elson and Pearson's (1989) edited collection demonstrates the unevenness of the European experience, as European and US-based transnationals invest in the peripheries of the European Community. Jean L. Pyle in her work on Ireland (1990a, 1990b and 1990c) and Singapore (1994) posits that the state plays an essential role in determining whether new employment opportunities favor the employment of women or men. Seung-kyung Kim (1992) provides examples of workers' resistance to state policy (including martial law) in South Korea. Susan Tiano (1990, 1994) returns to the subject of *maquiladora* women and, using case-study data from assembly-processing work in several Mexican communities, addresses the debate as to whether this is a new kind of employment. Does it exacerbate the relative unemployment of men? Does it alleviate the lack of income owing to the displacement of husbands, brothers and fathers from US agricultural employment, or are these women who have always made economic contributions to their household now simply working at new locations? Diana Tamar Wilson's (2002) overview piece analyzes the masculinization of Mexican *maquiladoras*.

Readings This section's readings are classic contributions to the literature about women's experiences in the internationalization of labor. Elson and Pearson (Chapter 22) critique the supposedly 'natural womanly' qualities of 'nimble fingers', docility and subordination, noting that these attributes result from specific socialization processes. They pose the key question of whether wage work liberates women from gender subordination and discuss women's resistance to workplace and familial subservience. Fernández-Kelly's account (Chapter 23) of her anthropological fieldwork in a US–Mexico border *maquiladora* allows us to see the labor process from the vantage point of the workers themselves, as well as to glimpse their impressions of the anthropologist. Working at the plant and studying the labor force, the author learns to appreciate how skilled this work is.

B: Women in the informal sector

The process of industrialization and the mechanization of agriculture in many Third World countries has resulted in unemployment and underemployment (people whose jobs do not fully occupy them, compensate them or use their skills), as well as migration from the countryside to the cities and emigration abroad. Especially vulnerable to unemployment, women in the countryside and the cities create self-employment outside the formal sector, which has not provided a sufficient number of secure, stable and well-paid jobs. Portes et al. (1989) differentiate formality from informality by counting as formal sector employment only those jobs that provide regulated wages, pensions and benefits. There is an extensive debate in the development literature about definitions and their applicability to different situations (Peattie 1987; Kabra 1995). Lourdes Arizpe (1977) was one of the first to integrate a feminist analysis into discussions of the informal economy.

Women in the informal economy are located primarily in particular interrelated areas: preparation of goods for sale in the market and marketing, domestic service, sex work (often as trafficked workers), and subcontracting and home production. Anthropologist Florence E. Babb's fieldwork on market women in the Andean city of Huarez in north-central Peru reveals a range of food preparation and clothing processes that, in part, move traditional housework out of the home. Babb also notes new tasks of buying and selling, transporting and bulk ordering that must be learned from other market women. Unlike domestic workers, market women perceive themselves, even under the stress of structural adjustment, as a group with different interests from the male market entrepreneurs, the government and consumers, and they act accordingly.

Gracia Clark's work on the relationship between Ghanaian women producers and marketers suggests that the market women's flexible arrangements allow them to continue to supply food 'through stresses of political upheaval, economic crisis, and seasonal and extended drought' (1992: 21). Market women play an important role in Jamaican 'higgling' (trading); Witter's anthology (1989) and Faye V. Harrison's (1991) study present a range of experiences and theoretical insights. A special issue of *Cultural Survival Quarterly* (Rothstein

1992) contains contemporary reports on the key role of women's market activities in Africa, Nicaragua and other parts of Latin America; Stephen, Sullivan, Trask and Trask raise the problem of indigenous women in Mexico and Hawaii 'marketing' their 'ethnicity'. Nash's (1993) anthology continues this debate on the role of craft production and marketing in the lives of peasant artisans.

Elisa M. Chaney and Maria Garcia Castro's edited collection (1989) presents a theoretical model for understanding the situation of domestic workers. The authors note that: the work of domestic workers is undervalued; domestics are recruited from among poor and often indigenous women with minimal education, who are considered inferior in culture, language, dress, and race; they work in isolation and are 'invisible' to other domestic workers, to trade unions, and to society; they are not protected by labor legislation; and they are distrustful of women in professional and feminist groups owing to their ambivalent relationship with their middle-class women employers. This collection includes five chapters written by domestic workers. The film *Maids and Madams*, made in South Africa in 1985 for British television, illustrated the complex relationships between domestic servants and their employers, other domestic workers, trade unions, and society.

Ximena Bunster and Elisa Chaney (1985) provide a case study of fifty women in Lima, Peru, who have tried various domestic- and market-employment opportunities in a capital city that has experienced enormous in-migration. Chapters focus on the different ages of women involved in the extensive rural-to-urban movement. Since the 1990/91 Gulf War, the international press and feminist scholars have raised questions, similar to those posed in Chaney's two co-authored books, about ethnic difference and the isolation of young Filipina and Southeast Asian women who are hired as domestic workers and then stranded and abused in Kuwait and the Arab Emirates (Rodriguez 2009).

Another type of informal sector work is industrial home work, in which women produce industrial goods at home or in small workshops. Large formal sector firms often subcontract portions of their production process to smaller firms or to workshops which may operate outside the auspices of the state. Benería and Roldan (1987) and Benería (1987) reveal an extensive network of non-traditional home work and workshops in Mexico City. They note that TNCs take advantage of women workers' vulnerability by using this type of production (without the costs of higher factory wages, machinery and plants) to increase their profits. The women move through various subsectors of formal and informal employment because of familial and household responsibilities, their lives vividly detailed over the course of the 1980s. Economic downturns in the Mexican economy in the 1990s have, however, resulted in lower wages for factory workers, making this cost-cutting strategy less common and virtually eliminating this type of informal sector work as a source of employment (Rendon and Salas 1995).

Sometimes women themselves, especially under the pressure of economic crisis such as structural adjustment or the transformation from a planned economy, begin small entrepreneurial activities (e.g. garment production and repair). These micro-enterprises often begin as a method of self-employment but may grow to employ other workers. They are usually started with small infusions of capital. Blumberg (1995) and Osirim (1996) provide analysis and examples of this phenomenon. More commonly, rotating savings societies, found in many cultures and consisting of daily or weekly private collections of funds which are distributed to the members in rotation, provide lump sums of small capital to initiate or expand small enterprises (see Part 1 readings on microfinance by Visvanathan and Yoder and K. Kalpana).

While social scientists find it useful to make a distinction between formal and informal sectors, between enterprise zones and local entrepreneurs, or between home and marketing work, over the course of their working lives women move in and out of these areas without paying much heed to the differences, seeking to support themselves and their families. Firms in free trade zones often prefer younger and more formally educated women, and to avoid paying social benefits (such as state-mandated maternity leaves or pension plans) have dismissed pregnant women or those over age thirty-five. Market women combine motherhood and selling responsibilities. Older women often make handicrafts and processed foodstuffs to be sold by others. For example, particular women in Nicaragua worked in a free trade zone in their youth, but later found employment in sales or the production of garments in their homes or small shops (Wiegersma 1994).

Readings Chapter 24 by Barbara Ehrenreich and Arlie Hochschild introduces the reader to global 'care-giving chains' that span the world, which in some cases are part of a government's specific development plan for 'exported workers' to remit earnings home to their family members. Chapter 25 by Beth Herzfeld is a concise introduction to the incidence of slavery, focusing on bonded labor, the most widespread form of slavery today, as well as on the worst forms of child labor. In Chapter 26, a well-researched piece on globalization and transnational care work, Jean Pyle looks at who is and who is not receiving care. She finds deficiencies in the level of care that international care workers and their families receive, including deficits in the working and living conditions of most international domestic and healthcare workers. There are often deficiencies also in the care that families of these workers receive at home.

C: Structural adjustment and women

The debt crises experienced by most less-developed countries in the 1980s led to cutbacks in international lending. In order to ensure loan repayment, the bilateral and multilateral international lending agencies, predominantly the International Monetary Fund and the World Bank, proceeded to develop a number of political-economic strategies, known collectively as structural adjustment, which were then pressed upon less-developed countries seeking the refinancing of loans. These policies have taken economic directions which the IMF/World Bank hoped would put countries experiencing financial trouble on a more solid financial footing in the short run and improve their long-term international market positions. They have included: (1) cutbacks in public spending in order to balance government budgets and service past debts; (2) monetary policies designed to fight inflation by restricting the money supply (all incomes); (3) the selling of government enterprises (privatization) in an attempt to balance government budgets and improve business production efficiency; and (4) the shift of manufacturing and agricultural sectors toward production for export instead of for the domestic market, in order to improve international currency balances. The export processing zones, described above, have been further developed because of this export orientation.

Developmental goals such as improvements in health and education have been adversely affected by these policies, as have short-run food balances and nutrition. Publications by UNICEF (Cornia et al. 1987) and the United Nations (1989) describe how women and children have suffered unequally under structural adjustment policies (SAPs). The claim and hope of UN officials that carefully designed policies could change this situation – that is, give SAPs a human face – were overly optimistic. This view was shared by Manuh (1994).

The assumptions concerning resources, choices and market perfection underlying the SAPs, even in their more humanized form, are inconsistent with the inequalities and market imperfections which constitute actual conditions in less-developed countries. The clearly unequal impact of the adjustment process is predictable if we analyse the disadvantages for women under structural adjustment: (1) the largest cutbacks in the public sector are in health and education programmes which affect women (both as teachers and health workers and as consumers) and their children particularly; (2) decreases in real wages and employment and increases in prices of necessities affect women and children worst because they are already the poorest of the poor.

A major geographic region of special concern relative to the impact of structural adjustment is sub-Saharan Africa. Food balances have been negatively affected in several countries when export crops have been favored over subsistence production. Adding to the misery of the countries which have followed SAP directives, the increases in the availability of coffee and cocoa on international markets caused price declines and reductions in the value of crops grown at the expense of subsistence crops so that the change did not even earn the planned extra income for these countries.

The impacts of structural adjustment on women are detailed in *Unequal Burden* (1992) edited by Benería and Feldman. The particular repercussions of

SAPs in the Caribbean were described in *In the Shadows of the Sun* by Deere et al. (1990).

Reading Chapter 27 by Haejin Kim and Paula B. Voos is a case study of the indirect impacts of structural adjustment (IMF conditionality) on the South Korean labor force, focusing on Korean women's labor market position and the spread of contingent work.

References and further reading

Women and industrialization

Acevedo, L. A. (1990) 'Industrialization and employment: changes in the patterns of women's work in Puerto Rico', *World Development*, 18(2).

— (1995) 'Feminist inroads in the study of women's work and development', in C. E. Bose and E. Acosta-Belen, *Women in the Latin American Development Process*, Philadelphia, PA: Temple University.

Acker, J. C. (1988) 'Gender and the relations of distribution', *Signs*, 13(3).

Bacon, D. (2003) 'Maquiladora bosses play the China card – companies in Mexico threaten to relocate to China', *Dollars and Sense*, September/October.

Bell, P. E. (1991) 'Gender and economic development in Thailand', in P. and J. van Esterik (eds), *Gender and Development in Southeast Asia*, XX(II), Canadian Council for Southeast Asian Studies.

Benería, L. (1989) 'Gender and the global economy', in A. MacEwan and W. K. Tabb (eds), *Instability and Change in the World Economy*, NY: Monthly Review.

Benería, L. and S. Feldman (1992) *Unequal Burden: Economic Crises, Persistent Poverty and Women's Work*, Boulder, CO: Westview Press.

Boserup, E. (1970) *Women's Role in Economic Development*, NY: St Martin's Press.

Brown, W. (1992) 'Finding the man in the state', *Feminist Studies*, 18(1).

Buang, A. (1993) 'Development and factory women: negative perceptions from a Malaysian source area', in J. H. Momsen and V. Kinnaird (eds), *Different Places, Different Voices*, London: Routledge.

Cagatay, N. (1996) 'Gender and international labor standards in the world economy', *Review of Radical Political Economics*, 28(3).

Cagatay, N. and G. Berik (1990) 'Transition in export-led growth in Turkey: is there feminisation of employment?', *Review of Radical Political Economics*, 16(1).

Chakravarty, D. (2007) '"Docile Oriental women" and organized labor: a case study of the Indian garment manufacturing industry', *Indian Journal of Gender Studies*, 14(3).

Chapkis, W. and C. Enloe (eds) (1983) *Of Common Cloth: Women in the Global Textile Industry*, Amsterdam: Translation Institute.

Dalsimer, M. and L. Nisonoff (1984) 'The new economic readjustment policies: implications for Chinese urban working women', *Review of Radical Political Economics*, 16(1).

Ecevit, Y. (1991) 'Shop floor control: the ideological construction of Turkish women factory workers', in N. Redclift and M. T. Sinclair (eds), *Working Women: International Perspectives on Labour and Gender Ideology*, London: Routledge.

Elson, D. (ed.) (1991) *Male Bias in the Development Process*, NY: St Martin's Press.

Elson, D. and R. Pearson (1981) 'Nimble fingers make cheap workers: an analysis of women's employment in Third World export manufacturing', *Feminist Review*, 7.

— (eds) (1989) *Women's Employment and*

Multinationals in Europe, Basingstoke: Macmillan.

Enloe, C. H. (1983) 'Women textile workers in the militarization of Southeast Asia', in J. Nash and M. P. Fernández-Kelly (eds), *Women, Men and the International Division of Labor*, Albany, NY: SUNY Press.

Fernández-Kelly, M. P. (1983a) *For We Are Sold, I and My People: Women in Industry in Mexico's Frontier*, Albany, NY: SUNY Press.

— (1983b) 'Mexican border industrialization, female labor-force participation and migration', in J. Nash and M. P. Fernández-Kelly (eds), *Women, Men and the International Division of Labor*, Albany, NY: SUNY Press.

Fernández-Kelly, M. P. and S. Sassen (1995) 'Recasting women in the global economy: internationalization and changing definitions of gender', in C. E. Bose and E. Acosta-Belen (eds), *Women in the Latin American Development Process*, Philadelphia, PA: Temple University Press.

Fuentes, A. and B. Ehrenreich (1983) *Women in the Global Factory*, INC Pamphlet no. 2, Boston, MA: South End.

Gallin, R. S. (1990) 'Women and the export industry in Taiwan: the muting of class consciousness', in K. Ward (ed.), *Women Workers and Global Restructuring*, Ithaca, NY: ILR Press.

Gray, L. (director and producer) (1983) *The Global Assembly Line*, Los Angeles, CA: Educational TV and Film Center.

Hewamanne, S. (2003) 'Performing the dis-respectability: new tastes, cultural practices, and performances by Sri Lanka's free trade zone garment-factory workers', *Cultural Dynamics*, 15(1).

Humphrey, J. (1987) *Gender and Work in the Third World: Sexual Divisions in Brazilian Industry*, London and New York: Tavistock.

Inter-American Development Bank (1990) *Economic and Social Progress in Latin America*, Washington, DC: Johns Hopkins University and I-ADB.

Kamel, R. (1990) *The Global Factory: Analysis and Action for a New Economic Era*, Philadelphia, PA: American Friends Service Committee.

Kim, S.-K. (1992) 'Women workers and the labor movement in South Korea', *Anthropology and the Global Factory*, New York: Bergin and Garvey.

Lim, L. Y. C. (1990) 'Women's work in export factories: the politics of a cause', in I. Tinker (ed.), *Persistent Inequalities*, Oxford: Oxford University Press.

— (1993) 'Capitalism, imperialism, and patriarchy: the dilemma of Third World women workers in multinational factories', in J. Nash and M. P. Fernandez-Kelly (eds), *Women, Men and the International Division of Labor*, Albany, SUNY Press.

MacEwen Scott, A. (1990) 'Patterns of patriarchy in the Peruvian working class', in S. Stichter and J. Parpart (eds), *Women, Employment and Family in the International Division of Labor*, Philadelphia, PA: Temple University Press.

Maurer, B. (1991) 'Symbolic sexuality and economic work in Dominica, West Indies: the naturalization of sex and women's work in development', *Review of Radical Political Economics*, 23(3/4).

Nash, J. (1988) 'Cultural parameters of sexism and racism in the international division of labor', in J. Smith (ed.), *Racism, Sexism and the World System*, New York: Greenwood Press.

Nash, J. and M. P. Fernández-Kelly (eds) (1983) *Women, Men and the International Division of Labor*, Albany, NY: SUNY Press.

Ngai, P. (2007) 'Gendering the dormitory labor system: production, reproduction, and migrant labor in South China', *Feminist Economics*, 13(3).

Ong, A. (1983) 'Global industries and Malay peasants in peninsular Malaysia', in J. Nash and M. P. Fernández-Kelly (eds), *Women, Men and the International Division of Labour*, Albany, SUNY Press.

— (1987) *Spirits of Resistance and Capitalist Discipline: Factory Women in Malaysia*, Albany, NY: SUNY Press

Pyle, J. L. (1990a) 'Export-led development and the underemployment of women: the impact of discriminatory development policy in the Republic of Ireland', in K. Ward (ed.), *Women Workers and Global Restructuring*, Ithaca, NY: Cornell University Press.

— (1990b) 'Female employment and export-led development in Ireland: labor market impact of state-reinforced gender inequality in the household', in S. Stichter and J. L. Parpart (eds), *Women, Employment and Family in the International Division of Labor*, Philadelphia, PA: Temple University Press.

— (ed.) (1990c) *The State and Women in the Economy: Lessons from Sex Discrimination in the Republic of Ireland*, Albany, NY: SUNY Press.

— (1994) 'Economic restructuring in Singapore and the changing roles of women, 1957 to present', in N. Aslanbeigui, S. Pressman and G. Summerfield (eds), *Women in the Age of Economic Transformation*, London and New York: Routledge.

Rendon, T. and C. Salas (1995) *The Gender Dimension of Employment Trends in Mexico*, Conference paper presented at URPE at ASSA, Washington, DC, 6–8 January.

Rios, P. N. (1990) 'Export-oriented industrialization and the demand for female labor: Puerto Rican women in the manufacturing sector, 1952–1980', *Gender and Society*, 4(3).

Rothstein, F. A. and M. L. Blim (eds) (1992) *Anthropology and the Global Factory: Studies of the New Industrialisation in the Late Twentieth Century*, New York: Bergin and Garvey.

— (1995) 'Gender and multiple incomes strategies in rural Mexico: a twenty year perspective', in C. E. Bose and E. Acosta-Belen, *Women in the Latin American Development Process*, Philadelphia, PA: Temple University Press.

Ruiz, V. and S. Tiano (eds) (1991) *Women on the US–Mexico Border; Responses to Change*, Boulder, CO: Westview Press.

Safa, H. I. (1981) 'Runaway shops and female employment: the search for cheap labor', *Signs*, 7(2).

— (1983) 'Women, production and reproduction in industrial capitalism: a comparison of Brazilian and US factory workers', in J. Nash and M. P. Fernández-Kelly (eds), *Women, Men and the International Division of Labor*, Albany, NY: SUNY Press.

— (1995) *The Myth of the Male Breadwinner: Women and Industrialization in the Caribbean*, Boulder, CO, and Oxford: Westview Press.

Salaff, J. W. (1981) *Working Daughter of Hong Kong: Filial Piety or Power in the Family?*, Cambridge: Cambridge University Press.

— (1990) 'Women, the family and the state: Hong Kong, Taiwan, Singapore – Newly Industrialized Countries in Asia', in S. Stichter and J. Parpart (eds), *Women, Employment and Family in the International Division of Labor*, Philadelphia, PA: Temple University Press.

Sinclair, M. T. (1991) 'Women, work and skill: economic theories and feminist perspectives', in N. Redclift and J. M. T. Sinclair (eds), *Working Women: International Perspectives on Labour and Gender Ideology*, London and New York: Routledge.

Standing, G. (1989) 'Global feminization through flexible labor', *World Development*, 17(7).

Stichter, S. and J. Parpart (eds) (1990) *Women, Employment and Family in the International Division of Labor*, Philadelphia, PA: Temple University Press.

Summerfield, G. (1994) 'Chinese women and the post-Mao economic reforms', in N. Aslanbeigui, S. Pressman and G. Summerfield (eds), *Women in the Age of Economic Transformation: Gender Impact of Reforms in Post-Socialist and Developing Countries*, London and New York: Routledge.

Tiano, S. (1990) 'Maquiladora women: a new category of workers?', in K. Ward (ed.), *Women Workers and Global Restructuring*, Ithaca, NY: Cornell University Press.

— (1994) *Patriarchy on the Line: Labor, Gender and Ideology in the Mexican Maquila Industry*, Philadelphia, PA: Temple University Press.

United Nations Development Programme (1995a) *Women in a Changing Global Economy: 1994 World Survey on the Role of Women in Development*, New York: United Nations.

— (1995b) *The World's Women 1995: Trends and Statistics*, New York: United Nations.

— (1995c) *Human Development Report 1995*, Oxford and New York: Oxford University Press.

Ward, K. (ed.) (1990) *Women Workers and Global Restructuring*, Ithaca, NY: Cornell University Press.

Ward, K. and J. L. Pyle (1995) 'Gender, industrialization, transnational corporations and development: an overview of trends and patterns', in C. E. Bose and E. Acosta-Belen (eds), *Women in the Latin American Development Process*, Philadelphia, PA: Temple University Press.

Wiegersma, N. (1994) 'State policy and the restructuring of women's industries in Nicaragua', in N. Aslanbeigui, S. Pressman and G. Summerfield (eds), *Women in the Age of Economic Transformation: Gender Impact of Reforms in Post-Socialist and Developing Countries*, London and New York: Routledge.

Wilson, T. D. (2002) 'The masculinization of the Mexican maquiladoras', *Review of Radical Political Economics*, 34.

Wolf, D. L. (1990) 'Linking women's labor with the global economy: factory workers and their families in rural Java', in K. Ward (ed.), *Women Workers and Global Restructuring*, Ithaca, NY: Cornell University Press.

Women in the informal sector

Aguilar, D. (1996) 'A half-hidden world of Filipina migrant labor: servants to the global masters', *Against the Current*, 11(1).

Arizpe, L. (1977) 'Women in the informal-labour sector: the case of Mexico City', *Signs*, 3(1).

Babb, F. (1984) 'Women in the marketplace: petty commerce in Peru', *Review of Radical Political Economics*, 16(1).

— (1987) 'From the field to the cooking pot: economic crisis and the threat to marketers in Peru', *Ethnology*, 26(2).

— (1989) *Between Field and Cooking Pot: The Political Economy of Marketwomen in Peru*, Austin: University of Texas Press.

Balakrishnan, R. (ed.) (2002) *The Hidden Assembly Line: Gender Dynamics of Subcontracted Work in a Global Economy*, West Hartford, CT: Kumarian Press.

Benería, L. (1987) 'Gender and the dynamics of subcontracting in Mexico City', in C. Brown and J. A. Pechman (eds), *Gender in the Workplace*, Washington, DC: Brookings Institution.

— (2008) 'The crisis of care: international migration, and public policy', *Feminist Economics*, 14(3).

Benería, L. and M. Roldan (1987) *The Crossroads of Class and Gender: Industrial Homework, Subcontracting, and Household Dynamics in Mexico City*, Chicago, IL: University of Chicago Press.

Blumberg, R. L. (1995) 'Gender, micro-enterprise, performance and power: case studies from the Dominican Republic, Ecuador, Guatemala and Swaziland', in C. E. Bose and E. Acosta-Belen (eds), *Women in the Latin American Development Process*, Philadelphia, PA: Temple University Press.

Bolles, A. L. (1992) 'Common ground of creativity', *Cultural Survival Quarterly*, 16(4).

Brennan, D. (2002) 'Selling sex for visas: sex tourism as a stepping-stone to international migration', in B. Ehrenreich and A. Hochschild (eds), *Global Woman: Nannies, Maids and Sex Workers in the New Economy*, Dallas, TX: Metropolitan Books.

Bunster, X. and E. Chaney (1985) *Sellers and Servants: Working Women in Lima, Peru*, New York: Praeger.

Castelberg-Koulma, M. (1991) 'Greek women and tourism: women's cooperatives as an alternative form of organization', in N. Redclift and M. T. Sinclair (eds), *Working Women: International Perspectives on Labour and Gender Ideology*, London: Routledge.

Chaney, E. M. and M. Garcia Castro (1989) *Muchachas No More*, Philadelphia, PA: Temple University Press.

Clark, G. (1992) 'Flexibility equals survival', *Cultural Survivor Quarterly*, 16(4).

Collins, J. L. and M. Gimenez (eds) (1990) *Work without Wages: Comparative Studies of Domestic Labor and Self-Employment*, Albany, NY: SUNY Press.

Ecevit, Y. (1991) 'The ideological construction of Turkish women factory workers', in N. Redclift and M. T. Sinclair (eds), *Working Women: International Perspectives on Labor and Gender Ideology*, London: Routledge.

Ehrenreich, B. and A. R. Hochshild (2002) *Global Woman: Nannies, Maids and Sex Workers in the New Economy*, Dallas, TX: Metropolitan Books.

Esim, S. (1992) *Improving the Involvement of Women in the Egyptian Informal Sector*, Middle East and North Africa Country Department II, Country Operations Division, World Bank.

Freeman, C. (2001) 'Is local : global as feminine : masculine? Rethinking the gender of globalization', *Signs*, 26(4).

Hamermesh, M. (writer and director) (1985) *Maids and Madams*, Produced by C. Wargler, London: Channel 4 Television Co.

Harrison, F. (1991) 'Women in Jamaica's urban informal economy: insights from a Kingston slum', in C. T. Mohanty, A. Russo and L. Torres (eds), *Third World Women and Politics of Feminism*, Bloomington: Indiana University Press.

Kabra, K. N. (1995) 'The informal sector: a reappraisal', *Journal of Contemporary Asia*, 25(2).

Koptiuch, K. (1992) 'Informal sectorization of Egyptian petty commodity production', in F. A. Rothstein and M. L. Blim (eds), *Anthropology and the Global Factory: Studies of the New Industrialization of the Late Twentieth Century*, New York: Bergin and Garvey.

Mohiuddin, Y. (1993) 'Female-headed households and urban poverty in Pakistan', in N. Folbre, B. Bergmann, B. Agarwal and M. Floro (eds), *Women's Work in the World Economy*, New York: New York University Press.

Nash, J. (ed.) (1993) *Crafts in the World Market: The Impact of Global Exchange on Middle American Artisans*, Albany, NY: SUNY Press.

Osirim, M. J. (1996) 'The dilemmas of modern development: structural adjustment and women microentrepreneurs in Nigeria and Zimbabwe', in J. Turpin and L. A. Lorentzen (eds), *The Gendered New World Order: Militarism, Development and the Environment*, New York and London: Routledge.

Peattie, L. (1987) 'An idea in good currency and how it grew: the informal sector', *World Development*, 15(7).

Portes, A. and R. Schauffler (1993) 'Competing perspectives on the Latin American informal sector', *Population and Development Review*, 19.

Portes, A., M. Castells and L. Benton (1989) *The Informal Economy: Studies in Advanced and Less Developed Countries*, Baltimore, MD: Johns Hopkins University Press.

Rodriguez, R. M. (2009) 'Migration, transnational politics, and the state challenging the limits of the law: Filipina migrant workers, transnational struggles in the world for protection and social justice', in L. Lindio-McGovern and I. Walliman (eds), *Globalization and Third World Women: Exploitation, Coping, and Resistance*, Surrey: Ashgate.

Rothstein, F. A. (ed.) (1992) 'Women's work, women's worth: women, economics, and development', *Cultural Survival Quarterly*, 16(4).

Rowbotham, S. and S. Mitter (1994) *Dignity and Daily Bread*, London: Routledge.

Saraceno, C. (1992) 'Women's paid and unpaid work in times of economic crisis', in L. Benería and S. Feldman (eds), *Unequal Burden: Economic Crises, Persistent Poverty, and Women's Work*, Boulder, CO, and Oxford: Westview Press.

Shah, S. (2003) 'Sex work in the global economy', *New Labor Forum*, 12(1).

Stephen, L. (1992) 'Marketing ethnicity', *Cultural Survival Quarterly*, 16(4).

Trask, H. K. and M. Task (1992) 'The Aloha industry', *Cultural Survival Quarterly*, 16(4).

Truelove, C. (1990) 'Disguised industrial proletarians in rural Latin America: women's informal sector factory work and the social reproduction of coffee farm labor in Columbia', in K. Ward (ed.), *Women Workers and Global Restructuring*, Ithaca, NY: ILR Press.

Witter, M. (ed.) (1989) *Higglering/Sidewalk Vending/Informal Commercial Trading in the Jamaican Economy: Proceedings of a Symposium*, Mona, Jamaica: University of West Indies.

Women and structural adjustment

Aguilar, D. D. and A. E. Lascamana (2004) *Women and Globalization*, Amherst, NY: Humanity Books.

Aslanbeigui, N., S. Pressman and G. Summerfield (eds) (1994) *Women in the Age of Economic Transformation: Feminist Critiques of Structural Adjustment*, London and New York: Routledge.

Cornia, G., R. Jolly and F. Stewart (1987) *Adjustment with a Human Face*, Oxford and New York: Oxford University Press for UNICEF.

Deere, C. D., P. Antrobus, L. Bolles, E. Melendez, P. Philips, M. Rivera and H. Safa (1990) *In the Shadows of the Sun: Caribbean Development Alternatives and US Policy*, Boulder, CO: Westview Press.

Elson, D. (1989) 'The impact of structural adjustment on women', in B. Onimode (ed.), *The IMF, the World Bank, and African Debt*, vol. 2, London: Zed Books.

Manuh, T. (1994) 'Ghana: women in the public and informal sectors under the Economic Recovery Programme', in P. Sparr (ed.), *Mortgaging Women's Lives*, London and New York: Zed Books.

United Nations (1989) 'Women, Debt and Adjustment', *1989 World Survey on the Role of Women in Development*, New York: United Nations Press.

22 | The subordination of women and the internationalization of factory production

Diane Elson and Ruth Pearson

World market factories: the latest phase of the internationalization of capital

Since the late 1960s, a new type of wage employment has become available to women in many Third World countries: work in 'world market factories' producing manufactures exclusively for export to the rich countries (Hancock 1980).

World market factories represent a relocation of production of certain kinds of manufactured product from the developed countries, where they continue to be consumed, to the Third World.[1] The factories typically produce on subcontract to the order of a particular overseas customer, and the customer arranges the marketing of the product. The world market factory may be owned by indigenous capitalists, be a wholly owned subsidiary of its overseas customer, or be a joint venture of some kind between Third World businessman and the overseas customer (Tang 1980).

Some factories producing final consumer goods do no more than assemble parts supplied by their customers. Through the provision of material inputs, design capacity or working capital, the customer may control the production process to the extent that though the supplier has formal autonomy, in practice the customer is operating a new and more sophisticated version of the 'putting-out' system. The transfer of the goods across national boundaries, though ostensibly organized through market sales and purchases, may in substance be a transfer between two departments of an integrated production process. In some cases there is some scope for local initiative, but in general the degree of autonomy enjoyed by the factories is limited for they lack the means to develop new technologies.

Labour-force requirements

A critical factor in the location of world market factories is the availability of a suitable labour force, one which provides a ratio of output to costs of employment superior to that which prevails at existing centres of capital accumulation in the developed countries. This has been achieved by a combination of much lower costs of employment, and matching or even higher productivity than that achieved in developed countries. This is not being achieved through superior technology: it is the result of greater intensity of work, greater continuity of production; in short, greater control over the performance of the labour force.

Many Third World countries which in the past had enacted progressive labour legislation, often as a result of the contribution of trade union struggles to the fight against imperialism, have by now incorporated the official trade union organization into the state apparatus; and either suspended, or failed to enforce, major provisions of that legislation. Workers in [these] factories have been left exposed by the abrogation of their rights on such matters as minimum wage payments, contributions to insurance funds, limitations on the length of the working day and week, security of employment, redundancy conditions and payments, and the right to strike. Free Trade Zones[2] have particularly stringent controls on the activity of workers' organizations, but in some countries, particularly in South-East Asia, such controls [are nationwide] and the power of the state is used vigorously to enforce them.

The employment of women

Why is it young women who overwhelmingly constitute the labour force of world market factories? The reproduction in the factories of the sexual division of labour typical of labour-intensive assembly operations in developed countries rests upon some differentiation of the labour force which makes it more profitable to employ female rather than male labour. Female labour must either be cheaper than comparable male labour, have higher productivity, or some combination of both; the net result being that unit costs of production are lower with female [workers]. In general, the money costs of employing female labour in world market factories do seem to be lower than would be the costs of employing men but direct productivity comparisons are hard to make, since so few men are employed in comparable operations. In the few documented cases where men have been employed – in Malaysian electronics and Malawi textile factories – their productivity was lower than that of women in the same plants. Firms running world market factories seem firmly convinced that this would generally be the case.

What produces this differentiation? The answers that companies give when asked why they employ women, as well as the statements made by governments trying to attract world market factories, show that there is a widespread belief that it is a 'natural' differentiation, produced by innate capacities and personality traits of women and men, and by an objective differentiation of their income needs; men need an income to support a family, while women do not.

Women are considered not only to have naturally nimble fingers, but also to be naturally more docile and willing to accept tough work discipline, and naturally more suited to tedious, repetitive, monotonous work. Their lower wages are attributed to their secondary status in the labour market, which is seen as a natural consequence of their capacity to bear children. The fact that only young women work in world market factories is also rationalized as an effect of their capacity to bear children – they will be either unwilling or unable to continue in employment much beyond their early twenties. Indeed, the phenomenon of women leaving employment in the factory when they get married or pregnant is known as 'natural wastage', and can be highly advantageous to firms which periodically need to vary the size of their labour force to adjust to fluctuating demand for their output in the world market. There is a real differentiation between the characteristics of women and men as potential workers in world market factories [but] in our view it is far from being natural.

Where do women get their skills?

The famous 'nimble fingers' of young women are not an inheritance from their mothers, in the same way that they may inherit the colour of her skin or eyes. They are the result of the training they have received from their mothers and other female kin since early infancy in the tasks socially appropriate to woman's role. For instance, since industrial sewing of clothing resembles closely sewing with a domestic sewing machine, girls who have learnt sewing at home already have the manual dexterity and capacity for spatial assessment required. Training in needlework and sewing also produces skills transferable to other assembly operations.

It is partly because this training is socially invisible, privatized, that the skills it produces are attributable to nature and the jobs that make use of it are classified as 'unskilled' or 'semi-skilled'. Given that manual dexterity of a high order is an admitted requirement for many of the assembly jobs done by women in world market factories, and that women working in the electronics industry have to pass aptitude tests with high scores, it is clear that the categorization of these jobs as unskilled does not derive from the purely technical characteristics of the job. The fact that the training period required within the factory is short, and that once this is over workers do not take long to become highly proficient, does not detract from this conclusion. Little training and 'on the job' learning is required because the women are already trained. 'It takes six weeks to teach industrial garment making to *girls who already know how to sew*' (Sharpston 1975: 105, emphasis added).

In objective terms, it is more accurate to speak of the jobs making a demand for easily trained labour, than for unskilled labour. But of course, skill categories are not determined in a purely objective way (Braverman 1974). In particular, jobs which are identified as 'women's work' tend to be classified as 'unskilled' or 'semi-skilled', whereas technically similar jobs identified as 'men's work' tend to be classified as 'skilled' (Phillips and Taylor 1980). To a large extent, women do not do 'unskilled' jobs because they are the bearers of inferior labour; rather, the jobs they do are 'unskilled' because women enter them already determined as inferior bearers of labour.

Women's subordinaton

The social invisibility of the training that produces these skills of manual dexterity and the lack of social recognition for these skills are intrinsic to the process of gender construction in the world today. This is not only an ideological process, a matter of people ascribing lesser value to women's gender roles. It is a material process which goes on in our practices.

In claiming that it is a material process we do not intend to reduce it to an economic process, to be analysed only in terms of labour, but rather to emphasize that it cannot be changed simply through propaganda for more 'enlightened' views, but requires practical changes in daily living. We would suggest that this process of subordination of women as a gender can be understood in terms of the exclusion of women as a gender from certain activities, and their confinement to others; where the activities from which women as a gender are excluded are some of those which are constituted as public, overtly social activities, and the activities to which women as a gender are confined are some of those which are constituted as private, seemingly purely individual activities.

The constitution of activities as public or private, social or individual, of course differs over time, and between different kinds of society, and is itself a matter of struggle, not a predetermined given. Activities in which the social aspect is dominant, which are overtly represented as social, confer social power. In our view it is a mistake to see private power as co-equal with social power. Social power is collective, reproducible through social processes, relatively autonomous from the characteristics of particular individuals; private power is individual, contingent on the specific characteristics of particular individuals, reproducible only by chance.

A distinction can usefully be made between relations which are gender ascriptive – that is, relations which are constructed intrinsically in terms of the gender of the persons concerned – and relations which are not gender ascriptive, but which can nevertheless be bearers of gender (Whitehead 1979: 11). An example of the first is the conjugal relation: marriage is a relation necessarily involving the unions of persons of definite and opposite gender; unions between persons of the same gender are not marriage. An example of the second is the sexual division of labour in the capitalist labour process. Though the capital–labour relation is not gender ascriptive, it is nevertheless a bearer of gender (Phillips and Taylor 1980).

Gender-ascriptive relations are clearly the fundamental sites of the subordination of women as a gender, and in them women's subordination may take a literally patriarchal form, with women directly subject to the authority of the father, their own or their children's. But male hegemony in gender-ascriptive relations does not always assume a patriarchal form. Rather it is a matter of the extent to which women's social being can only be satisfactorily established through the mediation of a gender-ascriptive relation, whereas the same is not true for men. This kind of gender subordination is not something which an individual woman can escape by virtue of choosing to avoid certain kinds of personal relation with men. For instance, it means that the absence of a husband is as significant as his presence for the establishment of a woman's social identity.

Behind the mirage of docility

It is in the context of the subordination of women as a gender that we must analyse the supposed docility, subservience and consequent suitability for tedious, monotonous work of young men in the Third World. This is the appearance that women often present to men, particularly men in some definite relation of authority to them, such as father, husband, boss. A similar appearance, presented by colonized peoples to their colonizers, was brilliantly dissected by Fanon, who showed how the public passivity and fatalism which the colonized displayed towards the colonizers for long periods concealed an inner, private rebellion and subversion. This passivity is not a natural and original state: to achieve it requires enormous efforts of self-repression (Fanon 1969: 48).

That self-repression is required for women to achieve an adequate level of docility and subservience can be demonstrated on an everyday level by differences in their behaviour when authority figures are present and absent. An example is the behaviour observed by Heyzer (1978) in a factory producing textiles in Singapore. Here the women workers were always on guard when the supervisors were around, and displayed a characteristic subservience; in the absence of supervisors behaviour changed. Far from displaying respectful subservience, workers mocked the supervisors and ridiculed them. The stress that such self-repression can impose and the 'non-rational' forms its relief may take are exemplified in the well-documented occurrence of outbreaks of mass hysteria among young women factory workers in South-East Asia. It is interesting that governments and companies are unwilling to trust completely the personal docility of women workers, reinforcing it with suspension of a wide variety of workers' rights. In spite of being faced with extensive use of state power to control labour unions and prevent strikes, women workers have at times publicly thrown off their subservience and taken direct action.

Secondary status in the labour market

A major aspect of the gender differentiation of the labour force available for employment in world market factories is what is generally referred to in the literature as women's 'secondary status' in the labour market (Lim 1978: 11): women's rates of pay tend to be lower than those of men doing similar or comparable jobs; women form a 'reserve army' of labour, easily fired when firms want to cut back on their labour force, easily rehired when firms want to expand again. This tends to be explained in terms of 'women's role in the family' or 'women's reproductive role'. In a sense this is true, but is an ambiguous explanation, in that for many people 'women's role in the family' is an ahistorical fact, given by biology. What has to be stressed is that women's role in the family is socially constructed as a subordinated role – even if she is a 'female head of household'. For it is the female role to do the work which nurtures children and men, work which appears to be purely private and personal, while it is the male role to represent women and children in the wider society. It is the representative role which confers social power.

> This kind of gender subordination means that when a labour market develops, women, unlike men, are unable to take on fully the classic attributes of free wage labour. A man can become a free wage labourer in the double sense that as a free individual he can dispose his labour-power as his own commodity and that, on the other hand, he has no other commodity for sale ... he is free of all the objects needed for the realisation of his labour-power. (Marx 1976: 273)

A woman is never 'free' in this way. She has obligations of domestic labour, difficulties in establishing control over her own body, and an inability to be fully a member of society in her own right. She may also obtain her subsistence from men in exchange for personal services of a sexual or nurturing kind, thus realizing her labour-power outside the capitalist labour process. It is this gender difference which gives women a 'secondary status' in the labour market. Our purpose is not to deny the social reality of this secondary status. It is to take up a critical stance towards it: nature does not compel the tasks of bringing up children to be the privatized responsibility of their mother while depriving her of the social power to secure, in her own right, access to the resources required for this, forcing her into a dependent position.

This secondary status arising from women's subordination as a gender means that women workers are peculiarly vulnerable to super-exploitation, in the sense that their wages may not cover the full money costs of the reproduction of their labour-power, either on a daily or a generational basis. It means also that women tend to get lower wages than men, even when those wages contribute to the support of several other people, as do the wages of many of the young women who work in world market factories (or indeed of many women workers in developed countries). Sending a daughter to work in such a factory is in some cases the only remaining strategy for acquiring an income for the rest of the family.

The limits to liberation through factory work

Ever since large numbers of women were drawn into factory work in the Industrial Revolution in nineteenth-century England there has been a strong belief that wage work can liberate women from gender subordination. The fact that the social relations of factory work are not intrinsically gender ascriptive but rooted in an impersonal cash nexus gives some plausibility to such views. The end result would be a labour force undifferentiated by gender, with women and men doing the same jobs, in the same conditions, for the same wages, modified only by personal preferences or prejudices for this or that kind of employment or employee. There would be no objective basis for gender differentiation.

This argument fails to consider how it is that women have acquired the characteristics that make them initially the preferred labour force. If men are to compete successfully, they also need to acquire the 'nimble fingers' and 'docile dispositions' for which women are prized. For this, they would be required to undergo the same social experience as women. In order to compete successfully, men would need to experience gender subordination. But since men and women cannot both experience gender subordination simultaneously, this could happen only if women were to be freed from gender subordination; i.e. a reversal, rather than an elimination of gender differentiation. Competition between women and men in the labour market can tend to produce, in certain circumstances, signs of such a reversal (Engels 1976: 173–4), provoking the traditionalist critique of women's participation in wage work as an overturning of the natural order of things. But these signs of the reversal of gender roles are themselves a demonstration of the fundamental interdependence of the labour force characteristics of women and men. Though, as competitors in the labour market, women and men may at first appear as atomized individuals, they are never so completely separated. They are always linked through gender-ascriptive relations, and their labour market relations become bearers of gender. The important point about the development of capitalism is that it does offer a form of interdependence – the cash nexus – which is not gender ascriptive. But though capitalist production is dominated by the cash nexus, in the sense that it must be organized to make a profit, it cannot be organized solely through cash relations (through wages and prices) but requires a specific hierarchal managerial organization: the capitalist labour process. It has to be organized through the giving of orders, as well as the making of payments. Typically, [this] is defined as a male prerogative, while the role of women is defined as the carrying out of orders.

A great deal of the labour required to provide the goods and services needed for the reproduction of labour power can be socialized through the cash nexus. The monetization of labour processes formerly carried out domestically, and socialized through the gender-ascriptive relations of marriage, is one of the hallmarks of capital accumulation (Braverman 1974: ch. 13). But the establish-ment of the social identity of children, their social integration, cannot be accomplished solely through the cash nexus. One implication of this is that the de facto position of women workers as major contributors to the family income does not automatically mean that they will become socially recognized as 'breadwinners', their secondary status in the labour market ended. The position of breadwinner is not constituted purely at the economic level; it is also constituted in the process of establishing the connection of the family with the wider society. The breadwinner must be the public representative of the family. Whitehead (1978) suggests that the wage itself, though clearly not a gender-ascriptive form, tends to become a bearer of gender, in the sense that wages of male and female family members are not treated as interchangeable but are earmarked for different things.

The recognition of this limitation does not mean that we must therefore deny capitalism any liberating potential: the alternative, cash-based, forms of socialization it entails tend to undermine and disrupt other forms of socializa-tion. They provide a material basis for struggle against the subordination of women as a gender; but there is no way that capitalist exploitation of women as wage workers can simply *replace* gender subordination of women. Exploitation of women as wage workers is parasitic upon their subordination as a gender.

The dialectic of capital and gender

We would like to distinguish three tendencies in the relation between factory work and the subordination of women as a gender: a tendency to *intensify* the existing forms of gender subordination; a tendency to *decompose* existing forms of gender subordination; and a tendency to *recompose* new forms of gender subordination.

There is evidence of all three at work in the case of women employed in world market factories. One way existing forms of gender subordination may be *intensified* is the case of a multinational corporation which believes in deliberately trying to preserve and utilize traditional forms of patriarchal power.

The enhanced economic value of daughters certainly provides a motive for fathers to exert more control, including sending them to work in the factories whether they wish to or not. On the other hand, the ability to earn a wage may be an important factor in undermining certain forms of control of fathers and brothers over young women. This does not mean that there is a reversal of the authority structure of the family. There is considerable empirical evidence that their wages do not confer greater status or decision-making power on the women, even though they may be the chief source of family income.

An example of the way existing forms of gender subordination may be *decomposed* is posited in Blake's observation (1979) of the importance of factory work as a way of escaping an early arranged marriage. But the ability to resist

arranged marriage and opt for 'free-choice' marriage is two-edged. In the conditions of a society dominated by the capitalist mode of production, 'free-choice'
marriage tends to take on the characteristics of the dominant form of choice in
such societies, a *market* choice from among competing commodities. It is
women themselves who take on many of the attributes of the competing
commodities, while it is men who exercise the choice. This 'commoditized'
form of making marriages is actively encouraged by the management styles
of some of the large American multinational electronics companies, which
appeal naturally to the 'feminine interests' of the young women workers. Such
interests are indeed 'feminine' [when] many young women are competing in
a marriage market. A young woman's face may quite literally be her fortune.

Though one form of gender subordination, [that] of daughters to their
fathers, may crumble, another form, that of women employees to male factory bosses, is built up. Young female employees are almost exclusively at the
bottom of [the] hierarchy; the upper levels are almost invariably male. The
sexual element in the relation between female employee and male boss is not
contained and shaped by kin relations. This is one of the reasons why factory
girls are often regarded as not quite 'respectable'.

This *recomposition* of a new form of gender subordination can also intensify
more traditional forms of subordination of wives to husbands. The fact that,
if his wife works in a factory, she will be subject to the authority of other
men may be a powerful reason for a husband wishing to confine his wife to
the home.

Instability of employment

The problem is not simply that young women may, through factory work,
escape the domination of fathers and brothers only to become subordinate
to male managers and supervisors, or escape the domination of managers
and supervisors only to become subordinate to husbands or lovers. There is
also the problem that the domination of managers and supervisors may be
withdrawn – the woman may be sacked from her job – while the woman is
without the 'protection' of subordination to father, brother, husband.[3] She
may be left dependent on the cash nexus for survival, but unable to realize
her labour-power in cash terms through working in the factory.

This problem is particularly acute for women who work in world market
factories. The fact that the mass of capital continues to be accumulated in
developed countries means that market demand, technical know-how and
finance continue to be concentrated there, so that the factories, representing
relatively small dispersions of capital accumulation, are inherently vulnerable
to changes in the conditions of accumulation in developed countries.

The hiring and firing of particular firms add to the inherent precariousness
and instability of employment. The preference of firms for young workers

means that workers in their early twenties who have not left voluntarily are the first to be dismissed if it is necessary to retrench the labour force. Pregnancy is often grounds for dismissal, or women are dismissed on the grounds that they can no longer meet productivity or time-keeping norms. A deterioration in performance is, in fact, often the result of some disability caused by the work itself. Women employed in the garment industry on the Mexican border tend[ed] to suffer from kidney complaints and varicose veins. Women using microscopes every day in the electronics industry suffer eye-strain and their eyesight deteriorates. The shift work which is common in electronics and textile factories can produce continual fatigue, headaches and general deterioration of health. The net result is that it is quite often workers who have already acquired new consumption patterns, responsibilities and, in many cases, debts who lose their jobs, rather than those who have just entered factory life.

If a woman loses her job after she has reshaped her life on the basis of a wage income, the only way she may have of surviving is by selling her body. There are reports from South Korea that many former electronics workers have no alternative but to become prostitutes (Grossman 1979: 16). A growing market for such services is provided by the tourist industry, especially in South-East Asia.

Struggle as workers

In our view the development of world market factories provides a material basis for a process of struggle for self-determination. It does this by bringing together large numbers of women and confronting them with a common, cash-based, authority: the authority of capital. This is not the effect of most alternative forms of work for young Third World women.

The most obvious possibility for struggle which this suggests is a struggle as *workers* around such issues as wages and conditions of work. It is therefore, at first sight, disappointing to find a low level of formal participation in trade union activities by women employed in world market factories. But we need to bear in mind both the *limitations*, as well as the possibilities, of factory-based struggle about work-related issues, and the *shortcomings* of official trade union organizations in many parts of the world.

The limits within which workers in world market factories are confined are particularly narrow because of the ease with which operations might be relocated, and because the management so often enjoys the backing of particularly coercive forms of state power.

The ability to secure improvements tends to be conditioned by particular rates of accumulation at particular localities. It is noticeable that it is in countries like Hong Kong and Singapore where the rate of investment has been high that wages tended to rise. A higher proportion of married, and older, women tends to be found in the factories in these countries, symptomatic of a tighter labour market.

An important consideration is the extent to which other social groups will support workers in particular factories in campaigns for better pay and conditions of work. [But] no matter how effective and far-reaching the support given to the workforce, the struggle of better pay and conditions of work remains contradictory. To a considerable extent, the success in this struggle is predicated upon the success of management in making profits.

Struggle at the level of the factory cannot be judged solely in terms of its effect on pay and conditions of work. It has to be judged [also] as a way of developing the capacities of those involved in it, particularly the capacity for self-organization. In this context, participation in collective action in the factory itself, even of a sporadic and spontaneous character, is more important than purely formal membership of a trade union. It also helps factory workers to understand the worldwide structure of the forces which shape their lives, and helps prepare them for struggle, not just in the factory where they work, but against the economic system of which it is a part.

Struggle as women

Struggles arising from the development of world market factories will, however, remain seriously deficient from the point of view of *women* workers if they deal only with economic questions of pay and working conditions, and fail to take up other problems which stem from the recomposition of new forms of the subordination of women as a gender: how to attract a husband or lover; how to deal with the contradictions of female sexuality – to express one's sexuality without becoming a sex-object; how to cope with pregnancy and childcare (Blake 1979: 12). The concern of women workers with these problems is not a sign that they are 'backward in consciousness' as compared with male workers, but that for women, it is gender subordination which is primary, capitalist exploitation secondary and derivative.

The forms that workers' organizations have traditionally taken have been inadequate from women's point of view because they have failed to recognize and build into their structure the specificity of gender. New forms of organization are required that will specifically take up these problems, offering both practical, immediate action on them, and also revealing the social roots of what at first sight appears to be a series of individual, personal problems whose only common denominator lies in the supposed 'natural' propensities and capabilities of women as a sex.

The employment of women in world market factories does provide a material basis for 'politicizing the personal' because of the way it masses together women not simply as workers but as a gender.

A practical reality is given to the concept of women as a gender in the same way that a practical reality is given to the concept of labour in general (Marx 1973: 103–5). This creates a basis for the struggle of women factory workers

222

as members of a *gender*, as well as members of a class. Women workers in various parts of the Third World have formed sector-based organizations which link women in different factories operating in the same industry, and 'off-site' organizations to tackle issues like housing, education and sanitation, which remain the responsibility of women.

Of course, limitations and contradictions similar to those discussed in the case of activity to improve pay and working conditions in the factory beset the struggle to ameliorate other aspects of women workers' lives. Accordingly women's struggle as a gender should not be judged in purely instrumental terms. The development of conscious cooperation and solidarity between women on the basis of their common experience of gender subordination is even more important a goal than any particular improvement in the provision of jobs or welfare services to women, than any particular reform of legal status, than any particular weakening of 'machismo' or 'patriarchal attitudes'. Improvements which come about through capital accumulation or state policy or changing male attitudes can be reserved. Lasting gains depend upon the relationships built up between women themselves.

The most important task of sympathetic personnel in national and international state agencies is to work out how they can facilitate access to resources for organizations (and for activities) which are based on an explicit recognition of gender subordination and are trying to develop new forms of association through which women can begin to establish elements of a social identity in their own right, and not through the mediation of men. Such organizations do not require policy advisers to tell them what to do, supervise them and monitor them; they require protection from the almost inevitable onslaughts of those who have a vested interest in maintaining both the exploitation of women as workers, and the subordination of women as a gender.

Notes

1 The forces underlying the process of relocation are discussed in greater detail in Elson and Pearson (1980, 1981).

2 Free Trade Zones are special areas which are exempt from normal import and export regulations, and also from any other kinds of regulation, such as protective labour legislation and tax laws.

3 It may seem paradoxical to talk of the protection afforded by subordination, but the paradox lies in the social relations themselves. When the social identity of women has to be established through their relation with men, the absence of father, brother or husband is often disadvantageous.

References

Blake, M. (1979) 'Asian women in formal and non-formal sectors – review and proposals for research – education – mobilisation', Occasional Paper no. 2, United Nations Asian and Pacific Centre for Women and Development.

Braverman, H. (1974) *Labor and Monopoly Capital*, London and New York: Monthly Review Press.

Elson, D. and R. Pearson (1980) 'The latest phase of the internationalisation of capital and its implications for women in the Third World', Discussion Paper no. 150, Institute of Development Studies, University of Sussex.

— (1981) 'Nimble fingers make changed

workers: an analysis of women's employment in Third World export manufacturing', *Feminist Review*, 7.

Engels, F. (1976) *The Condition of the Working Class in England*, St Albans: Panther.

Fanon, F. (1969) *The Wretched of the Earth*, Harmondsworth: Penguin.

Grossman, R. (1979) 'Women's place in the integrated circuit', *Southeast Asia Chronicle*, 66, joint issue with *Pacific Research*, 9(5/6).

Hancock, M. A. (1980) 'Women and transnational corporations: a bibliography', Working Paper for the East–West Culture Learning Centre, Honolulu.

Heyzer, N. (1978) 'Young women and migrant workers in Singapore's labour intensive industries', Paper presented to Conference 133 on the Continuing Subordination of Women in the Development Process, Institute of Development Studies, University of Sussex.

Lim, L. (1978) 'Women workers in multinational corporations in developing countries – the case of the electronics industry in Malaysia and Singapore',

Women's Studies Program Occasional Paper no. 9, University of Michigan.

Marx, K. (1973) *Grundrisse*, Harmondsworth: Penguin.

— (1976) *Capital*, vol. 1, Harmondsworth: Penguin.

Phillips, A. and B. Taylor (1980) 'Sex and skill. Notes towards a feminist economics', *Feminist Review*, 6.

Sharpston, M. (1975) 'International subcontracting', *Oxford Economic Papers*, March.

Tang, S. L. (1980) 'Global reach and its limits: women workers and their responses to work in a multinational electronics plant', Mimeo, Department of Sociology, Chinese University of Hong Kong.

Whitehead, A. (1978) 'The intervention of capital in rural production systems: some aspects of the household', Paper presented at Conference 133 on the Continuing Subordination of Women in the Development Process, Institute of Development Studies, University of Sussex.

— (1979) 'Some preliminary notes on the subordination of women', *IDS Bulletin*, 10(3).

23 | *Maquiladoras*: the view from the inside

María Patricia Fernández-Kelly

Along the Mexican side of the United States–Mexico border, there has been a huge expansion of manufacturing activities by multinational corporations. This has incorporated large numbers of women into direct production in the last fifteen years. As a result of implementation of the Border Industrialization Program since 1965, more than one hundred assembly plants, or *maquiladoras*, have sprung up in Ciudad Juarez, across the border from El Paso, Texas. This set of programmes has made it possible for multinational firms to collaborate with Mexican state and private enterprise to foster the emergence of a booming export industry along the border. More than half of the plants are electric or electronic firms. Most of the rest are apparel assembly plants (see Newton and Balli 1979).

The importance of the programme in recent years may be appreciated by noting that *maquiladoras* account for about half of US imports from underdeveloped countries under assembly-industry tariff provisions, as compared with only 10 per cent in 1970. The objective circumstances that have determined the growth of the *maquiladora* industry are the availability of what appears to be an inexhaustible supply of unskilled and semi-skilled labour, and extremely high levels of productivity.

The plants themselves are small, and most subcontract from corporations with their headquarters in the United States. Although nationally recognized brands are represented in Ciudad Juarez, the vast majority of these industries are associated with corporations that have regional rather than national visibility. The low level of capital investment in the physical plant often results in inadequate equipment and unpleasant working conditions.

While all *maquiladoras* employ an overwhelming majority (85 per cent) of women, the apparel industry hires women whose position in the city makes them especially vulnerable to exploitative labour practices. They tend to be in their mid-twenties, poorly educated and recent migrants to Ciudad Juarez. About one third of the women head households and are the sole supports of their children.

Looking for a job: a personal account

What is it like to be female, single and eager to find work at a *maquiladora*? Shortly after arriving in Ciudad Juarez, and after finding stable lodging, I began looking through the pages of newspapers, hoping to find a want ad. My intent was to merge with the clearly visible mass of women who roam the streets and industrial parks of the city searching for jobs.

My objectives were straightforward. I wanted to spend four to six weeks applying for jobs and obtaining direct experience of the employment policies, recruitment strategies and screening mechanisms used by companies to hire assembly workers. I was especially interested in how much time and money an individual worker spent trying to get a job. I also wanted to spend an equal amount of time working at a plant, preferably one that manufactured apparel. This way, I expected to learn more about working conditions, production quotas and wages at a particular factory. I felt this would help me develop questions from a worker's perspective.

In retrospect, it seems odd that it never entered my head that I might not find a job. Finding a job at a *maquiladora* is easier said than done, especially for a woman over twenty-five. This is due primarily to the large numbers competing for jobs. At every step of their constant peregrination, women are confronted by a familiar sign at the plants – 'no applications available' – or by the negative responses of a guard or a secretary at the entrance to the factories. But such is the arrogance of the uninformed researcher, I went about the business of looking for a job as if the social milieu had to conform to my research needs.

By using newspapers as a source of information, I was departing from the common strategy of potential workers in that environment. Most women are part of informal networks which include relatives, friends and an occasional acquaintance in the personnel-management sector. They hear of jobs by word of mouth.

Most job seekers believe that a personal recommendation from someone already employed at a *maquiladora* can ease the difficult path. This belief is well founded. At many plants, managers prefer to hire applicants by direct recommendation of employees who have proved to be dependable and hard working. By resorting to the personal link, managers decrease the dangers of having their factories infiltrated by unreliable workers, independent organizers and 'troublemakers'.

Appearing to take a personal interest in the individual worker at the moment of hiring, management can establish a paternalistic claim on the worker. Workers complain that superintendents and managers are prone to demand 'special services', like overtime, in exchange for granting personal 'favours' such as a loan or time off from work to care for children. Yet workers acknowledge a personal debt to the person who hired them. A woman's commitment to the firm is fused with commitment to the particular personnel manager or superintendent who granted her the 'personal favour' of hiring her. Anita expressed the typical sentiment: 'If the group leader demands more production [without additional pay], I will generally resist because I owe her nothing. But if the *ingeniero* asks me to increase my quota on occasion, I comply. He gave me the job in the first place! Besides, it makes me feel good to know that I can return the favour, at least in part.'

One firm advertised for direct production workers in the two main Juarez newspapers throughout the year, an indication of its high rate of turnover. I went into its tiny office in the middle of summer to apply for a job. As I entered, I wondered whether my appearance or accent would make the personnel manager suspicious. He looked me over sternly and told me to fill out a form [there and then] and to return the following morning to take a dexterity test. Most of the items were straightforward: name, age, marital status, place of birth, length of residence in Ciudad Juarez, property assets, previous jobs and income, number of pregnancies and general state of health. One, however, was unexpected: what is your major aspiration in life? All my doubts surfaced – would years of penmanship practice at a private school in Mexico City and flawless spelling give me away?

I assumed the on-the-job test would consist of a short evaluation of my skills as a seamstress. I was wrong. The next morning I knocked at the door of the personnel office where I filled out the application, but no one was there. In some confusion, I peeked into the entrance of the factory. The supervisor, Margarita, a dark-haired woman wearing false eyelashes, ordered me in and led me to my place at an industrial sewing machine. That it was old it was plain to see; how it worked was difficult to judge. I listened intently to Margarita's instructions. I was expected to sew patch pockets on what were to become blue jeans from the assortment of diversely cut denim parts on my left. Obediently, I started to sew.

The particulars of 'unskilled' labour unfolded before my eyes. The procedure demanded perfect coordination of hands, eyes and legs. I was to use my left hand to select the larger part of material from the batch next to me and my right to grab the pocket. Experienced workers did it on a purely visual basis. Once the patch pocket was in place, I was to guide the two parts under a double needle while applying pressure on the machine's pedal with my right foot.

Because the pockets were sewn on with thread of a contrasting colour, the edge of the pocket had to be perfectly aligned with the needles to produce a regular seam and an attractive design. Because the pocket was diamond shaped, I also had to rotate the materials slightly three times while adjusting pressure on the pedal. Too much pressure inevitably broke the thread or produced seams longer than the edge of the pocket. The slightest deviation produced lopsided designs, which then had to be unsewn and gone over as many times as it took to do an acceptable pocket. The supervisor told me that, once trained, I would be expected to sew a pocket every nine to ten seconds. That meant 360 to 396 pockets every hour, or 2,880 to 3,168 every day!

As at the vast majority of apparel-manufacturing *maquiladoras*, I would be paid through a combination of the minimum wage and piecework. In 1978 this was 125 pesos a day, or US$5. I would, however, get a slight bonus if I sustained a calculated production quota through the week. Workers are not allowed to produce less than 80 per cent of their assigned quota without being admonished, and a worker seriously endangers her job when unable to improve her level of output. Margarita [indicated] a small blackboard showing the weekly bonus received by those able to produce certain percentages of the quota. They fluctuated around 50 pesos (US$2.20) for those who completed 100 per cent. Managers call this combination of steep production quotas, minimum wages and modest bonuses an 'incentive programme'.

I started my test at 7.30 a.m. with a sense of embarrassment about my limited skills and disbelief at the speed with which the women in the factory worked. As I continued sewing, the bundle of material on my left was renewed and slowly grew in size. I had to repeat the operation many times before the product was considered acceptable. I soon realized I was being treated as a new worker while presumably being tested. I had not been issued with a contract and therefore was not yet incorporated into the Instituto Mexicano del Seguro Social (the national social security system), nor had I been told about working hours, benefits or system of payment.

I explained to the supervisor that I had recently arrived in the city, alone, and with very little money. Would I be hired? When would I be given a contract? Margarita listened patiently while helping me unsew one of my many defective pockets and then said, 'You are too curious. Don't worry about it. Do your job and things will be all right.' I continued to sew, aware of the fact that every pocket attached during the 'test' was becoming part of the plant's total production.

At 12.30, during the thirty-minute lunch break, I had a better chance to see the factory. Its improvised quality was underscored by the metal folding chairs at the sewing machines. I had been sitting on one of them during the whole morning, but until then I had not noticed that most of them had the Coca-Cola label painted on their backs. I had seen this kind of chair many times in casual parties both in Mexico and in the United States. Had they been bought, or were they being rented? In any event, they were not designed to meet the strenuous requirements of sewing all day. Women bought their own colourful pillows to ease the stress on their buttocks and spines. Later, I was to discover that chronic lumbago is a frequent condition among factory seamstresses (Fernández 1978).

My questions were still unanswered at 5 p.m. when a bell rang to signal the end of my shift. I went to the personnel office intending to get more information. Despite my overly shy approach to the personnel manager, his reaction was hostile. Even before he was able to turn the disapproving expression on his face into words, Margarita intervened. She was angry. To the manager she said, 'This woman has too many questions: will she be hired? Is she going to be insured?' And then to me, 'I told you already, we do piecework here; if you do your job, you get a wage; otherwise you don't. That's clear, isn't it? What else do you want? You should be grateful! This plant is giving you a chance to work! What else do you want? Come back tomorrow and be punctual.'

I finally got a job at a new *maquiladora* that was adding an evening shift. I saw its advertisement in the daily newspapers and went early the following morning to apply at the factory, which is located in the modern Parque Industrial Bemudez. Thirty-seven women preceded me. Some had arrived as early as 6 a.m. At ten, the door that separated the front lawn from the entrance had not yet been opened, although a guard appeared once in a while to peek at the growing contingent of applicants. At 10.30 he opened the door to tell us that only those having personal recommendation letters would be permitted inside. This was the first in a series of formal and informal screening procedures used to reduce the number of potential workers. Thirteen women left immediately. Others tried to convince the guard that, although they had no personal recommendation, they knew someone already employed at the factory.

One by one we were shown into the office of the personnel manager, where we were to take a manual dexterity test. Later on, we were given the familiar application form. Demonstrating sewing skills on an industrial machine followed. At 3.30 p.m., seven hours after we arrived at the plant, we were dismissed with no indication that any of us would be hired. A telegram would be sent to each address as soon as a decision was made. Most women left disappointed and certain that they would not be hired. Two weeks later, when I had almost given up all hope, the telegram arrived. I was to come to the plant as soon as possible to receive further instructions.

Upon my arrival I was given the address of a small clinic downtown. I was to bring two pictures to the clinic and take a medical examination. Its explicit purpose was to evaluate the physical fitness of potential workers. In reality, it was a pregnancy test. *Maquiladoras* do not hire pregnant women in spite of their greater need for employment. During the first years of its existence, many pregnant women sought employment in the *maquiladora* programme knowing they would be entitled to an eighty-two-day pregnancy leave with full pay. Some women circumvented the restrictions on employing pregnant women by bringing urine specimens of friends or relatives to the clinic. Plant managers now insist on more careful examinations, but undetected pregnant women sometimes get hired. The larger and more stable plants generally comply with the law and give maternity leave, but in small subcontracted firms women are often fired as soon as the manager discovers they are pregnant.

After my exam at the clinic, I returned to the factory with a sealed envelope containing certification of my physical capacity to work. I was told to return the following Monday at 3.30 p.m. to start work. After what seemed like an unduly long and complicated procedure, I was finally hired as an assembly worker. For the next six weeks, I shared the experience of approximately eighty women who had also been recruited to work the evening shift.

Working at the *maquiladora*

The weekday evening shift began at 3.25 and ended at 11.30 p.m. A bell rang at 7.30 to signal the beginning of a half-hour dinner break. Some women brought sandwiches from home, but most bought a dish of *flautas* or *tostadas* and a carbonated drink at the factory. On Saturdays the shift started at 11.30 a.m. and ended at 9.30 p.m., with a half-hour break. We worked, in total, forty-eight hours every week for the minimum wage, an hourly rate of about US$0.60.

Although wages are low in comparison to those of the USA for similar jobs, migrants flock to Zone 09, which includes Ciudad Juarez, because it has nearly the highest minimum wage in the country (only Zone 01, where Baja California is located, has a higher rate). Legally, *maquiladoras* are also required to enrol their workers in the social-security system and in the national housing programme (Instituto Nacional a la Vivienda). As a result, investment per work hour reached US$1.22 in 1978. For women who have children, the medical insurance is often as important as the wage.

Newcomers receive the minimum wage but are expected to fulfil production quotas. My new job was to sew a narrow bias around the cuff opening of men's shirts. My quota of 162 pairs of sleeves every hour meant one every 2.7 seconds. After six weeks as a direct production operator, I still fell short of this goal by almost 50 per cent.

Sandra, who sat next to me during this period, assured me that it could be done. She had worked at various *maquiladoras* for the last seven years. Every time she got too tired, she left the job, rested for a while, then sought another. She was a speedy seamstress who acted with the self-assurance of one who is well acquainted with factory work. It was difficult not to admire her skill and aloofness, especially when I was being continuously vexed by my own incompetence.

One evening Sandra told me that she thought my complaints and manner of speech were funny and, at the end of what turned out to be a lively conversation, admitted to liking me. I was flattered. Then she stared at my old jeans and ripped blouse with an appraising look and said, 'Listen, Patricia, as soon as we get our wage, I want to take you to buy some decent clothes. You look awful! And you need a haircut.' So much for the arrogance of the researcher who wondered whether her class background would be detected. Sandra became my most important link with the experience of *maquiladora* work.

Sandra lived with her parents in *las lomas* on the outskirts of the city. The area was rugged and distant, but the house itself indicated modest prosperity. There were four ample rooms, one of which was carpeted. The living-room walls were covered with family photographs. There were an American television and comfortable chairs. There were two sinks in the kitchen as well as a refrigerator, blender, beater and new American-made washing machine (waiting until the area got its hoped-for running water). Sandra's father was a butcher who had held his job at a popular market for many years. Although in the past, when his three daughters were small, it had been difficult to stay out of debt, better times were at hand. He had only two regrets: his failing health and Sandra's divorce. He felt both matters were beyond his control. He considered Sandra a good daughter because she never failed to contribute to household expenses and because she was also saving so she could support her two children, who were currently living with her former husband. Sandra had left him after he beat her for taking a job outside the home.

Even with Sandra's help, I found the demands of the factory overwhelming. Young supervisors walked about the aisles calling for higher productivity and greater speed. Periodically, their voices could be heard throughout the workplace: 'Faster! Faster! Come on, girls, let's hear the sound of those machines!'

My supervisor, Esther, quit her job as a nurse for the higher wages as a factory worker because she had to support an ill and ageing father after her mother's death three years earlier. Although her home was nice and fully owned, she was solely responsible for the remaining family debts. She earned almost one thousand pesos a week in the factory, roughly twice her income as a nurse.

The supervisor's role is a difficult one. Esther, like the other supervisors, often stayed at the plant after the workers left, sometimes until one in the morning. She would verify quotas and inspect all garments for defects, some of which she restitched. She would also prepare shipments and select materials for the following day's production. Managers held supervisors directly responsible for productivity levels as well as for workers' punctuality and attendance, putting the supervisors between the devil and the deep blue sea. Workers frequently believed that supervisors were the ones responsible for their plight at the workplace and regarded abuse, unfair treatment and excessive demands from them as whims. But while workers saw supervisors as close allies of the firm, management directed its dissatisfaction with workers at the supervisors. Many line supervisors agreed that the complications they faced on their jobs were hardly worth the extra pay.

Although my supervisor, Esther, was considerate and encouraging, she still asked me to repair my defective work. I began to skip dinner breaks to continue sewing in a feeble attempt to improve my productivity level. I was not alone. Some workers, fearful of permanent dismissal, also stayed at their sewing machines while the rest went outside to eat and relax.

I could understand their behaviour; their jobs were at stake. But presumably my situation was different. I had nothing to lose by inefficiency, and yet I was compelled to do my best. I started pondering upon the subtle mechanisms that dominate will at the workplace, and about the shame that overwhelms those who fall short of the goals assigned to them. As the days passed, it became increasingly difficult for me to think of factory work as a stage in a research project. My identity became that of a worker; my immediate objectives, those determined by the organization of labour at the plant. I became one link in a rigidly structured chain. My failure to produce speedily had consequences for others operating in the same line. For example, Lucha, my nineteen-year-old companion, cut remnant thread and separated the sleeves that five other seamstresses and I sewed. Since she could only meet her quota if we met ours, Lucha was extremely interested in seeing improvements in my level of productivity and in the quality of my work. Sometimes her attitude and exhortations verged on the hostile. As far as I was concerned, the accusatory expression on her face was the best work incentive yet devised by the factory. I was not surprised to find out during the weeks I spent there that the germ of enmity had bloomed between some seamstresses and their respective thread cutters over matters of work.

Although [this] relationship was especially delicate, all workers were affected by each other's level of efficiency. Cuffless sleeves could not be attached to shirts, nor could sleeves be sewed to shirts without collars or pockets. Holes and buttons had to be fixed at the end. Unfinished garments could not be cleaned of lint or labelled. In sum, each minute step required a series of preceding operations completed effectively. Delay of one stage inevitably slowed up the whole process.

From the perspective of the workers, the work appeared as interconnected individual activities rather than as an imposed structure. Managers were nearly invisible, but the flaws of fellow workers were always present. Bonuses became personal rewards made inaccessible by a neighbour's laziness or incompetence. One consequence of these perceptions was that workers frequently directed complaints against other workers and supervisors. In short, the organization of labour at any particular plant does not automatically lead to feelings of solidarity.

On the other hand, the tensions did not inhibit talk, and the women's shared experiences, especially about longings for relief from the tediousness of industrial work, gave rise to an ongoing humorous dialogue. Sandra often reflected in a witty and self-deprecatory manner on the possibility of marriage to a rich man. She thought that if she could only find a nice man who would be willing to support her, everything in her life would be all right. She did not mind if he was not young or good looking, as long as he had plenty of money. Were there men like that left in the world? Of course, with the children it was difficult, not to say impossible, to find a godsend. Then again, no one kept you from trying. But not at the *maquiladora*. Everyone was female. One could die of boredom there.

Sandra knew many women who had been seduced and then deserted by engineers and technicians. Other women felt they had to comply with the sexual demands of fellow workers because they believed otherwise they would lose their jobs. Some were just plain stupid. Things were especially difficult for very young women at large electronic plants. They needed guidance and information to stay out of trouble, but there was no one to advise them. During the first years of the *maquiladora* programme, sexual harassment was especially blatant. There were *ingenieros* who insisted on having only the prettiest workers under their command. They developed a sort of factory 'harem'. Sandra knew of a man – 'Would you believe this?' – who wanted as much female diversity as possible. All of the women on his crew, at his request, had eyes and hair of a different colour. Another man boasted that every woman on his line had borne him a child. She told me about the scandals, widely covered by the city tabloids, about the spread of venereal disease in certain *maquiladoras*. Although Sandra felt she knew how to take care of herself, she still thought it better to have only female fellow workers. The factory was not a good place to meet men.

Fortunately, there were the bars and the discotheques. Did I like to go out dancing? She did not think I looked like the type who would. But it was great fun. Eventually Sandra and I went to a popular disco, the Cosmos, which even attracted people from 'the other side' (the USA), who came to Juarez just to visit the disco. It had an outer-space decor, full of colour and movement, and played the best American disco music. If you were lucky, you could meet a US citizen. Maybe he would even want to get married, and you could go and live in El Paso. Things like that happen at discotheques. Once a Jordanian soldier in service at Fort Bliss asked Sandra to marry him the first time they had met at Cosmos. But he wanted to return to his country, and she had said no. Cosmos was definitely the best discotheque in Juarez, and Sandra could be found dancing there amid the deafening sound of music every Saturday evening.

The inexhaustible level of energy of women working at the *maquiladoras* never ceased to impress me. How could anyone be in the mood for all-night dancing on Saturdays after forty-eight weekly hours of industrial work? I had seen many of these women stretching their muscles late at night, trying to soothe the pain they felt at the wrist. After the incessant noise of the sewing machines how could anyone long for even higher levels of sound? But as Sandra explained to me, life is too short. If you don't go out and have fun, you will come to the end of your days having done nothing but sleep, eat and work. And she didn't call that living. Besides, where else would you be able to meet a man?

Ah, men! They were often unreliable, mean or just plain lazy (wasn't that obvious from the enormous number of women who had to do factory work in Ciudad Juarez?), but no one wanted to live alone. There must be someone out there worth living for – at least someone who did not try to put you down or slap you. Sandra could not understand why life had become so difficult. Her mother and father had stayed married for thirty years and they still liked each other. There had been some difficult times in the past, but they had always had each other. She knew a lot of older folks who were in the same situation. But it was different for modern couples.

At 11.15, Sandra's talks about men stopped, and we prepared to go home. We cleaned up our work area and made sure we took the two spools and a pair of scissors we were responsible for home with us to prevent their being stolen by workers the following morning. As soon as the bell rang at 11.30, we began a disorderly race to be the first to check out our time cards. Then we had to stand in line with our purses wide open so the guard could check our belongings. Women vehemently resented management's suspicion that workers would steal material or the finished products. The nightly search was an unnecessary humiliation of being treated as thieves until proved innocent by the guard.

Once outside the factory, we walked in a group across the park to catch our bus. There was a lot of laughing and screaming, as well as teasing and exchanging of vulgarities. Most of the time we could board an almost-empty bus as soon as we reached the main avenue. Sometimes, when we had to wait, we became impatient. In jest, a woman would push another worker towards the street, suggesting provocative poses for her to use to attract a passer-by to offer a ride. When a car did stop, however, they quickly moved away. To joke was one thing, but to accept a ride from a man, especially late at night, was to look for trouble.

Individually, the factory women appeared vulnerable, even shy, but as a group, they could be a formidable sight. One night a man boarded the bus when we were already in it. His presence gave focus to the high spirits. Women immediately subjected him to verbal attacks similar to those they often received from men. Feeling protected by anonymity and by their numerical strength, they chided and teased him; they offered kisses and asked for a smile. They exchanged laughing comments about his physical attributes and suggested a raffle to see who would keep him. The man remained silent through it all. He adopted the outraged and embarrassed expression that women often wear when they feel victimized by men. The stares of whistling women followed him as he left the bus.

Although I saw only one such incident, I was told that it was not uncommon. 'It is pitiful,' a male acquaintance told me; 'those girls have no idea of what proper feminine behaviour is.' He told me he had seen women even paw or pinch men while travelling in buses and *ruteras*. According to him, factory work was to blame: 'Since women started working at the *maquiladoras*, they have lost all sense of decorum.' The women see it as a harmless game fostered by the temporary sense of membership in a group. As Sandra liked to remind me, 'Factory work is harder than most people know. As long as you don't harm anybody, what's wrong with having a little fun?'

Conclusions

Textile and garment manufacturing are, of course, as old as factories themselves, but *maquiladoras* epitomize the most distinctive traits of the modern system of production. They are part of a centralized global arrangement in which central economies such as [that of] the USA have become the locus of technological expertise and major financial outflows, while Third World countries increase their participation in the international market via the manufacture of exportable goods.

This global system of production has had unprecedented political and economic consequences. For example, the fragmentation of labour processes has reduced the level of skill required to perform the majority of assembly operations required to manufacture even the most complex and sophisticated electronics products. In turn, the geographical dispersion of production has curtailed the bargaining ability of workers of many nationalities vis-à-vis large corporations. At times, workers in Asia, Latin America and the Caribbean seem to be thrust into competition against one another for access to low-paying, monotonous jobs. Labour unions and strikes have limited potential in a world where factories can be transferred at ease to still another country where incentives are more favourable and wages cheaper.

It is evident from the testimony of workers that women seek *maquiladora* jobs compelled by their need to support families whether they be formed by parents and siblings or by their own children. Male unemployment and under-employment play an important part in this. Multinationals tend to relocate assembly operations to areas of the world where jobless people automatically provide an abundant supply of cheap labour. Sandra's longing for male economic support and regrets over the irresponsibility of men represent a personal counterpoint to a structural reality where men are unable to find remunerative jobs while women are forced, out of need, to join the ranks of the industrial labour force.

The same testimony demonstrates that *maquila* women would prefer to withdraw from the exhausting jobs available to them and give full attention to home and children. Husbands and fathers frequently press women to leave their jobs to adjust to a conventional understanding of what gender roles should be. Nevertheless, when women retire from wage labour to become housewives and mothers, they often face dire alternatives. Later, they may have to seek new forms of employment because of the inability of their men to provide adequately for their families. Older and with children to provide for, they then face special constraints in a labour market that favours very young, single, childless women. The life profile of *maquiladora* women is a saga of downward mobility, a fate contrary to the optimistic expectations of industrial promoters.

The segregation of the labour market on the basis of sex tends to weaken the bargaining position of both men and women as wage earners. But perhaps more important is the observation that the same segregation produces a clash between ideological notions about the role of women and their actual transformation into primary wage earners. This has given rise to tensions perceived both at the household and community levels. *Maquiladora* workers have become notorious in that they challenge conventional mores and values regarding femininity. Concerns about young women's morality, virtue and sexual purity are, in part, reflections of widespread anxiety and fear that, as a result of wage earning, women may end up subverting the established order. *Maquiladora* workers may see their riotous behaviour towards a man in a bus as an innocuous diversion. Others, however, see it as a clear sign that women are losing respect for patriarchy.

Maquiladoras are hardly a mechanism for upward mobility, hardly the bold entrance to middle-class respectability, hardly the key to individual economic autonomy. All these are issues that should be of concern to government officials and social planners. Yet, while *maquiladoras* have taken advantage of women's vulnerability in the job market, they have also provided a forum where new forms of consciousness and new challenges are present. For young *maquila* workers who are living with parents and siblings and have few or no children of their own, wage labour offers the cherished possibility of retaining at least part of their income for discretionary purposes.

References

Fernández, M. P. (1978) 'Notes from the field', Mimeo, Ciudad Juarez, Mexico.

Newton, J. R. and F. Balli (1979) 'Mexican in-bond industry', Paper presented to the Seminar on North–South Complementary Intra-industry Trade, UNCTAD United Nations Conference, Mexico, DF.

24 | Global women

Barbara Ehrenreich and Arlie Russell
Hochschild

'Whose baby are you?' Josephine Perera, a nanny from Sri Lanka, asks Isadora, her pudgy two-year-old charge in Athens, Greece.

Thoughtful for a moment, the child glances toward the closed door of the next room, in which her mother is working, as if to say, 'That's my mother in there.'

'No, you're *my* baby,' Josephine teases, tickling Isadora lightly. Then, to settle the issue, Isadora answers, 'Together!' She has two mommies – her mother and Josephine. And surely a child loved by many adults is richly blessed.

In some ways, Josephine's story – which unfolds in an extraordinary documentary film, *When Mother Comes Home for Christmas*, directed by Nilita Vachani – describes an unparalleled success. Josephine has ventured around the world, achieving a degree of independence her mother could not have imagined, and amply supporting her three children with no help from her ex-husband, their father. Each month, she mails a remittance check from Athens to Hatton, Sri Lanka, to pay the children's living expenses and school fees. On her Christmas visit home, she bears gifts of pots, pans and dishes. While she makes payments on a new bus that Suresh, her oldest son, now drives for a living, she is also saving a modest dowry for her daughter, Norma. She dreams of buying a new house in which the whole family can live. In the meantime, her work as a nanny enables Isadora's parents to devote themselves to their careers and avocations.

But Josephine's story is also one of wrenching global inequality. While Isadora enjoys the attention of three adults, Josephine's three children in Sri Lanka have been far less lucky. According to Vachani, Josephine's youngest child, Suminda, was two – Isadora's age – when his mother first left home to work in Saudi Arabia. Her middle child, Norma, was nine, her oldest son, Suresh, thirteen. From Saudi Arabia, Josephine found her way first to Kuwait, then to Greece. Except for one two-month trip home, she has lived apart from her children for ten years. She writes them weekly letters, seeking news of relatives, asking about school, and complaining that Norma doesn't write back.

Although Josephine left the children under her sister's supervision, the two youngest have shown signs of real distress. Norma has attempted suicide three times. Suminda, who was twelve when the film was made, boards in a grim, Dickensian orphanage that forbids talk during meals and showers. He visits his aunt on holidays. Although the oldest, Suresh, seems to be on good terms with his mother, Norma is tearful and sullen, and Suminda does poorly in school, picks quarrels, and otherwise seems withdrawn from the world. Still, at the end of the film, we see Josephine once again leave her three children in Sri Lanka to return to Isadora in Athens. For Josephine can either live with her children in desperate poverty or make money by living apart from them. Unlike her affluent First World employers, she cannot both live with her family and support it.

Thanks to the process we loosely call 'globalization,' women are on the move as never before in history. In images familiar to the West from television commercials for credit cards, cell phones, and airlines, female executives jet about the world, phoning home from luxury hotels and reuniting with eager children in airports. But we hear much less about a far more prodigious flow of female labor and energy: the increasing migration of millions of women from poor countries to rich ones, where they serve as nannies, maids, and sometimes sex workers. In the absence of help from male partners, many women have succeeded in tough 'male world' careers only by turning over the care of their children, elderly parents, and homes to women from the Third World. This is the female underside of globalization, whereby millions of Josephines from poor countries in the South migrate to do the 'women's work' of the North – work that affluent women are no longer able or willing to do. These migrant workers often leave their own children in the care of grandmothers, sisters, and sisters-in-law. Sometimes a young daughter is drawn out of school to care for her younger siblings.

This pattern of female negotiation reflects what could be called a worldwide gender revolution. In both rich and poor countries, fewer families can rely solely on a male breadwinner. In the United States, the earning power of most men has declined since 1970, and many women have gone out to 'make up the difference.' By one recent estimate, women were the sole, primary, or coequal earners in more than half of American families. So the question arises: Who will take care of the children, the sick, the elderly? Who will make dinner and clean the house?

While the European or American woman commutes to work an average twenty-eight minutes a day, many nannies from the Philippines, Sri Lanka, and India cross the globe to get to their jobs. Some female migrants from the Third World do find something like 'liberation,' or at least the chance to become independent breadwinners and to improve their children's material lives. Other, less fortunate migrant women end up in the control of criminal employers – their passports stolen, their mobility blocked, forced to work without pay in brothels or to provide sex along with cleaning and childcare services in affluent homes. But in even more typical cases, where benign employers pay wages on time, Third World migrant women achieve their success only by assuming the cast-off domestic roles of middle- and high-income women in the First World – roles that have been previously rejected, of course, by men. And their 'commute' entails a cost we have yet to fully comprehend.

The migration of women from the Third World to do 'women's work' in affluent countries has so far received little scholarly or media attention – for reasons that are easy enough to guess. First, many, though by no means all, of the new female migrant workers are women of color, and therefore subject to the racial 'discounting' routinely experienced by, say, Algerians in France, Mexicans in the United States, and Asians in the United Kingdom. Add to racism the private 'indoor' nature of so much of the new migrants' work. Unlike factory workers, who congregate in large numbers, or taxi drivers, who are visible on the street, nannies and maids are often hidden away, one or two at a time, behind closed doors in private homes. Because of the illegal nature of their work, most sex workers are even further concealed from public view.

At least in the case of nannies and maids, another factor contributes to the invisibility of migrant workers and their work – one that, for their affluent employers, touches closer to home. The Western culture of individualism, which finds extreme expression in the United States, militates against acknowledging help or human interdependency of nearly any kind. Thus, in the time-pressed upper middle class, servants are no longer displayed as status symbols, decked out in white caps and aprons, but often remain in the background, or disappear when company comes. Furthermore, affluent career women increasingly earn their status not through leisure, as they might have a century ago, but by apparently 'doing it all' – producing a full-time career, thriving children, a contented spouse, and a well-managed home. In order to preserve this illusion, domestic workers and nannies make the house hotel-room perfect, feed and bathe the children, cook and clean up – and then magically fade from sight.

The lifestyles of the First World are made possible by a global transfer of the services associated with a wife's traditional role – childcare, homemaking, and sex – from poor countries to rich ones. To generalize and perhaps oversimplify: in an earlier phase of imperialism, Northern countries extracted natural resources and agricultural products – rubber, metals, and sugar, for example – from lands they conquered and colonized. Today, while still relying on the Third World countries for agricultural and industrial labor, the wealthy countries also seek to extract something harder to measure and quantify, something that can look very much like love. Nannies like Josephine bring the distant families that employ them real maternal affection, no doubt enhanced by the heartbreaking absence of their own children in the poor countries they leave behind. Similarly women who migrate from country to country to work as maids bring not only their muscle power but an attentiveness to detail and to the human relationships in the household that might otherwise have been invested in their own families. Sex workers offer the simulation of sexual and romantic love, or at least transient sexual companionship. It is as if the wealthy parts of the world are running short on precious emotional and sexual resources and have had to turn to poorer regions for fresh supplies.

There are plenty of historical precedents for this globalization of traditional female services. In the ancient Middle East, the women of populations defeated in war were routinely enslaved and hauled off to serve as household workers and concubines for the victors. Among the Africans brought to North America as slaves in the sixteenth through nineteenth centuries, about a third were women and children, and many of those women were pressed to be concubines, domestic servants, or both. Nineteenth-century Irishwomen – along with many rural Englishwomen – migrated to English towns and cities to work as domestics in the homes of the growing upper middle class. Services thought to be innately feminine – childcare, housework, and sex – often win little recognition or pay. But they have always been sufficiently in demand to transport over long distances if necessary. What is new today is the sheer number of female migrants and the very long distances they travel. Immigration statistics show huge numbers of women in motion, typically from poor countries to rich. Although the gross statistics give little clue as to the jobs women eventually take, there are reasons to infer that much of their work is 'caring work,' performed either in private homes or in institutional settings such as hospitals, hospices, childcare centers, and nursing homes [...]

Most women, like men, migrate from the South to the North and from poor countries to rich ones. Typically, migrants go to the nearest comparatively rich country, preferably one whose language they speak or whose religion and culture they share. There are also local migratory flows: from northern to southern Thailand, for instance, or from East Germany to West. But of the regional or cross-regional flows, four stand out. One goes from Southeast Asia to the oil-rich Middle and Far East – from Bangladesh, Indonesia, the Philippines, and Sri Lanka to Bahrain, Oman, Kuwait, Saudi Arabia, Hong Kong, Malaysia, and Singapore. Another stream of migration goes from the former Soviet bloc to western Europe – from Russia, Romania, Bulgaria, and Albania to Scandinavia, Germany, France, Spain, Portugal, and England. A third goes from south to north in the Americas, including the stream from Mexico to the United States, which scholars say is the longest-running labor migration in the world. A fourth stream moves from Africa to various parts of Europe. France receives many female migrants from Morocco, Tunisia, and Algeria. Italy receives female workers from Ethiopia, Eritrea, and Cape Verde.

Female migrants overwhelmingly take up work as maids or domestics. As women have become an ever greater proportion of migrant workers, receiving countries reflect a dramatic influx of foreign-born domestics. In the United

States, African-American women, who accounted for 60 per cent of domestics in the 1940s, have been largely replaced by Latinas, many of them recent migrants from Mexico and Central America. In England, Asian migrant women have displaced the Irish and Portuguese domestics of the past. In the French cities, North African women have replaced rural French girls. In western Germany, Turks and women from the former East Germany have replaced rural native-born women.

Why this transfer of women's traditional services from poor to rich parts of the world? The reasons are, in a crude way, easy to guess. Women in Western countries have increasingly taken on paid work, and hence need others – paid domestics and caretakers for children and elderly people – to replace them. For their part, women in poor countries have an obvious incentive to migrate: relative and absolute poverty. The 'care deficit' that has emerged in the wealthier countries as women enter the workforce *pulls* migrants from the Third World and post-communist nations, poverty *pushes* them.

In broad outline, this explanation holds true. Throughout western Europe, Taiwan, and Japan, but above all in the United States, England, and Sweden, women's employment has increased dramatically since the 1970s. In the United States, for example, the proportion of women in paid work rose from 15 percent of mothers of children six and under in 1950 to 65 percent today. Women now make up 46 percent of the US labor force. Three-quarters of mothers of children eighteen and under and nearly two-thirds of mothers of children age one and younger now work for pay. Furthermore, according to a recent International Labor Organization study, working Americans averaged longer hours at work in the late 1990s than they did in the 1970s. By some measures, the number of hours spent at work have increased more for women than for men, and especially for women in managerial and professional jobs.

Meanwhile, over the last thirty years, as the rich countries have grown much richer, the poor countries have become – in both absolute and relative terms – poorer. Global inequalities in wages are particularly striking. In Hong Kong, for instance, the wages of a Filipina domestic are about fifteen times the amount she could make as a schoolteacher back in the Philippines. In addition, poor countries turning to the IMF or World Bank for loans are often forced to undertake measures of so-called structural adjustment, with disastrous results for the poor and especially for poor women and children. To qualify for loans, governments are usually required to devalue their currencies, which turns the hard currencies of rich countries into gold and soft currencies of poor countries into straw. Structural adjustment programs also call for cuts in support for 'noncompetitive industries' and for the reduction of public services such as healthcare and food subsidies for the poor. Citizens of poor countries, women as well as men, thus have a strong incentive to seek work in more fortunate parts of the world.

But it would be a mistake to attribute the globalization of women's work to a simple synergy of needs among women – one group, in the affluent countries, needing help and the other, in poor countries, needing jobs. For one thing, this formulation fails to account for the marked failure of First World governments to meet the needs created by its women's entry into the workforce. The downsized American – and, to a lesser degree, western European – welfare state has become a 'deadbeat dad.' Unlike the rest of the industrialized world, the United States does not offer public childcare for working mothers, nor does it ensure paid family and medical leave. Moreover, a series of state tax revolts in the 1980s reduced the number of hours public libraries were open and slashed school-enrichment and after-school programs. Europe did not experience anything comparable. Still, tens of millions of western European women are in the workforce who were not before – and there has been no proportionate expansion in public services.

Secondly, any view of the globalization of domestic work as simply an arrangement among women completely omits the role of men. Numerous studies, including some of our own, have shown that as American women took on paid employment, the men in their families did little to increase their contribution to the work of the home. For example, only one out of every five men among the working couples whom Hochschild interviewed for *The Second Shift* in the 1980s shared the work at home, and later studies suggest that while working mothers are doing somewhat less housework than their counterparts twenty years ago, most men are doing only a little more. With divorce, men frequently abdicate their childcare responsibilities to their ex-wives. In most cultures of the First World outside the United States, powerful traditions even more firmly discourage husbands from doing 'women's work.' So, strictly speaking, the presence of immigrant nannies does not enable affluent women to enter the workforce; it enables affluent *men* to continue avoiding the second shift.

The men in wealthier countries are also, of course, directly responsible for the demand for immigrant sex workers – as well as for the sexual abuse of many migrant women who work as domestics. Why, we wondered, is there a particular demand for 'imported' sexual partners? Part of the answer may lie in the fact that new immigrants often take up the least desirable work, and, thanks to the AIDS epidemic, prostitution has become a job that ever fewer women deliberately choose. But perhaps some of this demand [...] grows out of the erotic lure of the 'exotic.' Immigrant women may seem desirable sexual partners for the same reason that First World employers believe them to be especially gifted as caregivers: they are thought to embody the traditional feminine qualities of nurturance, docility, and eagerness to please. Some men feel nostalgic for these qualities, which they associate with a bygone way of life. Even as many wage-earning Western women assimilate to the competitive culture of 'male' work and ask respect for making it in a man's world, some

242

men seek in the 'exotic Orient' or 'hot-blooded tropics' a woman from the imagined past.

Of course, not all sex workers migrate voluntarily. An alarming number of women and girls are trafficked by smugglers and sold into bondage. Because trafficking is illegal and secret, the numbers are hard to know with any certainty. Kevin Bales estimates that in Thailand alone, a country of 60 million, half a million to a million women are prostitutes, and one out of every twenty of these is enslaved [...] Many of these women are daughters whom northern hill-tribe families have sold to brothels in the cities of the south. Believing the promises of jobs and money, some begin to voyage willingly, only to discover days later that the 'arrangers' are traffickers who steal their passports, define them as debtors, and enslave them as prostitutes. Other women are kidnapped, or sold by their impoverished families, and then trafficked to brothels. Even worse fates befall women from neighboring Laos and Burma, who flee crushing poverty and repression at home only to fall into the hands of Thai slave traders.

If the factors that pull migrant women workers to affluent countries are not as simple as they first appear, neither are the factors that push them. Certainly relative poverty plays a major role, but interestingly, migrant women often do not come from the poorest classes of their societies. In fact, they are typically more affluent and better educated than male migrants. Many female migrants from the Philippines and Mexico, for example, have high-school or college diplomas and have held middle-class – albeit low-paid – jobs back home. One study of Mexican migrants suggests that the trend is toward increasingly better-educated female migrants. Thirty years ago, most Mexican-born maids in the United States had been poorly educated maids in Mexico. Now a majority have high-school degrees and have held clerical, retail, or professional jobs before leaving for the United States. Such women are likely to be enterprising and adventurous enough to resist the social pressures to stay at home and accept their lot in life.

Noneconomic factors – or at least factors that are not immediately and directly economic – also influence a woman's decision to emigrate. By migrating, a woman may escape the expectation that she care for elderly family members, relinquish her paycheck to a husband or father, or defer to an abusive husband. Migration may also be a practical response to a failed marriage and the need to provide for children without male help [...] And there are forces at work that may be making the men of poor countries less desirable as husbands. Male unemployment runs high in the countries that supply female domestics to the First World. Unable to make a living, these men often grow demoralized and cease contributing to their families in other ways [...]

To an extent, then, the globalization of childcare and housework brings the ambitious and independent women of the world together: the career-orientated upper-middle-class woman of an affluent nation and the striving woman from a crumbling Third World or postcommunist economy. Only it does not bring them together in the way that second-wave feminists in affluent countries once liked to imagine – as sisters and allies struggling to achieve common goals. Instead, they come together as mistress and maid, employer and employee, across a great divide of privilege and opportunity.

25 | Slavery and gender: women's double exploitation

Beth Herzfeld

For many people, the word slavery conjures up images from history – of the transatlantic slave trade, the practice of buying and selling people that the modern world is supposed to have left behind, and of the nineteenth-century abolitionist movement. But the reality is that not only does slavery exist today, it is expanding. An estimated 27 million women, children and men are currently enslaved around the world (Bales 1999: 8): eastern European women are bonded into prostitution in western Europe; children are trafficked between West African countries; and men are forced to work as slaves on Brazilian agricultural estates. Contemporary slavery can affect people of any age, sex, or race on every continent and in most countries. This article is an introduction to what constitutes slavery. It focuses on bonded labour (the most widespread form of slavery today), and on the worst forms of child labour. It provides examples of the way in which socially constructed expectations can increase women's and children's vulnerability to slavery-like practices.

What is slavery?

Contemporary slavery takes many forms: bonded labour, forced labour, forced and early marriage, the worst forms of child labour, human trafficking, and 'traditional' slavery. All types of slavery share some of the following key elements, with persons being:

- forced to work through the threat or use of violence;
- owned or controlled by an 'employer', usually through mental, physical or threatened abuse;
- dehumanized, treated as a commodity, or even bought and sold as 'property';
- physically constrained or having restrictions placed on their freedom of movement and freedom to change employment.

A person can be subject to more than one form of slavery at a given time. In some cases, a person is enslaved for several months, in others they may be enslaved for their whole lives, passing the status on to their children. For example, in the case of bonded labour (also known as debt bondage), a debt that keeps individuals or families enslaved can be passed on from generation to generation.

Gender-specific forms of slavery

Poverty, greed, marginalization – particularly of women and girls and of minority groups – social complicity and lack of political will to address the issue are central to slavery's existence. Although slavery affects men, women and children, there are particular slavery-like practices that are gender-specific.

Female ritual servitude, which is found in West Africa, is one example of this. Under the system of *Trokosi* in south-eastern Ghana, girls as young as seven are given by their family to a shrine in order to atone for a family transgression. The family believes that if they do not do this, they will be cursed; this 'contract' can last for generations.

As one former *Trokosi* recounted:

> I was sent to the shrine when I was nine years old because my grandmother stole a pair of earrings. I was made to work from dawn until dusk in the fields and when I came home there was no food for me to eat. When I was 11, the priest made his first attempt to sleep with me. I refused and was beaten mercilessly. The other girls in the shrine told me it was going to keep happening and if I refused I would be beaten to death and the next time he tried I gave in. The suffering was too much so I tried to escape to my parents but they wouldn't accept me and sent me back to the shrine. I couldn't understand how my parents could be so wicked. (Anti-Slavery International 2000: 11)

Although the girls themselves have not committed any crime, they are obliged to work all day in the priest's fields and are forced to act as a wife to him, including providing sexual services. The priest keeps several *Trokosi* at a time. In effect, the priest exercises ownership over them.

More generally, social and cultural factors play a role in gender decisions over whether girls or boys are sent out to work in order to send money back to the family. Because it is expected that girls in many societies will leave the home at a future date by marrying into another family, girls are often less valued and seen as more dispensable than boys. In some cultures, dowry payments are considered a financial drain, meaning that a daughter is seen as a burden to (and by) her family. Sending young girls away to work is a way of lightening the burden of a poor household. The work they go to do is seen as suited to girls and women; often it is house-based work (domestic labour), involves making and selling food, or is sex work. In all forms of slavery, women and girls are subject to particular abuse and treatment because of their gender. In the next section, bonded labour, and the additional hardships faced by women who are bonded, are examined.

Bonded labour and gender issues

According to the United Nations Working Group on Contemporary Forms of Slavery, at least twenty million people around the world are affected by bonded labour (United Nations 1999: 36). Bonded labour is most prevalent in South Asia, but it is also found in other regions including the Americas and Europe.

People become bonded when their labour is demanded as a means of repayment for a loan, or for money given in advance. Usually they are forced by necessity or are tricked into taking a loan in order to pay for such basic needs as food, medicine, and for social obligations such as the costs of a wedding or funeral. Some take loans in order to finance their migration, in search of a higher income elsewhere. To repay the loan, bonded labourers are typically forced to work long hours regardless of their age or health, sometimes for seven days a week, 365 days a year.

In South Asia, entire families can be bonded, requiring children, as well as adults, to work. And once the loan is taken, bonded labourers are deprived of their rights to negotiate terms and conditions of work. They are charged high rates of interest, and because they do not even receive a minimum wage, the cycle of interest and debt keeps them enslaved. Most have no proof of their agreement and, if a contract exists, few can read it, leaving them vulnerable to continued exploitation.

The practice has its roots in South Asia's caste system, and a disproportionate number are Dalits (those at the bottom of the caste hierarchy) and members of tribal groups. In industries such as agriculture and quarrying, in some South Asian countries, the vast majority of those working as bonded labourers come from those groups.

Women's additional hardship Although all bonded labourers are vulnerable to abuse, women suffer additional hardship owing to their low social status. They not only have to work long hours in the fields and undertake domestic chores in their husband's employer's home, but they must also fulfil domestic duties in their own home.

When a husband becomes a bonded labourer, it is not unusual for his wife's labour to be automatically included with the man's as repayment by an employer. And among bonded labourers, women and girls are particularly vulnerable to rape by landlords.

Pultalingamma, aged forty-five (interviewed in 1999), has worked as a bonded labourer in India for more than twenty-five years.

> My husband died five years ago as a bonded labourer. Now I bear the responsibility of repaying both of our loans. I go to work at 6am, cleaning the cattle shed and performing domestic chores in the landlord's house. Then I go to work in the fields, and return at the end of the day to resume domestic chores. I return home betweens six and eight pm to cook for my own children ... I will make sure my daughter stays in school. I won't let her go and work for the landlord because he will 'spoil' her. (Anti-Slavery International 1999)

The feudal aspect of bonded labour means that the person who owes the debt is effectively owned while the debt is held. While a man may nominally take a loan himself, his wife and children may in fact be included in the contract. The slave-owner sees the slave as there to satisfy all of his needs – labour and otherwise – meaning that women are particularly vulnerable to abuse.

In addition to women, children are also vulnerable, as they are seen as easy to control. They are subject to exploitation that can harm their health and welfare. Work in this category constitutes the worst forms of child labour.

The worst forms of child labour

The International Labour Organization estimates that of the 250 million (ILO 1996) children aged between five and fourteen who work in developing countries, 120 million (ibid.) work full-time, and 80 million (ibid.: 2) are in work that is harmful to their mental and physical well-being. These figures do not include the number of children who are engaged in the worst forms of child labour in Europe and North America.

According to the International Labour Organization's Convention No. 182, on the Worst Forms of Child Labour (1999), a child includes anyone under the age of eighteen, with no exceptions (Article 2) (Brown 2001: 5). The definition of the worst forms of child labour includes:

- all forms of slavery or similar practices, such as debt bondage, trafficking, and forced or compulsory recruitment of children for use in armed conflict;
- the use of children for prostitution and pornography;
- the use of children for illicit activities, such as the production and trafficking of drugs;
- all work which is likely to endanger the health, safety or morality of children (Article 3) (ibid.).

Although some types of work can contribute positively to a child's development as well as providing a vital source of income helping to sustain the child and their family, millions of children around the world are forced into work that is damaging or extremely exploitative. They are denied their right to education, and their physical and mental health – and even their lives – are put at risk.

Gender differences in labour practices Exploitative employers often prefer children to adults because they are more vulnerable, easier to control, cheaper and less likely to demand better working conditions and higher wages. Most working children around the world work in agriculture, although the single largest form of employment for girls worldwide is domestic work in the homes of strangers. This reflects the general cultural view that girls are well suited for employment in domestic work. They also sell food in open markets, and are 'sold off' into sex work. Boys are more likely to be involved in farming and animal herding, quarries (though girls in Nepal also work as stone-breakers), fishing and some factory work. In South Asia, however, girls make bangles, and both boys and girls make carpets in small 'factories'.

In some cases the children or their parents are tricked by traffickers' false promises of good, well-paid work and training, in others they are abducted, as is the case with some child camel jockeys and the children forced to fight for Uganda's main insurgent group, the Lord's Resistance Army (LRA). Boys as young as four from Pakistan, Bangladesh and parts of Africa are abducted and taken to the Middle East to be camel jockeys. Desired because they are small and light, they are not paid. Before a race, they are deprived of food to keep them as light as possible. There are examples of abuse, severe injuries and death.

In northern Uganda, abducted children – boys and girls – are believed to constitute 90 per cent of the LRA (Coalition Against the Use of Child Soldiers 1999: 114). Boys are used for fighting, looting villages, and abducting other children. Girls, who are also trained as soldiers, are mainly distributed to LRA soldiers as sex slaves (or 'wives') (ibid.: 115). If they refuse, they are killed.

Children who work away from their families are particularly vulnerable because they are under the complete control of their employer. They work long hours for little or no pay and in many cases they sleep where they work. Roushan [not her real name], now fourteen, was trafficked from Bangladesh to India when she was ten years old. She was taken to the border and sold to a woman for 500 taka (US$6), who then sold her to a bangle factory. 'I didn't know how to make the bangles very well, which caused me to be beaten up. There were also older girls there who were threatened that if they didn't work well, they would bring men who would abuse them ...'

Between 100 and 150 girls and young women were locked in the house where they worked. They worked long hours and slept there. No beds or pillows were provided, so Roushan slept sitting against the wall, she said (Anti-Slavery International 2001).

Working towards ending slavery

Despite the scale of slavery, change is possible. Anti-Slavery International, the world's oldest international human rights organization, works at the local, national and international levels to eliminate forms of slavery around the world.

At the international and national levels, Anti-Slavery International presses governments that are not enforcing existing legislation to implement it. International and domestic laws prohibiting slavery do exist. Key international standards include the 1948 Universal Declaration of Human Rights, which applies to all United Nations member states. It prohibits the practice of slavery in all of its forms. The UN Supplementary Convention on the Abolition of

Slavery, the Slave Trade, and Institutions and Practices Similar to Slavery (1956), which most states have ratified, and the International Labour Convention No. 29 concerning Forced or Compulsory Labour (1930), form the key international instruments banning bonded labour. But the lack of political will to enforce these laws and develop or implement domestic legislation allows such slavery as bonded labour to continue.

Children are further protected under Article 32 of the UN Convention on the Rights of the Child (1989), which states: 'States Parties recognize the right of the child to be protected from economic exploitation and from performing any work that is likely to be hazardous or to interfere with the child's education or to be harmful to the child's health or physical, mental, spiritual, moral, or social development.' In 1999, the International Labour Organization's Convention No. 82 on the Worst Forms of Child Labour defined which of 'the worst forms of child labour' it is an absolute priority to eradicate. Anti-Slavery International works with local partner organizations around the world to encourage governments to ratify and implement this measure.

In cases where legislation does not exist, we urge governments to develop workable laws and advocate their enforcement. In many cases, slavery such as bonded labour and the practice of using children as domestics or to sell items in the market is so established it is not perceived to be a problem. Raising awareness in the countries concerned is crucial if the public is to support initiatives to end this abuse. There are a number of examples where raised awareness has led to significant changes. Anti-Slavery International's partner in Togo, WAO Afrique, for example, has enabled communities to realize the dangers of child domestic labour by educating employers and children about children's rights. It also provides former child domestics with training to give them alternatives and to help them to avoid abusive employment.

Conclusion

If the elimination of slavery is to be effective, viable alternatives need to be made available for freed slaves, and the issue of poverty needs to be addressed. In Nepal, where in 2000 the government declared bonded labour illegal, thousands of freed bonded labourers were forced off the land. They have had to live in makeshift camps, on roadsides and in forests because the government has both failed to provide assistance and to allocate land despite its promises. As a result their freedom has little meaning.

Slaves need to be empowered to free themselves. This is particularly relevant in the case of women and girls who are enslaved and who live in societies where women have low social status. In such situations it can be effective to challenge society's views of women and girls, as well as providing training programmes and poverty alleviation schemes to empower women and develop their confidence in themselves.

The forces of poverty, marginalization and social complicity which lead to exploitation need to be addressed if slavery is to be eliminated. Solutions must take into account the super-exploitation of women, particularly where families are enslaved, and also the underlying low status of women in many countries, which helps provide the conditions in which slavery can flourish.

References

Anti-Slavery International (1999) *Interview with Pultalingamma*, India: Anti-Slavery International, April.

— (2000) *Reporter*, Series VIII, 6(1), January.

— (2001) *Interview with Roushan*, London: Anti-Slavery International, November.

Bales, K. (1999) *Disposable People*, Berkeley: University of California Press.

Brown, P. (2001) *The New ILO Worst Forms of Child Labour Convention 1999: Do You Know ...?*, Geneva NGO Group for the Convention on the Rights of the Child Sub-Group on Child Labour, Geneva: Anti-Slavery International.

Coalition Against the Use of Child Soldiers (1999) *The Use of Child Soldiers in Africa: A Country Analysis of Child Recruitment and Participation in Armed Conflict*, London: Coalition Against the Use of Child Soldiers.

ILO (International Labour Organization) (1996) Press release, Geneva: ILO, 12 November.

— (1999) *A New Tool to Combat the Worst Forms of Child Labour: ILO Convention 182*, Geneva: ILO.

United Nations (1999) *Report of the Working Group on Contemporary Forms of Slavery*, 24th Session, E/CN.4/Sub. 2/1999/17, Geneva: United Nations Economic and Social Council, 20 July.

26 | Globalization and the increase in transnational care work: the flip side[1]

Jean L. Pyle

This chapter focuses on the relationship of the recent period of globalization with flows of transnational caring labor, looking specifically at who is (or is not) receiving care.[2] This issue has distinctly gendered dimensions and complicated inequities that also involve class, age, national origin, sexual orientation, race/ethnicity, and culture. It has economic, political, social, ethical, and moral aspects and implications. It is a critical matter for all involved: the individuals migrating to provide caring labor, their families, the households and institutions in which they work, and both the sending and receiving countries. Caring labor – and who does or does not receive it – is also an essential concern for sustainable human development. As the United Nations Development Program points out:

> Studies of globalization and its impact on people focus on incomes, employment, education and other opportunities. Less visible, and often neglected, is the impact on care and caring labour – the task of providing for dependants, for children, the sick, the elderly ... Human development is nourished not only by expanding incomes, schooling, health, empowerment and a clean environment but also by care. ... Care, sometimes referred to as social reproduction, is also essential for economic sustainability. (UNDP 1999: 77)

Typically, women from lower-income regions provide caring labor – domestic services, childcare, and healthcare services – to households in higher-income areas. It is, however, not necessarily the lowest-income women who migrate. For example, many Filipinas migrating are considered middle-class in the Philippines (Parreñas 2001b). They are often well educated and speak English (Lan 2003; Cheng 2004). Some leave their own children in the care of others, forming global care chains (Hochschild 2000; ILO 2004a). Their families become transnational families; their parenting must occur across national borders (Asis et al. 2004; Parreñas 2001a).

Governments often encourage workers to migrate for employment – particularly lower-income developing countries, often with large debt burdens. Women are a valuable 'labor export' since research indicates they are more likely to send remittances home than men (Blue 2004; Connell and Brown 2004; Samarasinghe 1998).

There is an extensive literature on domestic workers, focusing chiefly on Asia, the United States (USA), and western Europe. Research documents the perceived positive and negative aspects of migration (Pyle 2006). Other studies examine the often low wage levels and adverse working/living conditions. There are policy analyses that develop strategies to improve the situation of these workers (Heyzer and Wee 1994; Piper and Ball 2001; Villalba 2002; ILO 2003a, 2003b, 2004a; IOM 2005).

Some scholars explore how female transnational domestic workers reconstitute their identities and their relationships to their own families and establish themselves distinctly from their employers (Asis et al. 2004; Lan 2003; Yeoh and Huang 2000; Barber 2000; Cheng 2004). Some focus on how immigration alters gender relations between women and men (Menjívar 1999). Others reveal the problems these women encounter when they return home (Constable 1999; Siddiqui 2003; Surtees 2003).

In addition, some examine the representation of female domestic workers. They have been stereotyped as heroes or victims (Santos 2002; Gibson et al. 2001), as 'others' who are inferior (ILO 2003b; Cheng 2004), as immoral (Chin 1997; Chang and Groves 2000), as a drain on society (Chang 2000), and as commodities (Tyner 1996; Chin 1998, 1997). Representations are often used by a country in marketing its workers for employment in other countries (Tyner 1996) or by receiving-country brokers who channel women into different labor market segments by nationality (Loveband 2004). They are also a means to control the options workers face and deny them their due rights (Chin 1997).

Much research reveals the immigrants' range of reactions to situations in which they find themselves – showing that these workers, although on the disadvantaged side of unequal power relations, have varying degrees of agency and creatively resist the constraints of their situations (Constable 1997; Yeoh and Huang 1998; Gamburd 2000; Barber 2000; Chang and Groves 2000; Lan 2003; Cheng 2004).

The different aspects of social reality explored in these widening literatures on workers are all important for understanding transnational caring labor. It is only within the last decade, however, that multilevel approaches to understanding the political economy of transnational migration for such work have been explored (Heyzer and Wee 1994; Pyle 2001; Pyle and Ward 2003; Parreñas 2001a, 2001b; Misra et al. 2006; Oishi 2005).

Furthermore, no overarching analysis of the relationship of globalization to who *is* or *is not* receiving care has been undertaken. In this article, I initiate this project. I examine the flip side of the increased flow of transnational caring labor into higher-income areas. At the same time women migrate to provide caring labor, there are deficiencies in the levels of care they and their families obtain – a care deficit.[3] This can undermine health, violate human rights and dignity, and undercut possibilities for sustainable development.

In the next two sections, I examine the dual aspects of the flip side. First, I provide an overview of the research on the working and living conditions of transnational migrant care workers (domestic workers and healthcare workers), showing the care deficit that most encounter.[4] Second, I survey research on the experiences of their families – looking at the economic and psychological aspects of the care that family members receive when women emigrate. In the third section, I examine the double bind that many national governments encounter as they seek to balance the advantages of having women emigrate with the need to counter the adverse conditions the migrants may encounter. I examine several different approaches to female migration, ranging from relatively open migration to very restrictive, and critique governments' ways of addressing the abuse of migrating women. In the last section, I outline initiatives at the international level begun since 2000 to address the problems migrant workers face (up to 2006 publication date). I point out that what is missing in these approaches is an understanding of how forces of globalization and the international power structure have shaped migrant flows – the actual numbers and their gender, class, and other demographic characteristics.

The flip side: female transnational workers – what care do they receive?

Economic issues are a primary reason for women workers to emigrate. Women typically earn a wage abroad that exceeds their alternatives at home. Others leave to escape oppressive home situations and feel empowered. Some view migration as an opportunity to see more of the world and meet people from other cultures (Villalba 2002; ILO 2004a; Oishi 2005).

These benefits notwithstanding, there is, however, wide evidence that many transnational care workers find themselves in situations where others possess most of the power, leaving them limited grounds to negotiate the terms of their employment and existence (ILO 2003b). They face wide-ranging problems that affect their mental and physical health. There are countless examples of how they strive to improve their circumstances, but the level of care they experience in their own lives is often seriously deficient.

What women migrating for caring labor experience and the actions they take in response are complex and shaped by many dimensions of social reality, including the particular economic, social, political, legal, and cultural conditions of the receiving countries. Women originating from the same country encounter similarities and differences across host countries. On one level, Parreñas (2001b) found that Filipina domestic workers in the different contexts of Los Angeles and Rome experienced similar problems – painful separation from their families, reduced occupational status, social exclusion from host communities, and quasi-citizenship. On a more micro level, Filipinas had better protections in Hong Kong than in Singapore, although the latter is considered somewhat more democratic (Bell 2001; Buckman and Saywell 2004). Not surprisingly, they preferred working in Hong Kong. But their experiences also differed within Hong Kong, depending on whether they worked in Chinese or Western households. They believed Western employers offered better work environments with more equal treatment and personal space (Cheung and Mok 1998). Nurses also experienced sharply different circumstances. Ball (2004) compared Filipina nurses' access to institutionalized ways of raising concerns (at the workplace or societal levels) in Saudi Arabia and the USA, finding much less recourse in Saudi Arabia.

Multiple types of workplace discrimination Discrimination affects health and well-being and is therefore a major factor in the levels of care people experience in their lives. Women migrating transnationally for caring labor can experience multiple forms of discrimination[5] – based on ethnicity, race, nationality, class, religion, perceived morality, gender, or because they are undocumented or trafficked workers (ILO 2003a, 2003b). Instead of building bridges across nations, migration can reinforce and augment many forms of inequality (Cheng 2004; Ehrenreich and Hochschild 2002). For example, Ball (2004) documented how Filipina nurses in Saudi Arabia are multiply disadvantaged: as foreign nationals, as women, and as females in occupations that cross taboos of touching between unmarried members of opposite sexes. To resist, they move to other countries for work once they gain experience in transnational employment.

In terms of ethnicity, Gamburd (1999) described how local agencies placing Sri Lankan women abroad charged higher fees for Sinhala women than Muslim women. Hierarchies based on race and nationality disadvantage many. For example, Indonesian women in Taiwan are channeled into the more demanding jobs (caring for the very sick and elderly), while the Filipinas receive the easier domestic positions (Loveband 2004). Filipina domestic workers in Singapore received one or two days off a month, Sri Lankans one or none, and Indonesian domestic workers none (Yeoh and Huang 1998). McNeil-Walsh reported nurses of the racial minority may be assigned less desirable shifts and have fewer opportunities for training and promotion (2004). Immigrant nurses in the USA and Saudi Arabia often felt talked down to by patients and colleagues – and were reprimanded in circumstances that would not result in criticism of a white colleague (Ball 2004). Although workers are aware of these injustices, their vulnerability makes them reluctant to report them.

Class differences between employer and domestic worker can be reinforced by either maternalism (the female employer intruding on workers' personal lives or disclosing her personal life to the domestic worker) or the creation of a more distant hierarchical relationship. Both can control and demean the domestic worker. Although in the less powerful position, workers can influence the employer–employee boundary by refusing to share details of their personal lives (Lan 2003).

Oishi (2005) reminds us that employers may seek domestic employees of the same religion. Arab households prefer Muslim domestic workers, even though those of other faiths may be readily available, because they don't want their children exposed to different value systems.

Discourse has also centered on the morality and sexuality of domestic workers. Responses and resistance of groups of transnational migrants vary. For example, some Filipinas challenged the portrayal of them as prostitutes by establishing organizations with ethical rules for domestic workers' behavior, thus hiding sexuality; others flaunted their sexuality to mock the accusers (Chang and Groves 2000).

Gender is, however, a major basis upon which discrimination occurs, often overlapping these other forms of discrimination. In most countries, cultural and traditional attitudes devalue women and restrict their economic and political rights, their social and cultural roles, and their opportunities for education and access to information and resources (ILO 2003a). Gendered hierarchies exist (Wee and Sim 2004). Transnational women domestic workers typically have few occupational choices in the gender-stratified labor markets, limited mobility between employers, and often must live at their workplace. Migrating nurses may encounter barriers regarding licensing, fees, language tests, and approval of their qualifications (Bach 2003; Hawthorne 2001; ILO 2003b).

Although women often migrate because higher wages are promised abroad, nevertheless many receive relatively low hourly pay and find their wages withheld for months (Lim and Oishi 1996; Surtees 2003; Buckman and Saywell 2004). Recruitment agencies, arguing that they must recoup the costs of placing the women abroad, often garnish wages for the first few months on the job (Perlez 2004). Wage hierarchies exist (ILO 2004a). Gender, race, and nationality interact in ways that disadvantage many. Female domestic workers from countries such as Indonesia, Sri Lanka, India, and Nepal, for example, earn less than Filipinas in Singapore and Hong Kong (Buckman and Saywell 2004; Oishi 2005). Women have begun resisting. Wee and Sim (2004) describe how Filipinas in Hong Kong have more power to negotiate with employers – many have networks of family and friends already employed there, numbers of Filipino-dominated NGOs have been established in Hong Kong, and many workers have cell phones, facilitating organizing. Filipina nurses in the USA have challenged discrimination by filing lawsuits under US equal employment law (Ball 2004).

Women often take jobs of lower status than the occupations for which they trained (Piper 2005). This is commonly the case for Filipinas who become domestic workers. Moving lower in the occupational hierarchy diminishes their class status, fosters alienation, and can result in loss of skills (Parreñas

2001b). The skills of trained healthcare workers are also often underutilized (ILO 2004a). Bach (2003) highlighted the ways they are deskilled – some visas curtail job options and past experience and skills are often overlooked in assigning jobs and setting pay rates. McNeil-Walsh (2004) reported that healthcare workers from South Africa are treated as 'different' and staffed in positions that underutilize their skills.

Migrating domestic workers may have few labor rights – limits on hours worked or overtime, specified days off and vacation time, a minimum wage, or the right to organize – because they are typically in occupations not covered by labor laws (ILO 2003a, 2003b; Abu-Habib 1998; Silvey 2004). Furthermore, there may be no contract stipulating the terms of their employment or they may have been forced to sign a document that restricts their rights. If a contract exists, it may not be enforced, allowing widespread violations. Women typically have few welfare rights and health benefits. They may be in forced labor or bound to an employer by debt.

In addition, domestic workers may be exploited by recruitment agencies. Wee and Sim (2004) document the differences Filipinas and Indonesian women experience during the recruitment process, with the latter encountering more abusive conditions. Surtees (2003) observed the long confinement of Indonesian women in crowded 'holding centres' awaiting emigration. She also pointed out how return migrants may be extorted by immigration officials and charged high rates for currency exchange or transportation home. Bangladeshi women traveling through the airport to their homes have been harassed, extorted, robbed, even killed (Siddiqui 2003). To avoid the abuses of private agencies and some official channels, Sri Lankan women established recruitment structures that worked through personal networks (Gamburd 2000).

In the event of an economic crisis, immigrant women are particularly vulnerable. After the Asian economic crisis of 1997, both Thailand and Malaysia wanted to expel 500,000-plus foreign emigrants (Lund and Panda 2000).

Households – the domestic black box In some cases, women migrate with their families and live separately from their workplaces. Nevertheless, problems can arise in their own households. Menjívar's research (1999) on largely undocumented El Salvadorean and Guatemalan immigrants in California revealed that women often have better chances of finding employment (in households, where they are not seen) than the men. The men, frustrated by not fulfilling their cultural roles as 'male provider,' often drink excessively and beat their wives/partners. Such outcomes temper the argument that a woman's bargaining power and position in the household will be enhanced in the short run by earning money.

Women migrating alone transnationally for live-in domestic work may be discriminated against because they are isolated within households, with their living and working conditions hidden from view. They are reduced from whole social beings to commodified labor (Yeoh and Huang 1998). Working conditions vary, depending on how the domestic workers are regarded in the household. According to Chin (1997), many Malaysian employers view their domestic workers as 'girl-slaves.' In sharp contrast, the Filipina and Indonesian migrants in Malaysia wanted to 'be perceived and treated as human beings deserving of respect'. Cheng (2004) tells how Filipina domestic workers and their Taiwanese female employers struggle to reconstitute their respective identities around ideologies of domesticity, womanhood, and motherhood. Each woman in the employer–employee dyad tries to enhance her own self-image, the way the other sees her, and her image in the larger society.

Domestic workers may experience poor working conditions that include excessive work demands or being on call continuously, with little time to themselves (Constable 1997). Yeoh and Huang's (1998) interviews with employers and immigrant domestic workers in Singapore, a nation considered modern, showed how the government and the employer severely limit employees' time and ability to go outside the household (by lack of regulations, by guiding them into 'appropriate' activities on their day off such as dressmaking, and by verbal suasion, couched paternalistically in terms of 'protecting' the workers from the 'ills' of society). Workers resisted by meeting on playgrounds while caring for small children, at churches (an employer-approved activity), or by ignoring the employer's warnings and frequenting public areas where their compatriots gather on any day off acquired. Similarly, Chin's research (1997) revealed that Malaysian employers sought to curtail their domestic workers' movement outside the home, fearing the women would pick up 'bad habits.' Workers resisted, adopting a more stylish persona on days off to demonstrate an identity distinct from that of a domestic worker (ibid.).

Transnational domestic workers are typically unable to change employers because a national (i.e. the employer) must sponsor their visa (ILO 2003a). What occurs in households is often outside the purview of the law. For example, Silvey reported, in her study of Indonesian women domestic workers in Saudi Arabia, that both the Indonesian and Saudi governments considered the household 'beyond their respective jurisdictional scopes' (2004). Given such isolation, immigrant domestic workers often endure health and safety risks that include verbal abuse, physical or sexual violence, and harmful exposures (Chin 1998; Lim and Oishi 1996; Villalba 2002; ILO 2004a). Employers' criticism is common and domestics even experience humiliating treatment from the children they care for (Cheng 2004). Many have been beaten by employers; some have been murdered or died under suspicious circumstances (Rosca 1995; Buckman and Saywell 2004; US Department of State 2005). The Indonesian embassy in Saudi Arabia documented '1105 migrant workers who suffered physical abuse, 2182 who were abused psychologically and 612 who were sexually abused' from 1994 to 1997 (Surtees 2003: 102, citing a 2002 report). Waldman (2005) reported that the bodies of 100 Sri Lankan women a year were returned home; many others were raped. Prosecution is infrequent and penalties tend to be light. For example, the US Department of State (2005) reported that the Lebanese government did not look into suspicious deaths of Philippine and Ethiopian domestic workers or prosecute employers, even though evidence of their sexual or physical abuse of domestic workers existed. Working conditions can be dangerous in other ways. Almost a hundred maids a year died in falls from high-rises in Singapore. Although some were believed to have committed suicide, many slipped while washing windows or hanging laundry (Buckman and Saywell 2004).

In addition, although they reside in relatively affluent households, domestic workers may not be provided adequate food, a healthful place and enough time to sleep, or personal privacy to maintain their own lives and customs. For example, Lan (2003) said Filipinas in Taiwan typically are allotted a small, poorly ventilated room in the attic or basement of homes that have spacious bedrooms. Chin (1998) reported Malaysian employers want domestics to work long work hours, with little time for eating or sleeping. Constable revealed that domestic workers in Hong Kong were told to eat less and lose weight when they requested more food (Constable 1997). Sri Lankan domestic workers that Abu-Habib (1998) interviewed in Lebanon stated the food was unfamiliar and they were often unable to practice their own religious customs.

The flip side: their families – what care do they receive?

In evaluating the 'flip side' of the flows of transnational caring labor, we must also assess the impact on the levels of care received by care workers' families. Many women migrate transnationally because they believe their increased earnings will allow them to better provide for their families or communities. They hope to fund improved housing for their families, finance a small family business, reduce family debts, or furnish children with a better education (Barber 2000; Gamburd 2000; Frank 2001). They feel positively about such contributions (Ehrenreich and Hochschild 2002). In doing this, however, they are supplying important domestic services and giving daily care to the children of *others* – which can be painful emotionally when there is a long separation from their own children (Hochschild 2002; Parreñas 2002; Yeoh and Huang 2000).

Women may be away from their families for years (DeAlwis 2002; ILO 2003a). The way they are evaluated 'back home' can be both positive and negative. This evaluation, in turn, affects their psychological and physical well-being. On the one hand, they may be thought of positively because they remit significant amounts of money and therefore 'care' for their families (including children, spouses, parents, siblings, and even wider familial networks). This type of care is skewed to the material and away from care provided face to face.

On the other hand, those migrating transnationally for caring work are often accused of neglecting their care-giving roles at home. Women are deemed responsible for the well-being of their families, even though hundreds of miles away for extended periods of time. They are blamed for the adverse things their family members do (or that happen to them) in their absence (Parreñas 2002; ILO 2004a; Oishi 2005). The evaluations of married/partnered women with children often are contradictory. Women are simultaneously expected to be on-site mothers as well as helpmates to their husbands/partners (earning money if necessary, migrating to do so if that is the best option). If children remain at home, grandmothers may be overburdened by being substitute care-givers (DeAlwis 2002). Children may suffer emotionally (Hochschild 2002), be sick more often, be abused, or 'go astray' in the absence of a mother (lag in their schoolwork or drop out, get involved with drugs, enter the labor market too young) (ILO 2003a). Other studies, however, suggest that some mothers and children maintain linkages that overcome the problems of distance (Asis et al. 2004; Parreñas 2002).

Women are often seen as corrupted by their new lives (DeAlwis 2002; Gamburd 1999). In spite of the fact that many Bangladeshi husbands or fathers made the decision that women in their family should work abroad, the men infer that returning women are a cause of the spread of HIV/AIDS. They believe that women tend to become part-time sex workers (Dasgupta 2003).

Masculine identities may be threatened. Some husbands drink, philander, or squander the money their wives send home (Gamburd 2000; Ehrenreich and Hochschild 2002). Issues regarding the gendered division of labor within households surface in the immigrants' households as well as the employers' homes. There are mixed conclusions regarding whether men pick up the housekeeping and childcare duties when the wife/mother migrates. According to Parreñas (2002) and Gamburd (2000) respectively, few Filipino or Sri Lankan men took over childcare and household responsibilities when their wives migrated. Asis et al. (2004) found, however, that all husbands in their small sample assumed domestic duties when their wives migrated from the Philippines to Singapore.

The lack of demographic information on women migrating presents obstacles for understanding the problems. Ogaya (2004) says the emphasis on women with children may not be truly representative since she believes single women predominate. She argues that the focus on mothers distorted the discourse. Chin (1997) found that Filipinas in Malaysia in the mid-1990s were largely single, but suggested that the marital status of migrants may change over time. More longitudinal data – that includes gender, marital status, occupation, age, and number of children – would provide a clearer portrait of who is migrating.

In sum, the increasing flow of women moving transnationally to provide caring labor is, ironically, often accompanied by *diminished* levels of care in the lives of the migrating workers. Although many find innovative ways to actively resist the negative aspects of migration, nevertheless many experience deterioration in their own physical or psychological health. Their families may also suffer. There are very different stressors in the lives of those buying care, those providing it, and the families of the care-givers. There are also dramatic disparities in whose fundamental rights are preserved or violated in this process (ILO 2003a).

The state's double bind

Redress for the problems of emigrants typically involves the national level, whether a government alone or in agreements with other countries. Although many non-governmental organizations (NGOs), ranging from local to regional in scope, assist migrants, they operate within the constraints of the legal frameworks of national governments.

To examine how the state addresses emigration problems it is critical to use a gendered perspective. Many governments experience a double bind. On the one hand, they have strong economic incentives to encourage emigration. They can stave off social unrest by exporting labor, thereby reducing unemployment or underemployment. In addition, emigrants' remittances provide funds to support family members at home as well as the foreign exchange needed to improve the balance of payments and service the debt owed large international financial institutions. In many cases, given occupational segregation, it is female labor that is wanted abroad. Because these economic reasons to encourage out-migration are compelling, labor export often appears in countries' multi-year economic development plans. However, economic reasons can be problematic at the social level. The ILO recognizes that the state's desire to increase foreign exchange may 'leave migrant workers exposed to exploitation and abuse' (ILO 2003a).

Therefore, on the other hand, a government may be pushed to regulate emigration. It has the putative goal of protecting the rights of citizens who become migrant workers *and* its public image may require steps in this direction, especially given the often well-publicized abuse of its citizens abroad. A government may also want to protect society's perception of 'family' and keep women home. Governments address abuses female emigrants experience in several ways – by banning women's emigration to 'protect' the women (or to force receiving countries into adopting protective policies), by promoting male migration, by training programs to teach a few occupational, language, and coping skills, or by attempts at bilateral or multilateral agreements to establish better standards for treatment of foreign workers. These strategies range from weak and ineffectual to misleading and discriminatory. They can also have unintended consequences.[6]

It has been economically expedient for some countries to export women. In some cases, female migrants are more 'marketable' abroad than men. But abuses occur. Governments' strategies to address the abuses are problematic. Governments have either tried to change the gender composition of the emigrant stream by bans or by incentives, attempted to shift responsibility for welfare and economic outcomes onto the individuals migrating, or tried to develop bilateral or multilateral agreements.

First, banning female emigration to 'protect' the women often results in protests by the women themselves (who need to migrate to earn incomes in spite of the risks) and challenges from recruiting agencies and NGOs. Workers prevented from emigrating by protective policies may leave through illegal channels where the probability of abuse is greater (Alegado 1997; Oishi 2005; Siddiqui 2003). Bans are discriminatory to women; men do not encounter similar obstacles. Although not as blatant, promoting only male migration also disadvantages women.

Second, the approach of addressing abuse by shifting responsibility onto individuals migrating is often disingenuous. Domestic workers are trained in basic skills, at least partly to avoid angering employers. This can lead maids to the misleading conclusion that abuse may be their own fault. Changing the rhetoric to convince migrating workers they are overseas foreign investors transforms 'citizens with rights into entrepreneurs who can be held responsible for their own failures' (Weekley 2004).

Last, countries can try to negotiate agreements with receiving countries that include worker protections. Sending governments have little incentive or leverage to accomplish this, however, since they are trying to promote their workers abroad and face competition in the labor export industry. There are other governments willing to send workers without seeking protection for them (Alegado 1997; Oishi 2005). Sri Lanka has expressed such fears of Indonesia and the Philippines (Gamburd 1999; Waldman 2005). Given the double bind just discussed, it is unlikely that governments will enforce policies (if they even formulate them) to substantially address the inequities faced by transnational care workers. Policies may be more for public relations.

In short, none of these strategies allows women the same access to emigration as men and none provides a transnational environment that ensures their rights to safe work.

Conclusion: what are the options?

We have seen how women's transnational migration to provide caring labor has a flip side. Flows of care are not symmetrical. Women migrating provide care but, in return, they and their families often experience care deficits. Migrating women can encounter a range of economic, social, and political abuses that involve discrimination based on ethnicity, race, nationality, class, religion, and age. They resist these injustices but have limited power. The state is often in a double bind and ineffective in addressing abuses. What can be done?

At the broadest international level, there has been increased attention to migration issues since 2000. The goal is to manage migration in a way that addresses the concerns of migrants and those of sending and receiving countries, while contributing to growth and development (ILO 2004a, 2004b).

Some suggest a multilevel approach (local, national, and international) that strives for policy coherence among economic and social policies relating to migration (GCIM 2005; ILO 2003a, 2004b). This requires policy coordination across nations, among international organizations with different but overlapping mandates, as well as coordination among levels. It also requires large organizations such as the UN and the ILO to have integrated internal approaches to migration (ILO 2004a). Policy coherence is a step toward a global consensus on migration, although the process is complicated, fraught with unintended consequences, and even more difficult post-9/11 when security issues regarding migrants became prominent.

This approach is part of a wider movement advocating a fair globalization, in which benefits of globalization would be distributed more justly. The ILO's World Commission on the Social Dimension of Globalization argued that to be sustainable, globalization must meet the needs of people. There is a global economy but not a global society. Economic benefits and social costs are not distributed equally among groups. It is critical to see the human side of globalization and focus on the social as well as economic aspects (ILO 2004b).

The human side is fundamentally based on human rights, including the right to a safe livelihood and to migrate (Jolly 2003). Many ILO and UN documents or conventions uphold migrant workers' human rights, often specifying women or even domestic workers (GCIM 2005; ILO 2004a, 2003a; Oishi 2005).[7] Two key examples are the UN Migrant Workers Convention,[8] adopted in 1990, which sets standards for both documented and undocumented workers and their families (few countries ratified it at first, so it became effective only in 2003) and the UN Resolution on Violence Against Women Migrant Workers, adopted in 2000 (Oishi 2005). The conventions are, however, widely ignored.

Several other global initiatives on migration have been launched since 2000. The Berne Initiative of 2001 helped governments develop effective migration policies and structures. The Declaration of the Hague on the Future of Refugee and Migration Policy advocated including civil society, the private sector, and academia in the discussion. Many international organizations made migration a major theme of conferences or action. The Global Commission on International Migration's final report urged countries of origin and destination to revise their national laws, policies, and practices so migrants can exercise the human rights that international law grants them (GCIM 2005). It recommended that the UN form an international agency focused on migration, recognizing that too many organizations have a role in addressing migration issues; policies are piecemeal, sometimes conflict, and gaps exist (ibid.). Most recently, the UN General Assembly scheduled a High-Level Dialogue on Migration and Development for September 2006 to develop ways to maximize the benefits of migration and reduce its adverse aspects.

At a gendered level, some international institutions have focused on the problems female labor migrants face (ibid.; ILO 2003a, 2003b; ILO 2004a; UNIFEM 2005). The UN's publication *The World's Women 2005* called for better migration data by gender. The ILO and UNIFEM advocate multilevel approaches. The ILO's comprehensive document *An Information Guide – Preventing Discrimination, Exploitation and Abuse of Women Migrant Workers* (2003a) espouses a rights-based, gender-sensitive approach. The United Nations Development Fund for Women (UNIFEM 2005) specifies several other important components of an effective approach – unionization, public awareness campaigns, and provision of services.

While it is encouraging that migration has become a prominent issue and some helpful strategies have been developed, there are problems with these approaches to improving migrants' conditions, particularly female trans-national care workers. First, developing coordinated policies across countries may be very difficult given many nations' double bind regarding women's migration, the inequities in relative power among nations, and the sometimes conflicting goals among social actors (government, recruiters, women migrants, and their families). Enforcing policies is even harder, especially when workers are isolated in households.

Second, a larger context is missing here – recognition of the structure of power internationally and the effect globalization has on factors influencing women's migration. The goal of these approaches is only to *manage* the flows that occur. They do not address or alter the dimensions of globalization that shape the numbers migrating and their demographic characteristics (gender, class, age, or nationality). The ILO (2003a) states it is important to focus on the reasons underlying the demand for and supply of migrant workers, but merely lists a few causal factors without exploring them further. To fully understand and address transnational workers' lives and concerns, these factors must be analyzed.

This project is underway. I have argued elsewhere that women have been increasingly drawn into several types of work, including domestic labor and the migration often necessitated for it, because of characteristics of this period of globalization: the increasing role of markets and correspondingly diminished role of governments in many of the world's economies; the 'opening up' of nations internationally as many developing countries adopted export-oriented strategies and liberalized financial markets; the spread of multinational corporations (MNCs) into new tiers of countries and sectors; and the widespread adoption of structural adjustment policies (SAPs) required by the International Monetary Fund (IMF) as a condition for granting countries loans. Each of these characteristics has affected women. (Pyle 1999, 2001, 2005).

In addition, I pointed out that the structure of power internationally has shifted dramatically, with an increase in the influence of institutions that profess to support market-determined economic outcomes (MNCs, IMF, World Bank, and the World Trade Organization, WTO) relative to those that are more people-centered and concerned with sustainable human development [non-governmental organizations (NGOs) and many United Nations agencies, particularly the International Labour Organization] (Pyle and Ward 2003; Pyle 2005). The language of 'free markets' and 'liberalization' hides the reality that markets are not free and competitive, but are dominated by powerful institutions whose goals are profit-making or repayment of loans. In fact, rather than freely choosing, many national governments have been pushed to embrace these four aspects of globalization outlined above by powerful international institutions (IMF, World Bank, WTO, and MNCs) (Pyle and Ward 2003).

We must develop our multilevel approach within the larger context of the global political economy. Successful strategies to improve the lives of transnational migrants require a realistic understanding of the structure of power internationally and the impact of globalization on the gendering of labor migration. If we do not shift to this new way of thinking and take actions to strengthen the power of organizations focused on sustainable human development, we may have limited success. Working within the existing power structure may result in marginal gains and not fundamentally address the inequities that foster much migration.

Notes

1 Reprinted from *Globalizations*, 3(3), 2006, pp. 297–315. The original version had additional text incorporating issues regarding women who had been trafficked.

2 I refer to the last three and a half to four decades. Other periods include the latter nineteenth century to World War I and the period after World War II.

3 Which Hochschild identified (1995; Ehrenreich and Hochschild 2002).

4 Given that the literature on female domestic workers is substantial and space is limited, I focus mainly on those migrating from Asian countries.

5 The ILO Convention entitled Discrimination (Employment and Occupation) Convention, 1958 (No. 111), defines discrimination as 'any distinction, exclusion or preference made on the basis of race, colour, sex, religion, political opinion, national extraction or social origin, which has the effect of nullifying or impairing equality of opportunity or treatment in employment or occupation' (ILO 2003a).

6 These conflicts and the gender inequalities that arise are illustrated by the Philippines, Sri Lanka and Bangladesh. These three cases are examined in the original article.

7 The foundations of a human rights approach rest in documents such as the UN charter, the UN Universal Declaration

of Human Rights (1948), seven UN human rights treaties, and various conventions on refugees, trafficking, and crime (GCIM 2005; ILO 2004b).

8 The full name is The 1990 International Convention on the Protection of the Rights of all Migrant Workers and Members of their Families.

References

Abu-Habib, L. (1998) 'The use and abuse of female domestic workers from Sri Lanka in Lebanon', *Gender and Development*, 6(1): 52–6.

Alegado, D. T. (1997) 'The labor export industry and post-1986 Philippine economic development', *Pilipinas*, 29: 19–38.

Asis, M. M. B., S. Huang and B. S. A. Yeoh (2004) 'When the light of the home is abroad: unskilled female migration and the Filipino family', *Singapore Journal of Tropical Geography*, 25(2): 198–215.

Bach, S. (2003) 'International migration of health workers: labour and social issues', Working Paper in Sectoral Activities Programme, Geneva: International Labour Office, www.ilo.org/public/english/dialogue/sector/papers/health/wp209.pdf.

Ball, R. E. (2004) 'Divergent development, racialised rights: globalised labour markets and the trade of nurses – the case of the Philippines', *Women's Studies International Forum*, 27(2): 119–33.

Barber, P. G. (2000) 'Agency in Philippine women's labour migration and provisional diaspora', *Women's Studies International Forum*, 23(4): 399–411.

Bell, D. A. (2001) 'Equal rights for foreign resident workers? The case of Filipina domestic workers in Hong Kong and Singapore', *Dissent*, Fall, pp. 26–34.

Blue, S. A. (2004) 'State policy, economic crisis, gender, and family ties: determinants of family remittances to Cuba', *Economic Geography*, 80(1): 63–82.

Buckman, R. and T. Saywell (2004) 'Domestic disputes: for Asia's maids, years of abuse spill into the open', *Wall Street Journal*, 19 February, p. 1A.

Chang, G. (2000) *Disposable Domestics: Immigrant Women Workers in the Global Economy*, Cambridge, MA: South End Press.

Chang, K. A. and J. M. Groves (2000) 'Neither "saints" nor "prostitutes": sexual discourse in the Filipina domestic worker community in Hong Kong', *Women's Studies International Forum*, 23(1): 73–87.

Cheng, S.-J. A. (2004) 'When the personal meets the global at home: Filipina domestics and their female employers in Taiwan', *Frontiers*, 25(2): 31–52.

Cheung, T. S. and Bong Ho Mok (1998) 'How Filipina maids are treated in Hong Kong – a comparison between Chinese and Western employers', *Social Justice Research*, 11(2): 173–92.

Chin, C. B. N. (1997) 'Walls of silence and late twentieth century representations of the foreign female domestic worker: the case of Filipino and Indonesian female servants in Malaysia', *International Migration Review*, 31(2): 353–85.

— (1998) *In Service and Servitude: Foreign Domestic Workers and the Malaysian 'Modernity' Project*, New York: Columbia University Press.

Connell, J. and R. P. C. Brown (2004) 'The remittances of migrant Tongan and Samoan nurses from Australia', *Human Resources for Health*, 2(2): 1–21.

Constable, Nicole (1997) *Maid to Order in Hong Kong: Stories of Filipina Workers*, Ithaca, NY: Cornell University Press.

— (1999) 'At home but not at home: Filipina narratives of ambivalent returns', *Cultural Anthropology*, 14(2): 203–28.

Dasgupta, A. (2003) 'Rights – Bangladesh: returning women migrants get no warm welcome', 25 July, ipsnews.net/interna.asp?idnews=19401.

DeAlwis, M. (2002) 'The changing role of women in Sri Lankan society', *Social Research*, 69(3): 675–91.

Ehrenreich, B. and A. R. Hochschild (2002) *Global Woman: Nannies, Maids, and Sex Workers in the New Economy*, New York: Metropolitan Books (Henry Holt and Co.).

Frank, R. (2001) 'For a Philippine town, monthly allowances pave a road to riches', *Wall Street Journal*, 22 May, pp. A1, A6.

Gamburd, M. R. (1999) 'Class identity and the international division of labor; Sri Lanka's migrant housemaids', *Anthropology of Work Review*, XIX(3): 4–8.

— (2000) *The Kitchen Spoon's Handle*, Ithaca, NY: Cornell University Press.

GCIM (Global Commission on International Migration) (2005) *Migration in an Interconnected World: New Directions for Action*, Switzerland: SRO-Kundig, www.gcim.org.

Gibson, K., L. Law and D. McKay (2001) 'Beyond heroes and victims: Filipina contract migrants, economic activism and class transformations', *International Feminist Journal of Politics*, 3(3): 365–86.

Hawthorne, L. (2001) 'The globalisation of the nursing workforce: barriers confronting overseas qualified nurses in Australia', *Nursing Inquiry*, 8(4): 213–29.

Heyzer, N. and V. Wee (1994) 'Domestic workers in transient overseas employment: who benefits, who profits', in N. Heyzer, G. Lycklama a Nijcholt and N. Weerakoon, *The Trade in Domestic Workers: Causes, Mechanisms and Consequences of International Migration*, London: Zed Books, pp. 31–101.

Hochschild, A. R. (1995) 'The culture of politics: traditional, postmodern, cold-modern, and warm-modern ideals of care', *Social Politics*, pp. 331–46.

— (2000) 'Global care chains and emotional surplus value', in W. Hutton and A. Giddens (eds), *On the Edge: Living with Global Capitalism*, London: Jonathan Cape.

— (2002) 'Love and gold', in B. Ehrenreich and A. Hochschild (eds), *Global Woman: Nannies, Maids, and Sex Workers in the New Economy*, New York: Metropolitan Books (Henry Holt and Co.), pp. 15–30.

ILO (International Labour Organization) (2003a) 'Booklet 1: Introduction: why the focus on women international migrant workers', in *An Information Guide – Preventing Discrimination, Exploitation and Abuse of Women Migrant Workers*, Geneva: International Labour Office.

— (2003b) 'Booklet 4: Working and living abroad', in *An Information Guide – Preventing Discrimination, Exploitation and Abuse of Women Migrant Workers*, Geneva: International Labour Office.

— (2004a) *Towards a Fair Deal for Migrant Workers in the Global Economy*, Report VI, International Labour Conference, 92nd Session, Geneva: International Labour Office.

— (2004b) *A Fair Globalization: Creating Opportunities for All*, World Commission on the Social Dimension of Globalization, www.ilo.org/public/english/wcsdg/docs/report.pdf.

IOM (International Organization for Migration) (2005) *World Migration Report 2005*, Geneva: International Organization for Migration.

Jolly, S. (2003) 'Gender and migration in Asia: overview and annotated bibliography', Paper presented at the Regional Conference on Migration, Development and Pro-Poor Policy Choices in Asia, Dhaka, 22–24 June.

Lan, P.-C. (2003) 'Negotiating social boundaries and private zones: the micropolitics of employing migrant domestic workers', *Social Problems*, 50(4): 525–49.

Lim, L. L. and N. Oishi (1996) *International Labour Migration of Asian Women: Distinctive Characteristics and Policy Concerns*, Geneva: ILO.

Loveband, A. (2004) 'Positioning the product: Indonesian migrant women workers in Taiwan', *Journal of Contemporary Asia*, 34(3): 336–48.

Lund, R. and S. M. Panda (2000) 'The Asian financial crisis, women's work and forced migration', *Norsk Geografisk Tidsskrift* [Norwegian Journal of Geography], 54: 128–33.

McNeil-Walsh, C. (2004) 'Widening the discourse: a case for the use of post-colonial theory in the analysis of South African nurse migration to Britain', *Feminist Review*, 77(1): 120–24.

Menjívar, C. (1999) 'The intersection of work and gender: Central American immigrant women and employment in California', *American Behavioral Scientist*, 42(4): 601–27.

Misra, J., J. Woodring and S. N. Merz (2006) 'The globalization of care work: neoliberal economic restructuring and migration policy', *Globalizations*, 3(3): 317–32.

Ogaya, C. (2004) 'Social discourses on Filipino women migrants', *Feminist Studies*, 77(1): 180–85.

Oishi, N. (2005) *Women in Motion: Globalization, State Policies, and Labor Migration in Asia*, Stanford, CA: Stanford University Press.

O'Neill, K. (2004) 'Labor export as government policy: the case of the Philippines', *Migration Information Source*, 1 January.

Parreñas, R. S. (2001a) 'Mothering from a distance: emotions, gender, and inter-generational relations in Filipino transnational families', *Feminist Studies*, 27(2): 361–90.

— (2001b) *Servants of Globalization: Women, Migration, and Domestic Work*, Palo Alto, CA: Stanford University Press.

— (2002) 'The care crisis in the Philippines: children and transnational families in the new global economy', in B. Ehrenreich and A. R. Hochschild (eds), *Global Woman: Nannies, Maids, and Sex Workers in the New Economy*, New York: Metropolitan Books (Henry Holt and Co.), pp. 39–54.

Perlez, J. (2004) 'Asian maids often find abuse, not riches, abroad', *New York Times*, 22 June.

Piper, N. (2005) 'Gender and migration', Paper prepared for the Policy Analysis and Research Programme of the Global Commission on International Migration, www.gcim. org/attachements/TP10.pdf.

Piper, N. and R. Ball (2001) 'Globalisation of Asian migrant labour: the Philippine–Japan connection', *Journal of Contemporary Asia*, 31(4): 533–55.

Pyle, J. L. (1999) 'Third World women and global restructuring', in J. S. Chafetz (ed.), *Handbook of the Sociology of Gender*, Plenum Publishing, pp. 81–104.

— (2001) 'Sex, maids, and export processing: risks and reasons for gendered global production networks', *International Journal of Politics, Culture, and Society*, 15(1): 55–76.

— (2005) 'Critical globalization studies and gender', in R. P. Appelbaum and W. I. Robinson (eds), *Critical Globalization Studies*, New York: Routledge, pp. 249–57.

— (2006) 'Globalization, transnational migration, and gendered care work: introduction', *Globalizations*, 3(3): 283–95.

Pyle, J. L. and K. Ward (2003) 'Recasting our understanding of gender and work during global restructuring', *International Sociology*, 18(3): 461–89.

Rosca, N. (1995) 'The Philippines shameful export', *The Nation*, 260(15): 522–3.

Samarasinghe, V. (1998) 'The feminization of foreign currency earnings: women's labor in Sri Lanka', *Journal of Developing Areas*, 32(3): 303–25.

Santos, A. (2002) 'The Philippines: migration and trafficking in women', in J. Raymond et al. (eds), *A Comparative Study of Women Trafficked in the Migration Process*, Coalition Against Trafficking in Women, action.web.ca/home/ catw/attach/CATW%20Comparative %20Study%202002.pdf.

Siddiqui, T. (2003) 'Migration as a livelihood strategy of the poor: the Bangladesh case', Manuscript presented at the Regional Conference on Migration, Development and Pro-Poor Policy Choices in Asia, Dhaka, www.eldis. org/go/topics/dossiers/livelihoods- connect&id=17526&type=Document.

Silvey, R. (2004) 'Transnational migration and the gender politics of scale: Indonesian domestic workers in Saudi Arabia', *Singapore Journal of Tropical Geography*, 25(2): 141–55.

Surtees, R. (2003) 'Female migration and

trafficking in women: the Indonesian context', *Development*, 46(3): 99–106.

Tyner, J. A. (1996) 'The gendering of Philippine international labor migration', *Professional Geographer*, 48(4): 405–16.

UNDP (United Nations Development Program) (1999) *Human Development Report 1999: Globalization with a Human Face*, New York: Oxford University Press.

UNIFEM (United Nations Development Fund for Women) (2005) *Progress of the World's Women 2005*, New York: UNDP.

United Nations (2006) *The World's Women 2005: Progress in Statistics*, New York: United Nations.

US Department of State (2005) *Trafficking in Persons Report (2005)*, www.state. gov/g/tip/rls/tiprpt/2005/.

Villalba, M. A. C. (2002) 'Philippines: good practices for the protection of Filipino women migrant workers in vulnerable jobs', ILO GENPROM Working Paper no. 8. Geneva: International Labour Office, www.ilo.org/wcmsp5/ groups/public/---ed_emp/documents/ publication/wcms_117953.pdf.

Waldman, A. (2005) 'Sri Lankan maids' high price for foreign jobs', *New York Times*, 8 May.

Wee, V. and A. Sim (2004) 'Transnational networks in female labour migration', in A. Ananta and E. N. Arifin (eds), *International Migration in Southeast Asia*, Singapore: Institute of Southeast Asian Studies, pp. 166–99.

Weekley, K. (2004) 'Saving pennies for the state. A new role for Filipino migrant workers?', *Journal of Contemporary Asia*, 34(3): 349–63.

Yeoh, B. S. A. and S. Huang (1998) 'Negotiating public space: strategies and styles of migrant female domestic workers in Singapore', *Urban Studies*, 35(3): 583–602.

— (2000) '"Home" and "away": foreign domestic workers and negotiations of diasporic identity in Singapore', *Women's Studies International Forum*, 23(4): 413–29.

27 | The Korean economic crisis and working women

Haejin Kim and Paula B. Voos

The Asian financial crisis in the late 1990s dramatically affected Korea's economic structure and its labour markets. A serious recession in Korea was precipitated by the Asian financial market crash and the weakness of the domestic Korean institutions, particularly financial institutions. The liberalization of Korean financial markets earlier in the 1990s had brought considerable foreign capital into the Korean stock market, which contributed to an unprecedented stock market boom and a strong economic expansion. In late 1997, foreign investors rapidly withdrew their money from the Korean stock market in response to the financial crisis in other Asian countries. This, in combination with policies designed to stabilize the currency by the International Monetary Fund (IMF) and Korean government, threw the economy into a serious recession.

The financial crisis officially ended in 2001 after Korea repaid all the funds loaned by the IMF. Nonetheless, the economic crisis had an enormous impact on Korean society. The divorce rate rose owing to economic difficulties; emigration increased to countries such as the USA and Australia; and social bonds based on Confucianism weakened (A. Kim 2004).

The most significant changes produced by the financial crisis occurred in the labour market. The IMF imposed conditions for the loan of recovery funds and these conditions had both direct and indirect effects on the labour market. As D. Kim and S. Kim (2003: 352) explain, 'The Korean government was required to provide containment of inflationary pressure through tight monetary and fiscal policy, fundamental restructuring of the financial sector, and reduction of corporations' excessive reliance on short-debt financing.' The IMF demanded structural adjustments including legalization of lay-offs, relaxation of limits on the worker dispatch system (of temporary or leased workers), and strengthening unemployment insurance (I. Kim 1998). These demands were, in short, to enhance flexibility in the labour market. Real wages fell 9.3 per cent in 1998 in response to these policies (D. Kim and S. Kim 2003). Numerous reports during the period (e.g. Shin 1999) described instances of human suffering – Korean news carried many grim stories of male household heads who were unemployed, deserted their families, or became homeless.

However, behind these headline stories was a simultaneous reality: the suffering of women. Women workers were the first to be let go in the restructuring of banks and financial institutions. Part-time and temporary work spread rapidly among women workers (Cho 1999). Women, even more than men, experienced difficulty finding work, particularly college-educated women. During the first year of the crisis, labour market non-participation among college-educated women increased by 31.8 per cent as they became 'discouraged workers' who had given up actively looking for jobs because they believed none was available. On the other hand, many housewives had to take whatever work they could find in order to maintain households, given their husbands' reduced earnings (Shin 1999).

This article investigates changes in women's labour market status between 1997 and 2002 to evaluate the overall impact of the economic crisis and subsequent recovery on women along a variety of dimensions: employment; earnings; returns to education; unionization; and so forth, using a 'before and after' research design. Data from the first year, 1997, largely reflect the economic situation before the crisis (at the end of that year); by 2002, Korea had recovered almost fully in a macroeconomic sense, but nonetheless there were permanent changes in its labour markets.[1]

Status of women workers in Korea

Traditional Korean society was highly patriarchal. For instance, daughters were granted the same legal rights to inheritance as sons only a few years ago. Even today, when Korea's birth rate is lower than that of most industrialized countries, sons are still preferred to daughters.

Korean industrialization initially took advantage of this social situation. Women workers, mostly young girls from rural areas, were the majority of the labour force in light manufacturing industries in the 1960s – the textile, garment, shoe and electronics industries. Young women were attracted to factories by the opportunity to study beyond the mandatory Grade 6 education level (it is now Grade 9). Special industry-affiliated schools were built for young women workers to attend after working hours. However, it was not uncommon for a young girl with a sixth-grade education to work eighty hours a week in order to send her family money for her brothers' college education. Most women workers in the 1960s and 1970s worked in factories established in Export Processing Zones or in sweatshops in big cities. During this industrialization period, union density among women was the same as that among men in Korea (Seoul Women Workers' Association and Korean Women Workers Associations United 1997).

Traditional Korean society had sharply delineated gender roles, and employment roles initially reflected this social context. In the 1970s heavy manufacturing industries, such as steel, auto and shipbuilding, developed in Korea – here men were typically employed. As the economy shifted from female-dominated light manufacturing to male-dominated heavy manufacturing, Korean women continued to experience various forms of discrimination, including occupational/industrial segregation, lower earnings than men in similar jobs, less opportunity for education or on-the-job training, and fewer promotion opportunities. The labour division by gender, with men as primary breadwinners and women as primary caregivers, played an ongoing role inside and outside the workplace (ibid.).

Nonetheless, the situation was not static. The gender wage gap continuously narrowed over the course of development. Simple wage ratios, unadjusted for hours, education, occupation or other productivity-related attributes of workers, indicate this long-run trend. The male–female wage ratio rose from 44.5 per cent in 1980 to 53.4 per cent in 1990; 58 per cent in 1995; 61 per cent in 1997; and 62.8 per cent in 2003 (Korean Women's Development Institute 2000, 2004).

The decrease in the gender wage gap was accompanied by changing ideas about women's role and by Korean women's increased labour force participation. The labour force participation rate among women aged fifteen and above increased by 22.9 percentage points between 1960 and 2002, while that for men increased by only 1.3 percentage points. As a result, in 2002, women were 41.6 per cent of the Korean workforce (Korean National Statistical Office 2004).[2] One of the factors having the strongest influence on the narrowing of the gender wage gap has been education. The number of women with no more than an elementary school education shows a 54.3 percentage point decrease between 1970 and 2000, while that of their male counterparts shows a 36.1 percentage point decrease. Moreover, the percentages of women with a high-school/college degree or more have increased about six times and eleven times, respectively; for men, it has increased about three times for both groups (Korean Women's Development Institute 2002).

Hence, prior to the economic crisis in 1997, Korean women worked in a context where there was a considerable legacy of economic/social discrimination, but with a more recent history of rising education, greater social equality, and rising economic opportunities for women. It was also a context in which all workers had benefited from a democratization of government and society in the 1980s and 1990s and from the growth of the Korean labour movement, particularly after 1987.

Effects of the crisis on women workers

Employment As noted above, the financial crisis had a large negative impact on employment. Both men and women were affected, but employment dropped more in percentage terms for women than for men at the outset of the crisis. After being laid off in the downturn, more women than men gave up looking for jobs. Kang (1999) finds that the 'discouraged worker effect' occurred primarily among young, single, pink-collar women and it outweighed the 'added worker effect' among middle-aged, married women who entered the labour market to maintain family income levels as the crisis affected their husbands' earnings.

Furthermore, the initial decline in employment happened somewhat differently between women and men. For men, it occurred in manufacturing industries and small-sized companies. Women suffered the severest decline in service industries (particularly pink-collar occupations) and in both small- and large-sized companies (ibid.).

Data on the number of employees by gender tend to support the view that women were used as a buffer during the economic crisis. They were laid off first and 'encouraged' to withdraw from the labour market during the economic crisis. Shin (1999) finds that 86.2 per cent of employers targeted women for 'voluntary' resignation, especially women from double-income families or married women with children. Anecdotal evidence supports the statistical picture: according to a Korean study that does not list corporate names, two advertising companies eliminated a female-dominated department and targeted college-educated female employees for resignation; furthermore, an insurance company and a construction company transferred to remote locations female employees who had not resigned voluntarily (Workers' Institute for Management Analysis 2001).

Casual, non-standard employment in Korea soared as a direct consequence of the structural adjustments demanded by the IMF. Even though temporary employment increased for both women and men, it increased more for women. The regular employment to total wage employment ratio among women reportedly decreased by 22 per cent between November 1997 and March 1999, compared to a 10 per cent decrease among men (Cho 1999). Many banks during the crisis forced female tellers to resign and then rehired them as temporary employees (Y. Kim 1998).

One study (Workers' Institute for Management Analysis 2001) reports that 86.7 per cent of temporary agency/leased workers worked continuously for one employer doing the same job. Furthermore, Korean temporary workers had few opportunities to move to regular jobs; about 70 per cent of temporary workers could not escape this status after five years as temporary workers. This was especially true for women (Keum 2000).

Regarding the degree to which women workers are affected by recessions, scholars (e.g. Rubery 1988) have suggested three different theories based on empirical studies in developed countries. The first is the buffer hypothesis. According to this theory, women are typically a labour reserve, whom employers turn to in economic upturns and expel in economic downturns (Benston 1969). The second theory is the job segregation or segmentation hypothesis. This perspective suggests that women's employment is not affected much by economic recessions because segregated, female-dominated occupations are relatively insulated from business cycles. The last theory is the substitution hypothesis. During recessions, this theory predicts, employers substitute women for men as a cost-saving strategy. It can be direct substitution of women for men as in the USA (Humphries 1988), or indirect substitution of unstable jobs (for women) for stable jobs (for men), as in Britain (Rubery and Tarling 1988).

When the Korean case was assessed against these different models, the buffer theory and the substitution theory each received some support. Women were hit harder by the crisis and hence played a role as an overall buffer in the labour market. However, five years after the economic crisis, women's rates of employment and labour market participation had recovered almost completely. Proportionally, women's employment grew more than men's over the five-year period from 1997 to 2002. This could be interpreted as employers substituting female employees for male over the longer term. This can be understood as a combined outcome of the mandates of the IMF, the response of the Korean government, and the actions of Korean employers to restructure the economy at the expense of job security.

Occupational sex segregation and pay Recessions can affect not only the number of women who are employed, but also other aspects of women's employment, including sex segregation and the gender wage gap.

Occupational sex segregation in Korea changed markedly after the economic crisis. Before 1997, even though the proportion of workers in female-dominated occupations decreased, the changes were modest. However, after 1998, the proportion of employees in gender-integrated occupations (those with 40–59 per cent women) increased substantially. The trend towards integration was particularly noted among teaching professionals, office clerks and certain categories of labourers and salespersons.

According to crowding theory, given gender stereotyping of economic roles, women are crowded into female-dominated jobs, lowering wages owing to oversupply (Bergmann 1986; Sorensen 1989a). Therefore, this theory predicts that if occupational sex segregation is reduced, women's crowding in female-dominated occupations will be lessened and the gender wage gap will decline. Did that, in fact, occur in Korea, given the events of the financial crisis?

For our analysis of the effects of the financial crisis on women's wages, we used the 1997 and 2002 Wage Structure Surveys administered by the Korean Ministry of Labour. In 1997 there were 40,536 persons in the 10 per cent random sample, and in 2002, 36,755. In this data set, as in the aggregate data, the overall wage gap between men and women in Korea decreased between 1997 and 2002, as women's wages rose from 58 per cent to 62 per cent of men's.[3]

In order to investigate pay differences between Korean women and men, we estimated conventional earnings equations for men and women in each year, with controls for education, other individual characteristics (tenure, career,

TABLE 27.1 Regression results

	Female		Male	
	1997	2002	1997	2002
Education				
High school	0.1471[3]	0.0847[3]	0.1018[3]	0.0459[3]
College – 2 yrs	0.2085[3]	0.1083[3]	0.1828[3]	0.1006[3]
College – 4 yrs or more	0.4733[3]	0.3467[3]	0.3565[3]	0.3363[3]
Experience	0.0104[3]	0.0087[3]	0.0319[3]	0.0317[3]
Experience – 2	−0.0003[3]	−0.0002[3]	−0.0006[3]	−0.0007[3]
Married	0.0118	0.0131	0.0382[3]	0.0713[3]
Union	0.0523[3]	0.0372[3]	−0.0180[1]	−0.257[3]
Tenure	0.0422[3]	0.0074[1]	0.0282[3]	0.0082[3]
Tenure – 2	−0.0006[3]	0.0006[3]	−0.0003[3]	0.0002[3]
Career	0.0637[3]	0.0342[3]	0.0589[3]	0.0279[3]
Career – 2	−0.045[3]	−0.0010	−0.0037[3]	−0.0010[2]
Skill level				
Engineers/Master craftsmen	−0.0367	0.0649	−0.0398[2]	−0.0245[1]
Craftsmen	0.0938[3]	0.0063	0.0498[3]	−0.0263
Other certificate holders	0.0247	−0.0481[2]	−0.0003	−0.0670[3]
Establishment size				
30–99	0.0461[2]	0.0343[2]	0.0003	0.0388[3]
100–299	0.0886[3]	0.0591[3]	0.0572[3]	0.0537[3]
300–499	0.1243[3]	0.0642[3]	0.1186[3]	0.0842[3]
500+	0.2389[3]	0.1022[3]	0.2280[3]	0.1064[3]
Industry controls (9)				
Occupation controls (6)				
Constant	7.9612[3]	8.3669[3]	8.1066[3]	8.3825[3]
N	10864	9048	29672	27707
R-squared	0.6216[3]	0.5135[3]	0.6042[3]	0.5477[3]

Notes: The dependent variable is the natural logarithm of hourly earnings. Tenure is the number of years with the same employer; career is the number of years in the same occupation. 1. Significant at the .10 level on a 2-tailed t test. 2. Significant at the .05 level on a 2-tailed t test. 3. Significant at the .01 level on a 2-tailed t test.

skill level, experience and marital status), union representation, establishment size, industry and occupation, using an ordinary least squares estimating procedure.[4] The resulting estimates are presented in Table 27.1.[5]

The Oaxaca decomposition indicates the degree to which the overall pay difference is 'explained' by personal and job-related variables in the equation. The residual, or 'unexplained', portion of the pay difference is often used as a proxy for wage discrimination (Oaxaca 1973). It is a reasonable indicator of changes in discrimination over time – under the assumption that unobserved individual characteristics explain a constant proportion of the wage differences in both years.

TABLE 27.2 Oaxaca decomposition of the gender wage gap in 1997 and 2002

Panel A: Based on estimates in Table 27.1

	1997		2002	
Total wage gap	0.5465	100.0%	0.4669	100.0%
Education	0.0671	12.3%	0.0554	11.9%
Other individual characteristics	0.2148	39.3%	0.0168	35.9%
Union	−0.0119	−0.4%	−0.0037	−0.8%
Establishment size	0.0119	2.2%	0.0042	0.9%
Industry	0.0030	0.6%	−0.0107	−2.3%
Occupation	0.0417	7.6%	0.0780	10.3%
Total explained		61.6%		55.8%
Unexplained/'discrimination'		38.4%		44.2%

Panel B: Adding percentage female categories

	1997		2002	
Total wage gap	0.5465	100.0%	0.4669	100.0%
Female percentage categories	0.0326	5.9%	0.0230	4.9%
Education	0.0673	12.3%	0.0545	11.7%
Other individual characteristics	0.2130	39.0%	0.1672	35.8%
Union	−0.0021	−0.4%	−0.0037	−0.8%
Establishment size	0.0119	2.2%	0.0044	0.9%
Industry	0.0020	0.4%	−0.0121	−2.6%
Occupation	0.0257	4.7%	0.0458	9.8%
Total explained		64.1%		59.8%
Unexplained/'discrimination'		36.0%		40.2%

Note: The decomposition is based on estimated coefficients in the male earnings equations.

According to these estimates, pay discrimination against women, as measured by the residual, increased between 1997 and 2002 in Korea (see the upper panel of Table 27.2 for the proportion of the wage gap not explained by the variables listed in Table 27.1). An increase in the residual is surprising in light of the decline in occupational segregation in this period: according to these estimates, it actually rose from 38 per cent to 44 per cent of the overall pay differential. Korean women improved their productive characteristics, such as education, and their aggregate pay grew more equal to that of Korean men over this period, but they experienced no lessening of wage discrimination as measured by the residual. If anything, wage discrimination appears to have intensified.

This is unexpected in light of crowding theory. According to crowding theory, if occupational sex segregation is reduced, then the wage gap between male and female workers based on occupational differences should be reduced. And occupational segregation did fall overall in Korea between 1997 and 2002.

In order to explore the role occupational segregation may have played in the evolving Korean wage structure, we evaluated a further set of equations that included variables measuring the degree to which a particular job is gender-segregated, with the 0–19 per cent female category taken as the base. The resulting Oaxaca decomposition is presented in the lower panel of Table 27.2. It indicates that even though pay differences due to occupational segregation decreased from 1997 to 2002, overall discrimination against women still increased, at least as measured by the residual.

While there was an overall reduction in occupational segregation between 1997 and 2002, the Korean women who moved into integrated occupations suffered a larger wage gap than before. Entry of women into integrated occupations led to a *lower* relative wage of women in these occupations in 2002 than in 1997. One explanation might be that women who entered these non-traditional occupations did so into the lower echelons. That possibility has encouraging implications in the longer run – once Korean women move into higher echelons in the integrated occupations (assuming such upward movement is not hindered by 'glass ceilings'), their earnings should improve relative to men's.

The return to education The consequences for women of structural adjustments, triggered by the IMF or the World Bank, have received special attention in several studies. Based on experiences in some Latin American and African countries, many researchers (e.g. Stewart 1992) argue that women are excluded from structural adjustment processes, both as participants and beneficiaries. During economic crises, women workers suffer from reduced employment opportunities, especially in the public sector, and their real wages fall even more than men's. Structural adjustment programmes often focus on financial matters, rather than on improving education or other infrastructure, which affects women more adversely because education has been an important vehicle for enhancing women's economic status. Since education has played a critical role for women's labour market status in Korea, it is important to examine the effect of the crisis on women's return to education.

In general, workers' education level is highest in integrated occupations and lowest in female-dominated occupations in Korea (Hwang 2003). In 1997, more highly educated women worked disproportionately in gender-integrated or male-dominant occupations, where the return to education was higher than in female-dominated occupations (H. Kim 1999). When the occupational sex segregation structure changed owing to the economic crisis and restructuring, what happened to the return to education for women? A partial answer to this question is contained in Table 27.1. Whereas there was a markedly higher return to education for women than for men in 1997, by 2002 the patterns of educational returns were similar. This is true both for women with four or more years of college and those with a two-year college degree. In 2002, there was still a slightly higher return to high-school education for women than for men, but for all college graduates the higher return to education for women had almost disappeared. Simply put, as more Korean women obtained higher education, their rate of return to education fell to male levels. The decrease in the return to education in Korea between 1997 and 2002 disproportionately affected highly educated women in female-dominated occupations.

Women and unions One final aspect of the economic crisis and women that is important is the relationship between gender and union organization. In the 1970s, workers began to challenge traditional, government-dominated unions in Korea and women workers played a major role in the resulting 'democratic union movement'. At that time, women workers in democratic unions enjoyed union premiums such as higher wages and better benefits than non-union workers; however, they also faced serious oppression both from employers and the dictatorship that then governed Korea.

The democratic union movement expanded in the 1980s to include workers in the auto, steel and shipbuilding industries, most of whom were men, and the slight gap in the unionization rate between men and women in Korea began to widen. At the same time, the union movement made itself a major force for change in Korean society. In the early 1990s, a second national union federation, the Korea Confederation of Trade Unions, was organized to represent this strengthening democratic union movement. That development played an important role in making the existing national union federation, the Federation of Korean Trade Unions, more independent from government control and more focused on its members' interests.

An interesting aspect of the Korean situation involves the union wage premium. In comparison to the USA, the impact of union membership on earnings in Korea has been estimated to be very small, non-existent or even negative. Previous studies indicate that Korean women typically received higher union wage premiums than men: 3.4 per cent versus 2.8 per cent in 1988, for instance (J. Kim 1991). Our results are similar (see Table 27.1): in our cross-sectional analysis, the wage coefficient on union membership was negative for men in both 1997 and 2002, but small and positive for women, in the range of 3–5 per cent.

We interpret the small differences between union and non-union wages in Korea as the product both of a substantial 'threat effect' on non-union employers and a particular political strategy on the part of Korean unions. With the emergence of the union movement as a driving force in Korean society, its demonstrated militancy had a strong threat effect on non-union workers' wages, at least in large corporations. H. Kim (2001), using 1997 data, finds a negative relationship between threat effect factors (the unionization rate and the ratio of democratic union members to total union members in industries) and the union wage effect: her research supports the notion of a strong threat effect in this time period.

Furthermore, since 1987 the Korean union movement has not confined itself to wage and economic gains – rather it has enlarged its activities into the political arena. One example would be the general strike of 1997 over labour law reform. Given the politicized and militant nature of the union movement, Korean employers may have felt so threatened by possible labour disputes beyond their control that they were willing to pay union-comparable wages to avoid unionization.

Korean unions, in general, used the economic crisis to recruit more members and form twenty industrial (as opposed to single-enterprise) unions, a move to overcome worsening working conditions (D. Kim and S. Kim 2003). At the national level, the union movement also tried to reduce contingent employment and its associated problems. In the midst of this, a new approach to unionism among women workers emerged. At the time, proportionally fewer women workers were represented by unions (6.9 per cent in 1997 and 6.7 per cent in 2002) than men (17.3 per cent and 18.9 per cent, respectively) (Korean Women's Development Institute 2005); and the crisis threatened to further reduce the proportion of women who were organized, insofar as stable union jobs were being replaced by unstable, contingent jobs, particularly for women.

This reality stimulated a new approach to organizing women workers and led to the formation of the Korean Women's Trade Union (KWTU) in 1999, to solve issues facing contingent women workers and women who work in small firms.[6] The KWTU began by organizing temporary school personnel (assistant cafeteria personnel, traffic assistants, science-class helpers and librarians), leased or subcontracted workers (janitors in universities and hotels) and independent contractors (golf club caddies and door-to-door tutors); it negotiated a number of contracts with employers for its members. Since its establishment with 400 members, the KWTU has expanded to twelve regional branches and five occupational branches (Korean Women's Trade Union 2006). This is the first time that any union has explicitly targeted contingent workers for membership since industrialization began in Korea.

The economic crisis worsened Korean women's working conditions. However, at the same time, it accelerated a strategic approach to unionism among working women. The new KWTU emphasis on organizing contingent workers and workers in small firms is an example of such new approaches, with the potential to improve Korean women's economic situation, particularly at lower levels in the labour market.

Conclusion

During the economic crisis in the late 1990s, the employment structure changed substantially in Korea. At the outset of the crisis, more women lost jobs than men -- a fact that supports the theory that women's employment is often an economic 'buffer', at least in the short run. However, as the structural adjustment period continued and recovery set in, women's employment rose more than men's – an outcome congruent with substitution theory. In the process many jobs became casual both for women and men. Furthermore, occupational sex segregation was reduced considerably in the period of structural adjustment.

As a whole, the reduced sex segregation did not have the expected outcome in terms of its effect on male/female earnings differentials. One would expect reduced differentials with a less segregated occupational structure. However, even after we controlled for the characteristics of employees and of jobs, there was no lessening of pay differences between women and men in Korea between 1997 and 2002.[7] Furthermore, as more women became more educated, the return to education fell – more precipitously for women than for men – especially for women with the highest educational attainment in Korea. We were struck by the persistence of, and seeming intensification of, wage discrimination against women. The economic crisis in Korea was a context unfavourable to women's advancement.

We recognize that our study is not a tight 'test' of any above-mentioned theories because so many things changed simultaneously between 1997 and 2002 in Korea. Nonetheless, we would argue that our research provides valuable policy implications for those working to advance the status of Korean working women. The first policy implication is that higher education alone probably will not improve the status of Korean women workers in the future to the same extent that it has done in the past. Increased education of women needs to be combined with policies that provide women with equal opportunities to ascend job ladders in all occupations, even non-traditional ones. Breaking 'glass ceilings' and allowing women to reach higher echelons within integrated occupations are especially important for highly educated women and would do much to further reduce the gender wage gap.

This leads to the second implication for Korean working women: the necessity of advocating for more effective enforcement of equality-related laws. Korea has an Equal Employment Law that requires equal treatment in recruitment, hiring, wages, training, promotion and lay-off, but its provisions were not followed during the financial crisis, particularly at its outset. It may be advisable to position demands for enforcement of women-specific laws within a context of general policies to improve the treatment of all workers, men and women. One example might be efforts to reduce the use of contingent employment. As long as increasing numbers of Koreans are forced to work as temporary workers, women will suffer more from precarious employment arrangements because women are more likely to work as temporary workers. A further example would be to modify Korean labour law to make it easier for workers to exercise their core labour rights.

Finally, Korean women need to continue to explore the benefits of union organization. Even though union/non-union wage differentials are small in Korea, this does not mean women workers cannot make gains through further organization. In fact, a new unionism among Korean women workers arose in the context of the economic crisis, as a response to issues like contingency that became increasingly salient during the crisis. Union involvement appears to be one way Korean women can advance their status in the labour market. Hence, a further policy recommendation would be for those who support the advancement of Korean women also to support efforts to build a new type of unionism in Korea.

The economic crisis of 1997 created setbacks for gender equality in Korea. At the same time, it encouraged long-run forces for change – reduced occupational segregation and exploration of new approaches by the labour movement – that bode well for ultimate improvements in Korean women's economic status.

Notes

1 Knowledgeable researchers (Keum and Choi 2001; Park and Kim 2002) have found that labour market changes in this period were dominated by the demand side (the crisis) rather than the supply side, so our research is predicated on this interpretation. However, labour market developments over a five-year period reflect various secular, cyclical and structural trends, and we do not attempt to disentangle those influences.

2 The labour force participation rate among Korean women (49.7 per cent) in 2002 was similar to that of Austria (49.9 per cent), France (49.6 per cent) or Germany (48.7 per cent) – albeit lower than that of the United States (57.8 per cent) or Canada (59.3 per cent) (Organisation for Economic Co-operation and Development 2002).

3 It should be noted here that use of this data implies that our findings will not reflect changes in wages in very small firms or in the informal sector.

4 The control variables are fairly standard except for two that are specific to this Korean data set: career and skill level. Career is the number of years a worker has been working in a specific occupation. Skill level is a set of 0–1 variables indicating technical certification.

5 The means, standard deviations and other statistical details are contained in the full version of this article, published in the *Journal of Contemporary Asia*, 37(2), May 2007, pp. 190–208.

6 The KWTU estimates that about two-thirds of all Korean women workers are contingent and that 64 per cent work for small employers.

7 At the same time, the entry of women into integrated occupations resulted in a bigger wage gap between these occupations and male-dominant ones.

References

Benston, M. (1969) 'The political economy of women's liberation', *Monthly Review*, 21(4).

Bergmann, B. (1986) *The Economic Emergence of Women*, New York: Basic Books.

Bettio, F. (1988) 'Sex-typing of occupation, the cycle and restructuring in Italy', in

J. Rubery (ed.), *Women and Recession*, London: Routledge & Kegan Paul.

Blau, F. and A. Beller (1988) 'Trends in earnings differentials by gender, 1971–81', *Industrial and Labor Relations Review*, 41(2).

Chae, C. (1993) *The Union Effect on Relative Wages in Monopoly Sector and Non-monopoly Sector*, Dissertation, Seoul National University (in Korean).

Chang, D. and J. Chae (2004) 'The transformation of Korean labour relations since 1997', *Journal of Contemporary Asia*, 34(4).

Cho, S. (1999) 'Sex-unequal structure in structural adjustment', *Korean Industrial and Labour Research*, 5(2) (in Korean).

Eurostat (2005) 'Gender pay gap in unadjusted form', epp.eurostat.cec.eu.int, accessed 8 April 2005.

Gupta, M., J. Zhenghua, L. Bohua, X. Zhenming, W. Chung and H. Bae (2003) 'Why is son preference so persistent in East and South Asia? A cross-country study of China, India, and the Republic of Korea', *Journal of Development Studies*, 40(2).

Ha, S. and S. Lee (2001) 'IMF and the crisis of the marginalized urban sector in Korea', *Journal of Contemporary Asia*, 31(2).

Humphries, J. (1988) 'Women's employment in restructuring America: the changing experience of women in three recessions', in J. Rubery (ed.), *Women and Recession*, London: Routledge & Kegan Paul.

Hwang, S. (2003) *Women's Occupational Choice and Employment Structure*, Research Report Series 2003-03, Seoul: Korean Labour Institute (in Korean).

Johnson, G. and G. Solon (1986) 'Estimates of the direct effects of comparable worth policy', *American Economic Review*, 76(5).

Kang, E. (1999) 'Economic crisis and trends of female labour market change', *Trend and Prospect*, 40 (in Korean).

Keum, J. (2000) 'Does there exist a trap of non-regular employment?', *Analysis of Labour Trend*, 13(4) (in Korean).

Keum, J. and J. Choi (2001) 'Study on the instability of the labour market around the financial crisis', *Korean Labour Economic Association Dissertation*, 24(1) (in Korean).

Kim, A. (2004) 'The social perils of the Korean financial crisis', *Journal of Contemporary Asia*, 34(2).

Kim, D. and S. Kim (2003) 'Globalization, financial crisis, and industrial relations: the case of South Korea', *Industrial Relations*, 42(3).

Kim, H. (1999) *The Effect of Education on the Wages of Women in Korea*, Master's thesis in Labor and Industrial Relations, New Brunswick, NJ: Rutgers University.

— (2001) 'The union wage effect in Korea', Unpublished paper presented at the Industrial Relations Research Association Annual Meeting, 5–7 January, New Orleans, LA.

Kim, I. (1998) 'The characteristics of the financial crisis and IMF', in *Assessment of IMF System from the Social Science Perspective*, Seoul: Seoul National University Publishing (in Korean).

Kim, J. (1991) 'Union wage effect: difference in wage determination between the union sector and the non-union sector in Korean manufacturing', *Kyong Jae Hak Yon Gu*, 39(1) (in Korean).

Kim, K. and S. Kwon (2003) *Five Years after the Exchange Crisis: What's Changed in Korean Economy?*, Seoul: Samsung Economic Research Institute (in Korean).

Kim, W. (2003) 'Economic crisis, downsizing and "Layoff Survivor's Syndrome"', *Journal of Contemporary Asia*, 33(4).

Kim, Y. (1998) 'Employment arrangements among women after IMF loan: cases of financial institutes', in Equal Employment Centre of Korean Womenlink, *Women's Right to Employment Is Suffering, What Are Alternatives?*, Workshop Proceedings, Seoul: Equal Employment Center of Korean Womanlink (in Korean).

Korean Ministry of Labour (2004) 'Employees by sex and occupation', laborstat.molab.go.kr/html/X7b82_r2c22.html, accessed 29 June 2004.

Korean National Statistical Office (2004) 'Overview of labour force participation by sex', kosis.nso.go.kr/cgi-bin/html_out.cgi?F=X6e68_r28c2e.html, accessed 29 June 2004.

Korean Women's Development Institute (2000) 'Wage, tenure, working hours, and turnover rate by sex', www.kwdi.re.kr/board/view.php?db=wifaq&category=5&no=310, accessed 7 April 2005.

— (2002) 'Composition of population by educational attainment and sex (25 years old and over)', www.kwdi.re.kr/d/stat_find_n_modify.php, accessed 8 April 2005.

— (2004) 'Monthly wage by sex and occupation and gender wage gap', kwdi.re.kr/stat_n_modify.php, accessed 7 April 2005.

— (2005) 'Union membership and union density by sex', kwdi.re.kr/d.stat_fnd_n_modify.php, accessed 17 February 2006.

Korean Women's Trade Union (2006) 'Introduction of KWTU', www.kwunion.or.kr/Intro, accessed 15 February 2006.

Milkman, R. (1976) 'Women's work and economic crisis: some lessons of the Great Depression', *Review of Radical Political Economy*, 8(1).

Monk-Turner, E. and C. Turner (2001) 'Sex differentials in earnings in the South Korean labor market', *Feminist Economics*, 7(1).

— (2004) 'The gender wage gap in South Korea: how much has changed in 10 years?', *Journal of Asian Economics*, 15(2).

Oaxaca, R. (1973) 'Male–female wage differentials in urban labor markets', *International Economic Review*, 14(3).

Organisation for Economic Co-operation and Development (2002) 'Labour market statistics – indicators', www1.oecd. org/scripts/cde/DoQuery.asp, accessed 7 April 2005.

Park, K. and Y. Kim (2002) 'Changes in labour force and wage structure around the 1997 economic crisis', *Korean Labour Economic Association Dissertation*, 25(3) (in Korean).

Rubery, J. (1988) 'Introduction', in J. Rubery (ed.), *Women and Recession*, London: Routledge & Kegean Paul.

Rubery, J. and R. Tarling (1988) 'Women's employment in declining Britain', in J. Rubery (ed.), *Women and Recession*, London: Routledge & Kegan Paul.

Seoul Women Workers' Association and Korean Women Workers Associations United (1997) *Wild Flowers! Flames! Your Name Is Women Workers*, Seoul: Seoul Women Workers' Association and Korean Women Workers Associations United (in Korean).

Shin, K. (1999) 'Where did many unemployed women go?' Female-unemployment in a paternalistic society', *Trend and Prospect*, 40 (in Korean).

Shin, Y. (1998) 'IMF policy toward Korea: from the World System Theory perspective', *Assessments of IMF System from the Social Science Perspective*, Seoul: Seoul National University Publishing (in Korean).

Sorensen, E. (1989a) 'The crowding hypothesis and comparable worth', *Journal of Human Resources*, 25(1).

— (1989b) 'Measuring the effect of occupational sex and race composition on earnings', in R. Michael and H. Hartmann (eds), *Pay Equity: Empirical Inquiries*, Washington, DC: National Academy Press.

— (1989c) 'Measuring the pay disparity between typically female occupations and other jobs: a bivariate selectivity approach', *Industrial and Labor Relations Review*, 42(4).

Stewart, F. (1992) 'Can adjustment programmes incorporate the interest of women?', in H. Afshar and C. Dennis (eds), *Women and Adjustment Policies in the Third World*, New York: St Martin's Press.

US Census Bureau (1987) 'Male–female differences in work experience, occupation, and earnings: 1984', *Current Population Reports*, Series P-70, vol. 10, Washington, DC: GPO.

— (2004) 'Income, poverty, and health insurance coverage in the United States: 2003', *Current Population Reports*, P60-226, Washington, DC: GPO.

Workers' Institute for Management Analysis (2001) 'The neo-liberalistic attacks of IMF and employment issues', Seoul: Workers' Institute for Management Analysis (in Korean).

PART FOUR

International women in social transformation

Introduction to Part Four

Nan Wiegersma

Our world is faced with dual crises in this period that are unparalleled since the Great Depression of the 1930s. A globalized economy has pushed a financial crisis originating in the USA to the farthest outreaches of the globe. This has slowed, stopped or reversed growth in less developed countries, causing unemployment and decreases in public services. An outmoded and broken international financial system is causing great hardship globally.

Meanwhile environmental crises involving energy resources and global warming are plaguing the planet. Increasingly unstable weather with floods, hurricanes and heat waves impact the less developed countries particularly harshly.

With these crises underlying other issues, there are global changes in women's health, public health policy and reproductive rights. Population control appears to many to be an answer to global crises and population control policies are developed that endanger the reproductive rights of women.

With a rapidly changing, destabilizing and hard to understand globalization process occurring, people look for answers to life's questions in fundamentalist religions. These fundamentalisms impact women's rights and are an area of concern for global women and local women's groups.

But other trends in women's political involvements show progressive movement. Women's involvements in peace movements and politics in Africa and in solidarity movements and politics in Latin America show progressive trends. Given these contrasting and conflicting trends, finally, we must ask 'what are the political systems of the future that could bring liberation and equality?'

A: Economic crises

Crises in finance, food and energy and the environment are at the forefront of current global changes that affect women and especially women from poor countries. Financial crisis affects the global system and those most vulnerable are generally hurt most. In Part 1, Chapter 2, Ghosh links increases in global financial crisis to other destabilizing aspects of the neoliberal (free trade, less government) development program of the past forty years.

In the current period of crisis for the global system, the glaring inadequacies of our international financial governing agencies are exposed. United Nations agencies formed to help poor countries have lost power as rich countries, such as the USA, have delayed dues payments in a political move to discredit and undercut these agencies.

Since our last edition, there has been a clear and distinct break between the United Nations agencies that pay attention to the policies of the UN General Assembly and an expanded Security Council, such as the UN Development Program, and the international financial institutions (IFIs) that follow what has been termed 'The Washington Consensus.' Based in Washington, the World Bank and the International Monetary Fund (IMF) and the US Agency for International Development have formed almost identical neoliberal economic policies and forced small countries to accept conditions in order to engage in international trade and finance.

Meanwhile, political struggles involving the international financial infrastructure have intensified over the last decade and a half. The World Bank, the International Monetary Fund and the World Trade Organization have, as a group, worked for the benefit of their financiers, the richest countries and the largest global companies. They have followed neoliberal policies and, through conditionalities, have usurped power over global finance and development programs. They have been wielding global financial power well beyond what their original mandates set out.

The power of the IFIs has been challenged by a movement that is generally known as 'the anti-globalization movement.' The IFIs have been picketed and challenged by demonstrations at their international meetings by representatives of groups left out of the conversation about global futures as these financial institutions assert more and more control over countries, especially small countries, and influence the lives of global citizens in general.

The impact of the 2008 global financial crisis has caused increased hardship for people in less developed countries, particularly women. After two decades of a gradual reduction in global hunger and malnutrition, the financial crisis brought a global shortage of food for the hungry. The Millennium Development Goal of eliminating global hunger by 2015 is very much at risk because of the crisis. Since females are 60 per cent of those hungry and malnourished, they suffer more. Women also suffer differentially in economic crisis because government cutbacks are most often in the fields of health and education.[1] Women experience more cutbacks as consumers of healthcare and education and they are also more likely to be laid off as the majority of workers in these fields in many countries.

Globally, decreases in consumption and trade have impacted job access for export industries. Women have lost employment in the industries that employ mostly women such as the garment and textile field. Other women have newly entered the workforce to try to replace some of the income lost because of their husband's job loss.

Readings In Chapter 28 Diane Elson gives us a perspective on global financial dealings in the modern era and their implications for women, particularly women in the South. Ever since the financial crisis in East and Southeast Asia in 1997/98, there have been calls for a better integration of social and economic policy; greater transparency and accountability in the governance of finance. This chapter discusses these issues from a gender perspective and proposes a view from the kitchen in order to show the effects of high-level policy on ordinary people.

Chapter 29 shows the effects of the global crisis on employment through changes in exports, domestic production and consumption. Crisis means a shift in the direction of more vulnerable jobs in Turkey and elsewhere. There is an 'added worker effect' as women try to enter the workforce to make up some of the income lost by unemployed husbands. Effects by province show differentials by extent of industrialization and trade and the identification of who the trading partners are. Moves forward in openness for women workers where there are patriarchal constraints are set back by economic crisis.

B: Environmental crisis

Global warming is increasingly impacting many countries of the global South and endangering their populations. Countries with warmer climates are enduring record heat, undergoing water shortages, extreme weather conditions and flooding. Women and children are particularly vulnerable under these conditions.

Global warming is already affecting agricultural producers in the global South with greater future effects anticipated. Women's greatest employment sector in Africa and much of Asia is in agriculture. The crises in agricultural production and the availability of drinking water greatly endanger women in their efforts to care for their families.

The rich countries of this world, which have the most power and could best afford to shift to renewable energy rapidly, are not taking responsible corrective action. The power and influence of those with a vested interest in fossil fuel industries appear to have considerable influence over these decisions.

The World Bank has been put in charge of the Climate Investment Funds (CIFs) that are supposed to help less developed countries counter effects of climate change. But they are criticized by environmentalists for continuing to invest in dirty energy and extractive industries, undermining the United Nation's Framework Convention on Climate Change (UNFCCC). Meanwhile Gender Action (2009) criticizes the Bank's approach to gender equality which marginalizes women's rights and overlooks crippling effects on women of loan conditionalities.

Reading Chapter 30 presents women's unique concerns and problems with global warming and then describes their intentional roles in Senegal in choosing and building projects with international partners that are effective in protecting water resources and increasing production.

C: State policy and women's health and reproductive rights

Environmental challenges often lead to population control issues and this is true in the present case. Population control efforts frequently use force or bribes (such as money in exchange for sterilization) to control women's and men's reproductive potential. Governments attempt to control population in both directions, depending on the circumstances. European countries concerned with decreasing population have offered family incentives. Countries with large populations – for example, China – have tried to control reproduction, through promoting the one-child family, using both incentives and penalties. See the article by Dalsimer and Nisonoff (1997) in our first edition.

Jean Larson Pyle (1990, 1994) has produced studies of two capitalist countries using public policy to influence population in different directions. In Ireland, the state kept women out of the labor force and denied birth control, reinforcing a traditional pro-natalist female role. In Singapore, the government moved from anti-natalist policies when labor was plentiful to a pro-natalist stand when there was a shortage of female labor for export processing.

Reproductive freedom with available family planning and health services is an obvious direction for a reasonable and fair population program, but this freedom has often been thwarted by government policies of the left and right. A phenomenon under the foreign aid policies of Ronald Reagan and later G. W. Bush was to end the funding of family planning programs if abortion was in any way considered an option or even discussed. President Obama quickly changed this policy, restoring family planning funding, upon entering office.[2]

The important real factors affecting population growth are level of income and access to family planning. Assuming a development process for poor countries (although now at risk because of our deep recession) we can even chart the future maximum global population and the decline in population growth that comes naturally with development. Reproductive health and family planning respect the rights of women and men to control their own reproductive potential.

HIV/AIDS has been a global health epidemic especially threatening to women and men in Africa and South Asia. AIDS drug treatments have greatly reduced the mortality of AIDS patients but at first only in the developed world. Then, with the successful replication of the drugs by Brazilian scientists, these drugs became available in Latin America, Asia and Africa.

Although HIV/AIDS remains a global problem, it has been a great advantage that the epidemic became more manageable with drugs. But as AIDS treatments become more available in poor countries, other issues came to the fore.

Caretaking work in a large number of affected families has increased greatly and most of this work is done by women.

Readings Chapter 31 by Hartmann and Barajas-Román discusses the arguments linking population and global warming. They present the case for reproductive rights and healthcare over population control policies that impinge on physical reproductive rights and also rights to social reproduction. Social reproduction ensures that individuals and communities can fulfill their basic needs and sustain themselves. So there is a convergence of reproductive rights and sustainable climate politics shown here.

In Chapter 32 Makina explores the issue of women providing unpaid care for family members living with HIV/AIDS in South Africa and Zimbabwe. In the context of insufficient health systems, state policies rely on women providing home-based care. This policy has the effect of impoverishing women and reinforcing gender stereotypes.

D: Women and ideological change

Religious ideologies have, in the late twentieth and early twenty-first centuries, often challenged women's progress toward equality. It was from Protestantism that the 'fundamentalist' terminology was first derived to describe a return to basic biblical tenets. Protestant fundamentalism has become an important religious tendency in the South and in the North. Several Latin American countries, such as Guatemala, have substantial fundamentalist movements. An important contribution for understanding how these Protestant fundamentalisms encourage US hegemony is the book *Exporting the American Gospel* by Brouwer, Gifford and Rose (1996).

The second-most significant global religion numerically is Islam, and fundamentalist tendencies in that religion are widely recognized, and often exaggerated, in the Western press. Part of the reason for this focus has to do with extremist attacks in the USA and Europe. Another part is clearly related to the veiling of women being associated with fundamentalist beliefs in the global popular press. It is clearly not true that all who are veiled are fundamentalist but the association is often made. See the article by Hoodfar (1991), 'Return to the veil: personal strategy and public participation', in our first edition.

Protestant fundamentalists, although more numerous, do not stand out from their general populations in an obvious way. These fundamentalists have been increasing their power and influence globally but relatively little is written about their restrictions on women's rights.

A reverse direction in ideological change has brought greater participation and leadership for women in peace movements and governments in Africa and solidarity movements and governments in Latin America. Promotion of women's rights through United Nations programs and UN agencies has influenced domestic politics around the globe and supported these areas of increased rights for women.

The interconnection of efforts toward women's liberation and socialist political directions is an ongoing story. With little knowledge of how class and patriarchy operate together, socialist leaders have often made policy decisions affecting the relations of production that have had unintended and contradictory effects on class and family structure. The influence of Chinese patriarchy on the development of Chinese socialism, for example, is discussed by Stacey (1983). An analysis of how Vietnamese patriarchy subverted collective agriculture is included in works by Wiegersma (1988, 1991). Women have often enthusiastically supported socialist goals but been disappointed by socialist policies. With new socialist directions in Latin America, we will witness another chapter in this story.

As the world moves through this critical period of distress in finance and in climate change, there will be attempts to change our global political and environmental systems. Women's rights and participation must be part of any just future direction.

Readings Chapter 33 by Shankaran on the 'right to have rights' demonstrates the similarities between the world's fundamentalist leaders in their absolutist rhetoric. She discusses the similarities in the challenges these religions pose for women's rights and freedoms and also pose, more specifically, for women's rights activists in the field.

Chapter 34 shows that African women's movements have played an important part in working for peace and are continuing to play a central role in politics in post-conflict societies. Women's percentages for political representation in post-conflict African societies have become some of the highest in the world. These representatives have pressed for greater rights in new constitutions and laws.

Chapter 35 shows the advances for women of recent educational programs and employment opportunities in Brazil. Lula's Workers' Party has sponsored life-changing opportunities and the prospects for African-American women have improved greatly in the present period.

In Chapter 36 Benería discusses the intersection of women's interests and socialist visions. In this classic piece, Benería develops a set of questions that feminists need to ask about alternative societies that could help us envision a truly feminist and socialist form of social and political organization of the future.

Notes

1 Secretary-General Ban Ki-moon announced the reversal of a two-decade trend in hunger reduction because of the economic crisis in a UN report, 'Economic and food crises threaten recent development gains', 2009, p. 1,

www.un.org/apps/news/printnewsAr.
asp?nid=31369.

2 This was reported by Barbara Crossette in *The Nation*, 25 January 2009, www.
thenation.com/doc/20090209/crossette/
print?rel=nofollow.

References and further reading

Aguilar, D. D. and A. E. Lascamana (2004) *Women and Globalization*, Amherst, NY: Humanity Books.

Antonopulos, R. (2009) 'The current economic and financial crisis: a gender perspective', Working Paper no. 562, Levy Economics Institute of Bard College, United Nations Development Programme.

Balakrishnan, R., D. Elson and R. Patel (2009) 'Rethinking macro economic strategies from a human rights perspective', Carnegie Council's Online Magazine for a Fairer Globalization, www.policyinnovaations.org/ideas/policy_library/data/01516.

Benería, L. (2003) *Gender, Development and Modernization: Economics as if All People Mattered*, New York: Routledge.

Birch, K. and V. Mykhnenko (eds) (2010) *The Rise and Fall of Neoliberalism: The Collapse of an Economic Order?*, London: Zed Books.

Brouwer, S., P. Gifford and S. D. Rose (1996) *Exporting the American Gospel: Global Christian Fundamentalism*, New York and London: Routledge.

Buechler, S. (2009) 'Gender, water and climate change in Sonora, Mexico: implications for policies and programmes on agricultural income-generation', *Gender and Development*, 17(1).

Croce-Galis, M. (ed.) (2008) 'Breaking barriers to HIV prevention, treatment, and care for women', New York: Open Society Institute.

Crossette, B. (2009) '"Global gag rule" lifted', *The Nation*, www.thenation.com/doc/20090209/crossette/print?rel=nofollow.

Dalsimer, M. and L. Nisonoff (1997) 'Abuses against women and girls under the One Child Family Plan in the People's Republic of China', *The Women Gender and Development Reader*, 1st edn, London: Zed Books.

Dankelman, I. (2002) 'Climate change: learning from gender analysis and women's experiences of organizing for sustainable development', *Gender and Development*, 10(2).

Denton, F. (2002) 'Climate change vulnerability, impacts and adaptation: why does gender matter?', *Gender and Development*, 10(2).

Gago, V. (2007) 'Dangerous liaisons: Latin American feminists and the left', *North American Congress on Latin America (NACLA) Report*, 40(2).

Gender Action (2009) 'Doubling the damage: World Bank Climate Investment Funds undermine climate and gender justice', Internet report, prepared by A. Rook, Programs Coordinator, Gender Action, February.

Goldberg, M. (2009) *The Means of Reproduction: Sex, Power and the Future of the World*, New York: Penguin Press.

Harcourt, W. (2009) *Body Politics in Development*, London: Zed Books.

Hoodfar, H. (1991) 'Return to the veil: personal strategy and public participation in Egypt', in N. Redclift and M. T. Sinclair, *Working Women: International Perspectives on Labour and Gender Ideology*, London: Routledge (also in 1st edn of *The Women, Gender and Development Reader*).

Kinoti, K. (2010) 'Copenhagen: did it do anything for women', Association for Women's Rights in Development, 15 January, awid.org/eng/layout/set/print/Issues-and-Analysis/Library/Copenhagen-Did-it-do-an...

Pyle, J. L. (1990) *The State and Women in the Economy: Lessons from Sex Discrimination in the Republic of Ireland*, Albany, NY: SUNY Press.

— (1994) 'Economic restructuring in Singapore and the changing roles of women', in N. Aslanbeigui, S. Pressman and G. Summerfield (eds), *Women in the Age of Economic Transformation*, London and New York: Routledge.

Reis, V. (2007) 'Black Brazilian women and the Lula administration', *North American Congress on Latin America (NACLA) Report: How Pink Is the Pink Tide?*, 40(2).

Smith, D. (2007) 'Media, politics and fundamentalism in Latin America', World Association for Christian Communications, www.waccglobal. org/en/20071-fundamentalism-revisited/445-Media-politics.

Stacey, J. (1983) *Patriarchy and Socialist Revolution in China*, Berkeley, CA: University of California Press.

Urdang, S. (2006) 'The care economy: gender and the silent AIDS crisis in southern Africa', *Journal of Southern African Studies*, 32(1).

Wee, V. (2006) 'Patriarchy in secular and religious varieties', *Development*, 49(1).

Wiegersma, N. (1988) *Vietnam: Peasant Land, Peasant Revolution, Patriarchy and Collectivity in the Rural Economy*, New York: St Martin's Press.

— (1991) 'Peasant patriarchy and the subversion of the collective in Vietnam', *Review of Radical Political Economics*, 23(3/4).

28 | International financial architecture: a view from the kitchen

Diane Elson

Introduction

Ever since the financial crisis in East and South-East Asia in 1997/98, there have been calls for a better integration of social and economic policy; greater transparency and accountability in the governance of finance; and the construction of a new reformed international financial architecture. This chapter discusses these issues from a gender perspective, with a particular concern for the implications for poor women living in the South. It proposes a view from the kitchen rather than the boardroom, the dealing room and the counting house.

Decontrol of the dealing room

The Asian financial crisis took place in the context of an international financial architecture in which the building regulations had been substantially changed from those agreed at Bretton Woods in 1944. The post-war architecture was built around international flows of public finance from the World Bank and the IMF [International Monetary Fund], both of which had social goals specified in their Articles of Agreement. In the case of the Bank, reference was made to investment in infrastructure 'thereby assisting in raising productivity, the standard of living, and the conditions of labour'. In the case of the IMF, reference was made to the promotion and maintenance of high levels of employment and real income. It was a system with a degree of public ownership, although the voting rights were not democratically distributed. However, there was from the beginning a tension between these goals and the interests of owners of private capital, who were interested in maximizing the returns to their assets, irrespective of social goals. One expression of that tension was the shifting balance between automatic access to the pooled resources of the IMF; and conditional access, with the conditions reflecting ideas about 'sound finance' that required countries with balance of payments deficits to cut public expenditure to reduce these deficits, irrespective of the implications for social goals. From the mid-1970s, conditionality dominated and was increasingly linked to neoliberal economic policies (Elson 1994; Harris 1988). At the heart of these policies was liberalization of international financial markets, first for 'developed' countries and then for 'developing' countries. It was argued that this would lead to the most efficient distribution of finance, but efficiency was judged only in terms of the use of marketed resources.

The IMF and World Bank as sources of finance became dwarfed by international banks borrowing and lending Eurodollars and petrodollars in offshore financial centres. For instance, Singh and Zammit (2000: 1250) point out that between 1984–89 and 1990–96, net official capital inflows to developing countries fell by nearly 50 per cent, from US$27.2 billion to US$16.8 billion. In the same period, net private capital flows increased by 700 per cent, from US$17.8 billion to US$129.4 billion. The most rapid increase in private capital flows to developing countries was in portfolio investment (bonds and equities), which was negligible in the 1970s and 1980s but which was US$51.1 billion in the period 1990–96. The operations of the IMF and the World Bank were increasingly geared to maintaining conditions which served the interests of international financial corporations (Harris 1988).

The period of capital market liberalization was also a period of growing inequality, both between and within countries (UNDP 1999). The delinking of social goals and international finance led to deep social divisions in many countries between the rentiers and the rest. A social structure emerged (see Elson and Cagatay 2000) in which the majority of households maintained themselves with a mixture of incomes earned in the public and private sectors, subsistence production, cash transfers authorized by the ministry of finance, public services provided by the public sector, and the unpaid care provided by family members; while wealthy households, which constituted a minority, received a large part of their income not from employment but from ownership of financial assets (bonds, shares, stock options, private pensions). These wealthy rentier households became almost as much 'offshore' as the international financial corporations. These households made very little use of public services, paid very few taxes, were not recipients of public transfers, derived wage earnings disproportionately from the financial sector, and undertook very little unpaid care for family members, relying instead on paid nannies, nurses, cooks, cleaners, drivers supplied by the other households (or similar households abroad). For women in these households, the kitchen was primarily a place where they gave orders to servants. The most important link from these rentier households to the national economy was through their ownership of financial assets and the return to these assets; but this link was always at risk of being weakened or even severed through capital flight. The majority of households were also linked to financial institutions – but in a different way, as net debtors rather than as creditors. In this, they were similar to the government and to the locally owned part of the private sector.

The positions of TNCs undertaking direct investment in mines, plantations and factories was somewhat different from that of the offshore corporations.

Many TNCs were under pressure from financial intermediaries to keep up their share prices or risk takeover bids, creating incentives for short-term time horizons. Unlike the 'offshore' corporations, the TNCs derived some benefits from public expenditure, through contracts, and provision of infrastructure, and from tax breaks (tax expenditures) – the hidden subsidies that corporations get from tax concessions, and which are not nearly as visible as the transfers to households in the shape of food subsidies, or child benefits, or maternity benefits, or pensions. TNCs have bargaining power to extract this 'corporate welfare' because they can threaten to leave – or not to come in the first place.

The non-wealthy majority of households do not have that luxury; the possibilities for permanent migration to become citizens of another country are highly circumscribed, and mainly available to the well-off and highly educated. International financial market liberalization has not been matched by international labour market liberalization. Poor people cannot migrate on the same terms as rich people. Poor and middle-income households, local firms and public sector agencies are much more 'locked in' to their country. (Many of the thousands of poor people who try to escape as undocumented migrants or asylum seekers are likely to find the alternative to being locked in at home is to be 'locked up' abroad.) Wealthy rentier households (who find they are much more welcome abroad than their poorer compatriots), TNCs and financial institutions are more footloose (with the latter the most footloose of all).

Decontrol of the dealing room has created a surreal financial architecture. Not only do different inhabitants have different experiences of space, but also of time. The clocks in the dealing rooms run very fast – five minutes is a long time during which a lot of money could change hands; whereas in the kitchen the clocks run slowly – five minutes is a tiny fragment of a human lifetime of cooking and eating. In the dealing room transactions are reversible; but in the kitchen they are not. The time horizons in the dealing room are short, whereas in the kitchen the horizon is that of the nurturing needed over the human lifespan. The whole building is precariously balanced. A key feature of the Asian financial crisis was massive inflows of short-term capital followed by a sudden reversal: 'Net financial inflows to Indonesia, Korea, Malaysia, the Philippines and Thailand totaled $93 billion in 1996. In 1997, as turmoil hit financial markets, these flows reversed in just weeks to a net outflow of $12 billion, a swing of $105 billion, or 11% of the pre-crisis GDPs of the five countries' (UNDP 1999: 40).

The gender implications of financial crises: downloading risks to the kitchen

International markets for money are inherently uncertain and liberalized international financial transactions are fraught with risks for which no objective probability distribution exists – such as currency risk, capital flight risk, fragility risk, contagion risk and sovereignty risk (Grabel 2000). Information is necessarily imperfect and available information is unequally distributed. Such markets are argued by heterodox economists to be intrinsically unstable (e.g. Spotton 1997; Singh and Zammit 2000). Periods of economic growth lead to exuberant risk-taking and the value of financial assets becomes inflated. But eventually the growing gap between financial values and real returns leads to a subjective re-evaluation of risks and holders of financial assets begin to sell them. Herd behaviour magnifies the propensity to sell and further stimulates the perception that risks have increased. The way is paved for crises in which the sudden drop in assets prices sparks panic selling; and the price of assets bought with loans drops below the value of loans outstanding, leading to collapse of credit markets and impending bankruptcy of banks and other private sector financial intermediaries. The crisis may be mitigated by intervention by governments or international public financial institutions to coordinate markets, restore confidence and bail out banks and other intermediaries. But such intervention can make things worse if the wrong advice is given and the wrong policies imposed; and bailing out failing firms shifts costs from individual actors in financial markets to other members of society. Moreover the expectation of being bailed out can lead to even greater excess financial risk-taking when the economy recovers.

It has been estimated that the average costs of government bailouts in banking crashes over the past twenty years amounts to about 9 per cent of GDP in developing countries and 4 per cent of GDP in developed countries (Caprio and Honohan 1999). The most immediately visible costs are to the taxpayers who fund the bailouts, and to the people who lose their jobs. But, as pointed out by Irene van Staveren (2000), the burden of excessive financial risk-taking is also shifted to the people, mainly women, who provide the unpaid care that keeps families and communities going. Particularly in poor and middle-income families, women are called upon to spend more time and effort in providing non-market substitutes for marketed goods that their families can no longer afford to buy, and providing substitutes for public services that are no longer available. In addition, women have to seek more paid work in informal employment, where new entrants making 'distress sales' tend to drive down returns. The burdens are thus not fully reflected in the GDP statistics but would show up in the additional stress and tiredness and ill-health experienced by women who are often working longer and harder.

The Asian financial crisis of the late 1990s is a good example of downloading risks to the kitchen. Attempts by the IFIs to manage the Asian financial crisis have been widely regarded as unsuccessful, not only by those outside the IFIs but also by some who were inside them at the time, most notably Joe Stiglitz, then the Chief Economic Adviser at the World Bank (Stiglitz 2000). The IMF in particular has been widely criticized for giving the wrong advice and imposing the wrong policies during the Asian financial crisis. It imposed cuts in public expenditure though the underlying problem was not a budget deficit; and instead of drawing attention to the strong real economies of most of the afflicted countries, it emphasized the need for much more thorough liberalization of markets and major changes in corporate governance, doing nothing to restore confidence among panicking investors. In the view of Singh and Zammit (2000: 1255), 'a relatively tractable liquidity problem was thus turned into a massive solvency crisis, with enormous losses in employment and output'. There was also a substantial increase in poverty, reduced public services and increased social stress (UNDP 1999: 40). In both Indonesia and the Philippines, the amount of work done by women increased, as women took up the role of provider of last resort. For Indonesia, relevant data are available from the Indonesia Family Life Surveys, which covered more than thirty thousand people in 1997/early 1998, and a follow-up survey of a 25 per cent sample in late 1998. Using this source, Frankenberg et al. (1999) calculate the percentage of the labour force employed in paid work in 1997 and 1998 and show that for men it decreased by 1.3 per cent, while for women it increased by 1 per cent. When unpaid work is also included, there is an increase for both men and women, but for men the increase is only 1.3 per cent, while for women it is 7 per cent. A nationally representative survey conducted by the Indonesian statistical office sixteen months after the onset of the crisis reveals the household coping strategies underlying these figures – especially increasing the labour market participation of older married women with children, and producing more goods for home consumption (de la Rocha 2000).

In the case of the Philippines, Lim (2000), using data from the Labor Force Survey, shows that both male and female unemployment rates rose between 1997 and 1998: for men from 7.5 per cent to 9.5 per cent and for women from 8.5 per cent to 9.9 per cent. However, mean weekly work hours for those employed moved in opposite directions for men and women, with those of men falling while those of women rose. Among the factors that may explain the increase for women is an increase in the hours of work undertaken by home-based women working on subcontract (Ofreneo et al. 1999). This increase in the average hours that women spend in paid work has occurred in a context in which women typically spend almost eight hours a day on housekeeping and childcare compared with about two and a half hours for men (UNDP 1997).

In South Korea, it was women who lost jobs more than men. Between 1997 and 1998, data from the National Statistical Office show that employment declined by 3.8 per cent for men and 7.1 per cent for women (Lee and Rhee 1999). In response, the Korean government promoted a national campaign under the slogan 'Get Your Husband Energized', calling on women to provide support for husbands who were depressed owing to unemployment or bankruptcy – husbands were not called upon to provide reciprocal support for wives (Tauli-Korpuz 1998).

Social policy, gender equality and financial policy

Singh and Zammit (2000) point out that one influential interpretation of the effects of the Asian financial crisis argued that the social impact was worse because governments in that region had not introduced selective social safety nets and targeted social insurance schemes in the period of rapid growth. If such schemes were in place, then, it was implied, the potential costs of instability and crisis arising from financial liberalization could be absorbed. In this view, a narrowly targeted social policy needs to be 'added on' to pre-existing financial policy, in order to protect vulnerable groups.

Following the Asian financial crisis, the World Bank/IMF Development Committee asked the World Bank to develop, in consultation with other institutions, some general principles to set standards for social policy. The resulting document, 'Managing the social dimensions of crises: good practices in social policy' (World Bank 1999), exemplifies the 'adding on' approach. Although there is much reference to households and communities, there is no systematic analysis of the way in which the principles of social policy need to take into account the different (and disadvantaged) position of women in comparison to men; and to take into account unpaid care work in households and communities. The principles focus on cutting public expenditure in ways that will not worsen the position of the worst off, but pay little attention to the question of whether cutting public expenditure is the appropriate strategy.

The IMF has also become more concerned with social policy. In explaining to the public its response to the Asian crisis, it states that it is concerned with 'strengthening and expanding the social safety net and encouraging a social dialogue among employers, employees, and governments' (IMF 1999).

An alternative approach, put forward by heterodox economists, is the creation of new international institutions to regulate global finance. For instance, Eatwell and Taylor (1998) call for the setting up of a World Financial Authority (WFA) to manage systemic risk and pursue both financial targets and social goals such as high rates of growth and employment. It would develop and impose regulations and coordinate national monetary policies. The IMF and the World Bank would both have roles to play, under the supervision of the WFA, which would have the responsibility of ensuring their transparency and accountability.

Three biases to avoid in building new economic architecture

One way of responding to the situation is to identify things that should be avoided in building any new system. In this section three biases are identified that would make the architecture very insecure from the point of view of most women and should thus be guarded against. They are 'deflationary bias'; 'male breadwinner bias'; and 'commodification or privatization bias' (see also Elson and Cagatay 2000).

Deflationary bias in macroeconomic policy is identified as an important issue for women in the recent UN *World Survey on the Role of Women in Development* (UN 1999). Using similar arguments to Singh and Zammit (2000), the survey defines deflationary bias as macroeconomic policies which keep paid employment and GNP growth below their potential. It is argued that liberalized financial markets pressure governments to keep interest rates high, inflation rates low, and taxation and expenditure low. Evidence is cited to suggest that the negative effects of these policies, which are used to attract private capital inflows, outweigh the benefits of the extra finance, and that these negative effects are disproportionately borne by women. Avoidance of deflationary bias is, however, necessary but not sufficient. As Aslanbeigui and Summerfield (2000) point out, growth of GNP and increased paid employment can have different implications for men and women. For instance, patterns of employment and the entitlements they bring can be built around a 'male breadwinner' model, which assumes that women and children will have, and should have, their livelihoods provided by the incomes earned by husbands and fathers. The counterpart to this is the assumption that typical workers will have few domestic responsibilities. Of course, in reality the majority of households have multiple livelihood strategies, which involve women earning money as well as undertaking unpaid care work. However, women's participation in the labour force is less visible because it is more often informal, home-based, part-time, seasonal, and low paid. So women's 'double day' of unpaid and paid work goes unnoticed. 'Male breadwinner' bias characterizes public policies that prioritize decent and remunerative employment for men while ignoring women's rights to decent jobs. 'Male breadwinner' bias relegates women to the status of secondary workers with fewer rights, even when they are playing a large role in maintaining family income. It excludes women from many state-provided social benefits, except as dependants of men. Full employment may reduce the chances of women experiencing material poverty but does not necessarily save women from patriarchal control.

In order to be gender-equitable, full-employment policies must be complemented by policies to ensure an equitable balance between work and family life; and state-based entitlements for the providers of unpaid caring labour as citizens in their own right. This suggests that a target of full employment needs to be supplemented by a target of decent jobs on comparable terms for both men and women, equally family friendly for both. The third bias to be avoided is privatization bias. This occurs when public provision is judged less efficient than private provision on the basis of incomplete and faulty measures of efficiency, which do not take account of unpaid work and quality of provision. This results in the replacement of public provision by market-based, individualized entitlements for those who can afford them – private pensions, private health insurance, private hospitals, private schools, private retirement homes, private paid care for children and old people, privatized utilities charging market rates for energy and transport. Rather than pooling and sharing risks and resources, with scope for the solidarity of cross-subsidy, there is separate insurance for specific contingencies. One point of continuity with 'male breadwinner' bias is that women are still often cast in the position of dependants. The insurable risk against ill-health or old age is constructed around male norms of labour market status; and the private system, just like the public system, is accessed by women through their male relatives.

The blueprints for privatization have been drawn up by the World Bank, and frequently involve sale of assets at knock-down prices; or prolonged subsidies to private corporations. This bias fuels the growth of financial corporations and the corporate welfare state, as is demonstrated in the experience of privatization of social insurance in Latin America (Laurell 2000). The privatization of pensions in Chile and Mexico will result in the largest transfer of public funds to national and transnational financial groups that has ever taken place in Latin America. It will be paid over a fifty-year period and is estimated to cost about 1–2 per cent of GNP in Mexico and 3.5 per cent in Chile. Given the pressure to balance the budget, this is likely to result in cuts in other social programmes (ibid.).

The private providers charge the insured workers higher administration costs than the public scheme and risks are shifted to the insured. Their future pensions are uncertain and at the mercy of financial markets (ibid.). In the case of health, the management of health funds rather than the provision of health services now drives the system, which is increasingly in the hands of health insurance companies, health management organizations and hospital corporations that are based in the USA or associated with US firms. There is increasing stratification in quality and access to services (ibid.) [...]

Thus privatization bias fuels the growth of financial intermediaries; and the growth of financial intermediaries fuels deflationary bias in macroeconomic policy, and leads to even more pressures to privatize. Rentier households and offshore financial institutions exert pressure for deflation and privatization, threatening to exit if their interests are not given priority. They have an immediate interest in minimizing tax payments, and keeping interest rates high and inflation close to zero, because they are not required to be permanent stakeholders in the country. Under this pressure, social policy becomes a branch of financial policy and can no longer take non-market criteria into account. Rather than the risks of liberalized international financial markets being offset by state-funded services in which risks and resources are pooled, the risks are compounded by funding social provision through financial markets.

To guard against privatization bias, we need a target of universal entitlement to basic services and benefits for women and men. One possible indicator to consider would be the proportion of women who have access, in their own right, to an adequately functioning primary healthcare clinic.

Putting social justice first: creating new spaces

A new financial architecture needs more than new institutions with new responsibilities. It needs to provide a supportive framework to enable women and men to exercise democratic oversight of how the building is operated. There must be spaces, accessible from the kitchen, for public dialogues on priorities and alternatives. The ability of different interests to exercise 'voice' on how financial policy and social justice should be linked is foreclosed not by the technical requirements of financial policy but by fear of pre-emptive exercise of the 'exit' option by private financial investors. Their ability to exit rather than join in a policy dialogue is, of course, a result of the openness of capital markets.

Ironically the openness of capital markets is conducive to an absence of openness in policy discussion, for fear that the wrong signals will be sent and the volatile 'sentiment' of capital markets will be disturbed. It is difficult to conduct a participatory consultation on how to put financial policy at the service of social goals when some of the key players have no stake in the outcome beyond the next few hours. A neglected argument for some form of capital controls is to ensure that financial institutions have more incentive to engage in discussions with other social interests in the country whose financial instruments they have purchased, and to prevent them from foreclosing discussion by a pre-emptive exit (Elson and Cagatay 2000).

Unfortunately, there is currently no sign of moves towards rebuilding along participatory and gender-equitable lines. There have been only a few minor repairs, concerned to improve the comfort of rich investors, not poor citizens. The repairs have been designed by a few rich governments (primarily the G7), though the work of carrying them out falls to the governments of poor countries (Griffith-Jones and Bhattacharya 2001). The Financial Stability Forum is a rich man's club, not a public meeting place. So we need a twin-track strategy. We need to keep alive a vision of what the international financial architecture should be, with the needs of the kitchen, the place of nurture, an important and integral part of the design. We also need to enlarge those small spaces that currently exist for the operation of socially responsible finance.

An example of what might be aspired to at national level is provided by the Canadian Alternative Federal Budget exercise, in which a large number of Canadian civil society groups have joined together to produce an alternative budget and an alternative financial framework that would be free of all three biases identified above (Loxley 1999). This is an example of a growing movement for gender-sensitive, democratically organized, public services and social insurance that rebuilds confidence in the principles of pooling and sharing through the state. (Women are particularly active in gender budget initiatives in more than twenty countries, analysing how government budgets are affecting men and women, and arguing for public finance to be free of the biases identified above. See Budlender 2000; Elson 2000.) At the international level there is a growth of ethical investment funds in which middle-income people can invest their savings in the knowledge that the money will be lent only to firms which operate in a socially and environmentally responsible way. There is a strong movement for the cancellation of the debt of poor countries and the rebuilding of the kind of development aid that supports human development. There is growing support for an international tax on currency transactions and for controls on short-term capital movements. Little by little, these initiatives, if they are interconnected, may liberate space from the malign flux of the dealing room and enable more of the kitchen to be a place of peaceful enjoyment.

References

Aslanbeigui, N. and G. Summerfield (2000) 'The Asian crisis, gender and the international financial architecture', *Feminist Economics*, 6(3): 81–104.

Budlender, D. (2000) 'The political economy of women's budgets in the South', *World Development*, 28(7): 1365–78.

Caprio, G. and P. Honohan (1999) 'Restoring banking stability: beyond supervised capital requirements', *Journal of Economic Perspectives*, 13(4): 43–64.

De la Rocha, M. (2000) 'Private adjustments; household responses to the erosion of work', Occasional Paper 6, Bureau of Development Policy, UNDP, New York.

Eatwell, J. and L. Taylor (1998) 'International capital markets and the future of economic policy', CEPA Working Paper Series 1II, Working Paper no. 9, New School University, New York.

Elson, Diane (1994) 'People, development and international financial systems', *Review of African Political Economy*, 62: 511–24.

— (ed.) (2000) *Progress of the World's Women 2000*, New York: UNIFEM.

Elson, D. and N. Cagatay (2000) 'The social content of macroeconomic policies', *World Development*, 28(7): 1347–65.

Frankenberg, E., D. Thomas and K. Beegle (1999) 'The real costs of Indonesia's economic crisis: preliminary findings from the Indonesia Family Life Surveys', Labor and Population Program Working Paper Series 99-04, RAND.

Grabel, I. (2000) 'Identifying risks, preventing crisis: lessons from the Asian crisis', *Journal of Economic Issues*, 34(2): 377–83.

Griffith-Jones, S. and A. Bhattacharya (eds) (2001) *Developing Countries and the Global Financial System*, London: Commonwealth Secretariat.

Gupta, S., B. Clements, C. McDonald and C. Schiller, (1998) 'The IMF and the poor', Pamphlet Series no. 52, Fiscal Affairs Department, International Monetary Fund, Washington, DC.

Harris, L. (1988) 'The IMF and mechanisms of integration', in B. Crow and M. Thorpe (eds), *Survival and Change in the Third World*, Oxford: Polity Press.

IMF (1998) *Distilling the Lessons from the ESAF Reviews*, www.imf.org.

— (1999) 'The IMF's response to the Asian Crisis', Washington, DC, www.imf.org/External/np/exr/facts/asia/htm.

IMF/World Bank (1999) *Heavily Indebted Poor Countries (HIC) Initiative – Strengthening the Link Between Debt Relief and Poverty Reduction*, Washington, DC.

Laurell, A. C. (2000) 'Structural adjustment and the globalization of social policy in Latin America', *International Sociology*, 15(2): 306–25.

Lee, J.-W. and C. Rhee (1999) 'Social impacts of the Asian crisis; policy challenges and lessons', Occasional Paper 33, Human Development Report Office.

Lim, J. (2000) 'The effects of the East Asian crisis on the employment of men and women: the Philippine case', *World Development*, 28(7): 1285–306.

Loxley, J. (1999) 'The Alternative Federal Budget in Canada: a new approach to fiscal democracy', Paper prepared for the workshop on Pro-Poor Gender- and Environment-Sensitive Budgets, UNDP and UNIFEM, New York, 28–30 June.

Ofreno, R., J. Lim and L. Gula (1999) 'Subcontracted women workers in the context of the global economy: the Philippine case', Paper commissioned by the Asia Foundation.

Singh, A. and A. Zammit (2000) 'International capital flows: identifying the gender dimension', *World Development*, 26(7): 1249–68.

Spotton, B. (1997) 'Financial instability reconsidered: orthodox theories versus historical facts', *Journal of Economic Issues*, 31(1): 175–95.

Stiglitz, J. (2000) 'What I learned at the world economic crisis: the insider', New Republic Online, www.thenewrepublic.com.

Tauli-Korpuz, V. (1998) 'Asia Pacific women grapple with financial crisis and globalisation', *Third World Resurgence*, 94.

Taylor, L. (1991) 'Varieties of stabilization experience: towards sensible macroeconomics in the Third World', *Wider Studies in Development Economics*, Oxford: Oxford University Press.

UN (1999) *World Survey on the Role of Women in Development*, Division for the Advancement of Women, Department of Economic and Social Affairs, United Nations, New York.

UNDP (1997) *Philippine Human Development Report*, Manila: United Nations Development Programme.

— (1999) *Human Development Report*, New York: Oxford University Press.

Van Staveren, I. (2000) 'Global finance and gender', Paper presented at the IAFFE conference, Istanbul, August.

World Bank (1999) 'Managing the social dimensions of crises: good practices in social policy', Paper prepared for the Development Committee of the Bank and the Fund, Washington, DC.

— (2000) *World Development Report 2000*, New York: Oxford University Press.

29 | 'One step forward, two steps backward' – from labor market exclusion to inclusion: a gender perspective on effects of the economic crisis in Turkey[1]

Gülay Toksöz

While the global economic crisis started in the USA as a financial crisis in 2007 and then spread to the rest of the world in 2008 and 2009, its effects were manifested in developing countries mainly through changes in investment, production and consumption. Shrinking demand and cessation of credit flows in export-oriented developing countries force these countries to face a serious risk of contraction and depression. This situation has important implications for employment and unemployment. A decline in formal employment and an increase in vulnerable employment and unemployment have resulted in the great majority of both industrialized and developing countries. This chapter addresses the effects of the crisis on women who generally have limited opportunities of access and therefore participation in labor markets. Women, even when they have access, often remain in disadvantaged positions in labor markets.

Effects of the crisis, from a gender perspective, reveal how differently the crisis affects males and females in a patriarchal sociocultural setting characterized by gender segregation in Turkey. Effects of the crisis on labor markets in Turkey will be shown based on comparative data of two provinces. The employment structure in these provinces will show two variations of the social construction of labor markets by gender.

Gendered effects on labor market outcomes of economic crisis

Taking a look at gender-related implications of Structural Adjustment Programs adopted by developing countries after 1980, it can be shown that the burden of adjustment has fallen on women disproportionately. As a result of these programs, women joined the labor market mostly in informal jobs without social protection. In addition, they extended unpaid labor time for domestic and care work owing to cuts in public expenditures on health and education. Various studies have demonstrated that adverse effects of Stability and Structural Adjustment Programs become especially apparent in periods of crisis with increasing unemployment. Being already disadvantaged in labor markets, women become more and more underprivileged as crises follow each other.[2]

The services sector offers the main employment area for women globally, whereas the agricultural sector still has an important, though diminishing, share. A small proportion of women are employed in the export-oriented branches of manufacturing industry, mostly in small-sized enterprises or informal production.[3] However, in the rapidly growing newly industrialized countries of Southeast and East Asia manufacturing industry outweighs other sectors in the composition of female employment. The industrial sector seems to be most immediately influenced by developments in the world economy.

The adverse effect of the crisis on the unemployment of women in developing countries is closely associated with the sector they concentrate in. When the female labor force is engaged mainly in export-oriented manufacturing industry, as in parts of Asia and Latin America, and/or in tourism, as in the Caribbean, job losses by women can exceed those of males. When both females and males lose jobs, consequences on women are often more adverse because women are employed at lower rates in full-time and protected jobs than males. Therefore women's opportunities for benefiting from social protection networks and unemployment insurance are limited.[4]

While dismissals constitute the first-wave effect of the crisis, the second wave is women's entrance into the labor force to partly remedy falling household income as a coping strategy. The relevant literature uses the term 'added worker effect' to describe situations in which other members of the household join the labor force when male household heads lose their jobs. According to the ILO Global Employment Trends, the largest impact of the crisis in developing countries will be an increase in vulnerable employment rather than an increase in unemployment. This includes own-account work in the informal sector or unpaid family labor. People in this type of work usually don't have any formal work arrangements, are confronted with higher economic risks and, in the case of contributing family workers, earn no direct income. More than a half of women (51.3 percent) and almost half of men (48.3 percent) worldwide were in vulnerable jobs in 2008. Although gender disparities vary according to regions, women usually concentrate in more precarious forms of informal work with unstable, low earnings, such as home-based production or street vending.[5]

To discuss the gendered effects of the recent economic crisis on a developing country we need to take into account the sectored composition of employment, the level of development, the place in the international division of labor, features of gender division of labor and the patriarchal sociocultural structures in which the economy operates. A fully comprehensive analysis including all these factors in Turkey is not within the scope of this article, written shortly after the crisis, but it can be seen as an effort in this direction.

Growth strategies and women's labor market situation in Turkey

Turkey, although considered to be a semi-industrialized developing country, is among the twenty largest economies of the world. While Turkey enjoyed a rapid growth prior to the recent crisis, what is in question now is economic growth that is not accompanied by growth in employment. For years, employment growth has lagged far behind growth in working-age population, and this imbalance has led to falling labor force participation and employment rates. Further, when labor force participation and employment rates are disaggregated by sex, we observe that women's participation in the labor force remains at very low levels. Being located in the Middle East region, where women's labor force participation rate is generally low owing to social and cultural in addition to economic factors, this situation is not surprising. However, it is astonishing that participation rates show a rising trend in the region in contrast to Turkey, where they are declining. Labor force participation rates in the Middle East have grown from 22.6 percent in 1999 to 25.4 percent in 2009, but declined from 32.4 percent in 1999 to 26 percent in 2009 in Turkey.[6]

This decline in women's participation is closely related with a decrease in agricultural employment with no compensatory increase in non-agricultural employment. Women migrating from rural to urban areas remain out of the labor force owing to a gender division of labor in more urban areas in which females are considered to be responsible for care work and household chores. Patriarchal structures, institutions and mentalities based on this gender division of labor either prevent women from participating in the labor market, or when they participate, determine the sectors and jobs that they can have. Women are expected to work in 'socially approved' occupations.

Although Turkey adopted export-oriented growth strategies after 1980, these were not successful in bringing any significant growth in employment. These strategies were accompanied by a new speculative accumulation model in which policies shifted priority from long-term fixed-capital investments in manufacturing to rent-earning activities like short-term financial investments with high interest rates.[7] In addition, in the 2000s industrialization depended increasingly on imports, which also contributed to low rates of growth in employment.[8] As a result the demand for labor has remained low compared to the huge labor supply associated with a labor force moving out of agriculture, and with new entrants into the urban labor market. People who cannot find waged work in the formal sector largely concentrate in own-account work or small family enterprises in services and manufacturing. Women joining the urban labor force face high rates of unemployment and often can find only informal employment.[9]

Looking at the sectoral composition of employment from a gender perspective, we observe that agricultural employment is based on the labor of both sexes in line with small-scale production of family-owned enterprises, whereas the male labor force is dominant in industrial employment. Agriculture still offers the main employment area for women as unpaid family workers. For females, non-agricultural employment is possible mostly in the services sector. Since labor markets and occupations in Turkey are segregated on a gender basis, women have no chance for employment in those industries and occupations regarded as 'for males.' Only one fifth of the industrial workforce is female and half of them are to be found in garments and textiles. In addition to these two subsectors there is demand, to some extent, for female workers in some branches of metal and machinery and food and beverage production.[10] The industrial female workforce is found mainly in big cities.

Impact of the crisis on the country's labor market

In Turkey, the current crisis has taken the form of a slowdown and contraction in growth, along with a contraction in manufacturing industry and services. The negative implications of this situation for the labor market became evident in the form of high unemployment rates and increases in informal employment. Whereas in July 2009 the overall rate of unemployment was 12.8 percent, the non-agricultural rate of unemployment reached 16.5 percent in urban areas.[11] These high rates were unprecedented in the history of Turkey.

As men lost their jobs and could not act as the sole 'breadwinner' for the family, more and more women joined the labor market in search of remuneration. Rates of female unemployment rose significantly, but at the same time the number of women employed increased modestly. The falling trend of the female labour force participation rate was reversed with an increase from 26 percent in July 2008 to 27.6 percent in July 2009.

The greatest difference between rates of female and male unemployment is in the urban rates. The number of urban unemployed women increased by 204,000 within a year and the rate of urban female unemployment, which was 16.6 percent in July 2008, rose to 20.6 percent in July 2009. In the same period, the number of unemployed males increased by 495,000, thus increasing their rate of unemployment from 10.6 percent to 14.5 percent. There has been a four-point increase in both, but the rate of female unemployment is much higher.

During this period total employment in Turkey grew by 50,000, mostly because of the increase in female employment. Increasing employment and unemployment figures for females confirm that the 'additional worker effect' observed elsewhere during crises holds true for Turkey as well. Of the 289,000 total female employment increase: 10,000 were in industry, 123,000 in services and 153,000 in agriculture. As a remedy for falling household income, agriculture still constitutes the main area of employment for women starting to work.

In the period mentioned, male employment declined by 391,000 in industry and by 63,000 in services but increased by 210,000 in agriculture. The contraction in industry caused by the economic crisis affected such branches of industry as textiles, garments, petroleum products, earth-stone [quarrying], basic metal and vehicle industries particularly heavily. Owing to the male-dominant nature of the labor force in these branches, they were the first to be affected by job losses. In the garments subsector, however, where the share of female workers is relatively high, it is difficult to reach a sound evaluation as informal employment is widespread.

Worldwide experience suggests that in cases where women enter labor markets in order to make up for falling household income, they often find vulnerable and informal jobs. To get an impression of the quality of these jobs, we can take a look at the job status of workers and whether employment is formal or informal. In the period July 2008–July 2009, only 28,000 of the 289,000 representing the increase in female employment were regular or casual wage earners. Own-account workers and unpaid family workers constitute the bulk of the increase in female employment. The number of female own-account workers increased by 146,000 and unpaid family workers by 124,000. As a traditional form of female employment in agriculture, unpaid family workers increased as a result of the crisis. Waged work out of agriculture increased very little and the greatest increase was in own-account workers. The increases in female employment were in various forms of vulnerable employment.

On the other hand, of the increase in male employment by 210,000 in agriculture, 145,000 were unpaid family workers and 75,000 were wage earners. It appears that agriculture also offers a means of subsistence in vulnerable forms of employment to males who have lost their jobs in the non-agricultural sectors. Some of the rural male population who have lost hope of finding urban jobs have had to move to unpaid family labor. Approaches of international finance institutions maintaining that agricultural employment has to shrink for its low level of productivity to rise have guided agricultural policies for decades. However, in a developing and highly populated country like Turkey, the employment that agriculture creates for the masses that are employed informally and deprived of any protection against unemployment is an important alternative. In 2009, when serious contractions were taking place in the sectors of industry and services, there was an increase, though limited, in value added in agriculture.

The prevalence of informal work with its lack of social protection is a major problem of the labor market in Turkey, and there is a large gender disparity with respect to informal work. As of July 2008, 61.6 percent of female and 39.3 percent of male employment in Turkey remained outside of any social security scheme. By July 2009, the number of informally employed persons had increased by 264,000. Of this total, 181,000 are females and 83,000 are males. Reflecting a rise in the vulnerability of labor in crisis conditions, the increasing employment is unregistered employment. Of own-account workers and unpaid family workers, an overwhelming majority do not have any social protection.

In gender-segregated labor markets women do not substitute for men, taking the jobs done by them. In a country in which the industrial sector's employment generation capacity is limited for women, they seem not to be directly affected by job losses or job gains in manufacturing. While men lose jobs mainly in the industry sector, new female entrants to the labor market either work in the services sector or in agriculture. Owing to lack of waged work, women in services mainly do own-account work at home in occupations deemed to be appropriate for women. In agriculture there is no competition among men and women because women work as unpaid family members. We can see this situation concretely in the following section on provincial labor markets.

Effects of the crisis on provincial economies and labor markets

Geographical regions in Turkey have been affected by the crisis in varying degrees. According to data provided by the Social Security Institution, in the first quarter of 2009 formal employment shrank, compared to the same period of the earlier year, in Istanbul, Western Marmara, Aegean, Eastern Marmara and Western Anatolia, as industrialized regions of the country. In the remaining regions, which are the south, north, center and east of Anatolia, employment continued to grow. In the second quarter of the same year, however, the picture worsened in almost all regions. While investigating the reasons for this regional variation in employment losses, it will be useful to analyze the sector-based composition of individual regions, the status of employment, the level of integration with the global economy and the situation in the various export markets where the goods of these regions are sold.[12] Those regions with relatively fuller integration into the global economy where exports are more important have been affected more by the crisis. In provinces where EU markets have higher shares, employment losses are also high, whereas other provinces that have larger export shares in Middle Eastern and North African markets faced relatively limited employment losses.[13]

In the following, the situation in two provinces of Turkey is considered to highlight the gendered effects of the crisis on local economies and labor markets. These provinces, in which a small survey was conducted, are Konya in central and Gaziantep in southeast Anatolia. Both provinces are considered to be at the medium level of socio-economic development and have very limited participation of women in non-agricultural employment. There are gender-segregated labor markets in both and women are underrepresented in manufacturing industry.

Females in Konya Province labor market The economy of Konya province depends on activities in agriculture, industry and services. In the composition of total employment, services lead the list, followed by agriculture and industry. Women's share is 26.5 percent, or 193,000 out of an employment total of 729,000 in 2008. As for the distribution of female employment, half of them are in agriculture followed by services with 31.1 percent and industry with 18.1 percent. On the other hand, almost half of employed males are in services, 26.9 percent in agriculture and 24.3 percent in industry.[14]

In Konya very few women are employed even in the subsectors of manufacturing such as garments, food and beverages, metal and metal products which are considered to be appropriate for women. There are many subsectors of manufacturing industry operating in Konya with a total absence of female employees, and the few women to be found in many enterprises are employed in service-related activities. The dominant patriarchal understanding considers locations where industrial production takes place, whether organized industrial districts or small industrial sites, not to be appropriate places for women, even in the case of an enterprise that would employ women only. This outlook is internalized not only by employers but by working people and job seekers as well. Consequently, employers provide for their labor needs with males and industrial employment is the last option to consider for unskilled females who have to work for subsistence. In addition to this, interviews show (1) that working hours in private enterprises were too long for women; (2) that it was difficult for women to adapt to shift work; and (3) that companies shied away from employing women because of prospective pregnancies and leaves.

With limited opportunities for waged employment, women in Konya move to own-account work. Women are eager to engage in remunerative activities, especially in poor households or when husbands have lost their jobs. These women mostly work at home processing food or preparing trousseaus for selling and earning income. The first problem women face in moving into own-account work is the unavailability of loans, and the second is marketing difficulties, since they all mostly produce the same items. Women are rarely employers or entrepreneurs.

Since industrial employment opportunities are very restricted for unskilled female labor, cleaning work in the services sector has become a significant area of employment. Of course, education, health and finance offer employment opportunities for qualified female labor. For Konya, women with low educational background move, if economic conditions force them, to lower-level jobs in the services sector while university and college graduates have a chance of finding more qualified jobs. Nevertheless, participation in the labor force of women with secondary education remains limited. The 'conservative norms,' as expressed by interviewees, prefer that women stay at home for household chores and care rather than get into remunerative work. These norms are influential for educated women and thus restrict female labor force supply.

The effect of the crisis in general caused a decrease in exports to industrialized countries and decreased production accompanied by dismissals. Nevertheless, a conclusion that can be drawn from interviews is that the crisis has not affected the overall economy of Konya much and not led to large-scale dismissals as exports from Konya are not large. Furthermore, exports mostly consist of intermediate goods and clients are mostly from Middle Eastern countries, which might have mitigated the negative effects of the crisis. Since companies were mostly family enterprises, based on equity capital rather than loans, this also made them more resistant to financial crisis.

In Konya there is no trade union organized in any private sector enterprise. Trade unions exist only in the public sector. Many workers in the private sector are employed informally to work long hours. The crisis has been influential in further spreading this kind of employment. Since informal workers are not covered by unemployment benefits they may not apply to the Employment Agency when they lose their jobs, and this situation prevents unemployment from being seen in its full dimensions. The impression that the effects of the crisis are not so heavy in Konya can be partly attributed to the commonness of informal employment.

Females in Gaziantep Province labor market In Gaziantep the total number of women employed was 108,000 in 2008 with a share of 20.4 percent in the total employment of 530,000. As the most developed province in south-eastern Anatolia, Gaziantep has an important place in industrial production. In total employment, services have the largest share, followed by industry and agriculture. As for the distribution of female employment, agriculture had the largest share with two-thirds, followed by services (23.1 percent) and industry (11.1 percent). For males, industry is at the top of the list with 38.4 percent, followed by services (37.9 percent) and agriculture (23.5 percent).[15]

Gaziantep has a large potential in industry and the top three industrial branches in terms of employment are textiles, foodstuffs and plastics. Textiles constitute the major exporting sector in the province. Looking at the destination of exported goods we see Iraq and other Middle Eastern countries at the top of the list. In spite of this industrially advanced status, informal employment here is widespread and the rate of unionization is very low.

In the industrial subsectors concerned, there are a limited number of female employees in machine knitting in the textiles subsector and some in food production and almost none in other industries. This situation is explained by the traditional cultural make-up of Gaziantep, which does not approve of women's presence in the labor market, and also women's own preference for not working outside the home. Industrial districts are not considered appropriate places for women. Unfavourable working conditions must be taken into account too, since interviews suggested that the risk of sexual harassment, particularly in small enterprises, dissuades women from working in such places. Larger enterprises are preferred; however, in some large food sector enterprises where women work in three shifts, many young girls quit these jobs after getting married. In cases where there is no commuting service after the night shift, many women leave their jobs because of concerns about their safety. Furthermore, in settings where all household work and care are expected to be provided by women, it is extremely difficult for women to reconcile their family responsibilities with the requirements of working life and husbands who also expect their wives to stay home. While some female higher-education graduates and professionals can find jobs, mainly in the services sector, the majority of women from higher-income groups prefer not to join the labor force.

Interviews showed that the textiles subsector was affected negatively by cheap imports from China and India even before the crisis, and many women lost their jobs upon the closure of some enterprises which used to produce goods that are now imported. In machine knitting, informal employment in small workshops is common, and a similar situation can also be observed in packing work in the food subsector. In this same subsector a specific seasonal job undertaken by women at home is pistachio cracking. Bead ornamenting on textile products is another example of outsourcing in which women are involved. In both of these home-based types of work women earn very low wages. On the other hand, home-based lacework by a few qualified women can be sold at rather high prices. But this type of engagement is unstable since it depends on irregular orders.

The segregation which was observed in the Konya labor market is also present in Gaziantep. Uneducated women are mainly employed in cleaning work in the services sector or as domestic workers. Women with higher education work in the management departments of enterprises, in the finance sector, education and health. However, women can rarely be seen in top management positions. High-school graduate young women are employed as intermediate personnel in private health clinics, which have recently mushroomed, or as sales personnel in markets.

Opinions about the effects of the crisis on the local economy diverge. There are some who maintain that the local economy is not affected much since exports are mostly to Middle Eastern countries. Yet interviews show that exports to the EU countries did fall, primarily affecting the textiles and automotive spare part subsectors, but not foodstuffs. Meanwhile there are also interviews stating that some employers consider the crisis as an opportunity to lay off senior workers and lengthen working hours. The number of unemployed people has increased and many people are ready to work at any pay and with unfavourable terms. This is also true of women who are searching for jobs owing to the unemployment of their male family members.

Conclusion

In Turkey, the most salient impact of the crisis is decreasing employment and increasing unemployment. As women's employment in general, and in industrial activities in particular, is limited, they are mainly affected by the crisis through the job losses of male family members. As economic conditions deteriorate, more women joined the labor force and female unemployment increased because of the new entrants. Their participation in employment mostly took the form of unpaid family labor and own-account work, both of which are without social protection. All these forms of increasing employment can be considered as an inclusion in the labor market that does not challenge the gender division of labor and is consistent with the patriarchal social structures.

The gender division of labor in the context of a macroeconomic growth policy with 'growth without employment' and the availability of huge surplus male labor are the main determinants of women's exclusion from remunerative activities in the labor market. Patriarchy has been defined as the systematic male control of women's labor and bodies.[16] Patriarchal control of female labor in today's Turkey confines the majority of women to care work and domestic chores in their homes. Control over their bodies confines women to working in certain types of sector and occupation. The potential risk of sexual harassment underlies the exclusion of women not only from mixed working teams in factories but even from industry settlements where men form the majority of the workforce. Increasing informalization of labor markets under neoliberal policies forces women either to take informal waged work in small workshops consisting of women workers only or to do home-based work or own-account work with irregular and insufficient income. Access to decent jobs is denied to the majority of women owing to the alliance or 'happy marriage'[17] of patriarchy with neoliberalism.

During times of crisis the state becomes the most important actor for solving problems. Turkey, being a state party in all international UN and ILO conventions on gender equality, is at least officially committed to including gender equality in mainstream politics. To end women's exclusion from labor markets and to support women newly entering the labor market the government is obliged to target gender equality in the macroeconomic policies guiding the public sector, designed to promote employment, and take measures to eliminate all the obstacles to women's participation. These measures should include safe working environments and decent working conditions, free from the fear of sexual harassment.

Notes

1 This paper is based on the findings of a survey conducted by the author in the last quarter of 2009 for the ILO Turkey Office.

2 Aslanbeuigi and Summerfield (2000: 87–8); Tutnjevic (2002: 4–6); UN (1999: 89–90).

3 ILO (2009: 10).

4 Seguino (2009: 3); Antonopoulos (2009: 16).

5 ILO (2010: 18, 53); Antonopoulos (2009: 19–20).

6 ILO (2010: 50); TurkStat, Household Labor Force Surveys, www.tuik.gov.tr, accessed 30 October 2009.

7 Şenses (1996); Yeldan (2001).

8 MAR (2009).

9 The situation of female labor in Turkey is analyzed more elaborately in the author's article 'Female labor force in Turkey in the impasse of neoliberal market and patriarchal family', in Dedeoglu and Elveren (eds), *Gender and Society in Turkey: The Impact of Neo-Liberal Policies, Political Islam and EU Accession*, I. B. Tauris, London, forthcoming.

10 Toksöz (2007: 32).

11 The reason for taking July 2008 and July 2009 as the basis of comparison is that, since the effects of the crisis became more manifest in the second half of the year, July 2008 was taken as the starting point, and the most update information available while the paper was being finalized was for July 2009. All data used are from the Household Labor Force Surveys of the Turkish Statistical Institute.

12 Kalkan and Başdaş (2009a: 3).

13 Kalkan and Başdaş (2009b: 2).

14 During the finalization of the report the updated information was for 2008.

15 During the finalization of the report the updated information was for 2008.

16 Hartmann (1981).

17 This metaphor is borrowed from Deniz Kandiyoti.

References

Antonopoulos, R. (2009) 'The current economic and financial crisis: a gender perspective', Working Paper no. 562, Levy Economics Institute of Bard College.

Aslanbeuigi, N. and G. Summerfield (2000) 'The Asian crisis, gender, and the international financial architecture', *Feminist Economics*, 6(3): 81–103.

Hartmann, H. (1981) 'The unhappy marriage of Marxism and feminism: towards a more progressive union', in R. Dale, G. Esland, R. Ferguson and M. Macdonald (eds), *Politics, Patriarchy, Practice*, vol. 2, Falmer Press.

ILO (2009) *Global Employment Trends for Women March 2009*, Geneva: ILO.

— (2010) *Global Employment Trends January 2010*, Geneva: ILO.

Kalkan, S. and Ü. Başdaş (2009a) *İşletme Büyüklüğü ve Bölgesel Farklılıkların Kriz Döneminde İstihdam Kayıpları Üzerindeki Etkileri*, TEPAV Politika Notu.

— (2009b) *Kriz Döneminde İhracat Yapısının İşsizlik Üzerindeki Etkileri*, TEPAV Politika Notu.

MAR (Mülkiye Araştırma Merkezi) (2009) '2008 Yılı Katılım Öncesi Ekonomik Programı', Makroekonomik Çerçevesinin Değerlendirilmesi, Kriz Çalışma Grubu, Temmuz.

Seguino, S. (2009) *The Global Economic Crisis, Its Gender Implications and Policy Responses*, UN Commission on the Status of Women, 7 March.

Şenses F. (1996) *Structural Adjustment Policies and Employment in Turkey*, Ankara: METU Economic Research Center.

Toksöz, G. (2007) *Women's Employment Situation in Turkey*, Ankara: ILO Office in Turkey.

TurkStat (n.d.) *Household Labor Force Surveys*, www.tuik.gov.tr.

Tutnjevic, T. (2002) 'Gender and financial/economic downturn', Working Paper 9, ILO Recovery and Reconstruction Department, Geneva.

UN (1999) *World Survey on the Role of Women in Development: Globalization, Gender and Work*, Report of the Secretary-General.

Yeldan, E. (2001) *Küreselleşme Sürecinde Türkiye Ekonomisi*, Istanbul: İletişim Yayınları.

30 | Gender, climate change and human security: lessons from Senegal[1]

The Women's Environment and Development Organization (WEDO)

Women and climate change

Although climate change affects everyone, it is not gender neutral. Climate change magnifies existing inequalities, reinforcing the disparity between women and men in their vulnerability to and capability to cope with climate change (UNDP 2007a; Mitchell et al. 2007).

Women, as the majority of the world's poor, are the most vulnerable to the effects of climate change (WEDO 2007). Poor women are more likely to become direct victims (mortalities and injuries) of climate change disasters such as hurricanes and flooding (Neumayer and Plümper 2007). During natural disasters, often more women die than men because they are not warned, cannot swim or cannot leave the house alone (UNFCCC 2005). When poor women lose their livelihoods they slip deeper into poverty and the inequality and marginalization they suffer from, because of their gender, increase. Therefore climate change presents a very specific threat to their security.

Women make up 55–70 percent of the Banda Aceh (Indonesia) tsunami deaths (UNIFEM 2005; Oxfam 2005). According to the BBC News online, of the 2003 French heat wave toll of 15,000, about 70 percent were women. And in the USA, Hurricane Katrina entrenched poor African-American women, who were already the most impoverished group in the nation, in deeper levels of poverty (WEDO 2007).

Women's responsibilities in the family make them more vulnerable to environmental change, which is exacerbated by the impacts of climate change. They are being affected in their multiple roles as food producers and providers, as guardians of health, caregivers and economic actors. As access to basic needs and natural resources, such as shelter, food, fertile land, water and fuel, becomes hampered, women's workload increases. Poor families, many headed by females (e.g. 15 percent in Bangladesh, 10 percent in Nepal and 35 percent in rural India), often live in more precarious situations, on lowlands, along dangerous riverbanks, or on steep slopes (Mitchell et al. 2007).

Drought, deforestation and erratic rainfall cause women to work harder to secure (natural) resources for their livelihoods. Girls regularly drop out of school to help their mothers gather wood and water. 'Loss of livelihood assets, displacement and migration may lead to reduced access to education opportunities, thus hampering the realization of Millennium Development Goal 2 (MDG2) on universal primary education. Depletion of natural resources and decreasing agricultural productivity may place additional burdens on women's health and reduce time for decision-making processes and income-generating activities, worsening gender equality and women's empowerment (MDG3) ...' (UNDP 2007b: 1).

Conflict that arises from a shortage of natural resources amplifies existing gender inequalities, while the relocation of people has severe impacts on social support networks and family ties – mechanisms that have a crucial value for women in their coping capacity (Patt et al. 2007).

Women's coping strategies: strengthening security

Too often women are primarily perceived as the main victims of climate change and not as positive agents of change and contributors to livelihood adaptation strategies. As highlighted by Enarson (2000) and O'Brien (2007), natural disasters could also provide women with a unique opportunity to challenge and change their gendered status in society. Women have been willing and able to take an active role in what are traditionally considered 'male' tasks in responding to disasters, e.g. following Hurricane Mitch in Guatemala and Honduras in 1998 (Schrader and Delaney 2000).

Women usually have fewer assets than men to recover from natural disasters, and usually do not own land that can be sold to secure income in an emergency. Among the problems women identify when having to adapt to climate change are lack of safe land and shelter, lack of other assets and resources, limited access to material and financial resources, lack of relevant skills and knowledge, high prices of agricultural inputs and other materials, and cultural barriers limiting women's access to services (Mitchell et al. 2007).

Nevertheless, worldwide women are starting to adapt to a changing climate and can articulate what they need to secure and sustain their livelihoods more effectively. Local strategies for adapting to climate change provide valuable lessons.

Case study: gender, human security and climate change in Senegal

This study gives an overview of the climate change situation in Senegal and draws out the implications for women's livelihood, security and gender equality. The position of women in Senegal is discussed in terms of how they manage to cope with the overall challenges of poverty and inequality, with specific reference to the consequences of climate change.

Senegal lies at the westernmost point of the African continent and is a country that belongs to the Sahel[2] group. Senegal has a Sudanic and Sahelian climate dominated by two very distinct seasons: a dry season from November to June and a rainy season from July to October.[3] The climate is governed by the dynamics of strong winds. The duration of the rainy season and the intensity of seasonal distribution of precipitations vary from north to south; the annual rainfall is estimated at between 1,200 and 200 millimetres in the north. In general, precipitation is unstable and irregular from one year to another and it can be very random in the northern part of the country.

There is climate insecurity characterized by recurrent droughts. The most devastating one that affected Senegal occurred between 1968 and 1972. It was during that period of great drought that the term desertification was born. This term explains the desolation and 'dramatic consequences on the ecological equilibrium and all human activities undertaken in regions North of the Saloum' (Sagna and Roux 2000). Rains are especially important for rain-fed agriculture, therefore climate insecurity is an important source of vulnerability for Senegal.

The issue of climate change has already become a reality today for local communities in Senegal. With temperatures rising all across the country, changes are felt by everyone.[4] Research on climate predicts that Sahelian Africa will experience a 4°C rise in average temperatures around 2100 and concurrently there will be a 20 percent decline in rainfall compared to present rainfall conditions. (Diagne Gueye 1997). Local populations recognize climate variability from what they experience on a daily basis and they look for ways to deal with the consequences.

Women's position and gender issues

In Senegal, significant advances have been made on gender issues despite constraints related to women's rights and social and economic empowerment. Senegal has signed[5] a number of international conventions and passed some laws advancing women's rights. They are reinforced by the new constitution of 2001 which reaffirms the principle of equity and gender equality and prohibits all forms of discrimination based on gender. Nevertheless, not much has been done to apply national laws in favor of women's advancement.

Yet Senegal is committed to halving gender inequalities through its National Action Plan on Women (1997–2001) that ended with an assessment leading to the adoption of the National Strategy on Equity and Gender Equality (SNEEG) in 2003, in compliance with recommendations from the Beijing Platform for Action, strategic orientations from the Poverty Reduction Strategy Paper (PRSP) and the Millennium Development Goals (MDGs). That strategy is the national gender reference framework and the operational instrument designed to integrate gender in the development of policies by sector.

In public and political life, as well as in the unions, there are a good number of women ministers, members of parliament and other public officials at all levels. In 2002, the president appointed the first woman prime minister and drafted and proposed a bill on gender equality in public office.

The most important challenge still remains in the daily lives of women who are confronted with hardships, especially in rural areas, where they constitute approximately 70 percent of the labor force. They operate with very limited resources and they generate 80 percent of agricultural production. Women are vulnerable to poverty owing to lack of resources and income.

With regard to women's access to social services, namely education and health, Senegal has been implementing programs for change. The government is trying to reach parity in school enrollment even though the large majority of women are illiterate: 67.9 percent of women are illiterate today (compared to 78 percent in 1995 and 72 percent in 2001). In the health sector, attaining all the set objectives has been particularly challenging owing to high maternal mortality and morbidity rates during childbearing (410 deaths for 100,000 childbirths). Access to social services is hampered by distribution of health centers and lack of health infrastructure.

Women have unequal access to employment despite their large number in the labor force. According to SNEEG, in rural and urban areas, among the 37.2 percent of unemployed population, 66.8 percent are women. In Dakar, 41.1 percent are men and 62.1 percent are women.

Although many women's activities are not really taken into account (according to the Gender Audit of Energy Policies in Senegal in 2007), they greatly support the livelihoods of the majority of households. The absence of gender-disaggregated data hampers a realistic interpretation of statistics related to the real contribution of women in the national economy.

Gender roles often tend to undergo transformation because of the changes that occur in people's lifestyles. As living conditions unfortunately worsen, and poverty escalates, there is also a greater need to generate earnings, thus reshaping relationships between men and women. Women also acquire more freedom to get involved in women's organizations. They sell in local markets, if they have capital. Today, women want to be able to meet their needs and look out for their own interests. Nevertheless they are still dependent on the environment, the opinion of their husbands and the expectations assigned to gender roles in public life.

Impacts of climate change and women: vulnerability in accessing resources

Women who were interviewed by ENDA in the field state the following: 'We walk for long hours to find wood. Our wells are empty. Goods for sale are hard to find. Our land becomes idle. We don't have money. It doesn't rain the way it used to before' (Denton et al. 2005). Women who have been exposed to hardships and environmental insecurity have changed their lifestyles owing to these issues. Today, we can see that they are the primary victims of climate change in light of all their responsibilities in the family and the community.

Rainfall is a big determinant of women's activities since most of their efforts to sustain livelihood revolve around the environment and depend on natural resources. Since 1996, there has been a 35 percent decline in rainfall and a shortening of the rainy season, making droughts more frequent (Diagne Gueye 1997). The relationship between gender and climate change can be assessed best through an overall development study. This encompasses all data related to health, education and women's training to improve their socio-economic conditions. To better analyze the impact of climate change on women, we need to consider sectors where women are most active, such as water and fuelwood collection, agricultural production, fishing and forestry.

Access to water The 35 percent decline in rainfall in Senegal – with a range of magnitude from 20 to 40 percent depending on the region – has been confirmed by a recent study on the impact of climate change on water resources (Ndiaye 2007). In this context, women experience great difficulty accessing water, particularly in areas where there are no bore-wells, electric wells or, worse, no connection to a water distribution network. Water collection has become a heavy burden that demands a lot of patience because women have to shuttle back and forth in order to keep checking the water level in the wells. Most wells have been drilled with a 45 to 50 meter depth because of the downward trend of the low water table, and sometimes they don't reach the drawing level. This is explained by the effect of climatic variability on underground resources, which are affected by the discharge process during rainfall shortage periods. The decline has been measured at up to 5 to 10 meters in the northwest and 15 to 20 meters in the south of the country, where the drinking water coverage ratio remains low and below the standards established by the World Health Organization (WHO) (Malou 1998).

Women have to walk long distances to fetch drinkable water because of challenges such as salinity, dry wells or water impurities. Despite the existence of 1,000 electric pumps, 1,500 manual pumps and more than 4,600 modern wells, women still have problems accessing water (Ndiaye 2007). Water quality and all the physical efforts involved in fetching water affect their health and their children's health. Since it is difficult to access water, women are unable to grow out-of-season vegetables for commercial use; neither is it usually possible to deal with reforestation or engage in other creative opportunities despite their willingness to do so.

In critical situations and when distances are too long, men pitch in and use donkey-driven carts, which women and children can use, too. That way, large quantities of water can be collected and stocked in casks.

Energy Because of the prevalence of traditional biomass as the main source of energy in Senegalese households, the energy sector remains one of the most critically affected by climate change, particularly for women. The 2005 annual report on the energy sector shows that wood and charcoal constitute 35 percent of total energy consumption, and 65 percent of household energy consumption. This is despite the government's introduction of butane gas, which contributed 7.8 percent of total energy consumption. The primary reason for introducing butane gas was to protect the country against the degradation of natural resources through tree-cutting, which exacerbates desertification. Urban populations are encouraged to adopt modern fuels like gas since they were the biggest consumers of charcoal. The overall burden on rural women was not lessened by the initiative.

Even though they encounter numerous problems in fuel supply and their health and their children's health is affected, rural women are still dependent on traditional biomass. Finding wood is an enterprise in itself in parts of the country where forest degradation has become a serious obstacle. Women don't have a choice but rely on non-conventional[6] use of fuels that cause continuous health hazards; the reason is a lack of other alternatives. The main causes of the extinction of forest resources in Senegal are of environmental and anthropogenic origins. Senegal has rainfall shortfalls, cyclic droughts and a low rate of vegetation regrowth. Deforestation undertaken to find fuelwood and to produce charcoal[7] along with exports of wood-made articles and increases in the cultivated area deplete forest resources. Consequences are dramatic for women, who face constraints related to accessing fuels and suffer financial loss because there is an increasing scarcity of forest products.

Problems related to energy within the framework of climate change are not limited to cooking but encompass a whole range of issues. Limited access to energy also impacts access to health services, water, education, and engagement in business development, productivity, and participation in decision-making.

Agricultural production In Senegal, beyond the flood zones and the intra-dune basins, over 90 percent of agriculture depends on the amount of precipitation, which varies from year to year. The unreliability of rain has resulted in loss of soil fertility and poor harvests, food shortages, and impoverished populations in rural areas. The poor conditions have led to outmigration of men in search of employment in urban areas. Women largely have been left to fend for themselves and their families, although they are now beginning to migrate too. Those remaining adopt intensive agriculture practices and extend the cultivation of land to combat the effects of climate change. Unfortunately, this type of agriculture has further diminished the productiveness of the soil.

Over 70 percent of women are active in the agriculture sector, yet they own only 13.4 percent of land.[8] They farm family lots. In addition, they are also responsible for agricultural processing. The annual report on the energy sector shows that agriculture in Senegal is not modernized. Farmers use only 6.4 percent of energy – 0.1 percent of the overall energy allocation in that sector. Women use rudimentary tools and are subjected to tough physical activities in the field and at home, where they have to do household chores.

Agricultural production takes up a lot of women's time because they have to deal with problems related to soil erosion and impoverished, unfertile land. Limited access to energy services exacerbates their predicaments.

Women's adaptation to climate change

Many strategies are being implemented in Senegal in sectors such as energy and forestry, agriculture, water resources, and trade. They contribute to sustainable development and generate earnings at different levels.

Reforestation and energy With the assistance of organizations, women draw lessons from their daily dealings with the environment and develop their own adaptation solutions, including reforestation and energy management. For a number of years, women have formed associations according to their field of work, cognizant that they have to use their own resources in order to cope in precarious situations. They have become very strong actors and can easily mobilize support for every action that they undertake.

The adaptation strategy adopted by the Regroupement des Femmes de Popenguine to control the degradation of natural resources and to protect their environment has drawn international attention and shown amazing results. This group lives between the mangrove area on the Atlantic coast and a region of stony soils inland. They wanted to regenerate the mangroves and regenerate part of the forest. They looked for partners to sustain their activities and received a lot of support. Their achievements contribute to combating desertification, protecting biodiversity, and mitigating the effects of climate change, even if it is low-scale.

Even though villagers engage in low-scale reforestation activities, they contribute to the strengthening of forest resources in villages. Reforestation is sometimes undertaken by the whole village, but women are the ones who initiate it and are joined later by men and young people. The upgrading of forest resources achieves three goals: (i) land regeneration, (ii) availability of fuelwood in the village, and finally (iii) availability of financial resources generated by log sales. However, in some cases, men have abused reforestation activities and the capital gained from selling logs.

To complement reforestation, some interesting initiatives, such as modernization of households and use of butane gas, were introduced. They were mostly funded by *tontines* – small, informal savings and loan associations – whereby the contributors pay premiums for a limited period, at the end of which the subscribers divide the total amount between them. In some villages, they set up gallery stores in order to ensure that local populations buy and become familiar with products like butane gas.

The use of some wind and solar-based energy technologies have helped women access water,[9] commercialize dry fruits and vegetables, and process agricultural products.

Adaptation in agriculture Women invest a lot in agriculture in areas characterized by problems related to frequent periods of food insecurity and erratic climatic conditions. Random agricultural yields exacerbate people's poverty and disturb the family equilibrium. Problems related to agriculture are different from one region to another, and women are often the ones who search for solutions. In the rural community of Keur Moussa (Pout), women have suffered a lot, but they have worked hard. Their efforts have paid off, and they are now reaping the benefits of their hard work. With the assistance of external partners, they acquired new techniques and knowledge in combating land degradation by improving the quality of soils and their productivity.

The community of Keur Moussa is composed of thirty-seven villages; seventeen villages are subjected to erosion and land degradation, which cause inadequate agricultural yields. Three villages (Santhie Serere, Kessoukhatte and Landow) have been selected as experiment sites dedicated to controlling erosion in the framework of the Agrobio Niayes Program by ENDA Ponat. The project has been initiated by local populations and women in particular, following consultations on problems of and solutions to erosion, disappearance of arable land, uprooting of crops and trees, water scarcity, and inaccessibility to villages. Committees were established according to priorities. The Anti-Erosion Committee, in which women are very active, is one example.

To control water flow, they built stone barriers and engaged in reforestation. Those barriers are built along the edge of the rainwater area and consist of stony borders, half-moon canals, vegetation fascines, infiltration ditches, and open trenches that slow water speed and direct it towards infiltration points.

Women are interested in solving the erosion problem because it is the greatest they encounter in agriculture and it makes it difficult to access drinking water. They are very active in building stony barriers. The impact of that hard work was immediately visible – groundwater is recharged, water bodies are created, soils are stabilized, rainwater flow is slowing down; the vegetation is regenerating and there is more diversity. The president of the organization said, 'Now, there is a lot of water in our wells, and this year we spend less time drawing water, meaning one to 1.3 hours to recharge the well compared to two to three hours last year. We will continue our anti-erosion campaign for better results.' Agriculture yields improved and women began trading herbal plants, which they had not done in a long time.

Notes

1 This chapter is part of a larger work that includes cases in Bangladesh and Ghana. The introduction was written by Irene Dankelman and the section about Senegal is based on a case study conducted by Yacine Diagne Gueye of ENDA (Environmental Development Action in the Third World).

2 From Senegal to Chad, these countries have one thing in common: drought and climate uncertainty. They are located in the south of the Sahara and the Sudanic regions of the South. These countries form the Permanent Interstate Committee for Drought Control in the Sahel (CILSS).

3 Seasonal distribution changes from one year to another depending on eco-geographical regions of the country.

4 January is usually a cool month with temperatures in Dakar between 16 and 22°, but this year the heat wave is alarming in the peninsula.

5 CEDAW – Convention on the Elimination of All Forms of Discrimination against Women in 1985; Provision of the African Charter on Human and People's Rights related to the rights of women in 2004.

6 Cow dung, plastics, crop residue.

7 Statistics from the Direction de l'Energie du Sénégal indicate that in 2002 104,000 tons of gas saved 337,500 tons of charcoal that would have demanded the deforestation of 40,500 hectares of forests. The increase in gas consumption continues to save approximately 700,000 cubic meters of forest woods.

8 Audit on Gender and Energy Policy and Programs in Senegal (ENDA-ENERGIA 2007).

9 In the region of Thiès, through the VEV program, wind pumps have freed women from heavy chores.

References

Denton, F. et al. (2005) *La Visage de la pauvreté énergétique à travers la femme au Sénégal*, Dakar: ENDA.

Diagne Gueye, Y. (1997) *Impacts potentiels des Changements Climatiques et sur la production alimentaire au Sénégal: synthèse des résultats*, Dakar: ENDA Programme Energie.

— (2008) *Genre, changements climatiques et sécurité humanes: le cas du Sénégal*, Dakar: ENDA Programme Energie.

Enarson, E. (2000) *Gender and Natural Disasters*, IPCRR Working Paper no. 1, Geneva: International Labour Organization.

Malou, R. (1998) *Etude de la vulnérabilité des ressources en eau, mesures d'adaptation et d'atténuation*, Unpublished.

Mitchell, T. et al. (2007) *We Know What We Need: South Asian Women Speak Out on Climate Change Adaptation*, Johannesburg/London: ActionAid International, November.

Ndiaye, G. (2007) *Impact du changement climatique sur les ressources en eau du Sénégal*, Unpublished.

Neumayer, E. and T. Plümper (2007) *The Gendered Nature of Natural Disasters: The impact of catastrophic events on the gender gap in life expectancy, 1981–2002*, London: London School of Economics, University of Essex and Max Plank Institute for Economics.

O'Brien, K. (2007) *Commentary to the paper of Úrsula Oswald Spring, Climate Change: A Gender Perspective on Human and State Security Approaches to Global Security*, Paper presented at the International Women Leaders Global Security Summit, New York, 15–17 November .

Oxfam (2005) *Gender and the Tsunami*, Briefing Note, Oxford: Oxfam, March.

Patt, A., A. Dazé and P. Suarez (2007) *Gender and Climate Change Vulnerability: What's the problem, what's the solution?*, Paper presented at the International Women Leaders Global Security Summit, New York, 15–17 November.

Sagna, P. and M. Roux (2000) *Atlas du Sénégal*, Jeune Afrique edn.

Schrader, E. and P. Delaney (2000) *Gender and Post-Disaster Reconstruction: The*

Case of Hurricane Mitch in Honduras and Nicaragua, Washington, DC: World Bank.

UNDP (2007a) *Human Development Report 2007–2008: Fighting Climate Change: Human Solidarity in a Divided World*, New York: Palgrave Macmillan.

— (2007b) *Poverty Eradication, MDGs and Climate Change*, Environment and Energy, UNDP, www.undp.org/climate change/adap01.htm.

UNFCCC (2005) *Global Warning: Women Matter*, Women's statement, UNFCCC COP, December.

UNIFEM (2005) *UNIFEM Responds to the Tsunami Tragedy – One Year Later: A Report Card*, New York: UNIFEM.

WEDO (Women's Environment and Development Organization) (2007) *Changing the Climate: Why Women's Perspectives Matter*, Fact sheet, New York: WEDO.

31 | The population bomb is back – with a global warming twist

Betsy Hartmann and Elizabeth Barajas-Román

Hunger, poverty, environmental degradation, violent conflict. Ever since the time of Malthus, rich elites have blamed these ills on the fertility of the poor. Now they've added climate change to the list. Population pundits and advocacy groups claim that overpopulation is the main cause of global warming and that only massive investments in family planning will save the planet. This argument threatens to derail climate negotiations and turn back the clock on reproductive rights and health. It's time for women's movements to defuse the population bomb – again.

When Stanford biologist Paul Ehrlich wrote *The Population Bomb* in the late 1960s, he argued that a population 'explosion' would wreak havoc on the environment and cause hundreds of millions to starve to death by the 1980s. His predictions did not come true. Instead world food production outpaced population growth, and birth rates started to fall for a variety of reasons, including declines in infant mortality, increases in women's education and employment, and the shift from rural to urban livelihoods. Yet his kind of dire forecast served as justification for the implementation of coercive population control programs that brutally sacrificed women's health and human rights.

When feminists won reforms of population policy at the 1994 UN population conference in Cairo, many thought family planning had finally been freed from the shackles of population control. The more immediate threat seemed to be fundamentalist forces opposing reproductive and sexual rights. But population control never went away. Mounting concern about climate change has provided a new opportunity for the population control lobby to blame the poor and target women's fertility.

Within the US population lobby, the influential Population Action International organization has taken the lead in linking population growth and climate change.[1] Paul Ehrlich is back on the circuit and popular media are spreading fear and alarm.[2] For example, a June 2009 ABC prime-time television documentary on climate change, *Earth 2100*, scared viewers with scenes of a future apocalypse in which half the world population dies of a new plague. And in the end, humans can get back into balance with nature again.

Unfortunately, even some feminists have jumped on board this fear-factor

327

bandwagon. Although their message tends to be softer – they believe investments in voluntary family planning will meet women's unmet need for contraception and reduce global warming at the same time – they are helping to legitimize the resurgence of population control.[3] They assume we live in a win-win world where there's no fundamental power imbalance between rich and poor or contradiction between placing disproportionate blame for the world's problems on poor women's fertility and advocating for reproductive rights and health.

The reasoning behind these views is fundamentally flawed. Industrialized countries, with only 20 percent of the world's population, are responsible for 80 percent of the accumulated carbon dioxide in the atmosphere. The USA is the worst offender. Overconsumption by the rich has far more to do with global warming than population growth of the poor. The few countries in the world where population growth rates remain high, such as those in sub-Saharan Africa, have among the lowest carbon emissions per capita on the planet.[4]

Moreover, the recent resurgence in overpopulation rhetoric flies in the face of demographic realities. In the last few decades population growth rates have come down all over the world so that the average number of children per woman in the global South is now 2.75 and predicted to drop to 2.05 by 2050. The so-called population 'explosion' is over, though the momentum built into our present numbers means that world population will grow to about nine billion in 2050, after which point it will start to stabilize. The real challenge is to plan for the addition of those three billion people in ways that minimize negative environmental impact, including global warming. For example, investments in public transport rather than private cars, in cluster housing rather than suburbia, in green energy rather than fossil fuels and nuclear, would do a lot to help a more populated planet.

Serious environmental scholars have taken the population and climate change connection to task,[5] but unfortunately a misogynist pseudo-science has been developed to bolster overpopulation claims. Widely cited in the press, a study by two researchers at Oregon State University blames women's childbearing for creating a long-term 'carbon legacy.'[6] Not only is the individual woman responsible for her own children's emissions, but for her genetic offspring's emissions far into the future! Missing from the equation is any notion that people are capable of effecting positive social and environmental change, and that the next generation could make the transition out of fossil fuels. It also places the onus on the individual, obscuring the role of capitalist systems of production, distribution, and consumption in causing global warming.

A second study to hit the press is by a population control outfit in the UK, Optimum Population Trust (OPT), whose agenda includes immigration restriction. OPT sponsored a graduate student at the London School of Economics to undertake a simplistic cost/benefit analysis that purports to show that it's cheaper to reduce carbon emissions by investing in family planning than in alternative technologies.[7] Although the student's summer project was not supervised by an official faculty member, the press has billed it as a study by the prestigious LSE, lending it false legitimacy. Writing on the popular blog RHRealityCheck, Karen Hardee and Kathleen Mogelgaard of Population Action International endorse the report's findings without even a blink of a critical eye.

Clearly, it is time for feminists to keep their critical eyes wide open to these developments. We also need to develop alternative frames and politics to address reproductive rights and climate change. We not only have to criticize the wrong links, but make the right ones.

Right links: reproductive justice/environmental justice/climate justice

Developed and advanced by women of color activists in the USA, the concept of reproductive justice strongly condemns population control, noting its long history of targeting the fertility of oppressed communities. At the same time it includes support for full access to safe, voluntary birth control, abortion, and reproductive health services. But reproductive justice goes far beyond the need for adequate services. According to Asian Communities for Reproductive Justice (ACRJ), reproductive justice 'will be achieved when women and girls have the economic, social and political power and resources to make healthy decisions about our bodies, sexuality and reproduction for ourselves, our families and our communities in all areas of our lives.'[8] Reproductive justice refers not only to biological reproduction but to social reproduction.

Feminist scholar Giovanna Di Chiro argues that the concept of social reproduction is crucial to understanding the possibilities for linking struggles for women's rights with environmental justice. Social reproduction includes the conditions necessary for reproducing everyday life (access to food, water, shelter, and healthcare) as well as the ability to sustain human cultures and communities.[9] Whether or not individuals and communities can fulfill their basic needs and sustain themselves depends critically on the extent of race, class, and gender inequalities in access to resources and power. Unlike the population framework with its focus on numbers, social reproduction focuses on social, economic, and political *systems*. It helps us to look more deeply at the underlying power dynamics that determine who lives and who dies, who is healthy and who is sick, whose environment is polluted and whose is clean, who is responsible for global warming and who suffers most from its consequences.

Looking through this lens leads to a much more liberatory understanding of the convergences of reproductive and climate politics. It encourages us to consider:

Connections between the local and the global: Some of the same powerful forces that drive environmental injustice at the local level contribute to climate change on the global level. While marginalized communities all over the world experience environmental injustices at the hands of powerful corporate and political actors, their experiences and concerns are diverse. Local battles against environmental injustice include coal-mining towns in rural Appalachia, indigenous communities of the Arctic and Subarctic, the oilfields of Nigeria and the oil refineries of the Gulf Coast. The task of confronting global climate change challenges us to build alliances, coalitions, and political solidarity across borders and among a wide range of communities. The global nature of climate change means our struggles are not in isolation from one another.[10]

Environmental dimensions of health: Communities subjected to environmental racism experience daily exposure to cancer-causing chemicals and other toxins that cause respiratory, reproductive, and skin disorders. Women experience this toxic burden twofold. They often must shoulder their own health concerns while taking on the role of caring for others in the community who have been harmed, particularly children and the elderly. Women are also physiologically more susceptible to the health effects of a number of common pollutants which can build up and be stored for long periods of time in the fatty tissue of their breasts. Women may then pass on concentrated doses of toxins to their infants during breastfeeding. Women have spearheaded many of the battles against environmental injustice. This stems largely from their roles as caretakers of their families and the fact that they are more often in a position to bear direct witness to the health impacts of toxic infrastructure on their community. The dialogue on climate change must open space for these women to contribute their knowledge and voice their concerns.

Food security: Climate-related scarcities of food and other natural resources such as water and firewood are likely to create burdens that fall disproportionately on poor people, especially women and girls whose domestic responsibilities include the management of these resources. In some families and communities, gendered food hierarchies in the household can put women at greater risk of malnutrition in times of crisis.[11] Achieving food security for all people should be a high priority in national and international responses to climate change. This means challenging present corporate food systems that appropriate land from peasant producers (many of whom are women) for large-scale luxury export crop production; engage in environmentally unsustainable mono-cropping and chemical-intensive agriculture; and draw down water supplies through inappropriate irrigation technologies. It also means opposing the transformation of lands that grow food crops into plantations of commercial biofuels.

The failure of corporate solutions to climate change: In the international arena, corporate needs outweigh human needs when it comes to official climate change agreements. Ironically, a number of the mechanisms put in place by the Kyoto Protocol are not only doing little to reduce carbon emissions, but are increasing poor people's vulnerability. Carbon trading schemes allow corporate energy guzzlers to maintain high levels of emissions if they invest in carbon sequestration projects in the global South. Many of these projects are huge monoculture tree plantations (also corporately owned) that reduce biodiversity and take over lands and forests from indigenous peoples, preventing women from collecting plants and firewood. These projects effectively shut the door on small-scale, non-corporate solutions such as systems that encourage local control of existing forests and improvements in their ability to sequester carbon and produce sustainable fuelwood supplies for community needs.[12]

The nature of disaster response: Early warning systems and disaster management schemes often neglect the needs of poor women and communities of color. In the USA Hurricane Katrina illustrated how race, class, and gender intersect in shaping who is most at risk during a disaster and who has the right to return afterwards. Activists should work together to press for more socially just and effective disaster responses, including those that take into account women's increased vulnerability to sexual and domestic violence and their need for safe reproductive health services in periods of dislocation. For strategic reasons, the US military presently wants to expand its role in disaster response in the USA and globally. We need to resist this development and insist that publicly accountable civilian institutions be strengthened to cope with climate-related natural disasters.

Saying no to nuclear power: The reproductive health effects of the release of radiation and toxic chemicals are a powerful reason to oppose the expansion of nuclear power as a solution to climate change. Plutonium, the most dangerous byproduct of nuclear energy, crosses the placenta in the developing embryo and can cause birth defects. Plutonium affects male reproductive health as well. Stored in the testicles, it can cause mutations in reproductive genes, increased incidence of genetic disease in future generations, and testicular cancer. Long ignored, the chemical byproducts of nuclear energy are also linked to genetic mutations, Down's syndrome, autism, and other serious health effects. The US nuclear industry has no regulations to protect women workers from the risk of early miscarriages and fetal malformations or men from potential harm to their ability to reproduce. A resurgence of nuclear power would also bring increased uranium mining on indigenous lands, with consequent environmental pollution and negative health impacts.[13] Nuclear power threatens both biological and social reproduction.

Immigrant and refugee rights: In the USA reproductive justice advocates have been some of the most vocal supporters of immigrant rights and effective organizers in immigrant communities. They point out how policies restricting immigration and blocking access to social services prevent immigrant women from getting the reproductive and basic healthcare they need. They also work with poor immigrant communities who suffer disproportionately from environmental racism.[14] Climate justice must include immigrant rights high on the agenda. In the event that people are displaced by global warming, we need to ensure that they are welcomed – not further traumatized and stigmatized.

Ending militarism: Militarism in all its forms, from the prison-industrial complex to wars of occupation, is one of the most powerful obstacles to the achievement of reproductive, environmental, and climate justice. Ending militarism is a point where our struggles can and should converge, where there are multiple overlaps. The list is long: Military toxins damage the environment and harm reproductive health. Militarism increases violence against women, racism, and anti-immigration activity. Militarism robs resources from other social and environmental needs. War destroys ecosystems, livelihoods, and health and sanitation infrastructure; it is the biggest threat of all to sustainable social reproduction.[15]

Militarism also stands in the way of effective solutions to climate change. Not only is the US military a major emitter of greenhouse gases – it burns the same amount of fossil fuel every day as the entire nation of Sweden – but it spends up to 30 percent of its annual budget on military actions to secure oil and gas reserves around the world. Imagine if those funds flowed instead to the development of renewable energy, green technologies, and programs to ensure that low-income people are not adversely affected by the transition to a new energy regime. Meanwhile, military research into controlling the climate poses a potentially grave danger to the environment.[16]

The resurgence of population control is a major roadblock on the route to effective and equitable climate policy and the achievement of reproductive health, rights, and justice. It is time to knock it down and get on our way.

Notes

1 www.populationaction.org/ Publications/Working_Papers/April_2009/ Summary.shtml.

2 e360.yale.edu/content/feature. msp?id=2041.

3 www.rhrealitycheck.org/blog/2009/ 07/10/world-population-day-important.

4 popdev.hampshire.edu/projects/ dt/57.

5 See, for example, e360.yale.edu/ content/feature.msp?id=2140; popdev. hampshire.edu/sites/popdev/files/ uploads/Satterthwaite%20pages%20545- 567.pdf.

6 blog.oregonlive.com/environment_ impact/2009/07/carbon%20legacy.pdf.

7 www.optimumpopulation.org/ reducingemissions.pdf.

8 Asian Communities for Reproductive Justice, *A New Vision for Advancing our Movement for Reproductive Health, Reproductive Rights and Reproductive Justice*, www.sistersong.net/documents/ ACRJ_Reproductive_Justice_Paper.pdf, accessed 7 January 2009. For a history of the reproductive justice movement and its opposition to population control, see Jael Silliman, Marlene Gerber Fried, Loretta Ross and Elena R. Gutiérrez, *Undivided Rights: Women of Color Organize for Reproductive Justice*, Cambridge, MA: South End Press, 2004.

9 popdev.hampshire.edu/projects/ dt/58.

10 The following sections draw on Stephen Blake Figura, Betsy Hartmann,

and Elizabeth Barajas-Román, 'Reproductive justice, climate justice, peace: a call for solidarity, not population control', Working Paper of the Population and Development Program, March 2008, popdev.hampshire.edu/blog/reproductive-justice-climate-justice-peace, accessed 7 January 2009.

11 For more on gender and climate change, see Irene Dankelman, *Gender, Climate Change and Human Security*, Women's Environment and Development Organization, May 2008, www.wedo.org/files/HSN%20Study%20Final%20May%2020,%202008.pdf, accessed 7 January 2009. See also WEDO's gender action link, www.genderaction.org/images/Gender%20Action%20Link%20-%20Climate%20Change.pdf, accessed 7 January 2009.

12 See the excellent resource *Carbon Trading: A Critical Conversation on Climate Change, Privatization, and Power*, Special issue of *Development Dialogue*, 48, September 2006, www.dhf.uu.se/pdffiler/DD2006_48_carbon_trading/carbon_trading_web.pdf, accessed 7 January 2009.

13 Meredith Crafton, 'Why a nuclear renaissance threatens our bodies, the environment and our future', *DifferenTakes*, 56, Winter 2009, popdev.hampshire.edu/projects/dt/56.

14 ACRJ, *A New Vision for Advancing our Movement for Reproductive Health, Reproductive Rights and Reproductive Justice*, www.sistersong.net/documents/ACRJ_Reproductive_Justice_Paper.pdf, accessed 7 January 2009.

15 See Population and Development Program, 'Ten reasons why militarism is bad for reproductive freedom', *DifferenTakes*, 20, Winter 2003, popdev.hampshire.edu/projects/dt/20, accessed 6 January 2009, and Simon Doolittle, 'Ten reasons why militarism is bad for the environment', *DifferenTakes*, 22, Spring 2003, popdev.hampshire.edu/projects/dt/22, accessed 6 January 2009.

16 On military consumption of oil, see Nick Turse, 'The Military-petroleum complex', *Foreign Policy in Focus*, 24 March 2008, www.fpif.org/fpiftxt/5097/, accessed 7 January 2009; on military costs of securing oil supplies, see Anita Dancs, *The Military Cost of Securing Energy*, National Priorities Project, October 2008, www.nationalpriorities.org/auxiliary/energy_security/full_report.pdf, accessed 7 January 2009; on military schemes of climate control, James R. Fleming, 'The climate engineers', *Wilson Quarterly*, Spring 2007, www.wilsoncenter.org/index.cfm?fuseaction=wq.essay&essay_id=231274, accessed 7 January 2009.

32 | Caring for people with HIV: state policies and their dependence on women's unpaid work

Anesu Makina

Introduction

This chapter focuses on unpaid care work in countries in which the HIV pandemic is creating a crisis. It argues that policy-makers in governments and development organizations should take a hard look at the economics of care work. The need to respond to HIV and AIDS necessitates that policy-makers, health professionals and community development workers acknowledge the increased labour, time and other demands placed upon households, support women carers, and challenge the assumptions made by some policy-makers about home-based care provision being available free of any cost. We need to challenge the norms and expectations about care and its provision (Ogden et al. 2004).

Exploring the concept of 'care work' Care encompasses the direct care of people and includes work such as feeding and bathing a young child – and the domestic tasks that are a precondition for caregiving, such as preparing meals, cleaning, organizing and purchasing food, or collecting water and fuel. It also extends to looking after those with intense and special needs, including young children, frail elderly people, and people with various illnesses and disabilities. These activities have been a function of society since time immemorial, but have now taken a political and economic meaning with problematic consequences, in particular for women.

This is because the care is commonly either given freely, or at a cost which the giver is willing or able to shoulder (Meyer 2000). Care work can be unpaid, undertaken for a family or community without remuneration or compensation. Alternatively, the same activities may be done by non-family members, or outside the home, and paid for, for example by nurses or domestic workers (Akintola 2004; Esplen 2009; Razavi 2007). Care work includes activities that are integral to the functioning of all economies, yet, unless it is performed within the formal sector, it remains unrecognized and unaccounted for in budgets and statistics.

In her discussion of unpaid care work, Debbie Budlender (2004) highlights the fact that this work is essential to society, even though it is not paid. Care work is critical to human well-being. The term 'care work' reminds us that all the activities women perform for family members at home are 'work', in an economic sense – that is, these activities have a cost, in terms of time and energy. Unpaid care work is exhausting, owing partly to its relentlessness: for the worker, there is no distinction between work and non-work time. Caring for a child or a sick person makes demands on the carer twenty-four hours a day. A person doing this by him/herself is always 'on call' (Elson 2005).

Women pay an opportunity cost when undertaking unpaid care work; they miss opportunities, including the more profitable kinds of income-generating work. These kinds of work are usually full-time, and take place away from workers' homes. They cannot easily be juggled with caring work. This leads to women missing out on recruitment and promotions in many areas of work. Women are also less likely to obtain such work because their caring responsibilities, which often start in childhood, have led them to miss out on education and training.

Care work's visibility to policy-makers

As stated in the last section, most of women's unpaid caring work for their families and dependants takes place in the home. The household is seen conventionally as a 'private sphere', and is hence 'out of the frame' for policy-makers; it is a realm that remains largely untouched by legal reforms, or other formal challenges to social norms and practices.

Women's unpaid work is an integral feature of social life in sub-Saharan countries that are struggling to cope with the HIV and AIDS pandemic. This work arises out of social and contractual obligations associated with marriage or other family relationships. The significance of women performing caring work to gender relations in sub-Saharan Africa, and elsewhere, is still only partly recognized. The fact that women do this work is connected to gender inequality: women still carry out most domestic work in the home and community, and female children continue to be socialized into the role of carer. The myth that women have a natural capacity and desire to care for others reinforces gender inequality by disproportionately burdening women with unpaid work, and on the other hand justifies employing them in low-paid care work outside the home (Meyer 2000: 5).

Over the past forty years, gender inequality and women's rights have been increasingly debated by policy-makers. From the Convention for the Elimination of All Forms of Discrimination against Women (CEDAW)[1] to the Beijing Declaration and Platform for Action,[2] women's rights have been slowly integrated into national laws, especially those pertaining to work and labour rights. Yet these debates, laws and declarations have not adequately addressed intra-household relations and unpaid workers. Women's labour rights are seen as an issue concerning paid work only, and unpaid care work is still unregulated.

In contrast, scholarly work and literature focusing on women's unpaid care work is extensive. However, most studies have a strong bias towards focusing on care work done by women, within the family, as opposed to care work provided by the state and private service providers (ibid.: 5). This is a problem, because this focus in the literature conflates caring with family; yet it can, of course, be provided by the state or the private sector. For example, former socialist countries were committed to socio-economic change, which they enacted through laws on labour and land. Women's subordination was acknowledged, and their emancipation from unpaid care work was seen as an important factor for development and the transformation of society. As a result, socialist states actively channelled women into the paid labour force. Although women remained responsible for most of the care work which needed to be done at home, state policies were formulated to significantly ease their burden (Molyneux 1984).

HIV and AIDS and the burden of care The debate on unpaid care work and women has taken on a new importance in the context of HIV and AIDS, especially in sub-Saharan Africa. This region accounts for nearly 67 per cent of those who live with HIV and 75 per cent of all AIDS deaths that occurred in 2007 (UNAIDS 2007).

Women are disproportionably affected by HIV infection themselves, because they are more likely to contract the virus owing to greater biological and social vulnerability – women currently comprise about 58 per cent of adult HIV infections (UNAIDS 2008). Yet whether or not they are *infected* themselves, women are also more adversely *affected*, because of their primary caregiving role. The workload at home rises dramatically when a family member begins to suffer from AIDS-related illness. When AIDS enters the home, more time needs to be allocated to household work for both women and men, but the burden of the former is at least twice as heavy. Women and girls are directly adversely affected, as the time they could have had to take part in paid labour, income generation, training and education is taken up by care work. In addition, the whole household is affected by women having less time to earn income. Upon a family member becoming ill, the role of women as carers, income-earners and housekeepers is stepped up as a coping and survival mechanism. In addition, infected women often find themselves caring for an ill relative or family member when they themselves also need care.

Policy and research debates on HIV and AIDS have tended to have a relatively narrow focus on the state provision of treatment; public education and reduction of stigma, rather than on other important issues including essential care, welfare and support to people living with HIV and AIDS. States are reliant on these services being provided at home or via community groups and NGOs. Some have never provided state services, or have now cut back on healthcare expenditure, and/or promoted the privatization of health services. This confinement of care, welfare and support programmes to the domestic sphere means that advocacy and policy efforts around these topics fall under the radar, because many of those responsible for these services are under-represented in the public sphere. Yet, despite this invisibility and silence in policy discussions and service provision, the costs of care do not disappear. They are quietly shouldered by the household, and particularly by women.

Home-based care as a policy option

Around the mid-to-late 1990s, programmers and policy-makers, realizing that the public sector was going to be unable to bear the costs of AIDS-related illnesses, began considering ways to shift the locus of clinical care from public health services to the community (Ogden et al. 2004). Research measuring the cost of AIDS care at government hospitals in Zimbabwe found that the cost of staying in hospital for patients with AIDS was on average twice as high as that of other patients (Hansen et al. 2000).

In this context, 'home-based care' has a new significance and meaning. The home-based care system is defined by the World Health Organization (WHO 2002) as the provision of health services by formal and informal caregivers in the home, in order to promote, restore and maintain a person's maximum level of comfort, function and health, including care towards dignified death. Home-based care was understood as part of the 'continuum of care' of patients with HIV or AIDS, and originated as an extension of the formal health system. However, it is now operated as an independent system on its own, with more and more hospitals discharging patients early to be 'taken care of' at home (Akintola 2004). Although the system is not limited to HIV and AIDS, it has taken up an association with the disease, because of the epidemic proportion that HIV and AIDS have reached in sub-Saharan Africa.

Supporters of home-based care emphasize the advantages: patients are cared for in familiar environments, and die with loved ones by their side. There is also the benefit of a reduction of the burden on public health facilities, and reduction in the cost of transport to hospitals by caregivers. However, this positive view is not shared by NGOs and caregivers, as the effectiveness and quality of home-based care are questionable in many contexts, and its costs have been greatly underestimated. Most patients and carers seem to have preferred home care during the last stages of AIDS, although this is not universal, especially when diseases grow burdensome (Iliffe 2006).

Caring for people with AIDS Providing home-based care for a person living with HIV/AIDS imposes considerable costs on the patient, his or her carer, and the wider family. These costs include financial resources, time resources, and opportunity costs. Research by Action Aid Southern Africa Partnership

Programme (SAPP) (2005), Olagoke Akintola (2004), and others, shows that the role played by women caring for people with AIDS-related illnesses intensifies poverty and insecurity for themselves and their dependants. The cost of women's time is not normally measured; yet caring for someone with an AIDS-related illness entails heavier work than usual. A South African study showed that caregivers in 40 per cent of the 312 households surveyed had to take time off to care for the ill. The majority of these had to take time off from other work in the household, while one in five had to take time off from school. Ten per cent took time off from formal employment (Steinberg et al. 2002).

Illness increases the amount of time and energy required to carry out care work. One study of caregivers found that carers spent up to three hours a day caring for patients with AIDS, a demand that grew as the disease progressed (Iliffe 2006: 110). Some tasks intensify, while others are new. Tasks include bathing and cleaning up after the sick person; obtaining food through purchase or agriculture; storing, preparing and serving meals; hand-feeding those too sick to feed themselves; washing clothes and bed sheets; escorting the sick person to and from the toilet; general assistance in walking (especially on stairs and uneven surfaces); house maintenance; emotional support; childcare; purchasing and administering drugs or remedies; and other work to ensure general household survival, including earning income and growing food (Ogden et al. 2004).

Another key issue is the impact of home-based caregiving on the welfare and rights of the girl child. Young girls are socialized into lifelong caregiving roles. They find themselves assisting with care work, at the expense of school work, leisure activities and important social development activities (critically, including HIV prevention activities), which are all essential to their well-being. In some households, the girls are expected to nurse a sick relative while the primary caregiver engages in income generation and other activities. The effects of playing secondary caregiver leave the girl too exhausted to carry out other activities. The situation is particularly grim if the girl child is heading a home as a result of being orphaned, or assisting a grandparent to bring up siblings. In such cases, many girls cannot go to school at all, renouncing their right to education – affecting their potential income and career choices, and ability to play a role in wider society.

The debate on the relationship between HIV/AIDS, work and poverty has often been simplistic, failing to encapsulate the gendered links between them. It is only in recent years that the gender dimensions of poverty have begun to be understood, and links with HIV/AIDS have begun to be considered by international and local organizations. Many advocacy campaigns by NGOs such as Oxfam and ActionAid, and even UNAIDS, are now underscoring the role of HIV/AIDS in increasing poverty.

Situational analysis – home-based care in South Africa and Zimbabwe

In this section, I briefly examine home-based care in two contexts: Zimbabwe and South Africa. With an inflation rate of over 231 million per cent (CNN International 2008), and a recorded 80 per cent unemployment rate (CIA 2008), Zimbabwe is a unique case. In contrast, South Africa has one of the strongest economies in Africa.

Zimbabwe In Zimbabwe, home-based care in the context of HIV and AIDS has become the only option for the majority. It gained pace from 1995, within the context of a deteriorating economy, and began to be institutionalized as an important response to HIV and AIDS (HDN and SAfAIDS 2008). The HIV rates in Zimbabwe are astronomically high, with one in seven adults recorded as having contracted the virus (UNAIDS 2008).

Zimbabwe's political upheaval and ongoing rapid economic decline, and the dilapidated infrastructure associated with this, have resulted in a grave state of affairs for everyone, but particularly for families living with HIV and AIDS. Zimbabwe lacks the systems and resources needed to provide an effective HIV and AIDS prevention, treatment and care programme. Not only is there a crisis in funding, but the healthcare sector has been badly affected by the migration of many skilled workers, who have left the country, further relegating most care work to the home and community. NGOs are unable to fill the 'care gap'. Care for Zimbabweans living with HIV is indeed a concern of many local and international NGOs, but the scale of need is huge, and the current turmoil in the country has affected the ability of NGOs to respond to the need, and led to reductions in humanitarian and foreign aid (Black and McGreal 2008).

Home-based care is the only option. The Minister of Health and Child Welfare, David Parirenyatwa, was quoted in 2008 as saying: 'Traditionally, our families and communities have taken on the responsibility of caring for chronically ill people, outside of the hospitals, clinics and medical institutions' (HDN and SAfAIDS 2008). This statement shows that the state is willing to invoke ideas of custom and tradition to put the burden of care on the shoulders of the community and families, without the relevant support structures in place.

In Zimbabwe, as elsewhere, the need for women to deliver home-based care creates an opportunity cost which compromises both individual and family well-being. Women are often unable to take up the opportunities which exist to earn cash, and households are trapped in a spiral of increasing poverty. An example of this is trading in imported goods, which is an obvious course of action for many Zimbabwean women. Traders make the journey into neighbouring countries to buy goods to sell at home (Kwidini 2009). However, travelling so far from home is not possible if there is an ill person in the home.

South Africa Despite its strong economy, South Africa faces the challenges of being the country with the highest number of people living with HIV/AIDS in the world.

Obviously, the state of healthcare is much better in South Africa than in Zimbabwe; here, the patients do have access to hospitalization and medical services, even in the early stages of displaying AIDS-related symptoms. However, South Africa, too, has intense stresses on its health systems. A survey of the impact of HIV/AIDS on the health sector in South Africa showed that 46.2 per cent of patients in the medical and paediatric wards of hospitals in that country were HIV positive (Shishana et al. 2002). As a result, South Africa, too, has handed over some of the caring to the household, justifying this by stating that patients are better off being nursed and then dying at home, in a dignified way, surrounded by those people with whom they are familiar (DoH 2001). Of course, these justifications contain much truth, but the issues are more complex than this, as we have seen.

Owing to poverty and strain on household resources, including time, the quality of care (e.g. nutrition) that patients receive at home is questionable. A national evaluation of home-based care found that 80 per cent of the family caregivers they interviewed reported that their income levels had reduced owing to care work (SAPP 2005) – a burden that should be borne by the state.

It is evident that care work impoverishes women, and also perpetuates existing gender inequalities. It is also a very inadequate policy response to the complex needs of people suffering from AIDS-related illnesses. Care work, therefore, has to be consolidated into public policy. The South African government has put enormous resources into scaling up home-based care services in general, by augmenting unpaid family care: training, and in some cases even paying, volunteers. Yet providing state-supported home carers is not the whole answer. Simple tasks such as cleaning, feeding and administering medication can be done by volunteers, but anything more complex poses a challenge. In addition, the services are not able to reach all of those in need. The Western Cape province of South Africa categorically states in its list of government-provided directory services that: 'Home-based care is not a 24-hour service, and does not replace the family as the primary caregiver. It is only meant to be a complementary and supportive service to prevent "burn-out" for caregivers who are forced to care for sick relatives' (www.capegateway.gov.za/).

Policy considerations and change

If no changes are made, there will be a continued failure to meet the needs of patients and further impoverishment of households. Equally importantly, from a gender perspective, women will continue to be treated as an inexhaustible supply of unpaid labour, young girls will forgo their chance of education and a better future, and there will be no change in gender-based power relations within households, communities and society at large.

In order to develop policies on care which deliver positive change for carers and the best possible care for people living with HIV and AIDS, there needs to be a complete overhaul of the methods used for assessing the economic cost of different policy options for caring. Approaches that fail to consider hidden social and economic biases lead to unsustainable healthcare policies which violate the rights of women and girls, and lead to the collapse of the household economy.

I will conclude by offering some policy recommendations, which are relevant to different levels of the economy. At the *macro-level* (that is, focusing on government budget allocation and policy), HIV and AIDS have absorbed considerable proportions of national budgets. Yet, while home-based care may appear to reduce the bill, it has hidden effects which affect other sectors of the economy. At the *micro-level* (focusing on household and intra-household processes and relations), the impact of home-based care on carers, patients and the wider family can sometimes be difficult to track, because it differs between households. However, it is true to say that for all households there is an increased burden, because of the extra work that needs to be done, and the extra expenditure incurred. It is at this household level that women and girls are most affected, because of the gendered expectations that they will provide the care work. At the *meso-level* (focusing on the policies, norms and practices of social institutions), perceptions about women's work coming at no cost persist, despite the lobbying and education efforts of gender specialists and advocates for women's rights, and women's organizations, and the existence of international conventions such as CEDAW and the Beijing Platform for Action.

HIV and AIDS budgets – both state and NGO – need to allocate more resources to care work. Currently, more resources are allocated to prevention, treatment and literacy. Some of the savings associated with reliance on home-based care should be passed on to carers, via the provision of emotional, financial and psychological support; this helps to make their work sustainable. The impact of home-based care on the girl child who is a carer must be acknowledged, and her needs must be taken into consideration – together with her right to education.

Future policies based on a recognition of the economic and social costs, and contributions, of home-based care work need to be developed accordingly. This acknowledgement should be accompanied by a valuation of the cost savings that governments make as a result of home-based care. In addition more focus is needed on the quality of care. Hospital discharge polices should be reviewed, so that patients are not discharged on the assumption that they will automatically receive first-class care at home. This not only burdens women and girls, but in many resource-poor settings the practice of sending people to be cared for at home results in home-based neglect, as the households do not have adequate resources to look after the patient effectively. Poor households need to be able to access subsidies and safety nets to ensure their survival. These can be in the form of food subsidies, medical supplies and other resources important for the care of patients.

We also need to see a shift in perceptions of care work as a professional career option which should allow workers to progress and develop. This would create a pool of trained, qualified professionals who are adequately compensated. In the long term, they would be able to alleviate the burden on women.

Finally, a key issue which is now coming up in debates about care is how better to engage men in care work. Action is needed to radically 'de-feminize' caregiving – challenging assumptions that care work is the domain of women and not men. This can help create the foundations for a more equal sharing of care responsibilities between women and men (Esplen 2009). If men and boys engaged more in care it would go a long way in lifting the burden off the shoulders of women and girls, and the long-term effects on gender equality and women's rights would be positive. But getting men to care is a challenge, because of the gender roles and stereotypes prescribed by culture and traditions. Professional nursing does now attract men, but the work of home-based care is still associated with women.

Notes

1 CEDAW, often described as an international bill of rights for women, is an international agreement adopted in 1979 by the UN General Assembly. The document defines what constitutes discrimination against women and sets an agenda for national action to end such discrimination. Taken from the web address www.un.org/womenwatch/daw/cedaw/, accessed March 2009.

2 Beijing Declaration and Platform for Action is a document that was adopted by the Fourth World Conference on Women: Action for Equality, Development and Peace held in Beijing, China, on 15 September 1995. It is the first broad-based agenda for promoting and protecting women's rights globally. It is distinct from CEDAW in that it advocates for shared responsibility not only between men and women but between civil society and governments. Taken from www.un.org/womenwatch/daw/beijing/platform/declar.htm, accessed March 2009.

References

Akintola, O. (2004) *A Gendered Analysis of the Burden of Care on Family and Volunteer Caregivers in Uganda and South Africa*, Durban: HEARD, University of KwaZuluNatal.

Black, I. and C. McGreal (2008) 'Mugabe suspends foreign aid agencies' work in Zimbabwe', *Guardian*, www.guardian.co.uk/world/2008/jun/06/mugabe.aid, accessed March 2009.

Budlender, D. (2004) *Why Should We Care about Unpaid Care Work?*, Harare: Southern Africa Regional Office, United Nations Development Fund for Women, www.sarpn. org.za/documents/d0000919/P1017-Unpaid_Care_Work.pdf, accessed December 2008.

CIA (2008) *World Fact Book*, www.cia.gov/library/publications/the-world-fact book/, accessed January 2008.

CNN International (2008) 'Hyperinflation forces Zimbabwe to print $200 million notes', www.cnn.com/2008/WORLD/africa/12/06/zimbabwe.currency/index.html?iref=mpstoryview, accessed 31 May 2009.

DoH (2001) *National Guidelines on Home-based Care and Community-based Care*, Pretoria: Department of Health.

Elson, D. (2005) 'Unpaid work, the Millennium Development Goals, and capital accumulation', Notes for a presentation at the Conference on Unpaid Work and the Economy: Gender, Poverty and the Millennium Development Goals, Levy Economics Institute of Bard College, Annadale-on-Hudson, New York, 1–3 October, www.levy.org/undp-levy-conference/papers/paper_Elson.pdf, accessed December 2008.

Esplen, E. (2009) 'Overview report', in *Gender and Care. BRIDGE Cutting Edge Pack*, Brighton: BRIDGE, Institute of Development Studies.

Hansen, K., I. Chapman, O. Kasilo and G. Mwaluko (2000) 'The costs of HIV/AIDS care at government hospitals in Zimbabwe', *Health Policy Planning*, 15: 432–40.

HDN and SAfAIDS (2008) 'Caring from within – key findings and policy recommendations on home-based care in Zimbabwe', www.hdnet.org/v2/file_uploads/ publications /hdn_publications /Caring_from_within_low-res_RGB.pdf, accessed December 2008.

Iliffe, J. (2006) *The African AIDS Epidemic: A History*, Oxford: James Currey.

Kwidini, T. (2009) 'Trade: middle-aged women keeping Zimbabwean economy afloat', ipsnews.net/news.asp? idnews =45991, accessed March 2009.

Meyer, M. H. (2000) *Care Work: Gender, Labor and the Welfare State*, New York: Routledge.

Molyneux, M. (1984) 'Women in socialist societies: problems of theory and practice', in K. Young, C. Wolkowitz and R. McCullagh (eds), *Of Marriage and the Market: Women's Subordination Internationally and Its Lessons*, London: Routledge.

Ogden, J., E. Simel and C. Grown (2004) 'Expanding the care continuum for HIV/AIDS: bringing carers into focus', Horizons report, Washington, DC: Population Council and International Center for Research on Women.

Razavi, S. (2007) *The Political and Social Economy of Care in a Development Context: Contextual Issues, Research Questions, and Policy Options*, Geneva: United Nations Research Institute for Social Development.

SAPP (2005) *Impact of Home Based Care on Women and Girls in Southern Africa, Implications for policy change*, Johannesburg: ActionAid.

Shishana, O. et al. (2002) *The Impact of HIV/AIDS on the Health Sector: National Survey of Health Personnel, Ambulatory and Hospitalised Patients and Health Facilities*, Pretoria: South African Department of Health.

Steinberg, M., S. Johnson, G. Schierhout and D. Ndegwa (2002) *Hitting Home: How Households Cope with the Impact of the HIV/AIDS Epidemic. A Survey of Households Affected by HIV/AIDS in South Africa*, Washington, DC: Henry J. Kaiser Family Foundation.

UNAIDS (2007) '2007 AIDS epidemic report', Geneva: UNAIDS, data.unaids.org/pub/EPISlides/2002/2007_epiupdate_en.pdf, accessed 1 June 2009.

— (2008) 'Report on the global AIDS epidemic', Geneva: UNAIDS.

WHO (2002) *Community Home-based Care in Resource-limited Settings: A Framework for Action*, Geneva: World Health Organization.

33 | The right to have rights: resisting fundamentalist orders

Deepa Shankaran

In a televised sermon[1] on 16 April 2010, a senior Iranian cleric, Hojjat ol-eslam Kazem Sediqi, declared a need for a 'general repentance,' warning of the 'prevalence of degeneracy' in the country. He pointed to the real consequences of immodesty and promiscuity among women, noting that 'many women who do not dress modestly lead young men astray and spread adultery in society which increases earthquakes.'

Sediqi's comments follow President Mahmoud Ahmadinejad's forecast that Tehran will be the site of an imminent and devastating quake. In the last ten years, earthquakes in Iran have claimed tens of thousands of lives, and the country rests upon some of the most earthquake-prone land in the world. 'What can we do to avoid being buried under the rubble?' Sediqi asked. 'There is no other solution but to take refuge in religion and to adapt our lives to Islam's moral codes.'

The proposal may seem far fetched, but it is far from isolated. Disaster and salvation are often linked in far-right interpretations of religion. For instance, soon after Hurricane Katrina ravaged New Orleans, Louisiana, Pat Robertson,[2] a prominent voice for evangelical Christianity in the United States, broadcast a theory linking the wreckage to the endurance of legalized abortion in the country. Citing an interpretation of the Old Testament about 'those who shed innocent blood,' he described the consequence: 'the land will vomit you out.' This discourse can be applied not only to natural disasters, but political disasters as well. With slogans like 'Thank God for Dead Soldiers,' Pastor Fred Phelps[3] and his followers in the Westboro Baptist Church have protested at more than two hundred military funerals of soldiers killed in Iraq and Afghanistan, insisting that God is punishing the United States for its tolerance of homosexuality.

What we see in the press is the hard-line face of religious fundamentalisms. This is a term that many women's rights activists use to identify religious actors who are absolutist and intolerant, who seek to impose a dogmatic worldview in society and politics, and who oppose democratic values, pluralism, and dissent. It can be tempting to dismiss these caricatures as an irrational element – somewhere out on the fringe. In reality, though, the fault-lines of this phenomenon are everywhere, and women across regions and religions bear the impact in very real ways.

The Association for Women's Rights in Development (AWID) launched its Resisting and Challenging Religious Fundamentalisms[4] initiative four years ago, following conversations with women's rights activists working on a range of issues – from reproductive rights and Lesbian, Gay, Bisexual, Transgender, Queer, Questioning, Intersex (LGBTQI) rights, to education, political participation and HIV/AIDS – that revealed the threat posed by fundamentalist movements to their work. Although they described very similar experiences, these activists felt isolated in their struggles without a clear view of whether and how religious fundamentalisms were active in other contexts.

Responding to the call for more international dialogue on the issue, AWID's initiative began as a research and advocacy program that sought to examine how the global rise of religious fundamentalisms was understood and experienced by women's rights activists within different regional and religious contexts. In 2007, we launched a global survey in English, French, Spanish, and Arabic, with responses from over 1,600 women's rights activists, and conducted a series of in-depth interviews with more than fifty key experts.

We learned that while religious fundamentalisms may vary according to the global context in which they operate, this diversity is far outweighed by the core characteristics, strategies, and impacts that they share. Across regions and religions, women's rights activists experience the rising influence of these movements in very similar ways. In our study, a number of key defining characteristics[5] of the phenomenon appeared to resonate across contexts. Among these, the most frequently mentioned by women's rights activists was 'absolutist and intolerant.' Throughout the world, fundamentalist movements are also experienced as 'anti-women and patriarchal,' 'about politics and power,' 'anti-human rights and freedoms,' and 'violent.'

Although the term often evokes particular and sensational imagery, women's rights activists caution against presumptions about who is a 'religious fundamentalist' and who is not. The main players in these movements may be active as political or religious leaders, charities and NGOs, religious organizations, missionaries, and ordinary members of communities and families. They can operate across local and global levels, within religious and secular institutions, and among the masses and the elite. Above all, the research affirms that there are no 'typical fundamentalists,' and that these players are better identified by their politics rather than their pretence.

In these politics, the key platforms are grounded in 'morality,' 'the family,' and gender roles, and fundamentalist campaigns often call for a return to 'traditional' values, speaking to the fear of social upheaval brought about by women's growing autonomy, sexual liberation, and the increasing visibility of LGBTQI people. According to women's rights activists, a major fundamentalist strategy in every region is the use of discourse that blames social problems on a 'decline of morality' or the 'disintegration of the family'; and that presents rigid gender roles within the family as 'natural.' As Alejandra Sardá in Argentina notes, among the 'three fundamentalist expressions that dominate the international debates: Islamists, Roman Catholics and Evangelical Christians ... the only issues on which they agree are those related to restricting the exercise of sexual rights on the part of women, but also of others with non-conventional identities and practices.'

As these discourses translate into fundamentalist campaigning on specific laws, policies, and practices, they give rise to concrete consequences for women's human rights. Among Muslim fundamentalisms, the focus on 'morality' and sexuality takes the form of campaigning on veiling, *Hudood* laws (which criminalize sex outside marriage), and restrictions on women's movement; while Catholic and Christian fundamentalisms campaign for abstinence and against premarital sex, politicizing the bodies of young people. In Nigeria, for example, some Christian colleges have introduced virginity testing as a precondition to academic scholarships or graduation. And in the United States, Southern Baptists introduced a university-level mandatory 'homemaking' course for women, 'to prepare them for their proper role.' As they work to reorder notions of masculinity and femininity, fundamentalist movements also pressure men to control their women, as Gita Sahgal writes, 'to push them back into the home, make them behave in ways that are acceptable – otherwise you're not a man.'

In the experience of eight out of ten women's rights activists surveyed from over 160 countries, religious fundamentalisms have a negative impact[6] on women's rights. The survey yielded over six hundred such examples, including reduced health and reproductive rights, reduced sexual rights and freedoms, reduced autonomy and rights in the public sphere, and increased violence against women. More than three-quarters of women's rights activists say that 'women in general' are frequently or sometimes targeted for verbal and physical attack – in short, that they are subject to fundamentalist violence simply because they are women.

Fundamentalist movements also exert a profound and long-lasting psychological impact – a reality that often goes unacknowledged. As Lucy Garrido in Uruguay remarks, 'the most serious impact is that many women believe and feel that they don't have the right to have rights; that decisions about themselves, their minds and bodies, are influenced by and can be made by others.' Describing the Indian context, one women's rights activist notes how the freedoms that previous generations of women enjoyed are increasingly suppressed by fundamentalist influence: 'Women were quite able to move freely in my childhood and youth. They would go to public parks on holidays and festivals, or to the two rivers to wash clothes. All of that has disappeared because of the growing influence of the fundamental reading of the holy book.' Susana Chiarotti in

Argentina recalls the Cairo Plan of Action and the Beijing Platform for Action in 1995: 'that's when we noticed extremely strong obstacles to activism, and the participation of religious fundamentalist groups. Since then, we have seen a constant rise in fundamentalism, both nationally and internationally.'

No matter how strictly they refer to a 'pure tradition' or 'glorious past,' religious fundamentalist movements are very much part of today's globalized world, shaping it and being shaped by it. For 76 percent of women's rights activists surveyed by AWID, the strength of religious fundamentalisms has increased globally in the past ten years. Wanda Nowicka in Poland observes the paradoxical shift: 'conservatism and religion are coming back as something in opposition to what has been for many years. So what is seen as conservative and traditional and old has now become a new, modern option.'

Fundamentalist agendas and strategies are to a degree built in reaction to global commitments to women's rights, human rights, and equality, but while this may be a sign of vehemence on their part, it is also a statement of weakness. There is no shortage of examples of rights advances in the face of religious fundamentalisms. For instance, in response to the spectacular extremism of the Westboro Baptist Church, there emerged a creative and collective counter-force, *The Pastor Phelps Project: A Fundamentalist Cabaret.* When the satirical production premiered at a 2008 Toronto theater festival it drew out a handful of Westboro members wielding hate-ridden picket signs, but it also mobilized the city's gay community to stage a broad counter-protest. As the playwright Alistair Newton[7] observed, 'by them showing up to picket my show, they're empowering me. When they show up, I get all this press. They have provided a platform for me to engage in these issues of fundamentalism and homophobia.' Across regions and religions, signs of resistance are visible everywhere along the spectrum – from public demonstration to discreet defiance. Indeed, as many reports of the repressive climate of Iran[8] also note, 'many young Iranians sometimes push the boundaries of how they can dress, showing hair under their headscarves or wearing tight-fitting clothes.'

Over the last two years, AWID's initiative has been working to document and share the broad range of feminist strategies to resist and challenge fundamentalist movements, and a series of case studies[9] was recently launched. These cases shed light on the numerous actions that women take up on a daily basis, as they reject fundamentalist dictates through individual choices or collective organizing, and cast lines to groups in different regional or religious contexts.

In news coverage of his recent earthquake sermon, the senior Iranian cleric described the violence and mass protests that followed the disputed presidential election of 2009 as no less than a 'political earthquake.' Just like the natural phenomenon, however, real solutions might begin from an understanding of why the ground shakes, and then move to mitigate the destructive potential, rather than wait with eyes shut until the end.

Notes

1 news.bbc.co.uk/1/hi/world/middle_east/8631775.stm.

2 edition.cnn.com/2010/US/01/13/haiti.pat.robertson/.

3 www.huffingtonpost.com/john-w-whitehead/fred-phelps-god-hates-fag_b_493156.html.

4 www.awid.org/eng/About-AWID/AWID-Initiatives/Resisting-and-Challenging-Religious-Fundamentalisms.

5 www.opendemocracy.net/20%Women%E2%80%99s%20rights%20activists%20define% 20religious%20fundamentalisms.

6 www.awid.org/eng/About-AWID/AWID-Initiatives/Resisting-and-Challenging-Religious-Fundamentalisms/What-s-new-from-this-initiative/Religious-Fundalmentalisms-on-the-Rise-A-case-for-action.

7 www.thestar.com/article/473577.

8 news.bbc.co.uk/2/hi/middle_east/8631775.stm.

9 www.awid.org/eng/About-AWID/AWID-Initiatives/Resisting-and-Challenging-Religious-Fundamentalisms/CF-Case_Studies.

34 | African women's movements negotiating peace

Aili Mari Tripp, Isabel Casimiro, Joy Kwesiga and Alice Mungwa

The steady end to a significant number of conflicts in Africa since the mid-1980s has been an important change in the African political landscape. Sometimes low-grade conflict continued in the aftermath of a negotiated peace agreement. Major settlements occurred after the end of national wars of liberation in Namibia and South Africa. Civil conflicts diminished or came to an end in countries such as Angola (2002), Burundi (2004), Chad (2002), the Democratic Republic of Congo (2002), Liberia (2003), Mozambique (1992), Rwanda (1994), Sierra Leone (2002), southern Sudan (2005), and northern Uganda (2007).

With the winding down of almost all these major conflicts, women's organizations vigorously pressed for increased political representation and changes in policy and legislation regarding women's rights. Unlike the post-conflict situations prior to the 1990s, and especially after 2000, women now were beginning to see many of their aspirations for greater rights addressed through new constitutions and the passage of legislation. International norms were changing, as evident in governmental commitments made at the 1995 Beijing United Nations Conference on Women and in other international and regional treaties and conventions.

One of the clearest examples of this change is in the area of women's legislative representation. In African countries where conflicts ended after 1985, women hold, on average, 24 percent of legislative seats compared with countries that did not experience conflict, where women account for only 13 percent of the legislative seats. Rwanda has the highest rate of representation for women in the world, with 49 percent of its parliamentary seats held by women. Women in post-conflict Burundi, Mozambique, South Africa, and Uganda claim over 30 percent of their countries' parliamentary seats in a continent where the average percentage of women-held seats is 17 percent. The higher rates are in large part due to the introduction of quotas aimed at increasing the representation of women. Women have also been running in presidential elections in increasing numbers throughout Africa, but noticeably in post-conflict countries, such as the Democratic Republic of Congo (2006), Liberia (2005), Rwanda (2003), and Sierra Leone (2002). Liberia's Ellen Johnson-Sirleaf became the first elected woman president in Africa in 2005.

There are a number of reasons for this heightened interest by women in political representation and policy change in post-conflict countries. First, the conflicts had a leveling effect as societies sought to re-create themselves through the writing of new constitutions and the implementation of new rules of governance. Women's organizations seized on this window of opportunity and demanded greater political representation. They did not have male incumbents to contend with or to oust from legislative seats (Tripp 2001).

Second, women themselves had experience mobilizing for peace during the conflict and during the peace talks. They came out of long periods of conflict determined to prevent a reversal of the peace process and to participate in the new political order to ensure that their rights were protected. They had the organizing skills, experience, and political muscle to assert themselves in the post-conflict context. They had tried both successfully (e.g. Burundi) and unsuccessfully to influence peace negotiations and wanted a place at the table in the new political arrangement.

Third, foreign donors and international agencies of the United Nations were putting pressure on governments to address women's rights in a concerted manner. New international norms had embraced the need for women's empowerment in post-conflict contexts through constitutional, legislative, and other means.

Finally, prolonged conflict also disrupted gender roles, thrusting women into new activities in the absence of men. In many cases, they ran businesses and sought new sources of livelihood, took over household finances and supported the household, learned how to drive, and played active roles in communities in new ways. These transformations continued in the post-conflict period.

This chapter explores the role of women's movements in the context of peace-building. It situates the Mozambican and Ugandan cases in the context of the broader trends, showing how conflict and peace and the emergence of peace and women's movements in these countries represented key moments and turning points in the history of women's activism. The end of Mozambique's war with its Portuguese colonizers (1964–74) produced some changes for women, but as in other conflicts ending at this time, the changes were not as far reaching as those that followed the end of Mozambique's conflict between Frente de Libertação de Moçambique (FRELIMO) and Resistência Nacional Moçambicana (RENAMO) (1974–92). This chapter examines the reasons for this shift, which occurred throughout Africa in the mid-1980s, beginning with the end of conflict in Uganda (1980–86). The more recent decline of conflict in northern Uganda after 2006 belongs to a later trend of decline in some of the deadliest and longest-lasting conflicts in Africa after 2000: Angola, Burundi, Democratic Republic of Congo, Liberia, Sierra Leone, and southern Sudan.

Turning point in women's mobilization

Uganda was the first of this new generation of post-conflict countries that introduced quotas and adopted measures to increase the political representation of women in the late 1980s and demanded gender-related policy changes. As mentioned earlier, increases in female representation did not occur after the end of wars of independence prior to 1985 (e.g. Angola [1974], Cape Verde [1974], Guinea-Bissau [1974], Mozambique [1974] and Rhodesia/Zimbabwe [1979]), even though women had sought greater representation at the time. What had changed in the intervening years was the holding of the UN conferences on women in Nairobi (1985) and Beijing (1995) and new pressures mounting from the international women's movement. The Ugandan example illustrates the way in which women were able to take advantage effectively of the window of opportunity afforded by the end of conflict.

Uganda had plunged into years of civil war, internal conflict, and institutionalized violence beginning with Idi Amin's takeover in 1971. Unrest in most of Uganda (the north excluded) lasted roughly until 1986, when the National Resistance Movement (NRM) came to power after waging a prolonged guerrilla war. Fifteen years of conflict left over eight hundred thousand people dead, two hundred thousand exiled, and millions displaced within the country (Watson 1988: 14). Out of these crises, new spaces for associational life emerged.

National women's organization leaders point to the 1985 Decade of Women conference in Nairobi as a watershed moment for Ugandan women's associations. Women activists in nongovernmental organizations – many of whom had attended the conference on their own, independent of the official delegation – returned from Nairobi with a new sense of urgency to begin revitalizing and creating autonomous women's associations. At the Nairobi conference of fifteen thousand women from 140 countries, the Ugandan participants got a sense of how far women in other countries had come. The Ugandan attendees felt that the women's movement in their country had been stalled by tyrannical regimes and was badly in need of a jumpstart. The women left Nairobi inspired and committed to changing the status of women. Upon their return, they immediately started to mobilize women and stepped up their efforts after the NRM takeover in January 1986 (Tripp 2000).

The new government led by President Yoweri Museveni did not have any particular program addressing women's concerns. Human rights activist Joan Kakwenzire recalls that one of Museveni's first speeches to women in 1986 was a 'disheartening speech,' in which he spoke of transforming women's status by bringing about changes in society more broadly and asked women to 'pull up their socks' and not to make too many pleas for help.[1] But gradually, as a result of women's lobbying efforts, Museveni changed his position regarding women's organizations. He also began to see possibilities for tapping into women's organizational capacity in order to promote his own goals and build his own base of support among women.

Shortly after 1986, twenty leaders of Action for Development, the National

Council of Women, and other women's organizations paid a courtesy call to the president, requesting that women be represented in government leadership. Many of their recommendations were adopted immediately, including the appointments of nine women ministers. In 1989, a quota system had been put in place, allowing women to run for a minimum of one seat per district. By 2007, women held 30 percent of all parliamentary seats in Uganda. A woman, Specioza Kazibwe, served as vice-president from 1993 to 2004. Thus, under pressure from women's organizations, Museveni encouraged women's leadership at all levels of the government, from local government on up. New women's organizations vigorously pushed for a provision that would allow women to contest all positions on the local councils (Ankrah 1996: 21; Tripp 2000).

The Ugandan case thus illustrates how women were inspired by the emerging norms that came out of the 1985 UN Nairobi Conference on Women to demand political representation. At the same time, one sees the beginning of a new strategy on the part of the NRM to use women's representation in these seats as a quid pro quo for women's votes and support. At times, this arrangement has reached cynical proportions, as when in 2005 Museveni allegedly cut a deal with women parliamentarians by following through on a constitutional provision to set up an Equal Opportunities Commission in exchange for their support for an effort to abandon presidential term limits.

The difference between the Ugandan women's experience in 1986 and the earlier post-conflict situations had in part to do with the emerging international norms that gave women new impetus to demand a political presence. Women had fought in the independence wars in Rhodesia and Mozambique, yet they were unable to capitalize at the time of their new roles to advance their status after the war and were proverbially told to 'go back to the kitchen and stay there until further notice.' The new international norms coming out of the UN Nairobi conference, combined with Museveni's own efforts to build a patronage system on a new footing and create new bases of support that drew heavily on women, resulted in a new political configuration. Thus, one has to look at a confluence of strategies of both internal and external women's movements as well as of the state or dominant parties. Although the Zimbabwean experience did not result in changes, it gave rise to an active women's movement that has persisted to this day.

Women's new peace activism

The end of the conflict in Mozambique marked another shift in women's activism, which began to incorporate peace mobilization, even at the national level. With most conflicts that ended in the 1990s and especially after 2000, women activists were involved in trying to bring an end to conflict through a variety of strategies. The fact that women activists had common goals around equal rights, opposition to violence against women, and increasing the number of women leaders brought them together as women and created a basis for unity often across so-called enemy lines. This common cause allowed women to engage in peacemaking activities at the national and local levels by building coalitions across ethnic and party differences in ways that were often distinct from men's peacemaking activities. Although rarely acknowledged by the press, academics, or policymakers, women and women's organizations in Africa have been actively engaged in peacemaking activities at both the national and local levels. Women activists have employed a wide variety of peacemaking tactics, organizing rallies and boycotts, promoting small arms confiscation, and negotiating with rebels to release abducted child soldiers. Women's rights advocates sought to become more active in formal peace initiatives, especially after the 1990s.

In the period leading up to the 1994 elections, the Association for Mozambican Women for Peace (MWFP) actively saw to it that the elections were carried out peacefully. These were the first democratic elections held after a ceasefire was reached following seventeen years of conflict between the FRELIMO (Liberation Front)-led government and RENAMO (Conservative Party). The women's peace group appealed to the competing parties to stop making threatening statements against each other. They organized a major peace rally in Maputo and negotiated with ex-combatant organizations that were threatening to disrupt the elections. They successfully convinced them to allow the elections to proceed without event. The meetings with the combatants were organized by the National Committee for Elections, including the MWFP and several Christian organizations (Snyder 2000).

Other remarkable efforts were mounted at this time. After 1992, demobilized combatants from the government army and RENAMO formed the Mozambican Association for the War Demobilized (Associação Moçambicana dos Desmobilizados de Guerra [AMODEG]). Women ex-combatants from both sides played a very important role in this organization in building bridges. Jacinta Jorge, a former soldier from the government side and one of the founding members of AMODEG, was also the head of Propaz (ProPeace), an organization of ex-combatants, including a group of disabled veterans. Propaz has worked in four provinces providing peace-building and conflict-resolution/transformation services.[2] These types of initiatives led Carolyn Nordstrom (1997: II) to observe in her book *A Different Kind of War Story*, 'The citizens in Mozambique demonstrated the most sophisticated country-wide conflict resolution practices and ideologies I have observed in the world.'

Women peace activists have had good reason to intervene. Even as many conflicts came to an end, some of the worst violence in Africa occurred during the period described in this section. Africa has been one of the most conflict-ridden parts of the world. The human cost of conflict has been staggering. Nowhere in the world have the death tolls related to civil war been as high as in Africa. It is estimated that 5.4 million died in the Democratic Republic of Congo between 1998 and 2008 from war-related causes, according to the International Rescue Committee (Polgreen 2008); roughly two hundred thousand have been killed in Burundi since 1993; about two million have died in the southern conflict since 1983 (Lacina and Gleditsch 2005); and over one million (mainly Tutsis) died in the 1994 Rwanda genocide and conflict according to the 2000 Rwandan census. Millions more have become refugees or displaced persons in their own countries. Large numbers of women were raped during the conflicts while men have also suffered untold sexual violence during and after these conflicts. Tens of thousands of children have been kidnapped and forcibly conscripted into conflicts in Angola, Burundi, Congo, Congo-Brazzaville, Liberia, Mozambique, Rwanda, Sierra Leone, Somalia, Sudan, and Uganda. They have made up over half of the fighting forces in these countries. These figures do not even begin to capture the consequences of these conflicts on the physical and psychological health of the affected populations, the disruptions to family life, the impact of war on the capacity to grow food, and other devastating consequences of warfare.

Women and formal peacemaking processes

In spite of women's brave and persistent efforts at grassroots peace activism, they have been largely left out of formal peace negotiations, even after the passage of UN Resolution 1325. In 2000, the United National Security Council adopted Resolution 1325 to provide women with a greater role in conflict prevention and resolution. The resolution gives strong support 'for States to include women in the negotiations and implementations of peace accords, constitutions and strategies for resettlement and rebuilding and to take measures to support local women's groups and indigenous processes for conflict resolution.' Although this resolution provides a basis on which to bring greater numbers of women into peacemaking processes and has had visible impacts, many have been disappointed with the slowness of its implementation.

In Uganda, women peace activists from around the country organized a Women's Peace Caravan in November 2006 that crossed the country from Kampala, to Kitgum, and then on to Juba, Sudan, where peace talks were being held between the Lord's Resistance Army (LRA) and Ugandan government representatives to bring an end to a conflict that had been dragging on for nineteen years.

At two different times in the history of the conflict, in 1993 and again in 2005, Betty Bigombe, the chief government negotiator with LRA head Joseph Kony, has been close to a settlement. On both occasions, she was unable to complete the task as fighting resumed. Her efforts, nevertheless, ultimately paved the way and were essential for the signing of a ceasefire in September 2006. However, women, who had suffered every bit as much as men from the conflict, were not represented in the final negotiations. For this reason, members of the Civil Society Women's Peace Coalition, the Uganda Women's Network, and the Uganda Women Parliamentary Association led a caravan to Juba to demand women's inclusion in the process. They carried a women's Peace Torch. As news commentator Mary Karooro Okurut said of the torch and women's absence from the peace talks:

> First it is a symbol of solidarity; a statement of togetherness – that the women of this country and region are fully behind the peace process ... The Peace Torch is the voice of women in the peace process, holding all players accountable to the women of Uganda and the Great Lakes region who have suffered most in the conflict. Lasting peace without the active input of women is unimaginable, which is why women must speak out as they are doing now. (Okurut 2006)

Up until 2006, the peace movement in Uganda was relatively small, as was women's role in it. Nevertheless, the insistence that women be part of all negotiations represented a change in women's movements that had already been evident for some time in Burundi, the Democratic Republic of Congo, Liberia, Sierra Leone, and Somalia. Women did eventually gain entry into the negotiations in Burundi, the Democratic Republic of Congo, Liberia, and Somalia after protracted lobbying.

International and regional mobilization

Women's movements in Africa have mobilized around peace issues not only domestically but also through regional and subregional networks. Women are coordinating their activities across state boundaries on an unprecedented scale. Peacemaking has been a central concern of networks such as the African Women's Committee for Peace and Development (AWCPD) and the Federation of African Women's Peace Networks (FERFAP). FERFAP, formed in 1997, includes representatives from sixteen countries and has been involved in activities ranging from petitions and peace marches to local alliance-building and national reconciliation conferences (Manuh 1998). Perhaps most significantly, the importance of women's participation in peace initiatives has gained recognition from African governments not previously evident in the post-independence era.

The formation of the African Union in 2001 was an important turning point in African women's regional mobilization around peace issues. However, the groundwork has been laid through a series of meetings and conferences. The Conference on Women and Peace that was held in Kampala, Uganda, in 1993 under the auspices of the Organization of African Unity (OAU), the UN Economic Commission on Africa (UNECA), and the government of Uganda resulted in the Kampala Action Plan on Women Peace, which was endorsed by the OAU heads of state and government in 1995. The principles were incorporated in the African Platform for Action and were later folded into the UN Platform for Action adopted at the 1995 Beijing Women's Conference. The Kampala Action Plan aimed to increase the participation of women in conflict resolution and decision-making; protect women living in conflict situations or under foreign occupation; reduce excessive military expenditures; control weapons availability; promote nonviolent forms of conflict resolution; protect human rights; encourage women's contributions in fostering a culture of peace; and provide protection, assistance, and training to refugee women and other displaced women.

In November 1996, the OAU and UNECA organized a Women Leadership Forum on Peace in Johannesburg, South Africa, which among other things discussed the participation of women in the OAU Mechanisms for Conflict Prevention, Management, and Resolution. A major outcome from this meeting was a recommendation for the formation of the African Women's Committee for Peace and Development (AWCPD). However, the lack of a clear policy environment and human and financial resource constraints hampered the committee. It did not have the necessary legal and policy framework and institutional supports to realize its mandate fully. Nevertheless, the AWCPD maintained strong and close partnerships with women's civil society organizations. Subsequent conferences organized by the OAU and UNECA in Kigali, Rwanda, in 1997 and another in Zanzibar in 1999 by OAU, UNESCO, and the Tanzanian government highlighted prevalent concerns regarding peace and women.

The African Union (AU) was formed in 2001 out of the unification of the OAU and UNECA. Gender equality was one of the founding principles of the AU. AWCPD seized the opportunity provided by the transition from the OAU to the AU to move gender issues to the forefront. Indeed, at the Fifth Extraordinary Summit of the OAU in Sirte, Libya, in March 2000, the AWCPD lobbied and engaged key foreign ministers on the need to highlight the gender components of the Constitutive Act of the AU. The AWCPD worked with the gender desks of UNECA's African Centre for Gender and Development, the African Regional Economic Communities, and the African Women's Development Fund (AWDF) to lay the groundwork for the establishment in 2002 of a Gender Directorate to be located under the office of the chairperson of the African Union and the Specialized Technical Committee on gender equality at the level of commissioners. These institutional arrangements ushered in a new era in gender mainstreaming within the AU, which would not have happened without years of mobilization on the part of women activists.

The AWCPD remained an active presence in addressing various conflict situations around the continent. Together with the AU, the AWCPD and associated organizations organized a Solidarity Mission to the Democratic Republic of Congo in December 2001. This mission, for example, supported Congolese women's preparations for effective participation in the Inter-Congolese dialogue hosted by South Africa early in 2002. The tribute marking the end of the OAU in July 2002 in Durban, South Africa, had particular meaning for the AWCPD, as the ceremony marked the transition to a new era of activism in the context of the AU.

Another concrete manifestation of women's heightened mobilization across the continent regarding peace issues was the passage of the UN Security Council Resolution 1325. Women's organizations met in May 2000 in Windhoek, Namibia, and helped draft a document that was to become the basis of the aforementioned UN Security Council Resolution 1325 detailing women's role in peacekeeping. On 21 July 2003, the African Union adopted the Protocol to the African Charter on Human and Peoples' Rights on the Rights of Women in Africa that recognizes 'the right of women to participate in the promotion and maintenance of peace.' This was preceded by a women's summit in Maputo, Mozambique, in June 2003, organized by the United Nations Development Fund for Women (UNIFEM) and Africa-wide women's associations.

One important West African network is the Mano River Union Women Peace Network (MARWOPNET) of women activists from Guinea, Sierra Leone, and Liberia. The network mediated an intense conflict between Guinea and Liberia in 2001 in spite of minimal resources and being excluded from the formal peace process. MARWOPNET was able to get the feuding heads of state to a regional peace summit. At one point, President Lansana Conte of Guinea had been adamant about not meeting with Charles Taylor of Liberia. Mary Brownell, a Liberian peace activist of the MARWOPNET delegation, told Mr Conte: 'You and President Taylor have to meet as men and iron out your differences, and we the women want to be present. We will lock you in this room until you come to your senses, and I will sit on the key.' Conte relented and met with Taylor as a result of the sheer audacity of a woman telling him what to do, saying 'What man do you think would say that to me? Only a woman could do such a thing and get by with it' (Fleshman 2002). As a result of their actions, the women were given delegate status at the twenty-fourth ECOWAS summit in December 2001, where they were able to make an appeal for African leaders to support women's peacemaking initiatives. They were also given observer status in the 2003 Accra talks that led to a ceasefire agreement and the establishment of an interim government in Liberia.

Conclusions

Women have sought to influence peace process and the post-conflict peace in a variety of ways at both the national and local levels. The cases of Mozambique and Uganda exemplify some of the constraints and opportunities that women have encountered since the 1970s. After Mozambique's liberation from Portugal, women had few opportunities to advance themselves in significant ways, especially as the country plunged into renewed conflict. It was not until

Uganda emerged from years of conflict in 1986 that women, energized by their experiences at the 1985 UN Nairobi conference, sought and gained greater political representation and expansion of their rights. Uganda was a turning point in post-conflict experiences as women united to push for a common agenda. Mozambique's experiences after 1992 were also critical, because from that time on we began to see women in various conflicts throughout Africa engaged in peace activism and linking these efforts with a common agenda of advancing women's rights and political representation in the post-conflict context. The activism most notably cut across party, ethnic, and other lines that had divided citizens during the conflicts.

After 2000, we witnessed many efforts by women to be represented in peace negotiations, some successful and others less so. The 2006 efforts by Ugandan women to be part of the northern Uganda peace settlements fall into this last phase of women's activism. Women, who had been totally shut out of formal peacemaking initiatives since independence in some cases, were now actively seeking a seat at the table after 2000, with moderate success in countries such as Burundi, the Democratic Republic of Congo, Liberia, Sierra Leone, and Uganda. Furthermore, they sought and often gained greater political representation in post-conflict governments. Their initiatives were linked to the growth of the women's movement throughout Africa that sought greater political representation for women at all levels. They were also indicative of the changing international norms regarding women's representation and rights. Preparations for the Beijing conference were one of the priorities of the newly formed Women's Forum in Sierra Leone in 1994, illustrating the importance of these international influences and linkages for the evolution of the women's movement.

Women's marginalization from politics and their outside status has, on the one hand, made them attractive contenders for power as the ends of the conflicts open up new political spaces. Their shared exclusion has given them a common agenda and capacity for being remarkably broad based regardless of partisanship, ethnicity, religion, or other factors, and many of the women's strategies in peacemaking are indeed shaped by the emergence from their marginalization in society. To what extent do these strategies simultaneously lock them into limited forms of peacemaking and keep them excluded from other roles? To what extent does their participation in these gendered structures perpetuate institutions that marginalize women rather than challenge them? These are some of the many questions women face as they rebuild their societies together with men.

Notes

1 Interview by Aili Tripp with Maxine Ankrah, Kampala, 19 June 1992.

2 Interviews conducted by Isabel Casimiro with Jacinta Jorge and Flora Ngoma, an ex-combatant from RENAMO, Maputo, 12 January 2005.

References

Ankrah, M. E. (1996) 'ACFODE: a decade and beyond', *Arise*, 17: 21–2.

Fleshman, M. (2002) '"Gender budgets" seek more equity: improved spending priorities can benefit all Africans', *Africa Recovery*, 16(1): 4.

Lacina, B. and N. P. Gleditsch (2005) 'Monitoring trends in global combat: a new dataset of battle deaths', *European Journal of Population*, 21(2/3): 145–66.

Manuh, T. (1998) 'Women in Africa's development: overcoming obstacles, pushing for progress', *Africa Recovery Briefing Paper*, 2 April.

Nordstrom, C. (1997) *A Different Kind of War Story (Ethnology of Political Violence)*, Philadelphia: University of Pennsylvania Press.

Okurut, M. K. (2006) 'Thank you women for the Peace Torch', *New Vision*, 2 November.

Polgreen, L. (2008) 'Congo's death rate unchanged since war ended', *New York Times*, 23 January, www.nytimes.com/2008/01/23/world/africa/23congo.html, accessed 31 January 2008.

Snyder, M. C. (2000) *Women in African Economies: From Burning Sun to Board-room*, Kampala: Fountain.

Tripp, A. M. (2000) *Women and Politics in Uganda*, Madison: University of Wisconsin Press, James Currey and Fountain Press.

— (2001) 'Women and democracy: the new political activism in Africa', *Journal of Democracy*, 12(3): 141–55.

Watson, C. (1988) 'Uganda's women: a ray of hope', *Africa Report*, July/August, pp. 26–33.

35 | 'I am somebody!': Brazil's social movements educate for gender equality and economic sustainability

Ruth Needleman

Brazil has become one of the fastest-growing economies in the Third World. This growth followed decades of military dictatorship and neoliberal economic policies that had destroyed the domestic economy and produced intolerable misery and poverty, especially for rural, Afro-Brazilian and indigenous women. But today foreign capital and investment no longer determine all economic policies. While transnational companies still dominate the landscape in industry and agriculture, grass-roots-led social movements are fostering an alternative, cooperative economy helping communities become more sustainable and, at the same time, contributing to meeting domestic needs.[1]

Economic development in Brazil is now being constructed from the grass roots as well as from the presidential palace, which is what accounts for the changes and contradictory trends in the direction of Brazil's development. Now there are policies that aim to close the gap between the very rich and the impoverished majority, to create jobs and open access to income, and to fight against Brazil's long history of neocolonial, racist and ethnic exploitation. While the government acknowledges the importance of and supports integration into the global economy, it does so through initiatives designed to integrate millions of Brazilians into the economic mainstream within the country.

Unfortunately much of the current industrial expansion has not significantly altered the lives of women still living on the margins of society, a subordinate status institutionalized through centuries of slavery, colonialism, and neoliberal economic policies.[2] For women in particular, marginalization translates into restricted access to education and employment. In fact, poverty and gender are inseparable.[3] Data on poverty in Brazil point to two general conclusions: women's poverty has increased with urbanization, and it is profoundly intensified by race/color.[4]

For most of the twentieth century, women of color, the majority of Brazilian women, could find little more than domestic work, which often lacked remuneration.[5] Live-in maids and servants might receive no more than room and board, while working a seven-day week. One Afro-Brazilian woman, now a leader of the Domestic Workers' Union in Bahia, explained that she had worked for eleven years as a domestic with the same family without ever receiving a penny, just room and board with a seven-day work week.[6]

When factory jobs opened for women, skin color worked like an invisible sieve; the lighter the woman, the greater the chance of employment. Although movements for greater social justice had begun to exert force in the late fifties and early sixties, a US-backed military coup in 1964 put an end to any progress in the status of women.[7]

The 1964 coup and establishment of a military junta stamped out two decades of progressive nationalist initiatives through widespread brutal and bloody repression. Murder, exile and imprisonment crushed democratic and progressive leadership and movements throughout the country. Many families were left with one or no head of household. Women who had fought for an equal voice and place in society faced the same repression as men. Once the ruling military junta consolidated its power, it invited Milton Friedman and the University of Chicago's economists to develop Brazil according to their model of free-market reforms.[8]

The military sold off public and private manufacturing to the highest corporate bidder, and allowed multinationals to buy up immense tracts of land. This led to the immediate dislocation of millions of peasant families, many indigenous and Afro-descendent, who moved to the outskirts of cities in search of housing and income. This transition led directly to the urbanization and feminization of poverty throughout the country through dramatically increasing the percentage of women-headed households.[9] This massive migration, in turn, led to the proliferation of slums or '*favelas*' encircling every urban center; abject poverty and desperation provided fertile ground for narco-trafficking and crime in these cardboard slums. For women, life became impossibly difficult. They lacked access to schools, jobs, and income, and increasing numbers of women were forced to raise their families in the *favelas*.

At the same time, the disruption in traditional lifestyles and family structure forced increasing numbers of women to seek jobs in urban labor markets. In 1970 only 18 percent of all women over the age of ten participated actively in the labor force. By 1978 35.5 percent of women were employed outside the home.[10] While the years of military dictatorship intensified poverty among women, they also increased labor force participation and inched women in the direction of greater economic independence.

At one time labeled an 'economic miracle,' Brazil's economic changes were, in fact, the testing ground for neoliberal economic policy or structural adjustments that would soon dominate global corporate economic strategy. After the junta's overthrow, the reins of government transferred into the hands of neoliberal economists. While the military had relied heavily on loans from the International Monetary Fund and World Bank, pocketing millions and putting Brazil into hopeless debt, the new Cardoso government in the 1990s attempted to pay back the funds by extensive privatization of the economy.[11] Areas of the economy sheltered in the public sector such as healthcare and education were among the first to go on sale, seriously undermining women's ability to access opportunities or social safety nets.

As in Argentina, Mexico and other nations, structural adjustments destroyed the economy and its middle class. Foreign investment was supposed to 'help finance balance-of-payments deficits, modernize industrial structures, develop advanced technology, promote productivity and promote the international competitiveness of Brazilian exports.'[12] Instead, foreign capital drained the nation of much of its wealth, first by taking over key sectors of the economy instead of making new investments for growth. Secondly, it forced the up-ward re-evaluation of the currency, making imports cheaper and exports more expensive.[13] Much of the domestic economy was wiped out, creating soaring unemployment and declining wages.

This growing poverty of the Brazilian people was denounced by the Catholic bishops, who recognized that without any purchasing power, the poor would become even more excluded, and the domestic economy would never recover its viability. They called for an end to transnational exploitation of the economy, and support for Brazil's millions of people suffering from homelessness, hunger and unemployment.

What had brought the military dictatorship down in the late 1980s – mass social movements – then forged a new national consensus and new economic initiatives, founded on the needs of Brazil's majority of poor, working and once middle-class families. By the early 1980s a new trade union movement had emerged, the CUT, Central Única dos Trabalhadores (United Workers' Federation). A rural workers' movement expanded as well, the MST, Movimento dos Sem Terra (Landless Workers' Movement), to fight against the landed oligarchy that owned but did not cultivate vast tracts of land. Along with many other social movements of women, Afro-Brazilians, and students, a coalition had been founded to create the Workers' Party of Brazil (Partido dos Trabalhadores, PT) in 1984.

Less than twenty years after its founding, the Workers' Party elected a president, a former rural migrant, auto worker, and union militant, Luiz Inacio Lula da Silva, or just Lula.[14] He was re-elected in 2006 for a second term. Women have positions of leadership in this party, and have won positions in federal and state government. In the 1988 elections, the Workers' Party put in thirty-six mayors, including a woman in São Paulo, Luiza Erundina.[15] The Workers' Party candidate, an economist and Lula's former chief of staff, Dilma Rousseff, was elected as Brazil's first woman president in October 2010.

Workers elected a president but did not control the government

Although the Workers' Party won the presidency in 2002, the people did not gain a majority in Congress nor in state governments. Lula's presidency, as a result, was a battleground, but one driven in part from the grass roots by powerful grassroots movements fighting for land, jobs, education, and housing. The cornerstone demand was 'access to income for all.' Emerging from four dark decades of repression and impoverishment, these movements easily found common ground.[16] They had been fighting the military and neoliberal economic policies openly for the previous twenty years, and one of their most effective instruments proved to be radically new forms of education, known as popular education or education for transformation. Since illiteracy was widespread, especially among women,[17] these programs have opened doors of opportunity that had never before existed.

While Lula had to maneuver to reconcile opposing political forces to push through every progressive economic reform, the new labor federation, the CUT, took up the battle for jobs in a very innovative fashion, by occupying abandoned plants, blocking attempts at factory shutdowns, and developing a whole new sector of the economy, known as the Solidarity Economy, built on cooperatives.

The cooperative movement or Solidarity Economy guarantees that economic development will not be primarily export-led and that communities throughout the country can achieve some measure of self-sustainability, despite a lack of jobs in the marketplace. Cooperatives take many different forms, although all are self-governed, with leadership elected from the workers involved. Income is used to develop the economic potential of the cooperative, and is shared equally to sustain the community. While few cooperatives can compete effectively with private-sector corporations, a few factories and older agricultural cooperatives have done so. A majority of women's cooperatives, in contrast, function at the margins of the market, but are developing skills applicable to any small business enterprise. They continue their education through various popular education vehicles, sponsored primarily by the social movements.

To enable these initiatives to succeed, the CUT and its affiliates designed innovative educational programs for workers, especially those most in need – the unemployed – not necessarily 'union members.'[18] The Solidarity Economy requires a new set of skills and knowledge for workers. If workers are to control production, they need literacy *and* business skills, along with an understanding of the economic and political system, including their place within it.

The process of education has been completely integral to the organizing work, according to the former Director of Education and Politics for the Metalworkers Union, Marino Vani. The union's approach, he stressed, was to design a process of education that would enable participants collectively to learn to administer cooperative production and handle finances as well as marketing within the basic literacy curriculum. For women this also meant tackling the forms of oppression that kept them in subordinate positions not only in society but also in their families and communities.[19]

Miracles are human creations: the popular education alternative

The real economic miracle in Brazil began in 2002, and is rooted in these 'citizenship schools,' programs of popular or 'integrated' education. All of the educational programs adapted the revolutionary approach of philosopher and educator Paulo Freire, but then took an additional step in 'integrating' multiple forms of learning and multiple disciplines into each unit or module. Freire had done his most important work in the fifties in Recife, prior to the military coup, developing literacy programs that built communities of activists who challenged the status quo, engaging in the struggle for social change.[20] He had stressed the importance of participants learning to read the world as well as the word, to understand why they had been illiterate and poor, and how the system itself would have to be changed to be more just and equal. For his work, the military junta exiled Freire. But this move encouraged him to bring his revolutionary philosophy or pedagogy to countries around the world.

His followers at home had already discovered that in times of great repression and violence, the most effective organizing work could be concealed and expanded through vehicles of education. Many activists forced underground in Brazil worked through the Catholic Church and in local communities as educators, using the principles of Freirean education: experience-based, participatory, student-centered, problem-solving and action-oriented. Every program began with the participants themselves, their stories, their experience, and the knowledge they had developed through life. Their stories determined the curriculum, providing the materials to be written, read and analyzed to teach literacy and vocational and critical thinking skills. In this way individual growth generated movement growth, and developed leadership. Short-term efforts to gain access to income contributed to the long-term struggle for a worker-run socialist economy. This work contributed centrally to the building of the movements that took down the military, and they continued to build power to elect and then push the Lula government forward.

Social movement education follows a spiral path from reflection on experience, to problem identification, followed by plans for action (problem resolution). Action is the goal of education, as well as the starting point for renewed reflection and analysis. Actions might involve setting up a health clinic or organizing a mass occupation of a factory. Many actions are designed to expand the cooperative movement to strengthen the Solidarity Economy. In addition to land and factories, movements have occupied housing developments, vacant urban land for housing, and unoccupied buildings and spaces. Today agricultural, manufacturing, and service cooperatives provide tens of thousands of people with education, income, and collective power, aimed at changing the economy to redistribute wealth throughout the country and among the previously marginalized sectors. Each cooperative is worker-run, in the interests of its members, who all participate in decision-making. For poor women who have been isolated from most traditional labor markets, these cooperatives have provided access to income along with education and confidence, enabling them to take on greater participation and leadership in political spheres as well.

New 'integrated' educational programs transform isolated individuals into communities, and turn victims into agents of change. Their activism has made it possible for Lula to pioneer programs such as 'Zero Hunger,' which pays parents to keep their children in school, for example. Lula is expanding educational opportunities through infrastructure-building, expansion of funding for vocational education, and also affirmative action programs that recognize that Brazil's most exploited poor, especially Afro-descendent and indigenous populations, require special measures to guarantee access to educational opportunities. Historically, for example, no more than 2 percent of college students were Afro-Brazilian.[21]

To illustrate the work at the grassroots level, especially among women, this chapter provides a few specific examples of how very poor and isolated groups of women gained education, citizenship, and economic sustainability through labor's 'integrated education programs.'[22]

How education transformed a community and built black pride

My first story begins in Africa, in the early years of the slave trade. The history behind Brazil's African rice, known as 'Arroz Quilombola,' is a story of cultural preservation, economic sustainability, and citizenship-building. I heard the story from the education director of the CUT, in Porto Alegre, in the state of Rio Grande do Sul, in southern Brazil.[23] When African women were seized as slaves in their homelands, according to the narrative, they were fearful for their survival. The women placed rice seeds in their hair to carry them along, so that they would have a means of sustenance wherever they landed. They held on to these seeds, and planted some on the plantations they worked, until the government outlawed the planting of African rice. When the chance came, many slaves escaped to the interior of Brazil and built *Quilombos. Quilombos* were/are villages built by escaped slaves, often including indigenous Brazilians and some European descendants, deep in the jungles or interior of the country for safety. Many *Quilombeiras*, women of the *Quilombos*, guarded their traditions and planted their African rice seeds.[24] In this manner they fed themselves, and handed a legend down from one generation to the next about their homeland and the African rice seeds.

Harvested long before the Asian rice strain was introduced into the Americas,

Quilombola rice provided sustenance for slaves and communities of escaped slaves. Nonetheless, Portugal's reigning queen outlawed this rice, once the Asian variety had established itself, in the late seventeenth and early eighteenth century, just as Portugal had outlawed many African and native traditions. Fines and jail terms awaited anyone who dared plant the African rice seeds.

After so many decades how did the legend resurface and transform the lives of the *Quilombeiras*? The CUT brought one of their education programs, 'All the Letters' (*Todas as letras*), to a small *Quilombo* in the state of Rio Grande do Sul. This basic literacy program follows the Freirean model. The classes take place five times a week, morning or evening, for three months, and are taught by educators from the communities themselves. Having a leader from their own community helps to dispel fears and insecurities many illiterate workers experience.[25]

As the women traced their origins, shared their histories and pinpointed current dilemmas, the story of African rice emerged. The *Quilombeiras* still planted and ate the rice descended from those seeds hidden in their ancestors' hair. With the CUT's help, they learned about the extraordinary nutritional value of this rice, compared to the more popular Asian variety. As part of the vocational component of the class, they began to discuss growing rice for the domestic market, packaging and commercializing the rice as a means of sustainability for the community. What they learned to read and write contributed directly to the formation of their own cooperative.

The educational process built awareness, confidence, and skills, as they explored the history of segregation and discrimination against African descendants in Brazil, the poverty and isolation of the *Quilombos*, and the importance of their own engagement in policy-making and national development. They learned to read and write as well as methods to increase the productivity of the land and expand production of the African rice. They learned accounting, marketing, and distribution skills, along with a growing sense of black pride.

Today this community of women sells African rice through its cooperative. They have become an active player in the Solidarity Economy, helping to promote domestic development, while also participating in the Afro-descendent and labor movements advocating equal opportunities, access to better education, and a voice at the policy-making tables throughout the country.

Women's power grows with the Solidarity Economy

Eunice Wolff used to work in a factory in Canoas, a small town outside of Porto Alegre. Under the military, she fought to build her local [collective bargaining unit] in the Metalworkers' Union, and as a leader brought her local into the movement to regain democratic rule in Brazil. Now she works for the statewide Workers' Party, but for the past decade she was responsible for the Solidarity Economy in the Metalworkers' Union in Rio Grande do

Sul. She introduced me to two cooperatives she had helped to form, the first being a community-based women's cooperative that grew out of a housing occupation.[26] The second, a catering cooperative, is known as the Association of Women Multiplying (Associação de Mulheres Multiplicar).

Since educational programs begin with the lives of the participants, the women identified many problems that restricted their opportunities: their marginalization from labor markets, family responsibilities, lack of education, gender stereotypes and male opposition. In the occupied housing development, Eunice helped the women organize themselves to do work in exchange for compensation, crafting, cooking, sewing, and caring their way into economic sustainability. The classes helped to dismantle a lot of fears that had kept them dependent and inactive.

The catering collective, *Multiplicar*, relied on the cooking skills of women brought together through education and with the assistance of the local Metalworkers' Union in Canoas. The union helped raise seed funds and carried out education on how to run a cooperative, everything from purchasing to sales, hand in hand, of course, with literacy and critical thinking. Supported by other metalworker women and wives, Eunice plays a very active role in the co-op. After the first few years, the women realized that they needed a center for their work and that the only way they could do it was by coalescing with other cooperatives to purchase a facility. Now six cooperatives have combined their efforts in 'A House for the Enterprising Woman' that provides catering, health services, sewing, art and dance (capoeira) classes as well. In taking charge of getting income, these women have taken charge of their lives, and interact comfortably with government officials, private sector representatives, and policy-makers.

Brazil's 'integrated education' serves long-run as well as short-term goals

The 'integrated' pedagogical approach has knocked down one additional barrier in adult education. The programs eliminate the compartmentalized education of the public school system. For adult learners, this final integration makes the education process a more comfortable place for personal and collective growth, based on what they know and how they learn best. For example, the metalworkers' elementary and secondary equivalency programs do not follow traditional education practices of teaching by discipline, which for many adults can be alienating and irrelevant. In my own adult education classrooms, workers often question why they have to take science or computers. The traditional way disciplines are taught – fragmented and compartmentalized – makes it hard for participants, especially adult learners, to understand how the disciplines might be useful in solving the problems of their day-to-day lives.

Instead of studying language, social studies, science, and math, participants study work, divided into five units: urban society, technology, environment, globalization, and the economy. Each unit integrates the disciplines so they are learned in the process of problem-solving, as applied and inter-connected skills, addressing issues such as pollution, price increases, or housing shortages.[27]

When I asked a participant how the program had affected her, she replied: 'It changed everything, everything. Now,' she added proudly, 'I am somebody. Even my son talks to me and I have warned him I may graduate high school before he does!' With this added education and confidence, women become somebody who matters, not a 'nobody' as they may have felt for most of their lives.

Final reflections

For many Third World nations where unemployment, illiteracy, and poverty continue to grow, as transnational corporations reshape economic development in their own interests, Brazil provides a model for grassroots economic development built on collective education and action. A full 40 percent of Brazil's agricultural output is produced by its 1,406 agricultural cooperatives. These member-owned and -operated cooperatives empower small and medium-sized producers by providing training and other forms of technical assistance.[28]

To put it simply, this 'integrated' education empowers participants, helping to eliminate the stigmas attached to poverty, and the barriers in the way of many women. The education brings previously marginalized populations into the economic and political mainstream, where they, too, can affect policy and advocate for their own interests.

Capital mobility has been a two-edged sword for women in developing nations, because on the one hand, it eliminates jobs with new technology, it moves jobs to where labor is cheapest, and leaves many women with declining or unreliable access to employment. On the other hand, women in the north who have never had market opportunities and have worked only as domestics are now taking low-skill, very-low-wage jobs in the newly arrived shoe factories. For these women a factory job means independence, compared to live-in seven-day-a-week domestic work. Eventually, however, as we have seen throughout the world, these opportunities will move again to other even lower-paid regions of the world, which is why the education component in economic development is so essential.

Short-term solutions must incorporate long-term goals, providing women with education, experience, and higher-level economic and political skills. 'Reading the world along with the word' prepares women to engage in collective struggle for change, at the same time that they gain access to income. In Brazil, only the power of social movements has been able to leverage the kind of changes needed for women to become equal and effective citizens.

Acknowledging the importance of the cooperative movement, the Lula government created a National Secretariat for the Solidarity Economy. Gatherings in all twenty-seven states of the nation have led to the establishment of a National Forum for the Solidarity Economy that includes a ninety-seven-member coordinating committee and a thirteen-member executive board. With education as its engine, this Solidarity Economy has transformed lives for hundreds of thousands of women in Brazil. Education plus income makes women fully engaged citizens, by raising their visibility and elevating their positions within society.

Notes

1 Economic development in Brazil has not broken the dominance of international capital and corporations, but what President Lula was able to do was facilitate new initiatives from the grass-roots organizations that brought him to power. For example, a recent issue of *The Economist* described the newer forms of land concentration for agricultural production as a model for other countries (28 September 2010, pp. 10–11). But the shift from plantation to agribusiness also has had devastating effects on rural workers, forcing hundreds of thousands to migrate to urban centers in search of jobs, which are not plentiful, growing the urban slums (*favelas*).

2 See Robert M. Levine and John J. Crocitti (eds), *The Brazil Reader: History, Culture, Politics*, Duke University Press, Durham, NC, 1999, for an excellent overview of the historical development of Brazil, as well as for the status of women, Afro-descendent and indigenous peoples.

It is important to note that the slave trade remained active in Brazil until 1850, and slavery itself was not abolished until 1888. Owing to a national policy called 'whitening' (*embranqueamento*), the federal government promoted European immigration and miscegenation as a means of limiting or eliminating the African descendent and indigenous populations. In reality, it meant that millions of people remained isolated from the job market and subject to widespread discrimination.

3 See Hildete Pereira de Melo, *Gênero e Pobreza no Brasil* [Gender and Poverty in Brazil], Final Report of the Project: Demo-

cratic Gender Policies in Latin America and the Caribbean, CEPAL, 2005.

4 Ibid., pp. 18, 25.

5 Historically domestic work was the main occupation for women; 80 percent of all women work in services today, and 20 percent as domestics. Well over half (56 percent) are Afro-descendent. Pereira de Melo, *Gênero e Pobreza*, p. 17.

6 Interviews done with three leaders of the Domestic Workers' Union in Salvador, Bahia, February 2008.

7 Brazil's women's movement has been quite strong, linked to women's organizations in Europe, in particular. It historically had been driven by middle-class, European descendent women. The problems of rural women and women of color have only recently become major areas of enquiry, and even within the labor movement contradictions and conflicts continue. There is a fine study put out by the CUT's Women's Department, Maria Ednalva Bezerra de Lima et al. (eds), *Mulheres na CUT: Uma História de Muitas Faces 1986–2006*, São Paulo, 2006. See also Silvano Aparecida Mariano, 'O sujeito do feminism e o pós-estruturalismo', *Revista Estudos Feministas*, 13(3), September–December 2005.

8 There is an excellent history of the impact of these 'free market reforms' in Naomi Klein's study, *The Shock Doctrine*. For an overview of economic policies, see Sue Branford and Bernardo Kucinski, *Lula and the Workers' Party in Brazil*, New Press, New York, 2003.

9 Mariano, 'O sujeito do feminism', p. 18.

10 *Mulheres na CUT*, p. 17.

11 Branford and Kucinski, *Lula and the Workers' Party*, p. 89.

12 Geisa Maria Rocha, 'Neo-dependency in Brazil', *New Left Review*, 16, July/August 2002, p. 7.

13 Branford and Kucinski, *Lula and the Workers' Party*, pp. 89–91.

14 A good biography and overview of his life and government can be found in Richard Bourne's *Lula of Brazil: The Story So Far*, University of California Press, Berkeley, 2008.

15 Branford and Kucinski, *Lula and the Workers' Party*, p. 27.

16 As might be expected, sectarian divisions have splintered the broad co-alition that originally brought Lula to power.

17 In 1970 36.7 percent of women were illiterate. By 1991 that had dropped to 20.3 percent, still a very high percentage. One of Lula's first initiatives was the *Programa Brasil Alfabetizado*. Over three million people were reached in the first year.

18 The fact that many unions in Brazil see their mission as fighting for all workers and not just members has made the labor movement very effective in reaching a large percentage of workers and assuming a national role capable of shaping policies. As unions attempt to put down stronger roots in developing countries, they will have to represent and address the interests of the class and not just narrow membership concerns.

19 The Lula government supported many of these programs during his first administration, and has created strong governmental departments to advocate for women, African descendants and indigenous peoples.

20 During his exile, Paulo Freire spent quite a bit of time in the United States, teaching pedagogy. His most famous work, *Pedagogy of the Oppressed*, analyzes how education has to serve the purpose of liberation or become a prop to continue the status quo.

21 José Jorge de Carvalho, *Inclusão Étnica e Racial no Brasil: a questão das cotas no ensino superior*, Attar Editorial, São Paulo, 2005.

22 Each movement or organization has its own education programs. Both the CUT and the Metalworkers refer to their programs as 'integrated.' The Metalworkers sponsor leadership programs for their members and elementary and secondary school equivalency programs for the unemployed. These equivalency programs are called '*Programa Integrar*.' The CUT launched a massive literacy campaign five years ago, called 'All the Letters,' '*Todas as letras*.' As described below in the text, this became a three-year program, reaching 80,000 people each year in some of the most remote areas of Brazil. The Education Department of the CUT published summaries of each year, including DVDs, photos, and analysis of accomplishments. The Landless Workers' Movement has expanded its education and been very innovative in its literacy work, now incorporating videos and distance computer education. The MST has promoted education in rural areas, through broad programs for adults, while also establishing special programs for youth and activists. For more information on the MST, see Luciola Andrade Maia, *Mistica, Educação e Resistência no Movimento dos Sem-Terra-MST*, Universidade Federal de Ceara, Fortaleza, 2008; Delze dos Santos Laureano, *O MST e a Constituição: Um sujeito historico na luta pela reforma agraria no Brasil*, Expressão Popular, São Paulo, 2007; and in English, *La Via Campesina: Globalization and the Power of Peasants*, Fernwood Publishing, Halifax, 2007.

23 I heard the story first in 2007, again in 2008, and have relied also on a brochure on the cooperative.

24 The official name of this rice is '*oryza glabberima*.'

25 In interviews with the coordinator of the program nationally, with the coordinator for Bahia and also with the one for Salvador, I found a strong consensus that instructors had to be members of the community and not outsiders. I attended the statewide coordinators' meeting in

Bahia, with more than three hundred participants, and it was clear that the instructors or facilitators had deep roots in the communities in which they taught. Peers create environments of equals, rely on participants to create knowledge, and most effectively create activist communities committed to social change. Myles Horton at Highlander in the US South in the 1950s adopted a similar approach, pushed by Septima Clark, a local teacher. She insisted that the literacy class taught on the Sea Islands, off the coast of Georgia, had to be led by residents, and she cajoled a relative, a local beautician, to figure out how to teach the classes. Her method proved effective and replicable, leading to thousands of 'Citizenship Schools' throughout the South that built the voter registration drives and civil rights movements. See Myles Horton, *The Long Haul*, Doubleday, New York, 1990; and Septima Clark with Cynthia Stokes Brown, *Ready from Within: Septima Clark and the Civil Rights Movement, a First Person Narrative*, Africa World Press, Trenton, NJ, 1990.

26 The story of the occupation is quite dramatic. Private developers had received public funds to build a community of small one-family houses, but had run into financial problems and could not complete the project. While debate went on in government about how to complete the project, a group of metalworkers, including Eunice, organized homeless workers to occupy the houses. A few days prior to the scheduled occupation, families walked through the project picking out a home for themselves, so that when the takeover began, families carried their possessions directly to pre-assigned houses. By the time the government realized what was happening, people had moved in and were setting up a new life.

27 At one time this 'integrated' equivalency program had centers in various states around the country, and did very successful work in Bahia as well as Rio Grande do Sul. Unfortunately, as the unions have become more recognized and established institutions, they have tended to cut back on educational programs.

28 Organization: Agricultural Cooperative Development International, ACDI-VOCA Brazil.mht.

36 | Capitalism and socialism: some feminist questions

Lourdes Benería

Why socialism anyway?

In this age of continued deregulation and privatization, to raise the issue of socialism seems almost a futile exercise. In the age of postmodernism and deconstruction this exercise seems almost out of fashion, even within progressive circles. Among feminists, there has always been a healthy mistrust of male-defined socialism, which is not to say that feminists have not been interested in progressive social change that might have a lot to do with what we loosely tend to call 'socialism'. Likewise, tired of the effort to deal with the unhappy marriage between Marxism and feminism, some feminists seem to be opting for their separation rather than reconciliation – thereby indirectly raising again the connection between socialism and feminism.[1]

Perhaps the time has come for socialism to be given a different name, or for asking, for the nth time, what we mean by the term. What can we, as feminists, say about it? More specifically, what might feminist socialism mean? Public ownership of the means of production or worker-owned firms? Elimination of hierarchies related to class and gender? Ecologically conscious production and consumption? Full employment? A centrally planned economy or market socialism? Equal share of domestic chores by men and women or collectivization of domestic work? Elimination of racism and homophobia? A moneyless utopia? All of the above? How relevant are these questions and how reconcilable, for example, with feminist utopias like Marge Piercy's *Woman on the Edge of Time*? I do not think that we can give up thinking about these questions if we want feminism to be a source of progressive social change.

More basically still we may want to ask why we need socialism at all. Capitalism has, after all, proved to be a very dynamic system, producing even larger amounts of goods and services with progressively less amounts of labour. In the industrialized Western countries, it has resulted in higher standards of living for the majority. The working class can now afford what would have been classified in the past as luxuries. For many, it has facilitated the acquisition of skills, access to knowledge and professional privileges, and a significant increase in individual freedoms. Why, then, are we talking about socialism?

About feminist socialism? Could we not achieve our goals within the existing capitalist structures?

What follows is not an attempt to answer these questions. It is instead a brief reflection on and a reiteration of some of the most basic criticisms of capitalism and, in particular, a discussion of directions for progressive social change with a feminist perspective. It is done with the conviction that, if feminism is to continue to be a source of inspiration for this change, women need to discuss, as much as ever, the overall economic and social aspects of this transformation.

One of the basic features of capitalism is its foundation on the private ownership and control of the means of production. This implies that social decisions are made on the basis of private (as opposed to social/public) interest. But private and social needs may be convergent or in conflict. For Adam Smith and subsequent advocates of a laissez-faire economy, the genius of the market mechanism is that the pursuit of individual self-interest results in the maximization of 'the wealth of nations'. But, as Fritjof Capra has pointed out, the word 'private' comes from the Latin verb *privare*, which means depriving, or taking from communal property.[2] This appropriation by private interests of what were in the past (and could be in the future) communal resources and production is at the heart of why capitalism (and not necessarily the market) produces negative as well as positive results.

Some of the most persuasive arguments for socialism come from the negative results of capitalism: great disparities in the distribution of income and wealth, with corresponding inequalities in control over resources and political power; the appearance and reappearance of poverty in the midst of an ever-increasing capacity to produce goods and services (witness the recent growth in the number of the homeless and beggars in the midst of the extreme affluence and lavishness displayed in the centres of world trade and finance); high levels of unemployment or underemployment with human costs that go far beyond economic survival; the all-encompassing hidden and not-so-hidden injuries of class and their connections with race and gender; the increasing disparities between rich and poor countries and the permanence, and even increase, of hunger and malnutrition despite the existence of food surpluses; the destruction of the environment and the disappearance of natural resources and ecological balances through exploitation of private profit.

Underlying these problems there is the fundamental role played by greed in capitalist institutions and its penetration into the realm of social and individual relations in everyday life. This is not to say that the social experiments of the so-called socialist countries have not created their own set of problems. However, this provides no argument against the need to transcend capitalism and move towards new social experiments that respond more closely to the objectives of a just society in which the gap between our values and real life is minimized.

Women have not played the same role as men in either the positive or negative aspects of capitalist societies. First, they have often been exceptions to the pursuit of individual self-interest by virtue of their *primary* responsibilities in the sphere of the household, where the pressures of the market have penetrated less directly and at a slower pace. Second, given the concentration of resources and power in male hands, men have benefited more than women from the ownership and control of private property and from the benefits derived from capitalism. This is not to say that women have remained outside of the system, but that they have been part of it in different ways.

Similarly, the inequalities generated by capitalism have a specific gender dimension. The feminist literature of the past twenty years has extensively analysed the specific forms that the subordination of women has taken in capitalist societies. To be sure, gender subordination can also be observed in countries that have moved away from capitalist institutions, despite the many achievements registered. As feminists, we want to make note of these achievements while, at the same time, asking critical questions about the reasons behind their limitations.

What directions for change?

The second wave of feminism has generated profound social criticisms, many of which have implications for any discussion of social change. In what follows, I summarize briefly what I think are fundamental aspects in a feminist consideration of alternative societies. My suggestions are not meant to be exhaustive, but simply to contribute some general points to this discussion:

1. The interaction between class and gender in determining women's lives should remain central to our understanding of what sort of changes we want. Thus, some feminist objectives of eliminating gender asymmetries can be met within the structures of a capitalist society. In the industrialized capitalist world, for example, we have recently witnessed much progress in women's access to traditional male strongholds, such as politics and the corporate world. Yet to the extent that women's position in society is determined by class and economic and social structures, some of the inequalities affecting women require basic changes in these structures and institutions. For example, affirmative action and comparable-worth policies have proved to be important instruments in the pursuit of gender equality in the countries where they have been implemented.[3] Yet the progress made through these policies at some levels is being undermined in the current restructuring of the economy through the creation of new structures of production – such as the low-paid service sector, part-time work and other practices of work flexibilization – that relegate women again to the lower echelons of the labour hierarchy.[4] This is because these policies cannot address the more basic questions of control, exploitation and organization of economic life.

Similarly, the permanence of structures and institutions that benefit from gender inequalities also explains the dangers of a backlash and tendencies towards retrogressive policies that wipe out previous gains – as has happened in the USA and other Western countries in recent years. In other words, it might be difficult to implement long-lasting changes towards equality between the sexes without structural changes to build a more egalitarian society.

2. The complexity of the interaction between the material and the ideological aspects of women's condition is a second factor to be underlined. Many of the debates on the transition to socialism as well as platforms of left regimes have been dominated by an economistic approach: their emphasis on economics tends to overlook other basic areas of human development and well-being.[5] To the extent that women's condition is affected by economic factors, the debates are relevant for a discussion of women and socialism. But to the extent that the debates neglect ideological dimensions and their interaction with the material, they cannot easily incorporate what Maxine Molyneux has called 'strategic gender interests' or short- and long-term feminist demands.[6] Thus, how gender roles are constructed and reproduced within the family and throughout the educational system, or through the media and other institutions, takes on a special meaning for women (as it does for racial and ethnic groups); not only do they effectively define women socially and politically, they also carry economic significance when translated into, for example, sex-typing of jobs, occupational segregation, lower wages, different promotional ladders and even job accessibility.

On the other hand, emphasis on the ideological only is likely to be ineffective unless it is accompanied by economic change. Campaigns challenging the traditional division of labour within the household are not likely to be very effective unless women have opportunities for employment in the paid labour market. Similarly, an effort to increase women's labour-force participation will be limited by the extent to which childcare is available and by the economy's capacity to generate jobs. In Cuba, for example, the government's effort to increase women's labour-force participation seems to have been limited by an insufficient industrial base and its corresponding lack of growth in industrial and service employment.[7] Similarly, campaigns against male violence are likely to be more effective if accompanied by policies that increase women's economic autonomy and self-esteem.

3. A fundamental obstacle to the elimination of gender inequalities has proved to be in the sexual division of labour at the domestic level. The evidence along these lines is overwhelming and cuts across countries and economic systems. In the USA, the lack of adequate childcare services for all working women and the limited or non-existent maternity leaves and maternity benefits continue to be a major handicap to the elimination of women's double pay, and to their participation in the labour market and in social life under conditions of equality with men.

In countries attempting to build socialist institutions, the commitment to these policies tends to be much greater. However, the evidence shows that the private sphere of the household is at the root of continuing asymmetries between men and women. In some of these countries, an attempt has been made to influence the household sphere through the introduction of family codes, as in the case of Cuba. What we can learn from the Cuban case is that, despite its intrinsic interest and worthy objectives, and despite the debate that the Family Code was subject to, its 'spirit' cannot be imposed solely from the top down. What is also needed is a vigorous questioning at the bottom, fed by women's concerns and channelled through women's own networks and organizations.

4. Feminism has many implications for the question 'What sort of alternative system?', or 'What form of socialism?' For example, given its emphasis on democratic and bottom-up processes of decision-making, feminism is less compatible with centralized planning and control of the economy than with more decentralized forms that emphasize individual or community control over resources. Thus, social ownership of the means of production does not necessarily imply government control and public enterprise. Other forms of collective ownership that allow control at the community level are likely to be more compatible with feminist processes of participatory decision-making and control. What specific forms these might take will depend on cultural specificity and traditions and might vary across countries.

Similarly, a preference for collective forms of ownership does not automatically have to exclude private ownership of the means of production, particularly when private accumulation is regulated to prevent the creation of inequalities and the concentration of resources in the hands of a small proportion of the population. For example, retail trade and small business in the service sector do not seem to function efficiently under socialized forms of ownership. Given that resources in the small-business sector are not very concentrated, a system that allows them to organize production privately does not pose a serious threat to socialist principles of equality. Since a characteristic of feminism is its lack of dogmatism with respect to 'solutions', it can opt for what seems more compatible with feminist objectives without having to adapt to a rigid model of social change.

In this sense, feminists should pay attention to the now fashionable debate on 'the global march to free markets', which argues that a new emphasis on the advantages of the invisible hand of the market can be found in both Western and centrally planned economies.[8] In both cases, is it argued, the state bureaucracies linked to public ownership and government regulation of the economy create inefficiency and distortions in the price system that slow down growth. Although such arguments need to be heeded, we should keep two points in mind. One is that even in the USA we hear many voices pointing to the serious problems created by the new emphasis on the market, deregulation, privatization, and cuts in government services and welfare funds. The new polarization of income and wealth is intensifying social inequalities at a point in history when the tolerance for them has been decreasing. Second, it is not clear whether the new trend towards the use of the market in non-capitalist countries such as those of the former Soviet Union and of China implies a return to capitalism. At the moment, they represent new experiments, the results of which cannot yet be fully evaluated.

As feminists, we want to pay attention to these experiments in order to best evaluate how compatible they are with our own objectives and practice. This might lead to contradictory conclusions. Thus, on the one hand, we want to be aware of the dangers of creating male-controlled bureaucracies and institutions insensitive to gender inequalities.[9] On the other, if these bureaucracies are eliminated through the market, we also want to be aware of possible negative consequences. For example, the reprivatization of land in China has eliminated the system of work points. This, together with a feminization of agriculture corresponding to men's tendency to take jobs in the towns, has meant that women's contribution to the household is no longer accounted for socially. The return to the market has, therefore, implied the re-emergence of old male privileges by eliminating mechanisms that decreased gender inequalities.[10] These contradictions, however, can be properly evaluated only at the level of each country's experience.

5. A fundamental aspect in the discussion of any alternative system is how production is organized and controlled and how its surplus is distributed. While this may appear to be a very economistic statement, here I want to emphasize the connections between what Burawoy has called 'the politics of production' and other aspects of everyday life.[11] Thus, hierarchical productive structures – beginning with the differentiation between those who own capital and those who need a wage to survive but including also the multiple dimensions of job differentiation – determine the distribution of income and wealth, shape class differences as well as social and political structures, and therefore have a bearing on individual and household location in society. Where we live and work, whether our children attend school or not and what kind of school, whether we eat at home or can afford to eat out, what we do with our leisure time, who our friends are and where we meet them, are all affected by where we are located within these productive structures.

Control over production and the sharing of the surplus also affected our lives in other ways. Thus, workers' control over production is likely to have an influence on the nature and direction of technological change and on the distribution of the firm's surplus. If women are involved, they are likely to press for day-care facilities and maternity leaves, and to stress policies affecting gender differentiation in the workplace.

Emphasis on the politics of production is also important in terms of evaluating proposals for social change. Maria Mies, for example, has called for a 'consumer liberation movement', to be led by women as primary consumers, that would aim at boycotting certain goods and struggling against business manipulation of consumers, and channel a social awareness about existing commodities in the market.[12] There is of course much ground to argue for actions that would create the true 'consumer's sovereignty' assumed by orthodox economic analysis of the market. Yet it seems naive to expect much from those actions alone. A more effective way to control what is being produced, and how, would be through the exercise of some form of collective control over production and surplus appropriation – hence creating the basis for future decisions on investment and growth. The question is how to do so without creating oppressive bureaucracies of centralized planning. If our objective is to move towards 'an emancipated society in which people make their own history' rather than having history being made 'behind their backs',[13] feminism is likely to emphasize its preference for a fusion of production politics and state politics that work from below. This requires a subtle combination of the need for collective work on the one hand, and respect for the individual and culturally determined social norms on the other.[14]

By way of a conclusion, production under socialism holds the potential to be organized so that it responds to social *need* rather than *profit* and to collective rather than individual planning. Thus, it opens the possibility of addressing those problems of concern to women whose solution may be in conflict with *private* profit-making production. How exactly a socialist collectivity might operate is not easy to establish by way of general principles and needs to be subject to new social experimentation. It is for this reason that socialism represents more a *direction* for change than a set of definitions.

Notes

1 See, for example, Michèle Barrett's Introduction to the 1988 edn of her book *Women's Oppression Today* (Verso, London, 1980).

2 Fritjof Capra, *Turning Point*, Simon and Schuster, New York, 1982.

3 Brigid O'Farrell and Sharon Harlan, 'Job integration strategies: today's programs and tomorrow's needs', in Barbara Reskin (ed.), *Sex Segregation in the Workplace*, National Academy Press, Washington, DC, 1984; and Heidi Hartmanni (ed.), *Comparable Worth: New Directions for Research*, National Academy Press, Washington, DC, 1985.

4 Barry Bluestone and Sarah Khun,

'Economic restructuring and the female labour market: the impact of industrial change on women', in L. Benería and C. Stimpson, *Women, Households and the Economy*, Rutgers University Press, New Brunswick, NJ, 1988.

5 There are of course exceptions and interesting efforts to include a wider range of topics. See, for example, Richard Fagen, Carmen Diana Deere and José Luis Coraggin (eds), *Transition and Development: Problems of Third World Socialism*, Monthly Review Press, New York, 1987.

6 Maxine Molyneux, 'Mobilization without emancipation? Women's inter-

ests, state and revolution', in Fagen et al., *Transition and Development*, pp. 280–320.

7 Margaret E. Leahy, *Development Strategies and the Status of Women: A Comparatiove Study of the United States, Mexico, the Soviet Union and Cuba*, Lynne Rienner, Boulder, CO, 1986.

8 Steve Greenhouse, 'The global march to free markets', *New York Times*, 19 July 1987.

9 Christine White, 'Socialist transformation of agriculture and gender relations', in John Taylor and Andrew Turton (eds), *Sociology of Developing Societies – South East Asia*, Macmillan and Monthly Review Press, London and New York, 1986.

10 Phillis Andors, personal communication.

11 Michael Burawoy, *The Politics of Reproduction*, Verso, London, 1985.

12 Maria Mies, *Patriarchy and Accumulation on a World Scale*, Zed Books, London, 1986.

13 Burawoy, *The Politics of Reproduction*, p. 157.

14 Many differences exist, for example, among countries of different cultural norms and traditions. Thus the emphasis on the individual by feminists in Western countries tends to be culturally biased and without meaning in societies where the collective, be it a household or a larger group, is more prevailing. The search for the right combination between the collective and the individual is therefore likely to be influenced by these factors.

Women organizing themselves for change: transnational movements, local resistance

Introduction to Part Five

Nalini Visvanathan

By design, Part 1 sketches the evolution of the development project into a worldwide industry and Part 5 provides women's alternative strategies for social justice and societal change. We begin by noting that after more than six decades, women continue to struggle for recognition of their rights as human rights even as their visibility increases in positions of leadership and structures of governance.[1] This expanded section on women organizing shows an evolving perspective both uplifting and dispiriting; it includes readings set in diverse geographical regions and accounts of multiple forms of collective action in resisting or alleviating oppressive policies and practices. The introduction briefly stresses authors and anthologies that conceptualize women's movements and resistance, historical and contemporary, local and global.[2] The critique of the development project begun in Part 1 continues in the following discussion, which highlights three overlapping areas:[3] movements and networks; community organizing and NGOs; and work-centered organizing.

What are social and transnational movements? How do they differ from transnational advocacy networks?

Social movements are 'collective challenges' by people held together by common goals and solidarity in opposing injustice (Tarrow 1998). Drawing from multiple authors, Moghadam (2009: 4) defines transnational social movements as 'a mass mobilization uniting people in three or more countries, engaged in sustained contentious interactions with political elites, international organizations, or multinational corporations.' Embedded in historical events and processes, Moghadam's work discusses diverse social movements and their challenge to globalization, linking transnational feminism with the global justice movement. Movements should be distinguished from a transnational advocacy network (TAN), where individual activists rather than a group take action. Keck and Sikkink (1998: 3) call TANs 'relevant actors working internationally on an issue who are bound together by shared values, a common discourse and dense exchanges of information and services.'[4] Women's TANs strengthen related movements when they are 'organized around principles of challenging gender hierarchy and improving the conditions of women's lives' (Sperling et al. 2001).

A: Transnational, regional and national movements

Countries in Africa, Asia and Latin America have a documented history of women's movements within nationalist and anti-colonialist struggles spanning two centuries and sometimes having transnational support (Jaquette 1994; Jayawardena 1986; Kumar 1993; Tripp et al. 2009). In her richly textured history of movements in different regions, Tripp (2006) discerns three waves of transnational mobilization; she observes that it was only with the third wave of activism starting in 1985 that women from the South asserted their agenda, directly challenging the leadership of Northern women at UN conferences.

Alvarez (2009: 182) maps the changing tide in Latin American women's movements recording the transformative and refashioned models of feminism found in the Third Wave that are being created by 'poor and working class women, indigenous and peasant women, Afro-descendent and Indigenous women, lesbians' once marginalized in a movement driven by elite women. Rural movements in this region also encompass indigenous women's groups and trans-border organizing (Deere and Royce 2009).

Following the 1995 Beijing Conference, two major transnational women's movements – for human rights and for sustainable development – coalesced to shape the rights-based approach (RBA) to development. The emergence of a rights-based development movement in settings where once the Western human rights agenda had been viewed as a liberal imposition has powerfully influenced advocacy by the women's movements and networks for reproductive rights and health, revisioned and regenerated around the Cairo Conference (Petchesky 2000; Harcourt 2009). Many Western bilateral agencies and international NGOs and donors have adopted the RBA in their development programming; Tsikata (2007) critically assesses the approach, balancing its positive features against its problematical aspects.

Harcourt and others criticize the 'development movement' for diluting its justice agenda in favor of 'efficiency and management,' repackaging women's complex experiences to re-present them as poor victims and conflating 'women' with 'family' (Harcourt et al. 2006). Moreover, the UN's distillation of several years of consultations with women's groups into the eight MDGs barely represents women's concerns with gender-based and sexualized violence, reproductive health and rights, reproductive work and other issues that manifest gender inequality and injustice. These themes are explored more fully in the context of the global women's rights movement (Harcourt 2006).

The UN conferences of the 1990s were concurrent with the diffusion of the Internet, which served to mobilize women's groups globally and facilitate cross-border collaborations. TANs address incipient issues such as transborder activism against NAFTA (Domínguez 2002) and the joint campaign by Japanese and Korean feminists against Japanese military sexual slavery (Piper 2001) and challenge the lack of accountability by global governance agencies (True 2008).

Readings In Chapter 37, Peggy Antrobus underscores the need for women's movements to go beyond gender and address the dimensions of class, race, ethnicity, and geographic location 'by transforming social institutions, practices and beliefs.'

In Chapter 38, Chandra Mohanty revisits the site of her classic essay 'Under Western eyes,' to address among other themes transnational feminism and the struggle against the politics and economics of capitalism. In asking for solidarity in the feminist opposition to neoliberal globalization and advocating for greater engagement by academics, Mohanty unambiguously rejects postmodernist relativism.

In Chapter 39, Aili Mari Tripp offers an instructive account of the outcomes of transnational advocacy when Western activists failed to consult with local players and domestic campaigns at the site of the problem; she responds by constructing guidelines that transnational feminist activists should consider in their advocacy work.

In Chapter 40, Annette Desmarais traces the evolution of women's leadership in a transnational peasant movement, La Via Campesina, traditionally dominated by men. Women's sustained efforts to take a greater role in decision-making processes illustrate the challenges they face even in progressive settings.

In Chapter 41, Ayesha Imam lays bare the contestation of feminism on the African continent, fractures within women's movements, and the creation of the African Feminist Forum (AFF) by feminists rejecting oppressive influences and embracing marginalized and stigmatized women.

B: Community organizing and non-governmental organizations

Communities organizing to protest local and extra-local sources of injustice are the bedrock of regional and national movements. The vibrancy of any large-scale women's movement depends on the resistance and fortitude of grassroots women who protest ways in which state-generated and neoliberal policies have negatively impacted their lives. During the structural adjustment crises in the global South, the heroic resistance of the poor and their response to the deprivations suffered in their daily lives were documented by such actions as community soup kitchens (Lima) and cooperative bulk purchases. These narratives of solidarity economics underscored women's agency and often overlooked the costs they paid in ensuring the survival of their families and communities. Thus Lind's (2005) retrospective analysis of the experience of Ecuadorian women's struggles in the 1990s goes beyond a critique of neoliberal policies and local implementing institutions to examine this irony. Emphasizing 'place' in the evolution of struggles for women's bodies and environmental rights, Harcourt and Escobar (2005) sift evidence of local knowledge and activism in shaping powerful movements against encroachment on vulnerable communities. In her exposition of transnational feminist praxis within the context of globalization, Naples (2002: 268) cites the emphases given to 'place' (locality) and 'localization' by feminist scholars such as Saskia Sassen and Vandana Shiva, as well as geographers and analysts who document the threats posed by globalization and the urgent need for resistance.

The 1980s and 1990s saw an explosion of civil society organizations in the global South, supported by international agencies that found them more effective in reaching grassroots communities. However, the amorphous and protean NGO sphere does not lend itself to facile categorization. Perceiving a growing trend in the 1990s for women's groups to professionalize and convert to institutionalized structures (vulnerable to co-option), Alvarez (1999) called attention to the growing NGO-ization of Latin American women's movements. A decade later, she re-evaluated this trend, noting the dissemination of 'feminist discursive fields' by these NGOs across the continent (Alvarez 2009: 177). However, the short-lived history of an independent Cuban transnational feminist network that emerged during the 1990s legitimizes her concerns across polities in the region (Fernandes 2005). Finally, faith-based organizations (FBOs) have engaged in social development work with some examples of visionary social change (Tyndale 2006); to just focus on the challenge to feminism from evangelical and fundamentalist groups would misrepresent the impact of FBOs on women's health and education services in marginalized communities.

Readings In Chapter 42, Amy Lind exposes the paradoxical situation of poor Ecuadorian women 'mothering' the crisis of neoliberal economic restructuring by their collective assumption of responsibilities relinquished by the state, thereby contributing to the success of a diminished welfare system.

Jennifer Fluri's lucid depiction of the Revolutionary Afghan Women's Association (RAWA) in Chapter 43 exemplifies an extraordinary women's organization delivering social and educational services to the refugee community, raising political consciousness and inducting men into its campaign for women's equality and a secular nation.

C: Work-centered organizing

Globally, only a small proportion of working women are found in the formal or salaried sector, whether manufacturing or service. However, in many areas of the informal economy where women dominate, unions and associations increasingly represent unskilled women workers. India's legendary Self-Employed Women's Association (SEWA) has fostered chapters in Indian cities and helped create Women in Informal Employment, Globalizing and Organizing (WIEGO), a global network of scholars, practitioners and activists working to improve the status of these women.

The informal economy encompasses a broad spectrum of workers from unincorporated business owners and street vendors to waste gatherers and ragpickers (Bhowmik 2005). The ILO is starting to document the conditions of millions of domestic workers, mainly women in the global South; and organized workers, local and migrant, are resisting punitive policies and demanding change (Swider 2006).

Within civil society, membership-based organizations, the backbone of social movements, are critical in mobilizing women often separated from fellow workers and isolated by illiteracy and poverty (Chen et al. 2007). NGOs advocating labor rights have also assumed many forms, including the hybrid 'worker centers' that serve as a hub for organizing and community services (see Reading below).

In China, the dominant global factory with 112 million manufacturing workers, 'stoppages, strikes and suicides' at electronics manufacturer Foxconn and other corporations pointed to an incipient labor resistance and revolt in the summer of 2010;[5] women and rural migrant workers are more likely to face exploitative conditions. Women's networks organizing to support women factory workers are not always supported by the labor movement.[6] The final reading records a successful collaboration.

Reading In Chapter 44, Samanthi Gunawardana presents a successful global campaign, at a Sri Lankan export processing zone, by a partnership between the workers' union and a local women's center with support from transnational groups, and draws lessons for cross-border organizing.

The selected readings embody models of progressive organizational structures and forums that women have envisioned for a just world. As Peruvian feminist activist Virigina Vargas stated:[7]

> Another world will not be possible without a different kind of economy, and another kind of economy will not be possible without a different kind of democracy ... The urgent battle against today's patriarchal system is to open the way for recognition of sexual diversity, for reproduction by choice instead of by obligation, to welcome the existence of different types of families, to value the reproductive economy, and the importance of democratization on all fronts – in the world, in countries, at home and in the bedroom.

Notes

1 Quota systems have elevated Rwandan women to the majority in parliament and brought impoverished rural women into local governance in India; www.un.org/ecosocdev/geninfo/afrec/vol18no1/181women.htm.

2 These works should also be valuable in planning course syllabi and for shaping exploratory research. See Fletcher (2005) and Rupp (2008).

3 Note the caveat that they are neither exhaustive nor fully representative of the literature.

4 Some of these transnational networks, such as DAWN, WEDO, Madre and Equality Now, have a long record of

campaigning for women's rights at major UN conferences (see list in Moghadam 2009: 71).

5 www.economist.com/node/16693397.

6 Jennifer Bickham Mendes discusses the challenges and pitfalls of transnational politics and the undue reliance on unions by Northern collaborators (Naples and Desai 2002: 137).

7 See Harcourt et al. (2006: 16).

References and further reading

Abu-Lughod, L. (2005) 'Is there a Muslim sexuality? Changing constructions of sexuality in Egyptian Bedouin weddings', in C. Brettell and C. Sargent (eds), *Gender in Cross Cultural Perspective*, 4th edn, Englewood Cliffs, NJ: Prentice Hall, pp. 247–56.

Alexander, M. J. and C. T. Mohanty (1997) *Feminist Genealogies, Colonial Legacies, Democratic Futures*, New York: Routledge.

Alvarez, S. E. (1998) 'Latin American feminisms "go global": trends of the 1990s and challenges for the new millennium', in S. E. Alvarez, E. Dagnino and A. Escobar (eds), *Cultures of Politics/Politics of Cultures: Re-visioning Latin American social movements*, Boulder, CO: Westview Press.

— (1999) 'Advocating feminism: the Latin American feminist NGO "boom"', *International Feminist Journal of Politics*, 1(2): 181–209.

— (2009) 'Beyond NGO-ization in Latin America', *Development*, 52(2): 175–84.

Anandhi, S. (2002) 'Interlocking patriarchies and women in governance: a case study of Panchayati Raj institutions in Tamil Nadu', in *The Violence of Development: The politics of identity, gender and social inequalities in India*, London: Zed Books.

Antrobus, P. (2004) *The Global Women's Movements: Origins, issues and strategies*, London: Zed Books.

Antrobus, P. and G. Sen (2006) 'The personal is global: the project and politics of the transnational women's movement', in S Batliwala and L. D. Brown (eds), *Transnational Civil Society: An introduction*, Bloomfield, CT: Kumarian Press.

Barlow, T. E. (2004) *The Question of Women in Chinese Feminism*, Durham, NC: Duke University Press.

Basu, A. (ed.) (1995) *The Challenge of Local Feminisms: Women's Movements in Global Perspective*, Boulder, CO: Westview Press.

Bhowmik, S. K. (2005) 'Street vendors in Asia: a review', *Economic and Political Weekly*, 28 May–4 June, pp. 2256–64.

Britton, H., J. Fish and S. Meintjes (eds) (2009) *Women's Activism in South Africa. Working across Divides*, Scottsville: University of KwaZulu-Natal.

Brooks, E. C. (2007) 'Unraveling the garment industry: transnational organizing and women's work', Minneapolis: University of Minnesota Press.

Buskens, I. and A. Webb (2009) *African Women and ICTs*, London: Zed Books.

Chen, M., R. Jhabvala, R. Kanbur and C. Richards (2007) *Membership-based Organizations of the Poor: Concepts, experience and policy*, New York: Routledge.

Crowell, D. W. (2003) *The SEWA Movement and Rural Development*, New Delhi: Sage.

Deere, C. D. and F. S. Royce (eds) (2009) *Rural Social Movements in Latin America*, Gainesville: University Press of Florida.

Desmarais, A. A. (2007) *La Via Campesina: Globalization and the Power of Peasants*, Halifax, NS: Fernwood Publishing.

Domínguez, E. R. (2002) 'Continental transnational activism and women workers' networks within NAFTA', *International Feminist Journal of Politics*, 4(2): 216–39.

El-Mahdi, R. (2009) 'Egypt's feminist movement: different or non-existent?', Cairo Papers for Social Sciences, Cairo: AUC Press, June.

Elson, D. (2006) *Budgeting for Women's Rights: Monitoring government budgets for compliance to CEDAW*, New York: UNIFEM.

Eschle, C. and B. Maiguashca (2010) *Making Feminist Sense of the Global Justice Movement*, Lanham, MD: Rowman & Littlefield.

Fernandes, S. (2005) 'Transnationalism and feminist activism in Cuba: the case of Magín', *Politics and Gender*, 1(3): 431–52.

Fletcher, Y. S. (2005) 'Teaching the history of global and transnational feminisms', *Radical History Review*, 92: 155–63.

Folbre, N. (2006) 'Nursebots to the rescue? Immigration, automation, and care', *Globalizations*, 1474-774X, 3(3): 349–60.

Gandhi, N. and N. Shah (1992) *The Issues at Stake: Theory and Practice in the Contemporary Women's Movement in India*, New Delhi: Kali for Women.

Gunawardena, N. and A. Kingsolver (2007) *The Gender of Globalization*, Sante Fe, NM: School for Advanced Research Press.

Harcourt, W. (2006) 'The global women's rights movement. Power politics around the United Nations and World Social Forum', Civil Society and Social Movements Programme Paper no. 25, UNRISD.

— (2009) *Body Politics in Development: Critical debates in gender and development*, London: Zed Books.

Harcourt, W. and A. Escobar (eds) (2005) *Women and the Politics of Place*, Bloomfield, CT: Kumarian Press.

Harcourt, W. with L. Horelli, K. Khan, K. Mumtaz, B. Murphy and Z. Randriamaro (2006) 'Feminist praxis: women's transnational and place based struggles for change', GTI Paper Series, Frontiers of a Great Transition, no. 11.

Ilumoka, A. (2006) 'Beyond human rights fundamentalism: the challenges of consensus building in the 21st century', Draft thematic paper, *What Next?* Dag Hammarskjöld Foundation, www.dhf.uu.se.

Jaquette, J. S. (ed.) (1994) *Feminist Agendas and Democracy in Latin America*, Durham, NC: Duke University Press.

Jayawardena, K. (1986) *Feminism and Nationalism in the Third World*, London: Zed Books.

John, M. (1999) 'Gender, development and the women's movement', in R. Sunder Rajan (ed.), *Signposts:Gender Issues in Post-Independence India*, New Delhi: Kali for Women.

Keck, M. E. and K. Sikkink (1998) *Activists beyond Borders: Advocacy Networks in International Politics*, Ithaca, NY: Cornell University Press.

Kumar, R. (1993) *The History of Doing. An Illustrated Account of Movements for Women's Rights and Feminism in India, 1800–1990*, London: Verso.

Leslie, A. N. (2006) *Social Movements and Democracy in Africa: The impact of women's struggle for equal rights in Botswana*, New York: Routledge.

Lind, A. (2005) *Gendered Paradoxes. Women's Movements, State Restructuring, and Global Development in Ecuador*, University Park: Pennsylvania State University Press.

Marchand, M. and A. S. Runyan (eds) (2000) *Gender and Global Restructurings. Sightings, Sites and Resistances*, London: Routledge.

McFadden, P. (2010) 'Challenging empowerment', *Development*, 53(2): 161–4 (special issue focus on empowerment).

Moghadam, V. M. (2005) *Globalizing Women: Gender, Globalization, and Transnational Feminist Networks*, Baltimore, MD: Johns Hopkins University Press.

— (2009) *Globalization and Social Movements. Islamism, Feminism, and the Global Justice Movement*, New York: Rowman & Littlefield.

Mohanty, C. T. (2003) *Decolonizing Theory, Practicing Solidarity*, Durham, NC: Duke University Press.

Molyneux, M. and S. Lazar (2003) *Doing the Rights Thing. Rights-based Development and Latin American NGOs*, London: ITDG Publishing.

Molyneux, M. and S. Razavi (eds) (2002) *Gender Justice, Development, and Rights*, Oxford: Oxford University Press.

Naples, N. A. (2002) 'Transnational

feminist praxis', in N. A. Naples and M. Desai (eds), *Women's Activism and Globalization. Linking Local Struggles and Transnational Politics*, New York: Routledge.

Naples, N. A. and M. Desai (eds) (2002) *Women's Activism and Globalization. Linking Local Struggles and Transnational Politics*, New York: Routledge.

Ngai, P. (2005) *Made in China: Women Factory Workers in a Global Marketplace*, Durham, NC: Duke University Press.

Petchesky, R. (2000) *Reproductive and Sexual Rights and Social Development: Charting the Course of Transnational Women's NGOs*, Occasional Paper 8, Geneva: United Nations Research Institute for Social Development.

— (2003) *Global Prescriptions: Gendering Health and Human Rights*, London: Zed Books, in association with UNRISD.

Piper, N. (2001) 'Transnational women's activism in Japan and Korea: The unresolved issue of military sexual slavery', *Global Networks*, 1(2): 155–70.

Rai, S. M. (2007) 'Local democracy and deliberative politics: Indian *panchayats* and the quota for women', *Hypatia: Journal of Feminist Philosophy*, 22(4) (Fall): 64–80.

Ram, K. (1999) '*Ná shariram nádhi,* My body is mine: the Urban Women's Health Movement in India and its negotiation of modernity', *Women's Studies International Forum*, 21:6.

Ray, R. (1999) *Fields of Protest. Women's Movements in India*, Minneapolis: University of Minnesota Press.

Ruiz, C. C. (2004) 'Rights and citizenship of indigenous women in Chiapas: a history of struggles, fears and hopes', in N. Kabeer (ed.), *Inclusive Citizenship*, London: Zed Books.

Rupp, L. J. (2008) 'Teaching about transnational feminisms', *Radical History Review*, 101: 191–7.

Silliman, J. (1999) 'Expanding civil society, shrinking political spaces: the case of women's nongovernmental organiza-

tions', in J. Silliman and Y. King (eds), *Dangerous Intersections: Feminist Perspectives on Population, Environment, and Development*, Cambridge, MA: South End Press.

Sperling, V., M. M. Ferree and B. Risman (2001) 'Constructing global feminism: transnational advocacy networks and Russian women's activism', *Signs*, 26(4): 1155–86.

Stephen, L. (1997) *Women and Social Movements in Latin America: Power from below*, Austin: University of Texas Press.

Swider, S. (2006) 'Working women of the world unite? Labor organizing and transnational gender solidarity among domestic workers in Hong Kong', in M. M. Ferree and A. M. Tripp (eds) (2006) *Global Feminism*, New York: New York University Press.

Tarrow, S. (1998) *Power in Movement: Social Movements and Contentious Politics*, 2nd edn, New York: Cambridge University Press.

Tripp, A. M. (2006) 'The evolution of transnational feminism: consensus, conflict, and new dynamics', in M. M. Ferree and A. M. Tripp (eds), *Global Feminism*, New York: New York University Press.

Tripp, A. M., I. Casimiro, J. Kwesiga and A. Mungwa (2009) *African Women's Movements. Changing Political Landscapes*, Cambridge: Cambridge University Press.

True, J. (2008) 'Global accountability and transnational networks: the Women Leaders' Network and Asia Pacific Economic Cooperation', *Pacific Review*, 21(1): 1–26.

Tsikata, D. (2007) 'Announcing a new dawn prematurely? Human rights feminists and the rights-based approaches to development', in A. Cornwall, E. Harrison and A. Whitehead (eds), *Feminisms in Development. Contradictions, Contestations and Challenges*, London: Zed Books.

Tyndale, W. R. (2006) *Visions of Development. Faith-based Initiatives*, Burlington, VT: Ashgate.

37 | The global women's movement: an introduction

Peggy Antrobus

The evolution of geopolitical events over the last century can be tracked by the pattern of social movements that emerged to challenge the most extreme forms of capitalist exploitation, militarism, dictatorship, sexism and racism. Since the collapse of the socialist alternative, new social movements are again emerging to challenge the excesses of unregulated capitalism.

Emerging out of the demonstrations that took place in Seattle around the Second Ministerial Meeting of the World Trade Organization (WTO) in November 1999, and facilitated by advances in information and communications technologies, a social movement, initially named the 'anti-globalization' movement,[1] has been gathering strength. The spread of neoliberalism as expressed through the operations of the WTO and international financial institutions (IFIs) was challenged wherever representatives of these organizations and those of the eight most powerful governments (the G8)[2] met in the years following Seattle.[3] Since that time these groups have begun to consolidate around the World Social Forum (WSF), initiated in January 2001 by Brazilian and European NGOs to counter the World Economic Forum (WEF) that had been meeting annually in Davos, Switzerland, for over thirty years. The WSF, meeting for the first time outside Brazil,[4] seems destined to be the coming together of social movements of the first decade of this new century. It is not a single movement but a 'movement of movements', an unprecedented alliance that has been growing around a diversity of issues over the past twenty years.

Catalysed by the UN conferences of the 1980s and 1990s, environmentalists, feminists and human rights activists have been joined by reinvigorated movements from the 1950s and 1960s – trade unionists, activists from the civil rights and peace movements, anarchists and liberation theologians. At the 2002 Forum, a campaign against fundamentalism – 'all of them', economic and political no less than religious – organized by Latin American women's movements, highlighted the ways in which women's lives and livelihoods are jeopardized by the convergences between the different social, economic, political and cultural processes unleashed or exacerbated by neoliberalism.

Only a few activists take the view that the objectives of the women's movement are similar to those of labour, human rights and student groups, which seek justice for their members. Many see the objectives of women's groups as broader, seeking changes in relationships that are more varied and complex. There are two entry points to concerns about a larger social project. One is recognition of the centrality of the care and nurture of human beings to the larger social project, and that to address this, given the primacy of women's gendered role in this area, requires addressing gender relations in all the complex interplay of their economic, social, political, cultural and personal dimensions.[5] It also involves locating gender inequality within other forms of inequality that shape and often exacerbate it. Another entry point is recognition that women cannot be separated from the larger context of their lived experience and that this includes considerations of class, race/ethnicity and geographic location, among other factors. This means that the struggle for women's agency must include engagement in struggles against sources of women's oppression that extend beyond gender.

The larger social project would therefore include transforming social institutions, practices and beliefs so that they address gender relations along with other oppressive relationships, not simply seeking a better place within existing institutions and structures. For this reason, women's movements in countries where the majority of women are marginalized by class, race or ethnicity must be concerned with the larger social project. This is often a point of tension between women's movements in the context of North–South relations, as well as in the context of struggles against oppression on the basis of class, race and ethnicity.

I believe that confusion about definitions of women's movements is also caused by failure to make distinctions between women's organizations as part of a wide spectrum of non-governmental organizations (NGOs) or civil society organizations (CSOs) and those that might be better understood as part of a politically oriented social movement. Similarly, the term 'women's movements' is sometimes used interchangeably with 'feminist movements', an error that confuses and misrepresents both feminism and the broad spectrum of women's organizations.

The following statements summarize my own views on women's movements:

- A women's movement is a political movement – part of the broad array of social movements concerned with changing social conditions, rather than part of a network of women's organizations (although many women's organizations may be part of a women's movement).
- A women's movement is grounded in an understanding of women's relations to social conditions – an understanding of gender as an important relationship within the broad structure of social relationships of class, race and ethnicity, age and location.
- A women's movement is a process, discontinuous, flexible, responding to

specific conditions of perceived gender inequality or gender-related injustice. Its focal points may be in women's organizations, but it embraces individual women in various locations who identify with the goals of feminism at a particular point in time.

- Awareness and rejection of patriarchal privilege and control are central to the politics of women's movements.
- In most instances, the movement is born at the moments in which individual women become aware of their separateness as women, their alienation, marginalization, isolation or even abandonment within a broader movement for social justice or social change. In other words, women's struggle for agency within the broader struggle is the catalyst for women's movements.

Notes

1 The current title, the 'movement for global justice', comes closer to capturing the wider agenda of the movement.

2 These include the USA, Canada, the UK, France, Germany, Italy, Russia and Japan.

3 The site of the second Ministerial Meeting of the WTO.

4 In Mumbai, India, from 16 to 24 January 2004.

5 I am grateful to Gita Sen for this analysis.

38 | 'Under Western eyes' revisited: feminist solidarity through anti-capitalist struggles

Chandra Talpade Mohanty

I write this essay at the urging of a number of friends and with some trepidation, revisiting the themes and arguments of an essay written some sixteen years ago. This is a difficult essay to write, and I undertake it hesitantly and with humility. It is time to revisit 'Under Western eyes,' to clarify ideas that remained implicit and unstated in 1986 and to further develop and historicize the theoretical framework I outlined then.

What are the challenges facing transnational feminist practice at the beginning of the twenty-first century? What are the urgent intellectual and political questions for feminist scholarship and organizing at this time in history?

First, let me say that the terms *Western* and *Third World* retain a political and explanatory value in a world that appropriates and assimilates multiculturalism and 'difference' through commodification and consumption. *Western* and *Third World* explain much less than the categorizations *North/South* or *One-Third/Two-Thirds Worlds*. *North/South* is used to distinguish between affluent, privileged nations and communities. As a political designation that attempts to distinguish between the 'haves' and 'have-nots,' it does have a certain political value.

I find the language of *One-Third World* versus *Two-Thirds World* as elaborated by Gustavo Esteva and Madhu Suri Prakash (1998) particularly useful, especially in conjunction with *Third World/South* and *First World/North.* These terms represent what Esteva and Prakash call social minorities and social majorities – categories based on the quality of life led by peoples and communities in both the North and the South.[1] The advantage of *One-Third/Two-Thirds Worlds* is that they move away from misleading geographical and ideological binarisms.

Under and (inside) Western eyes: at the turn of the century

There have been a number of shifts in the political and economic landscapes of nations and communities of people in the last two decades. Feminist theory and feminist movements across national borders have matured substantially since the early 1980s, and there is now a greater visibility of transnational women's struggles and movements, brought on in part by the United Nations world conferences on women held over the last two decades.

The rise of religious fundamentalisms with their deeply masculinist and often racist rhetoric poses a huge challenge for feminist struggles around the world.

My own present-day analytic framework remains very similar to my earliest critique of Eurocentrism. However, I now see the politics and economics of capitalism as a far more urgent locus of struggle. It is attentive to the micro-politics of everyday life as well as to the macropolitics of global economic and political processes. The link between political economy and culture remains crucial to any form of feminist theorizing – as it does for my work. Global economic and political processes have become more brutal, exacerbating economic, racial, and gender inequalities, and thus they need to be demystified, re-examined, and theorized.

'Under Western eyes' sought to make the operations of discursive power visible, to draw attention to what was left out of feminist theorizing, namely, the material complexity, reality, and agency of Third World women's bodies and lives. This is in fact exactly the analytic strategy I now use to draw attention to what is unseen, under-theorized, and left out in the production of knowledge about globalization. While globalization has always been a part of capitalism, and capitalism is not a new phenomenon, at this time I believe the theory, critique, and activism around anti-globalization has to be a key focus for feminists.

Feminist methodologies: new directions

What kinds of feminist methodology and analytic strategy are useful in making power (and women's lives) visible in overtly nongendered, nonracialized discourses? I believe that [an] experiential and analytic anchor in the lives of marginalized communities of women provides the most inclusive paradigm for thinking about social justice. If we pay attention to and think from the space of some of the most disenfranchised communities of women in the world, we are most likely to envision a just and democratic society capable of treating all its citizens fairly. Beginning from the lives and interests of marginalized communities of women, I am able to access and make the workings of power visible – to read up the ladder of privilege. It is more necessary to look upward – colonized peoples must know themselves and the colonizer. My view is thus a materialist and 'realist' one and is antithetical to that of postmodernist relativism. Methodologically, this analytic perspective is grounded in historical materialism.

Feminist scientist Vandana Shiva, one of the most visible leaders of the anti-globalization movement, provides a similar and illuminating critique of the patents and intellectual property rights agreements sanctioned by the World Trade Organization since 1995.[2] Along with others in the environmental and indigenous rights movements, she argues that the WTO sanctions biopiracy and engages in intellectual piracy by privileging the claims of corporate commercial interests, based on Western systems of knowledge in agriculture and medicine, to products and innovations derived from indigenous knowledge traditions. Thus, through the definition of Western scientific epistemologies as the only legitimate scientific system, the WTO is able to underwrite corporate patents to indigenous knowledge (as to the Neem tree in India) as their own intellectual property, protected through intellectual property rights agreements. As a result, the patenting of drugs derived from indigenous medicinal systems has now reached massive proportions.

The contrast between Western scientific systems and indigenous epistemologies and systems of medicine is not the only issue here. It is the colonialist and corporate power to define Western science, and the reliance on capitalist values of private property and profit, as the only normative system that results in the exercise of immense power. All innovations that happen to be collective, to have occurred over time in forests and farms, are appropriated or excluded. The idea of an intellectual commons where knowledge is collectively gathered and passed on for the benefit of all, not owned privately, is the very opposite of the notion of private property and ownership that is the basis for the WTO property rights agreements.

Shiva's analysis of intellectual property rights, biopiracy, and globalization is made possible by its very location in the experiences and epistemologies of peasant and tribal women in India. Beginning from the practices and knowledges of indigenous women, she 'reads up' the power structure, all the way to the policies and practices sanctioned by the WTO. This is a very clear example, then, of a transnational, anti-capitalist feminist politics.

It is especially on the bodies and lives of women and girls from the Third World/South – the Two-Thirds World – that global capitalism writes its script, and it is by paying attention to and theorizing the experiences of these communities of women and girls that we demystify capitalism as a system of debilitating sexism and racism and envision anti-capitalist resistance.

Since women are central to the life of neighborhoods and communities they assume leadership positions in these struggles. This is evident in the example of women of color in struggles against environmental racism in the United States, as well as in Shiva's example of tribal women in the struggle against deforestation and for an intellectual commons.

If these particular gendered, classed, and racialized realities of globalization are unseen and under-theorized, even the most radical critiques of globalization effectively render Third World/South women and girls as absent. Perhaps it is no longer simply an issue of Western eyes, but rather how the West is inside and continually reconfigures globally, racially, and in terms of gender. Without this recognition, a necessary link between feminist scholarship/analytic frames and organizing/activist projects is impossible. Faulty and inadequate analytic frames engender ineffective political action and strategizing for social transformation.

Globalization colonizes women's as well as men's lives around the world, and we need an anti-imperialist, anti-capitalist, and contextualized feminist project to expose and make visible the various, overlapping forms of subjugation of women's lives. Activists and scholars must also identify and re-envision forms of collective resistance that women, especially, in their different communities enact in their everyday lives. It is their particular exploitation at this time, their potential epistemic privilege, as well as their particular forms of solidarity, which can be the basis for reimagining a liberatory politics for the start of this century.

Anti-globalization struggles

Although the context for writing 'Under Western eyes' in the mid-1980s was a visible and activist women's movement, this radical movement no longer exists as such. Instead, I draw inspiration from a more distant, but significant, anti-globalization movement in the United States and around the world. Activists in these movements are often women, although the movement is not gender-focused. What does it mean to make anti-globalization a key factor for feminist theorizing and struggle? The site of anti-globalization scholarship I focus on is the emerging, notably ungendered and deracialized discourse on activism against globalization.

Anti-globalization scholarship and movements

Women's and girls' bodies determine democracy: free from violence and sexual abuse, free from malnutrition and environmental degradation, free to plan their families, free to not have families, free to choose their sexual lives and preferences. (Eisenstein 1998: 161) [3]

There is now an increasing and useful feminist scholarship critical of the practices and effects of globalization. I want to draw attention to some of the most useful kinds of issues it raises. I return to an earlier question: What are the concrete effects of global restructuring on the 'real' raced, classed, national, sexual bodies of women in the academy, in workplaces, streets, households, cyberspaces, neighborhoods, prisons, and in social movements? And how do we recognize these gendered effects in movements against globalization? Some of the most complex analyses of the centrality of gender in understanding economic globalization attempt to link questions of subjectivity, agency, and identity with those of political economy and the state. This scholarship argues persuasively for the need to rethink patriarchies and hegemonic masculinities in relation to present-day globalization and nationalisms, and it also attempts to retheorize the gendered aspects of the refigured relations of the state, the market, and civil society by focusing on unexpected and unpredictable sites of resistance to the often devastating effects of global restructuring on women.[4]

Women workers of particular caste/class, race, and economic status are necessary to the operation of the capitalist global economy. Particular kinds of women – poor, Third and Two-Thirds World, working-class, and immigrant/ migrant women – are the preferred workers in these global, 'flexible' temporary job markets. The documented increase in the migration of poor, One-Third/ Two-Thirds World women in search of labor across national borders has led to a rise in the international 'maid trade' (Parreñas 2001) and in international sex trafficking and tourism.[5] Many global cities now require and completely depend on the service and domestic labor of immigrant and migrant women. The proliferation of structural adjustment policies around the world has re-privatized women's labor by shifting the responsibility for social welfare from the state to the household and to women located there. The rise of religious fundamentalisms in conjunction with conservative nationalisms, which are also in part reactions to global capital and its cultural demands, has led to the policing of women's bodies in the streets and in the workplaces.

Global capital also reaffirms the color line in its newly articulated class structure evident in the prisons in the One-Third World. Just as the factories and workplaces of global corporations seek and discipline the labor of poor, Third World/South, immigrant/migrant women, the prisons of Europe and the United States incarcerate disproportionately large numbers of women of color, immigrants, and noncitizens of African, Asian, and Latin American descent.

Making gender and power visible in the processes of global restructuring demands looking at, naming, and seeing the particular raced and classed communities of women from poor countries as they are constituted as workers in sexual, domestic, and service industries; as prisoners; and as household managers and nurturers.

Marianne Marchand and Anne Runyan (2000) discuss the gendered meta-phors and symbolism in the language of globalization whereby particular actors and sectors are privileged over others: market over state, global over local, finance capital over manufacturing, finance ministries over social welfare, and consumers over citizens. They argue that the latter are feminized and the former masculinized and that this gendering naturalizes the hierarchies required for globalization to succeed.

In spite of the occasional exception, I think that much of present-day schol-arship tends to reproduce particular 'globalized' representations of women. Just as there is an Anglo-American masculinity produced in and by discourses of globalization,[6] it is important to ask what the corresponding femininities being produced are. Clearly there is the ubiquitous global teenage girl factory worker, the domestic worker, and the sex worker. There is also the migrant/ immigrant service worker, the refugee, the victim of war crimes, the woman-of-color prisoner who happens to be a mother and drug user, the consumer-housewife, and so on. There is also the mother-of-the-nation/religious bearer of traditional culture and morality.

Although these representations of women correspond to real people, they also often stand in for the contradictions and complexities of women's lives and roles. Certain images, such as that of the factory or sex worker, are often geographically located in the Third World/South, but many of the representations identified above are dispersed throughout the globe. The point I am making here is that women are workers, mothers, or consumers in the global economy, but we are also all those things simultaneously. Singular and monolithic categorizations of women in discourses of globalization circumscribe ideas about experience, agency, and struggle. There is a divide between false, overstated images of victimized and empowered womanhood, and they negate each other. We need to further explore how this divide plays itself out in terms of a social majority/minority, One-Third/Two-Thirds World characterization. The concern here is with whose agency is being colonized and who is privileged in these pedagogies and scholarship.

Because social movements are crucial sites for the construction of knowledge, communities, and identities, it is very important for feminists to direct themselves toward them. The anti-globalization movements of the last five years have proved that one does not have to be a multinational corporation, controller of financial capital, or transnational governing institution to cross national borders. These movements form an important site for examining the construction of transborder democratic citizenship. Anti-globalization movements have numerous spatial and social origins. These include anti-corporate environmental movements such as the Narmada Bachao Andolan in central India and movements against environmental racism in the US Southwest, as well as the anti-agribusiness small-farmer movements around the world.

While women are present as leaders and participants in most of these anti-globalization movements, a feminist agenda emerges only in the post-Beijing 'women's rights as human rights' movement and in some peace and environmental justice movements. In other words, while girls and women are central to the labor of global capital, anti-globalization work does not seem to draw on feminist analysis or strategies. Thus, while I have argued that feminists need to be anti-capitalists, I would now argue that anti-globalization activists and theorists also need to be feminists. Gender is ignored as a category of analysis and a basis for organizing in most of the anti-globalization movements, and anti-globalization (and anti-capitalist critique) does not appear to be central to feminist organizing projects, especially in the First World/North. In terms of women's movements, the earlier 'sisterhood is global' form of internationalization of the women's movement has now shifted into the 'human rights' arena. This shift in language from 'feminism' to 'women's rights' can be called the mainstreaming of the feminist movement – a (successful) attempt to raise the issue of violence against women onto the world stage.

If we look carefully at the focus of the anti-globalization movements, it is the bodies and labor of women and girls which constitute the heart of these struggles. Women have been in leadership roles in some of the cross-border alliances against corporate injustice. Thus, making gender, and women's bodies and labor, visible and theorizing this visibility as a process of articulating a more inclusive politics are crucial aspects of feminist anti-capitalist critique. Beginning from the social location of poor women of color of the Two-Thirds World is an important, even crucial, place for feminist analysis; it is precisely the potential epistemic privilege of these communities of women which opens up the space for demystifying capitalism and for envisioning transborder social and economic justice.

A transnational feminist practice depends on building feminist solidarities across the divisions of place, identity, class, work, belief, and so on. In these very fragmented times it is both very difficult to build these alliances and also never more important to do so.

Notes

1 Esteva and Prakash (1998: 16–17) define these categorizations thus: 'The social minorities are those groups in both the North and the South that share homogeneous ways of modern (Western) life all over the world. ... They are also usually classified as the upper classes of every society ... The social majorities have no regular access to most of the goods and services defining the average "standard of living" in the industrial countries.' (Ed.: Some notes are abridged.)

2 See Shiva et al. (1997). For a provocative argument about indigenous knowledges, see Dei (2000).

3 This book remains one of the smartest, most accessible, and complex analyses of the color, class, and gender of globalization.

4 The literature on gender and globalization is vast, and I do not pretend to review it in any comprehensive way. I draw on three particular texts to critically summarize what I consider to be the most useful and provocative analyses of this area: Eisenstein (1998); Marchand and Runyan (2000); and Basu et al. (2001).

5 See essays in Kempadoo and Doezema (1998) and Puar (2001).

6 Discourses of globalization include the pro-globalization narratives of neoliberalism and privatization, but they also include anti-globalization discourses produced by progressives, feminists, and activists in the anti-globalization movement.

References

Basu, A., I. Grewal, C. Kaplan and L. Malkki (eds) (2001) 'Globalization and gender', special issue of *Signs: Journal of Women in Culture and Society*, 26(4).

Dei, G. J. S. (2000) 'Rethinking the role of indigenous knowledges in the academy', *International Journal of Inclusive Education*, 4(2): 111–33.

Eisenstein, Z. (1998) *Global Obscenities: Patriarchy, Capitalism, and the Lure of Cyberfantasy*, New York: New York University Press.

Esteva, G. and M. S. Prakash (1998) *Grassroots Post-modernism: Remaking the Soil of Cultures*, London: Zed Books.

Kempadoo, K. and J. Doezema (eds) (1998) *Global Sex Workers: Rights, Resistance, and Redefinition*, New York: Routledge.

Marchand, M. H. and A. Runyan (eds) (2000) *Gender and Global Restructuring: Sightings, Sites and Resistances*, New York: Routledge.

Mohanty, C. T. (1986) 'Under Western eyes: feminist scholarship and colonial discourses', *Boundary 2*, 12(3): 333–58.

Parreñas, R. S. (2001) 'Transgressing the nation state: the partial citizenship and "imagined global community" of migrant Filipina domestic workers', *Signs*, 26(4): 1129–54.

Puar, J. K. (2001) 'Global circuits: trans-national sexualities and Trinidad', *Signs*, 26(4): 1039–67.

Shiva, V., A. H. Jafri, G. Bedi and R. Holla-Bhar (1997) *The Enclosure and Recovery of the Commons: Biodiversity, Indigenous Knowledge, and Intellectual Property Rights*, New Delhi: Research Foundation for Science, Technology, and Ecology.

39 | Challenges in transnational feminist mobilization

Aili Mari Tripp

The expansion and diversification of the international women's movement over the past three decades are a healthy development. But one of the biggest constraints on transnational feminism today comes from problems in *the manner in which* issues are treated and discussed, *how* to best achieve agreed upon goals, and *how* international support should be rendered. This chapter explores some of the continuing constraints on building and maintaining transnational ties that arise not only from the different agendas, strategies and priorities of women in different parts of the globe, but also from a lack of appreciation of the goals and strategies of others working in different contexts.

There have been many important initiatives from the global North that have exhibited strong transnational cooperation, for example, the '34 Million Friends' campaign started by Lois Abraham and Jane Roberts in 2002 and the Help Afghan Women campaign of the Feminist Majority. However, when international support is extended, it is not always offered in ways that reflect an understanding of other women's movements, their local contexts, and their needs.

Keck and Sikkink (1998) describe what they call the boomerang effect, in which non-governmental organizations bypass their own state and seek out transnational advocacy networks, such as those around human rights, indigenous rights, the environment and women's rights, in order to pressure their state from the outside to resolve a conflict. Such transnational networks provide local actors with access, leverage, information and resources that they otherwise would not have. The boomerang model assumes that local actors are the ones seeking support from the outside to strengthen their cause vis-à-vis their own state. Yet often transnational movements engage with local issues from the outside while remaining detached from the domestic movements mobilized around these and related causes.

Hubris in transnational assistance

Sometimes outsiders believe they are providing an unquestioned 'good' in taking action on behalf of another group of people, [... or] believe they know better than those on the ground what strategy should be adopted and thus wilfully ignore requests by local activists to desist in their activities. One such case was the transnational response to the introduction of Islamic sharia law in northern Nigeria in the last few years. These laws have especially serious negative repercussions for women, but international attempts to put pressure on the courts in northern Nigeria have often backfired.

In March 2002 a sharia court in Bakori, Katsina State, sentenced Amina Lawal Kurami to death by stoning, finding her guilty of adultery after she had given birth to a baby out of wedlock. In the Lawal case, thousands of petitions were launched to save her from stoning and about 33,800 websites mentioned her case. When she was finally acquitted, the news media outlets and petition websites gave almost full credit to international pressures. They failed to comprehend the reasons for her release or the potential damage their campaigns may have caused.

Nigerian activists and lawyers with BAOBAB for Women's Rights (a Nigerian organization which was working most closely with these cases) asked international activists to desist from sending letters of protest about the Lawal case. They were concerned that many of the letters were based on inaccurate information, which resulted in a loss of credibility for them and further setbacks because it was assumed that local activists had provided this inaccurate information to outsiders. BAOBAB pleaded in an email sent to various listserves that outsiders 'check the accuracy of the information with local activists, before further circulating petitions or responding to them'.

BAOBAB's work around the Amina Lawal case was also harmed by international activists who presented Islam and Africa as barbaric and savage in their petition campaign. To Nigerian activists these letters and petitions simply perpetuated racism and played into the hands of the Islamic political religious extremists.

Not all international organizations ignored BAOBAB's plea against international petitions. Women Living Under Muslim Laws (WLUML) and the International Association of Women Judges (IAWJ), for example, provided important support. WLUML told the Nigerian partners that they needed to provide up-to-date and accurate information to the international community. In cooperation with their Nigerian partners, they helped write and disseminate such information. When asked not to circulate the petitions, IAWJ then asked how it could better support the defence efforts, and instead helped raise funds to cover defence legal costs.

'Amnesty's International Secretariat and Amnesty USA similarly issued press releases disassociating themselves from the petitions. They negotiated with their Nigerian partners when they disagreed with their analysis and approach, and as a result changes in tactics on both sides occurred (Imam 2004).

Oversimplifications and disregard of context

When outsiders do not take the time to learn about or attend to the particulars of a situation, their efforts can backfire. This is particularly true in conflict situations, where one-sided support for a particular local group can have extremely harmful unintended consequences. As one example, consider the case of the article written by University of Michigan law professor Catherine MacKinnon in *Ms* magazine about pornography as the motivator for the rapes of Muslims and Croatians in former Yugoslavia during the war in Bosnia (1992–95).

Vesna Kesic and other local women's rights activists claim that MacKinnon made numerous unsubstantiated statements that could not be verified by people working with rape survivors in Bosnia. MacKinnon, who provided legal counsel to rape survivors in Bosnia, claimed that pornography had saturated Yugoslavia prior to the conflict. Yet Kesic notes that pornography was not openly permitted in Yugoslavia under socialism. MacKinnon also took a debate about pornography that came out of the US context and superimposed it on to a dramatically different context in an attempt to persuade a US audience that pornography sexualizes violence against women, being the 'theory' behind the practice of rape. For Kesic and others, MacKinnon trivialized the horrors of this genocide by equating its widespread rape and killing with pornography. But the biggest damage inflicted by the article was the way in which its arguments were used to stir ethnic hatred and promote revenge.

In general, transnational activists who ignore the local context of issues in favour of the way the concern is understood by their own constituents 'back home' do more to exploit the issue for their own political gain than to lay a groundwork for real alliance.

Rescue paradigm

A third problem is that some transnational feminist actors operate within a 'rescue paradigm' that seems to legitimize ignoring local actors altogether by stressing their neediness and backwardness. Concern about such ethnocentric attitudes has been especially raised by organizations throughout Africa which are fighting to abolish the practice of female genital cutting. Western organizations and individuals have often sought to champion this cause in a way that disregards and trivializes local efforts. Seble Dawitt, a Somali lawyer, and film-maker Salem Mekuria pointed [this] out in a 1993 *New York Times* editorial page article regarding Alice Walker's movie *Warrior Marks* and book *Possessing the Secret of Joy*. Mekuria explained further in a longer essay: '... Indeed, the depiction of the victims of this oppressive practice in *Warrior Marks* is so demeaning that the overall effect is one of denigration rather than empowerment.'

Another aspect of this problem in transnational advocacy comes from distancing others and making too much of differences between 'us', the privileged, and the 'other'. This approach refuses to recognize not only the common humanity of women but also the commonality of experiences of gender oppression despite the differences. Not only does this lead to fantasies of rescue that exaggerate Western women's power and freedom but often also to an inability to see local feminists as active, intelligent, competent partners for their efforts.

Homogenizing and essentializing partners

Stereotypes further complicate the ability to recognize and cooperate with partners. Outsiders sometimes homogenize and essentialize the other as 'all Africans', 'all Arabs', 'all Asians' and all peoples who are different from 'us'. 'All' of one group or another is reduced to a particular practice or belief, to which the entire society is depicted as mindlessly adhering. A good example of this overgeneralization and flattening out of complexity and conflict can be found in the reaction to veiling. In 1996, the Taliban took over Afghanistan and imposed harsh restrictions on women. The Feminist Majority and many celebrities, led by Mavis Leno, took up a well-intentioned petition campaign to 'save' the burqa-clad women who were victimized by this regime. The Feminist Majority has become more careful in the way it talks about the burqa in response to criticism, but initially this passive-victim image was one of the primary ways in which women in Afghanistan were depicted. The focus on the burqa collapsed women's experiences into a single practice and did not sufficiently allow for Afghan women's own experiences, choices, opinions and agency to matter.

In spite of the Feminist Majority's ethnocentric rhetoric, which included press releases referring to the USA as the 'civilized world' in contrast to 'barbaric' Afghanistan, used to build support for the cause, the campaign this organization launched was part of an important initiative. This was, as sociologist Valentine Moghadam (2003) explained, perhaps the first time a women's issue had generated so much interest as to influence US foreign policy. It demonstrated the power of transnational advocacy movements in putting the spotlight on and generating support for Afghan women's access to education, health services, employment, political participation and legal equality.

Conclusions

All four cases considered here – responding to the Islamic courts' punishments for alleged adultery in northern Nigeria, rape in the conflict in former Yugoslavia, female genital cutting in Africa, and women under the Taliban in Afghanistan – share many similarities. In all cases international support was welcomed, but the way it was being delivered was a problem. Local activists were not empowered by the interventions and in some cases women were endangered more than helped. If domestic feminist movements are to more effectively engage in global efforts to improve the status of women, there is much to learn from these cases. The most salient implications seem to be the following.

First, international actors should consider that local actors have the most intimate knowledge of issues, other players, conditions, laws and cultural sensitivities. Domestic actors often have greater legitimacy than outsiders. Taking action that affects another society requires consulting local organizations properly regarding the advisability of a strategy, its timing, and way in which the issues are framed in the international arena.

Working closely and learning from the expertise of local activists is not just a matter of respect; failure to do so can also endanger people on the ground and create unnecessary hostilities. This was the case in both Yugoslavia and Nigeria, where activists warned against the dangers of making statements in the international media that could prove inflammatory and exacerbate matters in an already very tense situation.

Second, international actors' selection of issues to highlight should reflect local priorities, not use the problems of women in one part of the world to recruit members or donors for themselves. Starvation does not grab headlines the way female genital cutting or honour killings do, yet a slow painful death by starvation is far more common than honour killings.

The selection of issues I fear sometimes reflects a fascination with the distant exotic. The Western feminist interest in difference has at times also led to an exoticization of that difference and a sense of superiority. As Vesna Kesic explains, this may be because we believe women in the West do not suffer the same brutalities that women elsewhere suffer as a result of their cultures.

Charlotte Bunch and Susana Fried (1996) argued that women across the globe were able to unite around the issue of violence against women because it was based on a universality of justice rather than a commonality of experience. I argue that it is the ability to recognize the commonality of experience in the other which makes it possible to conceive of a universality of justice. Greater transnational engagement by the North would create greater understanding of these commonalities and better bases on which cooperation can be built.

Third, to be taken seriously as global advocates for women's rights, women in the most powerful countries in the world have a particular role to play. They can play more of a role in trying to influence the International Monetary Fund, World Bank, World Trade Organization and other bodies that affect millions of women around the world. Without a fundamental change in the Northern movements and their re-engagement on a new basis with the global women's movements, we are not going to see fundamental changes in the global inequalities that underlie so many of the problems women face worldwide.

Fourth, movements in the North, in particular, need to be more engaged in transnational issues not just to improve conditions for women around the world, but for their own sake. Women in the USA, for example, can learn from strategies that have worked elsewhere and profit from international debates and lessons on issues we have not yet fully engaged.

The cautions raised in this chapter are not an excuse to withdraw from transnational engagement for fear of doing more harm than good. Rather, they are an appeal to work across international borders more collaboratively, with higher regard for local actors, and with greater understanding of the complexities of the issues involved.

References

BAOBAB for Women's Rights (2003) 'Please stop the international Amina Lawal protest letter campaigns', Signed Ayesha Imam (board member) and Sindi Medar-Gould (executive director), May, August and September, Lagos.

Bunch, C. and S. Fried (1996) 'Beijing '95: moving women's human rights from margin to center', *Signs*, 22(1): 200–204.

Imam, A. (2004) 'International solidarity strategies and women's rights under sharia law in Nigeria', Presented at the conference 'Women, Islam and transnational feminism', organized by the Women & Citizenship Research Circle, University of Wisconsin-Madison, 5 March.

Keck, M. E. and K. Sikkink (1998) *Activists beyond Borders: Advocacy Networks in International Politics*, Ithaca, NY: Cornell University Press.

MacKinnon, C. A. (1993) 'Turning rape into pornography: postmodern genocide', *Ms*, 4(1): 24–31.

Mekuria, S. (1995) 'Female genital mutilation in Africa: some African views', *ACAS Bulletin*, 44/45.

Moghadam, V. M. (2003) 'Global feminism and women's citizenship in the Muslim world: the cases of Iran, Algeria, and Afghanistan', Prepared for the Conference on Citizenship, Borders, and Gender: Mobility and Immobility, Yale University, 8–10 May.

40 | The international women's commission of La Vía Campesina

Annette Aurélie Desmarais

Rural people remain the poorest of the poor and women in rural households are often the most marginalized. A series of policy changes introduced in the 1980s exacerbated the situation in the countryside: structural adjustment programmes, and new trade agreements culminating in the creation of the World Trade Organization (WTO) in 1994, favoured corporate export agriculture, dismantled domestic support for small-scale farming, and dramatically increased rural poverty. These changes had a devastating impact on rural women (Razavi 2002). La Vía Campesina, a transnational peasant movement, was created in 1993 to respond to these challenges; it realized fairly quickly that to do so effectively required confronting the marginalized position of women in rural society. This chapter examines women's growing presence and influence within La Vía Campesina.[1]

Since La Vía Campesina emerged it has grown rapidly and is considered to be the most politically important transnational agrarian movement in the world (Borras and Franco 2010; Desmarais 2007). Initially bringing together forty-five farm organizations, La Vía Campesina now embraces 148 organizations of peasants, rural women, small-scale farmers, indigenous agrarian communities and rural workers from sixty-nine countries in Asia, the Americas, Europe and Africa.[2] Many national rural organizations are attracted to La Vía Campesina because it has strongly resisted the globalization of a neoliberal and industrial model of agriculture. By 'building unity within diversity' the movement creates much-needed political spaces in which men, women and youth from the North and global South engage in collective struggles against the violence, dispossession and disempowerment experienced in the countryside everywhere. An important part of these struggles includes developing alternatives to the increasing marginalization of peasants and small farmers.

Rural women play a critical role in agricultural production and in maintaining the economic and social fabric of rural communities, yet in most (if not all) countries peasant and farm organizations are very male-dominated. Because of their dominance of national organizations, all five of the initial Vía Campesina leadership – the regional coordinators elected in 1993 at the First International Conference of La Vía Campesina held in Mons, Belgium – were men. But women, who made up 20 per cent of participants in Mons, refused to accept a subordinate role and urged the newly established international peasant movement to tackle gender equality proactively. In the end, while the Mons conference voiced a commitment to strive for women's equal rights to resources and the need for equal participation, it failed to identify mechanisms to ensure the meaningful integration of women.

Consequently, three years later at the Second International Conference held in April 1996 in Tlaxcala, Mexico, women's representation had not increased. The women who attended this conference had struggled for years in their own communities and organizations to integrate gender issues in debates of agricultural policy. For most, this was an ongoing struggle waged at the local, national and regional levels. In Tlaxcala, women delegates demanded no less at the international level and they pushed La Vía Campesina to take concrete actions.

Thus, La Vía Campesina began to address gender issues in a systematic fashion during its Second International Conference. When it came to electing new representatives to the International Coordinating Commission (ICC), a body made up of seven regional coordinators from each of the seven regions of La Vía Campesina, there was much debate, partly because only one woman was elected. Eventually recognizing these highly skewed gender dynamics, conference delegates agreed to form a 'special committee', the International Women's Commission, whose mandate included developing strategies, mechanisms and a plan of action to ensure women's equal participation and representation at all levels of the movement (Vía Campesina Women's Working Group 1996: 1).[3]

Undoubtedly, there are very real limitations to women's auxiliaries and women's secretariats in mixed organizations. Nevertheless, the women delegates in Tlaxcala agreed that a Women's Commission was an important means to enhance women's integration into the growing transnational movement. Importantly, it created a much-needed international political space for women to organize among themselves with the ultimate aim of challenging male domination in rural organizations at the local, national and international levels.

Women quickly occupied their newly won space by meeting only four months after the Tlaxcala conference. This first women's planning session, held in San Salvador, set the tone for future collaboration among women of La Vía Campesina. In attendance were representatives from Europe, North America, South America and Central America.[4] As women spoke from their own experiences of working within peasant and farm organizations a real sense of camaraderie, sharing of insights, and respect for one another permeated the discussions of potential models for work within the Vía Campesina.[5] For many participants this was their first exposure to La Vía Campesina so they spent considerable time learning more about the movement, how it was formed, who was involved, and its goals and ideological foundations. In doing so, they established much common ground. This was especially the case as they worked collectively to broaden La Vía Campesina's concept of 'food sovereignty', broadly defined as the right of nations and peoples to define their own agricultural policies and control their own food systems as an alternative to the dominant model of corporate agriculture.

In studying the draft Vía Campesina Position on Food Sovereignty to be presented at the World Food Summit in Rome in November 1996, women inserted their insights, experiences and expertise to highlight additional issues. For example, to the concern for sustainable farming practices to ensure environmental sustainability women added a human health dimension. For women, as those primarily responsible for the well-being of their families, food sovereignty must include a move to organic production or certainly drastic reduction in the use of health-endangering chemical inputs and an immediate stop to the export of banned agrochemicals. Also, given the impact that agricultural policies were having on women's lives and their unequal access to productive resources (relative to men), women insisted that food sovereignty could be achieved only through women's greater participation in policy development. These and other concerns were subsequently integrated in the final document.

Over the years the International Women's Commission of La Vía Campesina has accomplished a great deal. Between 1996 and 2000 it concentrated its work in the Americas with the women leaders of three regionally based organizations – the Coordinadora Latinoamericana de Organizaciones del Campo (CLOC) in South America, the Asociación de Organizaciones Campesinas Centroamericanas para la Cooperación y el Desarrollo in Central America, and the Windward Islands Farmers Association in the Caribbean – to organize a series of exchanges and workshops. These activities were designed to enhance women's involvement in policy development and actions on food sovereignty and strengthen their capacity to organize at the international level; the ultimate goal was to increase women's participation and representation at all levels and activities of La Vía Campesina.

These activities were a huge success. By sharing ideas, information and experiences, women broadened their understanding of the agricultural realities in different countries and engaged in a collective analysis of the forces affecting the daily lives of people living in rural communities. The discussions ranged from human rights, struggles for genuine agrarian reform, biodiversity and genetic resources, management of natural resources, and the impact of agricultural trade, to different aspects of food sovereignty. Women also shared experiences about alternative production, marketing strategies and organizing in the countryside to address gender inequalities within their organizations. These face-to-face encounters were crucial in facilitating greater understanding and building unity among women of La Vía Campesina in the Americas. Similar exchanges were then held in Asia and Europe with very similar results.

This is not to suggest that the work within the International Women's Commission was without difficulty. The women acknowledged the existence of destructive power struggles among women themselves; cultural biases and lack of understanding sometimes led to cultural insensitivity; a longer history of organizing in some regions contributed to dominance of particular regional interests accompanied by the silencing of others; and some tensions and conflicts were left unattended as communication was often hampered by the lack of translation capacity. There were also organizational weaknesses. For example, initially, unlike the members of the ICC, the representatives to the International Women's Commission were not formally elected during the international conferences. The resulting somewhat informal selection process meant inconsistent representation within the International Women's Commission, and the subsequent lack of continuity hampered women's ability to build a strong, cohesive group of leaders. Perhaps most importantly, traditional gender roles meant that women remained primarily responsible for the care of families, thus making it more difficult to leave their homes and local communities to participate in international meetings. These and other challenges surfaced as the International Women's Commission went about its work of challenging unequal gender relations.

The women of La Vía Campesina believe that they must work together, on equal terms, with their male counterparts to build an alternative agricultural model. As they gained more experience and confidence in working beyond national borders, women increasingly joined the Vía Campesina delegations to international events. Organizing women's meetings prior to key Vía Campesina gatherings – a strategy first identified during the first meeting of the International Women's Commission and often used by the women of the CLOC – has been an especially successful mechanism to ensure women's greater participation and representation. For example, just prior to its Third International Conference held in Bangalore in October 2000, La Vía Campesina organized its First International Women's Assembly which meant that women then represented 43 per cent of the conference delegates.

The Bangalore conference was an important turning point for La Vía Campesina in terms of gender equality. The conference approved a 'Gender Position Paper' that provided a gender analysis of the restructuring and globalization of agriculture; elaborated some key principles and commitments regarding the roles, positions, needs and interests of women; stressed a gender perspective that includes class and ethnicity and the need to strengthen efforts to achieve gender parity at all levels of the movement (Vía Campesina 2000). Perhaps more importantly, the Bangalore conference unanimously agreed to a structural change to double the ICC to include two regional coordinators (one man and one woman) from each of its regions. Finally, La Vía Campesina had reached gender parity in its leadership, at least structurally.

Women have gained significant space and influence within the movement. At the Fifth International Conference of La Vía Campesina held in Maputo in October 2008, women represented 46 per cent of the conference delegates. Women are now more active in decision-making, visible in Vía Campesina actions, and the movement's positions reflect more of a gender analysis. At the time of writing, the ICC is made up of ten women and nine men because both the regional coordinators of the South American region are women.

Significantly, the Maputo conference – guided by the results of the Third Women's Assembly – argued that the violence of the corporate-led neoliberal model of agriculture cannot be separated from violence against women and placed the transformation of gender relations at the heart of the food sovereignty alternative by declaring that 'Food sovereignty means stopping violence against women'.[6] As the Maputo Declaration stated: 'If we do not eradicate violence towards women within our movement, we will not advance in our struggles, and if we do not create new gender relations, we will not be able to build a new society (Vía Campesina 2008).

Changing gender relations, of course, will be a huge challenge given that violence against women is not an issue that many of the male-dominated member organizations of La Vía Campesina ever discuss. Just how successful can an international movement be at tackling such a local issue? Paul Nicholson, former ICC member for the European region, puts it like this:

> Violence against women will now be taken up by national organizations. But it is going to be very difficult and complex because ... we're speaking about changing traditional family relationships and the need to develop a new type of relationship – men and women both at the family and the organizational level. This will be difficult for many organizations. But it is absolutely necessary.[7]

Notes

1 For a detailed exploration of gender dynamics within La Vía Campesina see Desmarais (2007: ch. 6).

2 See www.viacampesina.org.

3 Initially the 'special committee' was called the Vía Campesina Women's Working Group and later changed its name to the International Women's Commission of La Vía Campesina; this chapter uses the latter name throughout but for historical accuracy the references reflect the former.

4 Representatives from eastern Europe, the two Asian regions and South America were unable to attend.

5 As Technical Support to La Vía Campesina I participated in this meeting and the various Vía Campesina international conferences explored in the chapter. The following discussion reflects my observations and information from the written reports of each gathering.

6 One of the slogans used to introduce La Vía Campesina's International Campaign for an End to Violence against Women.

7 Interview conducted 19 November 2008, in Saskatoon, Saskatchewan, Canada.

References

Borras, S., Jr. and J. Franco (2010) 'Food sovereignty and redistributive land policies: exploring linkages, identifying challenges', in H. Wittman, A. A. Desmarais and N. Wiebe (eds), *Food Sovereignty: Reconnecting Food, Nature and Community*, Halifax, NS: Fernwood Publishing.

Desmarais, A. A. (2007) *La Vía Campesina: Globalization and the Power of Peasants*, Halifax, NS/London: Fernwood Publishing/Pluto.

Razavi, S. (ed.) (2002) *Shifting Burdens: Gender and Agrarian Change under Neoliberalism*, West Hartford, CT: Kumarian Press.

Vía Campesina (2000) 'Vía Campesina gender position paper', Position paper approved at the Third International Conference of the Vía Campesina, October, Bangalore.

— (2008) *Declaration of Maputo: V International Conference of La Vía Campesina*, 19–22 October.

Vía Campesina Women's Working Group (1996) 'Report of the Vía Campesina Women's Working Group meeting', held 6–8 August, San Salvador.

41 | Birthing and growing the African Feminist Forum

Ayesha M. Imam[1]

Introduction

The process of giving birth to the African Feminist Forum (AFF) has been long in gestation, including at least one miscarriage along the way.[2] The AFF is conceptualized as an autonomous space for African feminists, through the vehicle of a biennial pan-African meeting (Adeleye-Fayemi 2006). The objectives of the AFF are to develop an independent, self-directed, self-controlled arena where we can analyse our realities; develop our own priorities and strategies; and speak for ourselves. Autonomy and self-definition are integral to feminism, as a right and need in itself, and vis-à-vis patriarchal definitions and control. In the case of the AFF it is also a defence: against the pressures of external definitions (primarily from feminists in the global North); against externally defined agendas (primarily through donor conditionalities): and against accusations of imitating foreigners (primarily from conservative forces as a means of delegitimizing feminism in Africa).

Since the First African Feminist Forum in Accra 2006, there have been other feminist forums along similar lines. These include the Ghanaian Feminist Forum (Accra, 2007); the first Ugandan Feminist Forum (Kampala, 2008); the Nigerian Feminist Forum (Abuja, 2008); a series of reflections in Tanzania (2007/08); and the Second African Feminist Forum (Kampala, 2008).

The conception of the AFF

The AFF brings together African feminist activists to deliberate on issues of key concern to the movement. It was developed out of the growing concern that efforts to advance the rights of women on the continent were under serious threat from a number of sources. The women's movement seemed to have lost its focus and direction. Growing religious, ethnic and cultural fundamentalism had also developed within the movement. At the same time, new actors drawn from communities of marginalized women, such as lesbian and bisexual rights activists, women with disabilities and commercial sex workers, emerged to demand greater autonomy, accountability and representation of their issues among the mainstream women's movement. This often resulted in a reactionary and fundamentalist pandemic, worsening impoverishment, increasing violence against women and girls, and, together with the fact that funding for women's rights issues has been decreasing steadily over the years, the influence of the women's movement on the continent appeared to be in decline. Yet it is widely recognized that women's empowerment is central to development.

A group of feminist activists decided to develop an autonomous space for feminists from the continent to deliberate on these issues, internally reflecting on the current architecture for the advancement of women's rights, as well as assessing and developing strategies to address the external challenges to the movement.

AFF also built on lessons learnt from earlier attempts at cross-continent feminist movement-building. One, in particular, resulted in bitter arguments about what constitutes feminism and/or African feminism that displayed back-biting, appeals to regionalism or nationalism, intolerance, personal attacks, etc. This experience raised the question of how we must not let our own language and values (about democracy, inclusion, transparency) be used to undermine critical work we want to do, while at the same time upholding those values. The other fundamental point that it raised is how we need to be firmer about holding each other to account. These questions inspired the development of an African Feminist Charter as a road map for self-regulation and spelling out terms of engagement.

The Charter of Feminist Principles for African Feminists

The Charter is so named because it was developed by and for feminists who are African, rather than because we feel that these principles are or should be peculiar to Africa.

A key principle of the Charter is defining and naming ourselves publicly as feminists, celebrating feminist identities, rejecting fear of stigma, reclaiming historical struggles by African women against patriarchy, and developing feminist theory and practice to defend and (re)construct women's rights in Africa. In addressing patriarchy, the Charter recognizes the interlocking and often mutually supportive systems of exclusion, marginalization and oppression that must all be addressed.

Individual ethics begins with the assertion of the indivisibility, inalienability and universality of women's human rights. This specifically includes freedom of choice and autonomy regarding bodily integrity issues, including reproductive rights, the right to choose abortion, sexual identity and sexual orientation, as well as a critical engagement with discourses of religion, culture, tradition and domesticity, and recognition of the agency of African women.

However, the Charter goes beyond individual ethics to address collective principles on how we organize our institutions and exercise feminist leadership. It provides standards for the expressed commitment to 'walk the talk', addressing the patriarchal hierarchies in how we work and live. Hence the Charter also addresses using power and authority responsibly. It delineates accountability to women, to the movement, within institutions, to donors. It requires commitment to creating space to support, mentor and nurture, critically engaging and offering solidarity with other feminists.

Developed collectively and adopted at the end of the first AFF, the Charter is a declaration of our standards for accountability and self-regulation and has been used as a principle for inclusion in our feminist autonomous space.

Remaining challenges

The Charter sets out the collective values that we hold as key to our work and to our lives as African feminists. It charts the change we wish to see in our communities, and also how this change is to be achieved. In addition, it spells out our individual and collective responsibilities to the movement and to one another within the movement. There are still challenges in its operationalization. How do we use the Charter for improving our own accountability? What is our responsibility to sisters, who we feel are *not* living up to their stated principles? We also still need to do more to address homophobia and similar issues among ourselves.

Notes

1 With comments and suggestions from members of the African Feminist Forum Working Group: Bisi Adeleye-Fayemi, Jessica Horn, Muthoni Wanyeki, Hope Chigudu, Sylvia Tamale, Bene Madunagu.

2 Including, for example, the racism of a recent US reader on international feminisms, whose editors, when asked why it did not include any work from African feminists, replied that there was no African theorizing on feminism, completely ignoring the work of (a few examples in alphabetical order) Bolanle Awe, Bibi Bakare-Yusuf, Jane Bennet, Codou Bop, Aminata Diaw, Shireen Essof, Rudo Gaidzanwa, Shirin Hassim, Jessica Horn, Ayesha Imam, Patricia MacFadden, Amina Mama, Marjorie Mbilinyi, Charmaine Pereira, Vasu Reddy, Hanan Sabea, Elaine Salo, Fatou Sow, Sylvia Tamale, Dzodzi Tsikata, and of such journals as *Feminist Africa* and *Agenda* among others.

Reference

Adeleye-Fayemi, B. (2006) 'Background document', African Feminist Forum, www.africanfeministforum.org, accessed 8 March 2009.

42 | Women's community organizing in Quito: the paradoxes of survival and struggle

Amy Lind

[W]e vest great hopes in the 'resistance' everywhere in evidence in women's daily lives, household survival strategies, and collective struggles. Yet we too often ignore the less glorious, more contradictory, more paradoxical dimensions and sometimes ephemeral qualities of those struggles. (Sonia Alvarez, 'Concluding reflections: redrawing the parameters of gender struggle')

After the inception of the restructuring process in the early 1980s, Ecuadorian civil society was increasingly called upon to provide essential services for poor families. In many ways, it was poor families themselves which became the new civil society actors – particularly women. Either explicitly or implicitly, it was expected that civil society, including community associations, for-profit and non-profit organizations (e.g. NGOs), would pick up where the state left off. In general, a new model for social service delivery was being proposed, one that relied upon the traditional gender division of labor and assumed that women and families would 'absorb' the costs of restructuring and take on the new market-related responsibilities (Fisher and Kling 1993). The once-familiar public/private boundaries of the state, economy and civil society were being redrawn (Brodie 1994), leading not only to shifts in the broader economy but also to the restructuring of everyday life (Benería 1992): the organization of paid labor sectors, the intensification of domestic work (both paid and unpaid), changes in family structure (as in male migration to the United States and Spain, associated rise in female-headed households; and an increase in household size) and social relations, an evolution in cultural notions of play or vacation (e.g. fewer days off, fewer holiday get-togethers), and alternatives in community development strategies or initiatives. As a result of this restructuring, Ecuadorian business, NGOs and newly formed public/private partnerships began to play important roles in defining the country's social development agenda; this required, among other things, re-envisioning social policy and community development, two important areas of concern for poor neighborhoods.

During this same period, somewhere between five hundred and eight hundred grassroots women's groups were established during the 1980s, as a way for women to address the needs of their communities and families (Centro

María Quilla/CEPAL 1990). In many ways it was these grassroots women who 'mothered' the crisis, both individually and collectively. Through the process, they have gained some political visibility and have helped strengthen feminist demands for women's rights, although, I argue, often at a cost to their own survival. Constructions of femininity, particularly constructions of motherhood, have been central to their organizing strategies, just as they have been to the external actors and institutions that have helped mediate their forms of survival and struggle.

In this chapter I address the paradoxes that emerge through the process of women's community organizing. I discuss Ecuadorian women's responses to the foreign debt crisis and neoliberal restructuring in relation to how feminists, NGO activists, and development professionals intervened in the sphere of women's community organizing. Organized women have gained some political power, visibility and recognition as public actors. Yet in many ways their activism has been reduced to a new form of clientelism among their organizations and the developmentalist state, particularly in light of this neoliberal shift toward positioning poor women explicitly as clients (Schild 2000, 2002).

Organized women have been heralded as acquiring some economic 'empowerment' through their activism, yet overall it is clear that their livelihoods have eroded since the inception of neoliberal development policies, leading to the institutionalization of women's struggles for survival (to 'mothering the crisis') rather than to poverty alleviation or a significant transformation of gender relations. By 'mothering the crisis,' I am referring to the multiple material and symbolic ways in which women have utilized their traditional gender roles in community activism, whether it be to survive economically; to take care of their family; to preserve a tradition, set of values, role or activity; or to challenge traditions, values, and societal inequalities. Self-fulfillment or subjective 'empowerment' has been somewhat of a by-product, albeit an important one, that was 'directed' to some degree by the interventions of external actors such as feminist NGOs and neighborhood movements (Alvarez 1996; Bayard de Volo 2001). Their experiences of 'empowerment' have depended upon these interventions, as scholars such as Sonia Alvarez have observed:

> The interventions or mediations by the state, the church, political parties,
> NGOs, and international and national development and philanthropic agencies
> have many implications for women's 'empowerment.' These multiple actors
> hold agendas and stakes in poor women's struggles which can significantly
> reconfigure, redimension, and even redirect those struggles. (Alvarez 1996: 141)

Their collective political identity has emerged through this broader history of neighborhood organizing in Quito and through influences from the contemporary women's, popular education, liberation theology, and labor movements.

Community women's organizing in Quito, Ecuador

In Quito, women from poor sectors were motivated to organize around the growing economic crisis. Although many of them had never organized before, they worked together, with their neighbors, family members, and friends, to build houses, stake out pieces of land, buy food in bulk and share costs, establish community cooperatives or stores, develop a business, or simply to meet and discuss their lives as new urban settlers. They were not organizing to explicitly challenge or critique gender relations per se but rather to improve the gendered conditions of their daily lives; two very different things.

The possibility for their existence emerged historically through at least two sets of processes and discourses: that of neighborhood organizing and urbanization and that of WID [Women in Development] on the other. The institutionalization of the WID field paved the way for organized groups of women around the world to receive funding and ideological support for their struggles, which were often perceived by Western feminists as necessary and important challenges to entrenched forms of sexism, colonialism, class exploitation, and sometimes racism in poor countries (Kabeer 1994).

WID discourse allowed sectors of poor women to articulate their identities in ways that were actually heard by political institutions. It provided the framework for integrating women into various kinds of projects, including income-generation, microenterprise, rural agriculture, and education.

Community women's organizations came into being through these discourses and lived histories. In Chillogallo some women organized educational workshops to which they invited outside speakers to discuss topics such as women's small business ownership, alternative gardening, gender needs, herbal medicinal remedies, or the foreign debt crisis. The ideas for these types of workshops were often introduced by feminist NGOs influenced by WID discourse and funding. Most of these organizations have participated in marches, planned protests, and national mobilizations, including at the annual International Women's Day march in downtown Quito, protests against the government's adjustment measures, marches against political corruption, and protests against foreign banks, including Citibank and the World Bank. Today, many of the original groups continue to exist; others have been discontinued; and yet other, new groups have emerged.

During the mid to late 1980s, a combination of factors contributed to the increased politicization of urban poor women; these factors revolve around changes in the cost of living, including decreased state subsidies for infrastructure (e.g. roads, electricity, water, gas), higher transportation fares, higher costs of school books and supplies, lower wages because of inflation, the unavailability of well-paying jobs, informalization and 'flexibilization'[1] of the labor market, higher food costs, and heavier domestic burdens for women (Lind 1997).

In central and southern Quito, I interviewed fifty-five members of eight organizations[2] to find out about their backgrounds and reasons for participating during the 1989–93 period. Organizations varied in size, from eight to eighty-one members, partly reflecting the size of each district and the stage of each group's organizational development.[3] Participants came from a wide variety of backgrounds: they ranged in age from fifteen to over sixty years old, although the most active participants typically were in their thirties or forties. Most women were married, two were divorced or separated, nine were single mothers. Some had finished high school, others only the fourth grade; some speak Quichua as their first language, most speak Spanish. The majority identify as Catholic. Average income was almost US$80 per month. Each household spent an average of almost US$70 per month on 'household purchases,' which included food, household maintenance items, clothing, and school materials, among others.[4] A few women lived in extreme poverty with virtually no monthly income; the highest-earning household made approximately US$139 per month. Nine of the single women were single mothers; all of them spoke about the difficulties of simultaneously raising children and earning an income to support them. All the single mothers worked in the informal sector, either as street vendors or as domestic servants, usually six or six and a half days a week. Often, their oldest daughter (who, in one family, was as young as nine years old) took care of her younger siblings. Some mothers who were street vendors brought their youngest children with them to work. Some express relative contentment or perhaps resolution about their life situations, despite the fact that they have little money; others, often the women in their twenties, describe feeling hopeless and dream about 'making it' in college and/or finding a way to get to the United States.

While the members of the Centro Femenino 8 de Marzo come from a wide variety of backgrounds, they do share some experiences that make their sense of daily life and globalization a shared identity. One aspect of their shared identity concerns their socio-economic location in Chillogallo in the Quito metropolitan area. Several expressed feeling tired and worn out and/or feeling frustrated with their maternal/family roles and angry about the economic situation; these feelings were something that most of them identified with and shared as a group.

The majority of the women in Chillogallo that I interviewed (thirty-three out of fifty-five) depend upon some type of exchange such as ironing, washing, or tailoring clothes. Another common activity was taking turns going to the market, buying food in bulk, and distributing it among organization members. They all spoke of having less time and more household responsibilities, a situation that researchers have reported on in several countries undergoing adjustment measures (Dwyer and Bruce 1988; Benería and Feldman 2000; Menjivar 2002). They devoted more time to household chores, their daily routines had become longer, they worked longer days as a result of not being able to afford outside resources such as transportation, hiring someone to iron clothes, and affordable groceries (Lind 1990).

In relation to this, Centro Femenino 8 de Marzo members perceived changes in their gender identities and roles in the context of the economic crisis. In a sense, their elevated status as 'mothers' – a status ascribed to them, among others, through religious discourses of *marianismo* and political discourses of motherhood and family – was being challenged; the power they perceived to have in the private, reproductive sphere was under scrutiny and they felt marginalized from the public sphere of politics and decision-making.[5] Neoliberal discourse brought with it the emphasis on poor women as clients and volunteers for the free market.

Because motherhood was linked to family survival, national development, and women's societal status in neoliberal discourse, Centro Femenino 8 de Marzo members made use of their maternal roles to struggle for access to resources, including a challenge to development policies. In this regard, it was not out of sheer economic necessity that women organized in their so-called reproductive roles; rather, a combination of cultural, political and discursive factors played into their motivations for participating. They faced discrimination in society as a result of their location within structures of gender, race and class. Yet they also acknowledged that they had a certain status; with motherhood came certain benefits and forms of respect. This elevated status is the flipside of gender discrimination; the two occur hand in hand, an important aspect of constructions of femininity (and masculinity) in cultural contexts where motherhood and normative heterosexuality are glorified (Jetter et al. 1997; Kaplan et al. 1999; Lind and Share 2003).

The paradoxes of struggle and survival

The paradoxes of women's survival and struggle occur within the culturally constructed boundaries of the 'public' and 'private,' sometimes challenging or transgressing these boundaries, other times reinforcing them. They operate on various levels, including institutional, policy, cultural, political, economic, and identity production.

Indeed, many women have benefited personally from their participation in community organizations. They have learned new skills, such as organic gardening, arts and crafts, conflict resolution, local planning, and how to establish a small business. A few of them have received very small salaries for their roles as organizers and leaders. Some speak more comfortably about family issues that they had previously viewed as private and or shameful. Some felt empowered about speaking out loud, in front of a group; others felt empowered by sharing a personal experience or past form of victimization with other women (e.g. incest, sexual abuse by a local priest, domestic violence from a partner or in-law). These are forms of empowerment that cannot be taken away from them, nor can their new understandings of their gender roles and political and economic participation.

Similarly, as a group, the organization has gained political power and visibility through members' participation in protests, marches, and collaborations with their community, NGOs, and local politicians. Now the women are part of a much broader network of women's and feminist groups in civil society. Their own survival strategies have converged well with one of the goals of neoliberal economic and social development policies: to redistribute the responsibility and management of social welfare to private sectors. The women's political identities reflect and give meaning to these paradoxes. Neoliberal restructuring has exacerbated the paradox of their struggle since women have been galvanized to action because their perceived identities and roles as mothers are threatened by economic scarcity, foreign debt, and globalization. They struggle to address material needs such as food distribution, yet they have been increasingly positioned to absorb the largely invisible transfer of welfare responsibilities; in essence, to serve as mothers of the crisis. Thus simply increasing their roles in the development process and/or in the market does not necessarily translate into their 'empowerment.' Women's struggles for survival, then, are best viewed as paradoxical and as economic- or material-based, as well as cultural-political struggles over the meanings ascribed to their identities, citizen status, and 'roles in development.'

Conclusion

Chillogallo women's relationships with feminists and development professionals, along with global and regional feminist discourses, shaped their own political identities and strategies. It was also clear by 1990 that their struggle was becoming institutionalized and depoliticized by development planners. The 1997 political crisis in Ecuador created a new set of political and economic circumstances that led Chillogallo women to continue their protests against the state and foreign banks and institutions. While community-based women's organizations negotiated the terms of neoliberal social and economic policies in the local sphere, other groups of (primarily middle-class) women negotiated and helped implement these very policies at the state level, in NGOs, and internationally. Whereas elite feminist-issue networks became stronger during this period, poorer women's groups remained relatively marginalized, despite their increased participation in national networks. Because of these structural issues and paradoxes, it is difficult to say with certainty whether women's community mobilization entirely benefits them or is a disservice. The question remains, however, to what extent have their local struggles contributed to broader social change and to changes in their own lives?

Notes

1 'Flexibilization' (*flexibilización*), a term used widely in some Latin American countries, refers to the fragmented nature of global production processes, in which workers are increasingly hired as temporary or part-time employees, on a piecework basis, or in small workshops where labor conditions are less than optimal and pay is lower than in more formalized business or factory settings. Labor flexibilization has increased in Ecuador, particularly in sectors where employees are working indirectly for large regional or foreign corporations (e.g. Brazilian, Argentine, US and Japanese industries).

2 The eight organizations had a total membership of 214.

3 The Chillogallo women's organization was the largest. It was also the oldest and most established organization.

4 At the time of the study, the sucre was valued at 1,800 to one US dollar. The average for monthly purchases is based on a weekly average of S31,370.

5 According to some scholars, '*marianismo*,' the female corollary to '*machismo*,' is a cultural and religious concept 'where the ideal of womanhood is self-abnegating motherhood … [t]his is very much reinforced by the iconography of the Virgin Mary that is central to Catholicism' (Craske 1999: 12). The virgin mother is 'an impossible role model to follow,' as Nikki Craske points out, yet *marianismo*, with its emphasis on motherhood, has significantly shaped women's involvement in Latin American politics.

References

Alvarez S. (1996) 'Concluding reflections: redrawing the parameters of gender struggle', in J. Friedmann, R. Abers and L. Autler (eds), *Emergences: Women's struggles for livelihood in Latin America*, Los Angeles, CA: UCLA Latin American Center, pp. 153–84.

Bayard de Volo, L. (2001) *Mothers of Heroes and Martyrs: Gender Identity Politics in Nicaragua, 1979–1999*, Baltimore, MD: Johns Hopkins University Press.

Benería, L. (1992) 'Accounting for women's work: the progress of two decades', *World Development*, 20(11): 1547–60.

Benería, L. and S. Feldman (2000) (eds) *Unequal Burden: Economic Crises, Persistent Poverty and Women's Work*, Boulder, CO: Westview Press.

Brodie, J. (1994) 'Shifting the boundaries: gender and the politics of restructuring', in Isabella Bakker (ed.), *The Strategic Silence: Gender and Economic Policy*, London: Zed Books, pp. 46–60.

Centro María Quilla (1991) *Protagonismo de las mujeres en el levantamiento indígena*, Quito: Centro María Quilla.

Centro María Quilla/CEPAL (1990) *Mujeres, educación y conciencia de género en Ecuador*, Quito: Centro María Quilla.

Craske, N. (1999) *Women and Politics in Latin America*, Oxford: Polity Press.

Dwyer, D. and J. Bruce (eds) (1988) *A Home Divided: Women and Income in the Third World*, Palo Alto, CA: Stanford University Press.

Fisher, R. and J. Kling (eds) (1993) 'Mobilizing the community: local politics in the era of the global city', *Urban Affairs Annual Review*, 41, Beverly Hills, CA: Sage Publications.

Jetter, A., A. Orleck and D. Taylor (eds) (1997) *The Politics of Motherhood: Activist Voices from Left to Right*, Lebanon: University Press of New England.

Kabeer, N. (1994) *Reversed Realities: Gender Hierarchies in Development Thought*, New York: Verso.

Kaplan, C., N. Alarcón and M. Moallem (eds) (1999) *Between Woman and Nation: Nationalisms, Transnational Feminisms, and the State*, Durham, NC: Duke University Press.

Lind, A. (1990) *Economic Crisis, Women's Work and the Reproduction of Gender Ideology: Popular Women's Organizations in Quito, Ecuador*, MRP thesis, Cornell University.

— (1995) *Gender, Development and Women's Political Practices in Ecuador*, PhD dissertation, Cornell University.

— (1997) 'Gender, development and urban

social change: women's community
action in global cities', *World Development*, 25(8): 1205–24.

Lind, A. and J. Share (2003) 'Queering
development: institutionalized heterosexuality in development theory, practice and politics in Latin America', in
K.-K. Bhavnani, J. Foran and P. Kurian
(eds), *Feminist Futures: Re-Imagining
Women, Culture and Development*,
London: Zed Books, pp. 55–73.

Menjivar, C. (ed.) (2002) 'Structural
changes and gender relations in Latin
America and the Caribbean', Special
issue, *Journal of Developing Societies*,
18: 2–3.

Schild, V. (2000) 'Neo-liberalism's
new gendered market citizens: the
"civilizing" dimension of social programmes in Chile', *Citizenship Studies*,
4 (3): 275–305.

— (2002) 'Engendering the new social
citizenship in Chile: NGOs and social
provisioning under neo-liberalism',
in M. Molyneux and S. Razavi (eds),
Gender Justice, Development and Rights,
Oxford: Oxford University Press,
pp. 170–203.

43 | Feminist nation-building in Afghanistan: an examination of the Revolutionary Association of the Women of Afghanistan (RAWA)

Jennifer L. Fluri

> The freedom of a nation is to be achieved by itself – similarly the real emancipation of women can be realized only by themselves. If that freedom is bestowed by others, it may be seized and violated at any time. (RAWA statement, 8 March 2004)

Women-led political organizations that implement feminist and nationalist ideologies and operate as separate from, rather than associated with, male-dominated or patriarchal nationalist organizations are both significant and under-explored areas of gender, feminist, and nationalism studies. Theoretical and empirical feminist analyses of nationalism examine the various ways in which women have participated in nationalist struggles over time and across geographic space (Yuval-Davis 1996). Gender roles and behavioral norms are, therefore, malleable and altered for political purposes, particularly during times of heightened nationalism, war, and/or conflict (Mazurana et al. 2005). Feminism, in connection with nationalist identity politics, is often combined with and then subsumed into male-dominated nationalist groups (West 1997; Nelson 2001). Analyses that identify the success of feminism and nationalism underscore the inclusion of feminist ideologies or political positions within the scope and scale of nationalist politics (Herr 2003).

 This research on gender and nationalism has been particularly significant for critical examinations of nationalist and independence movements in post-colonial spaces and/or anti-modernist struggles that were complemented by the rise of political (and nationalist) Islam (Kaplan et al. 1999). These studies critically examine male-dominated and/or patriarchal nationalist struggles and the fluidity of women's inclusion or exclusion from active participation in these movements and in post-independence governments.

 The Revolutionary Association of the Women of Afghanistan's (RAWA) unique approach to political mobilization is both similar to and divergent from feminist nationalist groups in other socio-political contexts. RAWA remains outside the public political center while enacting reforms to patriarchal structures within kinship groups and through politically charged social programs within the spaces of its private and clandestine operations. This article examines the various methods of political resistance and mobilization implemented by RAWA to counter existing patriarchies and envision and (at times) experience feminist nationalism.

Data collection

A mixed-method approach was implemented for data collection.[1] This included email correspondences with RAWA and with their international support network in the United States between 2001 and 2005, and content analysis of the organization's website, political magazine (*Payam-e-Zan*), and other official publications and press releases. Additionally, the author conducted two field visits to their programs and facilities in Pakistan.

Afghanistan's revolutionary women from Marx to marginalization

In the 1960s and 1970s there were several forms of political philosophy from Marxism to hardline Islamic fundamentalism competing for ideological space within the growing intellectual class in Afghanistan's capital city, Kabul. Marxist intellectuals formed the People's Democratic Party of Afghanistan (PDPA), which eventually coordinated a successful and bloody coup known as the *Saur* (April) revolution in 1978. After its takeover of the central government, the PDPA (renamed the Democratic Republic of Afghanistan – DRA) initiated several social and political reforms in Afghanistan, including efforts to emancipate women.

Kandiyoti (1988) identifies Afghanistan's social structure as a form of 'classic patriarchy,' where the male head of household retains full authority over women and men in his kinship group. Efforts by former Kabul governments to 'modernize' and liberate and/or improve women's educational and economic opportunities throughout the twentieth century were largely limited to women of higher socio-economic classes, larger ethnic groups, and/or women living in Kabul.

Meena, who founded RAWA in 1977 at age twenty, was part of the largest and most politically powerful ethnic group (Pashtuns), from an upper socio-economic class, and a member of the student body at Kabul University. However, for Meena increasing women's status in Afghanistan included leaving the university and tackling various social inequities (Brodsky 2003). From the beginning, her organization actively recruited women from lower socioeconomic classes and ethnic minority groups. Irrespective of the DRA's promise of women's liberation, the *Saur* revolution and subsequent Soviet invasion and occupation made feminism marginal and women's rights[2] symbolically central. As resistance to emancipation efforts increased, women's rights organizations associated with the DRA were disbanded (Emandi 2002).

Despite the Soviet Union's 'promise' of women's emancipation, RAWA did not support the foreign presence/occupation of the USSR. Members organized demonstrations against the Soviet occupation, and became increasingly concerned with the amount of financial support the extremists were receiving from the United States over more politically moderate groups.

The growth of this organization continued and consisted of both private and public acts of defiance, including public marches and political demonstrations against the Soviet occupiers and the extremist groups. They also began publishing a political magazine, *Payam-e-Zan* (Women's Message), in 1980. This magazine continues to be published as a tool for political mobilization and a forum for presenting its ideological position and critiques of Afghan (and international) politics.

Their programs have expanded over time to include medical care facilities and mobile health teams, literacy programs, orphanages, income-generating projects, food aid, emergency medical services, and reconstruction.[3] The social projects are politically motivated and highlighted to demonstrate what the state/nation *should* do for its people and consequently what RAWA *does* for 'its' people and would do for the entire nation if it attained political power at the national scale.

RAWA after Meena In the mid-1980s Meena and several other RAWA members became targets of the extremist mujahideen/jihadi groups and the Khad (Afghan version of the KGB). Several members were imprisoned, tortured, and killed. In 1987, Meena was assassinated,[4] which both devastated RAWA and reaffirmed its commitment to political change in Afghanistan. Meena is positioned by the organization as its inspiration and martyred leader. Images of her are present in every program and she remains the only public and visibly identifiable leader of the organization. After Meena's death, in order to secure its existing membership and future, the organization operated completely underground. This clandestine approach to politics continues today and includes using pseudonyms, wearing the burqa/chadori[5] or other forms of veiling to conceal identities, avoiding being photographed or using images of current (living) members in its publications, moving 'safe houses' continually to avoid suspicion, and not publishing a physical location/address.

As conditions worsened for Afghans during the extremist mujahideen takeover and civil war (1992–96) and the rule of the Taliban (1996–2001), RAWA's resistance methods became more covert. These included the use of documentation as resistance by photographing and videotaping human rights abuses to discredit the political legitimacy of these extremist groups. Members refuse to compromise politically with any group or individual with ties to extremist/fundamentalist groups, which in one respect reinforces their political commitment to women's rights, secularism, and democracy, and in another respect marginalizes them from contemporary mainstream politics.

RAWA also experienced tremendous financial[6] difficulty during the civil war and the Taliban regimes. Late in 1996, as the Taliban militarily controlled the capital city, Kabul, RAWA members living in Pakistan began using email and developed a one-page website, which eventually grew into a multilingual award-winning site. This use of the Internet and email technologies facilitated the development of a transnational network of supporters (Fluri 2006).

Male supporters and counter-patriarchal gender politics

The integrity of the organizational structure prevents men from becoming members, while actively including them as supporters. Most male supporters are connected to the organization in three significant ways: through a kinship bond; as children growing up in RAWA-run orphanages or schools; or in political solidarity with the organization's nationalist goals. Once integrated into the organization, both female members and male supporters articulate feminist and women's rights discourses.

Men are also integrated as partners in political struggles and as evidence of successful feminist politics. Men associated with RAWA are not 'classic' patriarchs and do not obtain any decision-making or powerful position within the organization. Men participate in social and political programs and articulate the organization's feminist and nationalist vision, including bringing female family members into the organization. The strategic use of men as feminist partners helps to diminish patriarchal notions of women's inabilities and limited capacity in the Afghan family and larger social structures.

RAWA members articulate an understanding of the gains and losses experienced by women in male-dominated nationalist movements. 'We have learned from our Algerian and Iranian sisters, we cannot put the goals of the nation before women's rights' (RAWA personal communication, 2003). Negotiating within existing patriarchal structures (outside the organization) also requires male supporters to act as advocates who, because of their gender, have (at times) more influence and, subsequently, a greater ability to counsel and convince men (and sometimes women within kinship groups) to support RAWA's political platforms. This is particularly significant when the organization attempts to negotiate with families around issues such as: preventing a child marriage; domestic violence; and a women's membership in RAWA.

In addition to local male supporters, the organization also developed (largely through the use of the Internet beginning late in 1996) a cadre of transnational supporters (both men and women) who articulate a financial and/or political commitment to RAWA. Similarly to the restrictions on male membership, transnational female supporters are also prevented from becoming members. Membership remains contingent on nationality and location, which ensure women's leadership within the organization, autonomy from male-dominated nationalist groups, and a spatial fixity to the organization's on-the-ground commitment to the Afghan nation.

RAWA renegotiates patriarchal structures by working within the family as a prime site for the implementation of its feminist-nationalist ideologies. These renegotiations include partnerships with men and the bio-social reproduction of the organization as a mirror of its idealized nation.

RAWA's ideal nation is defined as secular and democratic with a focus on social programs and women's rights. Thus, it positions itself against the sovereign state and, by way of its programs, develops a collective Afghan feminist-national identity. Although RAWA does not retain a position of power within or outside the emerging Afghan state, its political goals include an ideal construction of the Afghan nation and remain nationalist in scope and scale.

RAWA also seeks to preserve Afghan 'culture' through its vision of Afghan national identity. The Cultural and Arts Committee produces audiotapes of patriotic songs, which are well-known national songs that have been altered to support its political ideology. Cultural teachings provide children with an understanding and remembrance of their *Watan* (homeland) under RAWA's rubric. Children in the orphanages are also required to speak the national languages of Afghanistan rather than the language of their respective ethno-linguistic groups.

Commitment to ethnic diversity and inclusion is evident in its orphanages and within the membership and leadership of the organization. Conversely, there is also a clear commitment to the national languages of Afghanistan (Persian – Dari and Pashto) over ethno-linguistic diversity. Cultural teachings are designed to celebrate its configuration of Afghan nationalism and ethnic plurality.

Spatial exclusion, control, and empowerment Empowerment for members mainly occurs in the private spaces of RAWA-run programs, which are clandestine and exclusionary. For example, in a refugee camp in Peshawar, Pakistan, members and supporters experience (to varying degrees) the organization's feminist-nationalist vision. The camp leadership consists of a men and women's leadership council, who are elected by the camp inhabitants.

RAWA negotiates within existing gender regimes by embracing and operating within certain gendered divisions of space and/or labor and by subverting or resisting others. The limits of women's empowerment are also bound by the physical structures and spaces they control. Regarding education, boys are an integrated aspect of socio-political philosophies and the development and reproduction of feminism. 'We know that boys and girls think differently about each other because of our schools. They realize they are equals. Yes we are a feminist and women's organization but we see education of boys as part of that process, to secure women's rights and change how men think of women' (Sahar, interview, 2004).

Education is an essential element of the organization's political project to alter men and women's epistemologies of gender norms and increase the value of women within and outside the family and household. Family and kinship networks are foundational and integral facets of its political structure. As RAWA argues, indigenous Afghan women are the only group able to bring forth women's true emancipation.

Feminisms within the structure of the family have the potential to destabilize patriarchal structures and to reconstruct gender-equitable systems through a feminist reworking of gender relations. Retaining the biological structure of the gendered family and several aspects of gendered divisions of labor allows space for negotiating within these structures, rather than rejecting the entire structure and ultimately alienating the potential for resistance and reconstruction.

(Re)politicizing women RAWA members, many of whom are wives and mothers, do not utilize these subject positions for social capital or political legitimacy in the public representation of the organization or as integral to its ideological construction of the Afghan nation. As an independent feminist-nationalist organization, RAWA retains autonomy from masculinist forms of nationalism and from the valorization of motherhood as integral to the symbolic and supportive roles of women as 'mothers of the nation.' Consequently, this organization politicizes, articulates, and envisions a space for women within a democratic and secular Afghanistan, as equal and active socio-political agents, citizens, participants, and leaders. Meena, for example, was married with three children; however, she is publicly positioned as a political leader, a courageous revolutionary and martyr; rather than a mother and/or wife.

Similarly, RAWA's emphasis on bravery explicitly links to both past and current threats against the organization and its membership. These risks have become benchmarks of individual membership and are used to illustrate their actions as both heroic and valorous. For members, their dedication to RAWA is interlinked with their devotion to the nation. The discourse of dedication, struggle, and sacrifice remains an entrenched aspect of membership. Courage and strength are linked to members' willingness to face death in the service of RAWA. However, there is no corresponding expectation to kill in the name of the organization.

Summary and conclusions

RAWA, as a women-led, feminist-nationalist organization working in conflict zones and riddled with a recent history of state-sponsored misogyny and patriarchal social regimes, engages in political acts that subvert, adopt, and rework these power structures. RAWA's resistance to the existing social and political configuration of Afghanistan focuses on a (re)articulation of women's capacity through leadership and empowerment programs, education, and their public representation of members as martyrs, revolutionaries, and agents; rather than wives, supporters, and mothers of the nation's potential future.

Negotiating and reworking gender norms create empowerment opportunities for women. Part of this reworking includes adopting certain aspects of conventional nation-building.

Future research on feminism and feminist activism is necessary to address the ability of independent feminist nationalist organizations to impact existing gendered configurations of nations and nationalism over time.

Notes

1 The data for this article were collected as part of my dissertation research on RAWA's political strategies at multiple scales and its transnational organizing.

2 Marxism, Maoism, feminism and other political ideologies present in Kabul also influenced Meena (RAWA).

3 The number of people RAWA serves varies over time and is contingent on the level of its financial resources. Many of its programs were focused on refugee areas in Pakistan (primarily Quetta, Rawalpindi, Islamabad, and Peshawar) during times of heightened conflict; comparable programs are also managed throughout Afghanistan.

4 RAWA believes that owing to their precarious position against both the Soviet occupiers and extremist mujahideen resistance, Meena was murdered by a coalition of the Khad and Gulbuddin Hekmatyar's Hizb-i-Islami party.

5 The burqa, known as the chadori in Afghanistan, is a garment worn by women in public space. This garment includes a cap that fits snugly on the head with a long flowing and pleated fabric that covers a woman's clothed body.

6 RAWA's primary forms of funding include membership dues, income-generating projects, and donations from supporters. After 1996 and its successful use of the Internet for generating funds, RAWA was able to increase the scope and scale of several projects.

References

Brodsky, A. (2003) *With All Our Strength: The Revolutionary Association of the Women of Afghanistan*, New York: Routledge.

Emandi, H. (2002) *Repression, Resistance, and Women in Afghanistan*, Westport, CT: Praeger.

Fluri, J. (2006) '"Our website was revolutionary": virtual spaces of representation and resistance', *ACME: An International E-Journal of Critical Geographies*, 5(1): 89–111.

Herr, R. S. (2003) 'The possibility of nationalist feminism', *Hypatia*, 18(3): 135–48.

Kandiyoti, D. (1988) 'Bargaining with patriarchy', *Gender and Society*, 2(3): 274–90.

Kaplan, C., N. Alarcón and M. Moallem (1999) 'Introduction: between woman and nation', in Kaplan et al. (eds), *Between Woman and Nation: Nationalisms, Transnational Feminisms, and the State*, Durham, NC: Duke University Press.

Mazurana, D. et al. (2005) *Gender, Conflict and Peacekeeping*, Lanham, MD: Rowman & Littlefield.

Nelson, J. A. (2001) 'Abortions under community control: feminism, nationalism, and the politics of reproduction among New York City's Young Lords', *Journal of Women's History*, 13(1): 157–82.

RAWA (2003) 'The voice of the voiceless', Organizational brochure, Islamabad.

West, L. (1997) *Feminist Nationalism*, New York: Routledge.

Yuval-Davis, N. (1996) 'Women and the biological reproduction of "The Nation"', *Women's Studies International Forum*, 19(1/2): 17–24.

44 | Struggle, perseverance, and organization in Sri Lanka's export processing zones

Samanthi Gunawardana[1]

The aim of this chapter is to examine the forms of organizing that have been possible in Sri Lankan export processing zones (EPZs),[2] where young women drawn from the rural poor make up approximately 85 percent of all workers (BOI 2003). These zones are state-demarcated production spaces where imported materials undergo some degree of processing before being re-exported. The number of these zones has grown exponentially over the past forty years with the growth of export-oriented industrialization among developing countries.

Although EPZ work has enabled the inclusion of women in formal work, workers commonly face 'low wages, poor working conditions and under-developed labor-relations systems,' where freedom of association, collective bargaining, and the right to organize have been constrained largely through the nonenforcement of labor laws (Gordon 2000). For global organizing, the challenge lies in finding and articulating a common context for struggle while accommodating local group-based needs and desires (Jonasdottir 1988).

I examine a successful global campaign at Jaqalanka Pty Ltd, an apparel manufacturer in the Katunayake EPZ (KEPZ). This involved a partnership between the democratic Free Trade Zone Workers Union (FTZWU) and a grassroots women's collective, the Women's Centre. This global campaign centered on the struggle for freedom of association and the right to organize. This chapter is based on ethnographic research since 2001. The main portion of research was carried out during twelve months of participant observation in 2003.

The creation of a gendered working class

In 1978, the United National Party (UNP) in Sri Lanka established the first EPZ at Katunayake, 20 kilometers north of Colombo, as part of a wider program of economic liberalization. By 2003, there were nine EPZs and two industrial parks in Sri Lanka employing approximately 139,000 workers (BOI 2003).

Eighty-five percent of workers are poor women, the majority of whom are unmarried and ethnically Sinhalese and identify themselves as Buddhist. Most are between nineteen and twenty-six years old, with a relatively high level of educational attainment. Despite the stress and degradation of the factory system, women reported feeling pride in their work and empowered through earning an independent income. Although EPZ wages were higher, the rising cost of living was unsustainable for EPZ workers, particularly if they were supporting their families in the village. As a consequence, workers relied heavily on overtime income and bonuses.

Struggle: the challenges of organizing workers

While Sri Lankan labor law guarantees freedom of association, the right to organize, and the right to collectively bargain, by 2003 only 4 percent of EPZ factories had recognized trade unions with varying degrees of functionality, and a collective agreement has yet to be reached. The challenges facing trade unions are outlined below.

First, the government has constrained trade union activity through the invocation of special laws.

Second, the government has enabled a system of industrial relations containment through the setting up of the Board of Investments (BOI), as well as banning May Day parades in Colombo.

The formation of in-house workers' councils was initiated after the 1994 presidential election, following mass labor agitation for trade union rights. However, workers' council representatives have limited influence.

While the masculinist orientation of political trade unionism in Sri Lanka traditionally hindered women's participation and prevented them attaining leadership positions (Caspersz 1998; Rosa 1994), EPZ workers did not join trade unions in great numbers or take an active part in them because of cultural and time restrictions and the rationalization that they would be there for only a short period of time (Rosa 1994). In summary, the challenges for organizing are manifold in EPZs, where local-level constraints combine with the challenge of coordinating and campaigning globally.

Freedom of association and organizing at Jaqalanka Apparels Pty Ltd

Jaqalanka Ltd operates three factories in Sri Lanka, two of which are situated in the Katunayake Free Trade Zone (KFTZ). The KFTZ factory is a British-owned company, which has several Sri Lankan expatriates on its board and Sri Lankan managers on site. At the time of the dispute, there were 400 workers. Until this particular dispute, the BOI work stoppages register does not record any disputes between 1994 and 2003.

In March 2003, the factory announced that the company was operating at a loss and would not be able to pay a bonus. Workers were surprised and angered by this announcement. By April the company still maintained that it would not 'pay even a single cent as a bonus for this year' (Anton Marcus, FTZWU, interview by author, 2003). As a result, the production sections stopped work after lunch and went on a half-day strike (FTZWU branch union secretary, interview by author, 2003). The BOI was informed, and senior officials from the BOI engaged in a discussion with the workers' council.

Several of the women workers had been taking part in the activities of the Women's Centre (FTZWU branch union secretary, interview by author, 2003). At this point, a number of workers approached the FTZWU at the Katunayake Centre and decided to form a branch union of the FTZWU at Jaqalanka. Two hundred and twenty members, a little over half of the total workforce, joined the trade union and elected officers, consisting of both men and women. Management agreed to take the workers back effective 8 April 2003 (TIE-Asia 2003), at which point workers requested that managers deal with the branch union. Management refused to engage with the union, attend meetings with the assistant commissioner of labor, or give leave for workers to attend the meeting (Anton Marcus, FTZWU, interview by author, 2003). Union members were verbally harassed and intimidated. The union then requested a referendum to be arranged under the provision of Section 56 of the 1999 Industrial Disputes Amendment Act for recognition of the union in the factory.

The global campaign A date for a referendum on the union was set with the labor commissioner, after which workers reported that a steady campaign was waged by managers to deter union membership. The trade union still faced difficulty in accessing and talking to workers at Jaqalanka to encourage them to take part in the referendum. To overcome this, the Women's Centre, along with trade union members, visited the boarding houses of Jaqalanka workers and distributed a letter outlining the situation to date. On the day of the referendum, 9 June 2003, a number of international observers from US and European labor groups were present. A report by the observers from the Fair Labor Association (FLA) concluded that 'the election was marred by the clumsiest of employer intimidation. The government of Sri Lanka did nothing about it' (Connor and Dent 2006: 23). Only seventeen workers, out of a total of 402, voted.

The Clean Clothes Campaign, global trade unions, and other international organizations managed a sustained letter-writing campaign in both Europe and the United States, targeting both Jaqalanka and its international brand-name clients, such as Nike and Vanity Fair. Many workers spoke about the continual intimidation by management and issues such as being forced to work after they had punched out for the day and to work overtime. The Women's Centre provided a safe and open space for workers to meet and discuss the campaign. Previous training and ongoing work with the Centre and the FTZWU enabled them to sustain their struggle.

Resolution Both the FTZWU and Nike lodged a request with the FLA, and subsequently FLA engaged with all key stakeholders to pursue 'an amicable nonconfrontational resolution.' They engaged a local NGO, the Centre for Policy Alternatives (CPA), to convene a roundtable discussion. The factory branch was recognized as 'representing the concerns of its members at Jaqalanka' (FLA 2004). The union then called off the global campaign.

Currently, the union functions and is working with management, which now allows union meetings in the factory (Connor and Dent 2006: 24), and union dues are being deducted by the factory. This case has led to a number of other positive outcomes for labor in the EPZs.

Perseverance: understanding forms of organizing found in Sri Lankan EPZs

To explain why the campaign was successful, I now examine how local trade unions and other groups have engaged in sustained organizing efforts.

Women organizing women: the importance of women's labor groups Women's organizations were among the first in Sri Lanka to work directly with EPZ workers. They have persistently worked with one another and other regional and international women's groups to articulate a common interest among Asian women workers, through a shared understanding of and confrontation of gender inequality as a basis for political action in the workplace. In doing so, they have focused on issues that have been overlooked by traditional Sri Lankan unions.

These include the Women's Centre, the *Da Bindu* (Drops of Sweat) collective, and *Kalape Api* (We in the Zone). All three of these groups are led either solely or jointly by women, some of whom have been workers themselves. Most are funded externally by international NGOs in the global North and supported by regional groups. These groups enable linkages between disparate women's labor organizations in the region and facilitate information sharing, capacity-building of local activists, and the development of alternative methods of organizing. From these early ad hoc beginnings, organized groups began to emerge.

The most proactive of the groups in Sri Lanka's EPZs is the Women's Centre, which originated from a strike at the Polytex garments factory in 1982 on an industrial estate next to the KEPZ. This strike was led by young women workers who instigated a community-based campaign, supported by local activists and other organizations, and faced off a coalition of police, state agents, management, and hired thugs (Jayakody and Goonatilake 1988). At this time a partnership was formed with the Industrial Transport and General Workers Union (ITGWU). The center was born from the workers' need to create a space to meet and plan their actions.

Currently, the center provides legal and medical assistance, library facilities, training, seminars, discussions, and education, as well as a much-needed space for women workers. Its aims and objectives are based on a discursive reorientation of women's work as a valuable service to the national economy. A key aim is to counter derogatory societal attitudes toward women through organization and collectivism. The Women's Centre engages in solidarity action with regional women's groups and trade unions and facilitates exchanges with other local women's labor groups, such as those working with migrant domestic workers and plantation workers, regardless of ethnic, religious, or caste differences. What differentiates this center from other NGOs mentioned above is that it seeks to actively involve its members in union activities; the center identifies and trains potential trade union leaders.

Because many women are neophyte workers, creative expression through writing and performance has been instrumental to the success of these groups. These practices seek to reorient workers as active agents. Issues of sexual harassment; the lack of labor rights, including freedom of association; and problems of substandard housing, sexual and reproductive health, and violence that workers face day to day – topics never broached by traditional unions – are addressed in these papers. Another form of creative expression that has been used by women's groups is the traditional *vedi natya* (street drama), which enables workers to express their grievances in an accessible and nonconfrontational, albeit powerful and expressive, way. Another area where women's groups have worked together across borders is in conducting strategic localized research that has in turn contributed to global campaigns. Organizations such as *Da Bindu* and the Women's Centre have been instrumental in documenting the conditions not only of EPZ workers but also other peripheral workers such as home-based workers in transnational commodity chains.

The trade union movement The first union to substantially concentrate on organizing EPZ workers as a distinct group was the ITGWU. The union offered informal worker education and training programs for EPZ workers in conjunction with the Women's Centre. The partnership with the Women's Centre enabled the union to highlight women's rights issues such as sexual harassment and living conditions in boarding houses through the 1990s, bringing them into the domain of trade union concern (Anton Marcus, FTZWU, interview by author, 2003).

At present, women make up more than 85 percent of the 14,000 members (Anton Marcus, FTZWU, interview by author, 2006). The union also organizes women in factories producing for export outside the zones. The union targets three strategic levels: the factory, the local/national, and the international. At the factory level the union, along with the Women's Centre, concentrates on identifying potential leaders and lobbying and agitating for the implementation of existing labor law and enforcement of ILO Conventions 87 and 89. At the national level, the FTZWU engages in advocacy for labor law reform. With the linkage with the Women's Centre remaining at the center, the union also engages in building solidarity links with other workers, such as workers in the plantation sector, and in people's movements. It is also part of a wider group of transnational trade union alliances and networks of NGOs. These networks include other local, regional, and international women's groups; trade union bodies; and human rights activists.

Lessons learned from the Sri Lankan experience

The successful partnership between the Women's Centre and FTZWU and their strategic mobilization of international networks in the Jaqalanka case offer insight into the possibilities for cross-border organizing. One concern with the top-down strategy of engaging the global North is that although international pressure campaigns can generate quick results, they do not resolve the issue of maintaining worker organization at the local level. Specifically in the Jaqalanka case, the Women's Centre provided localized support in reaching workers and sustaining the campaign.

Notes

1 The author thanks the following people for their assistance: Dr Darryn Snell, Monash University, and Dr Kate Bronfenbrenner, Cornell University, for their comments on earlier drafts of this chapter; two anonymous reviewers for their comments; Anton Marcus and Padmini Weerasoorriya for their assistance in conducting and participating in this research; the workers of Katunayake zone, who participated in this research; and all the other interviewees.

2 The term 'EPZ' has been used interchangeably with 'free trade zone,' 'free economic zone,' 'free ports special economic zone,' 'single industry zone,' 'single commodity zone,' and 'free trade geographical border.' Single enterprises can also be granted EPZ status.

References

BOI (Board of Investment) (2003) 'A profile of the zones', www.boi.lk.

Caspersz, D. (1998) 'Organizing export processing zone workers: some considerations for trade unions', Paper presented at the Association of Industrial Relations Academics of Australia and New Zealand Conference, Wellington.

Connor, T. and K. Dent (2006) 'Offside! Labor rights and sportswear production in Asia', Report for Oxfam International, www.oxfam.org.uk / what_we_do/issues/trade/offside_sportswear.htm.

FLA (2004) 'Fair Labor Association year two annual public report', www.fair labor.org/2004report.

Gordon, M. E. (2000) 'Export processing zones', in L. Turner and M. E. Gordon (eds), Transnational Cooperation among Labor Unions, Ithaca, NY: Cornell University Press.

Jayakody, S. and H. Goonatilake (1988) 'Industrial action by women workers in Sri Lanka: the Polytex garment workers', in N. Heyzer (ed.), Daughters in Industry: Work, Skills, and Consciousness of Women Workers in Asia, Kuala Lumpur: Asian and Pacific Development Centre.

Jonasdottir, A. G. (1988) 'On the concepts of interests, women's interests and the limitations of theory', in K. Jones and A. G. Jonasdottir (eds), The Political Interests of Gender, London: Sage.

Rosa, K. (1994) 'The conditions and organizational activities of women in

Free Trade Zones: Malaysia, Philippines, and Sri Lanka 1970–1990', in S. Rowbotham and S. Mitter (eds), *In Dignity and Daily Bread: New Forms of Economic Organizing among Poor Women in the Third World and the First*, London: Routledge.

TIE-Asia (2003) 'Victory for FTZWU workers at Jaqalanka Ltd Sri Lanka', tieasia.org.

Index

Banda Aceh tsunami, women's deaths in, 317

Bandung Conference, 15

Bangladesh: debt recycling in, 53; women's work in, 95

banks, 57; government bailouts of, 298; insensitive to women's needs, 59; lay-offs of women by, 273; protests against, 419; women's interface with, 58–9

BAOBAB for Women's Rights, 403

Basic Needs approach, 30, 31; theory of, 28

Bat Shalom organization, 79

Berne Initiative, 263

Bigombe, Betty, 354

biopiracy, 395

birth control, 28, 110

birth rates, falling, 110, 327

black pride, 365

Black voices, erasure of, 97

body, female: focus on, 44; used for advertising, 154; women's control of, 122

bogadi, payment of, 124, 125, 126

Bolivia, women's debt in, 53

bonded labour, 204, 245, 247; women in, 247–8

bonuses of factory workers, 232

Border Industrialization Program (US–Mexico), 225

Boserup, Ester, 85, 108, 114, 117; *Women's Role in Economic Development*, 7, 29, 38–42

Botswana, fatherhood in, 109; changing construction of, 121–36

Bramsen, Michelle Bo, 85

Brazil: as aid donor, 4; economic growth in, 360; factory work in, 200; gender equality in, 360–71

Brazil, Russia, India and China (BRIC), 4

breadwinner, position of, 219, 309

Bretton Woods system, 15, 295

bride-burning, 160, 161

bridewealth, payment of, 124

Brownell, Mary, 357

B'Tselem organization, 78

Bunch, Charlotte, 406

burqa, 76, 405, 427; as portable exclusion, 91

Burundi, women's involvement in peace negotiations, 350

Bush, Laura, 91; radio address, 89, 90

butane gas, introduced in Senegal, 322, 323, 324

Cairo population conference (1994), 327, 384; Plan of Action, 347

Canadian Alternative Federal Budget, 303

capability, 28, 31, 41, 175, 188

capital, dialectic with gender, 219–20

capital flight, 296

Capra, Fritjof, 373

carbon emissions, 328, 330–1

care: and the global economy, 41–2; as a feminine value, 80; changing methods of, 70; concept of, 7; economy of, 65; gendered division of labour in, 107; penalizing of, 42; provided by men, 123; provided by women and girls, 66 (in HIV/AIDS situations, 291); care deficit, 241

care diamond, 6

care economy, 24, 25

care work, 184, 231, 308, 312, 314, 377; as professional career option, 342; caring for the care workers, 259–61; concept of, 334; de-feminization of, 342; discrimination in the workplace, 255–7; for people with AIDS, costs of, 337–8; globalization of, 204, 252–69; impoverishes women, 340; in HIV contexts, 334–43; love as part of, 239; support for, 188; unpaid, 42, 296, 298, 301, 306; visibility of, 335–7

cash nexus, 218–19, 220

caste systems, 163, 164, 170, 247; permeability of, 166

casual employment, 273

casualization, 67

Catholic Church, 364

Central Única dos Trabalhadores (CUT) (Brazil), 362, 363, 365

Centro Femenino 8 de Marzo (Quito), 420–1

charcoal, production of, 322

chastity, female, 155, 157, 159

child camel jockeys, 249

child labour, 111, 204, 245, 248; gender differences in, 248–9

Child Line, 132

child soldiers, 249, 354; campaigning for, 353

childcare, 107, 118, 133, 160, 226, 238;

democratization, 18

demographic change, and burdens on women, 66

dependency theory, 18, 34

desertification, 319, 323; through tree-cutting, 322

development: adverse effects on women, 29; as a concept, questioned, 19, 33; encounter with sexuality, 102–4; gender and, 28–37; goals of, 205; history of, 14–37; neutrality of, challenged, 98; use of term, 95; women and, 85–8 *see also* sustainable development

difference, 100; acceptance of, 92; among women, 177; construction of, 98; cultural, 89

disability groups, 10

disaster response activity, 331

disciplining of children, 128–9, 131, 134; by women, 132

discouraged worker effect, 271, 272

discrimination, in the workplace, 255–7

division of labour: gendered, 28, 32, 41, 87, 107, 118, 126, 132, 213, 215, 236, 272, 274, 307, 308, 315, 417, 429 (in households, 260, 375); in African agriculture, 38–9; international, 138, 144–5

divorce, 68, 110, 242

docility of women, 139, 202, 213, 218, 242; analysis of, 216

domestic work: globalization of, 242; of women, 19, 114, 117–18, 157, 217, 247, 248, 301 *see also* household

domestic workers, 398; female, representation of, 253; globalized trade in, 398; in Arab Emirates, 203; morality of, 256; undervalued, 203; women as, 237, 360

Dominica, 200

domino theory, 14–15

dowry, 160, 161, 246; historical roots of, 163–4; increasing expectations of, 165; legislation not enforced, 169; negotiated by brokers, 164; recent developments of, 164–5; seen by Gandhi as corrupt, 164

Dowry Prohibition Act (1961) (India), 164, 165–6

dress of women, restrictions on, 156

drought, 319, 321

drugs, patenting of, 396

Earth 2100 film, 327

ecofeminism, 43

ecology *see* feminist political ecology

Economic Commission for Latin America and the Caribbean (ECLAC), 186

economic crisis, 287–9; effects on employment, 289; in Turkey, 306–16 *see also* financial crises

economic goods and services, definition of, 116

Ecuador: community organizing in, 417–24; women's struggles in, 385

education, 26, 75, 110, 170, 205, 223, 259, 320, 363, 430; access to, power dynamics in, 109; adult, 367; cutbacks of, 67, 288; expense of, 338; gender gap in, 20, 65–6; girls withdrawn from school, 26; integrated, in Brazil, 367–8; lack of gender sensitivity in, 66; married women banned from, 75; of boys, 429; of female migrants, 243, 252; of girls, 143, 317–18 (forgone, 340; right to, 341; seen as wasted, 144); of migrant women nurses, 256; of women, 271, 272, 280, 312, 327, 426 (in Afghanistan, 405; in Korea, 277–8); popular, 363, 364–5; programmes, 367

Egypt, 90, 91, 93; revision of marriage law in, 68

Ehrlich, Paul, *The Population Bomb*, 327

El-Bushra, Judy, 100

electronics industry, 199, 225, 271

employment of women, 48

employment patterns, 24

empowerment, 32, 421–2, 430; concept of, 10; measurement of, 8; of women, 8, 9, 48, 55, 75, 177, 186, 422, 429–30 (and microcredit, 52–3; economic, 418; limits of, 429)

energy management, by women, 323

enterprise-promotion loans, 59–60

entitlements, 30

entrepreneurial activities of women, 204

environmental crisis, 287, 289–90

environmental degradation, 31; burden on women, 330

environmental justice, 329

Equal Employment Law (South Korea), 280

Equal Opportunities Commission (Uganda), 352

financial architecture, time of, 297

financial crises, 5, 6, 287; Asian, 24, 270, 295, 297, 298, 300 (women's workloads in, 299); gender implications of, 297–300; impact on women of, 22–7; management of, 300; panic selling in, 298

Financial Stability Forum, 303

financial system, international, architecture of, 295–305

foeticide: in India, 162–73; methods of, 167–8

food, allocated to male children, 137

food security, 330

food sovereignty, concept of, 410

Forward-looking Strategies for the Advancement of Women, 114

Foxconn company, 387

France, heat wave, deaths of women, 317

Free Trade Zone Workers Union (FTZWU) (Sri Lanka), 432

free trade zones, 204, 213; women's employment in, 204

Freire, Paulo, 364, 366

Frente de Libertação de Moçambique (FRELIMO), 350, 353

Fried, Susana, 406

Friedman, Milton, 361

fuelwood, 322; collecting of, 318, 320, 322, 330

full employment policies, 301

fundamentalisms, 427; religious, 398; resistance to, 344–8

Gaborone (Botswana), fatherhood in, 126–33

Gambia, research into poverty programmes in, 174

garment industry *see* clothing industry

Gaziantep Province, Turkey, women's waged work in, 313–14

gender, 84, 215, 219, 392, 425; and climate change, in Senegal, 317–26; and development, 28–37; as category of analysis, 399; as determinant of health, 64–73; changing relations of, 412; construction of roles, 375; dialectic with capital, 219–20; implications of financial crisis for, 297–300; in neoliberal development, 99–101; institutionalization of, 32;

mainstreaming of, 71; roles disrupted by conflicts, 350; slavery and, 245–51; strategic gender interests, 375

Gender Action, 289

gender and development (GAD), 10, 99, 177, 183, 184, 188; criticized as cultural imperialism, 96; race in, 96–7

gender-ascriptive relations, 215–16

gender blindness, 14

gender budget initiatives, 304

gender discrimination, 23

gender equality and inequality, 5, 35, 48, 61, 64, 69, 71, 300, 318, 335, 340, 374, 377, 392; and poverty reduction, 183; in Brazil, 360–71; in Turkey, 315

gender ideology, analysis of, 149

gender justice, 80

gender lens, 95–8

gender mainstreaming, in UN, 7

gender stereotypes, challenging of, 68–9

gender subordination, recomposition of, 219, 220

Germany: East German migrant women in, 241; Turkish migrant women in, 241

Ghana: female ritual servitude in, 246; market women in, 202

Giddens, Anthony, 148

girls: as carers, 341; discrimination against, 65, 187; distributed as sex slaves to soldiers, 249; drop out of school, 317–18; education of, 66, 81; reduced education, food and healthcare for, 146; rights of, 338; socialization of, 144; undervalued, 165, 246 *see also* education, of girls

glass ceiling, for women's advancement, 280

Global Assembly Line, The, 200

Global Commission on International Migration, 263

Global South, use of term, 19

global warming, 289, 328

global women, 237–44

globalization, 19, 66–7, 81; critiques of, absence of women and girls in, 396; gendered dimensions of, 44; of care work, 252–69; of domestic work, 242; of systems of production, 235; study of, 41

governance, good, 18

Grama Sabha, women's participation in, 61

violence, 79; against children, 132; against women, 8, 9, 74–5, 179, 257, 352, 375, 397, 406, 412, 415 (exacerbated by affluence, 168; WHO report on, 69); domestic, 26, 78, 107, 110, 123, 421–2 (in India, 68); gendered, 26, 67; male monopoly of, 34; marital, 61; sexual, 79, 80 (class nature of, 159)
virginity testing, precondition for scholarships, 346
virtue, of women, perceptions of, 160
volunteer work of women, 114, 118–19, 184
vulnerable employment, 310; growth of, 307

Wachani, Nilita, *When Mother Comes Home for Christmas*, 237
waged work of women, 213–14, 239, 299, 306–16; in Korea, 270–84; instability of, 220–1
wages, 24, 25, 124, 142, 228, 270; decreases in, 205; differentials, 272, 280 (between tradable and non-tradable sectors, 41); minimum wage, 213, 257; of domestic workers, 241; of women, 198, 221–2, 254, 278 (declining, 277; low, 197, 201, 217, 230, 314)
Walker, Alice, *Warrior Marks*, 404
Wallerstein, Immanuel, 34
WAO Afrique, 250
war on terrorism, 89
wartime trauma, effects of, 79–80
Washington Consensus, 288
water: access to, 165, 289–90, 321, 324; collecting of, 318; fetching of, 320, 330
welfare, privatization of, 35
welfare responsibilities, transferred to women, 422
welfare state, 242
Westboro Baptist Church, 344, 347
Western, use of term, 394
widows, 66, 169, 178; in India, treatment of, 164; pensions denied, 61; prejudices against, 76
Windward Islands Farmers Association, 410
witchcraft, 130, 131
Wolff, Eunice, 366
women: abandonment of, 125; as analytical category, 84–5; as client category, 9; as fighters in

independence wars, 352; as providers of social services, 184; as reserve army of labour, 217; as victims, 184–5; as waged workers (effects of recession on, 273; relations with bosses, 220; status of, 271–2; struggles of, 221–2; vulnerability of, 217); bear brunt of poverty, 20; bodies of *see* body, female; burden of work borne by, 40; conflated with family, 384; contribution to the economy, 119; double day of, 301; equated with gender, 188; globalized representations of, 398; impact of financial crises on, 22–7; in India, treatment of, 154; in labour market, secondary status of, 216, 216; low status of, in India, 169; mobility of, 160 (dangers of, 170; restricted, 107, 156, 346); mobilization of, 89–91; poor, 420 (politicization of, 419); responsibilities of, for families, 260; role in economic development, 38–42; sexual control of, 154–61; struggles of *see* struggles of women; survival strategies of, 60–3; 'Third World' (image of, 84, 85, 88; not coherent group, 86); unpaid labour of *see* unpaid work; waged work of *see* waged work of women; Western (self-representation of, 84, 86; treated as sex objects, 154); work of (accounting for, 114–20; in export sector, 198; underestimated in statistics, 114–20; young, factory employment of, 138–53 *see also* agriculture, women's work in
women in development (WID), 28, 85, 419; critique of, 9, 32
Women in Informal Employment, Globalizing and Organizing (WIEGO), 386
Women Living Under Muslim Laws (WLUML), 403
women of cover, 92
Women's Centre (Sri Lanka), 435–6
Women's Leadership Forum on Peace, 356
women's movements, 114, 385, 406, 414, 417–18; global, 391–3; in Africa, 292, 349–59; in India, 170; in Latin America, 384; objectives of, 391–2
Women's Peace Caravan (Uganda), 354
work-centred organizing, 386–7
workers' control over production, 377
Workers' Party (PT) (Brazil), 292, 362, 363

About Zed Books

Zed Books is a critical and dynamic publisher, committed to increasing awareness of important international issues and to promoting diversity, alternative voices and progressive social change. We publish on politics, development, gender, the environment and economics for a global audience of students, academics, activists and general readers. Run as a co-operative, Zed Books aims to operate in an ethical and environmentally sustainable way.

Find out more at:

www.zedbooks.co.uk

For up-to-date news, articles, reviews and events information visit:

http://zed-books.blogspot.com

To subscribe to the monthly Zed Books e-newsletter, send an email headed 'subscribe' to:

marketing@zedbooks.net

We can also be found on **Facebook**, **ZNet**, **Twitter** and **Library Thing**.